THE HIDDEN PLACES OF
SCOTLAND

By David Gerrard

Regional Hidden Places

Cornwall
Devon
Dorset, Hants & Isle of Wight
East Anglia
Lake District & Cumbria
Lancashire & Cheshire
Northumberland & Durham
Peak District and Derbyshire
Yorkshire

National Hidden Places

England
Ireland
Scotland
Wales

Country Living Rural Guides

East Anglia
Heart of England
Ireland
North East of England
North West of England
Scotland
South
South East
Wales
West Country

Other Guides

Off the Motorway
Garden Centres and Nurseries
of Britain

Published by: Travel Publishing Ltd, 7a Apollo House, Calleva Park, Aldermaston, Berks, RG7 8TN

ISBN13 9781904434801

© Travel Publishing Ltd

First published 1994, second edition 1997, third edition 1999, fourth edition 2002, fifth edition 2004, sixth edition 2007, seventh edition 2010

Printing by: Latimer Trend, Plymouth

Maps by: ©MAPS IN MINUTES/Collins Bartholomew (2010)

Editor: David Gerrard

Cover Design: Lines and Words, Aldermaston

Cover Photograph: Glen Etive, Argyllshire
© www.picturesofbritain.co.uk

Text Photographs: © www.picturesofbritain.co.uk
and © Bob Brooks, Weston-super-Mare

Foreword

This is the 7th edition of *The Hidden Places of Scotland* taking you on a relaxed but informative tour of this wild and often wonderful country. The guide has been been fully updated and in this respect we would like to thank the Tourist Information Centres in Scotland for helping us update the editorial content. The guide is packed with information on the many interesting places to visit and you will find details of places of interest and advertisers of places to stay, eat and drink included under each village, town or city, which are cross referenced to more detailed information contained in a separate, easy-to-use section to the rear of the book.

Scotland has been inhabited for thousands of years and is rich in history and culture. It is blessed with some of the most impressive mountains in the British Isles and finest coastlines and offshore islands in the world. It is also full of "hidden places", which can enrich the visitor's knowledge of Scottish heritage and provide landscapes that astound the eye with their sheer beauty.

The Hidden Places of Scotland contains a wealth of interesting information on the history, the countryside, the towns and villages and the more established places of interest. But it also promotes the more secluded and little known visitor attractions and places to stay, eat and drink many of which are easy to miss unless you know exactly where you are going.

We include hotels, bed & breakfasts, restaurants, pubs, bars, teashops and cafes as well as historic houses, museums, gardens and many other attractions throughout the area, all of which are comprehensively indexed. Many places are accompanied by an attractive photograph and are easily located by using the map at the beginning of each chapter. We do not award merit marks or rankings but concentrate on describing the more interesting, unusual or unique features of each place with the aim of making the reader's stay in the local area an enjoyable and stimulating experience.

Whether you are travelling around Scotland on business or for pleasure we do hope that you enjoy reading and using this book. We are always interested in what readers think of places covered (or not covered) in our guides so please do not hesitate to use the reader reaction form provided to give us your considered comments. We also welcome any general comments which will help us improve the guides themselves. Finally if you are planning to visit any other corner of the British Isles we would like to refer you to the list of other *Hidden Places* titles to be found to the rear of the book and to the Travel Publishing website.

Travel Publishing

Did you know that you can also search our website for details of thousands of places to see, stay, eat or drink throughout Britain and Ireland? Our site has become increasingly popular and now receives over 500,000 visits annually. Try it!

website: www.travelpublishing.co.uk

Location Map

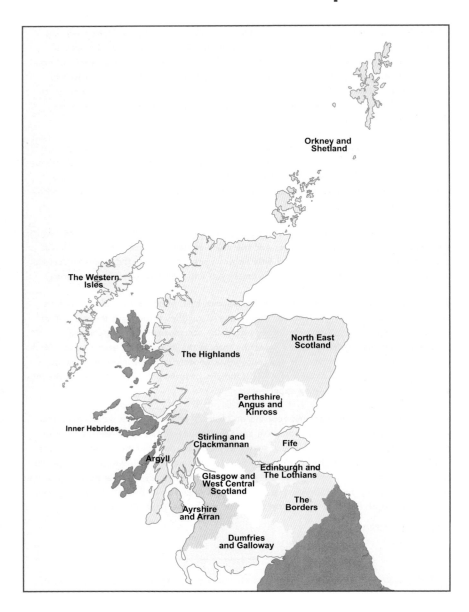

Orkney and
Shetland

The Western
Isles

The Highlands

North East
Scotland

Perthshire,
Angus and
Kinross

Inner Hebrides

Stirling and
Clackmannan

Fife

Argyll

Edinburgh and
The Lothians

Glasgow and
West Central
Scotland

The
Borders

Ayrshire
and Arran

Dumfries
and Galloway

Contents

The Borders

For centuries, the Borders area was the bloody cockpit in which the English and the Scots engaged in interminable warfare. Today, it is a peaceful pastoral region dotted with neat little market towns. Its 1800 square miles extends from the rocky Berwickshire coastline with its picturesque fishing villages, through the gentle valley of the River Tweed, to rolling hills and moorland in the west.

In medieval times, four great abbeys dominated the area: Jedburgh, Kelso, Melrose and Dryburgh, all of them now in ruins but magnificent in their shattered glory. The heart of Robert the Bruce is buried at Melrose Abbey;

Dryburgh Abbey was the last resting place of Sir Walter Scott whose beloved home, Abbotsford House near Melrose, is still lived in by his descendants. Traquair House, near Innerleithen, boasts an even longer record: the oldest continuously inhabited dwelling in Scotland, it has been lived in by the Stuart family since 1491. Floors Castle at Kelso, the hereditary home of the Dukes of Roxburghe, is a mostly Victorian, mock-medieval extravaganza of turrets and castellations, while by contrast, Paxton House and Mellerstain are gems of 18th century classical restraint, both masterworks the creations of the gifted Adam family. Perhaps the most august of all the great houses is Bowhill, the main Scottish residence of the Duke of Buccleuch, although multi-turreted Thirlestane Castle runs it a close second.

These historic houses are set in an inspiring landscape where grand vistas sweep across the majestic Eildon Hills or the crumpled masses of the Cheviots, broad green valleys unfold and huge tracts of forest shelter a varied wildlife. It's a largely unspoilt countryside that repays a leisurely exploration. And wherever your exploring takes you, you will come across still vivid memories of the area's most famous son, Sir Walter Scott, who celebrated the Borders in many a poem.

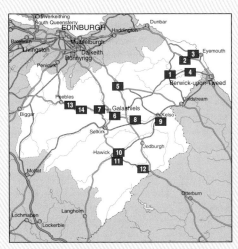

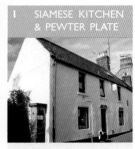

SIAMESE KITCHEN & PEWTER PLATE

Duns

Quality town centre tearoom and restaurant serving authentic Thai food.

see page 350

DUNS

Berwickshire is an unusual county, in that the town from which it takes its name has been part of England since 1482. Therefore Greenlaw, and then in 1853 Duns, was chosen as the county town. It is a quiet, restful place with a wide and gracious market square. On its outskirts is the 713 feet high **Duns Law** from whose summit there are magnificent views of the surrounding countryside. The Cheviot Hills to the south and the Lammermuir Hills to the north can be seen on a clear day, as can the North Sea, 12 miles away. In 1639 a Covenanting army of 12,000 men, which opposed the imposition of bishops on the Scottish church by Charles I, set up camp here under General Leslie, and a **Covenanter's Stone** commemorates this event. There are also the remains of an Iron Age fort, plus some defensive works built by the Covenanting army.

General Leslie was quartered in **Duns Castle**, built round the core of a 14th century pele tower owned by the Earl of Moray, who had been given the surrounding lands by Robert the Bruce. In 1696 it was bought by the Hay family, who enlarged it between 1818 and 1822, creating the Gothic Revival building we see today. The family has lived here ever since. Though not open to the public, it is a venue for weddings and corporate hospitality.

On the western edge of Duns Law is a cairn, which marks the original site of the town, now called The Bruntons, or "burnt towns". It was here that **John Duns Scotus**, known as "Doctor Subtilis", or the "subtle doctor", was supposed to have been born in about 1266 (though some people put his place of birth as Duns in Ireland). He was a Franciscan monk who became one of the greatest theologians and philosophers of his time. His followers were known as Scotists, and his influence is still felt within the Catholic Church to this day. However, his opponents had another, less flattering, name for them - "Dunses" - from which we get the word "dunce". He died at Cologne on November 8th 1308, and on his tomb are the words "Scotland bore me, England adopted me, Cologne holds". In 1991 Pope John Paul II pronounced him "Blessed", the first step on the ladder to sainthood (see also North Uist). In Duns Public Park there is a bronze statue of him and in the grounds of Duns Castle the modern Franciscan Order erected a cairn to his memory in 1966.

Also in the grounds of Duns Castle is the quaintly named Hen Poo, a lake which is the centrepiece of the **Duns Castle Nature Reserve**, owned and run by the Scottish Wildlife Trust. There is a bird hide on the northern shore, and from here you can see mallard ducks, tufted ducks, swans, and coots. Close by, the Mill Dam is also home to many bird species.

In the town itself there is a memorial to a famous man who

lived in more recent times. Jim Clark, the racing driver, was born in Fife in 1936, but from the age of six lived on Eddington Mains, a farm near Duns. He won 25 of his 72 Grand Prix races, and his win at the 1965 Indianapolis Grand Prix astonished the Americans, who considered that no one but an American could cross the finishing line first. He was world champion in 1963 and 1965. Jim Clark was killed at Hockenheim in Germany in 1968 aged 32, when a rear tyre burst during a Formula 2 race. He is buried in Chirnside Parish Church cemetery, about five miles east of Duns. In Duns itself, the **Jim Clark Memorial Trophy Room** in Newtown Street is dedicated to his memory and attracts motor racing enthusiasts from all over the world who make the pilgrimage to view the trophies (including the two world championship trophies he won) and other mementoes on display.

On the west side of Market Square is the 19th century Tolbooth House. The local council have recently laid out a town trail, guiding visitors to places of interest. A leaflet is available, linked to plaques at many places within the town.

Manderston House lies a mile-and-a-half east of the town in 56 acres of formal gardens and is open to the public. It was built between 1903 and 1905, and was the last great stately home built in Scotland. Designed by architect John Kinross, its opulence is quite astonishing incorporating features

such as a silver staircase that is said to be the only one in the world. Manderston was built for Sir James Miller and his wife, the Hon. Eveline Curzon, a member of one of the oldest families in the country. Nowadays Manderston is the home of the Palmer family, of the famous Huntly and Palmer biscuit empire, which explains why its contents include a large collection of biscuit tins.

AROUND DUNS

ABBEY ST BATHANS

5 miles N of Duns on a minor road off the B6355

The pretty village of Abbey St Bathans lies in the steep-sided valley of the Whiteadder Water, deep within the Lammermuir Hills, five miles north of Duns. It is truly a hidden gem, but its name is misleading, as there was never an abbey here. However, in 1170, Ada, Countess of Dunbar, founded the priory of St Mary in the village, and parts of the priory church have been incorporated into the present Parish Church.

The tombstone of a former prioress, which touchingly shows her pet dog, is preserved within the present church.

COCKBURNSPATH

13 miles N of Duns just off the A1

Two features of interest here: ruined **Cockburnspath Tower**, dating from the 15th and 16th centuries, and the **Mercat Cross** at the heart of the village which was erected in 1503 to celebrate the

•

To the south of Abbey St Bathans, at Cockburn Law, are the ruins of the Iron Age Edins Hall Broch, one of the few brochs (a round, fortified stone tower) to be found in Southern Scotland. It is named after Etin, a legendary giant with three heads who is said to have terrorised the area in olden times.

•

Reston

Village inn serving quality pub food and offering comfortable accommodation.

see page 350

Every year in July the Herring Queen Festival takes place in Eyemouth, when the gaily be-decked fishing fleet escorts the "Herring Queen" into Eyemouth Harbour.

marriage of James IV to Margaret Tudor, the daughter of Henry VII of England. The village sits close to **Pease Dean,** a Scottish Wildlife Trust Reserve, where you can see butterflies, lichens and rare mosses. Pease Bridge was built in in 1783 and at the time was the highest stone bridge in Europe. The village is also the eastern terminus of the Southern Upland Way.

AYTON

10 miles NE of Duns on the B6355

Ayton, a mile or so from the A1, is a pleasant village set beside the River Eye. Close by is **Ayton Castle** which was bought in 1834 by William Mitchell Innes, the governor of the Bank of Scotland. He commissioned James Gillespie Graham, a leading Gothic Revival architect, to design the present day Ayton Castle which was built between 1841 and 1846. It is reckoned to be one of the best examples in the country of the style of architecture dubbed "Scottish Baronial", and is surrounded by a 6000-acre estate. It is open from May to September by appointment, and houses fine paintings, furniture and porcelain.

EYEMOUTH

12 miles NE of Duns on the A1107

Scotland's second largest inshore fishing port, picturesque Eyemouth has long since abandoned its other main source of income in times past, smuggling. Contraband goods were furtively conveyed to Gunsgreen House, to the south of the harbour, and thence by way of

underground tunnels to eager purchasers in the town itself. The elegant 1750s house, designed by James Adam, has now retrieved its respectable status by becoming the headquarters of the local golf club.

Eyemouth stands at the mouth of the River Eye, five miles north of the Scotland/England border. The monks of Coldingham Priory founded it as a small fishing port sometime in the 13th century. That maritime origin is reflected in **World of Boats,** a collection of more than 400 historic boats from all over the world, from Alaska to Vietnam; the owner will show you around by appointment.

In the **Eyemouth Museum,** housed in the Auld Kirk built in 1812, the most poignant exhibit is a contemporary 15-feet long tapestry sewn in 1981 that depicts the traumatic disaster of 1881 when 189 fishermen, perished in one of the worst North Sea storms on record.

COLDINGHAM

13 miles NE of Duns on the A1107

The village of Coldingham, a mile from the coast, is visited mainly for the remains of **Coldingham Priory** which was founded in 1098 by King Edgar, son of Malcolm Canmore. It was blown up by Cromwell's men in 1648, with repairs being carried out in about 1670, though only the tower and a couple of walls were left standing. Between 1854 and 1855 the remains were restored, and today they are incorporated into the villages' parish church.

Four miles north west of the

4

village, on the coast, are the ruins of **Fast Castle**, perched precariously on a stack of rock 70 feet above the sea. It is barely accessible by a steep cliff path and is best viewed from above. Sir Walter Scott used the castle as his model for Wolf's Crag in his novel *The Bride of Lammermuir*.

ST. ABB'S

14 miles NE of Duns, on the B6438

The attractive fishing and holiday village of St Abb's is named after St Ebba and has a small, picturesque harbour. The village also serves as a centre for underwater diving because of the exceptionally clear waters.

The whole coastline here is rugged and spectacular, one of the most magnificent parts being **St Abb's Head** (National Trust for Scotland), a nature reserve with a large colony of seabirds located to the north of the village. The cliffs are more than 300 feet high, and are riddled with caves once haunted by smugglers. A monastery for monks and nuns was established on the cliff tops in the 7th century, and St Ebba eventually became a nun here. An old legend recounts that the nuns, instead of living a life of austerity and prayer, spent all their time eating, drinking and gossiping. This was because St Ebba had become too old and infirm to have control over them. The whole area is now managed by the National Trust for Scotland and is a National Nature Reserve. Offshore there is one of the best diving sites in the country.

CHIRNSIDE

6 miles E of Duns on the B6355

Chirnside sits on the south side of a low hill with wonderful views over the surrounding countryside. Nearby, Blackadder Water and the Whiteadder Water meet. The **Parish Church** was founded by King Edgar of Scotland in the 12th century, and is partly Norman, with an impressive Norman doorway at its west end. The substantial church tower was built in memory of Lady Tweedsmuir. Within the cemetery is the grave of Jim Clark the racing driver (see also Duns). The **Jim Clark Memorial Clock**, with a silhouette of a Lotus racing car on it, stands in the middle of the village.

FOULDEN

9 miles E of Duns on the A6105

The main attraction here is the old two-storey **Tithe Barn** (Historic Scotland), dating from medieval times, though it was restored in the 18th and 19th centuries. "Tithe" means a tenth, and each farmer in the parish was supposed to donate a tenth of his crops to the church. It was in the barn that it was stored. The barn can only be viewed from the outside.

PAXTON

10 miles E of Duns just off the B6460 and close to the Tweed

Near the village stands the impressive **Paxton House**, "the most perfect example in Scotland of the style now known as neo-Palladianism". A melancholy tale is

Coldingham

Traditional hostelry with great atmosphere offering appetising home-cooked food and comfortable accommodation.

see page 351

David Hume, the 18th century philosopher and historian, though born in Edinburgh, was educated at Chirnside School until he was 12 years old.

Chirnside

Delightful old coaching inn offering tasty home-cooked food, real ales and en suite rooms.

see page 352

•

Close to Paxton lies the Union Suspension Bridge across the Tweed, connecting Scotland and England, between Horncliffe in Northumberland and Fishwick in the Borders. It was built in 1820 by Sir Samuel Browne, who also invented the wrought-iron chain links used in its construction. It is 480 feet long and was Britain's first major suspension bridge to carry vehicular traffic as well as pedestrians.

•

attached to this gracious house, designed by the Edinburgh brothers John and James Adam in the 1750s. It was commissioned by Patrick Home, later the 13th Laird of Wedderburn, a rich and personable young man who while visiting Berlin on his Grand Tour of Europe bedazzled the court of King Frederick the Great of Prussia. The king's only acknowledged child, Charlotte de Brandt, became besotted with the smooth-talking Scotsman. She absolutely rejected her father's long-laid plans for a politically more useful dynastic connection with a plump and terminally boring Silesian prince. The king, surprisingly, finally agreed to her marriage with the wealthy, handsome but politically insignificant Scottish laird. Patrick gleefully returned to Scotland and spent lavishly on building a noble house at Paxton worthy of his intended quasi-royal bride. But Charlotte never entered its stately portals or passed through its sublimely decorated rooms. The only hint that she was the inspiration for its building is the pair of chamois leather gloves she gave Patrick as a token at their last meeting. These are now on display in the house.

Extraordinarily, the sad story of Patrick and Charlotte was to be duplicated a few years later when Patrick became engaged to Jane Graham of Dugaldstone. Their marriage did indeed take place, in Naples in 1771, and the couple spent three years touring Europe.

Once again, Patrick commissioned Robert Adam to design and build a new marital home, Wedderburn Castle. He returned to it alone; Jane stayed in Europe with a new lover.

No wonder the striking portrait of Patrick Home by John Hoppner, on display in the house, depicts an elderly man with a choleric complexion, a set jaw and a sour expression. It is part of a large collection which Patrick bequeathed to his nephew George who was then 77 years old. Despite his age, George enthusiastically set about building what is still the largest private picture gallery of any country house in Scotland. A rich collection of other paintings on display here are on loan from the National Galleries of Scotland (for whom Paxton House is an outstation) and are changed frequently.

Paxton House is also notable for its outstanding collection of furniture by Chippendale, more than 60 pieces ranging from the entire furnishing of the dining room (not just tables and chairs but window-seats, wine-coolers and knife boxes); pier tables with marvellous parquetry inlays; desks and secretaries; mahogany armchairs and sofas.

The house stands in 80 acres of grounds within a great loop of the River Tweed and were designed in the style of 'Capability' Brown by Robert Robinson in the 18th century. There are nature trails, woodland walks and a "Paxton Ted" teddy bear trail. From the award-winning red squirrel hide you can catch glimpses of what is rapidly becoming one of Scotland's rarest mammals. There is also a tearoom and shop, and in the Victorian boathouse on the banks of the Tweed is a museum dedicated to salmon net fishing.

GORDON

12 miles SE of Duns on the A6089

This pleasant village was the cradle of the Gordon clan which moved north into Aberdeenshire in the 13th century when Robert the Bruce granted them the lands of Strathbogie, which had been forfeited by the Earl of Atholl.

To the north of the village are the well-preserved ruins of **Greenknowe Tower** (Historic Scotland), built in 1581 by James Seton of Touch and his wife Janet Edmonstone. It is a typical L-shaped tower house, built originally as a fortified home.

COLDSTREAM

12 miles S of Duns on the A697

The town sits on the north bank of the Tweed and is linked to England by the graceful 5-arched **Smeaton's Bridge** built in 1766 to a design by John Smeaton. It replaced a ford that had been a natural crossing point for centuries - Edward I used it when he invaded Scotland in the 13th century. On the bridge is a plaque that commemorates the fact that Robert Burns entered England by this route in 1787. Nearby, a huge obelisk erected in 1832 to a little-known MP soars above the town.

In the 19th century, Coldstream rivalled Gretna Green as a place for runaway marriages. At the Scottish end of the bridge is the **Old Toll House**, where, in a 13-year period during the 19th century, 1466 marriages were conducted.

Coldstream's name is perhaps best known in connection with the Coldstream Guards. Officially designated the 2nd Regiment of Foot Guards, the regiment was formed here in 1659 by General Monk. In the following year he led them on the long journey south to London where they were instrumental in effecting the Restoration of Charles II. Within Henderson Park is a memorial stone which commemorates the regiment's foundation and the **Coldstream Museum** in the attractive, pedestrianised Market Square houses extensive displays on its history. The museum also has a children's section and a courtyard

Hirsell Country Park, Coldstream

Lauder

Traditional 18th century coaching inn offering quality cuisine and en suite rooms.

see page 351

with fountain and picnic area.

A mile north of the town is **The Hirsel**, home of the Earls of Home since 1611. The 14th Earl renounced his peerage to become the British Prime Minister, 1963-4, as Sir Alec Douglas Home. Though the house is not open to the public, the grounds can be explored. There is also a small museum, a crafts centre, a gem display and a tearoom.

About 4 miles southeast of Coldstream, just over the border in Northumberland and near the village of Branxton, is **Flodden Field,** the site of Scotland's most disastrous battle against the English. On 9 September 1513, at least 10,000 men perished, amongst them the Scottish leader, James IV, and "not a family of note in all Scotland was left without cause to mourn that dreadful day". In 1910, a tall Celtic cross was erected on the hill overlooking the battlefield. It is inscribed simply "Flodden 1513. To the brave of both nations".

GREENLAW

7 miles SW of Duns on the A697

Greenlaw was the county town of Berwickshire from 1696 to 1853, when Duns replaced it. It formerly stood near the "green law", or hill, a little to the southwest, and was given its burgh charter in 1596. The picturesque Market Cross dates from 1696, and there are many fine buildings within the town, including a town hall built in 1829.

Three miles south are the impressive ruins of **Hume Castle**, ancient seat of the Hume family and a rare example of a simple courtyard castle of the 13th century. The ruined curtain walls form the basis of a folly built in 1794 for the last Earl of Marchmont. It stands 600 feet above sea level, and provides an excellent viewpoint.

LAUDER

17 miles W of Duns on the A68

The main town in Lauderdale, the Royal Burgh of Lauder nevertheless has a population of little more than a thousand people. Surrounded on three sides by the gentle Lammermuir Hills, the town has preserved its medieval plan with a single main street widening into a Market Place dominated by the quaint old Tolbooth, or Town Hall.

Lauder's **Parish Church** of 1673 is decidedly unusual, built in the form of a Greek cross with the pulpit in the centre under the octagonal bell tower. The original box pews are still in place.

A short walk from the centre of the town brings you to the imposing pile of **Thirlestane Castle**. It's a flamboyant place, with turrets, pinnacles and towers, giving it the appearance of a French château. It was originally built in the 13th century but was extended and refurbished in the 16th century for the Maitland family. The most famous member of that family was John Maitland, second Earl and later first (and only) Duke of Lauderdale, who lived between 1616 and 1682. He was a close friend of Charles II and a member of the powerful and unpopular "Cabal Cabinet". The word "cabal" comes from the initial letters of the names of the five men who comprised it, Maitland's being "L" for Lauderdale. So powerful was he that he was soon regarded as the uncrowned king of Scotland.

In those days, political office meant rich pickings by way of bribes so the duke was able to spend lavishly on his opulent castle. The famous English plasterer, George Dunsterfield, was commissioned to create the marvellous ceilings, most notably in the Red Drawing Room where garlands of leaves and flowers cascade from the ceiling as if obeying the law of gravity. The castle's other wonders include a fascinating collection of historic toys which children are actually encouraged to play with, a Border Country Life Exhibition, and a superb park where the Scottish Championship Horse Trials are held in late August.

GALASHIELS

Galashiels (known locally as "Gala") sits beside the Gala Water, and is a manufacturing town at one time noted for its tweed and woollen mills. As a reflection of this, the town's textile manufacturers adopted the motto "We dye to live and live to die". The Scottish College of Textiles was established here in 1909 and today the **Lochcarron of Scotland**

Cashmere and Wool Centre, located within Waverley Mill in Huddersfield Street, offers tours which explain the processes involved in the manufacture of woollens and tweeds.

On the coat of arms of the old burgh appears the words "soor plooms" (sour plums), which refers to an incident in 1337 when some English troops were killed after crossing the border and found stealing plums in the town. In 1503, the betrothal of James IV to Margaret Tudor, Henry VII's daughter, took place at the town's old **Mercat Cross**. Its successor dates from 1695.

Old Gala House dates from the 15th century with later additions and at one time was the town house of the Pringles, Lairds of Gala. It is now a museum and art gallery. Its gardens have recently been re-established, with a pond, spring bulbs and rhododendrons. Exhibitions of local art are sometimes held in the house.

In Bank Street are the **Bank Street Gardens**, laid out shortly after World War II. In front of the town's war memorial (described by H.V. Morton as "the most perfect town memorial in the British Isles") is a reminder of the area's bloody past - a bronze statue of a border reiver, armed and on horseback.

Not to be missed by any devotee of Sir Walter Scott is a visit to his home for the last 20 years of his life, **Abbotsford,** a mile or so south of the town. It is a masterpiece of the Scottish

6 MAPLEHURST GUEST HOUSE

Galashiels

Magnificent Edwardian Arts & Crafts style house offering top quality en suite accommodation and excellent cuisine.

see page 353

7 CLOVENFORDS COUNTRY HOTEL

Galashiels

A beautiful hotel offering the very best in comfort and service, nestled in the heart of the Borders' countryside

see page 354

9

Every year, in July, the Braw Lads Gathering celebrates Galashiel's long history with the main event being a spectacular mounted procession. It is claimed that the event has its origins in a celebration the town mounted in 1503 to mark the marriage of James IV and Margaret Tudor, sister of Henry VIII.

Baronial style of architecture, surrounded by trim gardens and looking out over the River Tweed. Inside, visitors pass through a grand barrel-ceilinged Entrance Hall to the galleried and book-lined study where each morning at 6am Scott would seat himself at the small writing desk made of salvage from the wrecked ships of the Spanish Armada. His chair, his spectacles, the portrait of Rob Roy hanging on the wall - all remain just as he left them. In the superb Library next door, with a richly moulded ceiling copied from Rosslyn Chapel, are housed the 9000 books he collected during his lifetime along with a fascinating assortment of Scottish memorabilia, including Rob Roy's purse and skene dhu (knife), and a lock of Bonnie Prince Charlie's

hair. Elsewhere, there's a carriage clock once owned by Marie Antoinette and still keeping good time.

Perhaps the most poignant room in the house is the dining room. In September 1832, his health destroyed by overwork, Sir Walter's bed was placed here so that he could gaze out on his beloved River Tweed. On the 21st, his family was at his bedside, amongst them his son-in-law and biographer, John Lockhart: "It was a beautiful day - so warm that every window was open - and so perfectly still that the sound of all others the most delicious to his ear, the gentle ripple of the Tweed over its pebbles, was distinctly audible as we knelt around his bed, and his eldest son kissed him and closed his eyes".

The house is still lived in by Sir Walter's descendants.

The Southern Upland Way passes through Galashiels, and you can also join the 89-mile-long **Tweed Cycle Way**, which passes close by. It starts at Biggar in Lanarkshire and ends up in Berwick-upon-Tweed.

AROUND GALASHIELS

EARLSTON

12 miles E of Galashiels on the A68

The small town of Earlston is dominated by **Black Hill** which gives a good view of the surrounding countryside. One of Scotland's earliest poets, **Thomas Learmont of Earlston,** was born

Galashiels

here in about 1220. Also known as Thomas the Rhymer, Thomas of Erceldoune or True Thomas, he attained an almost supernatural status, as he was also a seer who could predict the future. His prophecies included Alexander III's death in 1285, the victory of Bruce over the English at Bannockburn in 1314 and Scotland's defeat by the English at Flodden in 1513. Some ruins in the town are supposed to be of his home, **Rhymer's Tower**.

MELROSE

3 miles SE of Galashiels just off the A6091

Melrose is an enchanting little town, set beside the River Tweed at the foot of the three peaks of the Eildon Hills. Behind the town square, the noble ruins of **Melrose Abbey** (Historic Scotland) stand in shattered glory. Founded in 1136 by David I, the original building was repeatedly attacked by the English; the present structure dates mostly from the late 1300s. Modelled on the abbeys of northern England, the building reflects the splendidly intricate Gothic style of that age. Look out for the curious gargoyle of a pig playing the bagpipes.

For centuries, tradition asserted that the heart of Robert the Bruce was buried near the abbey's high altar. In 1921, a casket was discovered beneath the Chapter House floor but not opened. Then, in 1996, using fibre optic cable, the casket was examined closely and found to contain a withered heart. It can't be proven to be the Bruce's heart but as there is no record, or legend, of any other heart being

buried at Melrose, the probability is very high. Two years later, the casket was ceremonially re-buried and a commemorative stone tablet erected.

Next door to the abbey, the inviting **Priorwood Garden** (National Trust for Scotland) specialises in growing plants suitable for dried flower arranging. The walled garden encloses an apple orchard walk, a picnic area and a shop selling the dried flowers. **Harmony Garden,** also run by the Trust, is close by. It is set around a 19th century house which is not open to the public, and has excellent views of the Eildon Hills. There are herbaceous borders, well

Harmony Garden, Melrose

A mile east of Melrose is Newstead, where there are the remains of Trimontium Roman Fort, covering 15 acres, and named after the three peaks of the Eildons. It was occupied between the late first century well into the second, and was the most important Roman settlement of the northern frontier. At its height, it housed 1500 Roman soldiers and supported a large town which covered a further 200 acres.

tended lawns and vegetable and fruit areas. It is renowned for its sense of peace and tranquillity. The house and small estate was built by Robert Waugh, a Melrose joiner, in the early 1800s after making his fortune from a Jamaica plantation called "Harmony".

Also within the abbey precincts is the 16th century Commendator's House, formerly the "Estate Office" for the abbey's extensive properties. It now houses a curious collection of ecclesiastical artefacts.

In the town itself, **The Three Hills Roman Heritage Centre**, in the Ormiston Institute in Melrose's Market Square, has displays on what life was like within a Roman settlement, and has artefacts that were found there. On Thursday afternoons (and Tuesday afternoons in July and August) a guided five mile, four hour walk to the fort leaves from the Centre.

During the second week of April each year, sedate Melrose

town is transformed when rugby fans and players from around the world gather for the **Melrose Sevens**. The game of Rugby 7s was invented here and the tournament has been held every year since 1883.

On a bend in the Tweed, two miles east of the town, is the site of **Old Melrose** (then called Mailros, meaning "bare moor"). Here, in about AD 650, Celtic monks from Iona established a monastery. Nearby, in about AD 635, a young shepherd was born. In AD 651, following a vision in which he saw the soul of St Aidan of Lindisfarne ascending to heaven, he entered the monastery to train as a monk. He eventually became Bishop of Lindisfarne, and died in AD 687. He is now known as St Cuthbert and is buried in Durham Cathedral. A 62-mile walking route called **St Cuthbert's Way** links Melrose and Lindisfarne.

The **100 Aker Wood Visitor Centre** is on the old Melrose to Newstead road, and has woodland walks, a childrens' play area, a coffee shop and car park.

DRYBURGH

9 miles SE of Galashiels off the B6356

The ruins of **Dryburgh Abbey** (Historic Scotland) must be the most romantically situated in all of Scotland, sitting as it does on a loop of the Tweed, which surrounds it on three sides. Nothing much remains of the great abbey church, except for the west door and parts of the north and

Thurlestain Caslte, Melrose

THE BORDERS

south transepts. However, the cloister buildings are remarkably well-preserved and the lovely surroundings create a sense of deep peace. Within the north transept is buried Sir Walter Scott and his wife Charlotte, as well as Field Marshall Earl Haig of Bemersyde. He was Commander-in-Chief of the British Expeditionary forces in France and Flanders during World War I.

The abbey now forms part of the 55-mile-long **Abbeys Cycle Route**, taking in the other three great Borders abbeys of Melrose, Kelso and Jedburgh. A short walk from the abbey is the 31 feet high (including pedestal) **William Wallace Statue** which depicts the great warrior rather incongruously in Roman garb. Wallace spent a lot of time in the Borders hiding from the English in Ettrick Forest. The Earl of Buchan commissioned the statue in 1814; it was the first monument erected to Wallace.

North of Dryburgh is **Scott's View**, which gives an amazing panorama of the Eildon Hills. Sir Walter Scott used to ride up here to get inspiration, and when his funeral cortege was making its way to Dryburgh, the hearse stopped for a short while. It is best accessed from the A68, where it is signposted from the Leaderfoot Viaduct that spans the Tweed.

ST. BOSWELLS
7 miles SE of Galashiels on the A68

This village is named after St Boisil, who was an abbot of the Celtic monastery at Old Melrose in the 7th century. The centrepiece of the village is its green, which hosts a fair on July 18th (St Boisil's Day) each year. In past times, this fair was one of the largest in the country, and attracted people - especially gypsies - from all over the Borders and beyond. At one time more than 1000 horses were offered for sale at the fair.

SELKIRK
6 miles S of Galashiels on the A7

The twin valleys of Ettrick and Yarrow present some of the most glorious scenery in the Borders. High on the hillside, the Ancient and Royal Burgh of Selkirk enjoys superb views across Ettrick Water. Sir Walter Scott had close connections with the town, serving as Sheriff of Selkirkshire from 1799 until 1832. There's a striking statue of him in front of the Courthouse where he presided so often and where visitors can see a video detailing Scott's associations with the area and its people.

Another statue in the High Street commemorates **Mungo Park**, the explorer and anti-slavery activist who was born in Yarrow, 7 miles to the east, in 1771. He was educated at Selkirk Grammar School and then trained as a doctor. After serving as a surgeon's mate on a ship sailing to the East Indies, he set off to map the River Niger, a project that occupied more than two and a half years. His account of that expedition, *Travels in the Interior Districts of Africa* became a best-seller. In 1806, he launched a second expedition but

A mile or so to the east of Dryburgh are Mertoun House Gardens. Though the house is not open to the public, the 26-acre gardens can be visited between April and September.

8 CLINT HOUSE COUNTRY LODGE

St Boswell's

Top class B&B or self-catering accommodation in beautifully refurbished former shooting lodge.

see page 355

13

Within Bowhill Country Park are the ruins of Newark Castle, dating from about 1450. In 1645 the Battle of Philiphaugh took place nearby, when Leslie's Covenanting army met and defeated a royal army commanded by Montrose. Leslie's prisoners were taken to Newark Castle and it was there, on September 13th 1645, that several hundred soldiers and camp followers of Montrose's army were savagely butchered. In 1810, when excavations were taking place beside the castle, bones were uncovered in a field known as "Slain Men's Lea". The tower can only be viewed from the outside.

disappeared without trace. That tragedy was mirrored 20 years later when his son followed him to Africa and also vanished.

The oldest building in Selkirk is **Halliwell's House and Robson Gallery**, just off the market square, where there is a small museum on the ground floor and an art gallery on the upper floor. The museum's most prized possession is the "Flodden Flag". Eighty men of Selkirk marched off to fight in the calamitous Battle of Flodden; only one of them returned. He stumbled into the Market Square bearing a captured English flag. Unable to express his grief, the soldier simply waved the flag towards the ground. His gesture is symbolically re-enacted each year in June during the Common Riding, one of the oldest of the Border festivals, dating back to the year of Flodden Field, 1513. As many as 500 riders take part in the ceremony.

Robert D. Clapperton Photographic in Scotts Place is a working museum and photographic archive. It traded for three generations under the family name of the founder Robert Clapperton, all using the original daylight Studio. They left a unique archive of photographic images of the life and times in which they worked and the Studio where they worked. The present proprietors, the fourth generation, demonstrate features of the studio which has been set up as a working museum and photographic archive,

At the **Selkirk Glass Visitor Centre** at Dunsdalehaugh you can see glass paperweights being made.

The Scottish Borders Archive and Local History Centre is within St Mary's Mill, and offers research facilities on local history, geography and genealogy, including the records of the old counties of Berwickshire, Selkirkshire, Roxburghshire and Peeblesshire.

BOWHILL
8 miles SW of Galashiels off the A708

The principal Scottish residence of the Duke of Buccleuch, **Bowhill** is a monumental building 437feet long, most of it built in the first half of the 19th century. The 4th Duke's kinsman and neighbour, Sir Walter Scott often travelled the 6 miles from his own home, Abbotsford, to visit the duke. He even advised on the early stages of the massive new construction. The famous portrait by Henry Raeburn of the affable poet and novelist with his beloved dog "Camp" at his feet hangs in the Scott Room at Bowhill, along with Sir Walter's plaid and the original manuscript of the *Lay of the Last Minstrel*.

Bowhill boasts a superlative collection of other works of art - family portraits by Lely and Reynolds, landscapes by Claude Lorraine and Ruysdael, as well as sumptuous French furniture and priceless displays of Meissen and Sèvres china.

The house alone provides a full and rewarding day but there's also the **Bowhill Country Park** where miles of footpaths and cycle trails criss-cross the estate. There's also a visitor centre, a restored Victorian kitchen, a display of Victorian fire engines, a tea room and the thriving **Bowhill Little Theatre**, housed in the former stables, which presents many professional plays.

ST MARY'S LOCH

16 miles SW of Galashiels on the A708

The largest loch in the Borders area, St Mary's Loch has attracted plaudits for its beauty from both Wordsworth and Sir Walter Scott. A narrow isthmus separates it from the smaller Loch of the Lowes, with a famous hostelry situated between them. Few public houses anywhere can boast such a long and well-recorded history as **Tibbie Shiel's Inn.** It takes its name from Isabella (Tibbie) Shiel, a doughty lady who in 1823 moved with her husband Robert into what was then known as St Mary's Cottage which occupied a lovely position beside the loch. Robert died the following year and Tibbie, determined to support herself and her six bairns, began taking in gentlemen lodgers. Thirteen beds were crowded into the attic and what is now the bar, but on special occasions as many as 35 were accommodated, the extra numbers being "made comfortable" on the floor. During the course of her long life (she died in 1878 in her 96th year) Tibbie became something of a national treasure, counting Sir Walter Scott amongst her friends and admirers. Her visitor's books have survived and they include such names as Robert Louis Stevenson, Thomas Carlyle

and William Ewart Gladstone. Since Tibbie's day the inn has been extended but the spirit of the place is unchanged - low-ceilinged, cosy , full of character, and hidden away in a place of incredible beauty and tranquillity. The inn is today a favourite stopping point for walkers on the Southern Upland Way which passes close by.

James Hogg, nicknamed "The Ettrick Shepherd", was also a frequent visitor to Tibbie Shiel's. He was born at nearby Ettrickhall Farm in 1770, became very popular in his time but only his macabre novel, *Confessions of a Justified Sinner*, still finds readers today. A red

Near Tibbie Shiels Inn

9   HAZEL LODGE TEA ROOM

Kelso

Popular town centre licensed tearoom/restaurant serving wholesome and appetising food.

see page 355

sandstone monument near Tibbie Shiel's commemorates his achievements.

KELSO

Sir Walter Scott considered Kelso "the most beautiful, if not the most romantic village in the land". Sir Walter was very familiar with this dignified little town, set around the meeting of the rivers Tweed and Teviot. As a boy he attended the Old Grammar School which was actually based within the melancholy ruins of **Kelso Abbey** (Historic Scotland). Founded in 1128 by David I, it became the richest and most powerful monastery in southern Scotland. Successive English invasions culminated in the Earl of Hertford's merciless attack in 1545 when all the monks were murdered and the abbey set on fire. The fine Norman and Gothic detail of the remaining transepts and façade give some idea of the glorious building that once stood here.

From Kelso's elegant and spacious cobbled **Market Square** (said to be the largest in Scotland), Bridge Street leads to John Rennie's fine 5-arched bridge over the Tweed. It was built in 1803 and Rennie was clearly pleased with his work since, some 8 years later, he used virtually the same design for his Waterloo Bridge in London.

There are grand views from the bridge of **Junction Pool,** the famous salmon fishing beat where the waters of the Tweed and Teviot mingle. If you want to try your angling skills here you must book years ahead and pay somewhere around £5000 per rod per week. Above the pool rises a high defensive mound, the site until 1550 of Roxburgh Castle. It was during a siege of the castle in 1460 that James II was killed outright when a cannon accidentally blew up in his face.

The **War Memorial Garden** in Bridge Street was part of the former abbey grounds. It has helped Kelso to win the Beautiful Scotland and Britain in Bloom competitions on several occasions. The garden was gifted to the town by the Duke of Roxburgh in 1921.

In July every year the **Kelso Civic Week** takes place, with many events that echo similar ceremonies in other Borders towns.

To the west of Kelso, within parkland overlooking the Tweed, stands the magnificent **Floors Castle**, Scotland's largest inhabited castle and the ancestral home of the Duke and Duchess of

Market Square, Kelso

Roxburghe. The original building, designed by William Adam and started in 1721, was a rather austere Georgian mansion. The mansion was transformed in the 1830s by the fashionable architect William Playfair into a dramatic masterpiece of the Scottish Baronial style, its roofs cape fretted with a panorama of stone pinnacles and turrets crowned by lead-capped domes. This palatial transformation was commissioned by the 6th Duke who had succeeded to the title at the age of seven. His father's succession had occurred under rather unusual circumstances. When the 4th Duke died childless, the inheritance was disputed between several claimants. After a 7-year legal battle, the House of Lords decided that Sir James Innes held the superior right to the title of 5th Duke. Sir James was then 76 years old and childless, prompting fears that on his death the succession would again be contested. Rising nobly to this challenge, the new duke married the youthful Harriet Charlewood and became a father for the first time in his 81st year.

The 6th Duke was a discriminating collector of works of art and the magnificent State Rooms of the castle display many fine paintings, amongst them portraits by Gainsborough, Reynolds and the Scottish artists Allan Ramsay and Henry Raeburn. The collection has since been supplemented by modern masters such as Matisse, Bonnard and Augustus John.

The extensive parkland and gardens overlooking the Tweed provide a variety of wooded walks and the walled garden contains splendid herbaceous borders. Queen Victoria visited the duke in 1876 and the summerhouse that was specially built for her can be seen in the outer walled garden.

Springfield Park is the venue, late in July each year, of the **Border Union Show** which features not only agriculture but fairground amusements, trade stands and sometimes parachutists.

Horse racing in Kelso began in 1822, and **Kelso Race Course** (known as the "Friendly Course") hosts horse racing all year.

AROUND KELSO

EDNAM

3 miles N of Kelso on the B6461

The village stands on the Eden, a tributary of the Tweed, and was the birthplace of two famous men. The first was **James Thomson**, born in September 1700, who wrote the words to *Rule Britannia*. It was written about 1740 for a masque called *Alfred*, and was soon adopted as a patriotic song. The other distinguished son of Ednam was **Henry Francis Lyte**, born in June 1793, who wrote *Abide with Me*. A plain stone obelisk to Thomson's memory has been erected at Ferniehill, to the south of the village, and the bridge over the river has a plaque commemorating Lyte, who died in Nice in France in 1847.

The Millennium Viewpoint, on the other side of the Tweed from Kelso and close to Maxwellheugh, was constructed in the year 2000, and is a vantage point for great views of the town and surrounding area.

Linton Church sits on a low mound of fine sand, which is almost certainly a natural feature. However, a local legend tells a different story. It seems that a young man was once condemned to death for murdering a priest. His two sisters pleaded for his life, saying they would carry out a specific task to atone for his crime. They would sieve tons of sand, removing all large grains, and from the small grains build a mound on which a church building could stand. The church authorities agreed to this, and the women set to work. Eventually, after many years, a mound of sand was created, and a church was indeed built on it.

KIRK YETHOLM

7 miles SE of Kelso on the B6352

The tiny conservation village of Kirk Yetholm lies little more than a mile from the Scottish-English border with the mighty Cheviot Hills rising to the south. The village is well-known to serious walkers as a stage on the 65-mile cross-border St Cuthbert's Way, and as the northern end of the gruelling 270-mile Pennine Way.

LINTON

6 miles S of Kelso on the B6436

Linton Church has Norman details, a fine Norman font and a belfry dated 1697. One Norman survival is the tympanum above the door which commemorates the killing of the **Linton Worm** by John Somerville in the 13th century. The Linton Worm was 12 feet long, and lived in a cave below the church. It terrorised the district, and the local people were powerless against it. John noticed that when it saw anything it wanted to eat, it opened its mouth wide. So he made a special spear that had inflammable materials instead of a point, and when he approached the worm on horseback with the spear blazing, it duly opened its mouth to devour him. John stuck the spear down the worm's throat, and the worm was killed. For this act the king granted him the lands of Linton.

SMAILHOLM

5 miles NW of Kelso on the B6397

Smailholm Tower (Historic Scotland) seems to grow out of a low, rocky outcrop, and is a four square 60 feet high tower which was once surrounded by a wall. Within it you can see a collection of costumed figures and tapestries connected with Scott's *Minstrelsy of the Scottish Borders*. Scott, as a child, spent a lot of time with his grandparents at the nearby farm of Sandyknowe and knew the tower well.

MELLERSTAIN

7 miles NW of Kelso on an unclassified road between the A6089 and the B6397

Ancestral home of the Earls of Haddington, **Mellerstain** is a grand mansion originally designed by William Adam in the 1720s, and completed by his son Robert in 1778. Although the exterior is rather austere, the interior is glorious. Robert Adam was at the peak of his powers and the Library at Mellerstain shows his genius at its most inventive, assured and appealing - "One of the most beautiful 18th century rooms in Europe" according to Nigel Nicolson. The lovely rooms house a remarkable collection of period furniture, family portraits and paintings by Van Dyck, Gainsborough, Allan Ramsay and many others. Outside, the attractive Italian terraces were laid out in 1910 by Sir Reginald Blomfield and give excellent views out over a small artificial loch towards the Cheviots.

HAWICK

The largest of the Border burghs,

Hawick (pronounced Hoyk) is a thriving community, its prosperity based on the manufacture of quality knitwear and carpets. The town is home to such names as Pringle of Scotland and Lyle and Scott, as well as many other smaller firms producing knitwear in cashmere, lambswool and Shetland yarns. Many of the mills in the town, such as Peter Scott and Company in Buccleuch Street and Wrights of Trowmill outside the town have visitor centres and guided tours. The Hawick Cashmere Company, based in Trinity Mills in Duke Street, has a viewing gallery and shop.

Like so many Border towns, Hawick was regularly attacked by the English. There was a particularly violent onslaught in 1570 which left scarcely a building standing. A notable exception was **Drumlanrig's Tower,** at that time a typical moated L-shaped Borders tower house. Later, the area between the two "legs" was filled in to convert it into an elegant town house. The basement was later used as a prison, and finally a wine cellar when it became a hotel. Now the tower has been restored and houses the towns' visitor information centre and an exhibition explaining the history of the Borders.

The **Hawick Common Riding** takes place in June each year, and commemorates yet another skirmish between the English and the Scots. This occurred in 1514, when some Hawick men beat off English soldiers and captured their banner.

A disagreement of a different kind took place in 1996, when two women riders tried to join what had traditionally been an all-male occasion. They faced bitter opposition but their claim was eventually upheld by the Sheriff Court.

On the edge of the town, the award-winning **Wilton Lodge Park** sits by the banks of the Teviot and has 107 acres of riverside walks, gardens, a tropical glasshouse, recreational facilities and a café. Within it is the **Hawick Museum and Scott Art Gallery**, which explains the history of the town and its industries. The gallery has a collection of 19th and 20th century Scottish paintings, and regularly hosts exhibitions of works by local and national artists.

AROUND HAWICK

DENHOLM

4 miles NE of Hawick on the A698

This pleasant small village was the birthplace of both John Leyden, poet, doctor, linguist and friend of Sir Walter Scott, and of Sir James Murray, editor of the *Oxford English Dictionary*. Leyden is commemorated by an obelisk on the green; Murray's monument is his ground-breaking dictionary of which millions of copies have been published.

MINTO

6 miles NE of Hawick off the B6405

Minto was founded in the late 1700s as a planned village by the

10 FINDLAY'S RESTAURANT

Hawick

Quaint, modern rustic restaurant offering outstanding cuisine based on fresh local produce.

🍴 see page 356

11 BRYDON'S BAKERY RESTAURANT

Hawick

Well-established town centre restaurant offering appetising selection of home-cooked food.

🍴 see page 356

12 THE STEADINGS

Chesters, nr Hawick

B&B or self-catering accommodation in beautifully converted farm outbuildings.

🛏 see page 357

A mile or so east of Ancrum, Monteviot House Gardens on the banks of the River Teviot offer a variety of gardens including a water garden of islands linked by bridges, an arboretum, greenhouses and plant stall. For a perfect family day out, combine Monteviot House with a visit to nearby Jedburgh Abbey.

2nd Earl of Minto. It was laid out by the architect William Playfair. The **Parish Church** was completed in 1831, and replaced an earlier building dating from the 13th century.

On top of Minto Crags sits the curiously named **Fatlips Castle**, built in the 16th century for the Turnbull family. It was restored in 1857 and used as a shooting lodge and private museum, though it is now ruinous.

To the east of Fatlips are the ruins of **Barnhills Tower**, another Turnbull stronghold. It was built in the 16th century, but now only a few decayed walls are left standing.

ANCRUM

13 miles NE of Hawick on the B6400

Prettily located beside Ale Water, a tributary of the River Teviot, Ancrum is a typical Borders village. Just to the north of village, one of the last of the major Border conflicts, the **Battle of Ancrum Moor,** took place in 1545. It part of what was known as the "Rough Wooing", when Henry VIII tried to force the Scots into allowing the young Mary, Queen of Scots to marry his son Edward. Three thousand English and Scottish horsemen under Lord Eure were ambushed by a hastily assembled army of Borderers. During the battle, the Scots horsemen changed sides when they saw that the Borderers were gaining the upper hand, resulting in a total rout for the English.

Harestanes Countryside Visitor Centre offers some beautiful woodland walks, activities and displays, all with a countryside theme, as well as a car park, gift shop and tearoom.

From Harestanes, it's an easy walk to the 150-feet high **Waterloo Monument** on Peniel Haugh. It was erected by the Marquis of Lothian between 1817 and 1824 to commemorate the Battle of Waterloo. Though there are stairs within the tower, it is not open to the public.

JEDBURGH

14 miles NE of Hawick on the A68

Approached along the lovely Jed valley, Jedburgh's glory is its **Abbey** (Historic Scotland)**,** magnificent even in its ruined state and still the most complete of all the Border abbeys. Built in glowing red sandstone, the abbey was founded in 1138 by David I but suffered grievously and frequently from English attacks during the interminable Border wars. In all, it was destroyed eight times by the invading English and each time, the monks painstakingly rebuilt it. But the final blow came in 1523 when the Earl of Surrey ordered the abbey to be burned.

In the abbey grounds, beside the River Jed, the **Cloister Garden** was planted in 1986, and shows what a typical monastic garden would have looked like in the early 1500s.

Some 40 years after the burning of the abbey, Scotland's monarch came to the town, a visit commemorated at **Mary, Queen of Scots House.** The name is rather misleading since Mary didn't own the house but stayed there as the guest of Sir Thomas Kerr. The exhibits include a death mask of the hapless queen and a rare portrait of her third husband, the Earl of Bothwell. The queen's host lived at **Ferniehurst Castle,** just outside the town and it is still the family home of his descendant, Lord Lothian. A magnificent example of defensive Border architecture, the castle and its Kerr Museum are open to the public during the summer months.

Every year at Candlemas (February 2nd) the **Fastern Even Handba'** game is played in the town, when the "Uppies" play the "Doonies" and chase beribboned balls through the streets of the town. Though the present game dates from the 18th century, it is thought that it had its origins in the 16th century, when the severed heads of English reivers were used instead of balls.

Five miles northeast of Jedburgh, off the A698, are the **Teviot Water Gardens**, planted on three levels above the River Tweed. There are three riverside walks, a bird hide and a café.

Jedforest Deer and Farm Park is five miles south of Jedburgh on the Mervinslaw Estate, just off the A68. It is a modern working farm with a deer herd and rare breeds. There are also birds of prey demonstrations using eagles, owls and hawks, and plenty of ranger-led activities.

Four miles beyond the Farm Park, the A68 reaches the English border at **Carter Bar** which is 1370 feet above sea level in the Cheviots. From here there is a wonderful view northwards, and it almost seems that the whole of southern Scotland is spread out before you. In the 18th century herds of sheep and cattle were driven over this route towards the markets in the south.

The last Borders skirmish, known as the **Redeswire Raid**, took place here in 1575. It took the arrival of a contingent of Jedburgh men to turn what was going to be a Scots defeat into a victory.

NEWCASTLETON

20 miles S of Hawick, on the B6357

Newcastleton, in Liddesdale, is a planned village, founded by the third Duke of Buccleuch in 1793 as a handloom-weaving centre. The **Liddesdale Heritage Centre Museum** is in the old Townfoot Kirk in South Hermitage Street, and has attractive displays about the history of the area and its people.

Every year, in July, the village holds the **Newcastleton Traditional Music Festival**, one of the oldest such festivals in Scotland. It was founded in 1970, and has concerts, ceilidhs and competitions. There are many informal music sessions held throughout the village. On the last day of the festival is the "Grand Winners Concert".

A mile from the village, off the Canonbie road, is the Millholm Cross, It has the initials AA and MA carved on it. The AA is

Jedburgh Castle Jail, in Castlegate, was a 19th century reform prison which now houses a display about the history of the town. Four miles northeast of Jedburgh are the Monteviot House Gardens which have a pinetum, a herb garden and a riverside garden linked by bridges.

The route of the present day A68 was at one time the main thoroughfare from Edinburgh to England, so Jedburgh saw many armies passing along its streets when Scotland and England were constantly at war with each other. The locals once called the town "Jethart", and it is still remembered in the expression "Jethart justice", meaning hang first and try later, a throwback to the bad old days of the reivers.

In June each year Peebles holds its Beltane Week, with the crowning of the Beltane Queen. The ceremony's origins go right back to pagan times though the present Beltane Week celebrations date only from the 19th century.

thought to be Alexander Armstrong, a reiver from nearby Mangerton Tower.

The **Dykescroft Information Centre and Newcastleton Historic Forest Walk** lie to the south of the village, off a minor road. It is closed in February and March each year. Within the forest can be seen one of the **7stanes,** seven mountain biking centres spanning the south of Scotland, from the heart of the Scottish Borders to Dumfries and Galloway. 'Stane' is the Scots word for stone, and at each of the 7stanes locations, you'll find a stone sculpture reflecting a local myth or legend. The sculpture at Newcastleton resembles the tail fin of an aircraft and faces north - south. On the north side, representing Scotland, *Auld Lang Syne* is inscribed and on the south side, representing England, the words of *Jerusalem.*

The highlight of this particular stane is that it stands right on the border between Scotland and England. The hole in the middle allows people to stand on either side of the border and shake hands through the stane.

Five miles north of Newcastleton is the massive bulk of **Hermitage Castle** (Historic Scotland). It dates from the 1300s and its imposing walls and stout defences reflect the bloody warfare that was common in this area before the union of Scotland and England. It belonged to the de Soulis family, who built the original castle of wood in the mid-13th century. However, in 1320 William de Soulis was found guilty of plotting against Robert the Bruce, and his lands and property were confiscated by the crown. The castle later became a Douglas stronghold.

While staying in Jedburgh, Mary Stuart covered the 50 miles between there and Hermitage and back again in one day to visit the Earl of Bothwell, whom she later married. During her journey, she lost a watch, which was recovered in the 19th century.

PEEBLES

The former county town of Peebles enjoys a superb position, surrounded by hills and with the River Tweed running through its centre. Spacious parklands extend along the river banks and the town itself has a genteel, almost demure charm, its houses presenting a pleasing medley of architectural styles. Though it looks peaceful enough nowadays, its history is anything but. It was burnt to the ground by the English in 1545, occupied by Cromwell in 1649, and again by Charles Edward Stuart in 1745.

The **Chambers Institute** was founded in 1859 by local man William Chambers who, with his brother Robert, went on to found the great Chambers publishing house in Edinburgh. Within the Institute is the **Tweeddale Museum and Gallery**, where the history of the town is explained. Here you can also see the extraordinary classical frieze commissioned by William Chambers which is based on parts of the Parthenon Frieze in the British Museum and on the Alexander Frieze commissioned in 1812 by Napoleon Bonaparte.

The ruins of the **Cross Kirk** (Historic Scotland), founded in 1261 as the church of a Trinitarian Friary, are to the west of the town. The Trinitarians were a monastic order founded in 1198 by St John of Math, a Frenchman, to redeem captives taken by the Saracens in the Holy Land during the Crusades. The tower of the former St Andrews Church still survives just off Neidpath Road. The present **Peebles Parish Church** is an imposing Victorian building at the west end of the High Street, a short distance from the quaintly named Cuddy Bridge over the Eddleston Water, a tributary of the Tweed. One of the hidden places of the town is to be found beyond an archway leading from the high street - the Quadrangle. Surrounding the town's war memorial are well laid out, colourful gardens.

Eastgate Theatre and Arts Centre is housed in a 19th century church. It has a programme of drama and exhibitions throughout the year, and there is a small café.

Natives of the town are known locally as "gutter bluids", while visitors or incomers to Peebles are called "stooryfits" - dusty-footed. Amongst stooryfits who made the town their home are John Buchan, the novelist, soldier and diplomat,

his sister Anna, the novelist "O. Douglas", and the surgeon and celebrated explorer of Aftica, Mungo Park.

Peebles also has the distinction of being ranked as the Top Independent Retailing Town in Scotland, and second in the UK, for its range of independent shops, in marked contrast to the ubiquitous 'cloned towns' predominant in other areas.

One mile east of Peebles off the A72 **Glentress Forest** stands. It is now the most visited tourist attraction in the Scottish Borders, and is said to have the country's best mountain biking course.

AROUND PEEBLES

KAILZIE GARDENS
3 miles E of Peebles on the B7062

Extending to 14 acres, **Kailzie Gardens** sit on the banks of the Tweed, surrounded by hills. The main part is contained in an old walled garden, plus there is a 15-acre wild garden and woodland walks among rhododendrons and azaleas. There is also a restaurant, gift shop and 18-hole putting green.

INNERLEITHEN
7 miles SE of Peebles on the A72

The Rivers Tweed and Leithen meet in this charming little town which was the model for Sir Walter Scott's St Ronan's Well. It used to be a spa town and the **St. Ronan's Well Interpretive Centre** at Well's Brae explains the history of the wells, whose waters were full of sulphur and other minerals. You

13 THE SHIELING GUEST HOUSE

Eshiels, nr Peebles

A beautiful guest house located in an idyllic rural area, close to the gateway of the Glentress Forest

see page 357

Innerleithen

Fine old hostelry offering cask-conditioned ales, good food and en suite rooms; also spacious beer garden.

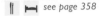

see page 358

River Tweed, nr Innerleithen

can even sample the water if you're brave enough.

In the High Street is **Robert Smail's Printing Works** (National Trust for Scotland). This was a genuine print works that still retained many of its original features and fittings when taken over by the Trust in 1987. Now you can see how things were printed more than a century ago, and even have a go at typesetting yourself.

TRAQUAIR

8 miles SE of Peebles on the B709

Traquair is a small village visited mostly for the magnificent **Traquair House,** set beside the River Tweed. It is the oldest house in Scotland to have been continuously inhabited by the same family, the first of the line being James Stuart who took up residence in 1491. In its time, 27 kings and queens have visited the place, including Alexander I in the 11th century, Edward I of England (known as the "Hammer of the

Scots") in the 13th, and Mary Stuart in the 16th. One laird of Traquair fell with his king at Flodden, and in the 18th century the then laird, the fifth Earl of Traquair, supported the Jacobite cause.

Charles Edward Stuart visited in 1745, and when he left, the laird closed the **Bear Gates** at the end of the long drive, vowing that they would never be opened until a Stuart ascended the British throne once more. They have remained firmly closed ever since.

The long and romantic history of the Stuarts of Traquair comes alive in every part of this fascinating house, - in the exquisite 18th century Library, in the corkscrewing stone staircases, and in family mementoes like the list compiled by the 4th Earl's wife detailing the 17 children, including two sets of twins, which she presented to her husband over a period of 14 years. The Stuarts reverted to Roman Catholicism in the early 17th century and within the house are secret passages and priests' holes.

In 1965, the then laird renovated the brewhouse which lies beneath the private chapel, and the **Traquair House Brewery** now produces a fine range of ales which can be bought in the estate shop. It is said that when Charles Edward Stuart visited, he too enjoyed a glass or two of Traquair Ale.

At the beginning of August each year the **Traquair Fair** is held, with music, dance, theatre, puppetry and children's entertainment.

Dawyck Botanical Gardens, Stobo

STOBO

5 miles SW of Peebles on the B712

Stobo Kirk, one of the oldest and most beautiful in the area, has a Norman tower, nave and chancel, with some later features and additions. The 19th century mansion, **Stobo Castle,** is set in some lovely grounds and is now one of Scotland's most luxurious health farms and spa.

Two miles south, along the B712, is the **Dawyck Botanic Garden and Arboretum**, an outpost of the National Botanic Gardens in Edinburgh. It sits beside the Scrape Burn, another tributary of the Tweed, and houses a unique collection of conifers, rhododendrons and other tree species within its 50 acres.

The original garden was laid out in the late 1600s by Sir James Naesmyth, who imported trees and shrubs from North America. In 1832 the garden was landscaped by Italian gardeners who built bridges, terraces and steps.

BROUGHTON

10 miles SW of Peebles, on the A701

Broughton is forever associated with the author and Governor-General of Canada, John Buchan, whose most famous work is undoubtedly *The Thirty Nine Steps.* Though born in Perth, his maternal grandparents farmed nearby, and his father, a Free Church minister, married his mother in the village. The old free kirk is now the **John Buchan Centre,** with displays about his life and writings. The village is also home to the famous Broughton Ales and to the excellent **Broughton Gallery,** housed in a castle-like mansion designed in 1937 by Sir Basil Spence.

NEIDPATH CASTLE

1 mile W of Peebles on the A72

Neidpath Castle stands dramatically on a steep bluff

One of the many streets in West Linton is quaintly called Teapot Lane, as a tap once stood here where the women of the village drew water into teapots to make tea.

overlooking the River Tweed. Its 14th century walls are more than 10 feet thick but when Cromwell's artillery relentlessly pounded them with cannon, the castle's owner, the Earl of Tweeddale, was forced to surrender.

In the 18th century the castle passed to the Douglas family, Dukes of Queensberry. In 1795, when the 2nd Duke found himself strapped for cash he ordered the felling of every marketable tree on the estate. This spectacular act of environmental vandalism resulted in the duke becoming the target of a wrathful sonnet by William Wordsworth which begins with the words "Degenerate Douglas…"

Sir Walter Scott visited

Neidpath frequently when his friend, Adam Ferguson, rented it at the end of the 18th century. It is the epitome of a Scottish tower house, and originally consisted of three great vaulted halls, one above the other (though the top vault was subsequently removed and replaced by a timber roof), reached by winding stone staircases. Below what was the guardroom, there is a genuine dungeon into which prisoners were sometimes lowered and in many cases forgotten about. Mary Stuart and James VI both visited the castle, and a series of Batik wall hangings depict Mary's tragic life.

WEST LINTON
12 miles NW of Peebles, just off the A702

West Linton is a delightful village, and one of the hidden gems of Peeblesshire. The picturesque **St Andrews Parish Church** of 1781 stands in the middle of the village, and the surrounding gravestones testify to the craftsmanship of the many stone carvers who used to live in the area. The local **Whipman Ceremonies** take place in June each year. They originated in 1803, when some local agricultural workers decided to form a benevolent society known as the "Whipmen of Linton". Now the weeklong festivities include honouring the Whipman (meaning a carter) and his Lass. In the centre of the village stands **Lady Gifford's Well**, with a stone carving of 1666 on one of its sides.

Neidpath Castle, Peebles

Dumfries & Galloway

Turn west off the A74(M) at Gretna Green and discover what the local Tourist Board calls "Scotland's best-kept secret". Well, they would say that, wouldn't they, but it's true that most visitors press on northwards and miss one of the most beautiful and unspoiled areas of the country.

More than 200 miles of superb coastline offer an infinite variety of beaches, bays and inlets. Inland stretch the vast expanses of the Galloway Forest Park where a patient observer may well spot a peregrine falcon or a golden eagle, and just within the Dumfries & Galloway border is the highest village in Scotland, Wanlockhead, 1500 feet above sea level.

The towns of Dumfries and Moffat are as appealing as any in Scotland and the region boasts more than its fair share of historic buildings, most notably romantic

Sweetheart Abbey, the mighty medieval fortress of Caerlaverock Castle, and the palatial 16th century Drumlanrig Castle, Dumfriesshire home of the Duke of Buccleuch.

The area also has strong literary connections. Thomas Carlyle was born at Ecclefechan and the even more illustrious Robert Burns spent the last 8 years of his life in and around Dumfries.

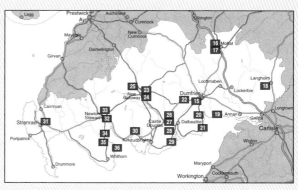

Dumfries

Unky Dunks is a must stop for a quick bite to eat in a cosy atmosphere or to sample some home made food.

see page 358

DUMFRIES

The Royal Burgh of Dumfries certainly lives up to its nickname of the "Queen of the South". It has a lovely location on the banks of the River Nith, and was once voted the town with the best quality of life in Britain.

The town is forever associated with Scotland's national poet, Robert Burns. Though born in Ayrshire, he moved to the town in 1791 to take up the improbable post of Excise Officer in charge of tobacco duties. At first, Burns lodged in a house in Bank Street, at that time a noisome alley leading down to the river which he nicknamed "Stinking Vennel", vennel being the Scots word for alley. He later moved to a more salubrious dwelling in Mill Street on the edge of town. He lived here from 1793 until his death from rheumatic heart disease in 1796 at the early age of 37. The building is now open to the public as **Burns' House.** Although not a grand house, it was nonetheless a substantial building for its day, showing that by the end of his life Burns had achieved some form of financial stability due to his work as an exciseman. On display are letters and manuscripts, the pistol he carried with him on his rounds and the chair in which he sat when he wrote his last poems.

Burns was buried in a simple grave in the churchyard of nearby St Michael's Church, a Georgian building only a few years older than himself. Twenty years later, his body was exhumed and re-interred in a splendid, columned **Burns Mausoleum** which also contains a finely-executed statue of Scotland's national bard communing with the Muse of Poetry. Also buried here are his wife, Jean Armour, and five of their family.

Another statue was erected to his memory in the Market Square, now also re-named as **Burns Statue Square**. This statue is a sentimental Victorian presentation of the roisterer and libertine as a clean-cut young fellow, clutching a posy of flowers in one hand and with a faithful canine curled around his feet.

A more authentic image of the partying poet is conjured up at the **Globe Inn** in the High Street. This down-to-earth hostelry first opened its doors in 1610 and was one of Burns' most favoured drinking dens, or "howffs" as they were called. His preferred armchair is still in place but before settling down in it, be warned that anyone who does can be called upon to buy a round of drinks for everyone present.

The most comprehensive record of Burns' five year residence in the town can be found at the **Robert Burns Centre** (free). Located on the west bank of the Nith and housed in an old water mill, it tells the full story of the poet and his connections with the town. There is a fascinating scale model of Dumfries in the 1790s and a haunting audio-visual presentation (for which there is a small charge), as well as a bookshop and a café-gallery with a lively exhibition programme.

Another writer associated with Dumfries is JM Barrie. Though not born here, he attended Dumfries Academy, a handsome building in Academy Street. While at the school, he stayed in a house in George Street and later admitted that the games of pirates he and his friends played in the garden sloping down to the Nith gave him the idea for Peter Pan and Captain Hook.

Dumfries boasts many handsome 18th century buildings. One of the most interesting is **Midsteeple** which dominates the High Street and was erected in 1707 as town hall, courthouse and prison. On its southern wall is a carving of an ell, an old Scots cloth measurement of about 37 inches. There is also a table of distances from Dumfries to various important Scottish towns. One of the towns however, is in England - Huntingdon. Three successive Scottish kings in medieval times held the earldom of Huntingdon, and it was one of the places where Scottish drovers took cattle to market in the 17th and 18th centuries.

In Shakespeare Street stands, rather appropriately, the famous **Theatre Royal**, the oldest working theatre in Scotland, dating from 1792. Burns regularly attended performances here. In contrast, Dumfries's newest attraction is **Organised Chaos** on Lockerbie Road. This activity centre has a paint ball arena and a purpose-built, all terrain 800 metre track for off-road buggies.

Dumfries proper sits on the east bank of the Nith. On the west, up until it was amalgamated into Dumfries in 1929, was the separate burgh of Maxwelltown, which was in Kirkcudbrightshire. Joining the two towns is **Devorgilla's Bridge**. Though the present bridge dates from 1431, the original structure was built by Devorgilla, Lady of Galloway, in the 13th century. Her poignant story of deep love and grievous loss is recounted later in this chapter under the entry for New Abbey.

At the Maxwellton end of the bridge is the **Old Bridge House Museum**, with exhibits and displays illustrating everyday life in the town. The museum building dates from 1660, and is built into the structure of the bridge. Also on the Maxwellton side of the river is **Dumfries Museum**, housed in an 18th century windmill, and with a Camera Obscura that gives fascinating views of the town.

Devorgilla's Bridge, Dumfries

To the east of Dumfries at Heathhall is the Dumfries and Galloway Aviation Museum, run by a group of amateur enthusiasts. It has three floors of displays in what was the control tower of the old airfield of RAF Tinwald Downs. It holds a fascinating collection of military aircraft, both propeller and jet driven, as well as engines, memorabilia and photographs.

On the northern outskirts of the town, but now surrounded by modern housing, are the beautiful red sandstone remains of **Lincluden College** (Historic Scotland). Built originally in 1164 as a Benedictine nunnery by Uchtred, Lord of Galloway, it was suppressed in the late 14th century by Archibald the Grim, third Earl of Douglas, and replaced by a collegiate church. The present ruins date from that time. One of its main features is the elaborate canopied tomb of Princess Margaret, daughter of Robert III.

Two miles out of town, the cathedral-style **Crichton Memorial Church** was designed by Sydney Mitchell and built between 1890-1897 as part of a mental hospital. It has an ornate oak roof, a striking floor of Irish and Sicilian marble, some impressive stained glass and a magnificent organ with richly carved screens.

For those interested in genealogy, the Dumfries and Galloway Family History Research Centre in Glasgow Street must be visited. There are archives, fiches and books about local history and families, though there is a modest fee for the use of the facilities.

AROUND DUMFRIES

AE

8 miles N of Dumfries on a minor road off the A701

The small village of Ae is famous for having the shortest name of any town or village in Britain, and for having the only place name with no consonant in it. It takes its name from the Water of Ae, and was founded in 1947 to house forestry workers. It is set in a great conifer forest which has some good walks and footpaths.

WANLOCKHEAD

28 miles N of Dumfries on the B797

People are usually surprised to discover that Scotland's highest village isn't in the Highlands, but in the Lowlands. Wanlockhead, in the Lowther Hills, is 1531 feet above sea level, and is a former lead mining village which is right on the Southern Upland Way. It is best approached from the A76, passing through one of the most beautiful and majestic glens in southern Scotland - the **Mennock Pass**. As you drive up, keep your eyes open for a small cross laid flat into the grass on the north side of the road. It commemorates Kate Anderson, a nurse who was killed here in 1925 when she was returning to Sanquhar after attending a patient. She fell off her bicycle in a snowstorm and broke her neck.

In the middle of Wanlockhead, in what was the village smithy, you'll find the **Museum of Lead Mining**, which explains all about the industry, and gives you the opportunity to go down the **Lochnell Mine**, a former working mine.

The **Miners' Library** is situated on a rise above the museum, and was founded in 1756 by 35 men. At the height of its popularity it had 3000 books on its shelves. The Library also houses detailed records of mining operations from 1739 and 1854, and a fascinating photographic collection that includes many pictures of the Leadhills and Wanlockhead Light Railway which had a precarious existence between 1901 and 1938. The Library was originally named after the poet Allan Ramsay who was born in the village around 1685 and whose son, also Allan, was to become one of Scotland's greatest painters.

Within the village you'll also find the **Beam Engine**, which has recently been restored. It used to pump water from one of the mines using, curiously enough, water to power it. Also in the village are the **Straitsteps Cottages** where you can experience what it was like to live as a miner in the 18th and 19th centuries. One cottage depicts a cottage interior around 1740 and the second around 1890. The artefacts on show, illustrate how the people of Wanlockhead lived, worked and played and the tour guide explains how the miners' families lived during these two time periods.

The **Leadhills and Wanlockhead Light Railway** is Britain's highest adhesion railway, reaching 1498 feet above sea level. It was originally built to take refined lead to Scotland's central belt, but finally closed in 1938. Now a length of two-feet gauge track has been re-opened between Wanlockhead and its twin village of Leadhills, and trips are available at weekends during the summer.

TORTHORWALD

4 miles NE of Dumfries on the A709

Within the village, on a narrow road off the A709, is the **Cruck Cottage**, an early 18th century example of a thatched cottage made in the traditional way, with "crucks", or thick, curved wooden supports. They were placed some yards apart within holes in the ground so that they leaned towards each other, forming the shape of an "A". This particular cottage was simply constructed on 3 massive oak cruck frames, fastened together with only oak pegs.

The ruined 14th century **Torthorwald Castle** was once a stronghold of the Carlyle and Kirkpatrick families. In 1544 Lord Carlyle destroyed the castle during a dispute with his sister-in-law.

LOCHMABEN

9 miles NE of Dumfries on the A709

Lochmaben is a small royal burgh in Annandale. In the vicinity are many small lochs in which is found the vendace, a rare species of fish with a stream-lined body and protruding lower jaw.

Near the Castle Loch stand the scant remains of **Lochmaben Castle** (Historic Scotland), which originally covered 16 acres. It can only be viewed from the outside.

About three miles to the southwest is Skipmyre, where **William Paterson** was born. He was the driving force behind the ill-fated Darien Scheme of 1698, which sought to establish a Scottish colony in modern day Panama.

Lead is not the only metal associated with Wanlockhead. In olden days, Wanlockhead was known as "God's Treasure House in Scotland" because of the gold found there. In fact, the Scottish crown was refashioned for James V in the 16th century from gold mined here. The largest nugget of gold ever discovered in the UK was found close to Wanlockhead. It weighed all of two pounds, and was the size of a cricket ball. Gold panning is still a popular activity in the local streams, and the UK National Gold Panning Championships are held here every May.

Lochmaben Castle

1988. On the evening of December 21st, Pan Am flight 103 exploded in mid-air after a terrorist bomb was detonated within its hold. The cockpit crashed into a field at Tundergarth, two-and-a-half miles east of the town, and its fuselage crashed into the town itself, killing all the passengers and crew, as well as 11 people on the ground. **Remembrance Garden** is situated within the town cemetery to the west of the motorway on the A709. It is a peaceful spot, though there is still an air of raw emotion about the place, and no one visits without developing a lump in the throat.

On December 6th, 1593 the **Battle of Dryfe Sands** took place on the banks of the Dryfe Water north of the town. The two great families in the area - the Maxwells and the Johnstones - were forever fighting about who should be the dominant family on the western border. Eventually the Maxwells brought things to a head by marching into Johnstone territory with 2,000 men. The Johnstones could only muster 400, and a Maxwell victory seemed to be a foregone conclusion. However, when they met in battle at Dryfe Sands, the Johnstones won the day, killing over 700 Maxwells.

To the south of the town is **Burnswark**, where 2nd century Roman forts are built on the site of an Iron Age fort.

Many Scots who went to Central America perished there, and it almost bankrupted the country. He was more successful in another venture - he proposed the creation of the Bank of England in 1690 and in the face of political hostility succeeded in 1694.

LOCKERBIE

12 miles NE of Dumfries off the M74

This quiet market town in Annandale is remembered for one thing - the Lockerbie Disaster of

MOFFAT

19 miles NE of Dumfries on the A701

Boasting one of the broadest High Streets in Scotland, Moffat is also one of the most pleasing small towns in the country. It stands beside the River Annan, surrounded by Lowland hills, at the heart of a thriving sheep-farming district. The town's dependence on sheep is symbolised by the striking **Colvin Fountain** at the top of the High Street. It is surmounted by a bronze sculpture of a sturdy ram although unfortunately it was accidentally cast without any ears.

Moffat has been attracting visitors ever since Rachel Whiteford, the minister's daughter, discovered Moffat Well in 1633 and its history as a spa town began. A steady stream of distinguished visitors sampled the 'magic waters', amongst them Robert Burns and James Boswell who came in 1766 "to wash off a few scurvy spots which the warmer clime of Europe had brought out on my skin".

In 1878 the grandiose Moffat Hydropathic was built. At its peak, the 300-bedroomed hotel was welcoming some 25,000 guests each year. Sadly, the Hydro was totally destroyed by fire in 1921 and Moffat's status as a spa town never recovered.

Moffat was the birthplace, in 1882, of Air Chief Marshal Lord Dowding, architect of the Battle of Britain. A statue of him can be found in Station Park. Though he wasn't born in the town, John Loudon McAdam, the great road builder, is buried in the old kirkyard at the south end of the High Street. He lived at Dumcrieff House, outside the town, and died in 1836. Dorothy Emily Stevenson,

better known as the novelist DE Stevenson, was born in Edinburgh but lived in Moffat and died there in 1973. She is buried in the local cemetery.

The small **Moffat Museum** at The Neuk, Church Gate, charts the history of the town and the people associated with it, including Dowding, McAdam and Stevenson.

The **Black Bull Inn** is one of the oldest in Dumfriesshire, and dates from 1568. Burns was a regular visitor, and Graham of Claverhouse used it as his headquarters while hunting Covenanters in the district. Another hostelry in Moffat that has a claim to fame, albeit a more unusual one, is the **Star Hotel** in the High Street. It is only 20 feet wide, making it the narrowest hotel in Britain. On the other side of the road is the former **Moffat House**, designed by John Adam for the Earl of Hopetoun and dating from 1750s. It, too, is now a hotel.

Two miles east of the town, on the A708, are **Craiglochan Gardens**, which are open during the summer months. They extend to four acres, and there is a small nursery.

TWEEDSWELL

24 miles NE of Dumfries, well off the A701

Tweedswell is the source of the Tweed, and sits 1250 feet above sea level. A topographical oddity here is that within an area of no more than a few square miles, three rivers rise. The Tweed flows east, the Annan flows south, and the Clyde flows north.

16 ANNANDALE ARMS HOTEL

Moffat

250-year-old town centre hotel with award-winning restaurant and recently refurbished en suite bedrooms.

🛏 ‖ *see page 359*

17 BUCCLEUCH ARMS HOTEL

Moffat

A comfortable and friendly hotel that has retained much of its original character and charm.

🛏 ‖ *see page 360*

33

Nearby is a great hollowed-out area among the hills known as the Devil's Beef Tub. In olden times, border reivers used to hide their stolen cattle here. To the east towers the 2651-feet high **Hartfell**, supposedly the seat of Merlin the Magician in Arthurian days.

ESKDALEMUIR

25 miles NE of Dumfries on the B709

Eskdalemuir, high in the hills, holds one of Dumfriesshire's hidden gems. The Samye Ling Centre, founded in 1967 by two refugee Tibetan abbots, is the largest Tibetan Buddhist monastery in Western Europe. Not only is it a monastery, it is a place where Tibetan culture, customs and art are preserved. To see its colourful Eastern buildings, its flags flying and its prayer wheels revolving in what is a typical Scottish moorland setting, comes as a great surprise.

Close by is **Eskdalemuir Geomagnetic Observatory**, opened in 1908. It was built here for an unusual reason. The observatory was originally at Kew in London, but the sensitive geomagnetic instruments used to measure the earth's magnetic field were affected by the overhead electricity lines used to power trams.

It was at Eskdalemuir in June 1953 that the highest short-term rainfall for Scotland was recorded - 3.15 inches in half an hour. This represents about 15 per cent of Scotland's average annual rainfall

GREY MARE'S TAIL

29 miles NE of Dumfries just off the A708

The A708 winds northeast from the town, and takes you past St Mary's Loch as you head for Selkirk. About eight miles along the road is a waterfall called **The Grey Mare's Tail** (National Trust for Scotland), fed by the waters of tiny Loch Skeen, high in the hills. The surrounding area has changed little since the 17th century, when it was a hiding place for Covenanters. It is now a 2150-acre nature reserve,

The Grey Mare's Tail

and is rich in fauna and flora, including a herd of wild goats. During the summer months there is a programme of guided walks starting from the visitor centre.

LANGHOLM

31 miles NE of Dumfries on the A7

Though within Dumfriesshire, the "muckle toon" of Langholm, in Eskdale, is more of a Borders town than a Dumfries and Galloway one. It was here, in 1892, that Christopher Murray Grieve the poet - better known as **Hugh McDiarmid** - was born, though it took many years for the people of the town to formally acknowledge his undoubted contribution to Scottish literature. Also born in the town, but not a native, was **James Robertson Justice** the actor and stalwart of 1950s and 60s British cinema. His mother was passing through and was forced to stop at the Crown Hotel, where he was delivered.

The **Armstrong Clan Museum** at Lodge Walk in Castleholm traces the history of one of the greatest Borders family. **Langholm Castle**, which is ruinous (though there has been some restoration work done on it) dates from the 16th century, and stands at the confluence of the River Esk and the Ewes Water. It can be accessed from the car park beside the museum. On the last Friday in July the annual **Common Riding Ceremony** is held in the town.

On a hillside to the east of the town is the **Malcolm Monument**, in memory of Sir John Malcolm, who died in 1833. He was born at Burnfoot, a farm near Langholm, in 1769, and became a major-general who distinguished himself in India.

WESTERKIRK

35 miles NE of Dumfries on the B709

The parish of Westerkirk lies a few miles north west of Langholm, and it was here that **Thomas Telford** the great civil engineer was born in 1757. The son of a shepherd, he left school at 14 and was apprenticed to a stone mason in Langholm. However, he was destined for greater things and rose to be the greatest civil engineer of his generation, building the Ellesmere Canal, the Caledonian Canal and the Menai Straits Bridge in Wales.

Within the parish is the unique **Bentpath Library**, founded in 1793 for the use of the antimony miners who used to work in the nearby Meggat Valley. It is still in use today, though only the people of the local parishes may borrow from its stock of 8000 books. On his death in 1834, Thomas Telford bequeathed money to it.

DALTON

9 miles E of Dumfries on the B7020

This little village has some picturesque cottages dating from the mid-1700s. Half a mile west, on a minor road, is **Dalton Pottery**, which sells a range of porcelain giftware. Young and old alike can also have fun decorating pots and tiles using ceramic felt-tipped pens,

Langholm is Armstrong country, and when Neil Armstrong, the first man to set foot on the moon, came here in 1972, he was given the freedom of the burgh.

18 ESKDALE HOTEL

Langholm

Former coaching inn with many amenities including varied dining facilities and quality en suite accommodation.

see page 361

which are fired in a small kiln and ready to take away the same day. You can also throw a pot on a wheel, though you have to return to collect it some time later.

ECCLEFECHAN

13 miles E of Dumfries on the B7076

This trim little village was the birthplace in 1795 of Thomas Carlyle, a towering figure in the literary life of 19th century Britain. Carlyle's strict Calvinist upbringing imbued his prolific writings with a stern moralism which, together with his intellectual rigour and often pedantic prose do not endear him to modern readers. He was born in The Arched House, now Carlyle's Birthplace (National Trust for Scotland), which was built on the main street by Thomas's father and uncle, who were both master masons. The three rooms of the museum contain many of Carlyle's possessions and provide a fascinating insight into nineteenth century life in a small Scottish town. The birthplace has been open to the public since 1883 and has changed very little in that time and so gives an authentic insight into a Victorian household.

KIRKCONNEL (KIRTLEBRIDGE)

18 miles E of Dumfries off J20 of the M74

In the kirkyard of the ruined Kirkconnel Church are said to be the graves of **Fair Helen of Kirkconnel Lee** and her lover Adam Fleming. Their story is a romantic one, and has been celebrated in a famous ballad..

Helen Irving was loved by two men, Adam Fleming and a man named Bell (whose first name isn't known) of nearby Bonshawe Tower. Helen found herself drawn towards Adam, and Bell was consumed with jealousy. He therefore decided to kill his rival. He waylaid the couple close to the kirkyard, and pulled out a pistol. As he fired, Helen threw herself in front of her lover, and was shot dead. There are two versions of the story after this. One says that Adam killed Bell where he stood, and another says he pursued him to Madrid, where he killed him. Either way, he was inconsolable, and joined the army. But he could never forget Helen, and one day he returned to Kirkconnel, lay on her tombstone, and died of a broken heart. He was buried beside her. It's a poignant tale, but there is no proof that the events actually took place.

CANONBIE

26 miles E of Dumfries on the B6357

Canonbie means the "town of the canons", because a priory once stood here. The English destroyed it in 1542, and some of the stones may have been used in the building of Hollows Bridge across the River Esk, Scotland's second fastest flowing river. This is the heart of the Debatable Lands, and was a safe haven for reivers. Beyond the bridge, and marked by a stone and plaque, is the site of Gilnockie Castle, home of Johnnie Armstrong, one of the greatest reivers of them all. So much of a threat was he to the relationship between Scotland and England that James V hanged him in 1530. The story goes that Johnnie and his men were invited to a great gathering at Carlanrig in Teviotdale where they would meet the king, who promised them safe passage. Taking him at his word, Johnnie and a band of men set out. However, when they got there, James had them all strung up on the spot. Perhaps the most amazing aspect of this tale is that the king was no world-weary warrior, but an 18-year-old lad at the time.

Gilnockie Tower, which dates from the 16th century, was a roofless ruin until 1980, but now it houses a small museum and Clan Armstrong library.

The Scots Dyke, two miles south of the village, was erected in the 16th century in an attempt to delineate the boundary between Scotland and England. It consists of a "dyke", or low, earthen wall and an accompanying ditch.

RUTHWELL
12 miles SE of Dumfries off the B724

Within the Parish Church of 1800 is the famous 18-feet high **Ruthwell Cross**. It dates from about AD 800 when this part of Scotland was within the Anglian kingdom of Northumbria. The carvings show scenes from the Gospels, twining vines and verses from an old poem called *The Dream of the Rood*, at one time thought to have been written by Caedmon of Whitby.

In 1810, the Revd Henry

Duncan founded the world's first savings bank in the village. The original Ruthwell Parish Bank is now home to the **Savings Banks Museum** (free). The eighteenth century building houses a collection of early home savings boxes, coins and bank notes from many parts of the world.

ANNAN
16 miles SE of Dumfries, on the A75

The picturesque old Royal Burgh of Annan, even though it is a mile from the coast, was once a thriving seaport, and had a boat-building yard. Even today there is a small, silted up quay on the River Annan. The Burns Cairn stands nearby commemorating the fact that Robert Burns visited here as an excise man.

The predominant stone in the town is red sandstone, epitomised by the handsome **Town Hall** of 1878, which dominates the High Street.

Hugh Clapperton the explorer was born in the town in 1788. At the age of 13 he became a cabin boy on a ship sailing between Liverpool and North America, and later went to the Mediterranean after being press ganged into the Royal Navy. He died in Nigeria in 1827 while searching for the source of the Niger. His notebooks and diaries have been published under the name *Difficult and Dangerous Roads*. . In Bank Street is the **Historic Resources Centre**, a small museum that puts on a programme of displays and exhibitions.

19 SAVINGS BANK MUSEUM

Ruthwell

A fascinating collection of early savings boxes, coins and bank notes.

 see page 360

Haaf Net Fishing is a means of catching fish that stretches back to Viking times, and it is still carried out at the mouth of the River Annan from April to August each year. The fishermen stand chest deep in the water wielding large haaf nets, which are attached to long wooden frames. In 1538 James V granted the haaf net fishermen of Annan a royal charter. In 1992 the rights of the fishermen were challenged in court by the owners of a time-share development further up the river, but the judge decided that the charter still held good today.

South of the town, at one time, was the **Solway Viaduct**, a railway bridge that connected Dumfriesshire to Cumbria across the Solway Firth. It was opened for passenger trains in 1870, and at the time was the longest railway bridge across water in Britain. In 1881 parts of the bridge were damaged when great ice flows smashed into its stanchions. The then keeper of the bridge, John Welch, plus two colleagues, remained in their cabin on the bridge as the lumps of ice, some as big as 27 yards square, careered into the bridges' supports. At 3.30 in the morning, when disaster seemed imminent, they were ordered to leave. Two lengths of the bridge, one 50 feet long, and one 300 feet long, collapsed into the firth, and 37 girders and 45 pillars were smashed beyond repair. However, unlike the Tay Bridge disaster, there was no loss of life. Finally, in 1934, the bridge was dismantled, and all that is left to see nowadays are the approaches on both shores, and a stump in the middle of the water.

POWFOOT
16 miles SE of Dumfries on a minor road off the B724

Today Powfoot is a quiet village on the Solway coast. But in the late 19th and early 20th centuries plans were laid to make it a grand holiday resort with hotels, formal gardens, woodland walks, a promenade, a pier, golf courses and bowling greens. The whole scheme eventually collapsed, though some of the attractions were actually built. Now the village is famous for its red brick housing and terraces, which look incongruous on the shores of the Solway but wouldn't look out of place in Lancashire.

EASTRIGGS
18 miles SE of Dumfries on the A75

A huge government works manufacturing explosives and gunpowder once stretched from Longtown in the east to Annan in the west, a total of nine miles. The **Eastriggs Heritage Project,** in St John's Church on Dunedin Road, traces the lives of the 30,000 workers who manufactured what Sir Arthur Conan Doyle called "The Devil's Porridge". At its height the whole complex employed more than 30,000 people from all over the United Kingdom.

KIRKPATRICK FLEMING
20 miles SE of Dumfries off the M74

This pleasant little village is visited mainly to see **Robert the Bruce's Cave**, where the great man is supposed to have seen the industrious spider, though similar claims are made for other caves in both Scotland and Ireland. Sir William Irving hid Robert the Bruce here for three months while he was being hunted by the English.

GRETNA GREEN
24 miles SE of Dumfries on the A75

This small village, just across the border from England, is the "romance" capital of Britain. In the 18th century it was the first stopping place in Scotland for coaches travelling north, so was the ideal place for English runaways to get married.

In 1754 irregular marriages in England were made illegal and the legal age at which people could get married without parental consent was set at 21. However, in Scotland matrimonial law merely required a declaration by the couple in front of any two witnesses. This relaxed attitude attracted many English runaway couples and since Gretna Green was the first village across the border, and the blacksmith's shop the closest dwelling to the coach stop, it was here that most of them "solemnised" their marriages in front of the anvil. The Anvil Priests, as they became known, charged anything from a dram of whisky to a guinea to conduct what was a perfectly legal ceremony. By 1856, the number of weddings had dropped, due to what was called the "Lord Brougham Act", which required that at least one of the parties to the marriage had to have been resident in Scotland for the previous 21 days. This act was only repealed in 1979.

However, couples still come from all over the world to get married before the anvil in Gretna Green, though the ceremony is no more than a confirmation of vows taken earlier in the registry office. The **Old Blacksmith's Shop** is still open and houses an exhibition on the irregular marriage trade.

Gretna Green was within the Debatable Lands, a stretch of land which, as its name implies, was claimed by both Scotland and England. It was therefore a lawless area in the 15th and 16th centuries, as no country's laws were recognised, and no one could adequately police it.

About a mile to the southwest is the Lochmaben Stone, a huge rock where representatives from the two countries met to air grievances and seek justice. It is also sometimes known as the "Clochmaben" Stone, Maben being a shadowy figure associated with King Arthur.

In the nearby village of Gretna is the Gretna Gateway Outlet Village, a complex of shops selling designer label fashions.

NEW ABBEY

6 miles S of Dumfries on the A710

The story of **Sweetheart Abbey** (Historic Scotland) and Lady Devorgilla has been told many times but remains as touching as ever. In 1230, Devorgilla, daughter of Alan, last of the Kings of Galloway, married John Balliol, a marriage that by all accounts was supremely happy. There were a few setbacks, however. John Balliol managed to offend the powerful Prince-Bishop of Durham and as part of his penance was obliged to finance a hostel for students at Oxford, a modest establishment that his wife later expanded into Balliol College.

John died in 1268 and Devorgilla, grief-stricken, had his heart embalmed and for the 21 years of her widowhood carried it with her in a casket of silver and

39

New Abbey

A fascinating establishment, housing a collection of unique costumes from Charles Stewart.

 see page 360

ivory. She was now one of the richest women in Europe, owning most of Galloway along with estates in England and Normandy. She spent lavishly on founding several religious houses in memory of her husband, amongst them Dulce Cor, "Sweet Heart", at New Abbey. It was here, in 1289, that she was buried beneath the High Altar together with her husband's heart. Sweetheart Abbey today is one of the finest sights in the country, a romantic ruin of rose-red stone that seems to glow in the setting sun.

New Abbey has been described as "the most perfect unspoiled village in Galloway". Take time to walk to the elegant bridge built in 1715 and then up through the avenue of Scots pines planted between 1775 and 1780 to enjoy the classically romantic views over the beck to Sweetheart Abbey.

In the village itself is the **New Abbey Corn Mill** (Historic Scotland), dating from the late 18th century. It is in full working order, and there are regular demonstrations on how a water powered mill works. The original mill on the site is thought to have belonged to the monks of Sweetheart Abbey.

Shambellie House is a large mansion designed by David Bryce on the outskirts of New Abbey, which houses the **Shambellie House Museum of Costume**, part of the National Museums of Scotland. The house and its collection were given to the National Museums in 1977 by the then owner, Charles Stewart, and the displays provide an absorbing record of our sartorial fads, fancies and extravagances over the centuries.

CAERLAVEROCK

8 miles S of Dumfries on the B725

Caerlaverock Castle (Historic Scotland) meets everyone's idea of a medieval fortress with its moat and mighty gatehouse flanked by blank-walled towers. In fact, Caerlaverock's ground plan is untypical of castles of the period since the design is triangular. Two sides are protected by the sea; the third by the moat. Edward I made a ferocious attack on the castle in 1300 and held it for 11 years. The king's balladeer, Walter of Exeter, proclaimed that "You will never see a more finely situated castle". Parts of the original structure of 1270 have survived but most of the present building dates from the 15th century, with Renaissance additions by the 1st Earl of Nithsdale in 1634.

Caerlaverock Wildfowl and Wetlands Trust is about three miles west of the castle, and is situated in a 1400-acre nature reserve. Here a wide variety of wildlife can be observed, including swans and barnacle geese. If you're lucky, you may also come across the extremely rare natterjack toad. There are three observation towers, 20 hides and a wild swan observatory linked by nature trails and screen approaches. There are also picnic areas, a gift shop, refreshments and binocular hire.

Some facilities are wheelchair friendly.

The place is on the well-signposted **Solway Coast Heritage Trail**, which stretches from Gretna in the east to Stranraer in the west.

KIRKBEAN

9 miles S of Dumfries, on the A710

About two miles south of the village are the famous, semi-tropical **Arbigland Gardens**, set around a secluded bay. They were originally laid out in the 1730s by a gardener named John Paul. One of his sons, also named John, was a lively youth who became a sailor boy at the age of 11 and later spent 5 years on an American slave ship. In Tobago he managed to get himself charged with murder and to avoid arrest changed his name to John Paul Jones, the name by which he is honoured in the United States as the "Father of the American Navy". The tiny white-washed cottage in which he was born in 1747 is now the John Paul Jones Birthplace Museum. The cottage has been restored to its mid-18th century appearance and houses some fascinating exhibits connected with the Admiral's eventful life. Outside stand two flagpoles, one flying the Stars and Stripes, the other carrying Scotland's St Andrew's Cross. The latter, incidentally, is identical to the Empress Catherine of Russia's flag under which the restless John Paul Jones sailed as Admiral of her Black Sea Fleet during the Russo-Turkish war of 1788-89.

Inside Kirkbean Parish Church, which was built in 1776, is a font presented by the American Navy in 1945. And to continue the American theme, **Dr James Craik**, Physician General of the United States Army during the American Revolution, was also born on the Arbigland estate. However, James was not born in the same humble circumstances as John Paul Jones. His father Robert was a Member of Parliament and owned the estate.

BEESWING

9 miles SW of Dumfries on the A711

This small village was laid out in the 19th century. The only remarkable thing about it is its name. It must be the only village in Scotland that is named after a horse. Beeswing was one of the most famous horses in the mid-1800s. Its finest performance was in the Doncaster Cup which it won in 1840. A local man won so much money on the race that he opened an inn called The Beeswing, and the village grew up round it.

CROCKETFORD

9 miles W of Dumfries on the A75

It was at Crocketford that the sorry tale of **Elspeth Buchan**, who founded a religious sect called the Buchanites, came to a macabre end. Part of the sect's beliefs was that Elspeth was immortal, and that she could bestow immortality on others by breathing on them. After having been driven out of Irvine, she and her followers headed south towards Dumfriesshire and settled there. Alas, Elspeth disappointed her

21 STEAMBOAT INN

Kirkbean, nr Dumfries

The Steamboat Inn, an amazing place to stay with magnificent views to the Lake Distric Peaks.

🍴 🛏 *see page 362*

22 BARNSOUL FARM

Dumfries

Barnsoul has nearly 300 acres of paddocks, woodland, ponds and so on, and is famous for its wildlife.

🛏 *see page 363*

The isolated farm of Craigenputtock in Dunscore, lies off an unmarked road five miles to the west. It was here that an unusual event took place concerning a small religious sect known as the Buchanites, founded by Mother Elspeth Buchan in Irvine, in the 18th century. She attracted a wide following, claiming she could bestow immortality on a person by breathing on them, and that she was also immortal. She also claimed that her followers would ascend to heaven in bodily form, without the inconvenience of death. The cult was eventually hounded from Irvine by the town magistrates, and it headed south towards Dumfries. In a large field near Craigenputtock she decided that it was time her followers went to heaven. So she had a wooden platform set up. She and her followers assembled on it, their heads shaved apart from a small tuft that the angels would grasp to lift them up to heaven. However, in the middle of the service the platform collapsed, throwing her followers to the ground. The sect eventually broke up when Elspeth died a natural death.

followers by dying a natural death, and the sect broke up.

But one man, who lived in Crocketford, still believed in her immortality, and that she would rise from the dead. He therefore acquired her body and kept it in a cupboard at the top of the stairs in his cottage, where it gradually mummified. Eventually he built an extension to the cottage, on the other side of the wall from the fireplace, and kept the corpse there. He even had a small opening cut through the wall so that he could examine the corpse every day to see if it had come alive again. Of course it didn't, but this never shook his belief in her resurrection, and the body remained in the cottage with him until his own death.

HOLYWOOD

4 miles NW of Dumfries off the A76

The present **Holywood Parish Church** of 1779 was partly built from the stones of a great medieval abbey which once stood here, of which nothing now remains above ground. To the west, on the other side of the A76, is a stone circle known as the **Twelve Apostles**, though one massive stone is now missing.

ELLISLAND

6 miles NW of Dumfries on the A76

Robert Burns brought his family south from Mauchline to Ellisland in June 1788. However, there was no farmhouse at the time, and he had to have one built, meaning that he couldn't move in properly until the following year. He leased the

170-acre **Ellisland Farm** from Patrick Millar of Dalswinton, but found the soil to be infertile and stony. So much so that by 1791 he gave up the unequal struggle to make a living from it and moved with his family to Dumfries.

The farm sits in a beautiful spot beside the Nith, and it was this romantic location which had made Burns choose it in the first place. Here he wrote some of his best poetry, including *Auld Lang Syne* and his masterpiece of the comic/macabre, *Tam o' Shanter.* Burns used to recount that Tam o' Shanter was conceived while walking the banks of the Nith, and he laughed out loud as he thought up his hero's adventures with the witches. Now the farmhouse houses a lively museum dedicated to his memory. To the north is Hermitage Cottage, which Burns used as a place to muse and write poetry.

DUNSCORE

8 miles NW of Dumfries on the B729

Dunscore (pronounced "Dunsker") is a small, attractive village with a neat, whitewashed Parish Church dating from 1823. When Robert Burns and his family stayed at Ellisland Farm, four miles to the east, they used to worship in its predecessor.

Not far from Dunscore is Lochenhead Farm, birthplace in 1897 of **Jane Haining**, the only British person to have died at Auschwitz during World War II. While still young she joined the Church of Scotland's Jewish

Mission Service, and was eventually appointed matron of the Jewish Mission in Budapest in 1932. In 1944 she was arrested, purportedly because she had been listening to BBC broadcasts, but actually because she had been working among the Jews. She was taken to Auschwitz, and on July 17th 1944 died there. Her death certificate gave the cause of death as cachexia, a wasting illness sometimes associated with cancer, but there is no doubt she was gassed.

Out of doors at **Glenkiln**, beside Glenkiln Reservoir four miles (as the crow flies) south west of Dunscore, is a collection of sculptures by Henry Moore and Rodin.

CLOSEBURN

13 miles NW of Dumfries on the A76

Closeburn sits in one of the most beautiful parts of Dumfriesshire - Nithsdale. To the north of the village the wooded dale closes in on either side, with the River Nith tumbling through it. To the south, it gradually opens out into a wide, fertile strath, dotted with green fields and old, whitewashed farms. The **Parish Church** stands some distance away from the village, and is an attractive Victorian building with a slim tower. Fragments of the older church, which date from 1741, can be seen in the kirkyard.

A small road winds up eastwards from just south of Closeburn into the moorland above the village. It makes an interesting drive, and takes you past the small but picturesque Loch Ettrick.

THORNHILL

15 miles NW of Dumfries on the A76

This lovely village, with its wide main street and pollarded trees, has a French feel to it, and was laid out in 1714 by the Duke of Queensberry. At the crossroads in the middle of the village is a monument surmounted by a winged horse, a symbol of the Queensberry family. In a field to the west of the village, and close to the bridge over the Nith, is the 15th century **Boatford Cross**, associated with the ferry and ford that preceded the bridge.

Three miles north of the village, and to the west of the A702, are the remains of 15th century **Morton Castle**, situated romantically on a tongue of land jutting out into Morton Loch. A castle of some kind has stood here since the 12th century, though the present castle was built by the Douglases, who were the Earls of Morton.

DRUMLANRIG CASTLE

17 miles NW of Dumfries on a minor road off the A76

One of Scotland's grandest great houses, **Drumlanrig Castle** is set in a 120,000-acre estate, and is the Dumfriesshire home of the Duke of Buccleuch. It was built by William Douglas, 1st Duke of Queensberry, and completed in 1691. It contains many fine paintings, including works by Gainsborough, Rembrandt and Hans Holbein. In the summer of

Against the wall of a building in East Morton Street in Thornhill, is the bust of Joseph Laing Waugh, Thornhill's own novelist and poet, who set some of his books, written in lowland Scots, in and around the village.

2003 the castle was the scene of a daring burglary when a painting by Leonardo da Vinci worth millions of pounds was stolen from it in broad daylight. Within the estate is a country park and gardens, the ruins of Tibbers Castle, craft workshops, a Cycle Museum, working forge and adventure play area. The **Drumlanrig Sycamore** is one of the largest sycamores in the country, and within the grounds is the first Douglas fir ever planted in the United Kingdom.

MONIAIVE

17 miles NW of Dumfries on the A702

Moniaive, caught in a fold of the hills at the head of Glencairn, through which the Cairn Water flows to join the Nith, must surely be one of the prettiest villages in Dumfriesshire. It is actually two villages, Moniaive itself and Dunreggan, on the northeast side of the river. Within the village is the Renwick Monument, which commemorates a Covenanting martyr who died in 1688.

James Paterson was a painter who was a member of that group known as the "Glasgow Boys". In 1882 he settled in the village with his wife, and lived there until 1906, when he moved to Edinburgh. Several of his paintings show scenes in and around the village.

Three miles east is the great mansion of Maxwelton House (not open to the public), formerly known as Glencairn Castle. It was here that Anna Laurie (her real name), of **Bonnie Annie Laurie** fame, was born in 1682. The song

was written by William Douglas of Fingland, though he later jilted her and joined the Jacobite army. Anna herself went on to marry Alexander Fergusson, 14th Laird of Craigdarroch.

Every September the village hosts the **Scottish Comic Festival**, with displays and exhibitions, as well as talks by cartoonists and comic illustrators. There is also the **Moniaive Folk Festival** in May each year.

PENPONT

17 miles NW of Dumfries on the A702

This small, attractive village is well worth a visit in the summer months to see the colourful gardens that surround some of the old picturesque cottages.

On a slight rise in a field just off the road to Moniaive is a piece of sculpture shaped like an egg. This is the work of **Andy Goldsworthy** the famous sculptor, who was born in Cheshire but now lives in the village.

KEIR

18 miles NW of Dumfries on a minor road off the A702

Keir is no more than a hamlet with a small Parish Church dating mainly from 1814. It was near here that Kirkpatrick MacMillan, inventor of the modern bicycle, was born in 1813. While his brothers all went on to become successful in their careers, Kirkpatrick was content to stay at home and ply the trade of a blacksmith.

Hobbyhorses, which relied on riders pushing themselves forward with their feet, had been around since the early part of the 19th century, but Kirkpatrick MacMillan's bicycle was the first to incorporate revolving pedals. On 6th June 1842 he set out on a 70-mile ride to Glasgow on his bicycle, and was greeted by crowds when he arrived there. However, while passing through the Gorbals, he knocked down a young girl, and even though she wasn't badly injured, he was fined five shillings by a Glasgow magistrate, the first recorded case of a cyclist being fined for a traffic offence. However, rumour has it that the magistrate offered to pay the fine out of his own pocket if Kirkpatrick would allow him to have a ride on the bicycle.

DURISDEER

*20 miles NW of Dumfries
on a minor road off the A702*

The tiny hamlet of Durisdeer sits at the end of a narrow road leading off the A702. It consists of a handful of cottages and a **Parish Church** built in 1699. The church is unusual in that it has, attached to it, the former parish school. It is also surprisingly large for such a small hamlet, but this is due to the fact that it is the church for the Queensberry estate. This explains the presence here of the wonderful **Durisdeer Marbles**. They are, in fact, an elaborate funerary monument constructed in 1713 for the 2nd Duke of Queensberry and his wife, who lie buried in the crypt beneath. They were carved in marble by the Flemish sculptor Jan Nost, and are said to be the best of their kind in the country.

TYNRON

*20 miles NW of Dumfries
on a minor road off the A702*

This small, pretty conservation village has only one building dated later than 1900. The **Parish Church**, which looks far too big for such a small place, was built in 1837 and was one of the last in Scotland to be lit by oil lamps.

ELIOCK HOUSE

*25 miles NW of Dumfries on a side road
running parallel to the A76*

Set deep in the heart of Nithsdale off a minor road, Eliock House (private) was the birthplace in 1560 of **James Crichton**, better known as the "Admirable Crichton". He was the son of the then Lord Advocate of Scotland, and was educated at St Andrews University. He travelled extensively in Europe, where he followed careers in soldiering and lecturing at universities. Though a young man, he could speak 12 languages fluently, and was one of the best swordsmen of his day. However, this didn't prevent him from being killed in Mantua in Italy in 1582 while a lecturer at the university there. The story goes that he was returning from a party one evening when he was set upon by a gang of robbers, and defeated each one in a sword fight. He then realised that one of the robbers was a pupil at the university, Vincentio di Gonzaga, son of the Duke of Mantua, ruler of the city. Realising

•

One of the more unusual cottage industries in Sanquhar during the 18th and 19th centuries was the hand knitting of gloves, and the intricate patterns soon made the gloves popular throughout the country. Up until the 1950s these patterns had never been published. Now it is possible once more to buy both hand and machine knitted gloves and garments made from the distinctive patterns.

•

what he had done, he handed Vincentio his sword and asked forgiveness. Vincentio, however, was a nasty piece of work. He took the sword and stabbed the defenceless James through the heart, killing him outright.

SANQUHAR

27 miles NW of Dumfries on the A76

Sanquhar (pronounced San-kar) is a small town in Upper Nithsdale that was created a royal burgh in 1598. The name comes from the language of the ancient Britons, and means "Old Fort". The site of this fort was on a small hill to the north of the town, close to **St Bride's Church** which was built in 1824. Within the church is a small collection of stone carvings, including one of St Nicholas and a medieval cross.

The **Sanquhar Tolbooth** was built to the designs of William Adam in 1735 as a town hall, schoolroom and jail, and now houses a small museum. It was in a house opposite the Tolbooth that

William Boyd, 4th Earl of Kilmarnock, lodged while on his way south to be tried and executed for his part in the Jacobite uprising. There is a plaque on the wall commemorating his stay. In Main Street is **Sanquhar Post Office**, dating from 1712, the oldest continuously used post office in the world. The Southern Upland Way passes through the burgh, and the **Sanquhar Historic Walk** takes you round many of the town's attractions and historic sites.

To the south of Sanquhar are the forlorn ruins of **Sanquhar Castle**, originally an old Crichton stronghold. It fell into the hands of the Douglases, and it was here that William Douglas, who wrote the original version of the song *Annie Laurie*, was born in 1672. The castle was founded in the 11th century, though what you see now dates from much later.

In the 17th century, Sanquhar was a Covenanting stronghold. Charles II had imposed bishops on the Church of Scotland, and the Covenanters took up arms to keep the church Presbyterian. These times were known as the "Killing Times", and many people were executed for following the dictates of their conscience. One of the most militant Covenanters was **Richard Cameron**, who rode into Sanquhar in 1680 and attached what became known as the "Sanquhar Declaration" to the Market Cross. This disowned the king, which was effectively treason. Cameron was subsequently killed at the Battle of Airds Moss in the same year.

Sanquhar Castle

The **Riding of the Marches** is an ancient ceremony, and takes place every August. The burgh boundaries are ridden by horse riders to ensure that adjoining landowners have not encroached onto burgh or common land - a common occurrence in olden times.

A series of plaques on various buildings takes you on a historic walk round the town, with a leaflet being available in the local tourist office.

KIRKCONNEL (UPPER NITHSDALE)

30 miles NW of Dumfries on the A76

This former mining village in upper Nithsdale is not to be confused with Kirkconnell House near New Abbey or Kirkconnel graveyard in Annandale. **St Connel's Church** dates from 1729, and is a fine looking building to the west of the village. Near the church is a monument to **Alexander Anderson**, a local poet who wrote under the name of "The Surfaceman". Though born in lowly circumstances, he rose to become chief librarian at Edinburgh University and subsequently the secretary of the Edinburgh Philosophical Union.

The Kirkconnel Miners Memorial commemorates the men who lost their lives in the Upper Nithsdale mining industry between 1872 and 1968.

KIRKCUDBRIGHT

"An irreproachable Scottish town...one of the most picturesque and fascinating Lowland towns I have seen". So enthused the travel writer HV Morton after visiting this enchanting little town (pronounced "Kirk-coo-bray") set beside the river Dee. It is still a working port with a small fishing fleet.

Morton was particularly impressed by the ruins of **MacLellan's Castle** (Historic Scotland) which towers over the tiny harbour. Built between 1569 and 1582, it was designed not for defensive purposes but as a private residence for Sir Thomas MacLellan. Its Great Hall is particularly striking and there's a curious feature in the enormous lintel over the fireplace. A spy-hole, known as the "Laird's Lug", has been cut into the lintel that looks into a small room behind it. Sir Thomas used to hide himself there and listen to what was being said about him in the Great Hall.

This part of Galloway has a very mild climate, thanks to the Gulf Stream washing its shores, and this, as well as the quality of light to be found here, encouraged the founding of an artists' colony. On a summer's morning, the edge between light and shadow can be as sharp as a knife, whereas during the day it becomes diffused and soft, and artists have been reaching for their paints and palettes for years to try and capture these two qualities. Even today, straw-hatted artists can be seen at the harbourside, trying to capture the scene.

Walk up the side of the castle into Castle Bank, passing the

Kirkcudbright was once the county town of Kirkcudbrightshire, also known as the "Stewartry of Kirkcudbright". It is a place of brightly painted Georgian, Regency and Victorian houses, making it a colourful and interesting place to explore.

DUMFRIES & GALLOWAY

Kirkcudbright was where the village scenes in the cult movie The Wicker Man were filmed, and indeed many locations in Dumfries and Galloway - and even Ayrshire - stood in for the fictional Summerisles, where the action is supposed to have taken place.

whitewashed **Harbour Cottage Gallery**, where there are regular exhibitions of work by local artists, and you arrive at the High Street. This must be one of the most charming and colourful streets in Scotland. The elegant Georgian and Regency houses - some of them quite substantial - are painted in bright, uncompromising colours, such as yellow, green and pink. Auchingool House is the oldest, having been built in 1617 for the McCullochs of Auchengool. **Broughton House**, dating from the 18th century, is now owned by the National Trust for Scotland, and was the home of AE Hornel the artist. He was one of the Glasgow Boys group of painters and died in 1933. The house is very

much as it was when he lived there. Behind the house are the marvellous **Japanese Gardens**, influenced by trips that Hornel made to the Far East.

Further along the street is Greengates Close, (private) which was the home of Jessie M. King, another artist. A few yards further on the High Street takes a dog leg to the east, and here stands the early 17th century **Tolbooth** which has been refurbished and now houses a museum and art gallery telling the story of the artists' colony. The Queen opened it in 1993. This was the former town house and jail, and John Paul Jones, founder of the American navy, was imprisoned here at one time for murder. He got his revenge in later years when he returned to the town aboard an American ship and shelled the nearby St Mary's Isle, where the seat of the Earl of Selkirk was located and a medieval priory of nuns once stood.

Kirkcudbright's Parish Church is a grand affair in red sandstone near the centre of the town, and dates from 1838. **Greyfriar's Kirk** is all that is left of a 16th century Franciscan monastery that once stood here. Within it is the grand tomb of Sir Thomas MacLellan of Bombie and his wife Grizzell Maxwell, which was erected in 1597. But the tomb isn't all it seems. The couple's son, in an effort to save money, used effigies from an earlier tomb within what is essentially a Renaissance canopy.

In St Mary's Street is the **Stewartry Museum**, which has

Tolbooth, Kirkcudbright

48

many artefacts and displays on the history of the Stewartry of Kirkcudbright. On the opposite side of the street is the Town Hall, where themed painting exhibitions are held every year.

The town also has its literary associations. The Selkirk Arms Hotel is an essential port of call for any devotee of Robert Burns. The poet stayed at the hotel in 1794 and it was here that he penned his much-quoted "Selkirk Grace":

Some hae meat and canna eat,
And some wad eat that want it,
But we hae meat and we can eat,
And sae the Lord be thanket.

Dorothy L. Sayers set her Lord Peter Wimsey whodunit *Five Red Herrings* among the artists' colony. It's not one of her best as it over-relies on a detailed knowledge of train times between Kirkcudbrightshire and Ayrshire, and of the paints found on an artist's palette.

A mile outside the town on the B727 is the Galloway Wildlife Conservation Park (formerly Wildlife Park Kirkcudbright), set in 27 acres of mixed woodland. The park is home to a varied collection of nearly 150 animals from all over the world.

AROUND KIRKCUDBRIGHT

NEW GALLOWAY

19 miles N of Kirkcudbright
on the A762/A712

With a population of just over 300, New Galloway holds the undisputed title of "Smallest Royal Burgh in Scotland". This picturesque place is a planned burgh, having been laid out in the early 1600s by Viscount Kenmure. Little more than a single street of attractive stone cottages, the village lies beside the River Ken, noted for its fine angling. There's a Town Hall and a church which is well worth visiting to see its unusual tombstones, an intriguing collection of curious carvings and some strange epitaphs.

Each year in early August New Galloway plays host to the **Scottish Alternative Games**. It's a refreshing antidote to all the traditional games held in Scotland, where tossing the caber, throwing the hammer, shot putting and Highland dancing take place. Instead there are sports such as gird and cleek (hoop and stick) racing, hurlin' (throwing) the curlin' stane, snail racing, flingin' the herd's bunnet (throwing the herdsman's bonnet) and tossin' the sheaf.

This part of Kirkcudbright is known as the Glenkens, an area combining the high drama of lonely moorland with fertile, wooded valleys. To the west of New Galloway stretches **Galloway Forest Park,** the largest forest park in Britain, covering 300 square miles of forested hills, wild and rugged moorland and numerous lochs. It's a vast and beautiful area criss-crossed by waymarked Forestry Commission trails and longer routes, such as the Southern Upland Way. It's also home to a rich variety of fauna, feral goats, red deer, falcons and even golden eagles.

A mile to the south of New Galloway, near Loch Ken, are the ruins of Kenmure Castle, which belonged to the Gordon family. To say that the building is unlucky would be an understatement, as it has been burnt down three times and rebuilt twice. After the last burning in the 1880s, it was left as a shell.

23 GLENLEE HOLIDAY HOMES

New Galloway

Quality self-catering accommodation in former farm buildings in peaceful woodland setting.

see page 363

24 THE CATSTRAND

New Galloway

Exciting contemporary performance and meeting space hosting a varied music, arts and exhibition programme.

see page 364

•

Earlston Castle, overlooking Earlston Loch to the north of the village of Dalry, was a Gordon stronghold. It was the birthplace of Catherine Gordon, later Mrs Catherine Stewart, who befriended Burns and encouraged him to write poetry when she lived in Stair Castle in Ayrshire. She was buried, along with two daughters, in Stair kirkyard in Ayrshire

•

25 GALLOWAY HYDROS

Tongland, nr Kirkcudbright

The visitor centre tells the story of the construction of the Galloway Hydros in the 1930s and the tour takes you into the power station, the control room and the turbine hall.

 see page 364

BALMACLELLAN

20 miles N of Kirkcudbright off the A712

This attractive little village was the home of **Robert Paterson**, a stonemason who was the model for Old Mortality in Scott's book of the same name. He travelled Scotland cleaning up the monuments and gravestones of the Covenanters, a group of men and women who fought Charles II's attempts to impose bishops on the Church of Scotland. Eventually he left home for good to concentrate on this work, leaving behind a no doubt angry wife and five children. Up to his death in 1800, he continued to travel the country, usually on an old grey pony. A statue of him and his horse sits inside the kirkyard of the whitewashed parish church.

Just outside the village you will find **The Balmaclellan Clog and Shoe Workshop**, where 20 styles of footwear are made by hand. Visitors can look round the workshop and see shoes and clogs being made.

ST JOHN'S TOWN OF DALRY

21 miles N of Kirkcudbright on the A713

St John's Town of Dalry, often known simply as Dalry, lies on the Southern Uplands Way, and is a picturesque Glenkens village with many old cottages. It got its name from the Knights Hospitaller of the Order of St John of Jerusalem, an order of military monks which owned the surrounding lands in medieval times.

Within the village is a curious chair-shaped stone known as St John's Stone. Local tradition says that John the Baptist rested in it. In the kirkyard is the **Gordon Aisle**, part of the medieval church that stood here before the present church of 1832. When a reservoir was created at lonely Lochinvar near Dalry in 1968, the waters of the loch were raised, covering the scant ruins of a castle owned by the Gordons. This was the home of the famous Young Lochinvar, written about by Scott in his famous lines from Marmion:

> *"O, young Lochinvar is come*
> *out of the west,*
> *Through all the wide border*
> *his steed was the best..."*

A cairn by the loch side, which is reached by a narrow track, records the existence of the castle. The cairn was built using stones from the castle ruins.

CARSPHAIRN

31 miles N of Kirkcudbright on the A713

Close to this quiet village there used to be lead mines. John Loudon MacAdam the roads pioneer, whose father came from near the village, experimented on his revolutionary road surfaces on what is now the A713 north of the village. The **Carsphairn Heritage Centre** has displays and exhibits on the history of the village.

TONGLAND

2 miles NE of Kirkcudbright on the A711

The small village of Tongland was once the site of the great **Tongland**

Abbey, founded in 1218 by Fergus, Lord of Galloway, and the scant remains - no more than a medieval archway in a piece of preserved wall - can still be seen in the kirkyard. The abbey's most famous inmate was Abbot John Damien, known as the "Frenzied Friar of Tongland", who achieved fame by jumping off the ramparts of Stirling Castle in an attempt to fly like a bird.

Tours are available of **Tongland Power Station,** the largest generating station in the great Galloway hydroelectric scheme built in the 1930s. Close by is **Tongland Bridge,** a graceful structure across the Dee designed by Thomas Telford and built in 1805.

THREAVE GARDENS

7 miles NE of Kirkcudbright, on the A75

Threave Gardens and Estate (National Trust for Scotland) surround a house built in 1872 by William Gordon, a Liverpool businessman. In 1948 the estate was given to the National Trust for Scotland by William's grandson. The gardens were created from scratch, and now house the Trust's School of Practical Gardening. The house itself is open to the public, with its interiors restored to how they would have looked in the 1930s when the place was owned by the Gordon family. The Maxwell Collection of local bygones is on display within the visitor centre.

LOCH KEN

9 miles NE of Kirkcudbright off the A713

Loch Ken is a narrow stretch of water almost nine miles long, and nowhere wider than a mile. It was created in the 1930s as the result of the great Galloway hydroelectric scheme, with the turbines being housed in the power station at Tongland, further down the Dee.

Loch Ken is a favourite spot for bird watching and sports such as sailing, fishing and water skiing, and round the shores are small nature reserves. Details about using the loch are available from the Loch Ken Marina, off the A713 on the eastern shore. At the Marina you will also find the Loch Ken Water Ski School.

CASTLE DOUGLAS

9 miles NE of Kirkcudbright off the A75

Castle Douglas is Scotland's food town, and offers real Scottish produce, such as meat, fish, vegetables, baking and drinks in its many small, specialist shops. It is a pleasant town based round what was a small village known as "Carlingwark". It was founded in the 18th century by William Douglas, a local merchant who earned his money trading with Virginia and the West Indies. He wanted to establish a thriving manufacturing town based on the woollen industry, and though he was only partly successful, he did lay the foundations for a charming town where some of his original 18th century buildings can still be seen.

On the edge of the town is Carlingwark Loch, where crannogs (dwellings built on artificial islands) have been discovered. It was joined to the River Dee in 1765 by

26 THREAVE ESTATE & GARDENS

Castle Douglas
A delightful garden, a grand restored house and large estate perfect for bird watching. Guided tours available.

🏛 see page 365

27 MAD HATTER

Castle Douglas
Cosy cafe with a difference, offering quality snacks and lunch, all prepared and cooked to a high standard.

🍴 see page 365

28 GELSTON CASTLE HOLIDAYS

Gelston, nr Castle Douglas
Self-catering accommodation on beautiful 4500 acre estate, with outstanding leisure facilities.

🛏 see page 366

Auchencairn, nr Castle Douglas

A beautiful B&B offering quality accommodation on the sea front.

see page 367

A mile south west of Dalbeattie is Orchardton Tower, the only round tower house in Scotland; it dates from the middle of the 15th century, and was built by a John Cairns. In the 17th century it passed to the Maxwells, one of whose members, Sir Robert Maxwell, was on the losing side at the Battle of Culloden. He was wounded, captured and taken to Carlisle for execution. However, among his papers was his commission in the French Army. As a result he was treated as a prisoner of war and later sent to France. He eventually returned to Orchardton, and his story became the inspiration for Sir Walter Scott's novel **Guy Mannering,** *or* **The Astrologer.**

Carlingwark Lane, a narrow canal. Marl, a limey clay used as manure, was dug from the bed of the loch and taken down river to Kirkcudbright on barges.

In Market Street is the **Castle Douglas Art Gallery**, gifted to the town in 1938 by the artist Ethel Bristowe. It hosts a continuing programme of painting, sculpture and craft exhibitions.

North west of the town, the **Ken Dee Marches Nature Reserve** follows the woodland and marshes along the River Dee and Loch Ken,

THREAVE CASTLE

9 miles NE of Kirkcudbright off the A75

A visit to **Threave Castle** (Historic Scotland) is something of an experience. It starts with a delightful 10-minute walk to the River Dee where the massive tower stands on an island. Visitors ring a brass bell and the castle custodian rows over to ferry them to the island. A forbidding building, the castle was built in the late 1300s by Archibald the Grim, one of the notorious "Black Douglases". The family earned this soubriquet by exhibiting a blood-thirstiness that was appalling even by the standards of that barbarous age. The stories of the clan's reign of terror throughout the area fit well with this brooding, gloomy fortress.

PALNACKIE

12 miles NE of Kirkcudbright on the A711

This small, attractive village on the west bank of the Water of Urr is a mile from the sea, though at one

time it was a thriving port. However, the meanderings of the river meant that ships were usually towed upstream by teams of horses. Each summer, the village hosts one of the most unusual competitions in Great Britain - the annual **World Flounder Tramping Championships**, held at the end of July. People come from all over the world to compete, making it a truly international event. The object is to walk out onto the mud flats south of the village at low tide, feeling for flounders hiding beneath the mud with your toes as you go. The person who collects the largest weight of flounders wins the championship. It may seem a light hearted and eccentric competition, but it has a firm basis in local history as this was a recognised way of catching fish in olden times.

The **North Glen Gallery** features glassblowing and interior and exterior design. It is also a good place to get advice on local walks and wildlife.

DALBEATTIE

12 miles NE of Kirkcudbright on the A711

This small town stands just east of the Water of Urr which at one time was navigable as far up-river as here. Ships of up to 60 tons could make the six-mile trip from the open sea beyond Rough Island, pulled by teams of horses. Now the "Pool of Dalbeattie" (the name given to the port area) is derelict, and the river has silted up.

Dalbeattie was a planned town, founded in the 1790s as a textile centre by two landowners - George

Maxwell and Alexander Copland, who sold feus, or tenancies, to various people so that they could build houses. Close by there were easily worked deposits of granite which also provided employment. The sparkling grey granite was of high quality and was used in the building of Sydney Harbour Bridge, Liverpool Docks and the Thames Embankment.

In Southwick Road you'll find the **Dalbeattie Museum** which has displays and exhibits about the history of the town. It has a particularly fine collection of Victoriana. Within Colliston Park is the **Dalbeattie Granite Garden**, designed by Solway Heritage to celebrate the beauty of the stone and the workers and craftsmen who mined it.

On the west bank of the Urr, about a mile from the town, is all that remains of **Buittle Castle and Bailey**, home to John Balliol, son of Devorgilla.

Robert I established a burgh here in 1325, and a recent archaeological dig has revealed that the castle's large bailey (an enclosed space next to the castle) may have housed it. A later tower house, the **Old Buittle Tower**, stands close by. It has occasional displays of arms and armour.

Three miles north of Dalbeattie is the Motte of Urr, a 12th century motte-hill and bailey that is the largest non-industrial man-made hill in Scotland. It stands close to the Water of Urr which at one time flowed by on either side, creating an island that was easily defended. Tradition says that Robert the Bruce fought an English knight called Sir Walter Selby at the Motte of Urr. The wife of a man called Sprotte who at that time lived within the motte saw the fight, and observed that Selby was gaining the upper hand. So she rushed out and jumped on him, bringing him to his knees in front of the Scottish king.

However, Bruce chose to spare Selby and both men retired to the woman's house. She produced one bowl of porridge and placed it before Robert, saying that she would not feed an Englishman. However, Robert told her to go outside and run as fast as she could. He would grant her and her husband all the land she could cover. The woman did so, and Robert and Walter finished off the porridge between them. Robert, however, kept his promise, and the Sprottes were granted 20 acres of land. They owned the land for more than 500 years, with the condition that if a Scottish king were to pass by, they were to give him a bowl of porridge.

Five miles southwest of Dalbeattie is **Scree Hill**, with marked walks through forest and woodland to its top, from which there are excellent views.

KIPPFORD

20 miles NE of Kirkcudbright off the A710

The tides in the Solway Firth are among the fastest in Britain, but this hasn't prevented the picturesque village of Kippford from becoming a great yachting

•

On the wall of the former town hall in Dalbeattie is the Murdoch Memorial to Lt William Murdoch, who was the First Officer aboard the Titanic when it sank in 1912. Over the years he has been unfairly accused of being, among other things, a coward who shot passengers attempting to leave the ship. He was also accused of not allowing third class passengers near the lifeboats and of accepting bribes from first class passengers to let them board lifeboats to which they were not entitled. The recent film also treated him unfairly, though the witness statements presented at the later official Board of Trade Enquiry cleared him of all these charges. In 1996 his name was finally and officially cleared of any wrongdoing.

•

centre. It was once a thriving port and fishing village, and it even had its own shipyard. Like its neighbour Rockcliffe, five miles away, it was also once a smuggling village.

ROCKCLIFFE

10 miles E of Kirkcudbright on a minor road off the A710

Rockcliffe was at one time a great smuggling centre but is now a quiet resort sitting on the Rough Firth, one of the smallest firths in Scotland. Off the coast is **Rough Island** (National Trust for Scotland), a bird sanctuary. It can be accessed at low tide. Close to the village is the great **Mote of Mark** (National Trust for Scotland), the site of a 5th century fort. Mark was a king featured in the story of Tristan and Isolde,

though there is no proof that the fort was ever his. It is more likely to have been built by a powerful Dark Ages chief.

There are a number of footpaths connecting Rockcliffe with Kippford, the two-mile long **Jubilee Path** (National Trust for Scotland) being the main one. There is a programme of ranger-guided walks along it in the summer months. Castlehill Point, a mile south of the village on a clifftop, can be reached by a pathway. It has the remains of an old fort.

DUNDRENNAN

5 miles SE of Kirkcudbright on the A711

This quiet village is now visited mainly because of the ruins of the once substantial **Dundrennan Abbey** (Historic Scotland). It was founded in 1142 by David I and Fergus, Lord of Galloway for the Cistercian monks of Rievaulx in Yorkshire, and was where Mary Stuart spent her last night on Scottish soil in 1568 before sailing for England and her eventual execution. Little of the grand abbey church now remains, though the chapter house and some of the other buildings are well worth seeing, as are some interesting grave slabs.

CAIRNHOLY

12 miles W of Kirkcudbright off the A75

Cairn Holy (Historic Scotland) comprises two chambered cairns dating from between 2000 and 3000 BC. The most remarkable

Rockcliffe Village

thing about their construction is how our ancestors managed to raise such huge stones. The place is supposed to mark the grave of an ancient, mythical king of Scotland called Caldus. About a mile north of the cairns are the ruins of **Carsluith Castle**, dating from the 16th century.

TWYNHOLM

3 miles NW of Kirkcudbright on the A75

Twynholm is the home village of David Coulthard the racing driver, and within the **David Coulthard Museum** in Burnbrae you can learn about the man's life. There is also a gift shop and tearoom.

GATEHOUSE OF FLEET

8 miles NW of Kirkcudbright off the A75

This neat little town was the original for the "Kippletringan" of Scott's *Guy Mannering*. It sits beside the Water of Fleet, about a mile from Fleet Bay, and was at one time a port, thanks to the canalisation of the river in 1823 by a local landowner, Alexander Murray of Cally House. The port area was known as Port MacAdam, though the site has now been grassed over**.** Cally House is now a hotel, though next to it are the **Cally Gardens**, laid out within a two-and-a-half acre walled garden.

Gatehouse of Fleet was established in the 1760s as a cotton-weaving centre by James Murray of Broughton, and today it remains more or less the way he planned it. He wished to create a great industrial town, though

nowadays it is hard to imagine "dark satanic mills" in such an idyllic setting. Within one of the former cotton mills is a museum called the **Mill on the Fleet**, which tells the story of the town's former weaving industry.

It was supposedly in Gatehouse of Fleet, in the Murray Arms, that Burns set down the words to *Scots Wha Hae*.

About a mile west of the town stand the substantial ruins of 15th century **Cardoness Castle** (Historic Scotland), former home of the McCullochs of Galloway. It stands on a rocky platform above the road, and is open to the public.

CREETOWN

17 miles NW of Kirkcudbright on the A75

Set at the mouth of the River Cree, the neat village of Creetown was once a centre for the mining of granite. Now it is visited chiefly because of the **Creetown Gem Rock Museum**, housed in a former school. It was established in 1971 and since then has amassed a remarkable collection of gemstones and minerals from all over the world. One of the finest privately owned collections of gemstones, crystals, minerals and fossils in Britain, its showroom galleries extend over 3000 square feet and contain almost every known gemstone and mineral from around the world including huge specimens from the quartz and fluorite crystal groups, exquisite geodes lined with amethyst, agates with spectacular colour bands, opals and even

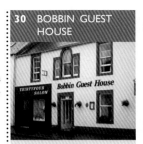

30 BOBBIN GUEST HOUSE

Gatehouse of Fleet

Great accommodation in the heart of a pretty town on the edge of Galloway Forest Park.

see page 367

•

Back in the 1950s, the citizens of Stranraer had a brilliant idea. Each would contribute a plant to help create a colourful public open space to be known as the Friendship Gardens. Half a century later, the Gardens are a splendid sight in summer, a living monument to the town's community spirit.

•

diamonds. There is also a fossilised dinosaur egg and meteorites from outer space.

The **Creetown Exhibition Centre** in St John's Street has exhibits on local history and wildlife, as well as occasional exhibitions by local artists. Over a weekend in September each year, the **Creetown Country Music Weekend** takes place, featuring the best in country music. There is also a street fair, parades and children's activities.

STRANRAER

Sitting at the head of Loch Ryan, and on the edge of the Rhinns of Galloway, that hammer shaped peninsula that juts out into the Irish Sea, Stranraer is a royal burgh and was at one time the only Scottish port serving Northern Ireland. A town of narrow streets and ancient alleyways, Stranraer was granted its royal burgh charter in 1617.

In the centre of the town is the **Castle of St John**, a tower house built by the Adair family in the 16th century. Claverhouse used it as a base while hunting down Covenanters in the area, and it was later used as the town jail. It is now a museum and interpretation centre. There is another museum in the **Old Town Hall**, which explains the history of the town and the county of Wigtownshire.

North West Castle is now a hotel, but at one time it was the home of **Sir John Ross** (1777-1856) who explored the legendary North West Passage north of Canada connecting the Atlantic and the northern Pacific. He was born near Kirkcolm, son of a minister, and joined the navy at the age of nine, reaching the rank of commander by the time he was 35 years old. On one of his expeditions he discovered the Boothia Peninsula, mainland America's northernmost point. He later served as British consul in Stockholm.

On the sea front is the **Princess Victoria Monument,** which commemorates the sinking of the car ferry Princess Victoria on 31st January 1953. It had left Stranraer bound for Larne with 127 passengers and 49 crew, and on leaving the shelter of Loch Ryan encountered a horrific gale. Though lifeboats were launched, it eventually sank with the loss of 134 lives.

Three miles east of Stranraer are the magnificent **Castle Kennedy Gardens**. They cover 75 acres between two small lochs, and

Glenwhan Gardens, Stranraer

56

are laid out around the ivy-clad ruins of Castle Kennedy, destroyed by fire in 1710. The 2nd Earl of Stair began creating the gardens in 1733. He was a field marshal under the Duke of Marlborough so he used soldiers to construct some of it. Also within the gardens is the relatively modern Lochinch Castle, the present home of the Earl and Countess of Stair. It is not open to the public.

South of the A75 is Soulseat Loch, where there is good fishing. A narrow peninsula with a few bumps and indentations on it juts out into the water - the site of Soulseat Abbey, of which not a stone now remains above ground.

Three miles beyond Castle Kennedy on the A75 is the village of Dunragit, where you'll find **Glenwhan Gardens**, overlooking beautiful Luce Bay. They were started from scratch in 1979 and now cover 12 acres.

AROUND STRANRAER

CAIRNRYAN

5 miles N of Stranraer on the A77

Cairnryan is strung out along the coast of Loch Ryan. Between the main road and the coast is a complex of car parks, piers, jetties and offices, as this small village is the Scottish terminus of the ferries to Northern Ireland. It was developed as a port during World War II, and had a breaker's yard. It was here that the famous aircraft carrier *HMS Ark Royal* was scrapped.

The Atlantic U boat fleet surrendered in Loch Ryan in 1945, and were berthed at Cairnryan before being taken out into the Atlantic and sunk.

GLENTROOL

25 miles NE of Stranraer on a minor road which leaves the A714 at Bargrennan

It was here, close to the lovely but lonely waters of Loch Trool, that Robert I defeated an English army in 1307, a year after his coronation. His soldiers had hidden themselves in the hills above the loch, and when the English troops went past, they rolled great boulders down on them before attacking. It was a turning point in the Wars of Independence, as up until then Robert had had little success. Bruce's Stone above the loch commemorates the event. It is said that Bruce rested here after the battle was over. The **Glentrool Visitor Centre**, three miles away, offers information about the surrounding forest walks, and has a small tearoom and gift shop.

Stranraer

Popular town centre restaurant serving appetising home-made food using traditional recipes and locally-sourced ingredients.

see page 368

Robert the Bruce's Stone, Glentrool

32 CAFÉ CREE

Newton Stewart

Exceptionally customer-friendly café serving excellent home-made food based on local produce.

¶ see page 368

33 FLOWERBANK GUEST HOUSE

Minnigaff

Attractive 18th century listed building in riverside setting offering quality B&B.

⊨ see page 369

GLENLUCE

11 miles E of Stranraer off the A75

The attractive little village of Glenluce has been bypassed by the A75, one of the main routes from southern Scotland and Northern England to the Irish ferries at Stranraer and Cairnryan. At one time it was the home of **Alexander Agnew**, nicknamed the "Devil of Luce". He was a beggar who, in the mid 1600s, asked for alms from a weaver named Campbell in the village, but was refused. He thereupon cursed the family and its dwelling, and strange things began to happen. Stones were thrown at their doors and windows when there was no one about, and stones came down the chimney. The bedclothes were even ripped from the children's beds as they slept. If this wasn't bad enough, Andrews was heard to say that there was no God but salt, meal and water - a clear case of atheism. He was eventually hanged for blasphemy at Dumfries.

A mile to the northwest are the ruins of **Glenluce Abbey** (Historic Scotland), founded in 1190 and occupying a site of great natural beauty. The abbey's best preserved feature is its 15th century chapter house, which is surprisingly intact. Its ribbed vault ceiling creates such an astonishingly clear acoustic that opera singers often practise here. Look out for the carvings of the "green men", always depicted with foliage sprouting from their faces. These pagan symbols of fertility were often incorporated into the fabric of medieval Christian churches - but always on the outer walls as a sign that they had been cast out by Mother Church. The end of the abbey came in 1560, with the advent of the Reformation. Unusually, the monks were allowed to live on within the abbey, the last one dying in 1602. Mary Stuart once visited, as did James 1V and Robert the Bruce. Immediately after the Reformation, the then Earl of Cassillis, head of the great Kennedy family, claimed the property and lands of Glenluce. He persuaded one of the monks to forge the abbot's signature on a document granting him the lands, then had the monk murdered. He then executed the men who had done the foul deed on his behalf in the name of justice.

Castle of Park is an imposing tower house built in about 1590 by Thomas Hay, son of the last abbot of Glenluce. A stone over the door commemorates the event. It is now owned by the Landmark Trust, and used as rented holiday accommodation.

Just outside the village, the **Glenluce Motor Museum** houses a splendid collection of vintage and classic cars, motor cycles, motoring memorabilia and even a vintage garage. There's also a shop and a tea room.

NEWTON STEWART

25 miles E of Stranraer on the A75

The burgh of Newton Stewart sits on the River Cree, close to where it enters Wigtown Bay. It is a pleasant, clean town, founded in the 17th century by William Stewart, son of the Earl of Galloway. A ford once stood where the present bridge crosses the Cree, and it was used by pilgrims to Whithorn and St Ninian's shrine.

Newton Stewart Museum is within a former church in York Road, and has displays and exhibits about the history of the town and immediate area. In Queen Street you'll find an unusual but internationally known little museum called **Sophie's Puppen Stube and Dolls House Museum**, which has 50 beautifully made doll's houses and room settings. The scale is 1:12, and all the exhibits are behind glass. There is also a collection of more than 200 exquisitely dressed dolls.

The **Wood of Cree Nature Reserve** is owned and managed by the Royal Society for the Protection of Birds, and lies four miles north of the town on a minor road running parallel to the A714. It has the largest ancient woodland in Southern Scotland, and here you can see redstarts, pied flycatchers, wood warblers and so on. There is a picnic area and nature trails.

Six miles west of Newton Stewart is the picturesque village of Kirkcowan, which has a church dating from 1834 with external stairs to the gallery.

WIGTOWN

30 miles E of Stranraer on the A714

Set beside the sands of the Cree Estuary, this small royal burgh has achieved fame as being Scotland's

Book Town, and has many bookshops and publishing houses. The focus for book activity, apart from the 20 or so shops, are the County Buildings of 1863. During the two book fairs held here every year - one in May and one in September - many of the readings, talks and events take place within the County Buildings.

In the kirkyard of Wigtown Parish Church are the remains of the medieval church, dedicated to St Machuto, who is known in France as St Malo, and gave his name to the French port. Also in the kirkyard are the **Martyrs' Graves**. In 1685, during the time of the Covenanters, two women - one aged 18 and one aged 63 - were tied to stakes at the mouth of the River Bladnoch for adhering to the Covenant and renouncing Charles as the head of the church. Rather than give up their principles, they drowned as the tide rose over their heads. The spot where the martyrdom took place is marked by the small Martyrs Monument on what are now salt marshes. On a small hill behind the town is another Covenanters' Monument, this time a slender column.

One mile west of the town is **Bladnoch Distillery**, Scotland's most southerly whisky distillery. There is a visitor centre and shop, and guided tours are available showing the distilling process.

Four miles west of the town, reached by the B733, is the Bronze Age **Torhouse Stone Circle**, built around 2000BC to 1500BC. It consists of 19 boulders forming a

34 LOCHANCROFT

Wigtown

A pleasant apartment containing a mix of antique furniture and modern appliances, perfect as a base for those wishing to explore Galloway.

🛏 *see page 369*

35 KIRKINNER INN

Kirkinner

A great family pub that provides the heart of this pretty village.

🍴 *see page 370*

36 THE HARBOUR INN

Garlieston

Waterside hostelry serving excellent food and offering comfortable en suite rooms.

see page 370

circle, with three other boulders in a line within it. It is of a type more commonly found in Aberdeenshire and north east Scotland.

CHAPEL FINIAN

17 miles SE of Stranraer on the A747

Beside the road that runs along the western shore of The Machars, the name given to that great peninsula that sticks out into the Irish Sea between Luce and Wigtown Bays, you'll find the foundations of a small church. The most interesting thing about them is their great age, as they probably date from the 10th century. Later on the chapel was probably used as a stopping off point for people making a pilgrimage to St Ninian's Shrine at Whithorn, 12 miles to the southeast.

Four miles inland from the chapel, and reached by a minor road off the A7005, is the Old Place of Mochrum, on the

northern edge of lonely Mochrum Loch. It was originally built in the 16th century by the Dunbar family, and was restored by the Marquis of Bute between 1876 and 1911. The gardens are particularly fine.

MONREITH

26 miles SE of Stranraer on the A746

This small village lies on Monreith Bay. The ruins of the old church of Kirkmaiden-in-Fernis can still be seen, the chancel a burial place for the Maxwells of Monreith.

The **Animal World & Gavin Maxwell Museum** has displays about local wildlife. It is named after Gavin Maxwell, author of *Ring of Bright Water*, who was born at nearby Elrig which features in his book *The House of Elrig*.

WHITHORN

35 miles SE of Stranraer on the A746

This tiny royal burgh (no bigger than a village) is often called the "Cradle of Scottish Christianity". A

Old Place of Mochum, Chapel Finian

century before Columba came to Iona, a monk called St Ninian set up a monastery here. He is a shadowy figure who may have been born in either Galloway or Cumbria , the son of a tribal chief. He almost certainly visited Rome, and stayed with St Martin of Tours, whom he greatly admired. Some sources say he died in AD 432.

The monastery would have been a typical Celtic foundation, with a high circular bank, or "rath", enclosing an area of monks' cells, workshops and chapels. This monastery was different in one respect, however. The main church was made of stone, not the more common wood, and was painted white. For this reason it was called Candida Casa, or "White House". When this part of Scotland was later absorbed into the kingdom of Northumbria, the name was translated into Anglo Saxon as "Hwit Aerne", from which Whithorn is derived.

The place was subsequently an important ecclesiastical and trading centre. In the 12th century Fergus, Lord of Galloway, founded **Whithorn Priory** (Historic Scotland), and its church became the cathedral for the diocese of Galloway. All that is left of the priory church is its nave and crypt. To the east of the crypt may be seen some scant foundations which may be all that is left of Ninian's original whitewashed church. The cathedral, with its relics of St Ninian, eventually became a place of pilgrimage, and many Scottish monarchs, especially James IV,

made pilgrimages to pray there.

The town's main street, George Street, is wide and spacious, with many small Georgian, Regency and Victorian houses. The Pend, dating from about 1500, is an archway leading to the priory ruins, and above it are the royal arms of Scotland. Close to the priory is the **Priory Museum** (Historic Scotland), with a collection of stones on which are carved early Christian symbols. One of them, the Latinus Stone, dates from the 5th century, and may be the earliest carved Christian stone in Scotland. Some years ago, excavations were undertaken at Whithorn, and at The **Whithorn Story**, owned by the Whithorn Trust, you can learn about the excavations and what was found there.

At Glasserton, two miles west of Whithorn, are the **Woodfall Gardens**, covering three acres within an old walled garden. They were laid out in the 18th century by Keith Stewart, second son of the earl of Galloway. He was an admiral in the British navy when he was given the 2000 acres of the barony of Glasserton in 1767. And at Garlieston, four miles north of the town, are the **Galloway House Gardens**, laid out informally at the ruined Cruggleton Castle, and with walks leading down to the shores of Cruggleton Bay. The medieval **Cruggleton Church** sits by itself in a field, and was built as a chapel for the castle. It was restored in the 19th century by the Marquis of Bute, and a key for it is available at nearby Cruggleton farm.

St Ninian's Cave is on the shore three miles southwest of Whithorn. It has incised crosses on its walls, and a legend states that St Ninian himself came to this cave to seek solitude and to pray.

Built as a hunting lodge in 1869 by Lady Hunter Blair, Knockinaam Lodge stands to the south of Portpatrick. It is now a hotel, but it was here, during the closing stages of the Second World War, that Churchill and Eisenhower planned the Allied strategy.

Three miles to the southeast is the tiny fishing village of Isle of Whithorn. On a headland are the 13th century ruins of the tiny **St Ninian's Chapel**. Though it sits on the mainland, the small area surrounding it may at one time have been an island, giving the village its name. It was probably built for pilgrims to Whithorn Priory who came by sea.

KIRKMADRINE

9 miles S of Stranraer on a minor road off the A716

In the porch of what was the tiny parish church of Toskerton are the **Kirkmadrine Stones**, thought to be the oldest inscribed stones in Scotland after those at Whithorn. They were discovered when the church was being rebuilt and converted into a burial chamber by a local family, the McTaggarts of Ardwell.

ARDWELL

11 miles S of Stranraer on the A716

Ardwell Gardens are grouped round the 18th century Ardwell House. They feature azaleas, camellias and rhododendrons, and are a testimony to the mildness of the climate in these parts. They feature a woodland and a formal garden, as well as good views out over Luce Bay from the pond.

PORT LOGAN

14 miles S of Stranraer on the B7065

Port Logan is a small fishing village with an unspoilt sandy beach situated on Port Logan Bay. Close by is the **Logan Fish Pond**, a remarkable tidal pond famous for its tame sea fish, which can be fed by hand. It was constructed in about 1800 as a source of fresh fish for the tables of nearby Logan House.

If anywhere illustrates the mildness of the climate in this part of Scotland, it is **Logan Botanic Garden**, part of the National Botanic Gardens of Scotland. Here, growing quite freely, are exotic plants and trees such as the tree fern (which can normally only survive in glass houses in Britain), eucalyptus, palm trees, magnolias and passionflowers. In fact, more than 40 per cent of all the plants and trees at Logan come from the Southern hemisphere. Within the garden are the Discovery Centre, which gives an insight into the plants that grow here and the Fish Pond which has a castellated keeper's house. In the 19th century ladies wishing to bathe in the pond could change in the adjacent bath house which is also castellated.

Port Logan achieved national fame when the TV series *2,000*

Coast, nr Portpatrick

Acres of Sky, supposedly set on a Hebridean island, was filmed in and around Port Logan.

KIRKMAIDEN

17 miles S of Stranraer on the B7065

Kirkmaiden is Scotland's most southerly parish. Four miles south of the village is the Mull of Galloway, Scotland's most southerly point. It comes as a surprise to some people when they learn that places like Durham in England are further north. The lighthouse was built in 1828 to the designs of Robert Stevenson, and sits on the massive cliffs, 270 feet above the sea. The lighthouse is open to visitors on summer weekends. In Drummore, half a mile to the east of the village, is the **Kirkmaiden Information Centre** which has displays and exhibitions about the area.

PORTPATRICK

6 miles SW of Stranraer on the A77

This lovely little village is at the western end of the Southern Upland Way. At one time it was the main Scottish port for Northern Ireland, but was in such an exposed position that Stranraer eventually took over. It sits round a little harbour that is always busy and, with its old cottages and craft shops,

Portpatrick Harbour

has become a small holiday resort.

On a headland to the south of the village are the ruins of **Dunskey Castle**, built in the early 16th century by the Adair family. The recently re-established **Dunskey Garden and Woodland Walk** is well worth visiting. Every Wednesday afternoon in summer, there are guided tours conducted by the gardener. Within the village is the ruined **Portpatrick Parish Church**. It was built in the 17th century, and unusually, has a round tower.

Portpatrick is the western terminus of the coast-to-coast **Southern Upland Way**; the first few miles of the walk to Killantringan Lighthouse are particularly stunning.

Ayrshire & Arran

ithin Ayrshire's 1200 square miles there's a marked contrast between north and south. In the north, there's a taste of the untamed Highlands while the south is more reminiscent of the Borders with rolling pasture lands and country villages. The long sandy shores and the popular resort of Largs in North Ayrshire, the rural nature of East Ayrshire with its wide open spaces, and the broad beaches, seaside towns and verdant hills of South Ayrshire, all add to the variety.

This is, of course, Robert Burns' homeland and wherever you go you'll almost certainly find that Scotland's national bard has been there before you and usually left behind a good anecdote - or a poem - to prove it. Pride of place in any Burns itinerary must go to the Burns Cottage & Museum at Alloway, near Ayr, where the poet was born. Homes of a statelier kind can be visited at Kelburn Castle, home of the Earls of Glasgow, and Culzean Castle, Ayrshire's top visitor attraction.

Twenty miles offshore is the island of Arran, a wonderful blend of wild scenery, pastoral views and rocky coastlines. Its history stretches right back into the mists of time as the many standing stones and ancient burial cairns testify. It is properly part of the Highlands, and Gaelic used to be the predominant language. A ferry connects it to Ardrossan on the Ayrshire coast.

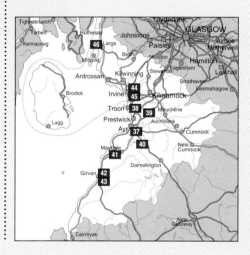

AYR

For centuries Ayr rivalled Glasgow as a major seaport. When its importance as a trading centre declined, the town's fine beaches provided a new lease of life as a popular Victorian resort. A whole new community of wide streets, boulevards, imposing public offices such as the County Buildings, and an esplanade sprang up making this part of Ayr stand in marked contrast to the narrow lanes and alleys of the Old Town - *"Auld Ayr"* as Robert Burns put it, *"wham ne-er a toun surpasses for honest men and bonnie lasses"*.

The most notable survivor of Ayr's medieval buildings is the **Auld Brig,** a sturdy 15th century construction made famous by Burns in his poem *Twa Brigs*. Elsewhere, the poet described the bridge as *"a poor narrow footpath of a street where two wheel-barrows tremble when they meet"*. Auld Brig was restored in 1910 and is now only open to pedestrians.

The second oldest building in the town is **Loudoun Hall,** in the Boat Vennel close to the New Bridge. It was built about 1513 as a fine town house for the Campbells of Loudoun, hereditary sheriffs of Ayr. It was due for demolition just after the war, but was saved when its importance was realised. South of Loudoun Hall, in the Sandgate, is **Lady Cathcart's House**, a tenement building which dates from the 17th century. Within it, in 1756, John Loudon McAdam, the roads engineer, is believed to have been born.

After the Battle of Bannockburn, Bruce held his first parliament in Ayr to decide on the royal succession after he died. That assembly was held in the ancient kirk of St John the Baptist of which only the tower still stands. Known as **St John's Tower,** it can be found among Edwardian villas near the shore. Oliver Cromwell dismantled the old church and used the stone to build Ayr Citadel. That too has gone, apart from a few feet of wall near the river and an arch

St John's Old Kirk Tower, Ayr

65

37 THE ROYAL CAFE

Ayr

The Royal Café is still producing the same high quality Italian ice cream it did when it opened almost nine decades ago.

🍴 *see page 371*

•

Ayr's most distinctive feature is the tall, elegant steeple of the Town Hall, built between 1827 and 1832 to the designs of Thomas Hamilton. Seen from the north, it blends beautifully with a cluster of fine Georgian buildings beside the river.

•

in a side street. To compensate, Cromwell gave the burgh £600 to build a new church, which is now known as the **Auld Parish Kirk**, situated on the banks of the river. It is now a mellow old T-plan building surrounded by tottering gravestones. Within the lych gate can be seen a couple of mort-safes, heavy iron grilles which were placed over fresh graves to prevent grave robbing in the early 1800s.

Robert Burns and Ayr are inseparable. He was born in Alloway village to the south of the town which has now become a well-heeled suburb, and his influences are everywhere. Ayr was the starting off point for Tam o' Shanter's drunken and macabre ride home after spending the evening at an inn, as portrayed in Burns's poem of the same name. In the High Street is the thatched **Tam o' Shanter Inn**, where the inebriated cobbler was supposed to have started his journey. At one time the pub was a small museum, but now it has thankfully reverted to its original purpose, and you can enjoy a drink within its walls which are adorned with quotations from the great poet. A few yards from the pub stands the 115 feet tall **William Wallace Tower** which commemorates the Scottish patriot who was imprisoned in the town in 1297 for setting fire to a barn with 500 English soldiers inside. About 400 yards to the south of the tower, Burns himself gazes thoughtfully over Burns Statue Square.

The bridges of Ayr take you to Newton upon Ayr on the north bank of the river, which was once a separate burgh with a charter dated to 1446, but now part of the town. Part of its old Tolbooth survives as **Newton Tower**, caught in an island in the middle of the street.

The **Belleisle Estate and Gardens** are to the south of the town, with parkland, deer park, aviary and pets corner. Nearby is **Rozelle House Galleries and Gardens**. There are art exhibitions within the mansion house, plus a tearoom and craft shop.

Ayr Racecourse is Scotland's leading racecourse, and is the venue for the Scottish Grand National in April and the Scottish Derby in July.

AROUND AYR

PRESTWICK

2 miles N of Ayr town centre, on the A79

Prestwick is one of the oldest towns in Scotland, having been granted its original burgh charter in the 12th century. With its long, sandy beach it was also one of the most popular holiday resorts for Glaswegians until Spain and Florida took over.

To the north of the town is Prestwick International Airport, at one time the main transatlantic airport for Glasgow. It is still a busy place, being a favourite starting point for those holidays in warmer climes that eventually saw off Prestwick as a holiday resort. On March 2nd 1960, the airport had possibly its most famous visitor - Elvis Presley. Having been discharged from the American army, his plane touched down at the airport for refuelling when he was returning home from Germany. He stayed at the American air force base (now gone) for just under an hour, and then re-boarded his flight. It was the only time that "The King" ever set foot in Britain. A plaque in the airport commemorates his visit, and people still turn up from all over Europe to pay their respects. In later life, someone asked Elvis what country he would like to visit, and he replied that he would like to go back to Scotland, possibly also because he had Scottish ancestors.

The name Prestwick means "priest's burgh", and the ruins of the ancient **Parish Church of St Nicholas** are near the coastline. At Kingcase was a lazar house where Robert the Bruce went to seek a cure for his leprosy. **Bruce's Well** can still be seen there.

The very first British Open golf Championship was held at Prestwick in 1860 (with eight competitors) and for 12 years after. A cairn near the golf course, unveiled in 1977 by Henry Cotton, commemorates the event.

MONKTON
4 miles N of Ayr on the A79

Traffic between Glasgow and Ayr used to thunder through Monkton, but now it is more or less bypassed. It sits on the edge of Prestwick Airport, and at one time the main road cut right across the main runway. This meant that traffic was held up every time an aircraft took off or landed - a magnificent sight, but inconvenient for cars and buses.

The **Muckle Stane** is an "erratic" (a boulder brought by an ice flow towards the end of the last Ice Age), and previously stood in a field outside the village. In 1998 it was relocated within the village.

To the north of the village is a curious monument known as MacRae's Monument that looks like the truncated top part of a church tower and spire. It commemorates James MacRae, Governor of Madras in the early 18th century. He was born in Ochiltree in humble circumstances, his father having died before he was born. He was then brought up by a carpenter called Hugh McGuire, and when MacRae returned from India in 1731 a rich man he bought the Orangefield estate (a site now occupied by part of Prestwick Airport). He also found his old benefactor living in poverty. He bought him the estate of Drumdow at Stair, east of Monkton, and introduced his daughters into polite society, each of them making good marriages. One of them even became the Countess of Glencairn. MacRae was buried in the churchyard at Monkton, though no stone now marks his grave.

TROON
6 miles N of Ayr, on the A759

This seaside resort is synonymous with golf since the British Open has been held here many times. It is a young town, having been laid out in the early 1800s by the 4th Duke of Portland who wished to create a harbour from which to export the

The ruins of 13th century St Cuthbert's Church stand at the heart of Monkton. At one time the Rev. Thomas Burns, Robert Burns's nephew, was minister here. William Wallace, it is said, once fell asleep in the church, and had a dream in which an old man presented him with a sword and a young woman presented him with a wand. He took it to mean that he must continue his struggle for Scotland's freedom.

38 ARRAN GARDENS B&B - SHELLDUN

Troon

Ground floor level accommodation, of the highest quality, situated in an ideal location for exploring the west coast of Scotland

🛏 see page 372

coal mined in his Ayrshire coalfields. It formed the western terminus of Scotland's earliest rail line, the Troon/Kilmarnock Railway, which was opened in 1812. In 1816 the Duke introduced a steam locomotive onto the line, and it started pulling passenger trains. The town is now the Scottish terminal for the Scotland/Ireland P&O express ferry service to Larne near Belfast.

On the shoreline is the Ballast Bank, created over the years by ships which discharged their ballast before taking on coal for Ireland.

SYMINGTON

6 miles N of Ayr off the A77

Symington is a pleasant village of old cottages, though a large estate of council housing on its northern edge has somewhat marred its picturesqueness. It is named after its Norman founder, Simon Lockhart, and at its heart is **Symington Parish Church**, Ayrshire's oldest church still in use. This Norman building, formerly dedicated to the Holy Trinity, was originally built about 1150, and has in its east wall a trio of delightful Norman windows. It has its original piscina in the south wall, and an ancient timbered roof.

On a hillside to the west of the village, at a spot called Barnweil, is the Victorian **Barnweil Monument**, looking for all the world like a church tower without a church. This marks the spot where Wallace watched the "barns o' Ayr burn weel" after he set fire to them. Next to it are the scant remains of Barnweil Church where John Knox once preached. The parish of Barnweil was suppressed in 1673, and the church, which may have been one of the oldest in Ayrshire, gradually became ruinous.

DUNDONALD

8 miles N of Ayr on the B730

Dundonald Castle (Historic Scotland) is one of Scotland's royal castles, and sits on a high hill overlooking the village. The hill has been occupied for at least 3000 years, and has been the site of at least three medieval castles. What

Dundonald Castle

you see nowadays are the remains of the third castle, built in the 14th century by Robert II, grandson of Robert the Bruce and the first Stewart king of Scotland, to mark his accession to the throne in 1371. It was here, in his favourite residence, that Robert died in 1390. When Boswell and Dr Johnson visited the castle in 1773 during their Scottish journey, Johnson was much amused by the humble home of "Good King Bob", though in the 14th century the castle was much larger than it is now, having stables, a brew house and a blacksmith's workshop.

At the top, now reached by a metal staircase, are what would have been the royal apartments, and it is here that Robert II no doubt died. There are fine views northwards and eastwards over central Ayrshire.

ST QUIVOX

2 miles NE of Ayr just off the A77

The tiny **Parish Church** is a small gem of a building. Though altered beyond recognition over the years, its basic fabric is still medieval. The church takes its name from a shadowy Celtic saint called variously St Kevock, St Kennocha, St Kenochis, St Cavocks and St Evox. It was restored by Lord Cathcart of Auchincruive - and no doubt altered to suit Protestant services - in 1595.

To the east is **Oswald Hall**, designed by Robert Adam for James Oswald in 1767. It is now a conference centre. The surrounding Auchincruive estate is one of the campuses of the Scottish Agricultural College.

TARBOLTON

7 miles NE of Ayr on the B744

Anyone following the Burns Trail will want to seek out this small village in order to visit the charming 17th century house known as the **Bachelors' Club** (National Trust for Scotland). Between 1777 and 1784, the Burns family lived at Lochlea Farm (private) near Tarbolton and during these years Burns was a leading light of the Bachelors' Club, a debating society where his ardent republican views ensured that discussions were never less than lively. As well as debating, drinking and pursuing pretty women (as his poem *The Tarbolton Lassies* confirms), another of Rabbie's passions was dancing. It was in this same house that he attended dancing lessons and was also initiated as a freemason. The thatched white-washed building contains a small museum with material relating to Burns' life in the area.

Tarbolton Parish Church is an elegant, imposing building of 1821, standing on a low hill.

MAUCHLINE

11 miles NE of Ayr on the A76

This little town is still vibrant with memories of Robert Burns. Following the death of his father in 1784, the 25-year-old Burns took a lease on nearby Mossgiel Farm (private) which is still a working farm today. Rabbie was hopelessly incompetent as a farmer and his

39 CROWN HOTEL

Tarbolton

Welcoming family run B&B offering appetising food based on local produce.

see *page 372*

69

To the north of Mauchline is the Burns Memorial, built in 1897. It is a tall, red sandstone tower with a small museum inside. From the top, you get good views of the rich agricultural lands of Ayrshire. Beside the memorial, and forming part of it, are some pleasant alms cottages for old people.

financial problems with the farm were compounded by his roller-coaster emotional relationship with Jean Armour, a sparky Mauchline lass. Jean lived in a house (now gone) in the Cowgate, daughter to a prosperous stone mason who, not surprisingly, originally disapproved of Jean seeing a penniless failed farmer who had a deserved reputation as a womaniser and who wrote verse. So much so that Jean's mother packed Jean off to her uncle in Paisley, even though the couple had signed a marriage pact that was legal under Scots law of the time. Not only that - she was pregnant. Despite these dual tensions, this was a period of extraordinary creativity for Burns. To his time in Mauchline we owe *To a Mountain Daisy*, *To a Mouse*, *Holy Willie's Prayer* and *The Holy Fair*. In 1786 his first volume of poems, now known as the Kilmarnock Edition, was published. The book became a best-seller and after savouring his literary triumph in the salons of Edinburgh, Burns returned to Mauchline in 1788 to marry Jean.

They set up house in Castle Street (which at that time was the main street of the village and was called Back Causeway) and their home now houses the **Burns House Museum**. The red sandstone building actually had four families living in it in the 18th century, but it has now been converted so that various displays and exhibitions can be accommodated. Robert and Jean's apartment has been furnished in much the same way as it would have

been in 1788 when they moved in. Across from it, but now a private house, was Nance Tinnock's Inn, Burns's favourite drinking place.

The Parish Church you see today is not the one that Burns knew. The old Norman church of St Michael was pulled down and rebuilt in 1826, though the kirkyard still has many graves connected with the poet (including the graves of four of his children). A chart on the church wall explains where each one is. Another one to look out for is that of **William Fisher**. William was an elder in Mauchline Kirk, and the butt of Burns's satirical poem *Holy Willie's Prayer*, in which he attacks the cant and hypocrisy of the church. Willie asks God's forgiveness for his own, understandable sins, while asking that he severely punish the sins of others. Opposite the church is **Poosie Nansy's Inn**. Though not a great frequenter of this inn, the poet still drank there occasionally, and Burns enthusiasts can still drink there today.

Burns' residence in Mauchline has rather overshadowed the town's two other claims to fame: the production of curling stones made from Ailsa Craig granite, and Mauchline Ware - highly collectable small boxes and other objects made from plane or sycamore wood, hand-painted with local scenes and varnished.

Gavin Hamilton was Burns's friend and landlord. His house can still be seen, attached to the 15th century **Abbot Hunter's Tower**. The tower looks like a small castle, but was in fact the monastic headquarters, or grange, of the Ayrshire estates owned by Melrose Abbey.

Burns used to wander through the Ballochmyle estates, which sit on the banks of the River Ayr. One day in about 1786 when he was strolling along the banks, he saw a Miss Wilhelmina Alexander. He was so taken by her that he wrote *The Lass o' Ballochmyle*, one of his most famous works, in her honour. He sent it to her, but so angry was she that she never replied. However, the anger was more to do with the fact that she was in her 40s at the time, and thought that Burns was having a joke at her expense. In later years, however, she cherished the poem.

SORN

13 miles NE of Ayr on the B743

Sorn is one of the most picturesque villages in the county and has won national and international awards for its tidiness and well kept gardens. It sits beside the River Ayr, with an 18th century bridge spanning it, and has many delightful cottages. **Sorn Parish Church** dates from 1658, and the lofts, or galleries, are reached by stairs on the outside of the walls. **Sorn Castle** dates from the 14th century, with later additions. It was built by a branch of the Hamilton family, and James VI once visited on horseback in the depths of winter to attend the wedding of Isobel Hamilton, the daughter of his Treasurer, Lord Seton. James VI's journey to Sorn so sickened him that he later said that if he

were to play a trick on the devil, he would send him from Glasgow to Sorn on a cold winter's day. The castle is open to the public from mid-July to early August each year.

Alexander Peden was born at Auchincloich near Sorn in 1626. Known as **Prophet Peden**, he was a Covenanter who held secret conventicles, or prayer meetings, at lonely spots all over central Ayrshire. The whole area abounds with places that have been named after him, such as "Peden's Pulpit" and "Peden's Table". There is even a field called "Preaching Peden".

MUIRKIRK

26 miles NE of Ayr on the A70

This former mining and iron-working town is surrounded by bleak but lovely moorland. To the west is the site of the **Battle of Airds Moss**, fought in 1680 and marked by a memorial. A Covenanting army was heavily defeated by Government troops. Just south of the town, and along an unmarked road, is a small monument to John Loudon McAdam the road builder, who owned a tar works in the vicinity.

FAILFORD

9 miles E of Ayr on the B743

Near this little village, in 1786, Burns took his farewell of Highland Mary, who would die soon after in Greenock. Burns, disillusioned by his treatment at the hands of Jean Armour's parents, had asked her to accompany him to Jamaica. They exchanged Bibles, which was seen as a marriage contract, and Mary set

The Ballochmyle Viaduct, to the south of Mauchline, carries the Glasgow to Dumfries line across the River Ayr, and is considered to be one of the finest railway bridges in the world. Work started on it in 1843, and it is still Britain's highest stone and brick railway bridge, being 163 feet above the river. It has three smaller arches at either end, and one long, graceful arch in the middle that spans 181 feet. One of the main scenes from the film Mission Impossible was filmed there with Tom Cruise, though in the film it was supposed to be on the London to Paris line. During the First World War, a pilot is said to have flown under the main arch.

71

AYRSHIRE & ARRAN

A mile east of Failford, in a field, are the remains of a tumulus known as King Cole's Grave. Legend tells us that Old King Cole of nursery rhyme fame was a real person - a British king called Coel or Coilus, who ruled in Ayrshire. In the Dark Ages, he fought a great battle against the Scots under their king, Fergus. Cole's army was routed, and he fled the battlefield. Eventually he was captured and killed. His supporters later cremated his body and buried it with some pomp at the spot where he died. The Kyle area of Ayrshire is supposed to be named after him. The tumulus was opened in 1837, and some cremated bones were discovered in two small urns. Up until not so long ago the nearby stream was referred to locally as the "Bloody Burn", and one field beside the stream was known as "Deadmen's Holm", as that is where those killed in the battle were supposedly buried. Tales were often told of bits of human bone and armour being turned up by men ploughing the field.

off home to Dunoon to prepare for the voyage. However, en route she died in Greenock. The Failford Monument, on a slight rise, commemorates the meeting.

It is in the Failford Inn that the guide centre for the 44-mile **River Ayr Way,** a long-distance footpath that follows the course of the River Ayr from its source at Glenbuck to the sea and passes through some of Ayrshire's most stunning scenery and sites of interest

OCHILTREE

13 miles E of Ayr on the A70

Ochiltree was the birthplace of yet another Ayrshire writer, **George Douglas Brown,** who was born here in 1869, the illegitimate son of a local farmer and a serving girl. He went on to write *The House with the Green Shutters*, a hard, unrelenting book about life in Scotland in the late 1800s. He wanted to banish the "kailyard school" of writing, which saw Scotland's countryside as being comfortable and innocent, full of couthy, happy people of unquestionable worth. He set his book in the fictional town of "Barbie", which is a thinly disguised Ochiltree, and not many characters in the book have redeeming features. One of the village's cottages (not open to the public) now has green shutters, and is itself known as the "House with the Green Shutters".

AUCHINLECK

16 miles E of Ayr off the A76

Burns is not the only famous

literary person associated with Ayrshire. Though born in Edinburgh, James Boswell was the son of a Court of Session judge who lived in **Auchinleck House,** perhaps the finest example of an eighteenth century country villa to survive in Scotland. The judge had the house built in about 1760 as his country seat, and Boswell brought the great Dr Johnson there to meet him when the pair were touring Scotland. They didn't hit it off.

Auchinleck House is now owned by the Landmark Trust and the ground floor of the house, including Museum Room, is open for visits by appointment on Wednesday afternoons during the season. The grounds are open throughout the spring and summer.

Boswell himself died in 1795, and lies in a small mausoleum attached to the old **Auchinleck Kirk,** which is no longer used for worship. It now houses a museum dedicated to the writer and biographer.

CUMNOCK

16 miles E of Ayr off the A76

Cumnock is a small industrial town which was granted its burgh charter in 1509. In the middle of its square stands **Cumnock Old Parish Church,** built in the mid-1800s. It's a foursquare building that seems to sprout transepts, apses and porches in all directions.

Two miles west of the town, at Lugar, is Bello Mill (private), birthplace in 1754 of William Murdoch, discoverer of gas lighting and, believe it or not, the man who

72

invented the wooden top hat. He conducted his gas experiments in a cave on the banks of the Lugar Water upstream from Bello.

The superb **Dumfries House**, one mile west of Cumnock, was designed for the 5th Earl of Dumfries in the mid-1700s by the brothers John, Robert and James Adam. It is one of their finest creations but for almost 250 years the house was not open to the public. Then in 2007, it was put up for auction by its former racing driver owner, the aristocrat and sportsman Johnny Bute. There was a real danger that the house's priceless collection of Chippendale furniture would be dispersed. Fortunately, the house was saved by a consortium of charities, trusts and the Scottish Executive, led by the Prince of Wales whose Charities Foundation provided almost half of the £45 million asking price.

Visitors can now join guided tours of this imposing Palladian mansion which sits in nearly 2000 acres of countryside.

NEW CUMNOCK

22 miles E of Ayr on the A76

The parish of New Cumnock was carved from the much older parish of Cumnock in 1650, with a church being built on the site of Cumnock Castle, once owned by the Dunbars. The ruins of this church can still be seen.

It was near here that the Knockshinnoch Mining Disaster took place in 1950. A slurry of mud and peat filled some workings that were close to the surface, trapping 129 miners underground. The rescuers showed great bravery and 116 men were eventually brought out alive. A feature film, *The Brave Don't Cry*, was made about the disaster in 1952.

To the south of the village is Glen Afton, through which flows the Afton Water. A cairn marks the spot where Burns was inspired to write *Flow Gently Sweet Afton*.

ALLOWAY

2 miles S of Ayr town centre on the B7024

Alloway is one of the iconic places on any **Robert Burns** journey of exploration. It was here, in 1759, that Scotland's national poet was born in a long, low thatched cottage that his father built with his own hands. Burns was not the uneducated "ploughman poet" from the peasant classes that his more romantic admirers would have us believe. His father was a tenant farmer, and although not well off, still managed to employ workmen and serving girls on his farm. Today, **Burns Cottage** is a place of pilgrimage with people coming from all over the world to pay their respects. Within the grounds of the cottage is the **Burns Museum** containing many of his manuscripts, letters and possessions, including his original manuscript for *Auld Lang Syne*.

Burns himself was a highly educated man for his time, thanks to his far-sighted father. He knew his Classics, he could speak French and some Latin, he could read music, he took dancing lessons, and

At the north end of Cumnock is the house that James Keir Hardie, the founder of the Scottish Labour Party, built for himself. Though born in Lanarkshire, he considered himself to be a Cumnock man. He was first of all MP for West Ham in London, and later for Merthyr Tydfil in Wales. His bust can be found outside the Town Hall.

40 KIRKTON INN

Dalrymple

Delightful village inn offering appetising food, en suite rooms, a Malt Room and beer garden.

 see page 374

Two miles south of Dalrymple, and straight out of a fairy tale as well, is Cassillis Castle (private), the home of the Marquis of Ailsa, head of Clan Kennedy. It is a wonderful concoction of pepper pot turrets and towers built originally in the 15th century but added to throughout the years.

he could play both the fiddle and, surprisingly, the guitar. When he went to Edinburgh in later life, he was possibly better educated than some of the gentry who patronised him. Two of his sons, James Glencairn Burns and W. Nicol Burns, attained the ranks of Lieutenant Colonel and Colonel respectively in the British Army.

At one time, Alloway was a small country village. Now it forms part of Ayr, and is full of large, impressive houses which illustrate the relative affluence of this part of Ayrshire.

Alloway Kirk is where Robert's father, William Burns, is buried, and it was the main setting for the poem *Tam o' Shanter*. It dates from the early 16th century, but even in Burns's day it was a ruin. Across the road, within some beautiful gardens, is the Grecian **Burns Monument**, built in the 1820s. Inside is a small museum.

Spanning the Doon is the graceful **Brig o' Doon**, a single arched bridge dating from the 15th century or possibly earlier. It was across the Brig o' Doon that Tam o' Shanter was chased by the witches he disturbed in Alloway Kirk. However, he managed to gain the keystone of the bridge and escaped unharmed, as witches cannot cross running water. In Burn's day the bridge lay on the main road south into Carrick, but a newer, wider construction now carries traffic south.

Across the road from Alloway Kirk is the **Burns National Heritage Park,** a visitor centre

with two audiovisual shows within its large auditorium. One illustrates Burns's life and times, while the other, the Tam o' Shanter Experience, recreates what happened to Tam o' Shanter after he left the inn and made his fateful ride south from Ayr.

East of Alloway is Mount Oliphant Farm (private) to which Burns and his family moved when he was seven years old.

DALRYMPLE

5 miles S of Ayr on the B7034

In this quiet little village of weavers' cottages Burns first received an education. While staying at Mount Oliphant, he and his brother Gilbert attended the Parish School on alternate weeks. The village sits beside the River Doon, and has a small Parish Church built in 1849.

Some people say it was the inspiration for the musical *Brigadoon,* about a mysterious Scottish village that only appears every 100 years. Alan Jay Lerner, who wrote the words, was looking for a way of turning a German fairy tale about a magical village called *Germelshausen* into a musical. One day while in Scotland he suddenly happened upon Dalrymple, which sits in a small glen, hidden until you're almost upon it. He immediately thought of locating his musical in Scotland, and called it Brigadoon because there really is a bridge over the River Doon in the village. He also called one of the characters Charlie Dalrymple.

MAYBOLE

This small, quiet town is the capital of Carrick, and sits on a hillside about four miles inland from the coast. It was here that Burns's parents, William Burnes (he later changed the name to Burns) and Agnes Broun met in 1756.

In 1562, a famous meeting took place in Maybole between John Knox, the Scottish reformer, and Abbot Quentin Kennedy of nearby Crossraguel Abbey. The purpose of the meeting was to debate the significance and doctrine of the Mass, and it attracted a huge crowd of people, even though it was held in a small room of the house where the provost of the town's collegiate church lived. Forty people from each side were allowed in to hear the debate, which lasted for three days. It only broke up - with no conclusion reached - when the town ran out of food to feed the thronging masses round the door.

The ruins of Maybole Collegiate Church (Historic Scotland) can still be viewed, though they are not open to the public. The church, dedicated to St Mary, was founded by Sir John Kennedy of Dunure in 1371 for the saying of daily prayers for himself, his wife Mary and their children. The clergy consisted of one clerk and three chaplains who said the prayers daily. The present ruins date from a rebuilding in the 15th century, when it became a full collegiate church with a provost and a "college" of priests. The present **Parish Church** dates from 1808, and has an unusual stepped spire.

At one time Maybole had no less than 28 lairds' town houses, each one referred to as a "castle". Now there are only two left, one at each end of the main street. The "upper" one is now part of the **Town Hall**, and was the 17th century town house of the lairds of Blairquhan Castle, about five miles to the east. The other is still referred to as **Maybole Castle** though it too was a town house, this time for the Earls of Cassillis. The largest and finest of the 28 town houses, it dates from the mid-1500s and was built in traditional 'Scottish Baronial' style with a sqaure tower and round turrets.

A few miles west of Maybole, near the farm of Drumshang, is the curiously named **Electric Brae**, on the A719 road between Ayr and Turnberry. Stop your car on the convenient layby at the side of the road, put it out of gear, let off the brake, and be amazed as it rolls uphill. Better still, lay a football on the layby's surface, and watch it roll uphill as well. The phenomenon has nothing to do with electricity, ley lines, earth magic, the "unseen world" of the earth's energy system or the same power displayed by poltergeists when they move objects, but everything to do with an optical illusion. The surrounding land makes you think that the road rises towards the west when it fact it descends.

KIRKMICHAEL

3 miles E of Maybole on the B7045

Like its neighbour Crosshill, Kirkmichael is a former weaving

41 MAYBOLE CASTLE

Maybole

A 16th century town house with many fascinating features, built originally for the Earls of Cassillis

 see page 373

Many of the scenes in the film The Match (also called The Big Game) were shot in Straiton, which became the fictional Highland village Inverdoune.

Dalmellington is the starting point for the new Scottish Coal Cycle Route which runs from Dalmellington to Coalburn, 40 miles away in Lanarkshire. It is part of the National Cycle Network.

village. However, its roots lie deep into Scottish history. The **Parish Church** dates from 1790, and the picturesque lych-gate from about 1700.

Every May, Kirkmichael is busy with the **International Guitar Festival** which draws musicians from all over the world. It covers everything from jazz to pop and country to classical. Huge marquees are erected, and local pubs host impromptu jamming sessions and folk concerts. It was founded by the internationally renowned jazz guitarist Martin Taylor, who lives locally.

STRAITON

8 miles SE of Maybole on the B741

A narrow road runs south from this lovely village called the **Nick o' the Balloch**. It doesn't go through the Carrick of gentle fields or verdant valleys, but over the wild hills and moorland that make the edges of this area so beautiful, and finally drops down into Glentrool.

Straiton itself sits beside the water of Girvan, and has picturesque little cottages facing each other across a main street, some with roses growing round the door. It was a planned village, laid out in 1760 by the Earl of Cassillis on the site of a small hamlet. The local pub, The Black Bull, dates from 1766, while parts of St Cuthbert's Parish Church date back to 1510.

Close to the village is **Blairquhan** (pronounced "Blair-whan"), a Tudor-Gothic mansion built between 1821 and 1824 to the

designs of the famous Scottish architect William Burn. It stands on the site of an earlier tower house dating to 1346 that was once a McWhirter stronghold before passing to the Kennedys. It is now owned by the Hunter Blair family, and is open to the public in summer. It has a fine collection of paintings by the Scottish Colourists. On a hill above the village stands the **Hunter Blair Monument**, built in 1856 to commemorate James Hunter Blair, killed at the Battle of Inkerman.

DALMELLINGTON

14 miles SE of Maybole on the A713

This former mining village sits on the banks of the Doon. Over the last few years, it has exploited its rich heritage, and created some visitor centres and museums that explain the village's industrial past. The **Dunaskin Open Air Museum** covers 110 acres and has many facets, each of which is well worth exploring. The **Dalmellington Iron Works** were first opened in the 1840s, and are now the largest restored Victorian Ironworks in Europe. Other attractions include the **Brickworks** and the **Scottish Industrial Railway Centre**, where steam trains run on a restored track. The **Cathcartson Centre** in the village is housed in weaving cottages dating from the 18th century and shows how weavers lived long ago.

A couple of miles beyond Dalmellington is a minor road that takes you to lovely Loch Doon, surrounded by lonely hills and moorland, and the source of the river that Burns wrote about. It was here, during World War I, that a School of Aerial Gunnery was proposed. Millions of pounds were wasted on it before the plans were finally abandoned. When a hydroelectric scheme was built in the 1930s, the water level of the loch was raised. **Loch Doon Castle**, which stood on an island in the loch, was dismantled stone by stone and reassembled on the shore, where it can still be seen.

In the late 1970s it was announced that 32 deep tunnels would be bored in the hills surrounding the loch to store most of Britain's radioactive waste. After many protests by local people, the idea was abandoned.

BARR

15 miles S of Maybole on the B734

Tucked in a fold of the Carrick hills, Barr is an idyllic village that was once the site of the wonderfully named Kirkdandie Fair. It was the largest annual fair in Southern Scotland during the late 18th and early 19th centuries, and was held on a strip of land where stood the long gone Kirkdandie (or Kirkdominae) Church. Its main claim to fame was the fighting that took place there every year, and it soon became known as the "Donnybrook of Scotland". People even came over from Ireland to participate in the great pitched battles. So famous did it become that a ballad was written about it, describing at least 63 tents, the sound of pipes and people

socialising, dancing, drinking and eating.

Above Barr is the estate of Changue (pronounced "Shang"), to which an old legend is attached. The cruel and wicked **Laird of Changue** was a smuggler and distiller of illicit whisky who enjoyed the fruits of his own still a bit to much and was therefore always penniless. One day, while walking through his estates, Satan appeared and offered him a deal. If he handed over his soul when he died, he would become rich. The laird, who was a young man, agreed, and duly prospered. But as he grew older he began to regret his rashness, and when Satan at last appeared before him to claim his soul - at the same spot where he had appeared all these years before - the laird refused to keep his side of the bargain.

Instead he challenged the Devil to fight for it. Drawing a large circle on the ground round both of them, he said that the first person to be forced out of it would be the loser. After a bitter struggle, the laird cut off the end of Satan's tail with his sword, and he jumped out of the circle in pain. The laird had won. Up until the end of the 19th century, a great bare circle on some grassland was shown as the place where all this took place. It's a wonderful story, but no one has ever managed to put a name or date to this mysterious laird. And it has often been pointed out that if Satan had bided his time, he would have had the soul of the laird in the usual way, so wicked was he.

COLMONELL

21 miles S of Maybole on the B734

The River Stinchar is the southernmost of Ayrshire's major rivers, and flows through a lovely glen bordered on both sides by high moorland and hills. In this valley, four miles from the sea, sits Colmonell. It's an attractive village of small cottages, with the romantic ruins of the old Kennedy stronghold of **Kirkhill Castle** standing next to the village hall. Knockdolian Hill, two miles west, was at one time called the "false Ailsa Craig" because of its resemblance to the volcanic island out in the Firth of Clyde.

CROSSRAGUEL ABBEY

3 miles SW of Maybole on the A77

The romantic ruins of **Crossraguel Abbey** (Historic Scotland) sit complacently beside the main Ayr-Stranraer road. They are very well preserved, and give a wonderful idea of the layout of a medieval abbey. Some of the architecture and stone carving, such as that in the chapter house, is well worth seeking out. Duncan, Earl of Carrick, founded it in 1244 for Clunaic monks from Paisley Abbey, though most of what you see nowadays dates from after the 13th century. The name is supposed to come from an old cross which stood here before the abbey was built, and it may mean the regal, or royal cross, or the cross of Riaghail, possibly a local chief.

To the north are the ruins of **Baltersan Castle**, an old fortified 16th century tower house built either for John Kennedy of Pennyglen and his wife Margaret Cathcart or as the residence of Quentin Kennedy, the Abbot of Crossraguel from 1548 until 1564.

OLD DAILLY

12 miles SW of Maybole on the B734

Old Dailly was originally called Dalmakerran, and was once an important village, with many cottages, a manse for the minister and a mill. Now it is a row of council houses close to the ruins of 14th century **Old Dailly Parish Church**. Within the kirkyard are two hefty stones called the Charter Stones, which men tried to lift in bygone days during trials of strength.

Buried in the kirkyard is the pre-Raphaelite artist **William Bell Scott**, who was staying at nearby Penkill Castle (private) when he died. Many members of the pre-Raphaelite Brotherhood visited the

Crossraguel Abbey

place, including Dante Gabriel Rossetti. Close by is the 17th century fortified mansion **Bargany House,** once a Kennedy stronghold. The house is private but the marvellous gardens are open to the public for a few weeks in late spring/early summer.

BALLANTRAE

28 miles SW of Maybole on the A77

When on a walking tour of Carrick in 1876, RL Stevenson spent a night in Ballantrae, a small fishing village. However, dour villagers took exception to his way of dressing, and almost ran him out of town. He got his revenge by writing *The Master of Ballantrae,* which confused everyone by having no connection with the place whatsoever.

In the churchyard is the **Bargany Aisle**, containing the ornate tomb of Gilbert Kennedy, laird of Bargany and Ardstinchar, who was killed by the Earl of Cassillis (also a Kennedy) in 1601. A bitter feud between the Cassillis and Bargany branches of the Kennedy family had been going on right through the 16th century, with no quarter given or taken. Matters came to a head when the two branches met near Ayr, and Bargany was killed. The power of the Bargany branch was broken forever, and the feud fizzled out. The ruins of **Ardstinchar Castle**, Bargany's main stronghold, can still be seen beside the river. It was built in 1421, and in August 1566 Mary Stuart stayed there.

KIRKOSWALD

4 miles SW of Maybole on the A77

It was to Kirkoswald, in 1775, that Burns came for one term to learn surveying. Though his poem *Tam o' Shanter* is set in Alloway, all the characters in it have their origins in the parish of Kirkoswald which was where his maternal grandparents came from.

Kirkoswald Parish Church dates from 1777, and was designed by Robert Adam while he was working on Culzean Castle. Dwight D. Eisenhower worshipped here twice, one of the occasions being when he was president of the United States. Another visitor is not so well known, though the airline he helped to found is. The late Randolph Fields, together with Richard Branson, founded Virgin Airlines. Randolph loved this part of Ayrshire, and when he died in 1997 he left some money for the restoration of the church. A year later his widow presented the church with a small table, on which is a plaque commemorating his donation.

The old parish **Church of St Oswald** stands at the heart of the village. It is a ruin now, but in its kirkyard are the graves of many people associated with Burns, including David Graham of Shanter Farm near Maidens, the real life "Tam o' Shanter".

The church also contains one interesting relic - Robert the Bruce's Baptismal Font. Both Lochmaben in Dumfriesshire and Turnberry Castle, within the parish

Three miles to the east of Old Dailly is the mining village of New Dailly with its T-shaped New Dailly Parish Church of 1766. Close by, on the opposite side of the Girvan Water, are the substantial ruins of Dalquharran Castle. It was designed by Robert Adam and built between 1780 and 1791 for Kennedy of Dunure. The castle is currently being renovated with plans to turn it and its estate into a luxury hotel and golf resort, with Jack Nicklaus designing the golf course. The ruins of the 15th century Old Dalquharran Castle are close by.

Glenapp Castle, a few miles south of Ballantrae just off the A77, was designed in 1870 by the noted Victorian architect David Bryce for James Hunter, the Deputy Lord Lieutenant of Ayrshire. It is now a luxury hotel surrounded by 30 acres of grounds and gardens.

Built onto the scant ruins of Turnberry castle is Turnberry Lighthouse, surrounded on three sides by the championship golf course. The elegant five star Turnberry Hotel is situated south east of the castle, just off the main road, and is one of the premier hotels in Scotland. It even has its own small runway for aircraft, and at one time had its own railway line from Ayr to bring guests. During World Wars I and II, all this area was an airfield, and the runways can still be seen. There is a War Memorial on the golf course dedicated to the men of the airfield who died in World War I. It is in the shape of a double Celtic cross, and was erected by the people of Kirkoswald parish in 1923. In 1990 the monument was altered so that the names of the airmen killed during World War II could be added.

of Kirkoswald, claim to have been the birthplace of Robert the Bruce. Turnberry is the more likely, as it was the ancestral home of the Countess of Carrick, Bruce's mother, and it is known that she was living there at about the time of the birth. The story goes that the baby was premature, and that he was rushed to Crossraguel Abbey for baptism in case he died. The abbey's font was used, and when Crossraguel was abandoned after the Reformation, the people of Kirkoswald rescued the font and put it in their own church.

Within the village you'll also find **Souter Johnnie's Cottage** (National Trust for Scotland). John Davidson was a "souter", or cobbler, and featured in *Tam o' Shanter*. Now his thatched cottage, built in 1785, has been turned into a small museum. One room at the back of the cottage is given over to the souter's workshop, complete with fire and all the tools needed for shoemaking. At the other end of the cottage is a room re-creating aspects of the parlour, with a large dresser and fire, and a bedroom complete with box beds along one wall. In the garden are life-size stone statues of a jovial-looking Souter Johnnie and other characters from Tam O'Shanter. They were carved in 1802 and exhibited around Scotland and England before being brought to the cottage in 1924.

TURNBERRY

7 miles SW of Maybole on the A719

Very little now survives of the 12th century **Turnberry Castle,** where Robert the Bruce is supposed to have been born. The story of how his parents met is an unusual one. Marjorie, Countess of Carrick, the young widow of Adam de Kilconquhar, saw a knight passing by her castle at Turnberry. She immediately became infatuated with him, and had him kidnapped and brought into her presence. He turned out to be Robert de Brus, son of the Lord of Annandale, and she persuaded him to marry her. The result of the marriage was Robert the Bruce, who himself became Earl of Carrick on his mother's death. Because Robert ascended the throne of Scotland as Robert I, the earldom became a royal one, and the present Earl of Carrick is Prince Charles.

GIRVAN

12 miles SW of Maybole on the A77

This pleasant little town is the main holiday resort in Carrick. It is also a thriving fishing port, with many boats in the harbour at the mouth of the Water of Girvan. Though there is a long, sandy beach, a boating pond and a small funfair in summer, the town is a quiet place overlooked by the bulk of Byne Hill to the south. From the top there is a fine view of the Firth of Clyde, and on a clear day the coast of Northern Ireland can be seen. The small Crauford Monument above Ardmillan House, on the western side, commemorates Major A.C.B. Crauford, who took part in the capture of the Cape of Good Hope in 1795.

Out in the Firth of Clyde, the bulk of **Ailsa Craig** rises sheer from the water. It is the plug of an ancient volcano, and is now a bird sanctuary. Trips around it are available from Girvan harbour.

Within the town, in Knockcushan Street, is a small, curious building with a short spire which has been given the nickname **Auld Stumpy**. It was built in the early 1800s as the town jail with cells on the 1st, 2nd and 3rd floors of the building with a clock tower above these cells. Exhibits in the tower include a 16th century wrought iron cannon and police memorabilia.

Behind Knockcushan House, near the harbour, are **Knockcushan Gardens**, the site of a court held by Robert the Bruce in 1328. There is a memorial commemorating this event and also an aviary.

At the **McKechnie Institute** in Dalrymple Street art exhibitions are sometimes held.

LENDALFOOT
18 miles SW of Maybole on the A77

Carleton Castle, now in ruins, was the home of Sir John Carleton who, legend states, had a neat way of earning a living. He married ladies of wealth then enticed them to Gamesloup, a nearby rocky eminence, where he pushed them to their deaths and inherited their wealth. Sir John went through seven or eight wives before meeting the daughter of Kennedy of Culzean. After marrying her, he took her to Gamesloup, but instead

of him pushing her over, she pushed him over, and lived happily ever after on his accumulated wealth. It is said that you can still occasionally hear the screams of the women as they were pushed to their death.

But if it's a gruesome tale you're after, then you should head for Sawney Bean's Cave a few miles south of the village, on the shoreline north of Bennane Head, and easily reached by a footpath from a layby on the A77. Here, in the 16th century, lived a family of cannibals led by **Sawney Bean** ("Sawny" being Scots for "Sandy"), which waylaid strangers, robbed them, and ate their flesh. They evaded capture for many years until a troop of men sent by James VI trapped them in their cave. They were taken to Edinburgh and executed. It's a wonderful story, but no documentary proof has ever been unearthed to prove that it really happened.

CULZEAN CASTLE
4 miles W of Maybole off the A719

Culzean Castle (National Trust for Scotland), perched on a cliff above the Firth of Clyde, is possibly the most spectacularly sited castle in Scotland. (Culzean, incidentally, is pronounced 'Cullane'). Magnificently furnished, the castle was designed by Robert Adam in 1777 and built round an old keep for the 10th Earl of Cassillis. The work took 15 years to complete but the result is one of Adam's finest creations, marked by dazzling features such as the Oval

42 CORRA-LINN

Girvan

Quality B&B en suite accommodation in handsome Victorian house with spectacular sea views.

🛏 *see page 374*

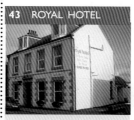

43 ROYAL HOTEL

Girvan

Friendly, family-run hotel close to the town centre offering excellent bar food, real ale and en suite rooms.

🛏 🍴 *see page 375*

Culzean Castle

Staircase and the Circular Saloon with its views out over the Firth. Surrounding the castle are the 560 acres of **Culzean Country Park** whose attractions include a Walled Garden, the Swan Pond, the Deer Park and the Fountain Court.

In gratitude for his part in World War II, the National Trust for Scotland presented General Eisenhower with the life tenure of a flat in Culzean. Eisenhower accepted, and spent a few golfing holidays here. The **Eisenhower Presentation**, within the castle, explains his connections with the area, and has exhibits about D-Day.

DUNURE

5 miles NW of Maybole off the A 719

This pretty little fishing village would not look out of place in Cornwall. Arriving by car, you drop down towards it, giving excellent views of the cottages and pub, all grouped round a small harbour.

To the south of the village are the ruins of **Dunure Castle**, perched on the coastline. This is the original castle of the Kennedys, and dates mostly from the 14th century. It was here that the famous **Roasting of the Abbot** took place in 1570. The Kennedys were at the height of their powers, and Gilbert Kennedy, 4th Earl of Cassillis, owned most of the land in Carrick. He was, as his contemporaries observed, "ane very greedy man", and coveted the lands of Crossraguel Abbey, which, at the Reformation, had been placed in the hands of Allan Stewart, commendator, or lay abbot, of the abbey. Gilbert invited Allan to Dunure Castle for a huge feast, and when Allan accepted, had him incarcerated in the Black Vault. He then stripped him and placed him on a spit over a great open fire, turning him occasionally like a side of beef. Eventually Allan signed away the lands, and was released. He immediately protested to the Privy Council and the Regent (James VI was still a child at the time), ordered Kennedy to pay for the lands. Such was Kennedy's power that he ignored the order.

KILMARNOCK

It was back in 1820 that a Kilmarnock grocer named Johnnie Walker began blending his own whisky at his shop on King Street. The whisky bottling business he founded grew to be the largest in the world and the town's main employer. Then in July 2009 its current owner, the multi-national company Diageo, announced that the plant would be closed in 2011. A vigorous campaign is at present under way to keep the company with its 700 jobs in Kilmarnock. The news broke just after council chiefs had launched a £21million 10-year town centre regeneration project.

Though it is now largely an industrial town, Kilmarnock has many Burns associations - the first edition of his poems was published in the town, at Star Inn Close (now gone) in 1786. Today, a copy from that first edition is worth many thousands of pounds but you can see one in the museum attached to the red sandstone Burns Monument in Key Park. **Burns Statue**, unveiled in the mid 1990s by the Princess Royal, stands at Kilmarnock Cross. It is the work of Sandy Stoddard, whose other works include the statue of David Hume on Edinburgh's Royal Mile and the sculptured friezes in the Queen's Gallery in Buckingham Palace.

Kilmarnock was granted its burgh charter in 1592, so its roots go deep into Scottish history. Legend says it grew up round a church founded by St Marnock, a Celtic saint, in the 7th century. The present **Laigh Kirk** (now called The Laigh West High Kirk) in Bank Street dates from 1802. In the previous year, during a service, 29 people were trampled to death when plasterwork started falling off the ceiling of the previous kirk, causing a mad rush for the doors. When the church was rebuilt, it was given 13 exits in case it ever happened again. The town's other old church is the **Old High Kirk**, which dates from the early 1730s.

In truth, Kilmarnock's shopping centre, notably Kilmarnock Cross and King Street, is dull and unattractive, due to uninspired modern developments. But if you go down Cheapside towards Bank Street and the narrow streets round the Laigh and West High Kirk, you get an idea of what the 18th century town looked like.

One place not to be missed is the **Dick Institute**, the town's museum, art gallery and library. It is housed in a grand classical building, and has impressive collections featuring geology, archaeology, biology and local history. The gallery is also impressive, with paintings by Corot, Constable, Turner and Kilmarnock's own painter, Robert Colquhoun. The area around the Dick Institute is particularly attractive, with a war memorial, Victorian houses, and the richly decorated façade of the old

*In 1862, at Crosshouse, a
mining village west of
Kilmarnock, was born
Andrew Fisher, who rose
to become Prime
Minister of Australia on
three separate occasions.*

technical college, now being
converted into flats. Across from
the Dick Institute is the statue of
Kilmarnock's own Dick
Whittington - James Shaw (known
affectionately in the town as
"Jimmy Shaw") who became Lord
Mayor of London in 1805.

To the north east of the town
centre is the town's oldest building,
Dean Castle. It was the home of
the Boyd family, who became Earls
of Kilmarnock, and is in fact two
castles within a curtain wall - the
14th century Keep and the later
Palace. Both are open to the public,
and house wonderful collections of
tapestries, historical musical
instruments, arms and armour.
Surrounding the castle(s) is **Dean
Castle Country Park** with many
walks and a small children's zoo.

Kilmarnock Academy, which
stands on an eminence overlooking
the town centre, is said to be one
of the few schools in the world
that has produced two Nobel Prize
winners - Sir Alexander Fleming
(1945, for Medicine) and Lord

Boyd Orr (1949, for Peace).

Across from the new sheriff
court building near the park is the
Old Sheriff Court of 1852, an
attractive building in neoclassical
style. Two miles west of the town
is the **Gatehead Viaduct**, built in
1807 to take the railway over the
River Irvine. Though it no longer
carries a railway line, it is still
Scotland's oldest railway bridge.
The viaduct was recently renovated
and is now accessible to the public.

AROUND KILMARNOCK

FENWICK

4 miles N of Kilmarnock off the A77

Fenwick (pronounced "Fennick") is
really two villages - High Fenwick
and Laigh Fenwick. They lie on the
edge of the Fenwick Moors, which
separate the farmlands of Ayrshire
from Glasgow and its suburbs, and
were originally weaving villages.
Some of the cottages still show
their weaving origins, with two
windows on one side of the door
to allow plenty of light to enter the
room containing the loom.
Fenwick Parish Church, which
dates from 1643, is an attractive
whitewashed building with a Greek
cross plan. On one wall hangs the
original jougs, where wrongdoers
were chained by their necks to the
wall.

Two miles south east of the
village is the quaintly named, and
often photographed, hamlet of
Moscow (pronounced "Moss-cow"
rather than "Moss-coe"), which
actually has a burn called the Volga

Dean Castle, Kilmarnock

flowing through it. And five miles to the north, off the B764, is **Lochgoin Farm**, which has a small museum commemorating the Covenanters.

Fenwick was the birthplace, in 1803, of John Fulton, a shoemaker who gained considerable fame throughout Scotland by making orreries - working models of the solar system where the planets revolve round the sun and satellites revolve round the planets, all synchronised by the use of gearing. Fulton built three such orreries, and one of them is still on show in the New Kelvin Galleries in Glasgow.

STEWARTON
5 miles N of Kilmarnock on the A735

Stewarton is famous as being the home of bonnet making in Ayrshire. It was the birthplace, in 1739, of **David Dale**, the industrialist and social reformer who founded New Lanark and later sold them to his son-in-law, Robert Owen. The **Parish Church of St Columba** dates originally from 1696, though it has been much altered.

DUNLOP
7 miles N of Kilmarnock on the A735

Dunlop is a delightful village of small weavers' cottages. The **Parish Church** dates from 1835, though it has fragments from the earlier church incorporated into the north aisle. In the kirkyard is the ornate early 17th century **Hans Hamilton Tomb**, contained within a small mausoleum. Hamilton was Dunlop's first Protestant minister, and was made Viscount

Clandeboye by James VI. The small Clandeboye Hall (private), beside the mausoleum, dates from 1641 and for almost two centuries served as the village's first school.

GALSTON
5 miles E of Kilmarnock on the A71

This pleasant little town in the Irvine Valley has a splendid **Parish Church** dating from 1808. One of its ministers, Perthshire-born Robert Stirling, was the inventor of the Stirling Engine. He died in 1878.

Another church not to be missed is **St Sophia's RC Church**, modelled on the Hagia Sophia in Istanbul. **Barr Castle** is a solid, 15th century tower house once owned by the Lockhart family. An ancient game of handball used to be played against the castle walls by the locals. The castle is now a small museum with many exhibits relating to local history.

On the edge of the town, Loudoun Gowf Club is unique in retaining the game's old Scots spelling. The course is open to visitors on weekdays.

To the north of the town are the impressive ruins of **Loudoun Castle**, ancestral home of the Campbells of Loudoun which burnt down in 1941. In their heyday, the Campbells entertained so lavishly that the castle was called the "Windsor of Scotland". Three ghosts reputedly haunt it - a Grey Lady, a Phantom Piper and a Benevolent Monk. At one time the great sword of William Wallace was kept within the castle, but it was sold in 1930. Beside its walls is the

It was in a farm near the village of Dunlop that the famous Dunlop Cheese was first manufactured in the 17th century by a farmer's wife called Barbara Gilmour. It is made from the milk of Ayrshire cattle, and closely resembles a Cheddar. Barbara now lies buried in the kirkyard, and her grave can still be seen. Cheese making was recently revived in the village, and Dunlop cheese, which is harder than the original variety, is made by Dunlop Dairy which also produces a range of sheep and goats cheeses.

Loudoun Castle was the birthplace of Lady Flora Hastings, who shook the monarchy and government to its core in 1839. Queen Victoria was 20 years old at the time, and had been on the throne for just two years. Lady Flora was a Lady of the Bedchamber who contracted a disease which so swelled her abdomen that she appeared pregnant. Gossip raged through the court, and she was shunned, even though doctors confirmed that she wasn't pregnant, but ill with an enlarged liver. Neither the government nor the Queen did anything to dispel the rumours, and people began to sympathise with the young woman. Soon it was the Queen's turn to be shunned, and she was shocked when people turned their back on her as she proceeded through London. It wasn't until Lady Flora was on her deathbed in 1833 in Buckingham Palace that a grudging reconciliation took place. The Campbells were so incensed by Flora's treatment that when postage stamps were introduced bearing Victoria's image, family members stuck them onto envelopes upside down.

Auld Yew Tree, under which Hugh, 3rd Earl of Loudoun, prepared the draft of the Treaty of Union between Scotland and England. Today the **Loudoun Castle Theme Park,** which claims to be the largest in Scotland, fills the grounds of the castle.

A mile or so away from Loudoun Castle are the ruins of the medieval **Loudoun Kirk**, at one time dedicated to St Michael. Flora now lies in the choir, which has been converted into a burial vault for the Campbells of Loudoun. A slim monument stands in the kirkyard to her memory. The Campbells coat-of-arms can still be seen on the choir walls, above the entrance to the vault. Attached to a wall of the ruined kirk is a plaque which commemorates the Belgian paratroopers who trained at Loudoun Castle during the Second World War.

NEWMILNS

7 miles E of Kilmarnock on the A71

Newmilns is a small lace making and weaving town in the Irvine Valley, which was granted its charter in 1490, making it the oldest inland burgh in Ayrshire. The small crow-stepped **Town House,** or Tolbooth, dates from 1739, and behind the Loudoun Arms, which itself dates from the 18th century, is Newmilns Tower (private), an impressive early 16th century tower house built by Sir Hugh Campbell, Earl of Loudoun. Sir Hugh was perhaps the most tragic member of the Campbell of Loudon family. After being involved in the murder of a member of the powerful Kennedy family during an ongoing feud, his wife and nine children were killed when the Kennedys besieged Loudoun Castle, a few miles away.

The Lady Flora Institute, built in 1877 as a girl's school, commemorates the tragic Lady Flora Hastings, a lady-in-waiting to Queen Victoria (see Galston above). The institute is now private housing.

During the American Civil War, the weavers of Newmilns sent a message of support to Abraham Lincoln, and he in turn sent back an American flag. This was subsequently lost, but in 1949 the American Embassy gave the town a replacement, which is now housed in the early 19th century Parish Church in the main street.

DARVEL

9 miles E of Kilmarnock, on the A71

Situated in the lovely Irvine Valley, Darvel is a small, attractive town which was laid out in the late 18th and early 19th centuries. Like its neighbour Newmilns, it is a lace making town, the skills having been brought here by the Dutch in the 17th century. It was in Lochfield, near Darvel, that Sir Alexander Fleming, the discoverer of penicillin, was born in 1881. To the east of the town rises the immense bulk of Loudoun Hill, the plug of a former volcano. Both William Wallace and Robert the Bruce fought battles at Loudoun Hill against the English, in 1297 and 1307 respectively. South of the town is the quaintly named Distinkhorn, the highest hill in the area.

IRVINE

7 miles W of Kilmarnock on the A71

The largest town in North Ayrshire, Irvine is an ancient seaport and royal burgh which, in the 1960s, was designated as Britain's first seaside new town. It is a mixture of old and new, and has many unattractive industrial estates surrounding it. However, the historical core has been preserved, though a brutally modern and totally unnecessary shopping mall straddling the River Irvine dominates it. Robert Burns learned flax dressing in Irvine in 1781 and lodged in a house in the cobbled Glasgow Vennel. A small museum has been created within both it and the heckling (flax-dressing) shop behind it. The national bard is also celebrated by an impressive 9 feet high statue on the bank of the River Irvine.

Irvine has other, more unexpected, literary associations.. In 1815 the American writer **Edgar Allan Poe**, spent a couple of months in the town, attending the local school. It is said that part of his lessons was to copy the epitaphs from the tombstones in the kirkyard of the Parish Kirk which may have prepared him for some of the macabre tales he wrote in later life. **Alexander MacMillan**, who founded the great publishing house, was also a native of the town.

In the nearby village of Dreghorn was born in 1840 yet another famous Ayrshireman - **John Boyd Dunlop**, who invented the pneumatic tyre. Born in 1840, he came from a farming background, and graduated from Edinburgh University as a veterinary surgeon. He practised in Edinburgh and then Belfast. He found the roads of Ulster to be stony and rough, and eventually invented an inflatable tyre to overcome the discomfort of travelling on them. Unfortunately, unknown to him, another Scot, Robert William Thomson, had patented the idea before him and only after a court case could he set up the Dunlop Rubber Company.

Dreghorn Parish Church, built in 1780, is unusual in that it is six-sided in plan. It was built by Archibald, the 11th Earl of Eglinton, and used to have the nickname of the "threepenny church", as its shape reminded people of the old threepenny bit.

The ruins of **Seagate Castle** date from the early 1500s and it is said that Mary Stuart lodged here briefly in 1563. Every August the town has its **Marymass Week**, which supposedly commemorates her visit. However, the celebrations probably have more to do with a pre-Reformation religious festival, as the parish church was formerly dedicated to St Mary.

In the 18th century, Irvine saw the founding of perhaps the most unusual religious cult ever seen in Scotland - the Buchanites. Elspet Buchan was the daughter of a publican, and claimed she could bestow immortality on a person by

Irvine

Popular town centre traditional inn with bar, restaurant and first floor cocktail lounge.

see page 376

Irvine

Here you will have the
opportunity for a guided
tour which includes a
restored 1920's shipyard
workers 'Tenement Flat' and
a collection of moored
vessels in the harbour, some
of which can be boarded.

 see page 376

breathing on them, and that she herself was immortal. She attracted a wide following, including a gullible Irvine clergyman, but was hounded from the town along with her followers. She eventually died a natural death, and the cult broke up.

Down by the harbour side is the Magnum Leisure Centre, one of the biggest centres of its kind in Scotland. It has a theatre and concert hall, an indoor bowling green, an ice rink, swimming pool and fitness and coaching areas.

Near the Magnum Centre is one of the three sites of the **Scottish Maritime Museum.** It houses a large collection of ships and small craft. There's also the Linthouse Engine Works, which houses a vast collection of maritime machinery, such as engines, winding gear and so on. In the Shipworker's Tenement Flat, a typical "room and kitchen" flat dating from the 1920s has been re-created, showing how shipyard workers lived in those days. Visitors can also board the *Spartan*, one of the last puffers in Scotland. These small cargo boats, immortalised in the *Para Handy* tales by Neil Munro, sailed the west coast of Scotland for many years.

In 1839, Irvine was the setting of the grand Eglinton Tournament, organised by the 13th Earl of Eglinton at his home, Eglinton Castle, on the outskirts of the town. Here, a great medieval tournament was to be re-created, with jousting, horse riding and other knightly pursuits for the great and the good. They attended from all over Europe,

but alas, the three-day event was a wash out due to colossal rainstorms. Little remains of the castle, but the grounds have been turned into **Eglinton Country Park**.

KILMAURS

2 miles NW of Kilmarnock, on the A735

Kilmaurs is a former weaving village, and though only a few fields separate it from Kilmarnock's suburbs, it is still a small, self-contained community with many small cottages. At its centre is the old 17th century **Tolbooth**, still with the jougs installed which were placed round wrongdoers' necks as a punishment.

St Maurs Glencairn Church dates from 1888 and is mainly notable for the **Glencairn Aisle**, the 16th century burial vault of the Earls of Glencairn which stands to the rear of the church. It has an ornate monument inside to the 7th earl and his family. It dates from around 1600, and carries an inscription that reads "nothing is surer than death, be therefore sober and watch in prayer".

The village takes its name from St Maura, daughter of a Scottish chieftain on the island of Little Cumbrae in the Firth of Clyde. **John Boyd Orr**, first director of the United Nations Food and Agricultural Organisation and Nobel prize-winner, was born in Kilmaurs in 1880.

KILWINNING

9 miles NW of Kilmarnock on the A737

Though nowadays a continuation of Irvine, Kilwinning was, up until

1975, a separate burgh. Its former name was Segtoune, meaning the "saint's town", as it was founded in the 7th century by St Winnin, whom some people associate with St Finnan of Moville, who taught St Columba in Ireland. In the 12th century the great Tironensian **Kilwinning Abbey** was built on the site, and its ruins still dominate the town centre, though they are not as extensive as those of Ayrshire's other great abbey, Crossraguel. The tower you see today was built in 1815 and replaced the original medieval one which fell down the year before. **Kilwinning Parish Church**, which sits within the ruins of the abbey, was built in 1775.

The Ancient Society of Kilwinning Archers is one of the oldest archery organisations in the world. Each year in August it holds the **Papingo Shoot**, where archers shoot upwards at a target (the papingo) held from a window of the tower. The papingo is usually a wooden pigeon, and such shoots were once common throughout Britain.

A few miles out of town, on the A737, is **Dalgarven Mill** dating from about 1620. It is now a museum dedicated to country life in Ayrshire.

ARDROSSAN, SALTCOATS & STEVENSTON

11 miles NW of Kilmarnock on the A78

These towns form a trio of holiday resorts along the Ayrshire coast. Ardrossan is the most industrialised and is the ferry terminal for Arran.

Kilwinning Abbey

It is a planned town, with its core being laid out in the early 19th century by the 12th Earl of Eglinton. The ruins of 15th century **Ardrossan Castle** stand on Castle Hill overlooking the main streets. Cromwell is said to have plundered some of its masonry to build the Citadel at Ayr. The ruins and the land surrounding them were given to the town by the Earl of Eglinton as a public park. The **Obelisk** at the highest point on the hill commemorates a local doctor,

Up until the 1930s, Ardrossan Docks, was one of the main supply ports for the Hudson Bay Company. The harbour then was crammed with ships loading supplies for North America and unloading furs, fish and sometimes animals.

Alexander McFadzean, who promoted piped water and gas supplies in the town. At the foot of the hill stands **St Peter in Chains**, designed by Jack Coia, one of Scotland's best-known architects, and built in 1938. It is reckoned to be one of the finest modern churches in Ayrshire.

Just off the coast is **Horse Island**, an RSPB reserve. Though it looks peaceful enough, it has been the scene of many shipwrecks over the years, and many sailors have found themselves marooned on it after their ships struck its submerged reefs. At the **Clyde Marina** is a sculpture park featuring works by the Japanese artist Hideo Furuta, who lives and works in Scotland.

In the 1500s, King James V dipped into his own pocket to establish the salt panning industry here from which the town takes its name. Saltcoats today is much better known for its picturesque harbour and golden, sandy beaches set around Irvine Bay. Visitors interested in the history of the area will find a comprehensive overview at the **North Ayrshire Museum** which is housed in a former church. The small harbour dates from the late 17th century with later alterations, and at low tide fossilised trees can be seen on the harbour floor. It was in Saltcoats, in 1793, that Betsy Miller, the only woman ever to have become a registered ship's captain, was born.

Stevenston is a straggling town with a High Church that dates from 1832. It has a good beach,

though it is some way from the centre of the town. Nearby, at Ardeer, the British Dynamite Company established a factory in 1873. It later became Nobel's Explosives Company, and in 1926 became part of ICI.

On the seawall of the beach is a portrait of Robert Burns which is 25 feet high and about 16 feet wide.

DALRY

11 miles NW of Kilmarnock on the A737

This small industrial town's square is dominated by the **Parish Church of St Margaret,** dating from the 1870s. The town's name comes from the Gaelic "Dal Righe", meaning the "King's Field", which indicates that at one time it must have had royal connections. To the south east of the town is Blair Castle, a large mansion centred on what was a typical Scottish tower house of the 12th century. The parkland which surrounds it was laid out by William Blair in the 1760s. It is the home of Clan Blair, who were supporters of both Bruce and Wallace. It was at one time the home of the daughter of the English King John, who had married William de Blare. Now the mansion can be hired as a venue for conferences and seminars.

BEITH

13 miles NW of Kilmarnock off the A737

Beith is a small attractive town, and at 500 feet is the highest town in Ayrshire. The remains of the **Auld Kirk** date from the late 1500s, while the impressive **High Church** dates from the early 19th century. Eglinton Street is the most attractive part of the town, with small, neat two-storey buildings dating from the late 18th and 19th centuries.

KILBIRNIE

15 miles NW of Kilmarnock on the A760

Kilbirnie literally means the "kil" or "cell" of St Birinus or Birinie, a West Saxon monk who died at Dorchester in Dorset in AD 650. Within the town you'll find the **Barony Parish Church**, dating from the 15th century. Inside is some wonderfully exuberant woodwork from the 17th and 18th centuries, including the extravagant Crawford Loft and the Cunninghame Aisle.

Standing next to the golf course are the ruins of the **Place of Kilbirnie**, a former castle of the Crawford family dating from the 15th century.

WEST KILBRIDE

17 miles NW of Kilmarnock off the A78

West Kilbride is a sedate village of Glasgow commuters, perched above its twin village of Seamill, on the coast. **Law Castle** was built in the 15th century for Princess Mary, sister of James III, on her marriage to Thomas Boyd of Kilmarnock, who became the Earl of Arran. However, the marriage was later annulled and he had to flee to the Continent where he died in Antwerp. Mary eventually remarried, this time to James Hamilton, first Lord Hamilton, and the Earlship of Arran passed to their son. The castle has been restored and modernised and is now available to rent as a holiday home.

At the hamlet of Portencross, out on a headland beyond Seamill, are the substantial ruins of 14th century **Portencross Castle**, another Boyd stronghold. Also on the headland is Hunterston Castle (not open to the public), ancestral home of Clan Hunter, and **Hunterston Nuclear Power Station**.

THE CUMBRAES

20 miles NW of Kilmarnock, in the Firth of Clyde

Little Cumbrae is privately owned, but Great Cumbrae can be visited by a frequent ferry from Largs, the crossing taking only ten minutes.

The only town on the island is Millport, a small, attractive holiday resort with a unique feature - the **Cathedral of the Isles**, Britain's smallest cathedral. It is sometimes referred to as Europe's smallest, but this honour is held by an even smaller cathedral in Greece. Nevertheless it is a real gem, and was completed in 1851 as part of a theological complex funded by George Boyle who later became the 6th Earl of Glasgow. Its nave is 40 feet by 20 feet, and can only seat 100 people. It was designed by William Butterfield, who also designed Keble College, Oxford. The ceiling is painted with all the wild flowers found on the island.

The **Museum of the Cumbraes** can be found at The Garrison, just off the seafront.

On the eastern shore of The Cumbraes, facing the mainland, is the University Marine Biological Station. It is an institution of both Glasgow and London Universities, and offers students research facilities, tuition in diving and in marine biology. It houses a museum, which is open to the public and has a magnificent aquarium.

91

46 THE BOSUN'S

Largs

This inn provides wonderful food, great ales and a comfortable nights sleep, what else is needed?

see page 377

•

Largs is a lively, attractive place and is the mainland terminal for the Cumbrae Ferry. It was south of here that the Battle of Largs took place in 1263 when the Scots defeated a force led by King Haakon IV of Norway and finally threw off the Norse yoke. A tall thin monument south of the town, affectionately known as the Pencil, commemorates the event. Within the town you'll find Vikingar! a museum and interpretation centre that explains the life and travels of the Vikings all those years ago. In addition to the Viking Experience, Vikingar! also houses a swimming pool, fitness studio, sauna and steam rooms

•

There are exhibits and displays on Millport's heyday as one of the Clyde holiday resorts.

LARGS

21 miles NW of Kilmarnock on the A78

Set against a spectacular backdrop of spreading woodland and hills rising up to 1500 feet, Largs has been a popular seaside resort for many years and was recently voted Scotland's Top Tourism Town. Standing just a few yards from the harbour, the superb **Skelmorlie Aisle** (Historic Scotland) is all that remains of the former parish church. In 1636, the aisle was converted into a mausoleum for Sir Robert Montgomerie and its elaborately painted barrel-vaulted ceiling and Montgomerie's intricately carved tomb are masterpieces of Renaissance art. Next to the Skelmorlie Aisle, is the Brisbane Vault, the final resting place of **Sir Thomas Brisbane** who died in 1860. He was born in Largs in 1773 and after a distinguished military career, he was appointed Governor of New South Wales in 1820. He gave his name to the city of Brisbane and the Brisbane River. There is also a crater on the moon named after him. In the local cemetery is buried **Sir William Burrell**, shipping magnate and millionaire, who gave the Burrell Collection to the city of Glasgow in 1944.

Largs Museum, with its local history collection, is also worth a visit.

Kelburn Castle stands to the south of the town, overlooking the Firth of Clyde, of which it has spectacular views. It is the ancestral home of the Boyles, Earls of Glasgow, and parts of it date back to the 13th century. Its grounds are now a country park, with gardens, an adventure playground, woodland walks, a pet's corner, craft workshops, licensed café, riding school and falconry centre. The castle itself is open for guided tours during July and August.

ISLE OF ARRAN

Arran (13 miles and 55 minutes from Ardrossan by ferry) is called "Scotland in miniature", as it is mountainous in the north, low lying in the middle and rises again towards the south. It is 19 miles long by about ten miles across at its widest, and within its 165 square miles it has history and spectacular scenery aplenty. The island is almost entirely owned by the Duke of Hamilton and the National Trust for Scotland. Together, they have successfully resisted any inappropriate development, ensuring that Arran is almost completely unspoilt. This is an island of Celtic saints, mysterious standing stones, craft workshops, cairns and old castles. It was a Gaelic speaking island up until the early 19th century, though the place names owe as much to the language of the Norsemen who settled here in the 10th and 11th centuries as they do to Gaelic. In fact, **Brodick**, one of the main settlements, comes from the Norse for "broad bay".

The northern portion can be every bit as spectacular as the Highlands, and for those with the stamina, a climb to the summit of **Goat Fell**, at 2866 feet the island's highest peak, is a must. There are two recognised routes to the top, with both routes eventually converging, and information on each can be had at the tourist office in Brodick.

Just north of Brodick is the **Arran Brewery**, which has a visitor centre and shop. There are also viewing galleries where you can see the brewing process. And at Home Farm, also near Brodick, is **Arran Aromatics**, Scotland's leading producer of body care products and scented candles. Again, you can watch the manufacturing processes from a viewing gallery.

Beneath Goat Fell, is **Brodick Castle** (National Trust for Scotland). This former Hamilton family stronghold occupies a wonderful location, surrounded by mature gardens. The present building dates from the 16th century and later, and inside there is a collection of paintings (by Watteau, Turner and Richardson amongst others), furniture and important collections of silver and porcelain. The castle grounds are particularly attractive. There's a formal walled garden, first laid out in 1710, and a woodland garden covering some 60 acres which was established in 1923 by the Duchess of Montrose, daughter of the 12th Duke of Hamilton.

The road from Corrie follows the coast north, then turns north

west and goes through the bleak but extremely beautiful **Glen Chalmadale** before bringing you to Lochranza ("Loch of the rowan tree river"). On the shores of this small village are the imposing ruins of **Lochranza Castle** (Historic Scotland), built in the 16th century as a hunting lodge for the Scottish kings.

At the entrance to the village is **Isle of Arran Distillers** which has guided tours with a tasting of the distinctive whisky and a visitor centre. In the summer months a small car ferry runs from the Mull of Kintyre to Lochranza, the crossing taking about 35 minutes.

Beyond Lochranza is the small village of Catacol, with a row of identical whitewashed cottages known as **The Twelve Apostles**. They were built in the 19th century to accommodate islanders cleared from Glen Catacol in favour of deer. From here you get a good view across to the Mull of Kintyre, which is only four miles away.

The magnificent cliffs at

On the northern outskirts of Brodick is the Isle of Arran Heritage Museum, housed in a former crofter's farm. Among its exhibits are a working smithy, an Arran cottage and a wide range of vintage agricultural tools. North of Brodick, on the A841 is the beautiful village of Corrie, with its small harbour, whitewashed cottages and gardens aflame with colour in the summer months.

Brodick Quay, Arran

Further on, and inland from Machrie Bay, is the wonderful Auchagallon Stone Circle, a Bronze Age burial cairn with a circle of 15 upright slabs surrounding it. There are several other ancient monuments in the area, including the Machrie Moor Stone Circle and the Moss Farm Road Stone Circle. It is said that this part of Arran has more stone circles per square mile than anywhere else in Scotland.

Drumadoon stand high above a raised beach and are spectacular. The **King's Cave** is close to the shore, and is supposed to be the cave where Robert the Bruce saw his spider, (though many other places in Scotland and Ireland make a similar claim). From the village of Blackwaterfoot, south of **Machrie Bay**, a road called The String cuts across the centre of the island towards Brodick. The village of Shiskine, on The String, has the lovely **St Molas Church**, with an ancient stone carving of the saint embedded in its wall. The Balmichael Visitor Centre is within a converted mill complex and has speciality shops and facilities for various outdoor activities.

South of Blackwaterfoot the road continues on towards Lagg, and if you need convincing about the mildness of the climate hereabouts, the palm trees in the gardens of the Lagg Inn should do the trick. The **Torrylinn Creamery**, which makes traditional Dunlop cheese in the old fashioned way, has a viewing gallery and shop. The tiny island of Pladda, with its lighthouse of 1790, can be seen about a mile

from the coast before the road turns north once more towards Whiting Bay, another small village and holiday resort. At one time it was a fishing port, and took its name from the whiting that were caught in the bay. A splendid walk starts from south of the village towards **Glenashdale Falls** and the prehistoric burial cairns known as the **Giants Graves**.

Lamlash sits on Lamlash Bay. Having the local high school, the hospital and the local government offices, it is the island's capital. In the bay rises the magnificent bulk of Holy Island, so called because the Celtic St Molas lived a life of austerity here in the 6th and 7th centuries. Nowadays it has regained its religious significance as it is home to a Tibetan Buddhist monastery and retreat. Roaming around the island are Eriskay ponies, Soay sheep and Saanen goats. Visitors are welcome to the island and there are regular ferries during the season. Near Lamlash is the factory Arran Provisions, the island's biggest employer. It makes a wide range of mustards, jams and preserves, and has a visitor centre and shop.

Glasgow & West Central Scotland

Glasgow and West Central Scotland was at one time the country's industrial hub. Heavy engineering, shipbuilding, coal mining and steelworks predominated, providing work for thousands and fortunes for the favoured few. But while it is still Scotland's most populous area, and where the bulk of its industry and commerce is located, it is now clean and attractive, with much to do and see.

The River Clyde has traditionally been a working river, its banks once ringing to the sound of shipbuilding. But there is another Clyde, one that isn't so well known. The upper reaches of the river, in rural Lanarkshire, present an altogether different picture. Within the verdant Clyde Valley, you'll find quiet orchards, green fields, woodland, small attractive villages and cosy pubs.

Loch Lomond is renowned the world over. From Glasgow, a train can take you straight to its bonnie banks in just under an hour, and it's a journey thousands of Glaswegians make. We're on the edge of the Highlands here, and indeed the Highland Boundary Fault, which separates the Highlands from the Lowlands, passes through the loch.

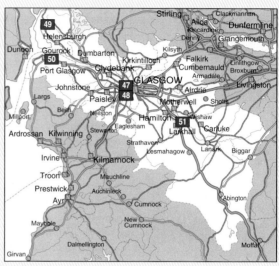

ACCOMMODATION

49	Green Kettle Inn, Garelochhead,	
	nr Helensburgh	p 107, 379
51	The Shawlands Park Hotel, Shawsburn,	
	nr Larkhall	p 113, 380

FOOD & DRINK

48	The Tall Ship at Glasgow Harbour,	
	Glasgow	p 96, 376
50	Conservatory Bar, Gourock	p 111, 378
51	The Shawlands Park Hotel, Shawsburn,	
	nr Larkhall	p 113, 380

PLACES OF INTEREST

47	Pollok House, Glasgow	p 96, 378
48	The Tall Ship at Glasgow Harbour,	
	Glasgow	p 96, 376

47 POLLOCK HOUSE

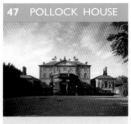

Glasgow

Visit Pollok House and capture the flavour of one of Scotland's grandest Edwardian country houses.

 see page 378

48 THE TALL SHIP AT GLASGOW HARBOUR

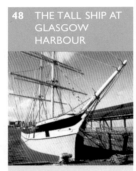

Glasgow

Explore the beautifully restored Glenlee and learn about the conditions aboard and the cargo she carried.

 see page 376

GLASGOW

Glasgow has worked hard on its image over the last few years. Gone are the constant references to gang fights, organised crime, drunkenness, ugly industrial townscapes and bad housing. A decade ago Glasgow was designated European City of Culture 1999, an appointment that provoked amused comment from those who only knew the city as the home of the Gorbals (once the worst slums in Europe), and as the originator of the "Glasgow Hello" (a head butt). Today, the image is of trendy nightspots, restaurants, pavement cafés and art galleries. It is home to Scottish Opera, The Royal Scottish National Orchestra, Scottish Ballet, and a string of theatres where you can see anything from serious drama to variety shows. It is also one of Britain's best dressed cities - it has been estimated that there are more Armani and Versace outfits worn here than anywhere else in Britain outside London.

But there is still the quirky Glasgow - the city of fish and chips shops, betting shops, working men's pubs, raucous laughter and street markets, including the famous Barras, held every Saturday and Sunday in the east end. The city is ringed by enormous council estates that took the families who used to live in the teeming tenements.

In fact, Glasgow has enjoyed a long history of cultural vitality, most notably during the Art Nouveau period when the architect and interior designer Charles Rennie Mackintosh (1868-1928) brought great prestige to the city. His career took off when he won a competition to design the **Glasgow School of Art,** generally considered one of his most impressive buildings - student-led tours are available. Mackintosh's most popular creation though was the **Willow Tea Rooms** in Sauchiehall Street for which he also designed the furniture, fixtures and fittings, cutlery and even the menu cards. The original building of 1908 closed in 1930 but half a century later Mackintosh enthusiasts funded a reconstruction faithful in every detail and standing on the original site.

Mackintosh was also the architect for the Glasgow Herald building off Argyle Street, the Queens Cross Church in the northwest of the city (now the headquarters of the Charles Rennie Mackintosh Society), and on the south side of the river the **Scotland Street School**, now a museum dedicated to education. Another school is the **Martyr's Public School** in Parson Street. It is no longer used as a school and is open to the public. At Bellahouston Park, on the south side, is the House for an Art Lover, which interprets some of the incomplete designs Mackintosh submitted to a competition in a German magazine. **The Lighthouse,** Scotland's centre for architecture, design and the city, is in Mitchell Lane and has a Mackintosh interpretation centre. It is housed in a Mackintosh-designed building that was once the home of Glasgow's daily newspaper, *The Herald*. In the **Hunterian Art Gallery** there is also the Mackintosh House, featuring the principal rooms from Mackintosh's own house, together with a collection of designs and watercolours.

Another Glasgow architect, formerly overshadowed by Mackintosh but now more widely known, was Alexander Thomson (1817-1875), known as **"Greek" Thomson** because of the Greek influences in his work. He designed St Vincent Street Church, as well as **Holmwood House** (National Trust for Scotland) in Netherlee Road, in the southern suburbs.

Perhaps Glasgow's most famous cultural attraction is the **Burrell Collection**, housed in a purpose built complex of galleries in Pollok Country Park, south of the river. The shipping magnate Sir William Burrell (1861-1958) was a lifelong collector of works of art and his interests ranged from 4000-year-old antiquities such as the splendid Mesopotamian lion's head, through Oriental art to mainstream European paintings. Unlike his close contemporary, William Randolph Hearst, Burrell was a discriminating collector, acquiring pieces because he admired them, rather than in deference to current fashions. In 1943, Burrell offered his fabulous collection to the city stipulating only that it should be housed in a rural setting, away from the then heavily polluted city

centre. It wasn't until the 1960s that his conditions could be met, and not until 1983 that the gallery was opened and it now contains more than 8000 items. A whole day could easily be spent going round the collection. Also in the park is **Pollok House** (National Trust for Scotland), a Georgian mansion that houses the Stirling Maxwell collection of decorative arts.

Art lovers will find it easy to overdose in the City of Culture. In addition to the inexhaustible treasures of the Burrell Collection, there is also an outstanding collection at the **Kelvingrove Art Gallery and Museum** which benefited from a £27.9m refurbishment before re-opening in 2006. It is housed in a grand red sandstone building that froths with detail. It has internationally important collections on archaeology, botany, zoology, geology and all the other ologies you can think of. There are Egyptian mummies, fossils, stuffed animals, dinosaur skeletons,

Glasgow has always been a city of museums and art galleries, even when it relied on industry for its employment. Like most large cities, its West End is where the well off built their mansions, as the prevailing south westerly winds carried the smells of the city away from them

Holmwood House, Glasgow

clothing and uniforms from all over the world, weapons, and a host of other material. The art collection is stunning, and is possibly the most comprehensive civic collection in Europe. The museum's magnificent organ was built at the turn of the last century by Lewis and Co Ltd, London and organ recitals have been a feature of Kelvingrove ever since the building opened.

The city has changed its image more than once over the years. It was founded in the 7th century by St Kentigern, also known as St Mungo, and started life in early medieval times as a small religious community grouped round a cathedral. In the 17th and 18th centuries it became a city of trade, dealing with the American colonies in such commodities as tobacco and cotton, which made many people very rich indeed. In the 19th century it became a city of industry, with shipyards and heavy engineering works. Now it relies mostly on tourism, the media, service industries and the arts for employment.

The area round the **Cathedral of St Mungo** (Historic Scotland) is where it all started. This was where St Kentigern, or Mungo, established a small church in the 6th century. The present cathedral was founded in the 12th century by David I, and the building shows work from this period onwards. It is the only Scottish mainland cathedral that escaped the Reformation of 1560 more or less intact. In its crypt is the Tomb of St Mungo, once a place of pilgrimage, but now visited by pilgrims of a different sort - tourists. The Blackadder Aisle is a wonderful piece of architecture added by Archbishop Robert Blackadder in about 1500.

In front of the cathedral is the modern (and looking anything but modern) **St Mungo Museum of Religious Life and Art**. Across from it is Glasgow's oldest house, **Provand's Lordship**, built in 1471

St Mungo's Cathedral, Glasgow

as a manse for the former St Nicholas Hospital.

The **Tall Ship at Glasgow Harbour** at Stobcross Road tells the story of the river and the industries it spawned. The centrepiece is the tall ship itself, the *S.V. Glenlee*, built in 1896. At Braehead, on the south side of the river, and a few miles downstream, is another museum that celebrates the Clyde - the award-winning **Clydebuilt**. It is part of the Scottish Maritime Museum and tells the river's story from the 1700s up to the present day.

The Clyde Waterbus Service takes you on a boat trip along the Clyde from the city centre to Braehead, with a commentary on the history of the river as you go.

Close to the Tall Ship is the Scottish Exhibition and Conference Centre, a mammoth complex of halls and auditoriums, including what Glaswegians now refer to as the Armadillo, a metal and glass creation whose design owes more than a little to Sydney Opera House. And across the river from it is the city's newest attraction, the **Glasgow Science Centre**. Built on the site of the Glasgow Garden Festival, it is a combination of museum, laboratory and hands-on exhibition area that explores science and discovery, and has four floors featuring more than 300 exhibits. The accompanying Glasgow Tower is Scotland's tallest freestanding structure at 412 feet, and there's also an IMAX Theatre.

The **Glasgow Museum of Transport**, with trains, carriages, motorcars and a marvellous collection of model ships, stands opposite the Kelvingrove Art Gallery and Museum. Perhaps the most striking display is the one on Glasgow's "underground" system. The system forms a simple loop round the city centre and West End. It was upgraded in the late 1970s with orange trains taking the place of the much-loved wood and metal ones. The Glaswegians immediately dubbed it the "Clockwork Orange" and the name

On a hill behind the cathedral of St Mungo, is the Necropolis, a wonderfully atmospheric wonderland of funerary extravagances. It was designed in 1833 by John Strong who modelled it on the Père Lachaise cemetery in Paris.

Time Clock at Clydebuilt

"The Clyde made Glasgow, and Glasgow made the Clyde", runs an old, but true, saying. In the 17th century, the city was seen as being wholly inland, and the river was so shallow that people could wade across it. But in 1768 a man called John Golborne began canalising and deepening it to allow large ships to sail right up into the city.

has stuck. More properly, it is known as the Glasgow Subway, rather than "underground" or "metro".

Also in the West End, just off Byres Road (the area's trendiest street) are the **Hunterian Museum** and the **Hunterian Art Gallery**, which form part of Glasgow University. The museum has fine collections covering geology and numismatics, while the gallery has paintings, furniture and interior design by Mackintosh and Whistler. At the top of Byres Road is the **Glasgow Botanic Gardens**, with at its centre the Kibble Palace, a huge greenhouse with plants from all over the world. It is named after its builder John Kibble, who erected it beside his house on the banks of Loch Long. It was rebuilt here in 1873, after being dismantled and sailed up the Clyde.

Within Victoria Park, further to the west, is the **Fossil Grove** (open between April and September only), undoubtedly the city's most ancient attraction. It consists of fragments

of an ancient forest more than 330 million years old which was discovered in 1887. They are housed within a small building to protect them.

The heart of Glasgow nowadays is George Square, a huge open space in front of the Victorian **City Chambers** (conducted tours available). There are statues galore, and it is a favourite place for city workers to relax in the sun. The City Chambers themselves reflect Glasgow's wealth and confidence in Victorian times, and so opulent are the interiors that they stood in for the Vatican in the film *Heavenly Pursuits*. Round the corner you'll find **Hutcheson's Hall** (National Trust for Scotland), founded in 1641 as a hospice, though the building itself is 18th century. It was designed by David Hamilton, and has a small exhibition about the Merchant City, that area that housed the homes and offices of the rich 17th and 18th century entrepreneurs who traded with America. Nowadays it is an area of expensive apartment blocks, smart bars, restaurants and pubs. Not far away, in Queen Street, is the **Gallery of Modern Art (GOMA)**, housed in an elegant, neo-classical building. It has four floors of work by modern artists such as Christine Borland and Toby Paterson. In Buccleuch Street near Charing Cross, is the **Tenement House** (National Trust for Scotland). A lady named Agnes Toward moved in here with her mother in 1911 and for more than half a century

Tenement House, Glasgow

its décor and furnishings remained unchanged. Agnes was something of a magpie so the rooms contain a marvellously random collection of ephemera such as ration books, framed religious mottoes and monochrome holiday snaps.

The **Centre for Contemporary Arts** (CCA) is at 320 Sauchiehall Street, and has a changing programme of events, performances and exhibitions. There are six galleries, small cinema, bookshop and bar/restaurant

The **Glasgow Police Museum** is in St Andrews Square (to the east of Glasgow Cross), with exhibits highlighting the Glasgow Police Force between 1800 and 1975. And at the Cross itself is the old **Glasgow Tolbooth Steeple**, dating from the 1620s. At one time it provided offices for the City Council, and had a jail incorporated into it.

Glasgow Green, a huge area of parkland in the city's east end, is "Glasgow's lung". It has been common land for centuries, and it was here that Charles Edward Stuart mustered his troops during the Jacobite Uprising when he occupied the city. Now it is the city's largest park, with its centrepiece being the People's Palace and Winter Gardens, a museum and glasshouse complex which tells the city's own story. Close to it is the **Doulton Fountain**, at 46 feet high and 70 feet wide the world's largest terracotta fountain. It was recently refurbished at a cost of £3.75m.

On the eastern edge of Glasgow Green is one of the city's most colourful buildings - **Templeton's Carpet Factory** (now a business centre). It is based on a Venetian design, with walls that incorporate multi-coloured bricks.

At Celtic Park in the Parkhead area of the city is the **Celtic Visitor Centre**, which traces the history of Celtic Football Club, one of Glasgow's "big two" football clubs. There are exhibits, a stadium tour and a shop selling Celtic memorabilia. Rangers Football Club is Glasgow's other major team, with Ibrox, in Govan, to the south of the river. The Rangers Tour Experience takes you on a guided tour of the stadium, including the Trophy Room.

If you want to immerse yourself in something typically

The Mitchell Library is an imposing domed building in North Street, not far from Charing Cross. It is Britain's largest municipal library, and has collections covering Scottish and local history, genealogy, and Robert Burns.

The Conference Centre, Glasgow

•

Glasgow is synonymous with football, and at the redeveloped Hampden Park, on the south side of the Clyde, is the Scottish Football Museum. It reveals the sights, sounds and stories of the world's most popular game, and tells how it almost shaped the history of Glasgow in the late 19th and 20th centuries. You can see such things as the oldest football ticket in the world, the Scottish Cup trophy and Kenny Dalgleish's 100th Scottish cap.

•

•

Within Glasgow city centre there are two exclusive retail developments. Princes Square, off Buchanan Street, is a mix of upmarket shops and cafés, while the Italian Centre is where you'll find the designer labels. At the other end of the shopping spectrum is The Barras, the famous weekend flea market where you can find anything from counterfeit designer clothing to genuine antique furniture. It dates back to the 1920s when one enterprising street trader had a roof built for her co-traders who until then had sold their goods from barrows.

•

Scottish, then the **National Piping Centre** in Otago Street has a small museum dedicated to Scotland's national instrument. Within the Caledonian University on Cowcaddens Road, not far away, is the **Heatherbank Museum of Social Work**. It has displays on housing, health and childcare, and looks at how socially excluded people were cared for in the past.

Glasgow is Britain's second largest shopping centre, the three main shopping streets being Argyle Street, Sauchiehall Street and Buchanan Street. There are also enormous shopping malls. The St Enoch Centre is just off Argyle Street, the Buchanan Galleries are at the corner of Buchanan Street and Sauchiehall Street, while the Braehead Shopping Centre is south of the river on the city's western fringes, near Renfrew. There's also the Forge at Parkhead, in the east end.

In Sauchiehall Street is the **Regimental Museum of the Royal Highland Fusiliers**. It is Scotland's second oldest infantry regiment, and was formed in the 1960s when the Highland Light Infantry amalgamated with the Royal Scottish Fusiliers.

AROUND GLASGOW

KIRKINTILLOCH

7 miles NE of Glasgow city centre on the A803

The old burgh of Kirkintilloch sits beside the Forth and Clyde Canal, which has recently been re-opened after a multi-million pound refurbishment. It connects the

Firth of Clyde and the Firth of Forth with a further canal, the Union Canal, connecting it to Edinburgh. The **Auld Kirk Museum** is housed in the former parish church, which dates from 1644. In Peel Park are some Roman remains from the Antonine Wall.

Craft Daft (On a Raft) is a craft studio on a canal boat moored in the Forth and Clyde Canal at Glasgow Bridge. Here you can paint a ceramic ornament to take away immediately, or a mug or plate to collect in a day or two. You can also try glass painting, silk painting, encaustic wax, pyrography or quilling.

KILSYTH

11 miles NE of Glasgow on the A809

Just to the east of Kilsyth, the council-owned **Walled Garden** at Colzium House contains an extensive collection of conifers, rare shrubs and trees, and also has woodland walks and a picnic area.

The **Battle of Kilsyth** was fought on the 15th August 1645 when the 1st Marquis of Montrose routed a Covenanting army led by William Bailiie of Letham. A reservoir is now located where Montrose's army camped, and a cairn marks the spot where the battle took place.

CUMBERNAULD

12 miles NE of Glasgow off the A80

Set on a hill above the A80, Cumbernauld is one of Scotland's new towns. It was created in 1956 as a population overspill for Glasgow City and was built partly on what was an old country estate. It is now the eighth most populous settlement in Scotland, the largest in North Lanarkshire, and also larger than two of Scotland's cities, Inverness and Stirling. In 1981, it provided the setting for the hit film *Gregory's Girl*. To the south east of the town, **Palacerigg Country Park** covers 750 acres and has an animal collection that is unique in Central Scotland. In addition to some friendly farm animals, the menagerie includes rare breeds such as Eriskay ponies, North Ronaldsay and Boreray sheep, Shetland and white park cattle, Bagot and Guernsey goats, Tamworth pigs and Scots grey and Scots dumpy poultry.

AIRDRIE AND COATBRIDGE
9 miles E of Glasgow on the A89

The twin towns of Airdrie and Coatbridge are industrial in character. In Coatbridge, in 1889, was born **John Reith**, first general manager of what was then the British Broadcasting Company. Single-handedly he shaped the character of the organisation.

The **Time Capsule** is one of the largest leisure centres in the area. In the **Drumpellier Country Park** there is a visitor centre, butterfly house, formal gardens, golf course and pets' corner.

RUTHERGLEN
2 miles SE of Glasgow city centre on the A749

This royal burgh is one of the oldest in Scotland, having been granted its royal charter by David I

in the 12th century. For a short while the burgh was incorporated into the city of Glasgow, something that was greatly resented by some of its citizens. Since 1997, the town has formed part of the local authority area of South Lanarkshire. A gable of its medieval Parish Church survives in the kirkyard of its more modern successor. Robbie Coltrane (Hagrid in the Harry Potter films) was born here, and for a short while Stan Laurel lived in the town and went to a local school.

NEWTON MEARNS
6 miles SW of Glasgow on the A77

Newton Mearns is a commuter town of smart bungalows and substantial houses. The foursquare Parish Church dates from 1755, and close by is **Greenbank House** (National Trust for Scotland) surrounded by beautiful gardens. The house is not open to the public but the walled garden and 16 acres of woodland are.

KILBARCHAN
11 miles SW of Glasgow, off the A761

This is undoubtedly the most picturesque village in Renfrewshire, a huddle of charming 18th century weaving cottages. **The Weaver's Cottage** (National Trust for Scotland) dates from 1723, and shows what a typical weaver's cottage (complete with working loom) was like.

In a niche on the wall of the Steeple Hall of 1755 is a statute to **Habbie Simpson**, the village's famous 17th century piper. It is a

Coatbridge is home to the Summerlee Heritage Centre, built on the site of the old Summerlee Ironworks. The Centre traces the history of the area's former industries - steel making, coalmining and the manufacture of heavy plant. Tramlines have been laid out in it and there is a small collection of trams from all over Europe. There is also a short section of the Summerlee branch of the Monklands Canal (now closed), which ran from Glasgow to the Lanarkshire coalfields. The canal was built between 1770 and 1794, and at one time was the most profitable in Scotland. The North Calder Heritage Trail runs from Summerlee to Hillend Reservoir, and passes many sites connected with the past industry of the area.

bronze reproduction of one made in wood by Archibald Simpson in 1822.

LOCHWINNOCH

16 miles SW of Glasgow on the B786

The **Clyde Muirshiel Regional Park** covers 106 square miles of magnificent countryside from Greenock to Inverkip and down into Ayrshire. It is ideal for walking, cycling, fishing and observing wildlife. There is also sailing on Castle Semple Loch. Near its shores are the ruins of **Castle Semple Church**, founded in the early 16th century by John Semple. He was later killed at the Battle of Flodden in 1513, and his tomb can be seen at the east end of the church.

The **Lochwinnoch Nature Reserve** is run by the RSPB, and has nature trails through woodland, with viewing areas and a visitor centre.

RENFREW

5 miles W of Glasgow on the A8

The ancient burgh of Renfrew was granted its charter in 1143, making it one of the oldest in Scotland. It was here, in 1164, that one of the lesser-known, but still important, Scottish battles took place - the **Battle of Renfrew**. It was fought between Somerled, Lord of the Isles, and the royal army of Malcolm IV led by Walter FitzAlan, founder of Paisley Abbey and first High Steward of Scotland. This battle brought the Western Isles fully under the control of the Scottish monarchy.

The **Renfrew Community Museum** in the Brown Institute in Canal Street was opened in 1997 to coincide with the 600th anniversary of the town being granted royal burgh status. It has displays of local history.

PAISLEY

7 miles W of Glasgow city centre on the A761

This famous textile manufacturing town grew up around its 12th century **Paisley Abbey**. The original was destroyed by Edward I in 1307 but rebuilt 7 years later after the Scottish victory at the Battle of Bannockburn. Victorian restorers gave the building a further mauling but the interior with its beautiful stained glass and fine stone-vaulted roof is still impressive. Within its walls are the tombs of most of the non-royal High Stewards, as well as that of Princess Marjory, daughter of Robert the Bruce. The abbey can legitimately claim to be the birthplace of the Stewart dynasty because Robert II, the first Stewart king, was born at the abbey in 1316. Marjory had been seriously injured in a riding accident at Knock, a

Coats Observatory Door, Paisley

Paisley Abbey

nearby hill, and she was brought to the abbey where she died soon after giving birth to her son.

Another famous Paisley church is the Baptist **Thomas Coats Memorial Church**, a giant red sandstone masterpiece which is generally considered the finest Baptist church in Europe. It was built in 1894 in memory of Thomas Coats of the Coats and Clark thread making firm. The same Thomas Coats gifted the Coats Observatory to the town's Philosophical Institution in 1883. It is now open to the public. Adjacent is **Paisley Museum and Art Galleries** where one of displays follows the development of the colourful Paisley "tear drop" design from its simple beginnings to the elaborate pattern now so familiar.

At the Corner of Shuttle Street and George Place are the 18th and 19th century weaving cottages known as **Sma' Shot Cottages**, housing an interpretation centre which gives an insight into the living conditions of Paisley weaving families in the past. Nearby, in New Street, is **Paisley Arts Centre**, housed in the former Laigh Kirk of 1738.

Paisley was the birthplace of many famous people. Tom Conti the actor was born here, as were John Byrne the artist and writer whose most famous work is undoubtedly the TV series *Tutti Frutti*, Andrew Neill, one-time editor of *The Scotsman,* Gerry Rafferty the singer and Fulton Mackay of *Porridge* fame.

In the 18th century, the town was famed for its poets, the most famous being Robert Tannahill who was born in Tannahill Cottage in Queen Street in 1774. He was a silk weaver who wrote the words to such beautiful songs as *Jessie the Flower o' Dunblane* and *The Braes o' Gleniffer*. The actual braes (hillsides) themselves now form part of the 1300 acre **Gleniffer Braes Country Park**, to the south of the town. There are spectacular views from

105

The Lillie Art Gallery, in Station Road, Milngavie, was founded by banker and amateur artist Robert Lillie, and opened in 1962. It has a collection of 20th century Scottish paintings, including works by the Scottish Colourists, Joan Eardley and Philip Reves.

the Robertson Car Park, and guide tours are available.

Jenny's Well Local Nature Reserve, on the south bank of the White Cart Water, is less than a mile from the centre of the town, and is locked between a council estate and a chemicals factory. For all that, it is a haven for wildlife with some pleasant walks. To the north of Paisley, on the other side of the M8, is Glasgow International Airport.

BEARSDEN AND MILNGAVIE

5 miles NW of Glasgow city centre on the A809 and A81

These two prosperous towns are firmly within Glasgow's inner commuting belt, and are full of large Victorian and Edwardian mansions as well as the more modest bungalows of the 1930s. The Antonine Wall (named after Roman Emperor Antoninus Pius) passes close by. It was built of turf in the 2nd century to keep out the warring tribesmen of the north, and stretched for 37 miles between the Clyde and the Forth. In Bearsden there are the remains of a **Roman Bathhouse.**

Mugdock Country Park sits off the A81 north of Milngavie (pronounced "Mull-guy") which is the starting point for the 95-mile long **West Highland Way**, which connects the Glasgow conurbation with Fort William.

CLYDEBANK

6 miles NW of Glasgow city centre on the A814

Clydebank is a former shipbuilding town, and it was here that the

Queen Mary, the *Queen Elizabeth* and the *Queen Elizabeth II* were built. The town suffered more damage in proportion to its size than any other British town from air raids in World War II. In early 1941, during the Clydebank Blitz, the centre of the town was flattened, other parts severely damaged and many people were killed. The **Clydebank Museum** at the Town Hall in Dumbarton Road has exhibits devoted to the Blitz, as well as to the famous Singer sewing machine factory which once stood in the town.

DUMBARTON

The town sits where the River Leven, fed by Loch Lomond, enters the Clyde. It is dominated by **Dumbarton Castle** (Historic Scotland), high on a volcanic plug 240 feet above the Firth of Clyde. This is one of the oldest fortified sites in Britain, and from the 8th to the early 11th centuries was the capital of the ancient kingdom of Strathclyde. The castle now mainly consists of modern barracks, but there is still plenty to see, including a 12th century gateway, a dungeon and a museum. From the top there is a splendid view out over the Firth of Clyde. It was from Dumbarton in 1548 that Mary Queen of Scots set sail for France and her eventual marriage to Francis, the Dauphin. This was considered to be much safer than leaving from an east coast port, as Henry VIII's ships were patrolling the North Sea. The English king had wanted Mary to marry his son Henry, and when the Scottish parliament refused to ratify such an agreement, Henry tried unsuccessfully to force the marriage, a period known as the "Rough Wooing".

The **Denny Tank Museum** in Castle Street forms part of the Scottish Maritime Museum. It is the oldest experimental water tank in the world, and is the length of a football pitch. It was built in 1882 as part of Denny's shipyard whose most famous ship was undoubtedly the tea clipper the *Cutty Sark*. It was here that hull shapes were tested in water using carefully crafted models before the ships themselves were built. On display are many of the models built by Denny craftsmen.

Though Denny was famous for its ships, it also has a place in aircraft history, as it built the first helicopter capable of flight in 1909, as well as the world's first hovercraft, half a century later.

In Church Street is an old archway called the **College Bow** once part of the long gone Collegiate Church of St Mary. On the hillside above the town is the beautiful **Overtoun Estate** which commands wonderful views over the Firth. It was bequeathed to the people of Dumbarton by Douglas White, a London doctor, in 1939. Old Kilpatrick, to the west of the town, is supposed to be the birthplace of St Patrick, who was captured by raiders and taken to Ireland in the 4th century.

AROUND DUMBARTON

BALLOCH

4 miles N of Dumbarton on the A811

This pleasant town sits at the point where the River Leven (at five miles long, Scotland's shortest river) leaves **Loch Lomond** on its way to Dumbarton and the Clyde. The loch is the largest expanse of fresh water in Britain and covers more than 27 square miles. The

49   GREEN KETTLE INN

Garelochhead

This B&B is a real hidden gem surrounded by beautiful rolling countryside.

see page 379

College Bow, Dumbarton

Loch Lomond and the Trossachs National Park was Scotland's first national park, opened in 2002, and Lomond Shores at Balloch includes the National Park Gateway.

The loch is at its widest to the south. It gradually narrows and gets deeper as it goes north, and at some points reaches a depth of more than 600 feet, making it the third deepest loch in Scotland. Many songs have been written about this stretch of water, the most famous being the *Bonnie, Bonnie Banks o' Loch Lomond*. The song was written by a Jacobite prisoner held in Carlisle Castle who was due to be executed. He is telling a fellow prisoner whose life had been spared that he (the condemned man) will be in Scotland before him because he will take the "low road", i.e., the road of death, while his colleague will take the "high road", or the road of life.

At the nearby village of Gartocharn is **Duncryne Hill**

Loch Lomond, Dumbarton

108

(nicknamed "The Dumpling" by locals), where you get a marvellous view, not just of the loch, but also of the surrounding countryside. The Highland Boundary Fault, which separates the Lowlands of Scotland from the Highlands, passes through Loch Lomond from Glen Fruin on the west to Balmaha on the east. The **Balloch Castle Country Park**, north east of Balloch, has lochside walks, gardens and a visitor centre. South from the town you can follow the **Leven Valley Heritage Trail**, taking you down the valley of the Leven to Dumbarton, passing such small industrial towns as Alexandria and Renton.

In Alexandria is the **Antartex Village Visitor Centre**. It incorporates a factory making sheepskin coats (with factory tours available), a mill shop and a small craft village. Close by is the Loch Lomond Factory Outlets and the Motoring Heritage Centre, housed in a magnificent building where one of Scotland's former makes of car, the "Argyll", was manufactured. The centre is currently closed while its exhibits are relocated in another part of the building. No date has yet been announced for the re-opening.

LUSS

12 miles N of Dumbarton off the A82

This beautiful little village - one of the loveliest in Scotland - was once the setting for Scottish Television's soap opera *High Road*, in which it was called Glendarroch. It's an estate village built in the 19th century by the Colquhoun family of nearby Rossdhu Castle, and sits on the bank of Loch Lomond. On the opposite shore, the mighty bulk of **Ben Lomond** can be seen. It is the most southerly of Scotland's "Munros", or mountains over 3000 feet, and is a comfortable climb if you're reasonably fit and active.

Luss used to be famous for the longevity of its residents. A visitor in 1769 found six people aged between 86 and 94, at that time an almost incredible age.

CARDROSS

3 miles NW of Dumbarton on the A814

Geilston Gardens (National Trust for Scotland) surround a late 17th century house (not open to the public) to the east of the town. It has a walled garden laid out with shrub borders, lawns and a herbaceous border that provides dazzling summer colour. Perhaps the most impressive feature is a spectacular Sequoiadendron giganteum.

Fruit, vegetables and cut flowers are grown in the kitchen garden and the Geilston Burn winds its way alongside some delightful woodland walks.

HELENSBURGH

9 miles NW of Dumbarton on the A814

Set on the north shore of the Firth of Clyde, Helensburgh was founded in the 18th century by Sir James Colquhoun of Luss and named after his wife Helen. It is a popular yachting centre and one of the ports of call in July and August for the *PS Waverley*, the world's last ocean-going paddle steamer. **John Logie Baird**, the inventor of television, was born at Helensburgh in 1888. He was buried in the town in 1945 and is commemorated by a bronze bust on the West Esplanade and a stained-glass window in the West Kirk.

In Upper Colquhoun Street you'll find one of Charles Rennie Mackintosh's masterpieces - the **Hill House**. It was commissioned by Walter Blackie, the Glasgow publisher, in 1902, and contains some of Mackintosh's finest work. Not only did he design the building, he also designed the interior decoration, the fittings and most of the furniture. There are also gardens surrounding the house.

North of Helensburgh is **Glen Fruin**, which has a narrow road that takes you over to Loch Lomond. It was the scene of a battle in 1602 when the MacGregors defeated the Colquhouns with much loss of life.

RHU

11 miles NW of Dumbarton on the A814

Rhu (pronounced "roo") is a small, attractive village at the entrance to the Gair Loch. It was originally called Row, and in the 18th century was one of the ports on the Rhu - Roseneath ferry. **Glenarn Gardens** off Glenarn Road is a sheltered woodland garden with a Himalayan atmosphere where visitors can walk under superb giant species of rhododendrons or gaze out across the Gareloch.

Renton has a special place in the hearts of all Scottish football supporters. Not only was Renton Football Club responsible for the founding of the Scottish League, it became "champions of the United Kingdom and the world" in 1888 when it beat West Bromwich Albion at Hampden Park.

GREENOCK

Situated on the south bank of the Firth of Clyde, at a point known as The Tail of the Bank, Greenock is a bustling industrial town and port. It was the birthplace, in 1736, of James Watt, who was to perfect the steam engine. The James Watt College was founded in 1907 with funds donated by Andrew Carnegie. Its most recent campus occupies a superb location on the waterfront at Greenock. He is also remembered in the name of the James Watt, one of the Wetherspoon chain of pubs housed in a spectacular building on Cathcart Street; and by a statue at the rear of the Town Hall.

Most of Greenock is built on steep north-facing slopes giving magnificent views across the Firth of Clyde to the mountains beyond. On the slopes of Lyle Hill is a huge **Cross of Lorraine** mounted on an anchor, which was built in 1946. It commemorates the Free French sailors who sailed from Greenock and lost their lives on the Atlantic during World War II.

Customhouse Quay was the departure point for thousands of Scottish emigrants sailing away to America in the 19th and early 20th centuries. The magnificent **Custom House**, built in 1810, reflects the port's importance in bygone days. It now houses a museum dedicated to the work of HM Customs and Excise. Another museum is the **McLean Museum and Art Gallery** on Kelly Street which features exhibits on local history as

well as paintings by Courbin, Boudin and the Scottish Colourists. The Watt Library in Union Street is named after the town's most famous son, and is the place to go for genealogical information.

AROUND GREENOCK

PORT GLASGOW

3 miles E of Greenock on the A8

Before the Clyde at Glasgow was canalised and deepened, this town was Glasgow's main port. **Newark Castle** (Historic Scotland) stands close to the riverbank, and dates from the 16th and 17th centuries. Up until the 1980s the castle was completely surrounded by shipyards, testament to the importance of this industry to the town at one time.

It was originally built by George Maxwell in the late 15th century, and upgraded in 1597 to what you see today by its most notorious owner, **Sir Patrick Maxwell**. He was an unsavoury man who was always quarrelling with other families, most notably the Montgomerys of Skelmorlie near Largs. In fact he murdered two of them - Montgomery himself and his eldest son - in the one day. He also treated his wife Margaret abominably. In 1632, in front of the local minister, he struck her on the face so hard that she had to take to her bed for six months. As soon as she had recovered, he attacked her again, this time with a sword.

In Greenock cemetery is the grave of Highland Mary, whose real name was Mary Campbell. Robert Burns had met her at a low point in his life in Mauchline and had asked her to accompany him to the West Indies when he thought of emigrating. However, on a trip home to Dunoon to make arrangements for her departure, she died. She was previously buried in the kirkyard of the former Old West Kirk, but was exhumed and reburied in 1920. When the Old West Kirk, which dated from the late 16th century, was dismantled in 1926, some of its stones were used to build the new Old West Kirk on the Esplanade. It has some wonderful stained glass and woodcarving.

Two miles west of Port Glasgow is the Finlaystone Estate, where the present head of the Clan Macmillan lives. It is open to the public, and features gardens and 140 acres of woodland. Finlaystone House, at the heart of the estate, dates back to the 14th century, though it has been extended over the centuries. It can be visited by special arrangement.

Many times Margaret had resorted to the law to have her husband restrained. Patrick even had his son ejected from the castle when he tried to intervene. Eventually, after 44 years of marriage and 16 children, Margaret left him, choosing a life of abject poverty rather than suffer any more. This caused the authorities to take an interest in Montgomery's conduct, but before he could be brought to trial in Edinburgh he died of natural causes.

GOUROCK

2 miles W of Greenock town centre on the A770

This little holiday resort is now effectively a suburb of Greenock though at one time it was a separate burgh. It is on a most attractive part of the Clyde, opposite Kilcreggan, the Gareloch and the entrance to Loch Long, where the mountains tumble down towards the sea. The Firth of Clyde is a famous yachting area, and the town is the home of the Royal Gourock Yacht Club, which is situated near the Promenade. At Cloch Point, four miles to the southwest, is the **Cloch Lighthouse** of 1797, a famous landmark for ships sailing on the Clyde. Between Castle Gardens and Kempock Street in the town is the curiously named **Granny Kempock's Stone** which dates from prehistoric times. It is shaped like a cloaked figure, and to walk round it is said to bring good luck.

The town is the one of the ferry terminals for Dunoon, across the Clyde in Argyll.

HAMILTON

Hamilton was once the county town of Lanarkshire, Scotland's most populous and industrialised county. It became a royal burgh in 1548, though it lost this status in 1669. It is very much connected with one of the most important families in Scotland, the Dukes of Hamilton, Scotland's premier dukes. Up until medieval times, the town was known as Cadzow, but gradually Hamilton took over as the family grew in importance. Up until the 1920s, when it was demolished, the immense Hamilton Palace, home to the dukes, was the grandest non-royal residence in Britain.

A two-mile long Grand Avenue once stretched from the palace all the way to **Chatelherault**, pronounced "Shattly-row"), a Hamilton hunting lodge east of the town. Most of the avenue is gone, but Chatelherault survives, having been refurbished in the 1980s in the largest refurbishment project of its time in Britain. It was officially re-opened in September 1987 by the Duke of Gloucester. Originally designed by William Adam in the 1730s, the lodge once also housed the Duke's hunting dogs, and was therefore known as the "Dog Kennels". Now it houses a museum and interpretation centre. The lodge got its name because the Dukes of Hamilton were also the Dukes of Chatellerault near Poitou in France. The title was bestowed in 1548 by Henry II of France in recognition

In Almada Street in Gourock you'll find the town's most prominent landmark - the County Buildings. They were built in the 1960s for the then Lanarkshire County Council, and were modelled on the United Nations building in New York. It is one of the few 1960s buildings in Scotland to be listed.

50 CONSERVATORY BAR

Gourock

A popular bar where you can relax and enjoy a drink as well as sample the delicious home cooked food on offer

see page 378

Not a stone now remains of Hamilton Palace above ground, though the Hamilton's burial place, the grandiose Hamilton Mausoleum, still remains. This bizarre building with an immense dome and full of Masonic symbolism was built by the eccentric 10th Duke in the 1850s and cost the huge sum of £150,000. A large portion of this was spent on the floor alone, a wheel mosaic containing almost every known variety of marble. The building is famous for its 15-second echo which made using it as a chapel, the original intention, impossible. When the duke died, he was laid to rest in the sarcophagus of an Egyptian princess. A curious tale tells of how the duke was found to be too tall to fit into the sarcophagus. Therefore his legs were broken and folded over. However, that's all it is - a tale. The duke was indeed too big for the sarcophagus, but he knew this long before he died, as he used to lie in it. So he had stonemasons enlarge it.

of the part the family played in arranging the marriage of Mary Stuart to his son Francis, the Dauphin. The spelling of the name changed over the years, and Chatellerault gradually became Chatelherault.

Surrounding the lodge is **Chatelherault Country Park**, with more than ten miles of woodland walks. The ruins of **Cadzow Castle**, the original home of the Hamiltons, and where Mary Stuart once stayed, can be seen within the park. There are also the remains of an old Iron Age Fort and the Cadzow Oaks, which are very ancient. In a field in front of Chatelherault is a small but famous herd of White Cattle.

Hamilton Parish Church, within the town, was designed by William Adam in the early 1730s at the same time as he was designing Chatelherault. It is an elegant building in the shape of a Greek cross, with a cupola over the crossing. The pre-Norman Netherton Cross stands at the church entrance, and in the kirkyard is the Heads Monument, commemorating four Covenanters beheaded in Edinburgh after the Pentland Rising of 1666.

Based in an old 17th century coaching inn once known as the Hamilton Arms is the **Low Parks Museum**, which has displays and memorabilia on local history. It also houses a large exhibit on Lanarkshire's own regiment - the Cameronians (Scottish Rifles). Raised as a Covenanting force in 1689, it took its name from Richard

Cameron, a Covenanting minister who opposed bishops in the Church of Scotland and the king being its head. It chose to disband itself in 1968 rather than amalgamate with another regiment. Most of the Low Parks, which at one time formed some of Hamilton Palace's parkland, has been given over to a huge retail development that includes a multi-screen cinema and supermarket

In the Bent Cemetery is the simple grave of one of Scotland's best-known entertainers, **Sir Harry Lauder**. Born in Portobello near Edinburgh in 1870, he at one time worked in the coalmines in Quarter, a village near Hamilton. He died in 1950. Nearby is the plot where the members of the Hamilton family who formerly lay in the mausoleum are now buried. The 10th Duke, who had the mausoleum built, still lies in his Egyptian sarcophagus.

Hamilton is the start of one of Scotland's ten national tourist routes, the Clyde Valley Tourist Route. It follows the Clyde Valley all the way south to Abington on the M74.

AROUND HAMILTON

MOTHERWELL AND WISHAW

3 miles E of Hamilton on the A721

The twin towns of Motherwell and Wishaw were steel making towns, though the steelworks at Ravenscraig have now gone. The award-winning **Motherwell Heritage Centre** on High Road has a number of exhibitions, and hosts varied activities with a heritage theme. To the west of Motherwell, adjoining the M74, is the 1100 acres of **Strathclyde Country Park**, developed from waste ground in the early 1970s. Within it there is an international-sized rowing lake where the rowing events of the 1986 Commonwealth Games were held. On its banks are the remains of a **Roman Bathhouse**. There are guided walks throughout the year, as well as nature trails and a camping and caravanning site. M&D's Theme Park is located near the north banks of the loch and offers more than 40 rides and attractions.

Amazonia is Scotland's only indoor rain forest attraction and houses reptiles, insects and animals connected with the Amazon rain forest.

A mile north east of Motherwell is the small industrial village of Carfin, where you will find the Lourdes-inspired **Carfin Pilgrimage Centre and Grotto**, created in the 1920s by Fr. Thomas Nimmo Taylor, the local priest, helped by out-of-work miners. There are displays and exhibits that help explain the notion of pilgrimage, not just in the Roman Catholic religion, but also in all major religions.

DALSERF

6 miles SE of Hamilton off the A72

Once a sizeable village with inns and a ferry across the Clyde, Dalserf has now shrunk to no more than a few cottages and a

church. **Dalserf Parish Church**, with its whitewashed walls, looks more like a house than a place of worship, and dates from 1655. The building is a rare survivor of a mid-17th century Scottish church. Most from that period were simply built with earth floors and a thatched roof. In the 18th and 19th centuries they were usually demolished to make way for something more imposing. Dalserf has lasted because the parish was a poor one and couldn't afford to rebuild, preferring instead to upgrade whenever it could. In the kirkyard is a pre-Norman "hogs back" grave slab, which was dug up in 1897.

STONEHOUSE

7 miles S of Hamilton on the A71

This former weaving village still has rows of 18th and 19th century weaving cottages. On one side of the main door is a large window, which allows plenty of light into the room which housed the loom, and on the other is a small window which allowed light to enter the main living quarters.

Patrick Hamilton, Scotland's first Protestant martyr, was born in Stonehouse in about 1503. He was burned at the stake in St Andrews in 1528. The **Alexander Hamilton Memorial Park** was opened in 1925, the gift of a local man. It has a bandstand which was originally made for the Great Glasgow Exhibition of 1911.

The remains of the **Old St Ninian's Parish Church** are to the north of the village, surrounded by an old kirkyard. A prehistoric burial

51 THE SHAWLANDS PARK HOTEL

Larkhall

Recently refurbished luxury hotel offering exceptional cuisine and quality en suite accommodation.

see page 380

To the west of Strathaven, at Drumclog, was fought the Battle of Drumclog, at which an army of Covenanters overcame government troops in 1679. A memorial on a minor road off the A71 commemorates the event. At the small village of Sandford, two miles to the south, are the lovely 50-feet high Spectacle E'e Falls on the Kype Water, a tributary of the Avon.

In the Calderwood area of East Kilbride is Hunter House, birthplace in the 18th century of the Hunter brothers, John and William, pioneering surgeons and anatomists who worked in both Glasgow and London. The house has a small display and museum about the two men and their lives. The Hunterian Museum in Glasgow is one of their legacies.

kist (coffin) was once dug up in the kirkyard, showing that the site may have had a religious significance long before Christianity came to the area.

STRATHAVEN

8 miles S of Hamilton on the A723

Strathaven (pronounced "Strayven") is a real gem of a small town that sits at the heart of Avondale. The ruins of **Strathaven Castle** (also known as Avondale Castle) are all that is left of a once large and powerful 14th century stronghold of the Douglas family. On the edge of the John Hastie Park is the **John Hastie Museum**, which has local history collections.

Close to the cemetery is the **James Wilson Monument**. James Wilson was born in Strathaven in 1760, his father being a weaver. He was a free thinker on the matter of religion, and was also a radical reformer, something of which the local landowners did not approve. In 1820 a band of reformers, of which he was a member, posted a bill on the streets of Glasgow that was held to be treasonable. He was arrested near Falkirk and executed in 1820.

EAST KILBRIDE

7 miles W of Hamilton on the A726

East Kilbride is the largest and undoubtedly the most successful of Scotland's new towns. Work started on laying it out in 1947 round an old village, and now it has a population of about 70,000. It is renowned for its shopping facilities, and has four shopping malls:

Princes Mall, the Plaza, the Olympia Centre and Centre West, which together make up the largest undercover shopping area in Scotland.

On the outskirts of the town is **Calderglen Country Park,** based on Torrance House (private). The 300-acre park has a boating pond, bowling green, mini railway, mini zoo, children's playground and many waymarked woodland and riverside walks.

To the north of the town is the **James Hamilton Heritage Park**, with a 16-acre boating loch. Behind it is the restored Mains Castle (private), which was built by the Lindsay family in the early 15th century. Up until the 1970s it was a ruin. Close by, the **Scottish Museum of Country Life** is based around Wester Kittochside Farm which was home to the Reid family since the 16th century. In 1992, the last of the family, Margaret Reid, gifted it to the National Trust for Scotland. Run jointly by the National Museums of Scotland and the National Trust, it explains rural life in Scotland throughout the ages and has a huge collection of farm implements and machinery. The elegant farmhouse of Wester Kittochside, which dates from 1783, is also open to the public.

EAGLESHAM

10 miles W of Hamilton on the B764

The conservation village of Eaglesham was planned and built by the Earl of Eglinton in the mid-1700s. It is shaped like a huge "A", with the point facing the moorland to the west of the village. Between the two arms of the "A" is a large village green area known as the "Orry", on which once stood a cotton mill. The lovely period cottages and houses in the village make a perfect picture of Scottish rural life, though the village has largely been colonised by commuters from Glasgow and Lanarkshire. The **Parish Church**, which dates from 1788, has the look of an Alpine church about it, and it is reckoned that while planning Eaglesham the 10th Earl was influenced by villages he had admired in northern Italy.

It was in a field near Eaglesham in 1941 that **Rudolph Hess**, Hitler's deputy, landed after he parachuted from an ME 110. He was found by a local farmer called David McLean, who took him home and treated him firmly but politely. Hess gave his name as Alfred Horn, but it was soon established that he was Hitler's deputy. He said he was on a secret mission to speak to the Duke of Hamilton. A map he possessed showed that he had been trying to reach Dungavel House, one of the Duke's hunting lodges near Strathaven.

Hess was then taken to Maryhill Barracks in Glasgow where one of his guards was Corporal William Ross who went on to become the Secretary of State for Scotland in the Wilson government. Hess was later moved to Buchanan Castle near Drymen in Stirlingshire, where he was interrogated.

BOTHWELL

2 miles NW of Hamilton off the M74

In the centre of this small town is **St Bride's Parish Church**, with a chancel dating from 1398. It was built as part of a collegiate church by Archibald the Grim, 3rd Earl of Douglas, and has a roof made entirely of stone. A year after it was built, the church was the scene of a royal wedding when David, son of Robert III, married Archibald the Grim's daughter Marjory. Outside the west end of the Victorian nave is a monument to **Joanna Baillie**, a playwright and poetess born at Bothwell manse in 1762. She was praised by Scott as being one of the finest writers of the 18th century. Her work, though at times filled with humour, is dark and often violent, with murderous, paranoid characters. More than one critic has wondered where a seemingly prim daughter of a minister found the material to write such stuff.

On the banks of the Clyde, some distance from the town, are the massive and impressive remains of **Bothwell Castle** (Historic Scotland) which historians have rated as one of the most important secular medieval buildings in Scotland. The mighty ruin stands dramatically on a hill above a loop in the river, its walls 15 feet thick. Started in the late 1200s, the oldest surviving part is the great circular donjon, or keep, 65 feet in diameter and 90 feet tall.

Upstream is Bothwell Bridge, the focal point in 1679 of the

In St Kentigern's kirkyard in Lanark is buried William Smellie (pronounced Smillie), the father of modern midwifery. He was born in Lanark in 1697 and was the first obstetrician to teach midwifery on a formal basis as a branch of medicine. He also pioneered the use of forceps. He began life as a doctor in Lanark, but then studied in Glasgow and Paris before establishing a practice in London, where he also lectured. He was a kindly man, and frequently delivered the babies of the poor of London without charging them. He died in 1763.

A lovely riverside walk from Lanark village leads to the famous Falls of Clyde, a series of picturesque waterfalls with drops ranging from the 30 feet drop at Bonnington, to Cora Linn's 90 feet descent in three scenic cascades. A hydroelectric scheme now harnesses the power of the water, and the falls are only seen at their most spectacular at certain times of the year.

Battle of Bothwell Bridge between the Royalist forces of the Duke of Monmouth and a Covenanting army. The Covenanters were heavily defeated, with more than 500 being killed and 1200 taken prisoner. The bridge you see today is basically the same bridge, though much altered and widened. A memorial on the Bothwell side of the bridge commemorates the event.

BLANTYRE

3 miles NW of Hamilton on the A724

Blantyre is now a suburb of Hamilton but in 1813 it was a mill town beside the River Clyde. In that year, David Livingstone was born in a one-room apartment in a tenement block built for the mill workers. Today, the block is the spruce, white-painted **David Livingstone Centre** (National Trust for Scotland). Visitors can see the cramped room in which he was brought up; other rooms have displays on the great explorer and missionary's life and work, including of course the legendary meeting with Henry Stanley. Outside, there's a themed garden. African playground, tearoom, gift shop and riverside walks.

LANARK

Set above the Clyde Valley near the upper reaches of the Clyde, Lanark is one of the original 4 Royal Burghs of Scotland created by David I who also built a castle here in the mid-1100s. It was at Lanark Castle that William Wallace began the war of independence by attacking the English garrison holding the fortress. Wallace is commemorated by a statue in front of St Nicholas Church which is itself notable for possessing the world's oldest bell, cast in 1130.

This small town, with a population of just over 8000, keeps alive several old customs. Every year, in June, the townspeople celebrate **Lanimer Day** which originated as a ceremony of riding the boundaries of the burgh. And on March 1 each year is held the **Whuppity Scoorie** celebrations when the children of the town race round the 18th century St Nicholas's Church waving paper balls above their head, and then scrambling for coins thrown at them. Nowadays it is the opening event in the Whuppity Scoorie Storytelling Festival, but it may have had its origins in pagan times, when it celebrated the arrival of Spring.

Another custom is the **Het Pint**, held on January 1st each year. Citizens of the town meet at 10am and are given a glass of mulled wine. Anyone wishing to do so can also claim a pound. The tradition goes back to the 17th century, when Lord Hyndford gave money to the town to be used each year for pious or educational purposes.

In the Westport you'll find the **Royal Burgh of Lanark Museum**, which recounts the town's history.

On the banks of the Clyde below Lanark lies the village and UNESCO World Heritage Site of

New Lanark. It was here, in 1785, that David Dale and Richard Arkwright founded a cotton mill. The Palladian-style mills and the workers' houses, by the standards of the time approached the luxurious. But it was Dale's son-in-law, Robert Owen, who had the vision of creating a "village of unity". Fair wages, decent homes, health care, free education for adults and children, a co-operative shop, and even the world's first day nursery would prove that a happy workforce was a productive workforce.

The mills were still in production up to 1968. Under the care of the New Lanark Conservation Trust, it has become one of the most popular tourist destinations in Scotland, even though people still live in some of the original tenements and cottages.

Attractions include a Visitors Centre (including a Textile Machinery Exhibition and the New Millennium Ride that introduces you to Robert Owen's original vision), the Millworker's House, the Village Store Exhibition and Robert Owen's House. Other buildings have been converted into craft workshops, and there is also a hotel housed in a former mill. A presentation called Annie McLeod's Story is shown in what was Robert Owen's School, and uses the latest in 3-D technology. The "ghost" of 18th century mill girl Annie Macleod returns to tell the story of her life in the days of Robert Owen. Also in the village is a **Scottish Wildlife Trust Visitors Centre**.

Lesmahagow Priory, Lanark

AROUND LANARK

BIGGAR

13 miles SE of Lanark on the A702

Biggar is a small, attractive market town that still has its original medieval layout. It sits among the rich agricultural lands of South Lanarkshire, and was granted its burgh charter in 1451.

It must have more museums per head of population than any other place in Britain. The **Biggar Gas Works Museum**, housed in the town's former gas works dating from 1839, explains how gas was produced from coal in former times, and the **Moat Park Heritage Centre** has exhibits and displays about the town and its immediate area from the time the landscape was formed millions of years ago right up to the present day. **Greenhill Covenanter's House** used to stand at Wiston, eight miles away, but was transported to Biggar stone by stone, and is now dedicated to the memory of the Covenanters. These

In Broughton Road in Biggar is the professionally run Biggar Puppet Theatre, which has a Victorian-style theatre seating up to 100 people, plus a museum. Purves Puppets, which owns it, is Scotland's largest puppet company and regularly presents shows all over Britain.

were men and women who, in the 17th century, resisted the Stuart monarchs' attempts to impose bishops on the Church of Scotland. They sometimes paid with their lives for their convictions. The **Gladstone Court Museum** has re-created a Victorian street, with a dressmaker's shop, boot maker's shop and even a schoolroom.

The Albion Building houses the **Albion Motors Archives**, which are the records of the Albion Motor Company, started up locally in 1899 by Norman Fulton and T.B. Murray before moving production to Glasgow. It soon grew to be the largest manufacturer of commercial vehicles in the British Empire.

At Brownsbank Cottage, a mile-and-a-half from the town, lived the Scottish poet Christopher Grieve, better known as Hugh McDiarmid. He died in 1978, and his wife Valda continued to live there until her death in 1989. Now the 'but and ben' (2-roomed cottage) has been restored to exactly how it looked when the poet lived there, and is now the base for a writer-in-residence. It can be visited by appointment only.

St Mary's Church was founded in 1546 by Malcolm, Lord Fleming, Chancellor of Scotland. It was formerly collegiate, and is a graceful, cruciform building. It was the last church to be built in Scotland before the Reformation. In the kirkyard is a gravestone commemorating the Gladstone family, forebears of William Ewart

Gladstone, British prime minister during Victorian times.

CARMICHAEL

5 miles S of Lanark on a minor road west of the A73

The small **Carmichael Parish Church** dates from 1750 and has an interesting laird's loft. One of the past lairds, the Earl of Hyndford, left a sum of money called the Hyndford Mortification to provide the local schoolmasters with a yearly pair of trousers and a supply of whisky. The **Carmichael Visitor Centre** is situated on the Carmichael Estate, and has a display of waxwork models (formerly housed in Edinburgh) that illustrate Scotland's history from the year AD 1000 to the present day. There are also displays about the history of the Carmichael family which has owned the lands of Carmichael since the 13th century, and others about wind energy.

LEADHILLS

27 miles S of Lanark on the B797

Like its neighbour Wanlockhead (which is in Dumfriesshire), Leadhills is a former lead mining village. It has the highest golf course in Scotland, and is full of old 18th and 19th century lead miners' cottages. It forms one terminus for the Leadhills and Wanlockhead Light Railway.

The **Allan Ramsay Library** is the oldest subscription Library in Scotland, and is named after the famous poet born here in 1684. In the graveyard is the grave of John

Taylor, a lead miner who lived to be 137 years old. Next to the cemetery is a monument to **William Symington**, who was born in the village in 1764. He worked as an engineer in the mines, and was a pioneer of steam propulsion in ships. His paddleboat the *Charlotte Dundas* was launched at Grangemouth in 1802.

DOUGLAS

14 miles SW of Lanark on the A70

It was in Douglas, in 1968, that the Cameronians (Scottish Rifles), a proud Scottish regiment, was disbanded. The ceremony took place in the grounds of Douglas Castle, better known as **Castle Dangerous** after publication of Sir Walter Scott's novel of that name which was based on the castle's history. Today, only a tower survives. It was at Castle Douglas in 1689 that the Cameronian regiment was raised by James, Earl of Angus. His statue now stands in the village.

The centre of Douglas is a conservation area, with many old cottages and houses. **The Sun Inn** of 1621 was once the village's Tolbooth, where justice was meted out. **Old St Bride's** is the choir of the former parish church dating from the 14th century. Within it are memorials to members of the Douglas family, including Archibald, the 5th Earl of Angus. He was killed at Flodden in 1513, and had the curious nickname of "**Bell the Cat**". There is also a memorial to "the Good Sir James of Douglas", killed by the Moors in

Spain while taking Robert the Bruce's heart to the Holy Land for burial. The clock in the clock tower was gifted to the church by Mary Stuart in 1565, and is the oldest working public clock in Scotland.

Douglas Heritage Museum, in Bell's Wynd, occupies the former dower house of the castle. It is open on Saturdays and Sundays by prior appointment. It has displays on the Douglas family and on the Cameronians (Scottish Rifles).

CROSSFORD

4 miles NW of Lanark on the A72

This lovely little village sits in the heart of the Clyde Valley, on the banks of the river. Above it you'll find the substantial ruins of **Craignethan Castle** (Historic Scotland) where Mary Stuart once stayed. It was built in the 1530s by Sir James Hamilton of Finnart, illegitimate son of James Hamilton, 1st Earl of Arran and ancestor of the present Dukes of Hamilton. He was the master of works to James V who gave him the lands of Draffan on which the castle was built. However, the king later suspected that Hamilton had been plotting against him (which was probably not true), and had him executed.

The castle then passed to the crown, and was subsequently given to the 2nd Earl of Arran, Sir James's half-brother and the Regent of Scotland.

Sir Walter Scott is reputed to have used the castle as a model for his "Tillietudlem Castle" in *Old Mortality*, though he later denied any link.

•

The Sulwath Brewery in King Street, Douglas, is a small, family-run micro-brewery producing 6 different beers which have found customers as far apart as Aberdeen in the north and Devon in the south. Guided tours of the brewery are available and end with a sample tasting.

•

Edinburgh & The Lothians

The Lothians consist of the three former counties of East Lothian, Midlothian and West Lothian. The land is generally low lying to the north, rising to moorland and hills in the south, with areas of industry to the west and expanses of good arable farmland to the east. Being close to Edinburgh, this area is at the heart of Scottish history, full of castles, grand houses and churches. It is also a place of quiet, pastoral villages and marvellous scenery. The only towns that could possibly be said to be industrial are Dalkeith, Bo'ness, Armadale and Bathgate, and even here industry never intrudes too much.

East Lothian (formerly "Haddingtonshire") is a farming county, a patchwork of fields and woodland dotted all over with small, neat villages. The land rises to the south where it meets the Lammermuir Hills. Here, the landscape changes though it never loses its gentle aspect. Haddington is the county town

and boasts many old buildings. The main Edinburgh-London railway line bypassed the town so it never developed as a place of industry. The town's main building is the cathedralesque St Mary's Church, the tower of which is sometimes called the "Lamp of the Lothians".

Mid Lothian was at one time called "Edinburghshire". Towards the south it meets the Moorfoot Hills, and has a string of small towns sitting like satellites round Edinburgh itself. Its most notable building is the world famous Rosslyn Chapel which, people claim (and Dan Brown's novel *The Da Vinci Code* supported), conceals a mystery that goes right to the heart of Christianity.

Before 1975, the county town of West Lothian was Linlithgow. It is an ancient burgh with a royal palace where Mary Stuart, better known as Mary, Queen of Scots, was born. West Lothian is more industrial in character than the other two Lothians but there are still plenty of tranquil places to be visited, such as Torphichen, with its preceptory of St John, and South Queensferry, in the shadow of the two Forth bridges. A full day could be taken up exploring Linlithgow itself, with its royal palace, medieval church, canal basin and old stone buildings. Then there are the county's grand houses, such as Hopetoun and The Binns, which deserve to be visited and explored.

	ACCOMMODATION	
56	Old Farm House, Gifford, nr Haddington	p 137, 383

FOOD & DRINK

53	Museum of Scotland, Edinburgh	p 124, 381
54	Volunteer Arms, Dunbar	p 136, 382
55	The Garvald Inn, Garvald, nr Haddington	p 137, 382
57	Ivy Tea Room, Bo'ness	p 140, 382

PLACES OF INTEREST

52	The Royal Yacht Britannia, Leith, nr Edinburgh	p 121, 381
53	Museum of Scotland, Edinburgh	p 124, 381

EDINBURGH

One of the world's great cities, Edinburgh is also one of the most attractive. Dramatically sited overlooking the Firth of Forth, like Rome the city drapes itself across seven hills. The most prominent of these is **Castle Rock**, a craggy outcrop which has been fortified since Stone Age times.

The present **Castle** dates back to 1230 although there have been many additions and alterations. The oldest part is St Margaret's chapel, an austere Norman place of worship which for 300 years was used as a gunpowder magazine. Its original function was recognised in 1845 but the chapel was not re-consecrated until 1924. The castle is part fortress, part Renaissance palace. In the palace visitors can see the room in which Mary, Queen of Scots gave birth to James VI (later also James I of England) and view the **Honours of Scotland,** the Scottish equivalent of England's Crown Jewels. The dazzling display includes the Crown, Sceptre and Sword of State plus, rather incongruously in the midst of such splendour, the Stone of Destiny, the plain sandstone slab on which 47 kings of Scotland were crowned.

Also within the castle is the **National War Museum of Scotland** which explores military service over the last 400 years. Another museum within the castle is the regimental **Museum of the Royal Scots Dragoon Guards**. The regiment is Scotland's only cavalry regiment, and was formed in 1971 when older regiments amalgamated.

The castle stands at the western end of the **Royal Mile,** the backbone of the medieval city. In herringbone fashion, narrow wynds and alleys skitter off this main road which is stacked for most of its length with lofty tenements. One of these, the 6-storey **Gladstone's Land (NTS),** is a splendid and authentic example of an early 17th century merchant's house. The Gladestan family occupied part of the tenement and rented out the remainder. If you are looking for an unusual holiday it's still possible to rent one of the floors. Nearby, in Lady Stair's House, you'll find the **Writer's Museum** with displays on Scotland's trio of great writers, Burns, Scott and Stevenson. The house is named after Lady Stair, who owned the house in the 18th century.

Allow plenty of time for exploring the Royal Mile. Its places of interest are too numerous to be listed here, but not to be missed are **St Giles Cathedral** with its magnificent crowned spire; the adjoining Thistle Chapel; **Outlook Tower** whose *camera obscura* has been delighting visitors with its glorious views of the city ever since it was installed in 1853; **John Knox's House** where the fiery reformer lived for a while; and the **Museum of Childhood** which, paradoxically, was created by a man who hated children. He dedicated his museum to King Herod.

52 THE ROYAL YACHT BRITANNIA

Edinburgh

Experience the splendour of the yacht used by Her Majesty the Queen and the Royal Family for over forty years.

 see page 381

From Edinburgh Castle every day except Sunday is fired the One o' Clock Gun. It booms out over the city, frightening tourists who are visiting the castle at the time. Another gun associated with the castle is Mons Meg. It is one of two huge siege guns presented to James II in 1457 by the Duke of Burgundy. Some people imagine that it is Mons Meg which is fired at one o' clock, but it is in fact a 25lb gun situated on Hill Mount Battery.

In Holyrood Road in Edinburgh is Our Dynamic Earth, an exhibition and visitors centre that takes you on a journey through the history of the universe, from the beginning of time and on into the future. It features dinosaurs, earthquakes, lava flows and tropical rainstorms.

Behind the cathedral is **Parliament House** where Scotland's parliament met up until the Treaty of Union in 1707. The building itself dates from the late 17th century, though the façade was added in 1829.

Across from the cathedral are the **Edinburgh City Chambers**, home to the city council. It started life as a royal exchange and was built between 1753 and 1761 to designs by John Adam, brother of the better-known Robert. Though it appears to have only two or three storeys if seen from the Royal Mile, it actually has 12 storeys, which tumble down the slope at the back.

At the eastern end of the Royal Mile stands the **Palace of Holyroodhouse,** most of which was built in the 1660s as a Scottish residence for Charles II who never in fact visited his elegant northern home. Of the medieval palace, only the Tower House remains, ingeniously incorporated into the present building. Here, visitors can see Mary, Queen of Scots private rooms, amongst them the study in which her private secretary, David Rizzio, was murdered. A group of Scottish noblemen, incited by Mary's husband, Lord Darnley, burst into the study, stabbed Rizzio 56 times, and dragged his body through her bedchamber.

Within the Palace grounds stand the romantic ruins of **Holyrood Abbey,** founded by David I in 1238. Most of it was destroyed in 1547 by English troops on the orders of Henry VIII when the Scots refused his demand to hand over the infant Mary, Queen of Scots.

The picture gallery at Holyroodhouse contains portraits of more than 100 Scottish kings. The recently opened **Queen's Gallery** is the first permanent exhibition space for the royal collection of paintings and sculpture in Scotland. It was designed by Benjamin Tindall Architects, and is housed in the former Holyrood Free Church and Duchess of Gordon's School at the entrance to the grounds.

Close to Holyrood is the new **Scottish Parliament Building**, designed by the late Catalan architect Enric Miralles. Officially opened in October 2004 by HM the Queen, it is a controversial building, having cost ten times the original estimate and opened four years late. Its appearance has also divided the nation, with some people loving it and others loathing it. Guided tours are available, and while Parliament is in session you can sit in the public galleries and watch the proceedings.

When King David built his abbey here, it was surrounded by

Holyrood Palace and Arther's Seat, Edinbugh

open countryside. Astonishingly, it still is. **Holyrood Park** covers 5 square miles of fields and lochs, moorland and hills, all dominated by **Arthur's Seat.** The crest of an extinct volcano, Arthur's 823 feet are easily scaled and the views from the summit are breathtaking.

Also within the Royal Mile is the **Canongate Tolbooth** of 1591, which held the council chamber, courtroom and burgh jail; it is a curious building with a clock that projects out over the pavement. It contains the **Museum of Edinburgh,** which gives an insight into the history of the city itself, and is packed with exhibits from its colourful past.

The **Canongate Church** of 1688 has Dutch influences, and in the kirkyard is buried Adam Smith the famous economist, Agnes McLehose for whom Burns wrote *Ae Fond Kiss*, and Robert Fergusson the poet. He was Burns's hero, and died aged 24 in a madhouse. When Burns visited his grave, he was disgusted to see that there was no grave marker, so he paid for the tombstone over the grave that we see now. **White Horse Close**, beyond the church, is the most picturesque of Edinburgh's closes, and it was from the White Horse Inn that the horse-drawn coaches left for London and York.

To the south of the Royal Mile, in Chambers Street behind Edinburgh University, are the **Royal Museum** and the new **Museum of Scotland**. They house internationally important collections relating to natural history, science,

Greyfriars, Edinburgh

the arts and history. On Nicolson Street is the **Surgeon's Hall Museum**, owned and run by the Royal College of Surgeons of Edinburgh.

Another famous church south of the Royal Mile is **Greyfriars**. Built in 1612, it was here that the National Covenant rejecting bishops in the Church of Scotland was signed in 1638. From this, the adherents of Presbyterianism in the 17th century got the name "Covenanters". In nearby Candlemaker Row is the famous **Greyfriars Bobby** statue. It commemorates a terrier that faithfully kept guard over the grave of John Gray, his former master, who died in 1858 of tuberculosis. He did this for 14 years, until he too died in 1872. Bobby became famous after an American author, Eleanor Stackhouse Atkinson, wrote a book about it and Disney turned it into a film. However, she sentimentalised the story somewhat by stating that Gray was a simple shepherd, when in fact he was a policeman.

One of Edinburgh's hidden gems can be found in the Cowgate - the Magdalen Chapel of 1547. It was built by Michael McQueen and his wife Janet Rynd, who are buried within it. It then passed to the Guild of Hammermen. The chapel contains pre-Reformation stained glass, and was where the very first General Assembly of the Church of Scotland was held in 1560, with 42 churchmen attending.

53 MUSEUM OF
SCOTLAND

Edinburgh

A superb museum tracing
the story of Scotland from
the dawn of time to the
present day.

 see page 381

By the 1790s the old town, or
"Royalty", had become so grossly
overcrowded, decayed and
dangerously insanitary that a New
Town was started on land to the
north. With its leafy squares and
handsome boulevards, Edinburgh's
New Town was an inspired
masterpiece of town planning.
Stately neo-classical public buildings
blend happily with elegant Georgian
terraces and the main thoroughfare,
Princes Street, was deliberately built
up along one side only so as not to
obstruct the dramatic view of the
Castle, high above. Some 40 years
later, the town's planners even
managed to make the huge expanse
of Waverley railway station almost
invisible by tucking it in against the
hillside.

A stroll along Princes Street
begins at **Register House,** a noble
neo-classical building designed by
Robert Adam in the 1770s to house
Scotland's historic documents and
records. It still does. A little further
west, the 200 feet high **Scott
Monument** celebrates one of the

country's greatest poets and
novelists with the largest memorial
to a writer anywhere in the world.
The monument's Gothic details
echo the architecture of Scott's
beloved Melrose Abbey.

The **Royal Scottish Academy**
is a grand Doric building which
hosts art exhibitions throughout the
year and the annual Academy
Exhibition from April to July. The
Academy was designed by William
Playfair who was also the architect
for the nearby National Gallery of
Scotland which houses a mouth-
watering display of masterworks.
They range from Hugo van der
Goes' lovely mid-15th century
altarpiece, the "Trinity Panels",
through exquisite Renaissance and
17th century European works, to a
comprehensive collection of
Scottish paintings.

Adding to the charm of Princes
Street (also renowned for its
shopping opportunities) are the
green open spaces of the extensive
gardens which border its length.
There always seem to be public
entertainers here, especially during
the last 3 weeks of August when the
Edinburgh International Festival
attracts around one million visitors
to the city. The Royal Mile also
becomes a colourful open-air
theatre where Fringe performers
and buskers take over every inch of
pavement to present drama,
juggling, classical music, magicians,
jazz, piping, folk music and a host
of other activities.

As in the old town, the New
Town has too many attractions to
list in full here. But you certainly

No 28 Charlotte Square, Edinburgh

shouldn't leave the city before sampling the **Scottish National Portrait Gallery,** housed in a curious building modelled on the Doge's Palace in Venice, and the **Georgian House**, restored by the National Trust for Scotland to its late-18th century elegance, complete with furniture of the period and some fine paintings by Ramsay and Raeburn.

On Calton Hill, to the east of Princes Street is the 106-feet high **Nelson Monument** from the top of which are views out over the city. It commemorates Nelson's death at the Battle of Trafalgar in 1805 and was designed by the architect Robert Burn. A time signal is installed at the top, consisting of a ball which drops at 12 noon in winter and 1pm in summer. It allowed ship's captains on the Forth to set their watches accurately.

Further north, off Inverleith Row, are the **Royal Botanic Gardens**, 70 acres of greenery and colour surrounded by the bustle of the city. They were founded in 1670 as a "physic garden" at Holyrood, but were transferred here in 1823. And at Leith, up until the 1920s a separate burgh, you'll find the **Royal Yacht *Britannia*** moored at the Ocean Terminal, a leisure and entertainment complex. The ship is open to the public.

In Pier Place in Newhaven, to the west of Leith, is the **Newhaven Heritage Museum** explaining the history of this former fishing village. It was in Newhaven that the largest fighting ship of its day, the *Great Michael* was built between 1507

and 1513 for James IV's Scottish navy. It is said that the whole fleet which sailed to America with Columbus in 1492 could fit comfortably into her hull. It was the envy of Europe, and Henry VIII even demanded that it be handed over to him, as it was far too good for the Scots.

Granton sits further west, and at one time was a busy harbour and industrial area, with a huge gas works. It is now undergoing a major redevelopment, though one of the huge gasometers has been preserved. At its centre is Caroline Park (private), an elegant mansion dating from the 17th century.

Craigmillar Castle (Historic Scotland) is on the southeast outskirts of the city. The extensive ruins date from the 14th century, with many later additions. Mary

At the west end of the New Town is one of Edinburgh's most spectacular churches - St Mary's Cathedral. It was built in Victorian times as the cathedral for the Episcopalian diocese of Edinburgh and is as large and grand as a medieval cathedral, with three soaring spires that have become Edinburgh landmarks. It was designed by the eminent architect Sir George Gilbert Scott and built in the 1870s, though the spires were added in the early 20th century.

Botanical Gardens, Edinburgh

Scottish Whisky Heritage Centre, Edinburgh

•

The Scotch Whisky Heritage Centre on Castlehill tells the story of Scotch, and brings three hundred years of its history to life. You'll learn about how it's made, and every Sunday afternoon there is a tasting session.

•

•

Further to the west of Edinburgh, at Corstorphine, are the Edinburgh Zoological Gardens, set in 80 acres. The zoo is famous for its penguins, and the daily "penguin parade" when the penguins march round part of the zoo. However, the parade taking place or not depends on the weather and the whim of the penguins themselves, who sometimes choose not to hold it.

•

Stuart stayed here for a short while after her Italian secretary Rizzio was murdered. **Lauriston Castle**, near Davidson's Mains, is also worth visiting. It is set in 30 acres of parkland. One of its owners was the father of John Napier, who invented logarithms. It now has a collection of furniture and decorative arts. The **Royal Observatory** sits on Blackford Hill, south of the city centre, and has displays and exhibits relating to astronomy.

Finally, and rather unexpectedly, Edinburgh also has a beach, at **Portobello,** once a stylish seaside resort but now somewhat down at heel.

AROUND EDINBURGH

MUSSELBURGH
6 miles E of Edinburgh on the A199

Musselburgh got its name from the beds of mussels that once lay at the mouth of the River Esk on which the town stands. Today, it is a dormitory town for Edinburgh.

The **Tolbooth** dates from the 1590s, and was built of stones from the former Chapel of Our Lady of Loretto, which in pre-Reformation times was served by a hermit. **Inveresk Lodge Gardens** (National Trust for Scotland), with their terraces and walled garden, illustrate methods and plants that can be used in a home garden. The **Battle of Pinkie**, the last battle fought between Scottish and English national armies, took place near Musselburgh in 1547 during the "Rough Wooing", when Henry VIII was trying to force the Scottish parliament to agree to a marriage between his son and the infant Mary Stuart. The Scots were defeated due to the incompetence of the Earl of Arran, Scotland's commander. Mary herself eventually married the Dauphin of France, heir to the French throne.

PRESTONPANS
9 miles E of Edinburgh on the B1348

Prestonpans sits on the south coast of the Firth of Forth and looks across a broad bay formed by this bank of the river towards Edinburgh, eight miles to the west. The town takes its name from the salt pans that were established here as long ago as the 1100s. The industry continued right up until 1959. Prestonpans also once had a busy harbour but that steadily declined from the 1930s and has now disappeared.

The town entered the history books in 1745 when the Jacobite army of Charles Edward Stuart defeated a Hanoverian army under

Sir John Cope at the **Battle of Prestonpans**. The whole battle only took 15 minutes, with many of the Hanoverian troops being trapped against a high wall (which can still be seen) surrounding Prestongrange House. Contemporary accounts tell of terrified Hanoverian troops trying to scale the wall and dropping into the comparative safety of the house's grounds. Even though it took place in the early 18th century, the site was largely an industrial one, with even a primitive tramway for hauling coal crossing the battle field. The Jacobite song *Hey Johnnie Cope* lampoons the English commander, though he was not wholly to blame for the Hanoverian defeat.

The **Prestongrange Museum** is at Morrison's Haven and tells the story of the local industries through the ages.

PORT SETON

10 miles E of Edinburgh on the B1348

A former fishing village and now a popular holiday resort, Port Seton takes its name from George Seton, 11th Lord Seton, who built the first harbour here between 1655-65.

Port Seton Collegiate Church (Historic Scotland) was built, but never completed, in the 14th century as a collegiate church served by a college of priests. It is dedicated to St Mary and the Holy Cross, and has some tombs of the Seton family, as well as fine vaulting. In 1544 it was looted and stripped by the Earl of Hertford and his English army. **Seton Castle**

dates from 1790, and was designed by Robert Adam. It replaced the former Seton Palace, one of the grandest Scottish buildings of its time. Mary Stuart visited the Palace after the murder of Rizzio by her second husband, Lord Darnley.

DALKEITH

6 miles SE of Edinburgh on the A68

This pleasant town is nowadays a dormitory for Edinburgh but at one time was an important market town on the main road south from Edinburgh to England. A busy little town, it has an unusually wide High Street at the eastern end of which are the gates of **Dalkeith Country Park.** This lovely wooded estate surrounds Dalkeith Palace, home of the Dukes of Buccleuch, a fine early-18th century mansion which can only be seen from the outside. Its former chapel, built in 1843 and now the parish Church of St Mary, is open however and well worth visiting to see its exceptionally fine furnishings and the only water-powered Hamilton organ in Scotland!

NEWTONGRANGE

8 miles SE of Edinburgh on the A7

The former Lady Victoria Colliery in Newtongrange houses the **Scottish Mining Museum** which tells the story of coal mining in Scotland from the earliest times right up until the present. The museum offers guided tours by former miners, award-winning "talking tableaux", a visitor centre, tea room and gift shop. Visitors can also marvel at the massive proportions of the largest steam engine in Scotland. It used to power the winding machinery which lowered workers down the mine shaft, 1625 feet deep. The Lady Victoria is one of the finest surviving Victorian collieries in Europe. It opened in the 1890s and closed in 1981. At its peak, it employed more than 2000 men.

ARNISTON

9 miles SE of Edinburgh off the A7

Standing just outside this small village, **Arniston House** is by common consent one of William Adam's finest buildings. It is a noble and dignified house built in a local sandstone that blushes pink in the clear Midlothian sun. The mansion was commissioned by Robert Dundas, lord President of the Court of Session, and a singularly unprepossessing person *"with small, ferret eyes, round shoulders, and a harsh croaking voice"*. But Dundas was also a fine example of that 18th century ideal - a Man of Taste and Judgement. Building at Arniston began in 1726 but four years later financial problems brought the work to a halt with one third of the house unfinished. More than 20 years passed before a judicious marriage to an heiress allowed it to be resumed although by this time both Dundas and William Adam were dead. The building was eventually completed in 1754 by William's son, John. Most of William Adams' glorious interiors have survived intact, along with some excellent period furniture. One of the most appealing features of the house is its comprehensive collection of family portraits, including several by Raeburn and Allan Ramsay.

BORTHWICK

11 miles SE of Edinburgh off the A7

Borthwick Castle is a massive twin-towered castle built by Sir William Borthwick in about 1430. It was to this castle that Mary Stuart and Bothwell came after their marriage in 1567. It was a marriage which displeased the Scottish people and more than a thousand Scottish nobles cornered the couple there. They demanded that Mary hand over Bothwell for his part in the murder of Lord Darnley, Mary's second husband. However, Bothwell escaped and fled to Dunbar.

On hearing of his escape, the nobles immediately retired from the Queen's presence, thinking that she had seen through his treachery. However, no sooner had they left her than she tore off her fine gowns and put on breeches and a pageboy's shirt, and made her escape so that she could rejoin her husband. The Red Room is said to be haunted by her ghost.

The Borthwicks were a powerful family, and when they took prisoners one of the games they played was to tie the prisoners' hands behind their backs and make them jump the 12 feet from the top of one tower to the other. If they succeeded they were set free.

In 1650 the castle was attacked by Oliver Cromwell's Parliamentarian army and it was abandoned not long after. In the early 20th century it was restored and during World War II it was secretly used to store national treasures. It is now a hotel.

The modern **Borthwick Parish Church** has a 15th century aisle with effigies of the first Lord and Lady Borthwick.

CRICHTON

11 miles SE of Edinburgh on the B6367

Crichton Castle (Historic Scotland) was probably built in the late 1300s by John de Crichton. It consisted of a simple tower house typical of the period. This was added to by his son William, an ambitious and unscrupulous man who became Lord Chancellor of Scotland. The most remarkable feature of renovation work carried out in the 1580s is the carved diamond-faceted red stonework facade on the north range. This remarkable piece of Italian-style architecture was the brainchild of the then owner, Francis Stewart, who had travelled widely throughout Europe.

Crichton Collegiate Church was built in 1449 by William Crichton and is remarkably well-preserved with only its nave missing. **Vogrie Country Park** lies to the north of the castle, and is centred on Vogrie House. It has woodland walks, picnic areas and a golf course.

SOUTRA

15 miles SE of Edinburgh off the A68

From Soutra, high in the Lammermuir Hills, it is reckoned that you get the best view in Central Scotland. On a clear day you can see the full sweep of the Firth of Forth with Fife beyond, and at least 60 Highland peaks. **Soutra Aisle** is all that remains of a medieval hospital. It was dedicated to the Holy Trinity, and it was here that Augustinian monks looked after travellers, pilgrims and the sick and wounded. A recent archaeological dig uncovered evidence of surgery and the treatment of patients by herbal remedies. Some pieces of bandage with human tissue still attached to them were even recovered.

ROSLYN

8 miles S of Edinburgh on the B7006

Roslyn (also known as Rosslin), has gained world renown through *The Da Vinci Code*, a thriller written by American author Dan Brown. According to some people, it is the most important place in Christendom, all due to **Roslyn Church**, an extravaganza of a building on which work began in 1446. Its founder was Sir William St Clair, third and last Prince of Orkney, who lived at nearby Roslyn Castle. In the choir of this unfinished church (still in use) are carvings with both Masonic and Knights Templar associations.

The carving in the interior is spectacular, and shows plants that only grow in the New World, even though Columbus had not yet sailed across the Atlantic when it was built. They tend to confirm the legend that the daring navigator Prince Henry of Orkney, grandfather of the Prince of

Legends abound about Roslyn church. One theory says that the writings of Christ lie in its unopened vaults. Another says that the bodies of Knights Templar lie in the unopened crypt, fully dressed in armour. A third says that the Holy Grail is embedded in one of the pillars. And yet another says it is a re-creation of Solomon's Temple in Jerusalem. There's even a theory that the body of Christ himself lies in the vaults. Whatever the truth of the matter, and the theories seem to get wilder and wilder with every new book written about it, there's no denying that it is one of the most beautiful buildings in Britain. There is certainly an aura about the place that can almost be felt.

Cramond Tower (private) dates from the 15th century, while Cramond House (private) dates from 1680. At one time, the village was famous for the manufacture of nails. Cramond Island lies one mile offshore. It is possible to walk to it via a causeway at low tide, though walkers should heed the notices about tide times before setting off.

Orkney who founded the chapel, did indeed set foot in America.

The carvings also include the pagan "Green Man", as well as the famous **Apprentice Pillar**. This was said to have been carved by an apprentice when the master mason working on the church was on the Continent seeking inspiration. When he returned and saw the workmanship, the mason is supposed to have murdered the apprentice in a fit of jealousy.

Nearby is the **Roslin Glen Country Park**, with woodland walks that go past old gunpowder works.

PENICUIK

9 miles S of Edinburgh on the A701

Penicuik was once a mining and paper making town, founded in 1770 by its laird, Sir James Clerk of Penicuik. To the west of the town rise the Pentland Hills, with Scald Law being the highest peak at 1898 feet. In the grounds of Penicuik House stands the Allan Ramsay Obelisk, dedicated to the memory of the poet **Allan Ramsay** who was born in Leadhills in Lanarkshire in 1685. Ramsay visited the town often, as he was a friend of Sir James Clerk, who raised the obelisk, and had a house nearby.

St Mungo's Parish Church dates from 1771, and has a 12th century detached belfry. The **Edinburgh Crystal Visitor Centre** at Eastfield has displays and exhibits about the history of crystal and glass making in Scotland, plus factory tours.

BALERNO

7 miles SW of Edinburgh off the A70

Malleny Garden (National Trust for Scotland) is a walled garden beside the 17th century Malleny House (private) extending to three acres and dominated by 400-year-old clipped yew trees. There are herbaceous borders, a fine collection of old-fashioned roses, and also the National Bonsai Collection for Scotland.

CRAMOND

5 miles W of Edinburgh off the A90

Cramond is a charming village of old whitewashed cottages on the banks of the River Almond where it enters the Firth of Forth. The **Parish Church** of 1656, with its medieval tower, sits within the ruins of a **Roman Fort** built about AD 142. The Rev. Robert Walker, who was painted by Raeburn skating on Duddingston Loch in the 18th century, was minister here.

INGLISTON

7 miles W of Edinburgh off the A8

Almost in the shadow of Edinburgh International Airport at Turnhouse is the Royal Showground, home each year of the Royal Highland Show, Scotland's premier country and farming fair.

RATHO

8 miles W of Edinburgh off the A8

Ratho sits on the Union Canal, and canal cruises are available from the Edinburgh Canal Centre. Parts of Ratho Parish Church date from the 12th century, though little of this can now be seen due to restorations over the years.

The **Adventure Centre** is billed as the "gateway to adventure", with the National Rock Climbing Centre having 2400 square metres of artificial wall surfaces, the largest climbing arena in the world. One other feature is the Airpark, Europe's largest suspended aerial adventure ropes ride.

SOUTH QUEENSFERRY

9 miles W of Edinburgh city centre off the A90

At times, South Queensferry lies literally in the shadow of the mighty **Forth Rail Bridge** which passes directly overhead. Completed in 1890, the cantilevered bridge was one of the greatest engineering triumphs of the Victorian age. A mile and a half long and 360 feet high, its construction absorbed more than 50,000 tons of steel. Close by, the **Forth Road Bridge** is a graceful suspension structure whose opening in 1964 put an end to the ferry service which had operated here since it was established in the 11th century by St Margaret, queen of Malcolm III, to carry pilgrims across the Forth to Dunfermline Abbey and St Andrew's Cathedral. Below the rail bridge is the historic **Hawes Inn** of 1683, which features in RL Stevenson's *Kidnapped*.

Each year in early August the quaint custom of the **Burry Man** takes place. Dressed from head to toe in plant burrs, he spends nine hours walking about the town on a Friday. While everyone agrees it is an ancient custom, no one knows how it originated or what purpose it served.

About 3 miles east of South Queensferry, **Dalmeny House** has been the home of the Primrose family, Earls of Rosebery, for more than three centuries. The splendid Tudor Gothic house seen today was built in 1815 by the English architect William Wilkins. Along with a hammerbeam roofed hall, vaulted corridors and classical main rooms, the interior also features some excellent family portraits, works by Reynolds, Gainsborough and Lawrence, tapestries, fine 18th century French furniture, porcelain from the Rothschild Mentmore collection and Napoleonic memorabilia amassed by the 5th Earl. Within the extensive grounds is a delightful 4-mile walk along the shoreline of the Firth of Forth.

Dalmeny Church, dedicated to St Cuthbert, is one of the best-preserved Norman churches in Britain. The south doorway is richly carved, as is the chancel and apse.

Flanking South Queensferry to the west, **Hopetoun House** lives up to its claim of being "Scotland's Finest Stately Home". Back in the late 1690s, the 1st Earl of Hopetoun built a grand house overlooking the Firth of Forth and a mere 20 years later commissioned William Adam to extend it enormously. Adam rose to the challenge magnificently, adding a colossal curved façade and two huge wings. The interior, completed after his death by his two sons, has all the elegance and panache one associates with this

South Queensferry has a glorious mix of cottages and houses dating from the 16th century onwards. Plewlands House (National Trust for Scotland) dates from 1643, and has been converted into private flats. The Queensferry Museum, in the High Street, has exhibits and displays on local history. There are also wonderful views of the two bridges from it.

The writer Samuel Smiles was born in Haddington in 1812. Though he wrote many books, he is best known for Self Help. Several of his observations have become very familiar, amongst them "A place for everything, and everything in its place", and "He who never made a mistake, never made a discovery".

gifted family. Their ebullient décor is enhanced by some superb 17th century tapestries, Meissen porcelain, and an outstanding collection of paintings which includes portraits by Gainsborough, Ramsay and Raeburn.

Surrounding the house is magnificent parkland extending to 150 acres, with a deer park and spring garden. The main approach to the house is by the Royal Drive which can only be used by royalty. George IV drove along it when he visited Scotland in 1822, and Elizabeth II also used it in 1988.

HADDINGTON

Fortunately, the A1 bypassed Haddington as long ago as 1920 and so allowed its picturesque market place, elegant streets and dignified buildings to remain unspoilt. More than 200 buildings in the town centre are listed. The classical **Court House,** designed by William Burn, dominates Court Street and, close by, the **Jane Welsh Carlyle House** was the childhood home of the girl who later married Thomas Carlyle. Only the dining room and garden are open to the public and both have been preserved as she would have known them.

Jane's sudden death in 1866 left Carlyle grief-stricken. His touching words mourning the loss of *"the light of his life"* can be seen on a plain slab in the choir of **St Mary's Church.** The largest parish church in Scotland, the "Lamp of Lothian" is also notable for the sumptuous alabaster tombs in the Lauderdale Aisle; for its concerts and art exhibitions of international standard, and for providing the unusual amenity of an excellent tea-room. The Lauderdale Aisle, owned by the Earls of Lauderdale, is unique in that it is a small Episcopalian chapel within a Presbyterian Church. This ecumenicalism continues every year in May with the Whitekirk and Haddington Pilgrimage when people from all the main Christian religions in Scotland walk between the two towns.

Also well worth seeking out is **Mitchell's Close,** a visually pleasing 17th century corner of the town where the houses with their crow-stepped roofs and cramped staircases were restored in the 1990s.

A mile south of Haddington, **Lennoxlove House** is the home of the Maitland family, Dukes of Hamilton. It's an impressive sight with its 14th century tower house. The interior is equally splendid and features a collection of fine and applied art, including some striking

Nungate Bridge, Haddington

family portraits, French furniture, and porcelain. One of the Maitland family was secretary to Mary, Queen of Scots at the time of her execution and it was he who obtain the death mask of the queen and one of her rings, both of which are on display. Lennoxlove acquired its name from one of its former owners, the Duchess of Lennox, also known as La Belle Stewart. An outstanding beauty, the duchess was the model for the figure of Britannia on British coinage. On her death in 1672 she bequeathed the house to Lord Blantyre, stipulating that it should be re-named in memory of her love for her husband. The house was comprehensively restored in 2007 and now offers accommodation and function rooms, as well as guided tours.

AROUND HADDINGTON

ABERLADY

5 miles N of Haddington on the A198

This pleasant village was the port for Haddington until the bay silted up. The **Aberlady Bay Nature Reserve** covers 1439 acres of foreshore and dunes, and is popular with bird watchers. The village was home to one of Scotland's most popular historical novelists, Nigel Tranter, who died in the year 2000 at the age of 90. During his long life he published more than 130 books. There is a small cairn to his memory close to Quarry House where he used to live.

Myreton Motor Museum

contains displays of motorcars, cycles and military vehicles dating from 1899. There is also a large collection of period advertising, posters, enamel signs, and toy vehicles. **Aberlady Parish Church** was remodelled in the 19th century, though an interesting 16th century tower still stands. In the High Street is the old **Mercat Cross** of 1780. To the east of the village is Luffness Castle, a T-plan tower house with Norman origins that was once the ancestral home of the Earls of Hopetoun and is now a hotel.

GULLANE

6 miles N of Haddington on the A198

This village sits inland from the Firth of Forth, but has fine views north towards Fife. Nowadays it is a small golfing resort with many large, imposing villas. The British Open is held here regularly, and the course at Muirfield is home to the Honourable Company of Edinburgh Golfers. The **Heritage of Golf** exhibition on the West Links Road traces the golfing history of the area.

The ruins of **St Andrew's Church** can be seen at the west end of the main street. They date from the 12th century, and were abandoned in 1612. On Gullane Bay, and signposted from the main street, is Gullane Bents, one of the best beaches on the Firth of Forth.

DIRLETON

7 miles N of Haddington off the A198

Many visitors consider Dirleton the prettiest village in Scotland. It is certainly a charming sight. Mellow

About four miles east of Haddington is Traprain Law from the top of which there are superb views. The summit was occupied from Neolithic times right up until the Dark Ages, and the outline of a fort can clearly be seen. It was the capital of a tribe the Romans called the Votadini, which roughly translated means "the farmers". More Roman finds have been made here, including a hoard of Roman silver, than anywhere else in Scotland.

Two miles off the coast from North Berwick rises the towering bulk of Bass Rock, a volcanic outcrop which is now home to many thousands of seabirds, mostly gannets but with colonies of puffins, fulmars, terns and razorbills. During the season, weather permitting, there are regular boat trips around the rock - but be prepared for the noise. Some 500 years ago the poet William Dunbar described the air near the rock as dark with birds that came

"With shrykking, shrieking, skimming scowlis
And meikle noyis and showtes".

From the Scottish Seabird Centre on a promontory near the old harbour you can use remote controlled cameras which are situated on the islands to study the birds without disturbing the colonies. The centre also provides powerful telescopes on a viewing deck, a film about Scotland's sea birds, and a café restaurant.

17th century cottages with red pantiled roofs nestle in well-tended gardens; there's an appealing corbelled church, and the impressive ruins of **Dirleton Castle** (Historic Scotland). To the west of the castle are some formal terraced gardens, first laid out in the 1500s, which are in the *Guinness Book of Records* as having the longest herbaceous border in the world. An unusual honey pot-shaped dovecot built with 1100 nests stands beyond the colourful borders and the geometric gardens provide a wonderful summer display.

ATHELSTANEFORD

3 miles NE of Haddington on the B1343

Athelstaneford has a special place in Scottish history. It was here that the Scottish flag, the Saltire, or St Andrew's Cross, was first adopted. Athelstan was a king of Northumbria who fought a combined army of Picts and Scots at Athelstaneford in AD 832. The Pictish leader, Angus mac Fergus, on the day before the battle, saw a huge white cross made of clouds in the sky, and took it as an omen. Athelstane was duly defeated, and a white cross on a blue background was adopted as the flag of Scotland, making it the oldest national flag in Europe.

This is why the Saltire on its own should be white and sky blue, whereas when it is incorporated into the Union Jack the blue darkens. The **National Flag Heritage Centre** in an old doocot ("dovecot") behind the village

church explains the story of the battle and the flag.

NORTH BERWICK

8 miles NE of Haddington on the A198

For grand views across the town and the Firth of Forth, follow the undemanding path to the top of **North Berwick Law** (612 feet). On top of this prominent hill stands a Watchtower built during the Napoleonic wars and an archway made from the jawbone of a whale which was first set up in the early 1700s.

Also on the promontory are the scant ruins of **St Andrew's Auld Kirk**, which date from the 12th century onwards. The kirk was the setting in 1590 for a gathering of witches and wizards who came to negotiate with the Devil (actually the Earl of Bothwell in disguise) to bring about the death of James VI. Despite completing the ceremony by kissing the Devil's bare buttocks, *("as cold as ice and hard as iron"),* the coven's efforts were in vain. Ninety-four witches and six wizards were tried and tortured. They were not executed however, James taking the view that their failure, even when in league with the Devil, demonstrated his own invincibility.

North Berwick town, which likes to describe itself as the "Biarritz of the North", is a popular family resort with safe, sandy beaches and a rather genteel atmosphere inherited from the mid-1800s when it was first developed as a holiday destination.

In School Road is the **North Berwick Museum**, housed in a

former school, which has displays and memorabilia about local history, wildlife and golf.

WHITEKIRK
9 miles NE of Haddington off the A198

St Mary's Parish Church dates from the 15th century and is the eastern end of the annual Whitekirk to Haddington Pilgrimage. Whitekirk had been a place of pilgrimage long before the church was built. In pre-Reformation times, people came to the village to seek cures at the Well of Our Lady, which used to be located nearby. An account of 1413 relates that more than 15,000 people of all nationalities visited yearly. Close to the church is the 16th century **Tithe Barn**, built to store the "tithes" (a tithe being a tenth part) given to the church as offerings from the parishioners' agricultural produce.

The place's most famous pilgrim - but one who did not come seeking a cure - was a young Italian nobleman called **Aeneas Sylvius Piccolomini**. He had set out from Rome in the winter of 1435 as an envoy to the court of James I. During the sea crossing, his ship was blown off course by a raging gale. Aeneas vowed that if he made it to dry land he would offer thanksgiving at the nearest church dedicated to Our Lady. The boat was eventually shipwrecked between North Berwick and Dunbar, and Aeneas survived. He therefore set out on a ten-mile pilgrimage in a snowstorm to Whitekirk where he duly offered

prayers of thanks. While in Scotland, he fell in love with a young woman, and made a pledge of love to her. However, he was ambitious, and soon gave her up. Twenty years later, Aeneas became Pope Pius II.

EAST LINTON
7 miles E of Haddington off the A1

Anyone travelling along the A1 should make a small detour to view this picturesque village. To the east is Phantassie, the mansion where John Rennie the civil engineer was born. He designed Waterloo, London and Southwark bridges over the Thames, and Rennie's Bridge at Kelso. Phantassie is now an organic market garden.

Preston Mill (National Trust for Scotland) is an old, quaint water mill that has been restored to full working order. It stands in an idyllic rural spot, and dates from the 18th century, though a mill has stood on the spot for centuries. With its conical roofed kiln and red pantiles, it is a favourite subject for painters and photographers.

Close by is **Phantassie Doocot** (National Trust for Scotland), which belonged to Phantassie House and could hold 500 birds. Also nearby is **Prestonkirk**, a small, attractive church. It was built in 1770, though the 13th century chancel still stands, as it was used as a mausoleum for the Hepburn family.

The **Scottish Museum of Flight** is situated at East Fortune, to the north east of the village. Formerly a World War II airfield, it

East of North Berwick is Tantallon Castle (Historic Scotland), spectacularly sited on a sheer-sided crag and surrounded by the sea on three sides. The castle was a fortress of the Douglas family for centuries until it was destroyed by General Monck in 1651. Only an imposing 50 feet high tower and a curtain wall 14 feet thick have survived. Together with the dramatic location and the Bass Rock in the background, Tantallon provides a good photo-opportunity but otherwise there is little to see within the ruins.

135

The ruins of Hailes Castle lie to the west of East Linton in a beautiful location. Its earliest masonry dates from the 13th century, though it was much altered in later years by the Hepburns, who acquired the castle in the 14th century. It was to Hailes Castle that James Hepburn, Earl of Bothwell, brought Mary Stuart after seizing her at Fountainbridge in 1567. He was later to become her third husband.

54 THE VOLUNTEER ARMS

Dunbar

A small family-run pub, which specialises in good homemade food at reasonable prices

¶ *see page 382*

now has 8 cavernous hangars housing a fascinating collection of aircraft, rockets, models and memorabilia. The most famous exhibit is Concorde, brought to the museum in 2004. Another is a Prestwick Pioneer, the only aircraft ever to have been wholly designed and built in Scotland. Also on display are a Soviet MIG, a Blue Streak rocket and a Lightning.

STENTON

8 miles E of Haddington on the B6370

This small conservation village still retains its old Tron, on which wool brought to the Stenton Fair by local sheep farmers was weighed. To the south of the village is Pressmennan Lake, one of the few lakes, as opposed to lochs, in Scotland (see also Lake of Menteith, Ellon and Kirkcudbright). This one, however, is artificial, created in 1819 by the local landowner. The **Pressmennan Forest Trail** runs along its southern shore, and from the highest point you can see Arthur's Seat in Edinburgh and the Bass Rock in the Firth of Forth.

Stenton Kirk is a handsome building designed by the noted architect William Burn in 1829. In the kirkyard is the Old Kirk, dating probably from the 14th century.

TYNINGHAME

8 miles E of Haddington on the B1407

Tyninghame is a small conservation village which formerly stood in what are now the grounds of Tyninghame House which has been divided up into private flats. In

1761 the village was moved to its present position by the then Earl of Haddington to improve the view from his house, though the remains of the former parish kirk, dedicated to St Baldred, still stand there.

DUNBAR

11 miles E of Haddington on the A1087

A Royal Burgh since 1370, Dunbar has a broad High Street, a ruined castle, a picturesque harbour, excellent beaches and more sunshine hours in which to enjoy them than anywhere else in Scotland. Dunbar was once a fishing and whaling port, but its main industries are now brewing and tourism. One of the oldest buildings in the town is the 16th century **Town House,** once a prison but now housing a small museum of local history and archaeology. A much newer "attraction" is situated south of the town, near the shore. **Torness Nuclear Power Station** was built in the early 1980s and has a visitor centre that explains how electricity is produced from nuclear power.

Americans especially will be interested in the **John Muir Centre** in the High Street, where the explorer, naturalist and founder of the American conservation movement was born in 1838. His family emigrated to America when John was 11 years old. He was later instrumental in the establishment of the Yosemite National Park, the first in the United States. Appropriately, Dunbar celebrates its most famous son with the **John**

136

Muir Country Park, located on a beautiful stretch of coastline to the north west of the town. Established in 1976, this was the first park of its kind in Scotland and covers 1760 acres.

Two miles south of the town, off the A1, is **Doonhill Homestead** (Historic Scotland), where once an Anglian hall dating from the 7th-8th century stood. Its site is marked out on the grass, and shows that this area of Scotland was once part of the mighty Anglian kingdom of Northumbria.

GARVALD

6 miles SE of Haddington off the B6370

This tiny red sandstone village lies on the northern slopes of the Lammermuir Hills. **Garvald Parish Church** dates partly from the 12th century, and has a sundial dated 1633. It is surprisingly light and airy inside.

South east of the village is the mansion of Nunraw in whose grounds Cistercian monks, who arrived here in 1946, began building the Abbey of Sancta Maria in 1952. It was the first Cistercian monastery in Scotland since the Reformation, and was colonised by monks form Tipperary in Ireland. A Cistercian nunnery, founded by nuns from Haddington, had previously been founded here in about 1158.

GIFFORD

4 miles S of Haddington on the B6369

Set at the foot of the Lammermuir Hills, this pretty village was mostly laid out in the early 1700s when the then Earl of Tweeddale began

building a new residence, Yester House (private). The settlement of Bothans lay too close to the house so Bothans was demolished and its inhabitants resettled at Gifford. Yester House was designed by James Smith and dates from 1745. From the 1970s until his death in 2007, the house was the home of the Italian-American composer Gian Carlo Menotti. He was persuaded to buy the house because of the superb acoustics in the 28 feet by 45 feet ballroom. In 2008, the house was put on the market for £15 million, making it Scotland's most expensive property up to that point.

Beyond Yester House are the ruins of Yester Castle (private), built by Hugo de Gifford in the late 13th century. He was known as the "Wizard of Yester". Beneath the castle is a chamber known as Goblin Ha' where he is supposed to have practised magic and called up goblins and demons. Scott mentions him in *Marmion*.

The whitewashed **Yester Parish Church**, which has Dutch influences, was built in 1708 and has a medieval bell. It was in Gifford that John Witherspoon, the only clergyman to sign the American Declaration of Independence, was born in 1723

The narrow road from Gifford up into the Lammermuir Hills is a fine drive and takes you past Whiteadder reservoir and down into Berwickshire.

PENCAITLAND

6 miles SW of Haddington on the A6093

The oldest part of **Pencaitland**

55 THE GARVALD INN

East Lothian

A beautiful inn, dating back to the 18th century, located in a stunning rural setting

see page 382

56 THE OLD FARM HOUSE

Gifford

Quality B&B and self-catering accommodation on working, mostly arable, farm in peaceful rural area.

see page 383

137

Parish Church is the Winton Aisle which dates from the 13th century. Close to the village is the 500-year-old Winton House. It was built for the Seton family by the king's master mason, and is famous for its "twisted chimneys". It overlooks the Tyne and has lovely terraced gardens. It is now a venue for private and corporate events. Glenkinchie Distillery, to the south of the village, was opened in 1837. It has a small exhibition and offers tours showing how whisky is distilled.

LINLITHGOW

The glory of this little town is the partly-ruined **Linlithgow Palace** (Historic Scotland) whose origins go back to the 1200s. The oldest surviving parts date from 1424 when James I began rebuilding after a catastrophic fire. His successors continued to extend the palace over the next two centuries. The palace has many royal associations. Mary, Queen of Scots was born here in 1542 and earlier her father, James V, had been married to Mary of Guise in a sumptuous ceremony during which the elaborate fountain in the inner court flowed with wine. Cromwell made Linlithgow his headquarters for a while and Bonnie Prince Charlie visited during the rebellion of 1745. The cavernous medieval kitchen is still in place, as is the downstairs brewery which must have been a busy place: old records show that an allowance of 24 gallons per day per person was considered just about adequate in the 1500s.

In the castle courtyard is the **King's Fountain**, built between 1536 and 1538 for James V. It is the oldest fountain in Britain, and is in three tiers, with elaborate carving that symbolises his reign. It was badly damaged during the fire. A restoration scheme of the 1930s used concrete to replace some of the carvings, and this introduced salts into the structure, which began its decay. Now, following a 5-year-long restoration project, the fountain has been restored to full working order.

The impressive Outer Gateway to the palace still stands. On it are the coats of arms of the four orders of chivalry to which James V belonged - the Garter of England, the Thistle of Scotland,

Loch Linlithgow

the Golden Fleece of Burgundy and St Michael of France.

Opposite the Palace is **St Michael's Parish Church**, one of the most important medieval churches in Scotland. It dates from the 15th century, though a church had stood here long before that. Within the church one of the most unusual incidents in Scottish history took place. The church was especially dear to **James IV,** who worshipped there regularly. In 1514, he had decided to take a large army into England in support of France, which had been invaded by Henry VIII's troops. Most of the Scottish court was against the idea, as was James's wife Margaret, sister of the English king.

But James held firm, and a few days before he and his army set out, he was at mass in St Michael's Church with his courtiers. A strange man with long, fair hair suddenly appeared in the church dressed in a blue gown tied with a white band and carrying a staff. Pushing aside the courtiers, he approached James and spoke to him. He had been sent "by his mother", he said, to tell James that no good would come of the invasion of England. Furthermore, he was not to meddle with other women.

Some of the courtiers tried to grab him, but before they could the man made good his escape. Confusion reigned, and people immediately took the man to be a ghost. The reference to his mother, they said, meant that he had been sent by Our Lady (of whom James

House of The Binns, Linlithgow

was especially fond). James took no heed, and marched into England. He, and all the flower of Scottish manhood, were wiped out on the field at Flodden. The "ghost's" prophecy came true.

People nowadays discount the ghost theory, and say that the whole thing had been orchestrated by James's wife with the help of some of the court. The reference to the king's meddling with other women was the Queen's own contribution to the event, as James was renowned for his philandering. One of the courtiers was Sir David Lyndsay, Lord Lyon and playwright, who knew all the tricks of the stage, and he may have been involved as well.

The **Town House,** in the centre of the town, dates from 1668, and replaces an earlier building destroyed by Oliver Cromwell in 1650. The Cross Well dates from 1807, and replaced an earlier structure.

It was in Linlithgow that the Earl of Moray, Regent of Scotland,

The Bo'ness' main attraction is the Bo'ness and Kinneil Railway, which has been developed since 1979 by the Scottish Railway Preservation Society. There is a Scottish railway exhibition as well as workshops and a working station. Trips on the steam trains, which run between Bo'ness and Birkhill Station are popular and trains can also be chartered for special occasions. At Birkhill are the caverns of the former Birkhill Fireclay Mine, which can be explored.

was assassinated in the street by James Hamilton of Bothwellhaugh, who later escaped to France. A plaque on the old County Buildings commemorates the event. In Annet House in the High Street is the **Linlithgow Story**, with displays and exhibits explaining the history of the town. There are also herb, fruit tree and flower gardens. At the **Linlithgow Canal Centre** in Manse Road is a small museum dedicated to the Union Canal, which links the Forth and Clyde Canal at Falkirk with Edinburgh. Trips along the canal are also available. **Beecraigs Country Park**, to the south of the town, covers 913 acres of land near the Bathgate Hills. It has a loch where you can fish, a deer farm and a camping and caravan park.

To the north of the town is the **House of the Binns** (National Trust for Scotland), ancestral home of the Dalyell family, the best known member of which is Tam Dalyell, the former MP. It was built in the early 1600s by another Tam Dalyell, one of the band of "hungrie Scottis" who accompanied James VI southwards to his coronation as James I of England. Less than a decade later, Tam returned to Scotland an exceedingly wealthy man. The outstanding feature of the tall, grey 3-storeyed house he built is the artistry of the ornate plaster ceilings. They were created in 1630 when it was hoped that Charles I would stay at The Binns before his coronation at Holyrood as king of Scotland.

It was Tam's son, General Tam Dalyell, who added the 4 corner turrets, a design feature apparently instigated by the Devil. The fearsome General was reputed to have frequent *"trookings (dealings) wi' the deil"*. During one of these trookings, the Devil threatened to *"blow down your house upon you"*, to which Tam retorted *"I will build me a turret at every corner to pin down the walls"*.

One of the great charms of the House of the Binns is the wealth of family memorabilia which has been amassed over the years and is displayed informally around the house. Outside, there are extensive grounds and a folly tower affording panoramic views over the Forth Valley.

AROUND LINLITHGOW

BO'NESS

3 miles N of Linlithgow on the A904

The town's real name is Borrowstoneness, though it is always referred to nowadays by its shortened name. It is an industrial town, and was formerly one of Scotland's leading whaling ports. It was near here that the eastern end of the Antonine Wall terminated. Near the town is the Kinneil Estate, with, at its centre, Kinneil House. It was built by the Hamilton family in the 16th and 17th centuries. It isn't open to the public, though it can be viewed from the outside. However, within the house's 17th century stable block is the **Kinneil Museum**, which tells the story of Bo'ness over the last 2000 years. There is also an exhibition called "Rome's Northern Frontier", which highlights the Antonine Wall and the Roman soldiers who manned it.

BLACKNESS

2 miles NE of Linlithgow on the B903

Blackness Castle (Historic Scotland) must be the most unusually shaped castle in Scotland. It sits on a promontory jutting out into the Firth of Forth, and from the air looks like a huge ship. It was a Crichton stronghold, with the first castle on the site being built in about 1449 by Sir George Crichton, Sheriff of Linlithgow and Admiral of Scotland. However, there is an intriguing but untrue story about how the castle eventually came to look like a ship.

By the early 16th century the castle had passed to the Douglases. James V appointed **Archibald Douglas** as Lord High Admiral of the Scottish fleet, but soon discovered that he had made a mistake, as every time Archibald went to sea he became sea sick.

The young James was enraged, and threatened to dismiss him. Archibald, who was making a fortune out of selling commissions in the navy, wanted to retain his position. So he promised his king that if he was allowed to keep his job, he would build him a ship that the English couldn't sink and on which he would never be sick. Mollified, the king agreed, and Douglas built Blackness Castle.

However, a more mundane explanation of its shape is the restricted shape of the site on which it was built.

MID CALDER

8 miles SE of Linlithgow on the B8046

The **Kirk of Mid Calder** has an apse built in the 16th century. One of the 17th century ministers of the church was Hew Kennedy, who was zealous in his persecution of witches. In 1644 several of them were burnt at the stake.

LIVINGSTON

6 miles S of Linlithgow off the M8

Livingston is one of Scotland's new towns, built round an historic village which has the **Livingston Parish Church** of 1732. At the 20-acre **Almond Valley Heritage Centre** in Millfield the visitor can find out about local history and the environment, including the Scottish shale industry which once thrived in West Lothian. There is also an 18th century water mill, a small railway line, a farm, a picnic area and teahouse.

The **Almondell and Calderwood Country Park** is three miles east of the town centre, and has woodland and riverside walks. Almondell was originally a private estate owned by the Erskine family. Many items from Kirkhill House, with which it was associated, have been relocated within the park, such as the entrance gates and the astronomical pillar. Calderwood was also a private estate and belonged to the barons of Torphichen. This area

Bo'ness Motor Museum displays an interesting mix of classic cars and James Bond 007 memorabilia including props from film and TV productions. There's also a soft play area ideal for keeping the children occupied whilst having a snack in Miss Moneypenny's or a refreshing drink in the Double "O" Bar.

While staying at Calder House (private) in 1556 (four years before the Scottish Reformation) John Knox first administered Holy Communion using the new reformed liturgy. In 1848 the Polish composer and pianist Frederic Chopin also stayed here.

Polkemmet Country Park, four miles west of Bathgate, has a golf course, a driving range, bowling green and picnic areas. The whole area was owned at one time by the Baillie family, and a mausoleum, built by Robert Baillie, fourth Lord Polkemmet, can still be seen.

has been deliberately left undeveloped to encourage wildlife.

The Oakbank Shale Bings are a reminder of the shale industry, and have been landscaped. A good view of the surrounding countryside, and even up into Fife, is available from the top.

TORPHICHEN
4 miles SW of Linlithgow on the B792

The unusual name of this picturesque village comes from Gaelic "Torr Phigheainn", meaning the "hill of the magpies", and is pronounced "Tor fichen". It is an ancient place, with its history going back to the founding of a church dedicated to St Ninian in the 6th century.

The Knights of the Order of St John of Jerusalem, or the Knights Hospitallers as they were more commonly called, was a monastic order of soldier monks formed in the 11th century to look after St John's Hospital in Jerusalem, and to offer hospitality and protection to pilgrims travelling to the Holy Land. **Torphichen Preceptory** (Historic Scotland) was one of only two such establishments in Britain, the other one being in London. It was founded in about 1124, when the lands of Torphichen were given to the monks by David I. The head of a Knights Hospitaller monastery was called a "preceptor", and for this reason a monastery was always known as a "preceptory".

The only parts left standing of the original preceptory are the

transepts and crossing of the monastic church. Above the crossing is a tower, which, no doubt because of the Knights' military role, looks more like a castle than a church tower. Within a small room is a display about the modern Order of St John, which was refounded in 1947 as a separate order in Scotland by George VI. Nowadays it runs old folks homes, mountain rescue units and hospitals in Scotland. Where the nave once stood is now **Torphichen Parish Church** which dates from 1756 though it incorporates masonry from the earlier building.

BATHGATE
6 miles SW of Linlithgow on the A89

Bathgate is a substantial industrial town, and was formerly a centre for the shale oil industry. Sir James Young Simpson, who introduced chloroform into midwifery, was the son of a Bathgate baker, and was born here in 1811, as was James "Paraffin" Young, who opened the world's first oil refinery in 1850, extracting paraffin from the local shale. **Cairnpapple Hill** (Historic Scotland), to the north of the town, is 1017 feet high, and was the site of a temple built about 2000-2500BC. Fragments of bone and pottery have been found. The view from the top is magnificent - on a clear day both the Bass Rock in the Firth of Forth and the mountains of Arran in the Firth of Clyde can be seen.

In Mansefield Street is the **Bennie Museum**, which contains collections relating to local history.

Fife

Surrounded on three sides by water - the Tay, the Forth and the North Sea - Fife has retained its identity ever since it was established as a Kingdom by the Picts in the 4th century. Its capital, then as now, is the small market town of Cupar, set in the fertile Howe of Fife, the pastoral heart of the kingdom. Also in the Howe is Falkland, a charming medieval town with a glorious Renaissance palace.

Over to the east, the handsome and dignified town of St Andrews is surrounded by unspoilt countryside and a coastline fringed with extensive sandy beaches. The most picturesque stretch of coast, however, lies to the south in the area known as the East Neuk (corner) of Fife. From Leven to Crail, there's a succession of

quaint old fishing villages with distinctive pantiled roofs.

Most of Fife's industrial towns are located in the south but this is where you'll also find the beautifully preserved 16th century village of Culross and historic Dunfermline with its grand old ruined abbey.

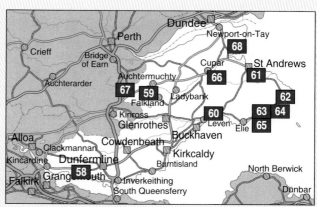

DUNFERMLINE

One other innovation is attributed to St Margaret - buttons on the sleeves of men's jackets. She had been disgusted to see that Scottish courtiers - in common with courtiers throughout Europe - wiped their noses on their sleeves, so set about making this habit as uncomfortable as possible. The buttons eventually became fashionable, and the fashion spread throughout Europe.

As the Fife Tourist Board points out, in Dunfermline you can walk through 900 years of history in a day. The capital of Scotland for six centuries until James VI succeeded to the English throne in 1603, the square mile of Dunfermline town centre is replete with history.

A good place to start your walk is, strangely enough, in Glen Bridge car park where you are just yards from **St Margaret's Cave**. In the late 11th century, the pious Margaret, queen to Malcolm III, frequently came to the cave to pray and here she would also wash the feet of the poor. In Margaret's time Scotland was a small kingdom, perched precariously on the edge of the known world. It was Margaret who brought refinement to the court and made the country think of itself as an integral part of Europe. Under Margaret and Malcolm, who was also a driving force, trade with the continent flourished. Malcolm revelled in this,

as though he could neither read nor write, he hankered after refinement and culture. He moved Scotland's capital from Perthshire to Dunfermline to be nearer the Fife ports that traded with Europe. Under Margaret, the centre of power shifted once more - this time to Edinburgh, which later became the nation's capital.

Just across the road from St Margaret's Cave is the **Town House,** a gloriously extravagant building presenting a heady mixture of Scottish Baronial and French Gothic styles. Nearby stands the impressive **Dunfermline Abbey,** originally founded by Queen Margaret and greatly extended by her equally devout son David I in the early 1100s. Only the nave of the medieval church has survived, its massive Norman columns reminiscent of Durham Cathedral. Robert the Bruce was buried in the abbey in 1295 but, astonishingly, his resting place was "lost" and not rediscovered until 1821 when the choir was being converted to serve as the parish church. The remains were re-buried beneath a fine memorial brass this ensuring it would not be mislaid again. (His heart, of course, remains at Melrose Abbey.)

The **Dunfermline Abbey Nave and Palace Visitors Centre** (Historic Scotland) tells the history of the abbey and of the later palace that was built on the site of the monastic buildings. A magnificent 200-feet long buttressed wall is all that now remains of the palace where

Dunfermline Abbey

Charles I was born. Within the abbey precincts is the 14th century Abbot House which was formerly the estate office for what was then the richest Benedictine Abbey in Scotland. After being neglected for many years, the house has been refurbished and the upper rooms are now dazzlingly colourful with brilliant murals and life-size models illustrating the town's history and people.

To the west of the abbey is a great mound known as **Malcolm's Tower**, all that remains of Malcolm's fortress. The town takes part of its name from the mound, as *Dunfermline* literally means "fort on the hill by the crooked stream".

Across the road from the abbey is the entrance to Pittencrieff Park, famous for its peacocks, which was gifted to the town by Andrew Carnegie in 1908. The park had always fascinated him as a boy, and as it was privately owned at the time, he was always denied access. So when he had the money, he bought it and threw it open to the people of the town. Also in the park is **Pittencrieff House Museum,** based in a 17th century mansion, which has an art gallery and displays on local history.

Dunfermline's most famous son, Andrew Carnegie was born in 1835 in a modest two up, two down cottage in Moodie Street which is now the **Andrew Carnegie Birthplace Museum**. As a young man, Carnegie emigrated to the United States where he rose from bobbin boy , telegraph operator and railroad developer to become

the "Steel King of America". When he sold his businesses in 1901 for $400 million he became the richest man in the world. He lavished most of his huge fortune on endowing schools, colleges and free public libraries. The Carnegie Library at Dunfermline was the first of an eventual 3000 such buildings. The various Trusts and Foundations established by Carnegie are still operating and dispensing around £100 every minute. In Pittencrieff Park, close to the Louise Carnegie Gates (named after his wife) is a statue of the great man.

It is not only New York that has a Carnegie Hall - Dunfermline has one as well, housing a theatre and concert hall. It can be found in East Port, near the **Dunfermline Museum and Small Gallery** in Viewfield. Here the history of the town is explained, including its time as a centre of manufacture for linen and silk, which continued right up until the 20th century. There are special displays from the Dunfermline Linen Damask Collection.

AROUND DUNFERMLINE

COWDENBEATH

5 miles NE of Dunfermline, off the A909

This small town was at the centre of the Fife coalfields, and though the mines have long gone, it still has the feel of a mining community about it. Its football team has perhaps the most unusual nickname of any senior team in Scotland -

To the north of Dunfermline, at Lathalmond, is the Scottish Vintage Bus Museum, housed in a former Royal Navy Stores depot. Opened in 1995, it is possibly the largest collection of vintage buses in Britain. The museum is open on Sunday afternoons during the season.

The famous crime writer, Ian Rankin, was born at Cardenden in 1960 and educated at Beath High School in Cowdenbeath.

the "Blue Brazils". **Racewall Cowdenbeath** has stock car racing every Saturday evening from March to November.

LOCHGELLY

7 miles NE of Dunfermline on the B981

Lochgelly is a small mining town, known throughout Scotland at one time for the manufacture of the "Lochgelly", the leather strap used to punish children in school.

Loch Gelly itself, after which the town is named, has water sports facilities. At one time, the loch was famous for the quality of its leeches, used by doctors for bloodletting.

Near the town is the **Lochore Meadows Country Park**, set in 1200 acres of reclaimed industrial land. The last pits closed here in 1966, with the park being created on the site in the early 1970s. The area is now a haven for wildlife, and at the west end of the loch is a bird hide with disabled access. The 260-acre Loch Ore, created as a result of mining subsidence, is stocked with brown trout. It is also used for water sports.

DALGETY BAY

4 miles E of Dunfermline off the A921

The ivy-clad ruins of **St Bridget's Church**, once the burial place of the Earls of Dunfermline, date from the 13th century. The church was first mentioned in a Papal Bull of 1178.

It was near Dalgety Bay that the murder of James Stewart, the **2nd Earl of Moray**, took place, an event which is remembered in one of the best known of Scottish songs, *The Bonnie Earl o' Moray*. Moray was the grandson of Regent Morton, regent of Scotland when Mary Stuart abdicated in favour of her infant son, later to be James VI. The earl was a popular nobleman, dashing and handsome, but he was also a staunch Protestant, and was always feuding with the Earls of Huntly, one of the great Catholic families of the time. The earl was implicated in a coup to overthrow James VI, though he probably had no involvement. But Huntly saw his chance and, armed with a king's warrant and a troop of soldiers, set out to seize the young earl. He eventually found him at his mother's castle at Donibristle, in what is now Dalgety Bay. He demanded that he give himself up, but Moray refused.

The troops therefore set fire to the building. Some men ran out from the front of the castle to distract Huntly's men while Moray ran out the back way, hoping to hide near the shore. Unfortunately, unknown to Moray, his bonnet had caught fire, and the smoke gave him away. He was hacked to death, with Huntly, it is said, striking the fatal blow. When James VI found out about the murder, he feigned outrage. When it later became known that Huntly had been armed with a king's warrant, James had to flee to Glasgow to escape the wrath of the public. Huntly spent a few weeks in Blackness Castle as a punishment, and was then released.

ABERDOUR

6 miles E of Dunfermline on the A921

Aberdour is famous for its silver sands and has even been dubbed the "Fife Riviera". The restored **St Fillan's Church** is partly Norman, with fragments that may date back to at least 1123, and has what is known as a "leper window". This was a window looking on to the altar through which lepers could see from a private room the mass being celebrated. It is said that Robert the Bruce, himself suffering from leprosy, used the window after his victory at Bannockburn in 1314. In 1790 the church was abandoned, and gradually fell into disrepair. However, in 1925 work began on restoring it, and it is now open for services once more. The town has two beaches, one of which, Silver Sands, has won a European blue flag for its cleanliness.

Aberdour Castle (Historic Scotland), close to the church, dates from the 14th century and has a spacious and attractive 17th century garden where there stands an unusual circular dovecote of the same period.

INCHCOLM

6 miles E of Dunfermline in the Firth of Forth

This small island was at one time known as the "Iona of the East". On it are the substantial ruins of **Inchcolm Abbey** (Historic Scotland), dedicated to St Columba. The story goes that Alexander I, son of Malcolm III and Queen Margaret, was crossing the Forth in 1123 when a storm blew up and the royal party had to seek refuge on the island, which had, for many years, supported a succession of hermits. The hermit of the time shared his meagre provisions with his guests for three days until the storm subsided. When Alexander reached the shore he vowed to build a monastery dedicated to St Columba on the island in thanksgiving for his safe passage, but before he could put his plans into effect he died. His younger brother David I, who succeeded him, founded a priory, which eventually became the Abbey of Inchcolm in 1223.

The abbey buildings as we see them now date mainly from the 15th century, and represent the most complete medieval abbey in Scotland, with most of the buildings remaining intact.

In the late 18th century, a military hospital was set up on the island to look after wounded sailors from the Russian fleet, which was using the Firth of Forth as a base. In the 20th century, it was fortified as part of the United Kingdom's sea defences, and some of these can still be seen. More than 500 troops were stationed on the island, and the first air raid of World War II took place close by in 1939 when German bombers dropped bombs not far from the Forth Rail Bridge.

INVERKEITHING

4 miles SE of Dunfermline off the A90

Inverkeithing is an ancient royal burgh which received its royal charter from William the Lion in

The Aberdour Festival is held every year at the end of July and offers 10 days of celebrations with arts, crafts, song, dance, puppetry, sports and much more.

about 1193. In medieval times it was a walled town with four "ports", or gates, though the walls were pulled down in the 16th century. From the 1920s, the town became known for its ship-breaking yards. Amongst the famous ships that met their end here were the battleship *HMS Dreadnought* in 1921, the *Titanic*'s sister ships the *Homeric* and *Olympic* in 1932, and the *Mauritania* in 1965. Over the years, countless aircraft carriers, battleships, and vessels of every other shape and size were also dismantled here.

The town lies close to the Forth Road and Rail Bridges, and has many old buildings. The Mercat Cross is 16th century, and the Old Town Hall opposite, with its outside staircase, dates from 1770. Of the 15th century St Peter's Church, only the tower remains, as the rest dates from 1826. Two other old buildings are Thomsoun's House dating from 1617 and Fordell's Lodging dating from 1670. **Inverkeithing Museum** housed in the hospitum of an old friary, tells the story of Inverkeithing and of Admiral Sir Samuel Greig, a local man born in 1735 in what is now the Royal Hotel in the High Street. He entered the service of Tsarina Catherine of Russia in 1764 and is credited with creating the modern Russian navy, manning it initially with Scottish officers. He died in 1788 aged only 53.

Near the town, in 1651, was fought the **Battle of Inverkeithing** between a Royalist force under Sir Hector MacLean of Duart and the Parliamentarian forces of Cromwell. The result was a victory for the Parliamentarians, and the death of MacLean. As a result of the battle the towns of Inverkeithing and Dunfermline were plundered, and the long-term result was the ascendancy of Cromwell in Scotland. A small cairn by the roadside opposite Pitreavy Castle (private), erected by the Clan MacLean, commemorates the event.

Mercat Cross, Inverkeithing

NORTH QUEENSFERRY

4 miles S of Dunfermline off the A90

Lying literally in the shadow of the two Forth bridges, North Queensferry acquired its name from the medieval Queen Margaret who regularly used the ferry on the way to her favourite palace at Dunfermline. The opening of the Forth Railway Bridge in 1890 meant that the ferries carried many fewer passengers across the river but it was the building of the Forth Road Bridge in 1964 that finally put them out of business.

The **Forth Bridges Visitors Centre** is housed within the Queensferry Lodge Hotel, and tells the story of the two bridges spanning the Forth. There is a magnificent scale model of the Firth of Forth, as well as photographs, documents and artefacts.

Deep Sea World is billed as "Scotland's Aquarium", and boasts the largest underwater tunnel in the world, some 120 yards long, made of specially toughened glass. More than 3000 fish swim above and beside you in a specially made tank containing a million gallons of water. As you stand within it you can see sharks, stingrays and electric eels. A special touch pool allows you to touch small friendly sharks, sea urchins and anemones. One of the most popular experiences on offer at the aquarium is the chance to dive with sharks.

CHARLESTOWN

3 miles SW of Dunfermline off the A985

This small village was established in 1756 by Charles Bruce, 5th Earl of Elgin, to exploit the large deposits of limestone in the area, including an easily worked crag facing the sea. It was Scotland's first planned industrial village, though Bruce died before the work was finished. It was finally completed by the 7th Earl (of Elgin Marbles fame). There were nine kilns here at one time producing lime for building, agriculture and the making of iron and glass. It was a self-sufficient community, with its own harbour, shops and school, and the houses were arranged in the shape of the founder's initials - CE, standing for Charles Elgin.

The works closed in 1956, having produced in their 200 years

•

North Queensferry is the start of the Fife Coastal Path, a 78-mile long path-way that passes through most of the small picturesque towns and villages on the Fife coast, ending at the Tay Bridge on the Firth of Tay.

•

58 THE ELGIN HOTEL

Charlestown

Beautiful country house hotel in tranquil and picturesque village offering quality cuisine and accommodation

🛏 🍴 see page 384

Limekilns, Firth of Forth

149

of existence more than 11 million tons of quicklime. Now guided walks round the complex are available in the summer months thanks to the Scottish Lime Centre in the Granary Building in Rocks Road.

CULROSS

7 miles W of Dunfermline off the A985

Culross, pronounced "Cooross", is an outstanding example of a 16th/17th century town, thanks partly to the National Trust for Scotland which since 1932 has been looking after its picturesque buildings with their crow-stepped gables and pantiled roofs. The streets are cobbled, and those around the old **Mercat Cross** (dating from 1588) have a feature known as the "crown o' the causie", a raised portion in the middle where only the wealthy were allowed to walk, while the rest of the townsfolk had to walk on the edges where water and dirt accumulated.

Culross is undoubtedly the most picturesque of Fife's old burghs - a situation that owes a lot to the town's relative poverty in the 18th, 19th and early 20th centuries when there was no money for modernisation.

The town's main industries were coalmining, salt panning and the making of baking girdles. Coal mining had been introduced by the monks of Culross Abbey at a time when coal was little known about, and wondrous tales spread round Scotland about the "stones that could burn". After the Reformation, the mines were taken over by **Sir George Bruce,** a descendant of Robert the Bruce. Between 1575 and his death 50 years later he revolutionised the industry. He was the first man to extend a coal mine beneath the sea, something which is taken for granted today. One of his mines had a tunnel that extended out under the waters of the Firth of Forth for more than a mile. James VI was fascinated by Culross's industry and paid a visit. Sir George took him on a tour of the mine, and led the unsuspecting king along the tunnel. When he emerged and found himself surrounded on all four sides by water, he panicked, shouting "treason!"

As an offshoot of the mining industry, salt panning became another major occupation in the town. It is reckoned that at one time there were 50 saltpans along the coast, all using inferior coal to heat salt water from the sea. Another industry was the making of iron girdles for cooking. Culross blacksmiths are said to have invented these round, flat utensils

Culross Palace

150

for frying and cooking after Robert the Bruce, in the 14th century, ordered that each one of his troops be given a flat pan for cooking oatcakes.

Nothing remains of Sir George's mining ventures. However, his home, now called **Culross Palace**, still stands, and is open to the public. Work started on it in 1597, and is a typical residence of its time for someone of Sir George's standing in society. It has splendid kitchen gardens.

Beside the Mercat Cross is **The Study**. It was built about 1610, and after the Palace, is Culross's grandest house. When the Church of Scotland was Episcopalian, the town formed part of the diocese of Dunblane, and it was here that Bishop Robert Leighton stayed on his visits. The quaint Outlook Tower housed his actual study, hence the name of the house. If you continue past The Study, along Tanhouse Brae and into Kirk Street, you will eventually reach **Culross Abbey**, dedicated to St Serf and St Mary. The choir of the church (restored in 1633) still stands, and is used as the parish church, though the other buildings have either completely disappeared or are in ruins. Off the north transept is the Bruce Vault, where there is an impressive alabaster monument to Sir George Bruce of Carnock, his wife and their eight children.

But Culross's attractions aren't all historical. Close to the town is Longannet Power Station, one of Scotland's largest. There are organised tours (which have to be pre-booked), and you can see the huge turbine hall from a viewing platform, as well as tour the visitors centre, which shows how coal produces electricity.

Stretching from Longannet past Culross to Combie Point on the shores of the Firth of Forth is the **Torry Bay Local Nature Reserve**, where there is a series of artificial lagoons built from the waste ash from Longannet. Here you can see many species of birds, such as shelduck, greenshank and great crested grebe.

KINCARDINE-ON-FORTH

10 miles W of Dunfermline, on the A985

This small burgh, which received its charter in 1663, sits at the north end of the **Kincardine Bridge**. Until the Forth Road Bridge opened in 1964, this was the only road crossing of the Forth downstream from Stirling. Opened in 1936, the middle section used to swivel to allow ships to pass up the river. It was controlled from a control room above the swivel section, and was, at the time, the largest swivel bridge in Europe. It allowed ships to sail up to Alloa, but has not opened since the 1980s when Alloa declined as a port.

The town is full of small, old-fashioned cottages with red pantiled roofs, and there are the ruins of the 17th century Tulliallan Church. The burgh's Mercat Cross also dates from the 17th century.

Sir James Dewar, inventor of the vacuum flask and co-inventor of cordite was born in the town in

The ruins of Ravenscraig Castle stand on a promontory to the east of the Kirkcaldy town centre. It was built in the 15th century by James II for his queen, Mary of Gueldres, who died there in 1463. James had a passion for weaponry - especially guns - and had the castle built so that it could withstand the latest artillery.

1842. It was not until 1904, however, that the vacuum, or Thermos, flask was produced commercially by a firm in Germany. The term "Thermos" was coined in Munich, and comes from the Greek word *therme*, which means "hot".

To the west of the town is Tulliallan Castle, now the main police training college in Scotland. During World War II, it was the base of the Polish Free Forces under the command of General Wladislav Sikorski who was killed in an air crash in Gibraltar in 1943.

SALINE

5 miles NW of Dunfermline on the B913

Knockhill Racing Circuit is Scotland's national motor sports centre for cars and motorbikes, and has meetings on most Sundays from April to October.

Kirklands Garden extends

over 2 acres and is surrounded by 20 acres of woodland. In spring it presents a spectacular display of rhododendrons, bluebells, wood anemones, hellebores and bulbs. There's also a walled terraced garden created in 1832, a bog garden, statues and a plant sales area.

KIRKCALDY

Kirkcaldy is the largest town in Fife, and is famous for the manufacture of linoleum. At one time it was known as the "Lang Toun", due to the fact that it appeared to stretch out along one main street. It was created a royal burgh in 1644, and one of the famous events held here every year in April is the **Links Market**, reckoned to be the longest street fair in Europe. The town's Esplanade is cordoned off from traffic and taken over by swings, roundabouts, dodgems, carousels, hoopla stalls and all the other attractions of a modern funfair. The very first Links Market took place in 1306 in Links Street in the town, hence its name.

Within **Kirkcaldy Art Gallery & Museum** in the War Memorial Gardens is an exhibition devoted to Wemyss Ware, a form of earthenware pottery that was produced in the town by the firm of Robert Heron and Son between 1882 and 1930. It is now much collected and is possibly the most sought after pottery ever made in Scotland. Its most distinctive feature was its decoration, which

Sailors Walk, Kirkcaldy

was bold, simple and direct. The firing methods caused a lot of waste, which meant that the pottery was always expensive. The museum also houses a local history collection, plus an extensive collection of Scottish paintings.

Overlooking the town harbour is the 15th century **Sailor's Walk**, the town's oldest house. The **Old Parish Church** sits at the top of Kirk Wynd, and dates from 1808. However, its tower is medieval.

In the town's Abbotshall Kirkyard stands a statue to another person born in Kirkcaldy, but an unusual one. Marjory Fleming was a child writer whose nickname was "Pet Marjory". She died in 1811, and yet her writings have intrigued and delighted people down through the ages. She kept a journal, in which she jotted down thoughts, poems and biographical scraps. She was, by all accounts, a "handful", and when her mother gave birth to another girl in 1809, Marjory was sent to live with her aunt in Edinburgh. This is where her writing began, encouraged by her cousin Isa, and she eventually filled three notebooks. Nobody knows what she might have achieved in adulthood, because, one month short of her ninth birthday, and after she had returned to Kirkcaldy, she tragically died of meningitis. Her last piece of writing was a touching poem addressed to her beloved cousin. Her writings were subsequently published, and found great favour with the Victorians, though some frowned on the absolute honesty she displayed when it came to describing her tantrums and innermost thoughts.

AROUND KIRKCALDY

GLENROTHES

5 miles N of Kirkcaldy on the A92

Glenrothes was one of the new towns established in Scotland in the late 1940s. In **Balbirnie Park**, which extends to 416 acres, is a late Neolithic stone circle dating from about 3000 BC. It was moved to its present site in 1971-1972 when the A92 was widened. The park was created in the estate of Balbirnie House, once owned by the Balfours.

Another attractive feature of Glenrothes is the array of modern sculptures dotted around the town. There are more than 130 of them, including giant flowers, totem poles and parading hippos.

About 2 miles east of Glenrothes, **Balgonie Castle** dates back to the 14th century with additions being made up until 1702. The castle is still the home of the Laird and Lady of Balgonie and as likely as not it will be one of them who guides you around the partly restored building. The informative tour provides interesting details about the castle's construction and its history which includes a visit by Rob Roy and 200 of his clansmen who were quartered at Balgonie in 1716.

FALKLAND

10 miles N of Kirkcaldy on the A912

Set in the Howe (Plain) of Fife,

● *Adam Smith, the founder of the science of economics, was born in Kirkcaldy in 1723. He went on to occupy the chair of moral philosophy at Glasgow University, and his famous book, The Wealth of Nations, was partly written in his mother's house (now gone) in the town's High Street. Also born in the town were William Adam the architect, and his son, Robert Adam.* ●

59 ROYAL PALACE OF FALKLAND

Falkland

This wonderful Palace was the country residence of Stuart kings and queens when they hunted deer and wild boar in the Fife forest. Mary, Queen of Scots spent some of the happiest days of her tragic life here, 'playing the country girl in the woods and parks'

🏛 See page 383

Royal Palace of Falkland

monarch was Marjory, daughter of Robert the Bruce). Six days later James was dead and Mary began her ill-fated reign.

Mary's experience of castles and palaces was generally pretty melancholy but she seems to have spent a happy childhood at Falkland, often playing in the splendid gardens, now restored. In later years, she frequently returned to the palace and enjoyed riding through the nearby Lomond Hills.

Falkland town has quaint old cobbled streets lined with 17th and 18th century cottages and was the first conservation area established in Scotland. The burgh's **Town Hall,** which dates from 1805, houses an exhibition about the town.

Falkland is a perfect gem, an unspoilt little burgh which grew up around a superb Renaissance mansion, **Falkland Palace** (National Trust for Scotland). Built between 1501-41, the palace was a favourite seat of the Stuart kings from the time of James V. He extended the building considerably, adding the beautiful Chapel Royal and also a Royal Tennis court in 1539. Both are still in use, with the tennis court believed to be the oldest in the world.

James V was on his deathbed at Falkland when he received news of the birth of his daughter, Mary Stuart. His two sons had died in infancy, now his turbulent kingdom would pass to a woman. He was filled with foreboding: the throne, he said "cam wi' a lass and it will gang wi' a lass". (The first Stuart

DYSART

NE suburb of Kirkcaldy on the A955

The harbour area of Dysart is very picturesque with whitewashed cottages and houses dating from the 16th, 17th and 18th centuries. At one time this was a salt panning area, and **Pan Ha'** (meaning "Pan Haugh") is a group of particularly fine 17th century buildings with red pantiled roofs (not open to the public). **St Serf's Tower** is the tower of the former parish church, and dates from the 15th century. It looks more like a castle than a tower, and reflects the area's troubled times when English ships prowled the Forth. In Rectory Lane is the **John McDouall Stuart Museum,** dedicated to the life of a locally born explorer who, in 1861-62, made the first return journey across the Australian continent.

The former **Harbourmaster's House** has been recently redeveloped and now provides visitors with an introduction to the features that make Fife's coastal area unique.

WEMYSS

4 miles NE of Kirkcaldy on the A955

Below the substantial ruins of **MacDuff Castle**, near the shoreline, are some caves in the sandstone cliffs with old carvings on the walls. They date mainly from between AD 400 to AD 800, though some may go back to before Christ. It has been claimed that there are more carvings within these caves than in all the other caves in Britain put together. However, due to erosion and subsidence, most of the caves can no longer be entered, though they may be viewed from the shore.

BUCKHAVEN AND METHIL

8 miles NE of Kirkcaldy on the B931

Buckhaven and Methil constituted one burgh which was created in 1891. Its motto was *Carbone Carbasoque*, which means "By Coal and by Sail", reflecting the fact that it used to export coal. As with other Fife ports, it also had saltpans, and by 1677 three pans were in operation, fuelled by coal. The Methil docks were opened in 1887. In Lower Methil's High Street is the **Methil Heritage Centre**, a lively community museum that explains the history of the area.

Buckhaven, to the west, was never as industrialised as Methil. It was once a fishing port and ferry terminal, and has some old, quaint cottages. In College Street there is the **Buckhaven Museum**, which has displays about the town's industries, including fishing.

LEVEN

9 miles NE of Kirkcaldy on the A955

The area to the northeast of Leven is known as the East Neuk (nook, or corner) of Fife. Its coastline is dotted with pretty villages and there's a long stretch of excellent sandy beaches around the broad curve of Largo Bay. Leven is the largest of the towns on the bay, popular with holiday-makers enjoying its fine beach, lively Promenade offering all the usual seaside attractions, and two peaceful public parks.

LARGO

12 miles NE of Kirkcaldy on the A915

There are two Largos - Lower Largo on the shores of the Forth and Upper Largo about half a mile inland, where the Parish Church, some parts of which date from the early 17th century, stands. It was here that Scotland's greatest seafarer and one time Admiral of the Fleet, **Sir Andrew Wood**, had his home. He died in 1515, and was buried in the kirkyard. He oversaw the building in Newhaven of the largest and most magnificent fighting ship of its day, the *Great Michael,* flagship of the Scottish fleet. All that remains of Wood's castle is a solitary tower.

The "real" Robinson Crusoe, Alexander Selkirk, was born in the

Wemyss Castle Gardens are open to the public during the summer months by prior arrangement. The six acre walled garden in its present form dates from the mid 18th century, with new heated walls and an Orangery added before 1800. Set high atop cliffs looking out across the Firth of Forth, Wemyss Castle (private) dates from the 13th century, although most of the present structure was built in the 16th century. It was at the castle that Mary Stuart first met Lord Darnley, her second husband, in 1565.

60 BALHOUSIE FARM

Leven

Family run B&B offering a peaceful and comfortable stay.

See page 385

Earthship Fife, at Kinghorn Loch, is an unusual building made of used car tyres and soft drink cans. It has its own heating, lighting, water supply and sewage works, and explains all about eco-buildings and sustainable lifestyles.

attractive seaside resort of Lower Largo in 1676. At the age of 19 he ran away to sea and a few years later was master of a pirate ship operating in the South Seas. After a dispute with his captain, William Dampier, Selkirk was put ashore on the uninhabited island of Juan Fernandez. He stayed there for 4 years and 4 months, never seeing another human being - Man Friday was Daniel Defoe's fictional addition. Then Dampier returned and rescued him. Lower Largo's most famous son is commemorated by a statue near the harbour showing Selkirk dressed as a castaway.

KINGHORN

4 miles S of Kirkcaldy on the A921

This quiet little royal burgh saw one of the most decisive events in Scottish history. In 1286, at the Pettycur Crags to the west of the town **Alexander III** was thrown from his horse and suffered fatal injuries. He was the last of the country's Celtic kings. The heir to the Scottish throne was now three-year-old Margaret, known as the "Maid of Norway". She was the daughter of Alexander's own daughter, who had married Eric II of Norway. But while crossing from Norway to Scotland, Margaret also died, leaving the country without an heir. In the resultant vacuum, noblemen jockeyed for position, putting forward many claimants to the throne. Edward I of England was asked to intercede, and he saw his chance. He tried to incorporate Scotland into his own kingdom by

installing a puppet king, and thus began the Wars of Independence.

A tall monument at the side of the road, erected in 1886, marks the spot where Alexander was killed.

Kinghorn Parish Church dates from 1774, though there are partial remains of an earlier church dating from 1243 in the kirkyard.

BURNTISLAND

6 miles SW of Kirkcaldy on the A921

This small royal burgh, called Portus Gratiae, or "Port of Grace" by the Romans, is overlooked by a 632-feet high hill called The Binn. In medieval times Burntisland was the second most important port on the Forth after Leith, and in Victorian times exported coal from the Fife coalfields. It is now more of a resort with a popular Blue Flag sandy beach.

St Columba's Parish Church is a four square building dating from 1592, and is possibly based on a Dutch design. It was the first church built in Scotland after the Reformation which is still in use today, and has a wealth of detail inside, including elaborate lofts and pews. The nave sits at the centre of the church, with the altar, or "Holy Table", sitting in the middle. The pews face it on four sides, emphasising the "equality of all believers". It is the birthplace of the Authorised Version of the Bible, as James VI attended a General Assembly of the Church of Scotland here in May 1601, and put forward the proposal for a translation of the Bible into English. The suggestion was enthusiastically received, but it was not until James had assumed the throne of Britain that work began.

James's son, Charles I, had good reason to remember Burntisland. In 1633, he lost most of his treasure, estimated to be worth more than £20m in today's money, when his baggage ship, the *Blessing of Burntisland*, foundered and sank just off the coast here. Nineteen witches who, it was claimed, had put a curse on the ship, were executed. In 1999 the wreckage was finally located, lying in a few metres of silt. Plans are afoot to explore the wreckage.

The **Burntisland Edwardian Fair Museum** is in the High Street, and features displays about Edwardian fairgrounds and local history. The highlight of the summer is the Highland Games in July, which attract around 30,000 visitors to the town. The annual Civic Week is held in June, and includes the crowning of the Summer Queen.

The restored Rossend Castle, at the western end of the town, was the scene of a bizarre incident concerning Mary Stuart and a love-struck French poet who broke into her room to declare his undying love for her. As he had attempted it once before at Holyrood, he was later executed. The castle has recently been modernised and is now used as offices.

ST ANDREWS

A measure of the historic importance of this elegant town is the fact that almost the whole of its town centre enjoys the protection of listed building status. The most striking of these buildings is the ruined magnificence of **St Andrews Cathedral.** Masons started to build it in 1160; their descendants finally completed the largest church ever built in Scotland in 1318. Robert the Bruce attended its consecration in that same year. Two and a half centuries later, this beacon of Christian faith was effectively snuffed out when John Knox arrived in St Andrews. On the 5th June 1559 Knox delivered a rabble-rousing sermon inciting his Protestant congregation to attack the Catholic church. The mob stripped the cathedral of its treasures (never recovered) and enthusiastically mutilated any stone image of saints and prophets within reach of their axes. The people of St Andrews never found the heart, money or will to restore their desecrated cathedral.

Standing alongside the ruins of the cathedral is **St Rule's Tower,** an extraordinary survival from around 1130 when, according to legend, it was built to house the sacred relics of St Andrew. No-one knows where those relics are nowadays. Within the tower, a 174-step corkscrew staircase leads to a platform from which there are grand views in all directions.

From the tower it's just a short walk to the rocky coastline and the ruins of **St Andrews Castle,** surrounded by the sea on three sides and by a moat on the fourth. The castle witnessed some grim

Open during the summer months, The Museum of Communication is the only museum in the UK that focuses on how our commuication systems have developed. It specialises in communications technology from the pre-electric telegraph to the present time. It has a major collection of artefacts covering Early Electrics, Telegraphy, Telephony, Radio, Television and Information Technology, together with a large number of supporting printed items.

61 BRITISH GOLF MUSEUM

St Andrews

A fascinating insight into the past of golf. A visit to the British Golf Museum is the perfect break from playing golf.

 see page 385

scenes during the turbulent years of the Reformation. In 1546 the Protestant reformer George Wishart was burnt at the stake in front of the castle while the Bishop of St Andrews, Cardinal Beaton, seated himself on the balcony *"to feed and glut his eyes with the sight of it"*. Less than three months later, Knox's supporters stabbed the Cardinal to death and hung his body from the castle wall. Later, it was dumped into the "bottle dungeon", a 24 feet-deep pit gouged out of solid rock which can still be seen in the Sea Tower.

Another Protestant who was executed in the town was **Patrick Hamilton** who was burnt at the stake in 1528. The spot is marked by his initials incorporated into the cobbles outside **St Salvator's Church** in North Street, part of St Salvator's College. The church was founded in 1450 by Bishop James Kennedy, not only to serve the college, but as a place of worship

for the people of the town.

It was on 28th August 1413 that Pope Benedict XIII issued six papal bulls authorising the founding of the university which is Scotland's oldest and the third oldest university in the English-speaking world. At first the classes were held in the cathedral, but this was found to be unsatisfactory. In 1450 Bishop Kennedy founded St Salvator's College, and classes moved there. In the 16th century two others were established, St Leonard's College and St Mary's College. **St Leonard's Chapel** was built long before the college came into being, its earliest parts dating from the 12th century.

St Mary's College is undoubtedly the loveliest of today's colleges. Step through the arch from South Street and you are in a grassed quadrangle surrounded by old, mellow buildings from the 16th century onwards. At the foot of the Stair Tower is **Queen Mary's Thorn**, said to have been planted by Mary Stuart in 1565. She visited the town five times and possibly lodged at what is now known as **Queen Mary's House** in South Street. It dates from about 1525, and was built by one of the cathedral's canons. Charles II also stayed in it in 1650.

The most recent addition to the university's amenities is **The Museum of the University of St Andrews** (MUSA) which opened in October 2008. It puts on display to the public for the first time some of the real treasures amongst the University's collection of more than

St Andrews Castle

112,000 artefacts. The museum has four galleries, a 'Leaning Loft' and a viewing terrace with panoramic views over St Andrews Bay.

Further along South Street, in front of Madras College, one of the town's schools, is all that remains of the **Dominican Friary**. This is the 16th century north transept of the friary church, with some wonderful tracery in its windows.

At the west end of South Street can be found the **West Port**, one of the original gates into the town. It was built about 1589 on the site of an earlier port. In North Street is the **St Andrews Preservation Trust Museum and Garden**, housed in a charming building dating from the 16th century. It has displays and artefacts illustrating the town's history. The **St Andrews Museum** at Kinburn Park also celebrates the town's heritage.

At the Scores, down near the shore, you'll find the **St Andrews Aquarium**, which not only lets you see lots of fish and animals from sea horses to seals and piranha to sharks, but lets you touch some as well. Also on the Scores is the **Martyr's Monument**, which commemorates the Protestant martyrs who were executed in St Andrews. It is a tall, needle-like monument, erected in 1842. Close by is the **British Golf Museum**, which illustrates the history of a game that Scotland gave to the world, with a particular focus on St Andrews. It has an array of exhibits from over 500 years of golfing history, and gives an insight

into "surprising facts and striking feats".

St Andrews and golf are inseparable. The town is still a place of pilgrimage, only today the pilgrims come wearing Pringle sweaters and weighed down by golf bags. The Royal and Ancient Golf Club is the world's ruling body on the game (with the exception of the United States), and formulates its rules as well as organising the yearly British Open Championship. The most famous of the town's courses is the **Old Course**, and it is here, in the clubhouse, that the Royal and Ancient has its headquarters.

Two of the greatest names in golf were born in St Andrews - **Tom Morris** and his son, also called Tom. Old Tom was made green keeper at the Old Course in 1865, and was one of the best golfers of his day. His son, however, was even better, and won the Open Championship three times in a row while still a teenager. He eventually died in 1875, aged only 24, some say of a broken heart after his wife died in childbirth. Memorials to both men can be seen in the cathedral graveyard.

Located in Queen's Gardens, **Fife Contemporary Art & Craft** provides opportunities for the people of Fife to experience quality exhibitions and take part in ambitious projects by local, national and international artists and makers.

Craigton Country Park sits about a mile outside the town to

In February 1563 a French poet called Pierre de Châtelard was executed in Market Street. He had accompanied Mary when she returned from France, and swore undying love for her. However, he went too far, twice breaking into Mary's bedroom - once in Holyrood and once at Rossend Castle near Burntisland. He was taken to St Andrews Castle, and there imprisoned. On February 22nd he was brought to trial and condemned to death. On the scaffold, he read out a poem called Hymn to Death, *then cried out* "Farewell cruel dame!".

62 THE GOLF HOTEL

Fife

A charming inn well known for its good food, good company and good service

 see page 386

63 THE SCOTTISH FISHERIES MUSEUM

Anstruther

This Museum tells and researches the story of the Scottish fishing industry and its people from the earliest times to the present.

 see page 385

the southwest. It has a small boating loch, miniature railway, aviary, pet's corner, glasshouses, restaurant and café. **Cambo Gardens** is a two-and-a-half acre walled garden within the Cambo estate at Kingsbarns. Cambo has been the home of the Erskine family since 1688, though the present mansion dates from 1881. There are also 70 acres of woodland, which is famous for its snowdrops.

The internationally recognised **St Andrews Botanic Garden** displays within its 7-hectare site an extensive range of rare and beautiful plants, both under glass and in the open.

St Andrews also boasts one of Scotland's best beaches at **West Sands** where scenes for *Chariots of Fire* were filmed.

AROUND ST ANDREWS

CRAIL

10 miles SE of St Andrews on the A917

The most ancient royal burgh in the East Neuk ("East Corner"), as this area of Fife is known, Crail is also one of the oldest ports. It is also possibly the most picturesque little town and its small harbour has featured on countless calendars and post cards. Artists flock to the place because of the light and the quaint buildings. Pretty as it is, this picture-postcard village is still a working port, home to Fife's crab and lobster fleet.

The **Tolbooth** dates from the early 16th century with a tower dated 1776, and has Dutch

influences. In the Marketgate is the **Crail Museum and Heritage Centre**, which traces the history of the town and its industries. During the summer months, the museum offers guided walks around the town.

The four star **Jerdan Gallery,** in Marketgate South, has a wide variety of paintings and craftwork from the 19th and 20th centuries, with exhibits changing on a monthly basis. There is a superb sculpture garden at the rear.

At Troywood, three miles west of the town, off the B9131, is perhaps the most unusual visitor attraction in Scotland. The **Secret Bunker** was Scotland's underground command centre in event of a nuclear attack. It has an amazing 24,000 square feet of accommodation on two levels, 100 feet underground and encased in 15 feet thick concrete walls. It was from here that the country was to have been run in the event of war with the Soviet Union. It is entered by an innocent looking farmhouse, and guarded by three tons of blast proof doors. As well as operations rooms, living quarters and six dormitories, it also contains two cinemas, a café and a BBC sound studio. Several similar bunkers were built around the country but this is one of the largest. It came off the Official Secrets list in 1993 at the end of the Cold War.

ANSTRUTHER

9 miles SE of St Andrews off the A917

Sixty years ago, the attractive port of Anstruther was so busy with fishing boats it was possible to walk from one side of the wide harbour to the other by stepping from boat to boat. Then the North Sea herring shoals which had brought prosperity to the town for centuries mysteriously disappeared and the vessels now rocking gently in the harbour are mostly pleasure craft.

Located in the 16th century St Ayles House, once a lodging house for the monks from Balmerino Abbey, is the **Scottish Fisheries Museum**, which was opened in 1969. Here you can follow the fleet with the "herring lassies", explore a typical fishing family's cottage and see skilled craftsmen at work. Also on display are two boats - a 78-feet long "Zulu" built in the early 1900s and based on an original African design, and the *Reaper*, a "fifie" herring drifter built in 1901. In a small private chapel is the poignant Memorial to Scottish Fishermen Lost at Sea.

In the town itself, collectors of curiosities will be pleased with

Kellie Castle, Anstruther

Buckie House. Its former owner decorated it inside and out with buckies, or shells, and as a final touch, stipulated that he should be buried in a shell-encrusted coffin.

Six miles southeast of Anstruther, in the Firth of Forth, is the **Isle of May**, measuring just over a mile long by a quarter of a mile wide at its widest. The whole place is now a national nature reserve managed by Scottish Natural Heritage. It was on this island that Scotland's first lighthouse was built

64 DREEL TAVERN

Anstruther

One of the area's oldest and most frequented public houses serving cask conditioned ales and excellent home-cooked food.

🍴 see page 387

65 THE WATERFRONT RESTAURANT

Anstruther

Outstanding harbourside restaurant offering superb cuisine, and B&B and self-catering accommodation.

🍴 🛏 see page 388

Isle of May, Anstruther

Every August since 1986, the Royal Burgh of Pittenweem in Fife has hosted a 9-day festival of visual arts. Houses, halls, galleries, churches, the fish market and the harbour all take on new roles. About 100 artists, resident, visiting and especially invited show and sell their work and more than 200,000 visitors thread their way through Pittenweem's cobbled wynds.

in 1635. It was no more than a small stone tower with a brazier atop it, which burnt coal. The present lighthouse was built in 1816 by Robert Stevenson, father of the author RL Stevenson. It is unusual in that it is designed to resemble a castle. Trips to the island are available from the pier at Anstruther and take about 45 minutes.

KILRENNY

9 miles SE of St Andrews on the A917

Kilrenny Parish Church has a tower dating from the 15th century, though the rest is early 19th century. In the kirkyard is a mausoleum to the Scotts of Balcomie. There are many picturesque 18th and 19th century cottages, formerly the homes of fishermen. The name "Kilrenny" actually means "the church of the

bracken", and the village may be one of the earliest settlements in the area.

PITTENWEEM

10 miles SE of St Andrews on the A917

The older houses in this small royal burgh crowd around the picturesque fishing harbour which is now the busiest of all the fishing harbours in the area. Like most of the houses in the East Neuk, they are whitewashed with red pantiled roofs and crow step gables. The Parish Church has a substantial tower (which looks more like part of a small castle than a piece of ecclesiastical architecture) dating from the 16th century, while the rest is Victorian.

Pittenweem means "the place of the cave", and the cave in question is **St Fillan's Cave** in Cave Wynd, which is supposed to be where St Fillan, an 8th century missionary to the Picts, used to go for private prayer. It was renovated and re-dedicated in 1935. Services are still held in this unconventional setting. The town also has many art galleries and antique shops, a testimony to the popularity of this area with artists and retired people.

A couple of miles inland, **Kellie Castle** (National Trust for Scotland) is an outstanding example of Lowland domestic architecture. It dates from the 14th century and contains superb plaster ceilings, murals, painted panelling and furniture designed by Sir Robert Lorimer, who refurbished the place in the late

East Neuk Port, Pittenweem

19th century. The Victorian nursery and kitchen are both fascinating while outside there are fine gardens with organically cultivated old roses and herbaceous borders.

ST MONANS
10 miles S of St Andrews on the A917

This little fishing port's motto is Mare Vivimus, meaning "From the Sea we Have Life". It is famous for the **Church of St Monans**, built by David II, son of Robert the Bruce, in thanksgiving after he survived a shipwreck on the Forth. It stands almost on the shoreline, and is a substantial building consisting of a nave, transepts and stumpy spire atop a tower. The chancel was never built.

The ruins of 15th century **Newark Castle** can also be seen near the shore. It originally belonged to the Newark family, but perhaps its most famous owner was General David Leslie, who fought for Cromwell in the 17th century.

Salt panning was once an important industry in the town, and the 18th century **St Monans Windmill** at one time formed part of a small industrial complex, which produced salt from seawater.

EARLSFERRY AND ELIE
11 miles S of St Andrews off the A917

These two villages are small holiday resorts surrounding a sandy bay. The older of the two is Earlsferry, which is a royal burgh. It was once the northern terminal for ferries which plied between it and ports on the south bank of the Forth.

The "earl" in its name comes from an incident concerning Macduff, who was the Earl of Fife. In 1054 he escaped from King Macbeth, took refuge in a cave at Kincraig Point near the town, and was then ferried across the Forth to Dunbar.

Gillespie House, in Elie, dates from the 17th century, and has a fine carved doorway. **Elie Parish Church** dates from 1639, though the unusual tower was added in 1729. At Ruby Bay are the scant remains of **Lady's Tower**, built in the late 18th century as a changing room for Lady Anstruther who bathed in the sea here.

CERES
8 miles SW of St Andrews on the B939

Ceres gets its name from the family which once owned the lands surrounding the village - the de Syras family. It is a small picturesque settlement with a village green and the hump-backed, medieval Bishop's Bridge. In the **Fife Folk Museum** you can find out about what everyday life was like in Fife in bygone days.

The village's Bannockburn Monument is close by the Bishop's Bridge, and was erected in 1914, 600 years after the Battle of Bannockburn took place, to commemorate the archers of Ceres who fell in it. The **Parish Church** was built in 1806 and its most unusual features are the communion tables which run the full length of the church. Built into a wall on the main street is a curious carving known as The Provost, said to have been the Revd

Thomas Buchanan, the last holder
of the title in 1578.

Pottery from the **Wemyss Ware
Studio** provides visitors with highly
collectable Scottish giftware. The
range consists of beautifully hand-
painted cats, pigs and other giftware,
decorative tableware and tiles.

CUPAR

8 miles W of St Andrews on the A91

This small town, sitting on the
River Eden, was once the county
town of Fife. It is a pleasant place,
and well worth strolling round just
to see and appreciate its many old
buildings. The **Mercat Cross**,
topped with a unicorn, was moved
from Tarvit Hill to its present
location in 1897 to commemorate
Queen Victoria's Diamond Jubilee.
In Duffus Park is the **Douglas
Bader Garden**, designed with the
disabled in mind. The Old Parish
Church dates from 1785, though
the tower is medieval.

**Hill of Tarvit
Mansionhouse & Garden**
(National Trust for Scotland) is a
fine Edwardian mansion that lies
two miles south of the town, and
was designed by Sir Robert
Lorimer in 1906. It has French,
Scottish and Chippendale
furniture, a collection of paintings,
an Edwardian laundry and fine
gardens. Close by is **Scotstarvit
Tower** (Historic Scotland). It was
built by the Inglis family around
1487 when they were granted the
lands of Tarvit. In 1612 it was
bought by Sir John Scott. He was
an advocate who was deprived of
his twin positions in the Scottish

judiciary as judge and director of
chancery by Cromwell in the 17th
century, and retired to Scotstarvit,
where he was visited by many
eminent men of the time.

A few miles west of Cupar, at
Rankeilor Park, is the **Scottish
Deer Centre** and **Raptor World**.
At the Deer Centre you can see -
and even feed - both species of
deer native to Scotland, the roe and
the red deer, plus other species
from around the world. At the
Raptor Centre there are exhibitions
about birds of prey such as owls,
hawks and falcons, plus there are
spectacular flying demonstrations.
There is also a small shopping
court, an indoor adventure play
area and picnic areas.

AUCHTERMUCHTY

16 miles W of St Andrews on the A91

Auchtermuchty is a typical inland
Fife town. It is small and compact,
and sits in a fertile area known as
the Howe of Fife ("Hollow of
Fife"). The **Tolbooth** dates from
1728, and it was here that the TV
series *Dr Finlay* was filmed, its town
centre being turned into a typical
townscape of the 1930s.

Though born in East Wemyss,
Jimmy Shand, the well known
Scottish dance band leader, lived in
the town for many years. There is a
statue of him, complete with kilt,
at Upper Glens in the town.

NEWBURGH

19 miles W of St Andrews on the A913

This small royal burgh stands on the
banks of the Tay. Close to it are the
red sandstone ruins of **Lindores**

Abbey, founded by David I in 1178 for Tironensian monks. It was the first abbey in Scotland to be sacked by Protestant sympathisers, 17 years before Scotland officially became a Protestant country. And the very first mention of whisky production in Scotland is contained in a document of 1494, when James IV commissioned John Cor, a monk at the abbey, to make the equivalent of 400 bottles of "aquavitae" for the king's table.

The **Laing Museum** in the High Street has displays on Newburgh's history from medieval burgh to industrial town.

LEUCHARS

5 miles NW of St Andrews, on the A919

Every September, the Royal Air Force puts on the **Leuchars Air Show**, held in one of Scotland's biggest RAF bases. The village is also famous for its **Church of St Athernase**, said by some to be the second finest Norman church in Britain. It was built in the late 12th century by Robert de Quinci

who lived in Leuchars Castle. The best parts are the finely carved chancel and apse, with the rather plain nave being Victorian. A bell tower was added to the apse in the 17th century.

Tentsmuir Forest, to the north of Leuchars, is a 3700-acre pine forest planted on sand dunes on the shores of the North Sea and the Firth of Tay. The whole area is rich in wildlife.

NEWPORT-ON-TAY

11 miles NW of St Andrews on the A92

This little town sits at the southern end of the Tay Road Bridge, and at Wormit, about a mile to the west, is the start of the Tay Rail Bridge. The ruins of **Balmerino Abbey** (National Trust for Scotland) stand five miles to the west. It was founded in 1229 by Queen Ermengarde, widow of William the Lion, king of Scotland, and colonised by Cistercian monks from Melrose. The ruins are not open to the public but can be viewed from close by.

68 HILLPARK HOUSE

Leuchars, St Andrews

Five comfortable rooms and a delicious breakfast are on offer at **Hillpark House.**

see page 389

165

Stirling & Clackmannanshire

The area of Scotland between the Firths of Clyde and Forth has always been strategically important. It is often referred to as Scotland's "waist"; before the Kincardine Bridge was built in 1936 the bridge at Stirling was the lowest crossing point of the River Forth. To the west of the town are the Campsie and Kilsyth Hills, and these, along with marshy bogland such as Flanders Moss, formed another natural barrier, so the bridge at Stirling became the gateway to Perthshire and the Highlands.

That's why so many battles have been fought in and around Stirling and Falkirk, including Scotland's most important, the Battle of Bannockburn, which secured Scotland's future as an independent nation. It is also the reason why Stirling Castle was built. This royal castle sits sentinel on a great rocky outcrop, with the town of Stirling laid out below it to the west. In medieval times it was almost impregnable, and from its top an approaching

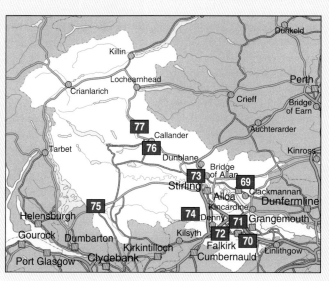

166

army could easily be seen miles away.

Clackmannanshire still proudly proclaims itself to be Scotland's smallest county, with an area of only 55 square miles. It sits in the shelter of the Ochil Hills to the north, which rise to well over 2000 feet in places, and was a centre for woollens and textiles. The string of "hillfoot villages" at the foot of the Ochils are all picturesque and well worth visiting for this alone.

Around Falkirk and Grangemouth, Stirlingshire is unashamedly industrial. This is the heart of Scotland's petrochemical industry, with great refineries lining the shores of the Forth, which is still tidal at this point.

Travel northwest from Stirling however, and you enter another world - the Trossachs, one of Scotland's most beautiful areas. Though its hills are not as high as those of the Grampians or the Cairngorms, and don't have that brooding majesty we tend to associate with Highland scenery, it is still Highland in character. The hills slip down to the wooded banks of lochs such as Loch Katrine, Loch Venachar and the wonderfully named Loch Drunkie, which are among the most picturesque in Scotland, and the skies seem endless and sweeping. The Loch

Lomond and Trossachs National Park takes in most of the Trossachs in its 720 square miles. It was the country's first national park, opened in 2002.

The town of Stirling is one of the most historic in Scotland, and has played a leading role in shaping the country's destiny. The castle has been fought over countless times by the Scottish and the English, and eventually became a favourite royal residence. Mary Queen of Scots stayed there, and her son, who became James VI, had his coronation in the town's Church of the Holy Rood. Falkirk, though more industrial in character, is also an ancient town, and has witnessed two important battles as Scotland's history was played out. Alloa, Clackmannanshire's largest town, is also industrial in character, though it too has history aplenty. At one time it was a thriving port, and Scotland's brewing capital, though only one brewery now remains.

The whole offers some memorable buildings: Dunblane Cathedral, Alloa Tower, the ruins of Camubuskenneth Priory, the Wallace Monument, and both Doune Castle and Castle Campbell are also well worth visiting.

CLACKMANNAN

This small town was granted its burgh charter in 1550. It was once a small port on the Black Devon, a tributary of the Forth, but the river silted up years ago, leaving it high and dry. In the centre of the town is the belfry of the old **Tolbooth**, built by William Menteith in 1592. He was the sheriff of the town, and objected strongly to holding felons in his own home, so he built the Tolbooth to hold them instead.

Beside it stands the **Mannau Stone**. Legend states that when St Serf came to this part of Scotland in the 6th century to convert it to Christianity, he found the locals worshipping the sea god Mannau, or Mannan, in the form of the stone (known as the "clach mannau"). From this, the town supposedly got its name. The stone can still be seen on top of a column close to the Tolbooth and the **Mercat Cross**, which dates from the 1600s.

Clackmannan Tower, on King's Seat Hill, dates from the 14th century, with later alterations, and was once owned by Robert the Bruce. Though in the care of Historic Scotland, the interior can only be viewed by special arrangement.

Robert Burns visited the area in 1787, and was "knighted" by a direct descendant of Robert the Bruce, a Mrs Bruce, who lived in a mansion house near the castle. She was in her nineties at the time, and a woman of "hospitality and urbanity". She still possessed her ancestor's helmet and two-handed sword, and she used the sword to carry out the ceremony, declaring that she had a better right to confer knighthoods than "some people" (meaning the Hanoverian kings who were on the throne in London).

Clackmannan's **Parish Church** dates from 1815. Inside is the beautiful Coronation Window, gifted to the church by its congregation to mark the

Mannau Stone, Clackmannan

coronation of Elizabeth II in 1953. The Queen visited the church specially to view it in 1997, so it seems that the loyalty of at least some Clackmannan people towards the monarchy in London is not in doubt any more.

Two miles north of the town is the **Gartmorn Dam Country Park**. It is centred on the 170-acre Gartmorn Dam, the oldest man-made reservoir in Scotland. It was constructed in the early 1700s by John Erskine, 6th Earl of Mar, to power the pumps which pumped water out of his coal mines at nearby Sauchie. Now a nature reserve, the park is popular with walkers and nature lovers, and the reservoir itself is stocked with brown trout.

AROUND CLACKMANNAN

TILLICOULTRY

5 miles N of Clackmannan on the A91

Tillicoultry is one of the "hillfoot villages" which relied on water tumbling down from the Ochils to power the mills in which most people were employed. Behind it is the picturesque **Tillicoultry Glen**, whose waters once powered eight mills in the town.

An old story says that the town got its unusual name from a Highlander who was driving some cattle along a road where the town now stands. He stopped at a stream to allow the cattle to drink. However, none of the cattle did so, and he exclaimed, "there's tiel a coo try", meaning "devil a cow is

thirsty!" However, a more prosaic explanation of the name is that it comes from the Gaelic, and means "hill in the back land".

DOLLAR

6 miles NE of Clackmannan on the A91

Just above the town, the spectacular ravine of Dollar Glen is dominated by the imposing bulk of **Castle Campbell** (National Trust for Scotland), a 15th century fortress that offers some stunning views from its parapet walk. It used to be, and locally still is, known as Castle Gloom. Visiting the town in the 1920s, the travel writer HV Morton was told "that in ancient times, the castle was called Castle Gloom (from the Gaelic Gloume), beside the waters of Griff (or Grief), in the Glen of Care, in the village of Dollar, or Dolour, surely the most miserable addresses on earth". Morton could have added that, for good measure, one of the mountain streams rushing down to the River Devon is called the Burn of Sorrow, completing a clutch of lugubrious names that seem totally inappropriate for such a superbly scenic corner of Clackmannanshire.

Within an old woollen mill now called Castle Campbell Hall in Dollar is the small **Dollar Museum**, which has displays on the history of the village and on the Devon Valley railway.

ALLOA

3 miles NW of Clackmannan on the A907

With a population of about 15,000, Alloa is the largest town in Scotland's smallest county. Though

Dollar is perhaps best known as the home of Dollar Academy. This private school (the equivalent of an English public school) was founded in the early 19th century thanks to a bequest by Captain John McNabb, a local herd boy born in 1732 who amassed a fortune in London as a merchant before his death in 1802. Eighteen years later the academy had been built, though if he came back today he might be puzzled to see it. He had intended it to be a school for the children of the poor in Dollar parish. The elegant, colonnaded building was designed by the eminent architect William Playfair, and was opened in 1819. In the 1930s McNabb's coffin was rediscovered in a London crypt. The remains were cremated, and the ashes now rest in a niche above the bronze doors of the school.

169

69 ALLOA TOWER

Alloa

Alloa Tower, the largest surviving keep in Scotland, dating from the 14th century.

 see page 391

an inland town, it sits on the River Forth at a point where it is still tidal. It was traditionally an engineering, brewing and glass-making town, though today these industries are less important than they once were.

St Mungo's Parish Church dates from 1817, though it incorporates the 17th century tower of an earlier church. **Alloa Tower** (National Trust for Scotland) dates from the 14th century and is all that is left of the ancestral home of the Erskines, one of the most important families in Scotland. They eventually became the Earls of Mar and as such were (and still are as the Earls of Mar and Kellie) Hereditary Keepers of Stirling Castle. The tower was built for Alexander Erskine, the 3rd Lord Erskine, in the late 1400s, and remodelled by the 6th Earl of Mar in the 18th century. It has the original oak roof beams, medieval vaulting and a dungeon.

The Erskines were custodians of Mary Stuart during her infancy, and she lived in the tower for a time. An old story says that when Mary gave birth to James VI in Edinburgh Castle in 1566, the baby was stillborn, and the Earl of Mar's infant son was substituted. Certainly, while still a boy, James stayed here, as did his mother.

The 6th Earl was an ardent Jacobite, and after the 1715 Uprising he was sent into exile. The story of the Erskines is told within the tower and the present Earl has loaned a superb collection of

paintings, including works by Raeburn and Kneller.

Alloa Museum and Gallery, in the Speirs Centre in Primrose Street, has exhibits tracing the history of the town.

TULLIBODY

5 miles NW of Clackmannan on the B9140

Legend says that Tullibody was founded by King Kenneth McAlpine, the first king of Scots, who united the kingdoms of Dalriada and the Picts in AD 843. He called it "Tirlbothy", meaning the "oath of the crofts", as he and his followers made an oath there that they would not lay down their arms until their enemies or themselves were killed.

Tullibody Auld Brig, which spans the River Devon, was built about 1535 by James Spittal, tailor to the royal family. In January 1560 the easternmost arch of the bridge was dismantled by Kirkcaldy of Grange to impede a French army which was in Scotland in support of Mary of Guise, mother of Mary Stuart and widow of James V. However, the French army dismantled the roof of **Tullibody Auld Kirk**, which dated from the early 1500s, and made a new bridge.

ALVA

5 miles NW of Clackmannan on the A91

Alva sits at the foot of the Ochils and is one of the "hillfoot villages" where weaving and spinning were the main industries. Its name means "rocky plain", as does that of its near neighbour Alloa. To the northeast is the Ochil Hills' highest peak, the 2363 feet Ben Cleuch. At the **Mill Trail Visitor Centre**, housed in the former Glentana Mill building of 1887, there are displays and exhibits that explain what life was like in mill factories over the last 150 years. There is also a shop and a café. **The Mill Trail** itself is a signposted route taking you to many mills with retail outlets. **The Ochil Hills Woodland Park** has attractive walks and a visitor centre. It is centred on what were the grounds of the long gone Alva House.

Alva Glen, also called the "Silver Glen", is very picturesque. Silver was once mined here in the 18th century, and **St Serf's Parish Church**, which dates from 1815, has some communion vessels made from local silver. It was the Erskine family that mined the silver, and according to them it was a hit or miss affair. A story is told of one member of the family, Sir John Erskine, showing two of the mines to a friend. "Out of that hole there I earned £50,000," he told him. "And in that hole there I lost it all again."

BLAIRLOGIE

6 miles NW of Clackmannan on the A91

Blairlogie is possibly the most beautiful of the "hillfoot villages", and was the first conservation village in Scotland. It sits in the shadow of the 1373 feet **Dumyat** which has the remains of a hilltop fort on its summit. The name derives from Dun Maetae, meaning the fort of the Maetae, a Pictish tribe. At the summit there are memorials to the Argyll and Sutherland Highlanders and superb views as far as Edinburgh.

MENSTRIE

6 miles NW of Clackmannan on the A91

Sir William Alexander, 1st Earl of Stirling, was born in Menstrie Castle in 1567. He was the founder of Nova Scotia, Scotland's only real colony in North America. The only part of the castle open to the public is the Nova Scotia Commemoration Room which has displays about the former colony. There are also the armorial bearings of the Nova Scotia baronetcies created in Scotland at the beginning of the 17th century. The baronetcies had nothing to do with chivalry or valour, but all to do with money as they were offered for sale at 3000 Scots merks each. In 1621, Sir William persuaded James VI to create the baronetcies, and when James realised how much money he could make from it, he readily agreed. In 1624, while at Windsor, he began the money making scheme. A year later he was dead but his son Charles I, not unnaturally, continued the practice. By the end of 1625 the first 22 titles had been conferred. Even today there are 109 titles still in existence. Sir William died penniless in London in 1644, and now lies buried in the Church of the Holy Rood in Stirling.

Menstrie Castle itself was built in the late 16th century and was a stronghold of Clan McAllister, a family that changed its name to Alexander as it adopted English

70 THE GRAEME HOTEL

Falkirk

The Graeme Hotel offers 14 extensively refurbished bedrooms of which 9 are en-suite and 5 with fully equipped bathrooms with shower or bath adjacent to rooms

 see page 390

•

Falkirk, like Stirling, is located in an important part of Scotland. Here the country narrows, with the Firth of Forth to the east and the Campsie and Kilsyth Hills to the west. This meant that any army trying to march north from the Lowlands or south from the Highlands had to pass close to the town. For that reason, there have been two battles fought at Falkirk. One was in 1298, when William Wallace and his Scottish army were defeated by the English army of Edward I.

•

customs. It gradually fell into a state of disrepair, but was refurbished in the 1950s.

FALKIRK

Falkirk is Stirlingshire's largest town, and sits at an important point on the road from Edinburgh to Stirling. Nearby Stenhousemuir was once the meeting place of various drove roads coming down from the Highlands. Here great herds of cattle were kept before being sold at "trysts" and taken further south to the markets of Northern England. It has been estimated that more than 24,000 head of cattle were sold annually at the three trysts held each year.

The second Battle of Falkirk was fought in 1746, when a Jacobite army defeated a Hanoverian army led by Lieutenant General Henry Hawley. After the defeat, Hawley was replaced by the notorious Duke of Cumberland.

The name of the town means the "kirk of mottled stone", a reference to its first stone built medieval church. The present **Old Parish Church** dates from 1810, and incorporates fragments of an earlier church. Its tower dates from 1734.

The **Town Steeple** was built in 1814, and was designed by the famous architect David Hamilton. It replaced an earlier building, which dated from the 17th century, and has traditionally been a meeting place for the people of the town. In 1927 the upper portion of the steeple was struck by lightning and

The Falkirk Wheel

had to be rebuilt.

Near Falkirk the two great Lowland canals - the Forth and Clyde and the Union Canal - meet. Thanks to the £84.5 million Millennium Link Project, they have recently been restored, and the magnificent new 120-feet high **Falkirk Wheel** at Rough Castle, which has become a tourist attraction in its own right, carries boats between one canal and the other (which are on different levels), within water filled "gondolas". It is the world's first (and as yet only) rotating lift for boats. It replaced a series of locks built in the early 19th century but which had been abandoned as the canals fell into disuse.

The town sits on the line of the Antonine Wall, a massive turf wall on a stone base built on the orders of the Roman emperor Antoninus Pius just after AD 138 in a doomed attempt to restrain the rebellious Picts. It stretched some 38 miles from the Firth of Clyde at Bowling to the Firth of Forth west of Bo'ness. **Rough Castle** (National Trust for Scotland) five miles from the town, is one of the best preserved of the wall's fortifications. Parts of the wall can be seen in the town's Callendar Park, in which you will also find **Callendar House**. This magnificent building has played host to many great historical figures over the centuries, amongst them Mary Queen of Scots, Oliver Cromwell and Bonnie Prince Charlie. There has been a house on this site since the 1300s but the present building, modelled on a

French château, was completed in the 1840s. It has now been restored by the local council as a heritage centre and museum, with a working Georgian kitchen, printer's and clockmaker's workrooms and a general store. In the ornate Victorian library is an extensive archive of books, documents and photographs on the history of the area, and the Major William Forbes Falkirk exhibition traces the history of the town. The **Park Gallery**, which runs a series of art exhibitions and workshop activities, is also located in Callendar Park.

AROUND FALKIRK

AIRTH

5 miles N of Falkirk on the A905

A huge royal dockyard founded by James IV once stood close to this small village. Now it is visited mainly because of one of the most unusual buildings in Scotland - **The Pineapple** (National Trust for Scotland) in Dunmore Park. It is a summerhouse, built in 1761, and on top of it is a huge, 45-feet high pineapple made of stone. The house is heated using an early form of central heating, as passages and cavities within the stone walls carry hot air through them. Now owned by the Landmark Trust, The Pineapple can be rented as a holiday home. Also at Dunmore are 16 acres of gardens.

Parts of the nearby **Airth Castle** (now a hotel and spa) date from the 14th century. An earlier castle stood on the site and it was here that William Wallace's uncle, a

71 THE PLOUGH HOTEL

Falkirk

The Plough Hotel offers 7 standard bedrooms which offer sky tv, tea & coffee making facilities, iron, shower cubical and wash hand basin.

see page 390

72 THE RED LION HOTEL

Larbert

The Red Lion Hotel offers14 comfortable, elegant and relaxed en-suite accommodation for those who require to stay in the area for either business or pleasure.

see page 390

Centred on the village of Bonnybridge, two miles west of Falkirk, is the Bonnybridge Triangle, so called because there have been more sightings of UFOs and unexplained phenomena in this area than anywhere else in the UK. It all started in 1992 when a cross shaped cluster of lights was seen hovering above a road. The sightings have continued up until the present day with mysterious football-sized lights, delta shaped craft and even spaceships with opening doors being recorded.

Zetland Park is the Grangemouth's main open area, and offers putting, crazy golf, an adventure playground, a boating pond and tennis courts.

priest, was held prisoner by the English before Wallace rescued him. The castle frontage as seen today dates from 1810, and was designed by David Hamilton. Close to the castle are the ruins of a 16th century church.

GRANGEMOUTH

3 miles E of Falkirk on the A904

Grangemouth is a modern town and the centre of Scotland's petrochemical industry. It was one of the country's first planned towns, having been established by Sir Laurence Dundas in the late 18th century to be the eastern terminus of the Forth and Clyde Canal. His son Thomas continued the work.

On Bo'ness Road is the **Grangemouth Museum**, which traces the history of the town up to the present day. The **Jupiter Urban Wildlife Garden** is off Wood Street, and was established in 1990 by Zeneca (formerly ICI) and the Scottish Wildlife Trust on a piece of land that was once a railway marshalling yard. Surrounded by industrial buildings and smokestacks, this oasis of green shows how derelict industrial land can be cleaned up and reclaimed for nature. It has four ponds, an area of scrub birch known as The Wilderness, a wildlife plant nursery and a formal wildlife garden, as well as meadows, marshland and reed beds.

STIRLING

Stirling is one of the most atmospheric of Scottish towns. Its imposing **Castle** (Historic Scotland) gives the appearance of growing naturally from the 250 feet high crag on which it stands. Long before the present castle was built, Stirling's strategic importance was recognised since it commands a "bottleneck" between southern and northern Scotland. Iron Age warriors established a garrison here; under the Stuart kings the fortification evolved over the years to become both a castle and royal residence. James III was the first of the Scottish kings to take an interest in its architecture, and built the **Great Hall** as a meeting place of the Scottish parliament and for great ceremonial occasions. James IV then began building a new palace in the Renaissance style, with his son James V finishing the work. In 1594, James VI had the Chapel Royal built, and these three buildings represent the most important architectural elements in the castle.

In recent years extensive restoration has been carried out at the castle and James IV's magnificent 125 feet long Great Hall now looks just as it would have been when it was completed in 1504, complete with the impressive King's Gold outer rendering which makes it visible for miles around.

A curious tale is told of Stirling Castle. It concerns James IV and John Damien, the Abbot of Tongland in Kirkcudbrightshire, who earned the nickname of the Frenzied Friar of Tongland. He was an Italian, and a learned man who spent a lot of time at court. In 1507 he convinced James IV that man could fly, and to prove it, he told him that he would jump from the walls of the castle and soar like a bird.

A date was set for the flight to take place, and a bemused James IV and his court assembled on the battlements. Meanwhile, Abbot Damien had told his servants to amass a large collection of feathers from flying birds and construct a large pair of wings from them. However, his servants could not collect enough feathers of the right kind in time, so incorporated some chicken feathers as well. The abbot duly presented himself on the battlements of the castle with the wings strapped to his back and wrists. Damien stood on the battlements, made a short speech, and began flapping his wings. He then jumped - and fell like a stone, landing in the castle midden, on which more than the castle's kitchen scraps were deposited. His fall couldn't have been that far, as all he succeeded in doing was breaking a leg. When he later discovered that his servants had incorporated chicken feathers in the wings, he blamed this for the failure of his flight. The court poet William Dunbar was present at this attempt at the world's first manned flight and wrote some verses about it.

The **Church of the Holy Rude** on St John Street is Stirling's parish church. The word "rude" in this context means "cross", and is also found in Holyrood Abbey in Edinburgh. It dates from the 15th century and was built at the command of James IV who, tradition says, worked alongside the masons during its construction. It is one of the finest medieval churches in Scotland and still has its original oak roof. Within the church, in 1567, the infant James VI was crowned king of Scotland in a Protestant ceremony at which John Knox preached a sermon. His mother, Mary Stuart, was unable to attend as she was being held prisoner in Loch Leven Castle. What is not generally known is that James (who later became James VI and I of Great Britain) had been christened Charles. James was chosen as his "royal" name to continue the tradition of having a "James" on the Scottish throne.

It is one of only two still functioning churches in Great Britain to have witnessed a coronation, the other one being Westminster Abbey. From just after the reformation until the 1930s a wall divided the church in two, with two independent congregations worshipping at the same time.

The kirkyard was once the castle's tilting ground, where great tournaments of jousting and horsemanship were held. One of the monuments in the kirkyard is the Star Pyramid which commemorates the Covenanting martyrs of the 17th century. Lady's Rock is next to the kirkyard and was where the ladies of the court sat and watched staged events take place on the fields below. Close by is **Cowane's Hospital**, on which work started in 1637 and finished

Stirling is Scotland's newest city, as in 2002 it was granted city status as part of the Queen's Golden Jubilee celebrations. A good introduction to the town is to follow the Back Walk, a scenic pathway around the castle and Old Town that takes in the medieval Church of the Holy Rude, the castle and Stirling Old Jail.

175

One bloody association with Scotland's past is to be found at the Beheading Stone, well to the north of the castle. It was here, in 1425, that James I took his revenge on Murdoch, Duke of Albany, his two sons and the Earl of Lennox, his father-in-law, by having them beheaded. The duke's father had controlled Scotland for 18 years while the English held James captive, and he and his cronies had brought the country to its knees by their greed and cruelty. Their lands were forfeited to the crown, and James gave them to his supporters.

in 1649. It is named after John Cowane, a Stirling merchant who bequeathed funds to establish an almshouse for 12 unsuccessful merchants, or "decayed guildsmen" of the town. It was later used as a school and an epidemic hospital and is now a venue for ceilidhs and concerts. Above the door is a statue of Cowane himself.

The King's Knot sits beneath the castle and church, on the south side, and is all that is left of a formal garden, originally planted in the 1490s, though the knot itself is much older - possibly early 14th century. It is in the shape of an octagonal stepped mound nine feet high, now grassed over.

The **Old Town Jail**, down the slope in the city itself, was opened in 1847 to take the prisoners that were formerly held in the Tolbooth. From 1888 until 1935 it was used as a military prison. Now it has been reopened as a tourist attraction and shows what life was like for prisoners and wardens in the 19th century. You'll also meet a

character called Jock Rankin, who was the town's hangman. If, during your visit, a prisoner should try to escape, you should remain calm and follow the advice of the warden!

Also in the town centre, in front of the Corn Exchange, is a memorial to another Scottish folk hero, Rob Roy Macgregor. The **Rob Roy Statue** faithfully depicts his famously long arms.

The intriguingly named **Mar's Wark** is in Broad Street, close to the parish church. It was the "wark" (meaning work, or building) of the sixth Earl of Mar, Regent of Scotland and guardian of the young James VI. In 1570 he began building a new Renaissance palace that would reflect his status and power; Mar's Wark was the result. In the 18th century it became a military hospital, but soon after fell into disrepair. Now all that is left of the building is a façade along the street front.

On the opposite side of the street is **Argyll's Lodging** (Historic Scotland), a charming Renaissance-style mansion built about 1630 by Sir William Alexander, the founder of Nova Scotia. It was further enlarged by the 9th Earl of Argyll in the 1670s, and is possibly the best example of a 17th century town house in Scotland. Most of the rooms have been restored, showing what life would have been like when the earl lived there.

Stirling is one of the few Scottish towns with parts of its old Town Wall still standing. The wall was built in 1547 as a defence

Argyll's Lodging, Stirling

176

against the English armies of Henry VIII when he was trying to force a marriage between his son Edward and Mary Stuart (a time known as the "Rough Wooing"). The remaining parts stretch along the south side of the town, from near the Old Town Jail to Dumbarton Road.

Incorporated into the Thistle Shopping Mall is the 16th century **Bastion**, one of the wall's defensive towers. It contains a vaulted guardroom above an underground chamber, and has a small display about the history of the town. There was no wall to the north of the town, as attacks never came from that quarter, though people who lived there were supposed to build thick, high walls at the backs of their gardens as a defence, and keep them in good repair.

The **Tolbooth** sits at the heart of the old town. It was built in 1704 by Sir William Bruce and was where the town council met and looked after the affairs of the burgh. A courthouse and jail were added in 1809. It is now used as a venue for concerts and rehearsals. The **Mercat Cross**, close to the Tolbooth, has the figure of a unicorn on top, and this is known locally as the "puggy".

Two famous battles have been fought near Stirling. The Battle of Stirling Bridge took place in 1297, when William Wallace defeated an English army under John de Warenne, Earl of Surrey, and Hugh de Cressingham. Wallace, who was a guerrilla fighter and a master tactician, used the bridge to divide

the English forces - leaving one contingent on each bank - before launching his attack. It was a major setback for Edward I, who more or less had to start his conquest of the country all over again. The bridge in those days was a wooden one; the present **Old Stirling Bridge**, which stands upstream from the original, was built in the late 15th century. Up until 1831, when Stirling New Bridge was built downstream, this was the lowest crossing point of the Forth, which made it one of the most important bridges in Scotland.

The other famous battle was the **Battle of Bannockburn**, fought to the south of the town in 1314. The actual site of the battle still arouses much debate, but there is no doubt that it was a defining moment in Scotland's history. Edward I had died by this time, and his son Edward II, a much weaker man, was in charge of the English army which was trying to reach Stirling Castle to relieve it. Robert the Bruce, one of Scotland's great

Scotland's other national hero, of course, is William Wallace, and on Abbey Craig, to the east of the town and across the river, is the National Wallace Monument. This spectacular tower is 220 feet high, with 246 steps, and from the top you get a panoramic view that takes in the Forth Bridges to the east and Ben Lomond to the west. Here you can learn about the Battle of Stirling Bridge, plus see a re-creation of Wallace's travesty of a trial at Westminster when he was charged with treason, even though he wasn't English. You can even gaze on his great two-handed broadsword, which is five feet six inches long.

Bannockburn Heritage Centre, Stirling

Bridge of Allan Parish Church (formerly known as Holy Trinity Church) was built in 1860. Inside it are some furnishings designed by the Glasgow architect Charles Rennie Mackintosh.

73 ALLANWATER CAFÉ

Bridge of Allan

A bright and spacious café offering a good selection of freshly made dishes and a variety of ice-creams.

see page 391

heroes, achieved a stunning victory - one that secured the country's status as an independent nation. **The Bannockburn Heritage Centre** (National Trust for Scotland), on the A872 two miles south of the town, commemorates this victory. There are exhibitions, an audiovisual display and a huge statue of Bruce on his warhorse.

The scant ruins of **Cambuskenneth Abbey** (Historic Scotland) also lie on the eastern banks of the Forth. David I founded it as an abbey in 1140 for Augustinian monks and in 1326 Robert the Bruce held an important parliament here. It suffered greatly at the hands of various English armies, and by 1378 was in ruins. It was rebuilt in the early 15th century through royal patronage. The detached bell tower of the abbey is more or less complete, though only the foundations of the rest of the buildings survive. James III and his queen, Margaret of Denmark, are buried before the high altar, and a monument marks the spot. In 1488 the king had been assassinated near Bannockburn after his defeat at the Battle of Sauchieburn, where his son, the future James IV, was on the opposing side.

The **Smith Art Gallery and Museum** in Albert Place chronicles Stirling's long history through displays, exhibitions and artefacts. It has a fine collection of paintings, including works by Naysmith and Sir George Harvey who painted great works depicting Scottish history. One of the more unusual exhibits in the museum is the world's oldest football, found in Mary Stuart's bedchamber in Stirling Castle and dated to the late 16th century.

AROUND STIRLING

BRIDGE OF ALLAN

3 miles N of Stirling off the M9

Bridge of Allan, which is almost a suburb of Stirling nowadays, was once a small spa town and watering place with a pump room and baths. Now it is chiefly known for being the home of Stirling University, based in the grounds of the Airthrie Estate, with its picturesque loch. In 1617, James VI wanted to establish a college or university at Stirling, but it was not until 1967 that his wish came true, when the first 180 students enrolled. Now it has more than 9000 students and is one of the premier universities in Scotland.

Airthrie was owned by Sir Robert Abercrombie who was instrumental in setting up the village as a spa, having had the waters of a local spring analysed. In 1844 the estate was bought by a Major Henderson, who developed the town even further. The **Fountain of Nineveh** (now dry) on Fountain Road was built by him in 1851 to commemorate the archaeological excavations going on at Nineveh at the time. Though healing waters are no longer taken, other, equally interesting, liquids are most certainly consumed. The Bridge of Allan Brewery Company, a microbrewery in Queens Lane, has tours showing how beer is produced.

DUNBLANE

5 miles N of Stirling off the M9

Before local government reorganisation, Dunblane (and most of the area north and north west of Stirling) was in Perthshire. This small town, or more properly city, is known for two things. The first is the horrific shooting that took place here in 1996 when 16 schoolchildren and their teacher were killed in a local school. The **Dunblane Memorial Garden** in Dunblane Cemetery was built in 1998 to commemorate the victims.

The second is the **Cathedral Church of St Blane and St Lawrence** (Historic Scotland) which stands on the site of a Celtic monastery founded by St Blane in about AD 602. He had been born on Bute where he had founded a great monastery. What you see nowadays dates mainly from the 13th century and was built by Bishop Clement who was elected bishop in 1233. He decided that the only part of the previous 12th century Norman church which would be left standing was the tower to which two extra storeys were added in the 15th century. It is not a cathedral in the style of Elgin, St Andrews or any of the great English establishments. Rather it is an intimate church with no side aisles or transepts.

In the 16th century, with the arrival of Protestantism, only the choir was used for worship, and the nave fell into decay, with the roof collapsing about 1600. The city also declined and became a small weaving centre. In 1898, the whole building was restored under the direction of Sir Rowand Anderson, a noted Scottish architect. In 1914, Sir Robert Lorimer did further work on the choir with the present choir stalls - one of the glories of the cathedral - being designed by him.

Within the **Dean's House**, built in 1624 by Dean James Pearson during the time the Church of Scotland was episcopal, is a small museum which explains the history of the city and its cathedral. **Bishop Leighton's Library** is housed in a building that dates from 1681. There are more than 4000 books, some of them priceless.

With the coming of the railways, Dunblane became a popular place in which to holiday and the city regained some of its former prosperity. Dunblane Hydro was built in 1875 to cash in on the tourist boom and it is still a luxury hotel to this day.

About three miles north east of the town is the site of the **Battle of Sheriffmuir**, one of the deciding battles in the 1715 Jacobite Uprising. It took place on 13th November 1715 and was an unusual battle in that the outcome was a stalemate.

FINTRY

14 miles SW of Stirling on the B818

This charming village sits on the northern slopes of the Campsies, that great range of hills that forms a northern backdrop for the city of Glasgow. There are some fine walks on the hills, which are popular with Glaswegians at

74 CARRONBRIDGE HOTEL

Carron Bridge

A former coaching inn, transformed into a small cosy family run hotel

see page 392

Fintry Parish Church dates from 1823 and is notable for its unusual method of building. The former church was too small for the growing congregation, so the present church was built around it. Only when it was complete was the earlier church, which had continued in use, demolished.

75 THE HAWTHORNS

Loch Lomond

A traditional Scottish B&B located in a picturesque village close to Loch Lomond

see page 391

weekends and holidays. The **Loup of Fintry**, east of the village, is an impressive waterfall caused by the Endrick Water tumbling down a 94-feet high slope.

Culcreuch Castle (now a country house hotel) is a 700-year-old tower house within a large estate that was once owned by the Galbraiths. The last Galbraith chieftain to live there was Robert Galbraith, who fled to Ireland in 1630 after killing a guest in his home. Carron Valley Reservoir, to the east of the village, was built in the 19th century to supply Falkirk and Grangemouth with a water supply. It now offers trout fishing (permit required).

KILLEARN

19 miles SW of Stirling on the A875

Killearn Glen is a picturesque area of deciduous woodland more than 250 years old with narrow footpaths. The village was the birthplace in 1506 of George Buchanan, Protestant reformer and tutor to James VI who greatly admired him. He was a noted linguist, and could speak Latin, Greek, French, Gaelic, Spanish, Hebrew and Italian. He also wrote plays, mostly in Latin, and now lies buried in the Greyfriars kirkyard in Edinburgh. The Buchanan Monument, an obelisk erected in the centre of the village in 1788, commemorates him.

DRYMEN

23 miles SW of Stirling off the A811

During World War II, **Buchanan Castle** was a military hospital. Its most famous patient was Rudolph Hess, Hitler's deputy, who was kept here after he parachuted into Scotland in 1941 on a secret mission to see the Duke of Hamilton. The castle itself dates from 1855 and was built by the 4th Duke of Montrose after the former castle was destroyed by fire three years previously. The roof was removed in 1955 to prevent the paying of taxes on it, and it is now partly ruinous, though it can be viewed from the outside.

Drymen is on the West Highland Way, the footpath that stretches from Milngavie on the outskirts of Glasgow to Fort William. It is also the gateway to the eastern, and less busy, shores of Loch Lomond, which lie three miles away. The small village of Balmaha (also on the West Highland Way) sits on the shore of the loch, and should be visited for the wonderful views it gives of Britain's largest sheet of water. Balfron, four miles east of Drymen, is an attractive village with a parish church that dates from 1832. Alexander "Greek" Thomson, the noted architect whose work can be seen in Glasgow, was born in Balfron in 1817.

KIPPEN

9 miles W of Stirling on the B822

This attractive little village sits to the south of that expanse of flat land called Flanders Moss. At one time it was a peat bog, then, in the 18th century, Lord Kames, a law lord and agricultural improver, began removing the peat to get at the fertile bands of clay beneath.

There are still a few remnants of the original peat bog left; these have been declared Areas of Special Scientific Interest.

Kippen Parish Church, built in 1825, is one of the finest post-Reformation churches in Scotland. The Carmichael Memorial Window was installed in 1985, and is the work of John K. Clarke. The ruins of the old church, built in 1691, still stand, surrounded by an old graveyard.

ARNPRIOR

11 miles W of Stirling on the A811

In the early 16th century, a man called John Buchanan, who had styled himself the **King of Kippen**, lived in this small village. One day a party of hunters was returning to Stirling Castle with some venison for James V's court, and passed John's castle. John captured them and confiscated the venison. The hunters told him that the meat was for the king, but John merely replied that if James was King of Scotland, then he was King of Kippen.

The king was duly informed of this, and instead of being angry, found the incident amusing. He and some courtiers rode out from Stirling one day to pay the King of Kippen a visit. He approached John's castle, and demanded that he be allowed to enter. His demand was refused by a guard, who told the king that John Buchanan was at dinner, and could not be disturbed.

James V had a habit of dressing up in peasant's clothes and slipping out of his palaces alone to meet and speak to his subjects and gauge their opinions of their king and country. When he did this, he assumed the guise of the "Guidman of Ballengeich" (meaning "The Goodman of Ballengeich"), Ballengeich being the name of a pathway he always took down from Stirling Castle when in disguise.

He therefore told the guard to tell Buchanan that the Guidman of Ballengeich was at his door, and he humbly requested an audience with the King of Kippen. When informed, John Buchanan knew who his visitor was, and rushed out in trepidation. But James greeted him cordially, and laughed at the escapade of the venison. Buchanan invited the king into his home to dine, and the king agreed. Soon the company was merry, and the king told Buchanan that he could take as much venison as he liked from the royal hunters that passed his door. He also invited the King of Kippen to visit his brother monarch at Stirling any time he liked. The "king" was later killed at the Battle of Pinkie in 1547.

To the east of Kippen, and off the A811, is the village of Gargunnock, with a picturesque parish church built in 1774.

PORT OF MENTEITH

14 miles W of Stirling on the B8034

This little village sits on the shore of the **Lake of Menteith**, sometimes erroneously called the only lake (as opposed to loch) in Scotland. However, there are several bodies of water in Scotland

In 1891, a man called Duncan Buchanan planted a vineyard in Kippen within a glasshouse, and one of the vines, later to be called the Kippen Vine, grew to be the largest in the world. When fully grown, it had an annual crop of more than 2000 bunches of table grapes, and in 1958 created a record by producing 2956 bunches. By this time it was enormous, covering an area of 5000 square feet and stretching for 300 feet within four large greenhouses. It became a tourist attraction, and people came from all over Scotland and abroad to see it. But alas, the vinery closed down in 1964 (when it could also boast the second and third largest vines in the world) and the Kippen Vine was unceremoniously chopped down by Selby Buchanan, Duncan's son. The land was later used for housing.

On the island of Inchmahome in the Lake of Menteith are the beautiful ruins of Inchmahome Priory (Historic Scotland), within which Mary Stuart was detained after the Battle of Pinkie in 1547. Within the re-roofed chapter house are many carved effigies and tombstones. The priory was founded in 1238 by Walter Comyn, Earl of Menteith, for Augustinian canons. In 1306, 1308 and 1310, Robert the Bruce visited the place, as the then prior had sworn allegiance to Edward I of England. No doubt Robert was pressurising him to change his mind. The priory can be reached by a small ferry from the jetty at Port of Menteith.

- some natural, some man made - which are referred to as lakes.

But there is no doubting that the Lake of Menteith is one of Scotland's most beautiful stretches of water. It is only a mile wide by a mile-and-a-half long, with low hills sloping down towards it northern shores. Its name is probably a corruption of Laigh (meaning a flat piece of land) as the land to the south of the lake, Flanders Moss, is flat.

ABERFOYLE

18 miles W of Stirling on the A821

Aberfoyle has been called the Gateway to the Trossachs and sits beside the River Forth after it emerges from beautiful Loch Ard. The six-mile long Duke's Road (named after a Duke of Montrose who laid out the road in 1886) goes north from the village to the Trossachs proper and has some good views over Lochs Drunkie and Venachar.

Standing close to the village's main road is a gnarled oak known as the **Poker Tree**. In Scott's novel *Rob Roy*, Baillie Nicol Jarvie, a Glasgow magistrate and cousin of Rob Roy, gets involved in a fight with a Highlander at a local inn, and draws the red hot poker from the fire to defend himself. A poker was later hung from the tree to remind people of the escapade.

The **Scottish Wool Centre** is situated within the village and tells the story of Scottish wool. You can visit the Spinner's Cottage and have a go at spinning wool into yarn. There are also occasional visits

from local shepherds who put on sheepdog demonstrations. There is also a shop where woollen items - from coats to blankets - can be bought. The Wool Centre is also the home of the **Scottish Sheepdog School** where you can watch local shepherds putting the dogs through their paces as they round up sheep and Indian Runner Ducks.

It was in Aberfoyle that the famous and mysterious disappearance of the **Rev. Robert Kirk**, minister at Aberfoyle Parish Church, took place. He was born in 1644, and had an abiding interest in fairies, even writing a book called *The Secret Commonwealth of Elves, Fauns and Fairies*.

Legend states that the fairies were none too pleased that Robert had revealed their secrets. In 1692, while walking on Doon Hill, well known in the area as one of the entrances to the fairy realm, Robert disappeared. People claimed that he had been taken to the fairy kingdom, and that one day he would come back, looking no older than he did when he disappeared. To this day, he has not returned.

Another legend states that Robert's wife was given the chance of getting her husband back. He would appear, she was told, during Sunday service in the kirk, and she had to throw a knife at him, which should penetrate his flesh. Robert did appear during the service, but his wife could not bring herself to throw the knife, so he disappeared once more.

Robert Kirk was indeed a

minister in Aberfoyle in the 17th century, and he did indeed disappear one day while out walking. Did the fairies take him? Or was he the victim of a more earthly crime? No one will ever know - unless he turns up again to give his account of what happened!

BLAIR DRUMMOND

6 miles NW of Stirling on the A84

Blair Drummond Safari and Leisure Park is one of the most visited tourist attractions in Scotland. You can tour the 1500-acre park by car or coach, and see animals such as elephants, lions, zebras, giraffes, white rhino and ostriches in conditions that allow them plenty of freedom. You can take a boat trip round Chimp Island, watch the sea lion show or glide above the lake on the "Flying Fox".

Right next door to the Safari Park, **Briarlands Farm** promises a great day out for all the family. Attractions include Giant Jumping Pillows, a Straw Mountain, go-karting and an Amazing Maize Maze, Also on site are a tea room and gift shop.

DOUNE

7 miles NW of Stirling on the A84

The bridge across the River Teith in this picturesque village was built by **James Spittal,** tailor to James IV. Legend has it that he arrived at the ferry that once operated where the bridge now stands without any money, and the ferryman refused to take him across. So, out of spite, he

had the bridge built to deprive the ferryman of a livelihood.

Doune Castle (Historic Scotland) is one of the best preserved 14th century castles in Scotland, and was the seat of the Earls of Moray. It stands where the River Ardoch meets the Teith, and was originally built for Robert Stewart, Duke of Albany, son of Robert II and Regent of Scotland during the minority of James I. Later, James had the Duke's son executed for plotting against the crown, and the castle passed to him. Later the castle was acquired by Sir James Stewart, the first Lord Doune, and then by the Morays. It has two main towers connected by a Great Hall with a high wooden ceiling. In 1883 the 14th Earl of Moray restored the castle. It is visited each year by many fans of Monty Python as some of the scenes in *Monty Python and the Holy Grail* were filmed here.

The village itself gained its burgh charter in 1611, and originally stood close to the castle. In the early 1700s, however, the village and its 17th century **Mercat Cross** were moved to their present position. The village was at one time famous as a centre of pistol making. The industry was started in about 1646 by a man called Thomas Cadell. So accurate and well made were his guns that they soon became prized possessions. By the 18th century Cadell's descendants were all involved in making guns and began exporting them to the Continent. It is said that the first pistol fired in the

South of Aberfoyle, near the conservation village of Gartmore, is the Cunninghame Graham Memorial (National Trust for Scotland). Robert Cunninghame Graham of Ardoch (born Robert Bontine) was a Scottish author and politician who died in 1936. The squat, cairn-like monument contains stones from Argentina, Uruguay and Paraguay, countries where Graham had lived as a young man and about which he had written.

On the B824 between Doune and Dunblane is the Sir David Stirling Memorial Statue, commemorating the founder member of the Special Air Services (better known as the SAS) during World War II. The striking life-size figure stands atop a boulder facing a grand view across the Spean Valley.

76 BRIDGEND HOUSE HOTEL

Callander

Great pub food, real ales and en suite rooms in 15th century listed building beside the River Teith.

see page 393

American War of Independence was made in Doune.

Just north of the village, **Argaty Red Kites** is central Scotland's only red kite viewing station. More than 100 bird species have been spotted at this wildlife friendly farm. Advance booking is recommended.

DEANSTON

7 miles NW of Stirling on the B8032

Deanston is a village on the banks of the River Teith, built round the Adephi Cotton Mill, founded in 1785 and designed by Sir Richard Arkwright. It passed through several hands before finally closing in 1965. Now the mill houses the Deanston Distillery which makes a range of whiskies using the same water that once powered the weaving machines. It is not open to the public.

CALLANDER

13 miles NW of Stirling on the A84

This pleasant holiday town stands to the east of the Trossachs and has some wonderful walking country on its doorstep. It is home to the **Rob Roy and Trossachs Visitor Centre**, housed in a former church in Ancaster Square and, as the name suggests, tells the story of both the Trossachs and its most famous son, Rob Roy MacGregor. His real name was Robert MacGregor (1671-1734) and even today people still cannot agree on whether he was a crook, a freedom fighter or the Scottish Robin Hood (though you don't have to guess which opinion the Visitor Centre prefers).

The Duke of Montrose confiscated his lands in 1712, and he was imprisoned by the English in the 1720s. He was made famous by two books - Daniel Defoe's *Highland Rogue* and Sir Walter Scott's *Rob Roy*, as well as by the recent film starring Liam Neeson and Jessica Lange. An earlier film, *Rob Roy the Highland Rogue*, was made in 1953, starring Richard Todd and Glynis Johns.

There's no denying that the man was an outstanding leader who could read and write in English and Gaelic, and possessed a large library. It was Sir Walter Scott who described him behaving dishonourably at the Battle of Sheriffmuir when in fact he acquitted himself with courage and honour fighting for the Jacobites. At his funeral on New Year's Day

Ben Venue, Trossachs

184

1735, people came from all over Scotland to pay their respects.

Also in Callander is the **Hamilton Toy Museum**, five rooms of model cars, planes, dolls, teddy bears and such TV collectables as Thunderbird, Star Trek and Star Wars figures.

The **Kilmahog Woollen Mill,** to the west of the town, is more than 250 years old and still has its original water wheel. A shop sells a wide range of Tweed and woollen garments.

LOCH KATRINE

23 miles NW of Stirling close to the A821

There is no doubt that Loch Katrine is one of the most beautiful lochs in Scotland. It is surrounded by craggy hills which in autumn blaze with orange and gold. But the loch as you see it today has more to do with man than nature. In the mid-19th century, the loch became a huge reservoir for the city of Glasgow and the depth of the water was increased considerably. In 1859 Queen Victoria opened the new reservoir and 90 million gallons of water a day flowed towards Glasgow, more than 30 miles away.

The engineering that made this happen was well ahead of its time and consisted of tunnels and aqueducts that relied purely on gravity to carry the water towards the city. The engineering surrounding the loch was equally as spectacular. The water from Loch Arklet, high in the hills between Lochs Katrine and Lomond, used to flow west into Loch Lomond.

By the use of dams, this was changed so that it flowed east into Loch Katrine. The whole scheme was the largest of its kind in the world for many years, and even today, Glasgow still gets its water from Loch Katrine.

The loch's name comes from the early welsh "cethern", meaning "furious", a reference to the many mountain torrents found in the area. It was made famous by Sir Walter Scott who set his poem *The Lady of the Lake* here. And at Glengyle, at the western end of the loch, Rob Roy MacGregor was born. It is still a remote place and cannot be reached by car.

The steamer *Sir Walter Scott* has been sailing the waters of the loch from the beginning of the 20th century and it still does so today. It was built in Dumbarton, and people always wonder how it got from there to the loch, The answer is that it was transported by barge up the River Leven onto Loch Lomond, then dragged overland by horses from Inversnaid. When it reached Loch Katrine, the engines were fitted.

The steamship takes you from the pier at the east end of the loch towards Stronachlachar, six miles away. The small islet at Stronachlachan is known as the Factor's Island, and recalls one of Rob Roy's exploits. He captured the Duke of Montrose's factor, who was collecting rents in the area, and imprisoned him on the island. He then sent a ransom note to the duke, but there was no response. So Rob Roy calmly relieved the

77 THE LADE INN

Callendar

A family run business offering fantastic food and excellent service to create a wonderful Scottish experience.

see page 394

man of the £3000 he was carrying and sent him on his way.

This is the heart of the Trossachs (the name translates as "bristly" or "prickly"), and there are other equally as attractive lochs nearby. Loch Lubnaig, to the east, is the largest. Loch Venachar, Loch Achray and Loch Drunkie (which can only be reached by a footpath through the forest) are well worth visiting. At the southern end of Loch Lubnaig are the spectacular **Falls of Leny**.

BALQUHIDDER

*26 miles NW of Stirling
on a minor road off the A84*

This small village sits to the east of the picturesque Loch Voil. It lies in that area of Scotland known as

Breadalbane ("uplands of Alban", as Alban is the ancient name for Scotland) and in the heart of Clan MacGregor country.

In the kirkyard of the roofless kirk , the "Highland Rogue" himself, Rob Roy is buried alongside his wife and two of his sons. **Rob Roy MacGregor's Grave** is marked by a rough-hewn stone on which is carved a sword, a cross and a man with a dog. Despite a sometime violent career - at one time there was a Government bounty of £1000 on his head - Rob Roy died peacefully in his bed at Balquhidder in 1734 at what was then the ripe old age of 65. He had received a royal pardon some eight years earlier.

Loch Voil, Rob Roy country

LOCHEARNHEAD

27 miles NW of Stirling on the A84

This small, attractive village is at the western end of Loch Earn, and is a centre for such pursuits as sailing, fishing, water skiing and diving. Walkers too are happy here since there's a delightful circular walk, about 12 miles long, around the shore of the loch.

KILLIN

33 miles NW of Stirling on the A827

At the western end of Loch Tay, the Breaadalbane Mountains provide a dramatic backdrop to the picturesque little town of Killin where the River Dochart rushes through its centre, tumbling on its way down the foaming Falls of Dochart. Opposite the falls, housed in a former mill, is the **Breadalbane Folklore Centre** which gives an insight into life and legends of the area.

Three miles north on a minor road are the **Falls of Lochay** on the River Lochay, though care should be taken when approaching them. The **Moirlanich Longhouse** (National Trust for Scotland) on the Glen Lochay road dates from the 19th century and is a rare surviving example of a cruck-frame Scottish longhouse, where a family and their livestock lived under the one roof. In an adjacent shed is a display of working clothes found in the longhouse, along with displays which explain the building's

history and restoration.

The ruins of **Finlarig Castle**, which date from the late 16th century, are to the north of the village. The castle was once a Campbell stronghold and was built by Black Duncan, one of the most notorious members of the clan. Within its grounds are the remains of a beheading pit and a Campbell mausoleum built in 1829.

CRIANLARICH

42 miles NW of Stirling on the A82

The name of this small village comes from the Gaelic for "low pass", and sits on the southern edge of Breadalbane. Surrounding it is some marvellous walking and climbing country, with the West Highland Way passing close to the village. The twin peaks of Ben More (3843 feet) and Stobinian (3821 feet) are to the south east, while the picturesque **Falls of Falloch** (with a small car park close by) lie four miles to the southwest on the A82.

TYNDRUM

47 miles NW of Stirling on the A82

This little village has a population of no more than 100 people, and yet has two railway stations - one on the line from Glasgow to Oban and the other on the line from Glasgow to Fort William. It sits at the head of rugged Strath Fillan which snakes south towards Crianlarich; the West Highland Way follows its course.

Argyll

This huge area with a population less than that of the City of York attracts large numbers of visitors in the summer months but apart from a few honey-pot centres Argyll is wonderfully empty and peaceful. It sits on the country's western seaboard, where long sea lochs penetrate deep into the interior and mountains tumble down towards fertile glens. Oban is the undisputed holiday centre with excellent road and rail communications and a generous choice of regular car and passenger ferries serving the main islands of the Inner Hebrides, as well as seasonal day trips to many of the smaller islands. The town stands at the heart of what was the 5th century Kingdom of Lorn, supposedly founded by the legendary Irish Celt of that name. Lorn later formed part of the great Kingdom of Dalraida whose kings were inducted at Dunstaffnage Castle, just north of Oban, on the hallowed "Stone of Destiny", later known as the Stone of Scone. Another historic site that should be on any visitor's itinerary is Rothesay Castle on the Isle of bute. Built in the early 1200s, the castle is generally regarded as one of the finest medieval fortresses in the country.

The climate in this area is mild, thanks to the Gulf Stream, and the place has many fine gardens such as Ardkinglas, Crarae and Arduaine, some with palm trees and other species you would not expect to thrive so far north.

Man has lived in Argyll for centuries. Around Kilmartin there are cairns and standing stones built long before the ancient Egyptians built the pyramids. A museum in the village of Kilmartin itself records the history of the area, and explains the many cairns, standing stones, stone circles, graves and henges that abound in the area.

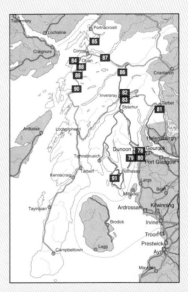

DUNOON

Dunoon is by far the largest town in Argyll with some 13,000 inhabitants. In the years following World War II, the town benefited greatly from the establishment of a US nuclear submarine base on nearby Holy Loch, and later suffered badly from the economic effects of the base's closure in 1992. But today Dunoon is once again a lively resort, well-known for the **Cowal Highland Gathering**, one of the largest in Scotland, where competitors take part in tossing the caber, throwing the hammer and other Scottish events. Held on the last Friday and Saturday of August, the event completely takes over the town with upwards of 150 bands, more than 2000 pipers and drummers, and 40,000 or more spectators.

On Castle Hill are the sparse remains of the 12th century **Dunoon Castle,** notorious as the setting for a grisly massacre in 1646 when the Marquis of Argyll had scores of his Lamont prisoners hanged from "a lively, fresh-growing ash tree" and their bodies tossed into a shallow communal grave. The grave was rediscovered in the 19th century during construction of a new road. A memorial marks the site. Forty years after that massacre, the castle was burnt down and it remained derelict until 1822 when James Ewing, Provost of Glasgow, cannibalised its stone to build Castle House, a castellated "marine villa" which is now used as council offices.

The upper floors of the house are occupied by the **Castle House Museum** which has an exhibition entitled "Dunoon and Cowal Past and Present". There are models, artefacts and photographs bringing the Dunoon of yesteryear to life. There are also furnished Victorian rooms and a shop.

At the foot of Castle Hill is an appealing **Statue of Highland Mary,** erected in 1896. Mary Campbell was a Dunoon-born lass who became one of Robert Burns' many lovers. It was an intense affair and, despite being already married. Burns became engaged to Mary. At that time he was obsessed with the idea of emigrating to the West Indies and poems such as *Will you go to the Indies, my Mary?* Make it clear that the poet's then-pregnant wife was not his preferred partner in the enterprise. Mary died at the age of 22, officially of a fever, but there has been persistent speculation that she dies giving birth to a stillborn baby.

Dunoon Grammar School merits a special mention since it is second only to Eton in the number of former pupils who became Members of Parliament, amongst them Ken Livingstone, Virginia Bottomley, Brian Wilson and the one-time leader of the Labour Party, John Smith.

Less than a mile to the north of the town, on the A885, the **Cowal Bird Garden** makes an ideal venue for a family outing. Set in some 10 acres of oak and birch woods, this award-winning attraction is home to a fascinating variety of exotic birds, amongst

•
Three miles north of Dunoon, on the A815, is Adam's Grave, the popular name for a 3500-year-old neolithic burial cairn, which still has two portals and a capstone intact at its entrance. At Sandbank, on the shores of the loch, is the two-mile long Ardnadam Heritage Trail, with a climb up to a viewpoint at Dunan.
•

78 THE SWALLOW CAFE

Dunoon

A popular café located on the main thoroughfare, with traditional home baking at its heart

see page 393

79 ABBOT'S BRAE HOTEL

Dunoon

A luxurious hotel surrounded by breathtaking scenery.

see page 395

189

80 BENMORE BOTANIC GARDEN

Benmore

Fantastic garden famous for its magnificent collections of trees and shrubs including some of the tallest trees in Britain

 see page 396

On a hillside just west of the Kilmun village is the Kilmun Arboretum, extending to 180 acres. First planted in 1930, it has a wide range of trees - some rare - from all over the world, and is maintained by the Forestry Commission, which does research work here. The Information Centre can provide you with copious details of the many forest walks throughout the Argyll Forest Park.

190

them macaws and parrots who, if they're feeling like it, may well croak back a "Hello!" in response to yours; brightly-hued budgerigars, karakiris from Australia, and many other species.

AROUND DUNOON

BENMORE

7 miles N of Dunoon off the A815

An outpost of Edinburgh's Royal Botanic Garden, **Benmore Botanic Garden** enjoys a magnificent mountainside setting on the Cowal Peninsula. This enchanting 120-acre garden boasts more than 300 species of rhododendron; Bhutanese and Chilean plantings and a spectacular avenue of Giant Redwoods. Within the Glen Massan Arboretum are some of the tallest trees in Scotland, including a Douglas fir more than 180 feet high (although there's an even loftier one near Cairndow which exceeds 200 feet). Within the garden there's also a café, a shop and a gallery that hosts various exhibitions and events. From the top of Benmore Hill there is a magnificent view across the Holy Loch to the Firth of Clyde and the Renfrewshire coast. **Puck's Glen** was once part of the Benmore Estate, but is now a delightful walk with great views and picnic areas.

To the north of Benmore is the seven mile long Loch Eck, with the A815 following its eastern shores towards Strachur on Loch Fyne. Near the head of the loch is Tom-a-Chorachasich, a low hill where, legend says, a Viking prince was once slain.

KILMUN

8 miles N of Dunoon on the A880

Kilmun stands on the shore of Holy Loch which, according to tradition, was given its name when a ship carrying soil from the Holy Land, destined for the foundations of Glasgow Cathedral, was wrecked here. It was taken for granted that the exotic soil had sanctified the loch. The village itself was an important early Christian site with a chapel founded here around AD 620 by St Mun, a contemporary of St Columba. The present church was built in 1841 but more impressive is the adjacent domed **Mausoleum** of 1794 which contains the earthly remains of all the Earls and Dukes of Argyll since 1442. Amongst them are the Earl Archibald who died at the Battle of Flodden, and the 8th earl who was beheaded in 1661. The building is currently undergoing much-needed restoration but is scheduled to open to the public for the first time in late 2009.

In the kirkyard is the grave of **Dr Elizabeth Blackwell** who, in 1849, was the first woman to graduate in medicine. Born in Bristol in 1821, she studied in Geneva (where she graduated), in the United States and at Paris and London. After returning to the United States, she opened (despite intense opposition) the first hospital staffed entirely by women. She died in 1910, and was buried in the churchyard as she regularly holidayed in the area.

ARDENTINNY

*12 miles N of Dunoon
on a minor road off the A880*

Ardentinny sits on the shores of Loch Long and is a small, attractive village made famous by the Sir Harry Lauder song *O'er the Hill to Ardentinny*. The mile-long **Flowers of the Forest Trail** takes you through oak woodland, where you can discover some of the native flowers and plants of the area.

TOWARD

7 miles S of Dunoon on the A815

The ruins of **Toward Castle** date mainly from the 15th century. It was a stronghold of the Lamonts who supported Charles II in his attempts to impose bishops on the Church of Scotland. The ruins are now in the care of the Clan Lamont. An episode in 1646 shows just how the Scottish clans took matters into their own hands when dispensing justice. The Campbells laid siege to the castle, and after unsuccessfully trying to blow it up, offered safe passage as far as Dunoon to the Lamonts sheltering within. The Lamonts duly left the castle, and were immediately rounded up and taken to **Tom-a-Mhoid** ("Hill of Justice") in Dunoon where 36 clansmen were hanged.

CAMPBELTOWN

Campbeltown occupies a very scenic position at the head of a deep bay sheltered by Davaar Island and surrounded by hills. In its 19th century heyday, when Campbeltown boasted a large fishing fleet and a thriving shipbuilding industry, it was said that there were 34 distilleries and almost as many churches in the town. A glance at the skyline here shows that most of the churches seem to have survived, although not always for religious purposes. The former Longrow Church for example is now the **Campbeltown Heritage Centre** and where the altar once stood there's now a beautifully crafted wooden skiff constructed in 1906. There are also displays on the area's whisky industry and exhibits relating to the 6th century St Kieran, the "Apostle of Kintyre". Kieran lived in a nearby cave which can still be visited at low tide. The saint believed in self-abnegation of an extreme nature. His food consisted of three equal parts of bread, herbs and sand; he heaped his body with heavy chains, and slept in the open air with a flat stone for his pillow. One is not surprised to learn that St Kieran died of jaundice at the age of 33 after sleeping outside during a snowfall.

Also on display in the centre are photos of the light railway that once connected the town with Machrihanish on the peninsula's west coast, where the town's airport now stands. Built during World War II for the RAF, the airport has one of the longest runways in Europe, though only one airline currently uses it - Flybe - and there's only one destination - Glasgow.

In the grounds of Campbeltown Library are the **Lady Linda McCartney Memorial**

A popular outing from Campbeltown is to Davaar Island which at low tide is linked to the mainland by a mile-long causeway known as The Doirlinn. The uninhabited island is used for grazing (so no dogs are allowed) and its main attraction is a cave in which a wall painting of the Crucifixion mysteriously appeared in 1887. Years later, in 1934, a local artist, Archibald MacKinnon, admitted that the painting was his work and in the following year, at the age of 85, he returned to renovate it.

81 MUASDALE HOLIDAY PARK

Muasdale

Peaceful beach-side family-run site with glorious views offering good and varied choice of accommodation.

see page 396

Gardens, named after the late wife of Sir Paul McCartney who has a holiday home on Kintyre. Campbeltown Picture House was built in 1913, and is the oldest cinema still functioning in Scotland.

AROUND CAMPBELTOWN

SOUTHEND

10 miles S of Campbeltown on the B842

This is the most southerly village in Argyll. It was near here, at Keil, that St Columba is supposed to have first set foot on Scottish soil in AD 563 before sailing north towards Iona. It's claimed that two footprints carved into a rock in the Kirk yard mark his first steps ashore, and that the ruined medieval chapel stands on the site of the one he founded here.

The nine feet tall **Knockstapple Standing Stone** can be seen from the Campbeltown - Southend Road. The remote Sanda Island, two miles south of the village, can be reached by boat from Campbeltown. Though it is remote, it still has a pub - the Byron Darnton Tavern which was built in traditional style and opened in 2003. It is named after the largest vessel to have been wrecked on the island, in 1946. Also opened in 2003, the **Sanda Bird Observatory** benefits from the fact that there are no rabbits, rats, mice or snakes on the island. Butterflies and moths abound, and more than 80 species have been logged.

Beyond Keil, a minor road leads to the most southwesterly point of the peninsula, the **Mull of Kintyre.** The road ends a mile short of the lighthouse of 1788 which stands 300 feet above sea level, exposed to the full force of Atlantic gales. It's a bleak, wild spot, but on a clear day worth the trek for the views across to Ireland, just 12 miles away.

SADDELL

9 miles N of Campbeltown on the B842

Saddell Abbey (Historic Scotland) was founded by Somerled, Lord of the Isles in 1148 for Cistercian monks, and completed by his son Reginald, who also founded Iona Abbey and Nunnery. Only scant remains can now be seen, most notably the presbytery and the north transept. As at other places in Argyll, stone carving once flourished here, and no fewer than 11 beautiful grave slabs, each one showing a knight in full armour or a monk, can be seen. After the Battle of Renfrew in 1164, the bodies of Somerled and his heir were brought to Saddell for burial. Saddell Castle (private) was built in 1508 for the Bishop of Argyll.

GLENBARR

11 miles N of Campbeltown on the A83

Visitors to Scotland are understandably fascinated by the clan system, and at **Glenbarr Abbey** they can enjoy a privileged insight into this unique element of Scottish society, as notable for its ferocious loyalties as for its sometimes barbarous feuds. The family seat of the Macalisters of Glenbarr, the abbey was built in the late 1700s and then greatly enlarged around 1815 with the addition of a striking west wing in the Gothic Revival style. This beautiful house is the home of Jeanne Macalister who personally conducts visitors around its many treasures. Guided by someone with such personal knowledge you will be introduced to a veritable wealth of exhibits: antique toys, an original Spode dinner service, a collection of Sevres and Derby china, family jewellery, 19th century fashions, wonderful patchworks, a unique thimble collection, and even a pair of gloves worn by Mary, Queen of Scots.

CARRADALE

14 miles N of Campbeltown on the B879

This quiet fishing village lies opposite Arran, on the east coast of the Mull of Kintyre. The **Network Carradale Heritage Centre**, in a former school, has displays about fishing, farming and forestry in the area, as well as hands-on activities for children. **Carradale House** dates from the 18th century, but was extended in 1804 for the then owner Richard Campbell. In its grounds are gardens noted for their rhododendrons, of which there are more than 100 varieties.

Torrisdale Castle, which has been converted into holiday accommodation, was built in 1815, and has a tannery which can be visited.

TARBERT

36 miles N of Campbeltown on the A83

At Tarbert an isthmus just one mile long links the Kintyre peninsula to the mainland. A venerable but true story recounts that in 1093 the wily Viking King Magnus Barelegs made a surprise attack on the west coast while the Scottish king, Malcolm Canmore, was away fighting the English. Malcom was forced to cede the Hebrides but, seeking to keep Magnus off the mainland, he stipulated that the 20-year-old invader might only retain any island he could navigate his ship around. Magnus coveted Kintyre, at that time much more fertile than the Hebridean islands, so he mounted his galley on wooden rollers and "sailed" his ship across the isthmus near Tarbert thus claiming the whole of the peninsula.

More than three centuries later, Robert the Bruce performed an identical manoeuvre while establishing his supremacy over the region. The Bruce was also responsible for building a castle at this strategic point but today only the ivy-covered ruins of the Keep remain, standing atop a 100 feet mound. This appealing little town was once a busy fishing port but nowadays it is pleasure craft that throng the harbour, particularly during the last week in May when the yacht races in the Rover series take place. They are followed the next week by the power boat Grand Prix.

Seven miles south of Tarbert is **Skipness Castle** (Historic Scotland), which dates originally from the 13th century. The first historical mention of it is in 1261 when the McSweens owned it,

An Tairbeart, to the south of Tarbert, is a heritage centre that tells of the place's history and people. North of the village is Stonefield Castle, built in 1837 and now a hotel. Attached is Stonefield Castle Garden, which is open to the public. As with so many gardens in the area, it is famous for its rhododendrons. There are also plants from Chile and New Zealand, and conifers such as the sierra redwood.

though it later came into the possession of Walter Stewart, Earl of Menteith. It finally came into the possession of the Campbells, and was abandoned in the late 17th century when a newer, more comfortable house was built close by. The ruins of **Kilbrannan Chapel**, near the foreshore, date from the 13th century, and were dedicated to St Brendan. Five medieval grave slabs are to be found inside the chapel walls and in the kirkyard. The church replaced an earlier building dedicated to St Columba.

LOCHGILPHEAD

This little town overlooking Loch Gilp is, rather surprisingly, the administrative centre for the sprawling district of Argyll and Bute. It is a planned town, laid out in about 1790, and is now the main shopping centre for a wide area known as Knapdale, that portion of Argyll from which the long "arm" of the Mull of Kintyre descends.

Kilmory Woodland Park, off the A83, surrounds Kilmory Castle, which has been turned into local government offices. The park contains many rare trees, plus gardens which were originally laid out in 1770 and during the season delight the eye with a dazzling display of more than 100 varieties of rhododendron.

The **Crinan Canal** (known as "Scotland's most beautiful shortcut") starts at Ardrishaig, a couple of miles south of Lochgiplhead, and skirts the town as it heads across the peninsula towards the village of Crinan on the west coast. Work started on the canal in 1794. However, it was beset with problems, and finally opened, albeit in an incomplete form, in 1801. By 1804 it still wasn't complete and had debts of £140,000. Then, in 1805, some of the canal banks collapsed and had to be rebuilt. It was finally opened in 1809, though in 1815 Thomas Telford, the civil engineer, inspected it and declared that even more work needed doing. In 1817 it reopened, this time to everyone's satisfaction.

It is nine miles long, has a mean depth of nine feet six inches and rises to 65 feet above sea level. Despite its short length, it has no fewer than 15 locks. In 1847 it got the royal seal of approval when Queen Victoria sailed its full length as she was making a tour of the Highlands. Perhaps the most unusual craft to have used it were midget submarines during World War II.

AROUND LOCHGILPHEAD

DUNADD

4 miles N of Lochgilphead off the A816

Dunadd (Historic Scotland) is one of the most important historical sites in Scotland. This great rock rises to a height of 175 feet from a flat area of land called Crinan Moss, and is where the ancient kings of Dalriada had their royal fort and capital. From here, they ruled a kingdom that took in all of modern day Argyll. It was founded by immigrants from Antrim in present day Northern Ireland in the 5th century, and gradually grew in importance. With them from Ireland they brought that great icon of Scottish nationhood, the Stone of Destiny.

The kings of Dalriada were special. Before this time, kings were looked upon more as great tribal leaders and warriors than as men set apart to rule a kingdom. But one man changed all that - **St Columba.** His monastery on Iona was within Dalriada, and on that island he conducted the first Christian "coronation" in Britain. In AD 574 he anointed Aidan king of the Dalriadans in a ceremony that relied on Biblical precedents. It also contained an element that is still used in today's coronations when the assembled crowds shouted out "God Save the King!" in unison. There is no doubt that Aidan sat on the Stone of Destiny during the ceremony.

Though it may now look austere and lonely, Dunadd in its heyday would have been a busy place. Excavations have shown that it traded with the kingdoms of present day England and the Continent. When the king was in residence, great flags would have fluttered from the wooden buildings, colourful banners and pennants would have hung from the ramparts and soldiers would have stood guard at its entrance. The River Add, no more than a couple of feet deep nowadays,

winds its way round the base of the rock before entering the sea at Loch Crinan. In olden days, before Crinan Moss was drained for agriculture, it would have been navigable right up to the rock itself. Boats would have been tied up at its banks, and there would have been a small township to house the king's retainers. There would also have been storerooms, stables and workshops where jewellery and weapons were crafted, cloth woven and pots made.

The other great kingdom north of the Forth and Clyde was the kingdom of the Picts, and for years it and Dalriada traded, fought, mingled and intermarried. Eventually, in AD 843, because of this intermarriage, Kenneth MacAlpin, king of Dalriada, also inherited the throne of the Picts. By this time the centres of power had moved to the west because of constant Norse raids, so Kenneth MacAlpin set off for Scone in present day Perthshire (taking the Stone of Destiny with him) and established his capital there. Thus

A climb to the top of Dunadd gives a wonderful view over the surrounding countryside, which is the reason the fort was established here in the first place. Parts of the ramparts can still be seen, and near the top, on a flat outcrop of rock, are some carvings of a boar, a footprint, a bowl and some ogham writing, which may have been connected to the inauguration of the Dalriadan kings.

Dunadd Fort

195

Behind the Kilmartin Parish church is the Glebe Cairn, a circular mound of stones dating from 1500-2000BC. It forms part of what is known as the linear cemetery, a collection of such cairns, which stretches for a mile along the floor of Kilmartin Glen. The others are Nether Largie North Cairn, Nether Largie Mid Cairn, Nether Largie South Cairn and Ri Cruin Cairn. All are accessible by foot. In addition, there is the Dunchraigaig Cairn, just off the A816, which doesn't form part of the linear cemetery.

was born the kingdom of Scotland, or Alba as it was known then, though it would be another 200 years before the kingdoms of the Lowlands - the Angles of the Lothians and the British of Strathclyde - were incorporated as well.

Dunadd survived for a few years after Kenneth left but it was no longer an important place and by the 12th century was largely abandoned.

KILMICHAEL GLASSARY

4 miles N of Lochgilphead on a minor road off the A816

In common with many other kirkyards in this part of Argyll, the kirkyard of the attractive 19th century **Parish Church** has a fine collection of carved, medieval and later, grave slabs.

The **Cup and Ring Rock** (Historic Scotland) lies within a small fenced off area in the village, and has some ancient cup and ring markings carved into it. No one knows the significance of such carvings, though there are many throughout Scotland.

KILMARTIN

9 miles N of Lochgilphead on the A816

The area surrounding Kilmartin is said to be Scotland's richest prehistoric landscape. Within a six-mile radius of the village over 150 prehistoric and 200 later monuments are to be found. The whole place is scattered with standing stones, stone circles, cairns, henges, burial mounds, forts, crannogs, cup and ring

markings, castles, carved grave slabs and crosses.

A church has stood in the village for centuries, though the present **Parish Church** was only built in 1835. Within it is a decorated cross that dates from about the 9th century, and within the kirkyard are three further crosses, dating also from the 9th century. Also in the kirkyard is the finest collection of carved medieval grave slabs in Western Scotland. Most date from the 14th or 15th century, though there are some which might be older. They might come as a surprise to people who imagine Scottish warriors to be wild Highlanders in kilts who brandish broadswords as they dash across the heather. These warriors are dressed in the kind of sophisticated armour found all over Europe at the time. Only the well-off could have afforded it. The other carvings on the slabs, such as swords, coats-of-arms and crosses, bear out their aristocratic lineage.

The **Temple Wood Circles**, south of Kilmartin, date from about 3500 BC. There are two of them, with the northern one possibly being used as a solar observatory when agriculture was introduced into the area. Burials were introduced at a later date. The Nether Largie Standing Stones are close to the Temple Wood Circle, and the Ballymeanoch Standing Stones are to the south of them. Of the seven stones, six still survive in their original positions.

If you find all these stone circles, cairns, castles, carvings and burial mounds hard to comprehend, then you should visit the award winning **Kilmartin House Museum** next to the church in the village. Using maps, photographs, displays and artefacts it explains the whole chronology of the area from about 7000 BC right up until AD 1100.

KILMORY

13 miles SW of Lochgilphead on a minor road off the B8025

North of Kilmory, on the shores of Loch Sween, stand the bulky ruins of **Castle Sween**, mainland Scotland's oldest surviving stone castle. Four massive, thick walls surround a courtyard where originally wood and thatch lean-tos would have housed stables, workshops and a brewery. It was started by one Suibhne (pronounced "Sween"), ancestor of the MacSweens, in about 1100, and in later years it became a centre of craftsmanship and artistry. This is shown by the **Kilmory Sculptured Stones**, at the 700-year-old Kilmory Knap chapel, a few miles south west of the castle. The symbols on the stones include men in armour, blacksmiths' and woodworkers' tools, swords and crosses. They probably all marked the graves of craftsmen and warriors associated with Castle Sween over the years.

The most spectacular stone is MacMillan's Cross, which dates from the 15th century. On one side it shows the Crucifixion, and on the other a hunting scene. There is a Latin inscription that translates,

"This is the cross of Alexander MacMillan". Across Loch Sween, at the end of the B8025, is **Keills Chapel**, which has another fine collection of grave slabs.

KILMARIE

On the B8002 10 miles NW of Lochgilphead

If you take the B8002 a few miles north of Kilmartin, you will find yourself on the Craignish Peninsula. Beyond the attractive village of Ardfern, a popular haven for yachtsmen, is **Kilmarie Old Parish Church**. This roofless ruin, dedicated to St Maelrubha, dates from the 13th century, and contains a wonderful collection of carved grave slabs dating from the 14th and 15th centuries.

INVERARAY

A striking example of a planned 'new town', Inveraray was built in the mid-1700s by the 3rd Duke of Argyll, chief of the powerful Clan Campbell. He demolished the old settlement to build his grand new castle and re-housed the villagers in the attractive Georgian houses lining Main Street. The duke also provided them with an elegant neo-classical church, **All Saints,** which was originally divided into two parts: one for services in English; the other for Gaelic speakers. A later addition, erected as a memorial to Campbells who fell in World War I, is the free-standing **Bell Tower,** equipped with ten bells which are reputedly the second heaviest in the world. During the summer months, the

To the north of Kilmartin are the substantial ruins of Carnassarie Castle (Historic Scotland), an outstanding example of a 16th century fortified house. Although the castle was sacked during the Monmouth rebellion of 1685, enough remains to give a good idea of what the house was like with features such as the huge open fireplace in the kitchen, large enough to roast a whole ox. The castle was originally built for John Carswell, Protestant Bishop of the Isles and the man who translated Knox's Book of Common Order (his liturgy for the reformed church) into Gaelic. It was the first book ever to be printed in that language.

197

82 INVERARAY JAIL

Inveraray

Inveraray Jail, the former County Courthouse and prison for Argyll, tells the story of the men, women and children who were tried and served their sentences here.

 see page 397

83 BANK HOUSE GUEST HOUSE

Inveraray

Striking 18th century house with large walled garden offering quality en suite B&B accommodation.

see page 397

tower is open to visitors and there are splendid panoramic views from the top.

Inveraray Castle stands to the north, and is an elegant, foursquare stately home. With its four turrets - one at each corner of the building - it looks more like a grand French château than a Highland castle, but this was the intention. It was designed to tell the world that the Campbells, Dukes of Argyll, belonged to one of the most powerful families in the land. Despite two major fires in 1977 and 1975, the most important treasures survived and include portraits by Gainsborough, Ramsay and Raeburn, superb furniture, and a mind-boggling array of weaponry which includes the dirk, or traditional Highland dagger, used by Rob Roy. Outside, the grounds are extensive with many pretty walks, some by waterfalls on the River Aray.

Moored alongside Inveraray Pier is the *Arctic Penguin*, a three-masted schooner built in 1911 which houses the **Inveraray Maritime Museum**. Here the maritime history of Scotland's western seaboard is vividly brought to life. There's an on board cinema with an archive of old film, and people can see what conditions were like aboard a ship taking them to a new life in America. The latest addition to the museum is the *Eilean Eisdeal,* a typical puffer built in Hull in 1944.

One of the most popular attractions in the area is Inveraray Jail, yet another of the 3rd duke's benefactions to the town. The

stately Georgian courthouse and the bleak prison cells were last used in the 1930s and have been converted into an award-winning and imaginative museum where costumed actors re-create the horrors of prison live in the past. Visitors can also seat themselves in the semi-circular courtroom and listen to excerpts from real-life trials that took place here.

One of the area's most famous sons was **Neil Munro** (1863-1930), the writer and journalist who wrote the ever-popular *Para Handy* books. On the A819 through Glen Aray towards Loch Awe is a monument that commemorates him. It stands close to his birthplace at Carnus.

AROUND INVERARAY

CAIRNDOW

11 miles NE of Inveraray on the A83

Standing at the head of Loch Fyne, this small village has a curiously shaped white-washed church. Built in 1816, the church is hexagonal with Gothic-style windows in pairs and a tower crowned by an elaborately carved parapet and four turrets.

Within the Arkinglas Estate, on the edge of the village, is the 25-acre **Arkinglas Woodland Garden**. High annual rainfall, a mild climate and light, sandy soil have created the right conditions for a collection of coniferous trees. The Callander family established the collection in about 1875, and it has seven champion trees that are either the tallest or widest in

Britain. There is also one of the best collections of rhododendrons in the country. Arkinglas House itself, designed by Robert Lorimer in 1907, is not open to the public.

At Clachan Farm near Arkinglas you'll find the **Clachan Farm Woodland Walks** which allow you to see many species of native tree, such as oak, hazel and birch. The walks vary from a few hundred yards in length to two-and-a-half miles, and take in the old burial ground of Kilmorich.

STRACHUR

5 miles S of Inveraray across the loch on the A815

Strachur sits on the shore of Long Fyne, on the opposite bank from Inveraray. **Strachur Smiddy** (meaning "smithy") dates from 1791, and finally closed in the 1950s. It has now been restored as a small museum and craft shop, and has some original tools and implements used by blacksmiths and farriers. **Glenbranter**, which was once owned by Sir Harry Lauder, has three short walks through mature woodlands. In the kirkyard at Strachur is buried **Sir Fitzroy MacLean**, diplomat and spy, who died in 1996, and was said to be the inspiration for Ian Fleming's James Bond.

Lachlan Castle (private), ancestral home of the MacLachlans, lies six miles south of Strachur on the B8000. The older 15th century castle, which is in ruins, is close by. Nine miles south of the castle, still on the B8000, is Otter Ferry. As the name implies, this village was once the eastern terminal of a ferry that crossed Loch Fyne, but it is long gone. The word "otter" comes from the Gaelic "oitir", meaning a gravel bank, and has nothing to do with the animal.

A single lane track, the Ballochandrain, leaves Otter Ferry and rises to more than 1000 feet before descending to Glendaruel. It has some wonderful views towards the Inner Hebrides.

ARROCHAR

22 miles E of Inveraray on the A83

Arrochar sits at the head of Loch Long. Two miles to the west is the small village of Tarbet, which sits on the shore of Loch Lomond. It sometimes surprises people who don't know the area that Britain's largest sheet of fresh water is so close to the sea. From the jetty at Tarbet small ships offer cruises on the loch. **Arrochar Parish Church** is a whitewashed building dating from 1847. It was recently saved from demolition by the concerted effort of the villagers.

Near the Jubilee Well in Arrochar are the **Cruach Tairbeirt Walks**. These footpaths (totalling just over a mile and a half in length) give some wonderful views over Loch Lomond and Loch Long. Though well surfaced, they are quite steep in some places.

AUCHINDRAIN

5 miles SW of Inveraray on the A83

Auchindrain Township is an original West Highland village which has been brought back to life

•

Some of Argyll's finest mountains are to be found close to Arrochar, such as Ben Narnain (3036 feet) and Ben Ime (3318 feet). This area could fairly claim to be the homeland of Scottish mountaineering, as the first mountaineering club in the country, the Cobbler Club, was established here in 1865. The road westwards towards Inveraray climbs up past the 2891 feet Ben Arthur, better known as The Cobbler, and over the wonderfully named Rest and Be Thankful. The modern A83 makes easy work of this pass along which, in 1803, William and Dorothy Wordsworth struggled "doubling and doubling with laborious walk". As they reached the summit, 860 feet above sea level, the Wordsworths noted with approval the plaque inscribed "Rest-and-be-thankful" placed here by the army troops when they repaired the old stone road in 1743.

•

199

84 SGEIR MHAOL GUEST HOUSE

Oban

A family run guest house, popular with those wanting to explore the beauty of its surroundings

⊨ *see page 398*

as an outdoor museum and interpretation centre. Once common throughout the Highlands, many of these settlements were abandoned at the time of the Clearances, while others were abandoned as people headed for cities such as Glasgow and Edinburgh to find work. Queen Victoria visited Auchindrain in 1875 when it was inhabited, and you can now see an approximation of what she saw. Most of the cottages and other buildings have been restored and furnished to explain the living conditions of the Highlanders in past centuries. The visitor centre also has displays on West Highland life, showing many farming and household implements.

CRARAE

10 miles S of Inveraray on the A83

Crarae Garden (National Trust for Scotland) was started by Lady Campbell in 1912, and includes the national collection of southern beech, as well as eucalyptus and eucryphia. It is one of the finest woodland gardens in Scotland, with rare trees and exotic shrubs thriving in the mild climate, and more than 400 species of rhododendron and azaleas providing a colourful display in spring and summer. A fine collection of deciduous trees adds colour and fire to autumn. There are sheltered woodland walks and a spectacular gorge. The Scottish Clan Garden features a selection of plants associated with various Argyll clans.

OBAN

The handsome and lively Victorian port of Oban is always busy with boat traffic criss-crossing between the islands of the Inner and Outer Hebrides. Protected by the length of the island of Kerrera, Oban's harbour is the finest on the west coast, with three piers and plenty of room for its still-active fishing fleet, a multitude of holiday craft and the ever-busy ferries. Tourism is by far Oban's most important industry but the town does have its own distillery. The **Oban Distillery** in Stafford Street produces a whisky that is one of the six "classic malts" of Scotland, and has tours showing the distillery at work. This is one of the smallest distilleries in the country, with just 2 pot stills. The whisky is a lightly peated malt, and the tour includes a free dram.

Oban

Another local industry is glass. **Oban Glass**, part of the Caithness Glass group, also welcomes visitors to watch the process of glass-making from the selection of the raw materials to finished articles such as elegant paperweights. Samples of their products are on sale in the factory shop.

By the North Pier, **World in Miniature** displays some 50 miniscule "dolls' house" rooms in a variety of historical styles, including two furnished in the manner of Charles Rennie Mackintosh and, like the others, built to a scale of one-twelfth.

The most striking feature of Oban however is a completely useless building. High on the hillside overlooking the town stands one of Britain's most unforgettable follies, **McCaig's Tower,** erected by John McCaig between 1897 and 1900. On the foundation stone McCaig describes himself as "Art Critic, Philosophical Essayist and Banker". He was motivated by a wish to provide work for unemployed masons in the area and, while a less romantic man might have built a Town Hall or a school, McCaig decided to build a replica of the Colosseum in Rome which he had admired on a visit there. His enormously costly project was designed from memory and its similarities to the original building are general rather than precise. McCaig had intended that a museum and art gallery would also form part of the complex and that large statues of his family would be stationed around the rim. None of this came to pass. He died in 1902 and his sister Catherine, who inherited his fortune, did not share her brother's taste for such a grandiose monument. John McCaig's Colosseum remained a dramatically empty granite shell, a wonderful sight when floodlit and adding an oddly Mediterranean aspect to this picturesque town.

The oldest building in Oban is **Dunollie Castle**, the ruins of which can be seen on the northern outskirts of the town beyond the Corran Esplanade. Much admired by both Sir Walter Scott and William Wordsworth, the castle was once the seat of the MacDougalls, Lords of Lorne, who still live nearby at Dunollie House (private). Little remains of the castle now apart from an impressive ivy-covered Keep rising majestically from a crag. North of the ruins, near the beach at Ganavan, is the *Clach a' Choin*, or Dog's Stone, where, legend has it, the giant Fingal tied up his dog Bran. The

Dunollie Castle, Oban

201

groove at the base is supposed to be where the leash wore away the stone.

On the Corran Esplanade is the **Oban War and Peace Museum**, which has photographs and military memorabilia. There is also a model of a flying boat with a 14 feet wingspan.

The **Oban Rare Breeds Farm Park** at Glencruitten has, in addition to rare breeds, a pets corner, a woodland walk, tearoom and shop. And at Upper Soroba is the **Oban Zoological World**, a small family-run zoo specialising in small mammals and reptiles. The **Puffin Dive Centre** at Port Gallanach is an award winning activity centre where you can learn to scuba dive in some remarkably clear water.

Armaddy Castle Garden, eight miles south of Oban off the B844 road for Seil Island, is another of the local gardens that benefit from the area's mild climate.

AROUND OBAN

DUNSTAFFNAGE

3 miles N of Oban off the A85

On a promontory sticking out into Ardmuchnish Bay, in the Firth of Lorne, is the substantial **Dunstaffnage Castle** (Historic Scotland). Seen from the east, it has a glorious setting, with the island of Lismore and the hills of Morvern behind it. Substantial parts of the castle 13th century fabric have survived, including walls 66 feet high and 10 feet thick in places, a curtain wall with 3 round towers, a large well surrounded by four small turrets, and a ruined chapel. The castle has a resident ghost, the Ell Maid. Sometimes on stormy nights she can be heard wandering through the ruins, her footsteps clanging off the stone as if shod in iron. If she is heard laughing, it means that there will be good news for the castle. If she shrieks and sobs, it means the opposite.

Dunstaffnage Chapel stands outside the castle, and also dates from the 13th century. It is unusual in that chapels were usually within the defensive walls of a castle. A small burial aisle built in 1740 for the Campbells of Dunstaffnage forms an eastern extension.

BARCALDINE

12 miles N of Oban on the A828

The **Scottish Sealife Sanctuary** is Scotland's leading marine animal rescue centre, and it looks after dozens of injured or orphaned seal pups before returning them back

Dunstaffnage Castle

into the wild. The sanctuary is set within a mature spruce forest on the shores of beautiful Loch Creran and is home to some of the UK's most enchanting marine creatures. In crystal clear waters you can explore more than 30 fascinating natural marine habitats containing everything from octopus to sharks. Every day there is a range of talks and feeding demonstrations from our team of marine experts.

Barcaldine Castle has associations with the Appin murder and the Massacre of Glencoe. There are secret passages and a bottle dungeon, and the castle is said to be haunted by a Blue Lady. Though not open to the public, it offers B&B accommodation.

Tralee Beach is one of the best beaches in the area. It lies off the unmarked road to South Shian and Eriska.

KINLOCHLAICH GARDENS

17 miles N of Oban on the A828

This old walled garden was created in 1790 by John Campbell. It sits on the shore of Loch Linnhe, in an area known as Appin, and it has one of Scotland's largest plant and nursery centres.

CONNEL BRIDGE

5 miles NE of Oban off the A828

Connel Bridge is a one-time railway bridge which now carries the A828 over the entrance to Loch Etive. The entrance to this sea loch is very shallow, and when the tide ebbs, the water pours out of the

loch into the Firth of Lorne over the **Falls of Lora**.

ARDCHATTAN

11 miles NE of Oban on a minor road on the north shore of Loch Etive

Ardchattan Priory (Historic Scotland) was built in about 1230 by Duncan McDougall, Lord of Lorne, for the Valliscaulian order of monks. The ruins of the church can still be seen, though the rest of the priory, including the nave and cloisters, was incorporated into Ardchattan House in the 17th century by John Campbell, who took over the priory at the Reformation. There are some old grave slabs which mark McDougall graves. **Ardchattan Priory Garden** is open to the public, and has herbaceous borders, roses, a rockery and a wild flower meadow.

TAYNUILT

12 miles E of Oban on the A85

Taynuilt lies close to the shores of Loch Etiven and is on the 128-mile long **Coast to Coast Walk** from Oban to St Andrews. Nearby, at Inverawe, is the **Bonawe Furnace**, which dates from 1753. Ironworking was carried out here for over 100 years, and the furnace made many of the cannonballs used by Nelson's navy. In 1805 the workers erected a statue to Nelson, the first in Britain, and it can still be seen today near Muchairn Church.

At Barguillean Farm you will find **Barguillean's Angus Garden**, established in 1957 on the shores of Loch Angus. It extends to nine acres, and was created in memory

85 BARCALDINE HOUSE HOTEL & COTTAGES

Barcaldine

Idyllic 18th century country house offering excellent cuisine and both hotel and self-catering accommodation.

 see page 399

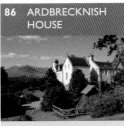

86 ARDBRECKNISH HOUSE

South Lochaweside

Overlooking Loch Awe and an ideal base for a family holiday, Ardbrecknish offers excellent self-catering accommodation.

see page 398

87 DALAVICH SHOP & WILD ROWAN CAFÉ

Dalavitch

Quality home-made food in wonderfully peaceful village set beside Loch Awe.

see page 400

of Angus Macdonald, a journalist who was killed in Cyprus in 1956.

ARDANAISEIG GARDEN

27 miles E of Oban on a minor road off the B845 on the banks of Loch Awe

Ardanaiseig is an extensive 100-acre woodland garden with a large herbaceous border. The garden is closed from January to mid February each year. Ardanaiseig House is now a hotel.

LOCH AWE

27 miles E of Oban on the A85

If you take the road east from Dunstaffnage Castle, passing near the shores of Loch Etive and going through the Pass of Brander, you will come to Scotland's longest loch, Loch Awe. This is its northern shore, and it snakes southwest for a distance of nearly 25½ miles until it almost reaches Kilmartin. Twenty crannogs, or artificial islands, have been discovered in the loch. On them defensive houses were built of wood, with a causeway connecting them to the mainland. They were in use in the Highlands from about 3000 BC right up until the 16th century.

Near the village of Lochawe are the impressive ruins of **Kilchurn Castle** (Historic Scotland), right on the shores of the loch. It was built around 1450 by Sir Colin Campbell, who came from a cadet branch of the great Campbell family. They were eventually elevated to the peerage as the Earls of Breadalbane.

St Conan's Kirk, also on the banks of the loch, is reckoned to be one of the most beautiful churches

in Scotland, though it dates only from the 1880s, with later additions. It was built by Walter Douglas Campbell, who had built a mansion house nearby. The story goes that his mother disliked the long drive to the parish church at Dalmally, so in 1881 Walter decided to built a church on the shores of Loch Awe. Not only did he commission it, he designed it and also carved some of the woodwork. The church was completed in 1887, but it proved too small for him, so in 1907 he began extending it. He died in 1914 before he could complete the extension and it was finally finished in its present state in 1930. It has a superb chancel, an ambulatory, a nave with a south aisle, various chapels and, curiously for a small church, cloisters. The Bruce Chapel commemorates a skirmish near the church, when a small force of men loyal to Robert the Bruce defeated John of Lorne, who had sworn allegiance to Edward I of England. The chapel contains a small fragment of bone from Bruce's tomb in Dunfermline Abbey.

The waters of Loch Cruachan, high on Ben Cruachan above Loch Awe, have been harnessed for one of the most ambitious hydroelectric schemes in Scotland. Not only does the **Cruachan Power Station** produce electricity from the waters of Loch Cruachan as they tumble down through pipes into its turbines and then into Loch Awe, it can actually pump 120 tons of water a second from Loch Awe back up the pipes towards Loch Cruachan by putting the turbines into reverse.

This it does during the night, using the excess electricity produced by conventional power stations. In this way, power is stored so that it can be released when demand is high. Cruachan was the first station in the world to use this technology, though nowadays it is commonplace.

The turbine halls are in huge artificial caves beneath the mountain, and there is an exhibition explaining the technology. Tours are also available taking you round one of the wonders of Scottish civil engineering - one that can produce enough electricity to supply a city the size of Edinburgh.

DALAVICH

25 miles SE of Oban on a minor road off the B845 on the banks of Loch Awe

If you follow the B845 south from Taynuilt, then turn south west onto a minor road near Kilchrenan, you will eventually reach the **Dalavich Oakwood Trail**. It is a two-mile long walk laid out by the Forestry Commission, with not only oaks, but also alder, hazel, downy birch and juniper. There are also small sites where 18th and 19th century charcoal burners produced charcoal for the Bonawe Iron Furnace near Taynuilt. Other woodland trails are the Timber Walk and the Loch Avich.

LERAGS

4 miles S of Oban off the A816

Lerags is a glen steeped in clan history with the burial grounds of the clan MacDougall, the ruins of Kilbride church, and the 16th century Campbell of Lerags Cross all within a one mile radius. The Cross, carved in 1562 with a depiction of the Crucifixion, was discovered centuries later lying in three pieces beside the ruined church. The figure of Christ escaped almost undamaged and is still a striking image.

KILMELFORD

14 miles S of Oban on the A816

In the kirkyard of the small **Parish Church** of 1785 are some gravestones marking the burial places of people killed while making the "black porridge".

It was at Loch Melfort, in 1821, that one of Scotland's most unusual weather phenomenons occurred - it rained herrings. The likeliest explanation is that the brisk south-westerly which was blowing at the time lifted the herring from the loch and deposited them on dry land.

ARDUAINE

18 miles S of Oban on the A816

The 50-acre **Arduaine Gardens** (National Trust for Scotland) are situated on a south-facing slope overlooking Asknish Bay. They are another testimony to the mildness of the climate on Argyll's coast and boast a wonderful collection of rhododendrons. There are also great trees, herbaceous borders and a diversity of plants from all over the world. The gardens were laid out by James Arthur Campbell, who built a home here in 1898 and called it Arduaine, which means "green point". The property was acquired by the NTS in 1992.

88 CLAN COTTAGES

Kilmore

A newly built self catering holiday village situated in five acres of grounds, each cottage accommodates from two to six visitors

see page 400 and Inside Front Cover

89 THE BARN AT SCAMMADALE FARM

Kilninver

Self catering accommodation on a 1000 acre family-run hill farm in a beautiful and picturesque corner of Scotland.

see page 400

90 CUILFAIL HOTEL

Kilmelford

Splendid former coaching inn near the shore of Loch Melfort offering excellent cuisine and en suite accommodation.

see page 401

BUTE

The island of Bute is the second largest of the islands in the Firth of Clyde, about 15 miles long by five miles wide. The island displays something of a split personality. Its sheltered east coast has been a popular holiday venue for Clydesiders since Victorian times; the west coast, however, never more than 5 miles distant, is sparsely populated, its most northerly minor road coming to a halt some 8 miles short of the northern tip of the island. Fortunately, there's no difficulty getting to the mile-long sands of Ettrick Bay on the west coast, regarded by many visitors and locals as the most beautiful place on the island.

Two ferries connect Bute to the mainland. The main one is from Wemyss Bay in Renfrewshire to Rothesay, while another, smaller one, runs between Colintraive on the Cowal Peninsula and Rhubodach on the north east tip of the island. The latter crossing takes only about five minutes, with the distance being only a third of a mile. At one time cattle, instead of being transported between the Bute and the mainland, were made to swim the crossing.

ROTHESAY

East Coast of Bute on the A886

The largest community on Bute is Rothesay, an attractive small town which displays its legacy as a popular Victorian resort in its tall colour-washed houses, trim public gardens and pedestrianised esplanade. Long before paddle-steamers brought 19th century holiday-makers here, Rothesay was a favourite refuge for Scottish kings in need of rest and recuperation. They would lodge at **Rothesay Castle** (Historic Scotland), built in the early 1200s and generally regarded as one of the finest medieval castles in the country. A picturesque moat surrounds the huge circular walls which in turn enclose the well-preserved Great

Rothesay Castle

Hall built by James IV. The Argylls sacked the castle in 1685 but did a less thorough job than usual, leaving much of it intact. Some 200 years later, the castle's hereditary guardians, the Marquesses of Bute, tidied the place up, opened it to the public and Rothesay Castle has been one of the region's major attractions ever since.

In Stuart Street, close to the castle, is the **Bute Museum**, which has displays and artefacts about Rothesay, the Firth of Clyde and the island of Bute itself. The ruins of the **Church of St Mary** (Historic Scotland), on the southern outskirts of the town, stand close to the present High Kirk built in 1796. St Mary's dates mainly from the 13th and 14th centuries and has two canopied tombs. One contains the effigy of a woman and child, and the other the effigy of a man. There is also the grave slab of an unknown Norman knight on the floor. The church has been recently re-roofed to protect them.

At one time Rothesay attracted thousands of Glasgow tourists during the "Glasgow Fair", which always takes place during the last two weeks in July. The town has a definite taste for festivals. On the last weekend in August it stages its own **Highland Games** at which the guest of honour may well be the Duke of Rothesay, a distinguished personage much better known as heir to the throne, Prince Charles. During the third weekend in July, the town hosts an **International Folk Festival,** and on May Day Bank Holiday the town resounds to the upbeat rhythms of a **Jazz Festival**.

Bute at one time was known by the nickname of "Scotland's Madeira", not just because it was an island, but also because palm trees flourish here due to the influence of the Gulf Stream. The gentleness of the climate can best be appreciated at **Ardencraig Gardens** in Ardencraig Lane, which were bought by Rothesay Town Council in 1970. They formed part of the original gardens designed by Percy Cane for the owners of Ardencraig House. Another popular spot is **Canada Hill**, to the south of the town, where there are spectacular views of the Firth of Clyde. From here, people used to watch ships sailing down the Clyde taking Scottish emigrants to a new life in North America, hence its name. On the sea front is a memorial to people who left Rothesay but never returned - the six hundred Bute bowmen who fought alongside William Wallace at the Battle of Falkirk in 1298.

The **Isle of Bute Discovery Centre** is housed in the town's Winter Garden (built in 1924), on the front. It contains an exhibition highlighting life on the island through interactive displays and plasma screens, as well as a cinema/theatre.

One of Rothesay's more unusual attractions is the complex of **Victorian Toilets** at the end of the pier, which date from 1899. They still work perfectly, and are

Rothesay

Well known for its quality food and good service, Brechin's Brasserie is popular with visitors and locals

see page 402

Mount Stuart House, near the lovely village of Kerrycroy, is the ancestral home of the Marquis of Bute. In 1877 a fire destroyed most of the old house, built during the reign of Queen Anne, and the third Marquis employed Robert Rowand Anderson to design the present Victorian Gothic one. It is an immense house, full of treasures, and reflects the history and importance of the family who owned it. When built, it was full of technological wonders. It was the first house in Scotland to be lit by electricity, and the first private house to have a heated indoor swimming pool. Surrounding the house are 300 acres of delightful gardens. The house achieved international fame in 2003 when Stella McCartney, daughter of Paul, got married here

full of ornate design. They were recently voted the second best place in the world to spend a penny. If you want the best place, you'll have to go to Hong Kong. Women can view the toilets at quiet times.

Scotland's first long distance island footpath, the 30-mile long **West Island Way**, starts at Kilchattan Bay and finishes at Port Bannatyne. Full details of the trail are available from the Isle of Bute Discovery Centre in Rothesay.

Close to Kilchattan Bay, at Kingarth, is **St Blane's Chapel**. The ruins of this Norman structure sit within what was a Celtic monastery, founded by St Blane in the sixth century (see also Dunblane). The whole area shows how such a monastery would have been laid out. The rath, or cashel, a low wall surrounding the monastery, can still be seen, as can the foundations of various beehive cells in which the monks lived. There are two old graveyards - one for men, and one for women. Close by is the **Dunagoil Vitrified Fort**, which dates from the Iron Age. Vitrified forts are so called

because at one time they were exposed to great heat, turning the surface of the stone used in their construction to a glass-like substance.

There are many other religious sites on Bute, some dating from the Dark Ages. At Straad (a name which tells you that the island once belonged to the Vikings) there are the scant remains of **St Ninian's Chapel**, which may go back at least 1500 years, and at Kilmichael there are the ruins of the old **St Macaille Chapel**.

Near Port Bannatyne, north of Rothesay, is Kames Castle, dating from the 14th century. Neither it nor its beautiful gardens are open to the public, but they can be viewed from the road. One place, which can be visited, however, is **Ascog Hall Fernery and Garden**, three miles south of Rothesay. It was built about 1870, and has a sunken fern house which houses more than 80 sub-tropical fern species. It was awarded the first ever Scottish prize by the Historic Gardens Foundation which promotes historic gardens and parks throughout the world.

Inner Hebrides

T he Inner Hebrides, unlike the Western Isles, is not a compact geographical unit. Rather it is a collection of disparate islands lying off the Argyll coast, and forming part of that county (apart from Skye, which is part of the Highlands). Each island has its own distinct character, with sizes ranging from the 87,800 hectares of Mull (the third largest of Scotland's islands) to the 33 hectares of Staffa and the 877 hectares of Iona.

Not all the islands are inhabited, and of those that are, most have seen a drop in

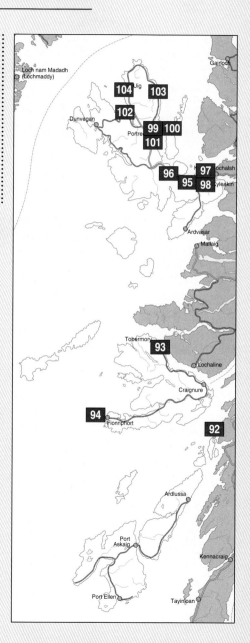

population over the years. Some of the now uninhabited ones were inhabited at one time, and the remains of cottages and even old chapels are still to be found. The names trip off the tongue like a litany, and some, to English speakers, are decidedly unusual. Mull; Muck; Rum; Eigg; Coll; Canna; Tiree; Islay; Jura; Colonsay - most have their origins in Gaelic, and in some cases Norse.

Even though most of the islands lie well away from the mainland, they have still been influenced by Lowland Scots and English sensibilities. Rum has changed its name three times over the last century. Originally it was Rum, then, when the Bullough family bought it in the late 19th century, they changed it to Rhum in deference to their teetotal beliefs. In 1957 the island was bought by Scottish Natural Heritage and the name changed back to Rum.

The Inner Hebrides can also claim to have the most sacred place in Scotland, if not Britain. Iona, off the west coast of Mull, was where St Columba established his great monastery, and from where missionaries set out to convert the northern lands. St Columba wasn't the first man to bring Christianity to Scotland - that honour goes to St Ninian - but he was the most influential. We know a lot about his life thanks to a biography written by St Adamnan, ninth abbot of Iona, almost one hundred years after he died. Though some of it is uncritical hagiography, there is enough to see the man behind the venerated saint that is Columba. He tells of a man who was all too human - vengeful yet forgiving, impetuous yet thoughtful, arrogant yet unassuming and boastful yet modest. Today Iona is still a place of pilgrimage, though most people now come as tourists to see and admire the later abbey buildings and experience that feeling of calm for which the island is famous.

GIGHA

17 miles NW of Campbeltown off the West Coast of Kintyre

This small island, no more than six miles long by two miles wide at its widest is reached by ferry from Tayinloan. It is best to see the island on foot, and the **Gigha Path Network** makes this easy. The name Gigha (pronounced gee-yah, with a hard "g") was given to the island by the Norse king Hakon, and means "God's island". It seems to have a climate of its own, and while the rest of Argyll is enveloped in cloud, Gigha is sometimes bathed in sunshine due to the Gulf Stream washing its shores. Its highest peak, at 330 feet, is Creag Bhan, where you can see a 4th century inscribed stone.

The 50-acre **Achamore Gardens**, near the ferry port at Ardminish, are open to the public. They were founded by Sir James Horlick, of bedtime drink fame, after he bought the island in 1944. They are famous for their rhododendrons and camellias. In 2001 the inhabitants of Gigha bought the island, and it is now managed by a trust.

ISLAY

35 miles SW of Inveraray in the Atlantic Ocean

Islay's relatively mild, wet climate has meant that the island has been inhabited for thousands of years. Clan Donald, which claims descent from Somerled, made the island the centre of their vast Lordship of the Isles, which at one time was almost a separate kingdom beyond the reach of Scottish monarchs. It is a truly beautiful island, with a range of hills to the east rising to 1500 feet, and low, fertile farmland. It is famous for its distilleries, with more than four million gallons of whisky being produced each year. Most of them have tours explaining the distilling process, and offer a dram at the end of it. An Islay malt has a peaty taste all of its own, due to the grain being dried over peat fires.

On islands in Loch Finlaggan, west of Port Askaig (where there is a ferry to Feolin Ferry on Jura and West Loch Tarbert on the Mull of Kintyre) you will find the ruins of the medieval centre of the Lordship of the Isles, with a visitor centre close by. The important remains are to be found on two of the islands in the loch, Eilean Mor (the Great Island) and Eilean na Comhairle (the Council Island). Ancient burial slabs are thought to mark the graves of important women and children, as the chiefs themselves would have been buried on Iona. Close to Port Askaig itself are the Bunnahabhain and the Caol Ila distilleries. To the east of Port Ellen (which also has a ferry to Tarbert) are the distilleries of Lagavulin, Laphroaig and Ardbeg.

The ruins of **Dunyveg Castle**, a MacDonald stronghold, sit near Lagavulin. At one time it was owned by a man called **Coll Ciotach,** or "left handed Coll". While he was away on business, the castle was captured by his enemies the Campbells, and his men taken prisoner. They then waited for Coll to return so that they could overpower him. But one of the

The scanty ruins of Kilchattan Church, behind the hotel, date from medieval times. In the kirkyard are some old grave slabs showing knights in armour. One is possibly of Malcolm MacNeill, Laird of Gigha, who died in 1493. And behind the church, atop the Cnoc A'Charraidh (Hill of the Pillar) is the Ogham Stone dating from the time the island formed part of the kingdom of Dalriada. It carries a carving that reads Fiacal son of Coemgen, and probably marks a burial.

Bowmore, on the A874 beside the shores of Loch Indaal, has one of only two round churches in Scotland. It was built in 1767 by Daniel Campbell, who reckoned that, having no corners, the devil could not hide anywhere within it.

prisoners was Coll's personal piper, and when he saw his master approach the castle, he alerted him by playing a warning tune. Coll escaped, but the piper had his right hand cut off, and never again could play the pipes. It's a wonderful story, though whether it is true or not is another matter, as the legend is also associated with other castles in Argyll, notably Duntroon.

At Ardbeg is the **Kildalton Cross and Chapel**. The incised cross dates from the 9th century, and is one of the finest in Scotland. Bowmore Distillery - the oldest (founded in 1779) and one of the most famous on the island - can be visited. North of Bowmore, near Bridgend, is an Iron Age fort with the wonderful name of **Dun Nosebridge** (Landrover trips can be arranged to visit and view it), and to the southwest of the village, at the tip of the Mull of Oa (pronounced "oh"), is the **American Monument**, which commemorates the 266 American sailors lost when Tuscania sank after being torpedoed in 1918 and the Otranto was wrecked. Many of the bodies were washed up at the foot of the cliff here.

On the opposite side of the loch is a peninsula called the Rhinns of Islay, and it is here that you will find the Bruichladdich Distillery, which, in 2003, found itself under surveillance by American intelligence agents as the whisky distilling process is similar to the one used in making certain kinds of chemical weapons. At Port Charlotte is the **Islay Natural History Trust**,

housed in a former whisky bond. It has a wildlife information centre, and provides information on the natural history and wildlife of Islay. Also in the village is the **Museum of Islay Life**, which tells of everyday life on the island through the ages, and has a special display on the many shipwrecks that have taken place off Islay's rugged coastline. Continue past Port Charlotte on the A874 and you will come to Portnahaven. About four miles from the village, and situated on the west side of the Portnahaven to Kilchiaran road, is the **Cultoon Stone Circle**. Not all the stones have survived, but three are still standing and 12 have fallen over at the point where they once stood. The ruins of **Kilchiaran Chapel**, on the west coast of the Rhinns can be reached by car via a narrow track. Though its fabric is basically medieval, its origins go right back to the time of St Columba, who founded it in honour of his friend St Ciaran. There is an old baptismal font and some carved gravestones. The nearby beach is a favourite place for seals to sun themselves. Further north is the **Kilchoman Church and Cross**, accessed by another narrow track, which leaves the B8018 and goes past Loch Gorm. The cross dates from the 15th century, and was erected by "Thomas, son of Patrick". The church is no longer in use and has lost part of its roof.

JURA

24 miles W of Inveraray in the Atlantic Ocean

Jura is an island of peat bogs, mists

and mountains, notably the Paps of Jura, to the south. The highest mountain in the range, at over 2500 feet, is Ben an Oir. The island's only road, the A846, takes you from Feolin Ferry, where there is a ferry to Islay, north along the east coast, where most of the island's population lives. You will pass **Jura House Garden** at Cabrach, with its collection of Australian and New Zealand plants. They thrive in this mild and virtually frost and snow free environment. Craighouse, with its distillery, is the island's capital. Behind the parish church of 1776 is a room with some old photographs and artefacts of life on Jura through the ages. On the small island of Am Fraoch Eilean, south of the village, are the ruins of **Claig Castle**, reputed to be an old MacDonald prison.

The road then takes you north to Ardlussa, where it peters out. Within the old burial ground is the tombstone of **Mary MacCrain**, who died in 1856, aged 128. They seem to have been long-lived on Jura, for the stone goes on to say that she was a descendant of Gillouir MacCrain, *"who kept one hundred and eighty Christmases in his own house, and died during the reign of Charles I"*.

Just under a mile off Jura's north cost is the small island of Scarba. It has been uninhabited since the 1960s, though in the late 18th century it managed to support 50 people. It rises to a height of 1473 feet, and has many Iron Age sites on its west coast. On the east coast are the ruins of **Cille Mhoire an Caibel**, surrounded by an old graveyard. Many miracles were supposed to have taken place within the kirk in early medieval times.

Between Jura and Scarba, in the Gulf of Corryvreckan, is the notorious Corryvreckan whirlpool. The name comes from the Gaelic Coire Bhreacain, meaning "speckled cauldron", and it is best viewed from the safety of the cliff tops on Jura (even though you have to walk about five miles from just beyond Ardlussa to get there) as it has sent many boats to the bottom. It is caused by the combination of an immense pillar of rock rising from the seabed and a tidal race, and the best time to see it is when a spring tide is running westward against a west wind. The sound of it can sometimes be heard at Ardfern on the mainland, more than seven miles away.

Legend tells us that the whirlpool's name has a different derivation. A Norwegian prince called **Breachkan** was visiting the Scottish islands, and fell in love with a beautiful princess, a daughter of the Lord of the Isles. Her father disapproved of the young man, but declared that he could marry his daughter providing he could moor his galley in the whirlpool for three days.

Breachkan agreed to the challenge, and had three cables made - one of hemp, one of wool and one from the hair of virgins. He then sailed into the Gulf of Corryvreckan, and while there was

A mile or so north of Craighouse on Jura is the ruined Chapel of St Earnadail. St Earnadail was St Columba's uncle, and the story goes that he wanted to be buried on Jura when he died. When asked where on the island, he replied that a cloud of mist would guide the mourners to the right spot. On his death, a cloud of mist duly appeared and settled where the ruins now stand.

a slack tide, moored his boat in the whirlpool. The tides changed, and the whirlpool became a raging monster. The hemp cable snapped on the first day and the wool one snapped on the second. But Breachkan wasn't worried, for he knew that the one made from virgins' hair would keep him safe.

But on the third day it too snapped, sending the prince to his death. It seems that some of the virgins from whom the hair had come were not as innocent as they had made out.

The whirlpool almost claimed the life of the writer George Orwell who lived in a cottage, Barnhill, on the north of the island while writing his novel *1984*. One day in 1947, Orwell (real name Eric Blair) had taken a day off from writing to sail with his nephews and nieces. They ventured too close to the whirlpool and their boat was sucked under the water. Fortunately, Orwell and the youngsters managed to reach a small rock where they were later picked up by a fishing boat.

COLONSAY AND ORONSAY

40 miles W of Inveraray in the Atlantic Ocean

The twin islands of Colonsay and Oronsay are separated by an expanse of sand called The Strand which can be walked across at low tide. Half way across the strand are the remains of the **Sanctuary Cross**. Any law-breaker from Colonsay who passed beyond it and stayed on Oronsay for a year and a day could escape punishment.

Colonsay is the bigger of the two islands, and has a ferry service connecting its main village of Scalasaig to Oban.

Oronsay is famous for the substantial ruins of **Oronsay Priory**, perhaps the most important monastic ruins in the west of Scotland after Iona. Tradition gives us two founders. The first is St Oran, companion to St Columba, who is said to have founded it in AD 563. The second is St Columba himself. When he left Ireland, the story goes, he alighted first on Colonsay, and then crossed over to Oronsay where he established a small monastery. However, he had made a vow that he would never settle where he could still see the coastline of Ireland. He could from Oronsay, so he eventually moved on to Iona.

John, Lord of the Isles, founded the present priory in the early 14th century, inviting Augustinian canons from Holyrood Abbey in Edinburgh to live within it. The church is 15th century, and the well-preserved cloisters date from the 16th century. A series of large carved grave slabs can be seen within the Prior's House, and in the graveyard is the early 16th century Oronsay Cross, intricately carved, and carrying the words *Colinus, son of Christinus MacDuffie*. Another cross can be found east of the Prior's Chapel, with a carving of St John the Evangelist at its head.

EILEACH AN NAOIMH

29 miles W of Inveraray in the Atlantic Ocean

This small island is part of the

Garvellochs, and is famous for its ancient ecclesiastical remains dating from the Dark Ages, which include chapels, beehive cells and an ancient graveyard. A monastery was founded here in about AD 542 by St Brendan, better known as Brendan The Navigator. This was before St Columba founded the monastery on Iona. In the 10th century the monastery was destroyed by Norsemen, and the island had remained unihabited since then. It is reputed to be the burial place of both Brendan and Columba's mother, Eithne. There is no ferry service to Eileach an Naoimh.

SEIL AND LUING

9 miles S of Oban on the B844

These two islands are known as the "slate isles" due to the amount of slate that was quarried here at one time. Seil is a genuine island, but is connected to the mainland by the **Bridge Across the Atlantic**, designed by Thomas Telford and built in 1792. It is more properly called the Clachan Bridge, with the channel below being no more than a few yards wide. It is a high, hump-back bridge to allow fishing boats to pass beneath.

It got its nickname because at one time it was the only bridge in Scotland to connect an island with the mainland. Now the more recent Skye Bridge dwarfs it. On the west side of the bridge, on the island itself, is a late-17th century inn called the Tigh na Truish, or **"House of Trousers"**. This recalls the aftermath of the Jacobite Uprising, when the wearing of the

kilt was forbidden. The islanders, before crossing onto the mainland by a ferry which preceded the bridge, would change out of their kilts here and into trousers.

On the west coast of the island is the village of Ellenabeich, with, facing it, the small island of Easdale. Ellenabeich was itself an island at one time, but the narrow channel separating it from the mainland was gradually filled up with waste from the local slate quarries. One of the biggest quarries was right on the shoreline, with its floor 80 feet below the water line. It was separated from the sea by a wall of rock. During a great storm, the wall was breached, and the quarry filled with water. Now it is used as a harbour for small craft.

An Cala Garden dates from the 1930s, and is behind a row of cottages that was turned into one home. There are meandering streams, terracing built from the local slate, and wide lawns. A 15-feet high wall of grey brick protects the garden from the worst of the

92 KILBRIDE CROFT COTTAGES

Balvicar, Seil Island

Quality self-catering accommodation in two traditional properties, both of which enjoy breath-taking views.

➥ see page 402

Bridge across the Atlantic, Seil

Lismore was a prized island, and it seems that St Moluag and another Celtic saint, St Mulhac, had a quarrel about who should found a monastery there. They finally agreed to a race across from the mainland in separate boats, with the first one touching the soil of Lismore being allowed to establish a monastery. As the boats were approaching the shore Moluag realised that he was going to lose, so took a dagger, cut off one of his fingers and threw it onto the beach. As he was the first to touch the soil of the island, he was allowed to build his monastery. This was supposed to have taken place at Tirefour, where there are the remains of a broch now called Tirefour Castle, whose walls still stand to a height of 16 feet.

On the west coast of Kerrera, facing the tiny Bernera Island, are the ruins of the 13th century Achadun Castle, where the Bishops of Argyll lived up until the 16th century, and further up the coast are the remains of Coeffin Castle, built by the MacDougalls in the 13th century.

gales that occasionally blow in from the Atlantic.

One of the former quarries' cottages in the village has been turned into the **Ellenabeich Heritage Centre** with a number of displays connected with the slate industry.

Offshore lies the small island of Easdale, connected to Ellenabeich by a small passenger ferry. This too was a centre of slate quarrying, and in the **Easdale Island Folk Museum** you can see what life was like when the industry flourished. It was founded in 1980 by the then owner of the island, Christopher Nicolson.

On Seil's southern tip is the small ferry port of Cuan, where a ferry plies backwards and forwards to Luing, to the south. This is a larger island than Seil, though it is more sparsely populated. Here too slate quarrying was the main industry. It is a quiet, restful place where seals can be seen basking on the rocks, as well as eagles and otters. Above the clachan of Toberonochy are the ruins of Kilchattan Chapel, with slate gravestones.

KERRERA

1 mile W of Oban, in Loch Linnhe

Offshore from Oban is the small rocky island of Kerrera, which can be reached by passenger ferry from a point about two miles south of the town. At the south end of the island are the ruins of 16th century **Gylen Castle**, another former MacDougall stronghold. It was built by Duncan MacDougall,

brother (or son) of the clan chief, Dougal McDougall. It was sacked by a Covenanting army under General Leslie in 1647 and all the inhabitants were slaughtered.

LISMORE

7 miles N of Oban, in Loch Linnhe

Lismore is a small island, no more than a mile-and-a-half wide at its widest and ten miles long. It's name means "great garden", and it is a low-lying, fertile island connected to Oban by a daily ferry. The main village and ferry terminal is Achnacroish, though a smaller pedestrian ferry plies between Port Appin on the mainland and the north of the island in summer. In the village is the **Commann Eachdraidh Lios Mor** (Lismore Historical Society), situated in an old cottage that re-creates the living conditions in the Lismore of yesteryear.

Lismore, before the Reformation, was the centre of the diocese of Argyll. **Lismore Cathedral** stood at Kilmoluaig, near the small village of Clachan. It was destroyed just after the Reformation, but the choir walls were lowered and incorporated into the present church in 1749.

The highest point on the island, at a mere 412 feet, is Barr Morr (meaning "big tip"), but from the top there is a wonderful panoramic view in all directions.

MULL

For ten months of the year, from September to June, the 3000 residents of Mull virtually have its 370 square miles to themselves - a spectacular landscape of moorland dominated by the massive bulk of Ben More (3140 feet), with a west coast gouged by two deep sea lochs and an east coast unusually well-wooded for the Hebrides. During July and August, it's quite a different story as visitors flock to this unspoilt island. Its charming "capital", the little port of Tobermory, becomes crowded and the narrow roads congested. But as always in the Highlands, one only has to travel a mile or so from the popular venues to find perfect peace and quiet. Getting away from the pestilent swarms of summer midges may not be quite so easy.

Duart Castle, Mull

Some 200 years ago, there were more than three times as many permanent residents on the island, but the infamous Highland Clearances of the early 19th century saw a constant stream of the destitute and dispossessed pass through Tobermory, boarding ships that would take them to an uncertain future in the slums of Glasgow or to the distant shores of America, Canada and Australia. The island is still scarred with the ruins of the crofts from which these refugees were driven or, quite often, even smoked out.

Today, Mull is well-served by vehicle and passenger ferries from Oban, either by the 40-minute crossing to Craignure on the southeastern tip of the island, or to Tobermory in the northeast.

On its north east side Mull is separated from Morvern on the mainland by the Sound of Mull, a deep sea trench that offers some of the best diving in Scotland. So much so that sometimes the wrecks can get very crowded with divers! One of the favourite dives is to the *Hispania*, sunk in 1954 and now sitting at a depth of 30 metres. She was sailing to Sweden from Liverpool with a cargo of steel and asbestos when she hit Sgeir Mor reef. A story is told that the captain refused to leave the sinking ship, thinking that he might be blamed for the accident. As the crew were rowing to safety in high seas, the last they saw of him was a figure standing on the ship saluting as it slowly submerged.

Another, unusual, wreck is of the *Rondo*. It sits vertically beneath the water, and though it is in two parts, its bow is 50 metres below the surface, embedded in the sea bed, and its stern just six metres below the surface.

TOBERMORY

This picture-postcard little town with its brightly painted houses is set within an amphitheatre of hills which cradle one of the safest anchorages on Scotland's west coast. Tobermory's potential as a port was not realised until 1786 when the British Society for the Encouragement of Fisheries decided to develop the harbour and build a quay. Despite the Society's encouragement, the fishing industry never really prospered - lackiing modern aids, the fishermen were baffled by the erratic movements of the herring shoals.

The British Society's development of Tobermory did however leave behind a charming legacy of (now) brightly painted, elegant Georgian houses ranged along the quayside. Combined with the multi-coloured pleasure craft thronging the harbour, they help to create an atmosphere that is almost Continental: bright, cheerful and relaxed. The town's other attractions include its arts centre, **An Tobar,** which stages exhibitions and live events; the tiny **Tobermory Distillery** where visitors are offered a guided tour and a complimentary dram of its famed single malt whiskys; and the **Mull Museum** on Main Street where one of the exhibits is devoted to the most dramatic incident ever recorded on the island.

It occurred in 1588 when a galleon of the routed Spanish Armada sough shelter in Tobermory harbour. The Spaniards were received with Highland courtesy; their requests for fresh water and victuals amply fulfilled. At some point, however, the people of Tobermory suspected that their guests intended to sail away without paying the bill for these provisions. Donald MacClean of Duart was deputed to go aboard the Spanish ship and demand immediate payment. The Spaniards promptly locked him up and set sail for their homeland. The ingenious Donald somehow managed to release himself, find his way to the ship's magazine, blow it up and consign himself, the crew and the ship's rumoured cargo of fabulous amounts of gold bullion to the deep. Ever since then, strenuous efforts have been made to locate this watery Eldorado. The first dive was in the early 17th century, when the Earl of Argyll sent men down to the wreck. Successive dives, including one by the Royal Navy, have recovered small items such as a skull, cannon shot, pieces of wood and even a gold coin. Sir Walter Scott owned a writing case made of wood from the wreck, and it is said that Queen Elizabeth II owns a snuff box made from the wood. The ship now lies completely covered in silt, and it is unlikely that anything will ever be recovered from her again.

A short walk from the museum is the headquarters of the **Hebridean Whale and Dolphin Trust**, a research, education and conservation charity. There is a small visitors centre with displays on whales and dolphins. Here you can watch videos of whales and dolphins in the Hebrides, as well as, in some cases, listening to their "songs".

AROUND TOBERMORY

GLENGORM

4 miles W of Tobermory off the A848

Glengorm Castle lies at the end of a single track road from Tobermory. It was built in 1860 for local landowner James Forsyth, who instigated the Clearances in the area, removing crofters from their land and replacing them with the more profitable sheep. It is not open to the public, though there is both a flower garden and a market garden here where you can buy plants and vegetables. There is also a coffee shop.

DERVAIG

6 miles SW of Tobermory on the B8073

From Tobermory, the narrow B8073 to Dervaig follows a tortuously twisting route through dramatic scenery - one of the more demanding stretches of the annual round-the-island **Mull Car Rally** held in October. Nestling at the head of Loch a'Chumhainn and reckoned to be the loveliest village on the island, Dervaig is home to the 38-seat **Mull Little Theatre**. According to the Guinness Book of Records, it is the smallest professional working theatre in the world, and puts on a season of plays every year to packed audiences. It opened in 1966 in the converted coach house of a Free Church manse and was established by Barrie and Marianne Hesketh, professional actors who had settled on Mull to bring up their children. Now it not only presents plays within the tiny theatre, it tours the Highlands and Islands as well.

CALGARY

8 miles SW of Tobermory on the B8073

From Dervaig, the B8073 continues on to the small village of Calgary, on Calgary Bay. The name in Gaelic means the "harbour by the dyke", the dyke being a natural basalt formation which can still be seen. Here you will find what is possibly the best beach on the island with vast stretches of white sand. In 1883 Colonel J.F. Macleod of the Royal North West Mounted Police holidayed in Calgary, and was so impressed by the scenery that when he later founded the capital of the province of Alberta, he christened the new settlement with the name of this remote Scottish village.

At the **Old Byre Heritage Centre**, which is about a mile from the village, Mull's visitors can learn about the island's history and heritage. There are also displays on natural history, and a half hour video.

OSKAMULL

27 miles S of Tobermory on the B8073

To summon the privately-owned ferry to Ulva, visitors slide back a small white panel to uncover a red panel which can be seen from the island. At the ferry point on the island is the small **Ulva Heritage Centre**, housed in a restored

93   MULL POTTERY

Tobermory

Well-stocked gallery showcasing ceramics and other crafts; also café/restaurant with fantastic views.

 see page 403

Craignure village itself offers a number of guest houses, an inn, and a part-time Tourist Information Centre but perhaps its most popular attraction is the Mull and West Highland Railway, a one-and-a-quarter mile long narrow gauge line, connects the castle with the pier. It has a gauge of 26 cm, and was opened in 1984 specifically to link the pier at Craignure with Torosay Castle. It passes through woodland and coastal scenery, and at one point it even crosses over a peat bog, which brought special problems when it was being built. The tiny engines that pull the carriages are a mixture of steam and diesel, with possibly the Lady of the Isles *being the prettiest of the lot. It was the first engine on the line, though there are now six operating.*

thatched cottage, with attached tearoom. To the west of Ulva is the smaller island of Gometra, connected to Ulva by a causeway. It has been uninhabited since 1983, though Gometra House can still be seen. Since early times, Gometra was owned by the monastery of Iona, and indeed was known as "Iona's granary" on account of the crops grown there.

The Treshnish Islands is a small chain of islands well to the west of Gometra. The main islands are Lunga, Fladda, Bac Mor, Cairn na Burgh Mor and Cairn na Burgh Beg. Now uninhabited, they are a haven for wildlife, with Lunga especially being a favourite nesting site for puffins, shags, guillemots, razorbills and kittiwakes. On Cairn na Burgh are early Viking and Iron Age fortifications. Autumn is the breeding season for grey Atlantic seals, and many can be seen on all the islands' beaches at that time. Boat trips to the Treshnish Islands leave from various ports on Mull and from Iona.

CRAIGNURE

As one approaches Craignure on the ferry from Oban, the great fortress on *dubh ard,* the "black height", becomes ever more imposing. **Duart Castle,** with its huge curtain wall, 30 feet high and 10 feet thick, was built in the 13th century by the Macleans of Duart to protect them from their inveterate enemies, the Campbells. A century later, around 1360, they added the massive Keep that still stands today.

Like many of the clans in the 16th century, the Macleans were a pretty blood-thirsty bunch. Lachland Maclean had taken as his second wife, Catherine, sister of the powerful Earl of Argyll. When Catherine failed to provide an heir, Lachland decided to dispose of her. One night, he bound her, took her to a rock in the Sound of Mull that becomes submerged at high water and abandoned her. The next day, he informed her brother of Catherine's death by drowning. In fact, she had been rescued by fishermen and taken to the earl's castle at Inveraray. A few days later, Lachlan arrived at the castle with his "late" wife's coffin and was ushered into the Great Hall to find Catherine sitting at the head of the table. Throughout the meal that followed no-one made mention of her astonishing resurrection but later that year, 1523, Catherine's family had their revenge. Lachland was visiting Edinburgh when he was surprised by her uncle, the Thane of Cawdor, and stabbed to death in his bed.

At low water, the skerry on which Catherine was marooned, now known as **The Lady Rock,** can be clearly seen from the Sea Room at Duart Castle.

In the Macleans long connection with the castle there is a huge gap of more than 200 years. In 1691, Duart was sacked by their relentless enemies, the Campbells, and then, following the Battle of Culloden, the Maclean estates were confiscated by the Crown and the castle was allowed to become increasingly dilapidated. It wasn't until 1911 that Sir Fitzroy Maclean,10th baronet and 26th Chief of the Clan Maclean, was able to buy Duart and begin the daunting work of restoration. To his eternal credit, Sir Fitzroy disdained any fake medieval additions - none of the extraneous castellations and pepper-pot turrets favoured by most Victorian and Edwardian restorers. When he died here at the age of 101 in 1936, he left behind a castle that was faithful in essentials to the uncompromising spirit of his forefathers who had laid its foundations some 700 years earlier.

At the railway's southern terminus is **Torosay Castle** with its fine gardens. The castle sits in 12 acres of grounds, and is a fine Victorian mansion built in 1858 to the designs of David Bryce in the Scottish Baronial style. The walls of the front hall are crowded with red deer antlers and there's an interesting collection of family portraits by artists such as Sargent and de Laszlo, along with wildlife paintings by Landseer, Thorburn and Peter Scott. Though it is open to the public, Torosay is still the family home of the Guthrie Jones family, who live on the upper floors. The castle was a favourite place of Winston Churchill in his younger years, and on display are photographs of him in the grounds. The castle is open to the public from April to October, while the gardens are open all year round.

Wings Over Mull is at Auchnacroish House, close to the castle, and brooded over by the island's second highest mountain, Dun da Ghaoithe. It is a conservation centre for birds of prey, with owls being especially well represented, though you can also see hawks, kites, eagles and even vultures. There are flying displays every day during the season and a display on the history of falconry.

AROUND CRAIGNURE

LOCHBUIE
18 miles SW of Craignure off the A849

A single track road leaves the A849 at Strathcoil, and heads south and then east towards Lochbuie. **Moy Castle,** built in the 15th century, sits on the shore of Loch Buie and was the family seat of the Macleans of Lochbuie. Inside is a dungeon that floods twice a day with the incoming tide. In the middle of the dungeon is a stone platform where the prisoners had to huddle to keep dry. Because of ongoing restoration work it is not possible to view the interior.

A small island a few miles south off the coast has possibly the most unusual name of any island in the Western Isles - Frank Lockwood's Island. It was named after the brother-in-law of a Maclean of Duart in the 19th century. During the Jacobite Uprising in 1745, the castle on the island was garrisoned by a troop of Campbells. In 1752 it was finally abandoned, and though it is still in a fine state of preservation, it is not open to the public. Close to the castle is one of the very few stone

When Johnson and Boswell were making their Highland tour in the 18th century, they were entertained on the island of Gruline by Sir Alan Maclean, chief of the Macleans of Duart. Johnson described it as a "pretty little island" - praise indeed from a man who disliked most things Scottish.

Inch Kenneth was a favourite haunt of Diana Mitford, whose father Lord Redesdale owned the island. She married the infamous Oswald Mosley, the British Nazi. When her sister Unity was recovering from a suicide bid (she had tried to shoot herself in the head), she stayed on the island until she died of meningitis brought on by the shooting in 1948. Another owner at one time was Sir Harold Boulton, who wrote perhaps the most famous Jacobite song ever- **The Skye Boat Song.** *Many people believe it is a traditional song, but in fact it was written in 1884.*

circles on Mull. There are nine stones, with the circle having a diameter of 35 feet.

BALNAHARD
24 miles SW of Craignure on the B3035

Mackinnon's Cave, on the Ardmeanach Peninsula near Balnahard, can only be reached at low tide, and great care should be taken if you visit. The cave goes hundreds of feet into the cliff face, and you'll need a torch if you want to explore it. It was visited by Dr Johnson, and is said to be the largest cave in the Hebrides, being over 90 feet high. A legend tells of a piper and his dog entering the cave in days gone by. The piper was killed by a witch who lived there, while his dog escaped. At the back of the cave is Fingal's Table, a flat rock used as an altar by early Celtic saints. Also on the Ardmeanach Peninsula is **McCulloch's Tree,** a huge fossil over 36 feet high and three feet in diameter. It is reckoned to be over 50 million years old. There is another fossil in a nearby cave. Part of the land here, including the fossils, is owned by the National Trust for Scotland. The cave can be reached by a track which branches off the A849. To the south of the Ardmeanach Peninsula is Loch Scridain, the largest of the island's sea lochs. Like other locations on Mull, it is famous for its bird life.

FIONNPHORT
38 miles SW of Craignure on the A849

At the end of the A849 is Fionnphort (pronounced "Finnafort", meaning "fair port"),

the ferry terminal for Iona. Before crossing, a visit to the four-star Columba Centre should prepare you for what you'll find on the island. On the shore stands Fingal's Rock, supposedly thrown by the giant Fingal while in a bad temper.

GRULINE
14 miles W of Craignure on the B3035

This small village is best known for the **Macquarie Mausoleum** in which lies Major General Lachlan Macquarie, Governor-General of New South Wales between 1809 and 1820, and sometimes called the "Father of Australia". His mausoleum is a square, cottage-like building of local stone surrounded by a high wall. Also buried here is his wife Elizabeth and their son, also called Lachlan. Born on the island of Ulva in 1762, he joined the army at the age of 14 and quickly rose through the ranks, serving in America, Egypt, Nova Scotia and India. In April 1809 he was appointed Governor of New South Wales, succeeding the highly unpopular William Bligh, former captain of *HMS Bounty*. However, Macquarie suffered frequent bouts of ill health and in 1820 he resigned, having turned New South Wales from a penal colony into a prosperous state.

He died in London in 1824, and his wife built the memorial above his grave in 1834. Now it is owned and maintained by the National Trust of Australia. In the year 2000 the Australian government spent $A70,000 on its refurbishment. So famous was

Macquarie in Australia that there are many towns, schools, universities, streets and even teashops named after him.

At this point Mull is no more than three miles wide, thanks to Loch na Keal, which drives deep into the island in a north easterly direction. Its shores are famous for their birdlife, which includes widgeon, Slavonian grebe, teal, golden eye, mallard, black-throated diver and shelduck. At the entrance to the sea loch is the 130-acre island of Inch Kenneth. Curiously enough, its geology is unlike that of Mull, and it is flat and fertile. The "Kenneth" in question is supposed to be St Cannoch, a contemporary of St Columba. The ruins of **St Kenneth's Chapel** date from the 13th century. In its kirkyard are many wonderfully carved grave slabs. A tradition says that ancient Scottish kings were buried here if the weather was too rough for the royal barges to travel to Iona. One of the best grave slabs is that of an armed man lying with his head on a cushion and his feet on an unnamed animal of some kind. In one hand is a cannonball and in the other is a shield. The shield once had a coat of arms on it, but it has long since been weathered away.

Mull only has two large fresh water lochs. One is the wonderfully named Loch Ba, close to Gruline, which has the remains of a crannog. The other, Loch Frisa, sits in inaccessible country in the north west of the island, and is famous for its bird life. Like Loch Ba, it has some good fishing.

IONA

36 miles W of Oban off the coast of Mull

No tourists' cars are allowed on Iona (National Trust for Scotland), but it is so small (no more than three miles long by a mile and a half wide) that everything on it can easily be visited on foot. It is one of the most sacred spots in Europe (and unfortunately, during the summer months, one of the busiest). This was where St Columba set up his monastery in AD 563. From here, he evangelised the Highlands, converting the Picts to Christianity using a mixture of saintliness, righteous anger and perseverance.

Columba's monastery would have been built of wood and wattle, and little now survives of it apart from some of the cashel, or surrounding wall. The present **Iona Abbey**, on the site of the original monastery, was founded in 1203 by Reginald, son of Somerled, Lord of the Isles, though the present building is early 16th century. It

94 IONA ABBEY & NUNNERY

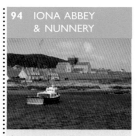

Iona

One of Scotland's most historic and sacred sites, Iona Abbey was founded by St Columba and his Irish followers in AD 563

 see page 404

St Orans Chapel, Iona

223

- • -

Tiree has the reputation of being the sunniest place in Britain, though this is tempered by the fact that it is also the windiest. This has made the island the windsurfing capital of Scotland. Near Vaul to the north east of the island is a curious marked stone called the Ringing Stone, which, when struck, makes a clanging noise. Legend says if it is ever broken the island will disappear beneath the Atlantic.

- • -

- • -

It was in Coll that an incident called the Great Exodus took place. In 1856 the southern part of the island, which was the most fertile, was sold to one John Lorne Stewart. In spite of protests from the crofters who farmed there, he raised their rents to a level they could not afford. So the tenants took matters into their own hands. Overnight, they all left their crofts and moved north to the less hospitable lands owned by the Campbells, where the rents were reasonable. Lorne Stewart was powerless to stop them leaving, and was left with no rent income whatsoever.

- • -

was a Benedictine foundation and later became a cathedral. By the 18th century it was roofless, and the cloisters and other buildings were in ruins. In the 20th century they were restored by the Rev George MacLeod, a Church of Scotland minister who went on to found the Iona Community.

Beside the cathedral is the Reilig Odhrain, or St Oran's Cemetery. Within it is the **Ridge of the Chiefs**, which is supposed to contain the bodies of many West Highland chiefs who were buried here in medieval times. Close by is the **Ridge of the Kings** where, it is claimed, no fewer than 48 Scottish, eight Norwegian and four Irish kings lie buried, including Macbeth. However, modern historians now doubt if any kings are buried there at all apart from some from ancient Dalriada. They say that the claims were a "marketing exercise" by the monks to enhance their abbey.

One man who does lie within the cemetery is John Smith the politician, who was buried there in 1994. **St Oran's Chapel**, near the cemetery, was built as a funeral chapel in the 12th century by one of the Lords of the Isles. The ruins of **St Mary's Nunnery** are near the jetty, and date from the 13th century. It too was founded by Reginald, and he placed his sister Beatrice in charge as prioress. A small museum has been established in the **Chapel of St Ronan** close to the ruins.

Just west of the cathedral is the Tor Ab, a low mound on which

St Columba's cell may have been situated. Of the many crosses on the island, the best are the 10th century St Martin's Cross, outside the main abbey door, and the 16th century MacLean's Cross.

In the former parish church manse (designed by Telford) is the **Iona Heritage Centre**, which traces the history of the people who have lived on the island throughout the years.

STAFFA
34 miles W of Oban in the Atlantic Ocean

The most remarkable feature of this small uninhabited island is **Fingal's Cave** which was visited in August 1829 by the composer Felix Mendelssohn. Though he found Edinburgh delightful, he was less enamoured of the Highlands which he declared to be full of "fog and foul weather". When he made the boat trip to see the cave, he was violently seasick and called the cave "odious". However, it later inspired one of his most famous works, the Hebrides Overture. The cliffs are formed from hexagonal columns of basalt that look like wooden staves, some more than 50 feet high. The Vikings therefore named the island *Stafi Øy* (Stave Island) from which it got its modern name.

Boat trips to the island are available from Mull and Iona.

COLL AND TIREE
50 miles W of Oban in the Atlantic Ocean

These two islands, lying beyond Mull, can be reached by ferry from Oban. They are generally low lying, and can be explored by car in a few hours. The ferry first stops at Arinagiour, Coll's main village before going on to Scarinish on Tiree.

Tiree means the "land of corn", as it is one of the most fertile of the Inner Hebridean islands. It is sometimes called Tir fo Thuinn, meaning the "land beneath the waves", because of its relative flatness. Its highest peaks are Ben Hynish (460 feet) and Ben Hough (387 feet). In the south eastern corner of the island is the spectacular headland of **Ceann a'Marra**, with its massive sea cliffs. They are home to thousands of sea birds, and on the shoreline you can see seals basking in the sun.

At Sandaig is the tiny **Sandaig Island Life Museum**, housed in a restored thatched cottage.

The **Skerryvore Lighthouse Museum** at Hynish tells the story of the Skerryvore lighthouse, ten miles to the south on rocks surrounded by open sea. It was designed by Alan Stevenson, uncle of Robert Louis Stevenson, and completed in 1842. The museum is within houses built for the Skerryvore workers.

SKYE

Skye is the best known and, at 50 miles long and up to 25 miles wide, one of the largest of the islands of Scotland. It is now linked to the mainland by the Skye Road Bridge, opened in 1995. Skye is one of the most beautiful and haunting of the Inner Hebrides, and the place has beauty and history aplenty. It is one

of the few Inner Hebridean islands that has seen an increase in population over the last few years, due to people from the mainland settling there to find a better quality of life.

Perhaps the most famous features on the island are the **Cuillin Hills**, a range of mountains in the south east of the island. They are divided into the Black Cuillin and the Red Cuillin. The former are made from hard rock that has been shaped into jagged peaks and ridges by the last Ice Age, while the latter are of soft granite which has been weathered by wind and rain into softer, more rounded peaks. Though not the highest, they are perhaps the most spectacular mountains in Scotland, and present a challenge to any climber. The highest peak is Sgurr Alasdair, at 3257 feet.

BROADFORD

Broadford has the distinction of being Skye's largest crafting township. It's a long straggling village set beside the bay of the same name and surrounded by dramatic hills - Beinn na Cailleach (2403 feet), the Red Hills and Applecross. The village is well-placed for exploring south Skye and has a number of good shops selling gifts or souvenirs.

A mile or so the east of Broadford, at Harrapool, is the **Skye Serpentarium Reptile World**, an award winning reptile exhibition. It suffered a serious fire in 2006 in which 149 reptiles

95 BEINN NA CAILLICH CAFÉ

Broadford

Superb restaurant serving appetising food; also Craft and Gift Shop.

🍴 see page 404

96 LUIB HOUSE BED & BREAKFAST

Broadford

A warm welcome awaits at this beautifully located B&B nestling in the shadow of the Red Cuillins.

🛏 see page 405

97 SAUCY MARY'S LODGE

Kyleakin

A comfortable and popular hostel surrounded by coastal and mountain views.

see page 405

98 THE MACKINNON COUNTRY HOUSE HOTEL

Kyleakin

Overlooked by the magnificent Sgurr na Coinnich mountain range and offering excellent cuisine and en suite rooms.

see page 406

99 CAFÉ ARRIBA

Portree

Lively town centre café/ bistro where good food and value for money go hand in hand.

see page 407

perished but since then it has been re-stocked. There are now more than 50 animals on display ranging from White's Tree Frogs to Large Green Iguanas.

From Broadford, the A87 passes through Sconser, the southern terminus of a ferry linking Skye to the smaller island of Raasay, before reaching the island's main settlement of Portree.

AROUND BROADFORD

KYLEAKLIN

7 miles E of Broadford on the A87

Kyleakin stands at the western end of the Skye Road Bridge and is notable for the **Bright Water Visitor Centre** which offers tours to the island nature reserve of *Eilean Ban* ("White Island") beneath the bridge. This was where Gavin Maxwell, author of *Ring of Bright Water*, once lived. Nearby are the ruins of **Castle Moil** , which was a stronghold of Clan Mackinnon. In the 17th century they abandoned the castle, and it gradually fell into disrepair.

ARMADALE

17 miles S of Broadford on the A851

Armadale lies on the Sleat Peninsula (pronounced "slate") in the southeast corner of Skye. This is the most fertile part of the island, an area which also goes by the name of the "Garden of Skye". An attractive village, Armadale is strung along the wooded shore and during the summer is linked to

Mallaig on the mainland by a regular vehicle ferry.

Just outside the village is the **Armadale Castle Gardens and Museum of the Isles**. It sits within a 20,000 acre Highland estate, once owned by the MacDonalds of Sleat, and was purchased by the Clan Donald Land Trust in 1971. The earliest parts of the castle date from the 1790s, when it was built by the first Lord MacDonald on the site of a farm and gardens where Flora MacDonald married in 1750.

PORTREE

In Gaelic, *port an righ* (now Portree), means "king's harbour", a name assumed after James V came here in 1540 to mediate a feud between the Macleod and Macdonald clans. A more melancholy visitor to Portree was Bonnie Prince Charlie as he prepared to leave for France and lifelong exile. Taking his leave of Flora Macdonald, the prince rather optimistically remarked "for all that has happened, I hope, Madam, that we shall meet in St James' yet". the room at McNab's Inn where he bade her farewell is now part of the Royal Hotel.

With a population of around 2000, Portree is the largest community on the island and its administrative centre. It's an attractive little town, enclosed by wooded hills with a deep, cliff-lined harbour busy with fishing boats and with whitewashed buildings all around. The harbour is well protected by the bulk of the Isle of

Raasay which is easily reached by one of the regular boat trips available.

One of the oldest buildings in Portree is Meall House, the former jail and courthouse. Until quite recently it housed the Tourist Information Centre with the manager's office located in what used to be the condemned cell. From here those sentenced to death would be taken to **The Lump,** overlooking the harbour. On this steep peninsula a flagpole marks the site of the gallows to which as many as 5000 would flock for the free entertainment of a public execution.

Much more pleasant entertainment (albeit for a modest charge) can be found at the **Aros Experience** on Viewfield Road on the south side of the town. This arts centre incorporates a theatre, cinema, shops and exhibition area. Nearby **An Tuireann Art Centre,** on Struan Road off the A87 to Uig, is a gallery that presents exhibitions of contemporary art and crafts.

The town is the gateway to the Trotternish Peninsula, which juts out for 20 miles into the Minch, the sea channel separating the Outer Hebrides from the mainland. A road from Portree follows its coastline right round until it arrives back at the town. **Dun Gerashader,** a prehistoric hill fort, lies about a mile north of Portree just off the A855. The fort still has some of its stone ramparts intact. Also off the A855, about seven miles north of Portree is the extraordinary 160 feet high pinnacle of rock known as the **Old**

Man of Storr which looks as if one vigorous push would topple it. It's actually part of a massive landslip from the face of the Storr mountain (2358 feet) which still occasionally sheds huge blocks of stone. The Old Man can be reached by an easy 30-minute walk from the car park on the A855. There are many other spectacular and eccentric rock formations to the north, most notably **The Quirking** (pronounced Crooking) with its outlandish forest of huge pinnacles and tortured rocks.

To the north, the **Lealt Falls** are possibly the most spectacular on the island. Though not visible from the road, there is a lay-by where you can park your car then walk the hundred yards or so to the gorge and the falls themselves. A few miles away is Kilt Rock, a formation of basalt rocks above the the shore that resembles the folds of a kilt. **Kilt Rock Waterfall,** which plunges down some cliffs into the sea, can also be seen.

100 THE ISLES INN AND THE PORTREE HOTEL

Portree

Well known for quality food using locally sourced ingredients, The Isles Inn and The Portree Hotel are both extremely popular establishments

🍴 🛏 *see page 407*

101 URQUHART CALEDONIAN HOTEL

Portree

Great accommodation in the heart of Wick, recently voted as one of the top six music venues in Scotland.

🛏 🍴 *see page 408*

Old Man of Storr, Skye

102 GRESHORNISH HOUSE

Edinbane, by Portree

A stunning white manor house secluded in a charming, loch-side setting

🛏 🍴 *see page 409*

103 THE BOTHY & BARN

Staffin

Quality self-catering accommodation in converted farm buildings set amidst spectacular countryside.

🛏 *see page 408*

104 THE FERRY INN

Uig

Superbly located with comfortable ensuite rooms, restaurant and friendly bars

🍴 🛏 *see page 410*

AROUND PORTREE

STAFFIN

21 miles N of Portree off the A855

The village of Staffin has the **Staffin Museum**, famous for its collection of dinosaur bones, the first ever discovered in Scotland. At An Corran, close to Staffin Bay, is a prehistoric rock shelter dating from 8000 years ago.

North of Staffin, within the grounds of the Flodigarry Country House Hotel, is **Flodigarry House**, where Flora MacDonald and her husband Allan MacDonald settled in 1751. Some people imagine Flora was a simple, Highland lass who helped Charles Edward Stuart, disguised as her Irish maid Betty Burke, cross from the Western Isles to Skye by boat. She came, in fact, from a wealthy family who were tenant farmers on South Uist, though she herself was brought up on Skye and went to school in Edinburgh. The sea crossing from Benbecula to Skye is remembered in the famous Skye Boat Song. However, it is not, as some people imagine, a traditional Jacobite song. It was written by an Englishman, Sir Harold Boulton, in 1884.

KILMUIR

22 miles NW of Portree off the A855

The **Skye Museum of Island Life** at Kilmuir is near the northern tip of the Trotternish Peninsula, and is a group of seven thatched cottages furnished very much as they would have been in times long past. Here you can also learn about the crofter rebellions of the 19th century, plus exhibits connected with Charles Edward Stuart and Flora MacDonald.

DUNVEGAN

16 miles W of Portree on the A850

Dunvegan is famous for **Dunvegan Castle**, perched above the waters of Loch Dunvegan. It has been the home of Clan MacLeod for eight hundred years and though much of it is Victorian, parts date back to the 13th century. In the drawing room is the famous **Fairy Flag,** revered by members of Clan MacLeod, which was supposed to bring success in battle. It is one of Clan MacLeod's most important possessions, and legends abound about its origins. Experts have examined the flag and say that the cloth is Middle East silk from either Rhodes or Syria. For this reason, some people have

Fairy Flag, Dunvegan Castle

connected it to the Crusades. But the fabric dates from about AD 400 to AD 800, many years before the Crusades took place. Another theory says it was the battle flag of King Harold Hardrada of Norway, who was killed in 1066. But how did he get hold of a flag from the Mediterranean?

The tower in which the flag used to be housed was consequently named the Fairy Tower, a dainty name for a building with massive walls 10 feet thick in places and still exactly as they were when built in 1500 by the 8th Chief, Alasdair "Crotach", or hunchback. The Chief's deformity resulted not from a birth defect but from having an axe driven between his shoulder-blades in battle.

Little changed at Dunvegan for almost 400 years but towards the end of the century, the 23rd Chief, Gen. Norman MacLeod, began a thorough overhaul of the castle in order to make it more inviting for his young second wife, Sarah, fresh from the pampered life of colonial India. He remodelled the Great hall into an elegant Georgian-style drawing-room, acquired some fine paintings by Ramsay and Raeburn, and generally transformed an uncompromising fortress into a gracious home. Half a century later, his grandson put the finishing touches to the castle as we see it today, adding battlements and the dummy pepper-pot turrets that give this sprawling building its remarkable unity.

In addition to this remarkable building, visitors can explore the 10 acres of gardens and woodland; take a boat trip on Loch Dunvegan to see the seal colony; charter a traditionally built clinker boat for a fishing trip or loch cruise; stay in one of the delightful estate cottages; sample the fare on offer at the MacLeod's Table or browse around the four shops.

COLBOST

22 miles NW of Portree off the B884

On the other side of Loch Dunvegan and reached by the B884, is the **Colbost Croft Museum**, based on a "black house" (a small traditional cottage of turf or stone, topped with a thatched roof). It shows the living conditions of islanders in the past, and features an illicit still. Black houses got their name, not because they were blackened inside by the peat fire, but to differentiate them from the "white houses" which were built in Victorian and later times, and which were more modern and usually painted white.

Travelling north from Colbost along a minor road brings you to Boreraig and the **MacCrimmon Piping Heritage Centre.** The MacCrimmons were the hereditary pipers to the MacLeods and reckoned to be the finest pipers in the country.

EIGG

42 miles NW of Oban in the Atlantic Ocean

In 1997 the island of Eigg was bought on behalf of its inhabitants by the Isle of Eigg Heritage Trust

Loch Chaluim Chille on the Trotternish Peninsula was at one time one of Skye's largest lochs, being over two miles long. It was drained in the early 19th century to create grazing land, and now you can walk across the old loch bed to what used to be islands to see the remains of an old Celtic monastery.

West of Colbost is the Glendale Toy Museum which as well as featuring antique toys also has displays of modern ones from films such as Star Wars, Barbie and Action Man. Many of the games can be enjoyed, demonstrated and played with. The small shop stocks the museum's own handmade games, traditional toys and crafts, plus a wide range of collectors items and well known stocking fillers at realistic prices.

from the German artist who called himself "Maruma". Its most famous feature is the 1277 feet high **An Sgurr**, which slopes gently up to a peak on one side, and dramatically plunges on the other.

Southwest of the main pier is St Francis's Cave, also known as the **Massacre Cave**. It got its name from a gruesome event in 1577, when nearly 400 MacDonalds took refuge there when pursued by a force of MacLeods. The MacLeods lit fires at the entrance, and every one of the MacDonalds was suffocated to death. The story was given some credence when human bones were removed from the cave in the 19th century and buried. A nearby cave, MacDonald's Cave, is also known as the Cathedral Cave, as it was used for secret Catholic church services following 1745.

At Kildonnan, on the west coast, are the ruins of a 14th century church, built on the site of an ancient Celtic monastery founded by St Donan. The saint and his 52 monks were massacred in AD 617 by a band of pirates.

MUCK

39 miles NW of Oban in the Atlantic Ocean

The tiny island of Muck's improbable name comes from "eilean nam muc", meaning "island of pigs", though in this case the pigs may be porpoises, which are called "sea pigs" in Gaelic. It is reached by ferry from Mallaig, and is a low-lying island with good beaches. Port Mor is

the main settlement and harbour, with, above it, an ancient graveyard and ruined church. On the south side of the Port Mor inlet are the scant remains of **Dun Ban**, a prehistoric fort. The highest point at 445 feet, is Beinn Airein, and from the top there is a good view of the whole of the island.

RUM

47 miles W of Fort William

When Sir John Bullough bought the island of Rum in 1888 he arrogantly changed its name to "Rhum", as he disliked the associations it had with alcoholic drinks. However, when the Nature Conservancy Council took over the island in 1957 they changed the name back to the more correct "Rum", meaning "wide island", and it has been that ever since. Nowadays it is a Special Site of Scientific Interest and a Specially Protected Area, as its plant life has remained almost unchanged since the Ice Age.

The main settlement is Kinloch, on the east coast. **Kinloch Castle**, overlooking Loch Scresort, was built by Sir George Bullough, John's son, as his main home on the island between 1901 and 1902. The **Bullough Mausoleum** in Glen Harris, to the south of the island, was built to take the bodies of Sir George, his father John and his wife Monica.

Kilmory, on the north coast of the island, has a fine beach and an ancient burial ground.

Isle of Canna

CANNA

60 miles NW of Oban in the Atlantic Ocean

Canna means the "porpoise island", and has been owned by the National Trust for Scotland since 1981 when it was given to them by Gaelic scholar John Lorne Campbell. It is about five miles long by just over a mile wide at its widest, and is usually sunny and mild. The remains of **St Columba's Chapel**, dating from the 7th or 8th centuries, with an accompanying Celtic cross, stand opposite the small island of Sanday, and have been excavated.

An Corghan, on the east coast, is all that is left of a small tower house where a Clanranald chief imprisoned his wife who was having an affair with a MacLeod clansman. At Uaigh Righ Lochlain can be seen remnants of Viking occupation, and at Camas Tairbearnais, a bay on the western side of the island, a Viking ship burial was uncovered. Sanday is a small island which lies off the south east coast and is joined to it by a bridge and, at low tide, a sand bar. Canna is reached by ferry from Mallaig.

Perthshire, Angus & Kinross

"Perthshire forms the fairest portion of the northern kingdom - the most varied and the most beautiful". That was Sir Walter Scott's opinion and few visitors to "Scotland in Miniature" would disagree.

It's an area renowned for the splendour of its noble mountains and romantic lochs. The country's tumultuous past is reflected in historic sites such as Loch Leven Castle, where Mary, Queen of Scots made a famous escape, ruined Dunkeld Abbey and Scone Palace where all 42 of Scotland's kings were crowned. Perth itself is one of the stateliest towns in

the realm and the great open spaces of the county make it ideal for a wealth of outdoor pursuits - shooting, fishing, skiing and, naturally, golf, with a total of 38 courses to choose from. And for lovers of good food, Perthshire represents a lavishly stocked outdoor

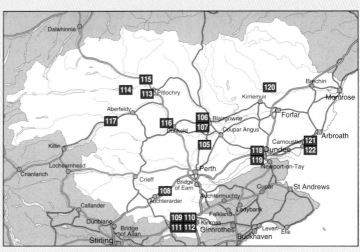

larder full of prime ingredients - salmon, trout, beef, game and venison.

Perthshire is a wholly inland county, the county of Loch Rannoch and Loch Tummel, and of possibly the loneliest railway station in Britain, Rannoch, deep within the bleak expanse of Rannoch Moor. It is also the county of the Gleneagles Hotel, one of Britain's most luxurious, and of rich farmland surrounding Perth itself. Blairgowrie is the centre of Scotland's fruit growing industry - fruit that once fed the Dundee jam makers.

Angus has a coastline that takes in high cliffs and sandy beaches. The coastal towns are famous. Carnoustie, where the British Open is sometimes held; Montrose and its almost land-locked basin where wildfowl can be seen; and of course Arbroath, with the ruins of an abbey where one of the momentous documents in Scottish history was signed - the Declaration of Arbroath. Inland, the countryside is gentle and pastoral, with the glens of Angus, such as Glen Prosen, Glen Clova and Glen Doll, being particularly beautiful as they wind their way into the foothills of the Cairngorms.

Kinross sits to the south east of Perthshire. It lies within a great saucer-shaped depression with, at its heart, Loch Leven. The main industry is farming, and the gentle countryside, ringed by hills, is well worth exploring if only for the sense of "getting away from it all". Loch Leven is famous for its fishing, and Vane Farm Nature Reserve was the first educational nature reserve in Europe.

PERTH

In the heart of the city stands the striking medieval St John's Kirk. From this church, the city took its earlier name of St Johnstoune, which is remembered in the name of the local football team. The kirk was consecrated in 1243, though the earliest part of what you see nowadays, the choir, dates from the 15th century, with the tower being added in 1511. It was at St John's, in May 1559, that John Knox first preached after his exile in Europe. His rabble-rousing sermon provoked an anti-Catholic riot in which four monasteries were razed to the ground, including the historic abbey at Scone, 2 miles north of the town. It was a defining moment in the movement for church reform in Scotland.

For a hundred years until 1437 the "Fair City of Perth" was Scotland's capital and it still carries an air of distinction. A regular winner of the "Britain in Bloom" competition, it has also received the accolade of providing the "Best Quality of Life in Britain".

Beautifully set beside the River Tay, it has a compact city centre framed by two extensive parks, the **North Inch** and **South Inch.** The North Inch was the site of a bloody tournament in 1396 which became known as the Battle of the Clans and later served as the background to Scott's novel *The Fair Maid of Perth.* The historical Fair Maid was Catherine Glover who in the 14th century lived in a house in Northport which is now the oldest dwelling in the city. The present **Fair Maid's House** (private) does not go back as far as the 14th century. However, it is more than 300 years old, and incorporates some medieval walls which may have belonged to the original house that stood on the site. In 1867 Bizet wrote his opera *The Fair Maid of Perth,* based on Scott's book, and the story became even more popular.

Just around the corner from the Fair Maid's House, the city's impressive **Art Gallery & Museum** is one of the oldest in Britain. It houses material whose scope goes beyond the city and its immediate area, as well as a collection of fine paintings, sculpture, glass and silver. There are also displays on local industries, with due prominence given to whisky since 3 major producers all had their origins here - Dewar's, Bells and Famous Grouse. There's more industrial heritage on display at **Stanley Mills,** a new visitor centre 4 miles north of Perth, which explains how the mill harnessed the power of the River Tay to drive cotton-spinning machines. And at the **Caithness Glass Visitor Centre** at Inveralmond there are viewing galleries from which you can see glass being blown into beautiful glass ornaments and vases.

Today, the area around St John's is the perfect place to pause and soak up the atmosphere in one of the many restaurants and coffee shops of what is now known as the Café Quarter. Also close by is the splendid **Fergusson Gallery,** a must for lovers of both fine art and striking architecture. It is housed in the former Perth Waterworks, completed in 1832 and now a Grade A listed building. Its impressive Rotunda is one of the most visually arresting sights in the city. The gallery boasts the largest single collection of works by Scotland's foremost "colourist" painter, John Duncan Fergusson (1874-1961).

Occupying a rather confined site in the north of the central area, **St Ninian's Cathedral** is easy to miss but is worth visiting to see its superb interior, designed by William Butterfield and looking much more venerable than its 19th century provenance. Consecrated in

1850, St Ninian's was the first cathedral to be built in Britain since the Reformation.

A recent addition to the city's cultural amenities is the new £20 million state-of-the-art **Perth Concert Hall** which stands on the site of the original Horsecross - Perth's 17th century horse market. Opened in 2005, it has an eye-catching glass-fronted foyer and copper-topped dome hall with a superb auditorium.

Bell's Cherrybank Gardens is an 18-acre garden on the western edge of the city. It incorporates the National Heather Collection which has more than 900 varieties of heather. On Dundee road is the **Branklyn Garden** (NTS), developed by John and Dorothy Renton since 1922. One of its more unusual plants is the rare blue Himalayan poppy. **Kinnoull Hill**, to the east of Perth, rises to a height of 729 feet above the Tay. If you are reasonably fit, you can walk to the summit, where there is a folly and get some wonderful views across the Tay to Fife, over to Perth and beyond, and down over the Carse of Gowrie.

AROUND PERTH

SCONE PALACE

2 miles N of Perth off the A93

Scone Palace is one of the most historic sites in Scotland. Between AD 840 and 1296, all 42 of Scotland's kings were "made" (not "crowned") on the Stone of Scone. The Stone, also known as the Stone of Destiny, was brought here by the first King of All Scotland, Kenneth McAlpin. Kenneth had acquired the throne by the rather sneaky method of inviting his Pictish enemies to a feast at Scone, waiting until they were helpless with drink, and then massacring the lot of them. An odd feature of the king-making at Scone was that all the nobles in attendance carried some earth from their own lands inside their boots. The mound on which the later abbey stood was supposedly formed as they emptied their footwear after the ceremony. The abbey no longer stands. It was one of those destroyed by the Perth mob after John Knox's inflammatory anti-Catholic sermon in 1559. Strangely, the rioters spared the Bishop's Palace and this forms the core of the present building. Since 1604, the Palace has been the home of the Murray family, later Earls of Mansfield. It was the 3rd Earl who, in 1802, began enlarging the house in the Gothic style popular at the time, creating what Queen Victoria was to call *"A fine-looking house of reddish stone"*.

The State Rooms of Scone Palace contain a magnificent array of objets d'art, including pieces that once belonged to Marie Antoinette. The treasures include a priceless collection of Meissen and Sèvres porcelain accumulated by the 2nd Earl during his assignments as Ambassador to Dresden, Vienna and Paris, along with exquisite sets from Chelsea, Derby and Worcester. With such a huge collection, the earl was able to

When Balhousie Castle was built in the 1400s, it stood well outside the city but now stands rather uncomfortably on the edge of a residential area. The castle was formerly the home of the Earls of Kinnoull but is now devoted to the Black Watch Regimental Museum, celebrating the exploits of the historic regiment founded in 1725 and now the senior Highland regiment.

105 MEIKLEOUR HOTEL

Meikleour, nr Blairgowrie

Come here for the imaginative locally-sourced bistro menu, stay for the welcoming lively atmosphere.

 see page 411

106 THE OLD CROSS INN & RESTAURANT

Rattray

Family-owned and family-friendly inn serving excellent home-made food, real ale and (soon) accommodation.

see page 411

107 DRUMELLIE MEADOW

Wester Essendy, by Blairgowrie

Providing 4 star Bed and Breakfast close to Blairgowrie, in Perthshire, **Drumellie Meadow** is a ranch style home set in three acres of wooded gardens

 see page 412

ensure that distinguished guests never dined twice off the same service. In the Ambassador's Room stands a magnificent bed presented to the earl by George III, its rich crimson hangings liberally sprinkled with the royal cypher and coat of arms. Nearby hangs Zoffany's enchanting portrait, *Lady Elizabeth Murray with Dido*. Elizabeth was the 1st Earl's daughter; Dido a black slave he had freed. His unprecedented action helped spark off the anti-slavery movement. Other fine paintings include major works by Reynolds and Allan Ramsay.

Within the grounds of the palace are some wonderful collections of shrubs, woodland walks through the 200-year-old pinetum which contains the original British Douglas Fir, a maze, adventure playground, picnic park, gift shop and coffee shop.

BANKFOOT

8 miles N of Perth off the A9

This small village sits just off the A9. The **Macbeth Experience** is a multi-media show that explains all about one of Scotland's most famous kings. It debunks the Macbeth of Shakespeare's play and instead concentrates on the actual man and his achievements.

MEIKLEOUR

10 miles N of Perth on A984

The **Meikleour Hedge,** just outside the village on the A93, is the world's largest, earning itself an entry in the *Guinness Book of Records*. It borders the road for

more than 600 yards and is now more than 85 feet high. It is of pure beech, and was supposed to have been planted in 1745 by Jean Mercer and her husband Robert Murray Nairne who was later killed at the Battle of Culloden. Jean immediately left the area, and the hedge was allowed to grow unattended for many years.

BLAIRGOWRIE

16 miles N of Perth on the A93

This trim town, along with its sister town of Rattray, became one burgh in 1928 by an Act of Parliament. It is noted as the centre of a raspberry and strawberry growing area. It sits beside the Ericht, a tributary of the Tay, and the riverside here is very attractive. Cargill's Visitor Centre, housed in a former corn mill, stands on its bank and has Scotland's largest water wheel. Within the library in Leslie Street is the Blairgowrie Genealogy Centre where you can carry out research on the old families of the area.

Craighall Castle, the earliest parts of which date from the 16th century, is perched on a cliff above the Elricht. Sir Walter Scott visited it, and he used it as a model for Tullyveolan in his book *Waverley*. It now offers B&B accommodation.

COUPAR ANGUS

12 miles NE of Perth on the A94

Situated in Strathmore, Coupar Angus is a small town which was given its burgh charter in 1607. The scant remains of the gatehouse of **Coupar Angus Abbey**, founded by

Malcolm IV for the Cistercians in the mid-12th century, stand in the kirkyard. At one time it was the wealthiest Cistercian abbey in Scotland. The town's **Tolbooth** dates from 1702, and was used as a courthouse and prison.

MEIGLE

17 miles NE of Perth on the B954

Tucked away at the foot of the Sidlaw Hills, the tiny village of Meigle has become a place of pilgrimage for anyone interested in Scotland's distant past. In the little churchyard here were found no fewer than thirty of the most remarkable early Christian and Pictish inscribed stones. They date from the seventh to the tenth centuries and it remains a mystery why so many of them should have been erected at Meigle. The most impressive of them all is an 8 feet high cross, delicately carved with both Biblical characters and mythological creatures. According to tradition, this graceful memorial - red sandstone at its base, merging into grey at the top - is the gravestone of Queen Guinevere but the meaning of the enigmatic symbols has yet to be deciphered. This striking collection is housed in the **Meigle Museum**.

ERROL

8 miles E of Perth off the A90

Set in the Carse of Gowrie, a narrow stretch of fertile land bordering the northern shore of the Firth of Tay, Errol is a peaceful village with a large **Parish Church** of 1831 designed by James

Gillespie Graham which is sometimes called the "cathedral of the Carse". It gives its name to an earldom, which means that there is an "Earl of Errol" (see Slains Castle). A leaflet is available which gives details of most of the old kirkyards and kirks in the Carse. The **Tayreed Company**, based in an industrial estate, harvests reeds for thatching from reedbeds on the nearby Tay. In the 1990s the **Errol Station Trust** opened the former railway station as a heritage centre. It is now a coffee and craft shop.

ELCHO

3 miles SE of Perth on a minor road

Elcho Castle (Historic Scotland) was the ancient seat of the Earls of Wemyss. The present handsome and complete castle was built by Sir John Wemyss in the 16th century on the site of an earlier fortification dating from the 13th century. By about 1780, the castle had been abandoned, and it gradually became ruinous. It was re-roofed in 1830.

ABERNETHY

7 miles SE of Perth on the A913

The pleasant village of Abernethy stands on the banks of the River Earn where it joins the River Tay. It is best known for the 75-feet high **Abernethy Round Tower** (Historic Scotland) which is one of only two round towers in Scotland (the other is in Brechin). It dates from the end of the 9th century and was used as a place of refuge for priests during times of trouble. At the foot of the tower is a carved Pictish stone.

The Cateran Trail is named after medieval brigands from beyond Braemar who used to descend on Perthshire to wreak havoc and steal cattle. It is a 60-mile long circular route centred on Blairgowrie, and uses existing footpaths and minor roads to take you on a tour of the area. It has been designed to take about five or six days to complete, with stops every 12 or 13 miles, and takes in parts of Angus as well as Perthshire.

237

108 SMIDDY HAUGH HOTEL

Aberuthven

A former traditional coaching inn that has a growing reputation for the quality service and delicious cuisine it offers, which is made using the finest, local, seasonal produce.

  see page 412

In 1072 Malcolm III met William the Conqueror here and knelt in submission, acknowledging him as his overlord. This was an act which had repercussions down through the ages - Edward I used it to justify his claim that Scottish kings owed allegiance to him. The **Abernethy Museum**, founded in the year 2000, explains the village's history, and is housed in an 18th century building.

In Main Street the oddly named Tootie House is a reminder of the days when the cowherd blew his horn as a signal for the villagers to release their cows to be driven to the common grazing.

DUNNING

9 miles SW of Perth on the B934

This quiet village is mainly visited because of **St Serf's Parish Church**, with its fine early-13th century tower. A couple of miles outside the village, near the road, is a monument topped with a cross which marks the spot where, according to its inscription, **Maggie Wall**, a witch, was burned in 1657. It is the only memorial to a witch in Scotland, though no record has ever been found about the trial or execution of someone called Maggie Wall.

AUCHTERARDER

12 miles SW of Perth on the A824

"A city set on a hill cannot be hid" was one of Auchterarder's promotional lines and although it's an 800-year-old Royal Burgh rather than a city, the town certainly enjoys an elevated position with the stunning scenery of the Grampian Mountains as a backdrop. Auchterarder is known locally as the Lang Toon because of its lengthy High Street. The town has been bypassed by the busy A9 and retains a quiet charm. At **Auchterarder Heritage**, within the local tourist office in the High Street, there are displays about local history. It was in Auchterarder in 1559 that Mary of Guise, mother of Mary, Queen of Scots, signed the Treaty of Perth acknowledging that Scotland was a Protestant country.

About three miles west of the town, near the A823, is the cruciform **Tullibardine Chapel** (Historic Scotland), one of the few finished collegiate chapels in Scotland that have remained unaltered over the years. It was founded by Sir David Murray of Tullibardine, ancestor of the Dukes of Atholl, in 1446.

The village nestles at the foot of the Ochil Hills whose springs are noted for the purity of their waters. Presumably this was why Scotland's first public brewery was built here. Records have survived showing that at James IV's coronation in 1488 beer from Tullibardine brewery was drunk. The site of the brewery is now occupied by the Tullibardine Distillery which produces a fine single malt whiskey. It has a visitors centre which is open from May to September each year.

MUTHILL

20 miles SW of Perth on the A822

Within Muthill (pronounced "Mew-thill") are the ruins of the former **Muthill Parish Church** (Historic Scotland), which date mainly from the early 1400s, though the tower was probably built four centuries earlier. The **Muthill Village Museum** is housed in a cottage built about 1760. It is open on Wednesdays, Saturdays and Sundays from June to September each year.

At Innerpeffray are the ruins of **Innerpeffray Castle**. It is a simple tower house dating from the 15th century which was heightened in 1610 for the 1st Lord Maddertie.

BRACO

20 miles SW of Perth on the A822

Just outside the quiet village of Braco, the **Phoenix Falconry** offers visitors the opportunity of handling and flying a selection of more than 80 spectacular hawks, owls, falcons and eagles. Sessions range from 1-hour tutorials in basic training to 5-hour safaris in the Perthshire hills pursuing game wit your own trained bird.

Drummond Castle Gardens are regarded as amongst the finest in Europe. They were first laid out in the 17th century, improved and terraced in the 19th, and replanted in the middle of the 20th. There's a magnificent Italianate parterre and a mile-long beech-lined avenue leading to an imposing ridge-top tower house (private). In 1842, Queen Victoria visited the castle and its gardens and planted two copper beech trees which are still standing and in good health.

FOWLIS WESTER

14 miles W of Perth
on a minor road off the A85

The first name of this small village (pronounced "fowls") comes from the Gaelic "foghlais", meaning "stream" or burn. However, there is another, more intriguing derivation. It seems that long ago three French brothers settled in Scotland - one at Fowlis Wester, one at Fowlis Easter near Dundee and one at Fowlis in Ross-shire. They each named their village after the French word for leaves, "feuilles". Above an archway in the **Parish Church of St Bean** in Fowlis Wester is a carving showing three leaves.

The church stands on a spot where a place of worship has stood since at least the eighth century. The present one dates from the 15th century, and is dedicated to an 8th century Irish saint, grandson of the King of Leinster, who preached in the area. The church has a leper's squint, a small window which allowed lepers to see the chancel area without coming into contact with the congregation. Two Pictish cross slabs from the 8th or 9th centuries are housed within the church - a ten-feet high cross slab and a smaller one. The larger one shows two horsemen and some animals on one side and a man leading a cow and six men on the other. The smaller slab shows two men - possibly priests - seated on chairs. A replica of the larger one stands on the village green. Also in the church is a fragment of the

•

Three miles east of Muthill, at Innerpeffray, is Innerpeffray Library, one of the oldest libraries in Scotland. It was founded in 1680 by David Drummond, 3rd Lord Maddertie and brother-in-law of the Marquis of Montrose, and is housed in a building specially built for it in 1750. It contains many rare books, amongst them a copy of the 16th century Treacle Bible, so called because the translation of Jeremiah chapter 8 verse 22 reads, "Is there not triacle (treacle) at Gilead". There is also a 1508 Ship of Fools, a medieval satire written by a German writer called Simon Brant. Before moving to its present building it was housed in Innerpeffray Chapel, (Historic Scotland), built in 1508.

•

The Baird Monument in Crieff stands on a hill and was erected by his widow in memory of Sir David Baird (1757-1829), the distinguished general whose achievements included taking South Africa from the Dutch.

McBean tartan, taken to the moon by American astronaut Alan Bean. He was the lunar module pilot on Apollo 12 during the second mission to the moon in November 1969, and the fourth man to walk on its surface.

CRIEFF

17 miles W of Perth on the A85

The second largest town in Perthshire with a population of around 6000, Crieff is an inland holiday resort and the "capital" of

Drummond Castle Gardens, Crieff

that area of Scotland known as Strathearn. Cliinging to a hillside above the River Earn, Crieff is a mellow town with peaceful flower-filled gardens and parks, and streets winding up the steep hill. At the centre of the town is St James's Square with an elaborate Victorian fountain. At the Crieff Visitor Centre on Muthill Road, in addition to copious information about the area, you can also see a display of paperweights, pottery and miniature animal sculptures.

Founded in 1775, the **Glenturret Distillery** at the Hosh, home of the famous "Grouse Experience", is Scotland's oldest, and tours (with a dram at the end) are available.

Lady Mary's Walk, a mile-long beech-lined avenue beside the River Earn, was gifted to the town in 1815 by Sir Patrick Murray of Ochtertyre in memory of his daughter Mary. Another popular feature is **Macrosty Park,** opened in 1902 and named after its benefactor, James Macrosty, who was Provost of the town. The park is one of the most picturesque in Scotland, with a fine collection of mature specimen trees and the Turret Burn flowing through it. The Victorian bandstand, gifted by the brother of James Macrosty, has brass band concerts in summer.

Crieff stands at the beginning of Glen Turret, within which are the picturesque **Falls Of Turret**. The 3480 feet high Ben Chonzie, eight miles north west of Crieff, has been described as the "most boring Munro in Scotland", though this is doing it an injustice. It can be climbed via a route leaving the car park at Loch Turret dam.

COMRIE
21 miles W of Perth on the A85

This village is often called the "earthquake capital of Scotland" and the "shaky toun" as it sits right on the Highland Boundary Fault. James Melville, writing in his diary in July 1597, mentions an earth tremor, though the first fully recorded one was in 1788. A 72-feet high monument to him - the **Melville Monument** - stands on Dunmore Hill. In 1874 it was struck by lightning, and the man who climbed to its top to repair it swore he could see Edinburgh Castle.

North of the village, in Glen Lednock, is the **De'ils Cauldron Waterfall,** overlooked by a granite obelisk commemorating Henry Dundas, 1st Viscount Melville (1742-1811).

In 1839 a major earthquake took place, causing the world's first seismometers to be set up in Comrie. The recently refurbished Earthquake House, built in 1874, now houses an array of instruments to measure the tremors. Large windows have been fitted so that visitors can observe both the old and new seismometers installed.

ST FILLANS
25 miles W of Perth on the A85

St Fillans stands at the eastern end of Loch Earn, where the River Earn exits on its way to join the Firth of Tay, and is a gateway to the Loch Lomond and Trossachs

National Park. It is named after the Irish missionary St Fillan. Two relics of the saint - his bell and his pastoral staff - are now housed within the National Museum of Scotland.

On an island in Loch Earn stand the scant ruins of **Loch Earn Castle**, which belonged to Clan MacNeish. From here they plundered the surrounding countryside before retreating to the safety of their castle.

At the top of Dunfillan Hill (600 feet) is a rock known as St Fillan's Chair. To the southwest, overlooking Loch Earn, is Ben Vorlich (3224 feet).

HUNTINGTOWER
3 miles NW of Perth on the A85

Huntingtower Castle (Historic Scotland) was the scene of the Earl of Gowrie's kidnapping of James VI in 1582. The earl had invited the 16-year-old king to his stern-looking 15th century castellated mansion and held him prisoner there for 9 months. The conspirators had planned to coerce him into dismissing his favourites. The plot failed and, justice in those days being rather prompt, the perpetrators were first executed, and then tried for treason. Today, the castle is notable for its richly painted walls and ceilings. The castle has no connection with the John Buchan spy yarn, also called *Huntingtower*, which was set in Ayrshire.

KINROSS

Once the main town in the tiny

To the south of Comrie, off the B827, is the Auchingarrich Wildlife Centre, home to a wide variety of animals, including Highland cattle, wallabies, llamas, raccoons, porcupines, otters, meerkats, maras, prairie dogs, chipmunks, deer and birds of prey. There's also a wild bird hatchery, woodland walks, soft play area and an adventure playground.

109 THE GREEN HOTEL

Kinross

A former eighteenth century coaching inn with a reputation for warn hospitality and excellent service.

 see page 413

110 THE WINDLESTRAE

Kinross

Delightful village inn offering appetising food, en suite rooms, a Malt Room and beer garden.

 see page 413

county of Kinross, which measures no more than 15 miles by nine, this small burgh now sits quietly on the shores of Loch Leven. The opening of the M90 motorway put the town within half an hour of Edinburgh and over the last two decades it has expanded to become a peaceful haven for commuters.

The town's **Tolbooth** dates from the 17th century, and was restored by Robert Adam in 1771. On the Mercat Cross are the "jougs", an iron collar placed round the neck of wrongdoers. **Kinross House,** built on a slight rose overlooking Loch Leven, dates from the late 17th century, and was built for Sir William Bruce, Charles II's surveyor and master of works. Bruce had been responsible for the fabric of the Palace of Holyrood in Edinburgh. Kinross House is an elegant Palladian mansion which is still a family home and not open to the public. However, the wonderful formal gardens are open to the public from April to September. An unusual feature within the grounds

is the decorative Fish Gate. Between a pair of overflowing cornucopias is an upstanding basket of fish containing, it is said, the seven varieties of fish that could be caught in the loch at that time. They have been listed as being salmon, char, grey trout, speckled trout, blackhead, perch and pike.

Loch Leven is one of Scotland's most famous lochs, not because of its size (it covers 3500 acres) or its spectacular beauty, but because of its wonderful trout fishing. Though this has gone into decline in recent years, the trout are still highly prized for their delicate pink flesh, caused by the small fresh water shellfish on which they feed. The whole loch is a National Nature Reserve, and on the south shore of the loch, close to the B9097, is the **Vane Farm Nature Reserve**, administered by the Royal Society for the Protection of Birds and part of the Loch Leven National Nature Reserve. It hosts a programme of events throughout the year, and was the first educational nature reserve in Europe.

On another island are the ruins of **Lochleven Castle** (Historic Scotland). It was a Douglas stronghold, the surrounding lands and the loch having been gifted to the family by Robert III in 1390. From June 1567 until May 1568 Mary, Queen of Scots, was held prisoner here, having been seized in Edinburgh for her supposed part in the murder of her husband Lord Darnley. She was 25 years old

Lochleven Castle, Kinross

at the time and married to Bothwell who was also implicated in Darnley's murder. While kept prisoner in the castle, she was constantly asked to abdicate and divorce Bothwell. She refused to do so as she was already pregnant by him. Shortly after she arrived on the island, she gave birth to stillborn twins, and eventually signed the deeds. But it was not her stay on the island that made the castle famous; rather it was the way she escaped.

The castle was owned by the Dowager Lady Douglas, mother of Mary's half brother, the Earl of Moray, who became regent when Mary abdicated. Both she and her other sons Sir William and George Douglas looked after Mary during her imprisonment. But George gradually fell under Mary's spell, and hatched various plans for her to escape. All failed, and he was eventually banished from the island.

But someone else had also fallen under Mary's spell - 16-year-old Willie Douglas, who was thought to be the illegitimate son of Sir William, and who was kept as a page. After the various attempts at escape, Mary was being held in the third storey of the main tower, above the Great Hall where the Douglas family dined. One evening young Willie "accidentally" dropped a napkin over the castle keys, which his father had placed on the table while dining. On picking up the napkin, he picked up the keys as well.

As the meal progressed, Mary and one of her attendants crept out of her room and made for the main doorway, where Willie met them. He unlocked the door, and they both slipped out. He then locked the door behind him and threw the keys into the water before rowing the two women ashore. There they were met by George Douglas, Lord Seton and a troop of loyal soldiers, and taken to the safety of Niddrie Castle.

In those days, the loch was much bigger and deeper than it is now, and the water came right up to the doors of the castle. Between 1826 and 1836 it was partially drained, reducing its size by a quarter, and the keys were recovered from the mud. Nowadays, trips to the island leave from the pier at Kinross.

Set beside the loch are the premises of Todd and Duncan, probably the best place in Scotland for cashmere bargains. The mill produces knitwear for Ballantyne, Chanel, Clements Ribeiro, Daks, Mulberry, Shelley Fox and others, and its shop is stocked with almost

THE MUIRS INN

Kinross

Traditional Scottish country inn in picturesque listed building; traditional cuisine; en suite accommodation.

🍴 🛏 *see page 414*

Loch Leven, Kinross

faultless seconds, samples and out-of-season stock. There's also a small exhibition called **Cashmere at Lochleven** which traces the history of this luxury cloth. The **Scottish Raptor Centre** at Turfhills has falconry courses and flying displays. Close to Kinross every year in July is held Scotland's biggest outdoor rock festival, **T in the Park**. And every Sunday the Kinross Market is held, the largest indoor market in Scotland. The Heart of Scotland Visitor Centre gives you a general introduction to the area, and is to be found near Junction 6 of the M90 motorway.

AROUND KINROSS

MILNATHORT

2 miles N of Kinross off the M90

Milnathort is a small, former wool-manufacturing town. To the east are the striking ruins of 15th century **Burleigh Castle**, built of warm red stone, which was a stronghold of the Balfour family. All that remains nowadays is a curtain wall and a substantial four-storey tower which is said to be haunted by the ghost of a woman called Grey Maggie.

There is an interesting story attached to the castle. In 1707 the heir to the castle fell in love with a servant girl, which so displeased his father that he sent him abroad. However, he declared his undying love for her, and swore that if she married someone else while he was away, he would kill her husband when he returned.

After a year or so he returned,

only to find that she had married a schoolmaster. True to his word, he shot him dead. He then fled, but was captured and sentenced to death. However, he escaped the gallows by changing places with his sister and donning her clothes. He later fought in the Jacobite army during the 1715 Uprising. For this, his castle and lands were taken from the family and given to the Irwins.

The **Orwell Standing Stones** are just off the A911. Two huge stones, dating to about 2000 BC, stand on a slight rise. One of them fell down in 1972, and during restoration work cremated bones were discovered buried at its foot.

SCOTLANDWELL

7 miles E of Kinross, on the A911

Scotlandwell takes its name from the springs that bubble up to the surface in this part of the county, which is on the western slopes of the Lomond Hills. In the early 13th century the Bishop of St Andrews set up a hospice here, and his successor gave it to the "Red Friars", or "Trinitarians". They exploited the springs and established a Holy Well. Soon it became a place of pilgrimage, bringing huge revenue to the monks. Robert the Bruce came here to find a cure for his leprosy, and held a parliament.

On the slopes above the village are the Crooked Rigs, remnants of a medieval runrig field system.

The local landowners, the Arnots of **Arnot Tower,** the ruins of which can still be seen, gazed enviously at the wealth of the Trinitarians, and decided to "muscle in" on the venture. They placed younger sons of the family within the order as fifth columnists, and when enough of them were in place, they occupied the friary and ejected those friars who weren't Arnots. They established Archibald Arnot, the Laird of Arnot's second son, as minister (the name given to the head of the friary), and began creaming off the vast wealth. At the Reformation, the lands and income of the friary were given to them, and the takeover was complete.

Today, the **Holy Well** still exists. In 1858 the Laird of Arnot commissioned David Bryce to turn it into a memorial to his wife Henrietta, and this is what can be seen today. The friary has completely disappeared, though a small plaque in the graveyard marks the spot where it once stood.

At Portmoak near Scotlandwell there's the **Scottish Gliding Centre**, where the adventurous can try an "air experience flight".

CROOK OF DEVON

5 miles W of Kinross on the A977

This small village has twice won an award for being the "best kept village in Kinross". An earlier claim to fame occurred in the 1660s when it achieved notoriety as a centre of witchcraft. A coven of witches had been "discovered" in the area, and in 1662 three women were tried and sentenced to be strangled to death and their bodies burnt at a "place called

Lamblaires". A few weeks later four women and one man were executed in the same manner, and not long after two women were tried, one of them escaping death because of her age. The other was burnt at the stake.

By this time the other members of the "coven" had fled from the area. But in July two further women were put on trial, one of whom was executed and the other, called Christian Grieve, acquitted. The acquittal was looked upon as an affront by the local people - especially the clergy - and she was retried and eventually executed.

There is no doubt that the trials were a travesty, and that many old scores were settled by naming people - especially old women - as witches. It was also not unknown in Scotland at that time for the accused, knowing their fate was sealed, to get their own back on the accusers by naming them as witches and warlocks as well. Thus Scotland seemed to be awash with devil worship, when in fact it was very rare.

PITLOCHRY

This popular resort is set in a particularly beautiful part of the Perthshire Highlands. To the west runs the lovely glen of Strathtummel while to the north the majestic peaks of the Grampians "pierce the heavens". Over the years, Pitlochry has added many other attractions to these natural ones. The **Blair Athol**

At the Pitlochry Visitor Centre, near the dam, there is the famous Salmon Ladder, which allows salmon to enter the loch from the River Tummel below. An underwater viewing chamber allows visitors to watch these noble fish flailing their way up the 1000 feet long tunnel during their annual migration.

113 FASGANEOIN COUNTRY HOUSE

Pitlochry

Picturesque Victorian family-run establishment offering wholesome food and 3-star en suite accommodation.

see page 416

114 DRUMNAKYLE FARMHOUSE

Foss, nr Pitlochry

Historic Highland farmhouse with spectacular views offering 5-star self-catering accommodation.

see page 415

Distillery, makers of Bell's whisky was founded in 1798 and is one of Scotland's oldest distilleries. Visitors are welcome and can watch the distilling process as crystal clear water from Allt Dour, the "burn of the otter", is transformed into amber nectar. Guided tours end with a complimentary dram and there are also a whisky and gift shop, coffee shop and bar.

Nearby stands the **Pitlochry Festival Theatre**. It was founded in 1951 and presented its first plays in a tent. Performances continued like this until 1981 when a purpose-built theatre was opened at Port-na-Craig on the banks of the Tummel. The theatre presents a varied programme of professional plays every summer, and is one of Scotland's most popular venues. In the town itself, the summer season brings pipe band concerts, country dancing displays, ceilidhs and many other events.

Nestling in the hills a couple of miles east of Pitlochry, Edradour Distillery is Scotland's smallest, and possibly its most picturesque distillery. It was established in 1837 and produces just 12 casks of its prized whisky each week. An old distiller's yardstick states that the smaller the still, the finer the taste and the Edradour stills are the smallest allowed under Excise regulations - any smaller, the theory goes, and they'd be hidden away on the hillsides. Conducted tours, finished off with a tasting, are available.

From Pitlochry, the B8019, the famous **Road to the Isles**, goes west towards beautiful Loch Tummel, whose waters have been harnessed for electricity. It passes the Forestry Commission Visitor Centre, which interprets the wildlife of the area. From the **Queen's View** there is a magnificent view west towards Loch Tummel and beyond. Queen Victoria stopped at this point during her Highland tour in 1866 and praised the scenery, though it is said that it was Mary Stuart who originally gave the place its name when she visited in 1564.

The A924 going east from Pitlochry takes you up into some marvellous scenery. It reaches a height of 1260 feet before dropping down into Kirkmichael and then on to Bridge of Cally. On the way, at Enochdhu, you will pass Kindrogan, a Victorian country house where the Scottish Field Studies Association offer residential courses on Scotland's natural history. The **Dunfallandy Standing Stone** stands south of the town near Dunfallandy House, and west of the A9. It dates from Pictish times, and has a curious legend attached to it. A nun called Triduana was being forced into marriage with the son of a Scottish king, but escaped to a small chapel at Dunfallady, where she erected this "praying stone" in gratitude.

There are many fine guided walks in the area, some organised by such bodies as National Trust for Scotland, the Scottish Wildlife Trust and the Forestry Commission. A small booklet about them is available.

Killiecrankie

AROUND PITLOCHRY

KILLIECRANKIE

4 miles N of Pitlochry off the A9

The rather unusual name comes from the Gaelic Coille "Creitheannich", meaning the aspen wood. On 27 July 1689, William of Orange's troops marched through the scenic Pass of Killiecrankie to attack the Highland forces massed on the hillside a mile away. A few hours later, the English soldiers were fleeing back through the Pass. The battle at Killiecrankie was the first military encounter of the Jacobite uprising and is commemorated at the **Killiecrankie Visitors Centre** (National Trust for Scotland) which has displays explaining the battle.

At the north end of the pass is a spot known as the **Soldier's Leap**, high above the River Garry. It is said that, after the battle, a government trooper called Donald McBean leapt across the 18-feet wide gap to escape from some Jacobites who were chasing him.

SPITTAL OF GLENSHEE

20 miles NE of Pitlochry on the A93

As the name suggests, a small

medieval hospital, or "spittal", once stood close to this village, which lies in the heart of the Grampian Mountains at a height of 1125 feet. It sits on the main road north from Perth to Braemar, surrounded by some marvellous scenery. The Glenshee skiing area (Britain's largest) lies six miles north of the village, and is dealt with in the North East Scotland section of this guidebook.

The Devil's Elbow on the A93 lies about five miles north. A combination of steep inclines and double bends made it a notorious place for accidents in days gone by, though it has been much improved. At Cairnwell the road reaches a height of 2199 feet, making it the highest public road in Britain. During the winter months the road can be blocked by snow for weeks on end.

DUNKELD

13 miles S of Pitlochry off the A9

Set in idyllic surroundings on the east bank of the Tay, Dunkeld has all the appearance of an attractive town, but is in fact a small cathedral city. **Dunkeld Cathedral** stands beside the river and consists of a ruined nave and a restored chancel which is now used as the

115 KILLIECRANKIE

Pilochry

A magnificent woodland with plenty of wildlife, much admired by Queen Victoria in 1844. It is designated a Site of Special Scientific Interest.

🏛 *see page 417*

116 THE COUNTRY BAKERY

Dunkeld

An endless amount of mouth-watering cakes and tasty delights to enjoy

 see page 417

•

In 1689 the town of Dunkeld was the scene of the Battle of Dunkeld when Jacobite forces were defeated by a force of Cameronians under William Cleland. This was an unusual battle as the fighting and gunfire took place among the streets and buildings of the town, and not in open countryside. Cleland was fatally wounded during the encounter, and now lies in the ruined nave of the cathedral.

•

From Dunkeld there are pleasant walks alongside the River Tay, which is spanned by an elegant bridge, designed by Thomas Telford, which leads to the tranquil village of Birnam. At the Birnam Institute is the Beatrix Potter Gardens, and within the Institute itself there is a small exhibition, which tells the story of the young Beatrix. She used to holiday in the area, and gained some of her inspiration from the surrounding countryside.

parish church. The cathedral as we see it nowadays dates from many periods.

Back in AD 850 Kenneth MacAlpin moved the religious centre of the country to Dunkeld from Iona and the town also became the seat of the royal court. The present cathedral was built between the 12th and 15th centuries. The leper's squint is still in place as is the striking tomb of the "Wolf of Badenoch", Alexander Stewart, Earl of Buchan. Notorious for his lawlessness he once sacked Elgin Cathedral as a measured response to the Bishop of Moray's criticism of the earl's marital infidelity.

Another, but not so famous, man lies in the nave of the cathedral. Curiously enough he lies beside William Cleland, and yet he was the grandson of the greatest Jacobite of them all, Charles Edward Stuart. The Prince's illegitimate daughter Charlotte had an affair with the Archbishop of Rouen, the result being two daughters and a son - Charles Edward Maximilien de Roehenstart, better known as Count Roehenstart (a name made up from "Rouen" and "Stuart"). On a trip to Scotland in 1854 he was killed in a carriage accident.

Most of the "little houses" in Dunkeld date from the early 18th century, as they were built to replace those that had been destroyed in the battle. Now the National Trust for Scotland looks after most of them. On the wall of one house in the square, the Ell

Shop, is portrayed an old Scottish length of measurement called the "ell", which corresponds to 37 inches. Also in the square is the Atholl Memorial Fountain, erected in 1866 in memory of the 6th Duke of Atholl.

This is the heartland of the "big tree country", and it was in Dunkeld, in 1738, that the first larches were planted in Scotland.

GRANDTULLY
11 miles SW of Pitlochry on the A827

Grandtully is pronounced "Grantly". Grandtully Castle, to the west of the village, dates from the 15th century, and was a Stewart stronghold. It is not open to the public but can be seen from the road.

St Mary's Church (Historic Scotland) was built by Sir Alexander Stewart in 1533, and was remodelled in 1633 when a painted ceiling was added that shows heraldic motifs and coats-of-arms of families connected with the Stewarts.

ABERFELDY
16 miles SW of Pitlochry on the A827

Now simmer blinks on flowery braes,
And o'er the crystal streamlet plays;
Come let us spend the lightsome days
In the birks of Aberfeldy.

In 1787 Robert Burns wrote a song called *The Birks of Aberfeldy*, and made famous this small town and its surrounding area. "Birks" are birch trees and the ones in question can still be seen to the south of the village, as well as the **Falls of Moness**.

The village sits beside the River Tay, and crossing it is **General Wade's Bridge**, built in 1733 by Major-General George Wade, Commander-in-Chief of North Britain from 1724 until 1740 ("Scotland" was not a name that was liked by the English establishment at the time). Designed by William Adam, architect father of Robert Adam, the 4-arched humpback bridge was the first to span the River Tay. The bridge was formally opened in 1735 and cost £3,596, which in today's terms is close to £1m.

General Wade's Bridge, Aberfeldy

At about the same time, six independent regiments were raised to "watch" the Highlands for signs of unrest. These six regiments later amalgamated to form the 43rd Highland Regiment of Foot under the Earl of Crawford, and it paraded for the first time at Aberfeldy in May 1740. The regiment later became the Black Watch, and the **Black Watch Memorial**, built in 1887, near the bridge commemorates the event.

Right on the A827 is **Dewar's World of Whisky**. Here you will find out about one of Scotland's most famous whisky firms, located in the distillery where Aberfeldy Single Malt is made.

A mile or so north west of the village, near Weem is **Castle Menzies**, home to Clan Menzies (pronounced Ming-iz in Scotland). The clan is not Scottish in origin, but Norman, with the name coming from Mesnieres near Rouen. James Menzies of Menzies, son-in-law of the then Earl of

Atholl, built the castle in the 16th century. In 1665 the clan chief was created a baron of Nova Scotia. The last member of the main line died in 1918, and the clan was left without a chief. In 1957 the descendants of a cousin of the first baron were recognised as clan chiefs, and the present one is David Steuart Menzies of Menzies.

The castle is now owned by the Menzies Charitable Trust. Parts of it are open to the public, and it houses a Clan Menzies museum. Charles Edward Stuart spent two nights within its walls in 1746 on his way to Culloden.

KENMORE

17 miles SW of Pitlochry on the A827

Kenmore sits at the eastern end of Loch Tay and was founded in about 1540 by the Earls of Breadalbane. The loch is the source of the River Tay, one of the most picturesque in Scotland. The loch is 14-and-a-half miles long, less than a mile wide, and plunges to a maximum depth of more than 500

117 LOCH TAY LODGES

Aberfeldy

Six beautiful self catering holiday lodges boasting some fantastic views overlooking Loch Tay

see page 418

Loch Tay, Kenmore

In a field next to the village of Fortinghall is the Cairn of the Dead, which marks the mass grave of plague victims during the galar mhor, or great plague. It is said that one old woman, who was still sufficiently healthy, carried the bodies to the field on a horse-drawn sledge.

---

feet. Overlooking it, on the northern shore, is **Ben Lawers** (4033 feet), with the **Ben Lawers Mountain Visitor Centre** (National Trust for Scotland) on a minor road off the A827. There is a nature trail, and a booklet is available at the centre.

The **Scottish Crannog Centre**, run by the Scottish Trust for Underwater Archaeology, explains how people in the past lived in crannogs, which were dwelling houses situated in the shallow waters of a loch that offered defence against attack. They were either built on artificial islands or raised on stilts above the water, and were in use from about 2500 BC right up until the 17th century. Off the north shore of the loch is Eilean nan Bannoamh ("Isle of the Holy Women") where once

stood a small Celtic nunnery. Alexander I's wife, Queen Sybilla, died here in 1122 and Alexander founded a priory in her memory.

FORTINGALL

19 miles SW of Pitlochry on a minor road off the B846

This little village has a unique claim to fame. It is said to be the birthplace of Pontius Pilate, the governor of Judea at the time of Christ's execution. It is said that his father, a Roman officer, was sent to Scotland by Augustus Caesar to command a unit which kept the local Pictish clans in check. Whether Pontius was born of a union between his father and a local woman, or whether his father had brought a wife with him, is not recorded. There is no proof that the story is true, but there was certainly a Roman camp nearby.

Sir Donald Currie laid out Fortingall as a model village in the 19th century and it has some picturesque thatched cottages that would not look out of place in a South of England village. In the kirkyard of the early 20th century parish church is the **Fortingall Yew**, said to be the oldest living thing in Europe. The tree looks rather the worse for wear nowadays, but as it may be as much as 3000 years old (a plaque next to it says 5000 years, but this is doubtful), perhaps this is not surprising.

The village sits at the entrance to **Glen Lyon**, at 25 miles long, Scotland's longest, and perhaps loveliest, glen. Tumbling through it is the River Lyon, which rises at Loch Lyon, part of a massive hydroelectric scheme. At Bridge of Balgie a minor road strikes south, rising into some wild scenery and passing Meall Luaidhe (2535 feet) before dropping down towards the Ben Lawers Mountain Visitor Centre and the shores of Loch Tay. Bridge of Balgie is also home to a gallery that houses prints and original paintings by renowned artist Alan Hayman.

On the B846 four miles north of Fortingall is the **Glengoulandie Country Park** within which is the Glengoulandie Deer Park with its herd of red deer, Highland cattle, goats and rare breeds of sheep.

KINLOCH RANNOCH

17 miles W of Pitlochry on the B846

This small village, laid out in the 18th century by James Small, a government factor, sits at the eastern end of Loch Rannoch, which has roads on both the northern and southern sides. It is overlooked by the conically shaped **Schiehallion** (3547 feet), from the summit of which there is a wonderful view as far south as the Lowlands.

An obelisk in the centre of the village commemorates **Dugald Buchanan**, who died here in 1786. He was one of the Highland's greatest religious poets, and was buried at Balquidder. The Parish Church is one of Telford's parliamentarian churches, and was built in 1829. Usually a parliamentarian church was nothing but a plain, T-shaped preaching box, but Kinloch Rannoch is more like a conventional church, with the Holy Table at the east end.

The B846 carries on westward past Kinloch Rannoch, and skirts the northern shores of Loch Rannoch. It eventually comes to an end at Rannoch Station. This station, on the Glasgow/Fort William line, is the loneliest railway station in Britain. Beyond it is **Rannoch Moor**, said to be the most desolate spot in Scotland, and "Europe's last great wilderness". In the winter, when snow covers it, it is treacherous, and no one should venture out onto it unless they're experienced. Even in summer, when it is hauntingly beautiful, it should still be treated with respect.

BLAIR ATHOLL

6 miles NW of Pitlochry off the A9

The village of Blair Atholl is dominated by the gleaming white walls and towers of **Blair Castle,** the most visited privately-owned home in Scotland. The hereditary seat of the Dukes of Atholl, the castle's oldest part is Cummings Tower, built in 1269. The 2nd duke transformed the castle into a gracious Georgian mansion and a century or so later the 7th duke remodelled the building in the flamboyant "Scottish Baronial" style. Most of the 32 rooms open to visitors date from this latter period, a marvellous sequence of grand apartments housing outstanding collections of furniture, painting, china, lace, tapestries, arms and armour. In the vast ballroom, where one whole

Rannoch moor's landscape isn't a natural one. Even here, man has made his mark. The whole of the moor was once covered with the trees of the old Caledonian Forest, but man gradually cleared them to use as fuel and for building. The whole of the moor is littered with large boulders, debris carried by the glaciers that once covered this area.

251

wall is festooned with antlers, look out for the portrait of the 7th duke. Beneath it lies his walking stick, scored with 749 notches, one for each stag he had killed.

Visitors to the castle may well find themselves greeted by a piper of the **Atholl Highlanders**, the duke's private army. This 80-strong force is unique in Europe, the legacy of a visit to Blair Castle by Queen Victoria in 1844. Enormously impressed by the Guard of kilted Highlanders assembled for her visit, Victoria conferred on them the right to carry the Queen's Colours, a privilege which also allowed them to bear arms. Every year, in May, they hold their annual parade for the Duke's Review and complete the Whitsun weekend with the famous **Atholl Gathering.** These historic Highland Games feature internationally known sportsmen, Highland dancing, traditional caber-tossing and local competitions. In August, the **Blair Castle International Horse Trials** have become a major event and are followed by Sheep Dog Trials.

In the kirkyard of St Bride's Kirk is the grave of John Graham, 1st Viscount Dundee, known as "Bonnie Dundee", who was killed at the Battle of Killiecrankie in 1689. At Bruar, four miles north of Blair Atholl, is the **Clan Donnachaidh Museum**. Though the name translates into English as Donnachie, it traces the history of the Clan Robertson, and shows their place in local and Scottish history. **The Falls of Bruar** are close by, and cascade through a picturesque ravine with footbridges over them.

DUNDEE

Approached by either the road or rail bridges over the Tay, Dundee presents a splendid panorama with the city sprawled across the twin hills of Balgay and Law, and framed by the often snow-capped Grampians in the distance. Opened in 1887. the **Tay Rail Bridge** stretches for two miles making it the longest rail bridge in Europe. It replaced the one which collapsed during a violent westerly gale on 28th December 1879 sending 75 passengers and crew to their deaths. The disaster inspired an out-of-work actor named William Topaz MacGonagall to write *Railway Bridge of the Silv'ry Tay* which includes the immortal lines:

Beautiful Railway Bridge
of the Silv'ry Tay!
Alas! I am very sorry to say
That ninety lives have been taken away
On the last Sabbath day of 1879,

Tay Rail Bridge, Dundee

*Which will be remember'd
for a very long time.*

Despite the poem's blithe disregard for metre and its banal sentiments, MacGonagall was lionised in Edinburgh's literary salons and his work still gives enormous, if rather guilty, pleasure to every new generation of readers.

Any visitor to Dundee will soon hear the term "The Three Js", a reference to the three pillars on which the city's past prosperity was founded - jute, jam and journalism. Throughout the 19th century, Dundee was Britain's leading producer of jute which was then widely used in the manufacture of coarse sacking, canvas and rope. The city's textile heritage is presented in a lively way at **Verdant Works** in West Henderson's Wynd. Here, in a former jute mill, visitors are taken on a tour of the industry, from its beginnings in India to the end product in all its forms. They see the processes involved in jute manufacture, the original machinery, and the living conditions of people both rich and poor who earned their living from the trade. There are interactive displays, film shows, and a guided tour.

The association with jam began in 1700 when a Dundee grocer named Keiller bought a cargo of Seville oranges very cheaply from a Spanish ship taking shelter from a storm. However, they were too bitter to eat so Keiller's wife made marmalade from them to sell in her confectionery shop. Several generations later, the Keiller family

McManus Galleries, Dundee

built a jam factory and a sweet-tasting success story followed. Sadly, Dundee marmalade has gone the way of jute.

The third J, journalism, is still flourishing, however. DC Thomson's publish the only wholly-owned Scottish daily newspapers as well as dozens of comics including the ever-popular *Beano* and *Dandy* which are still delighting children with such characters as Desperate Dan and Dennis the Menace.

Thomson's headquarters stand in Albert Square, across from the city's most imposing Victorian building, the **McManus Art Galleries and Museum.** Dundee's 19th century prosperity allowed its citizens to endow the gallery with a remarkable collection of Pre-Raphaelite and Scottish paintings. The museum has a significant display of artefacts from ancient Egypt and, closer to home, also has the table on which the Duke of Cumberland signed the death warrants of Jacobites captured at the Battle of Culloden.

The **Dundee Contemporary Arts Centre** in the Nethergate specialises in contemporary art and film, and has galleries, cinemas and workshops.

One of the city's most popular attractions is the *RSS Discovery*, which was built at Dundee in 1901 and used by Captain Scott in his expedition to the Antarctic in 1901-1904. . It was one of the last wooden three-masted ships to be built in Britain, and the first to be built solely for scientific research. You can explore the ship, "travel" to Antarctica in the Polarama Gallery and find out about one of the greatest stories of exploration and courage ever told. The ship now forms the centrepiece of the five-star **Discovery Point**, at Discovery Quay

A short walk along the waterside will bring you to another remarkable ship. *HM Frigate Unicorn*, a 46-gun wooden warship, was launched at Chatham in 1824 and is now the oldest British-built ship afloat. The ship has been restored to her original appearance and provides a fascinating insight into what life was like for its 300 officers and crew just 19 years after the Battle of Trafalgar.

The **Old Steeple** of St Mary's Church, in the heart of the city, dates from the 15th century, and is reckoned to be one of the finest in the country. The rest of the building dates from the 18th and 19th centuries, and was once divided into four separate churches.

Another reminder of Dundee's past is the **Wishart Arch** in the Cowgate. It is one of the city's old gateways, and from its top, George Wishart the religious reformer, is said to have preached to plague victims during the plague of 1544.

In recent years, Dundee has re-branded itself as the "City of Discovery", a programme that included the opening of **Sensation.** Located in the Greenmarket, it is a place where "science is brought to life" using specially designed interactive and hands-on exhibits. Here you can find out how a dog sees the world, how to use your senses to discover where you are, and why things taste good or bad. The latest exhibition is Roborealm, the only one of its kind in the world. It will give visitors a chance to interact with a team of robots.

RSS Discovery, Dundee

Located in picturesque wooded surroundings on Balgay Hill, the **Mills Observatory** in Balgay Park a mile west of the city centre also deals with matters scientific. It is Britain's only full time public observatory, and houses a 25mm Cooke telescope. It also has a small planetarium and display area.

Dudhope Castle, at Dudhope Park, dates originally from the 13th century, and was once the home of the Scrymageour family, hereditary constables of Dundee. The present building dates from the late 16th century. In its time it has also been a woollen mill and a barracks. It now forms part of the University of Abertay and is not open to the public, though it can be viewed from the outside. And at the junction of Claypotts Road and Arbroath Road is the wonderfully named **Claypotts Castle** (Historic Scotland), built between 1569 and 1588 by John Strachan. It can be viewed by prior appointment with Historic Scotland.

On the Coupar Angus Road is the **Camperdown Wildlife Centre**, with a fine collection of Scottish and European wildlife, including brown bears, Scottish wildcats, wolves and bats. **Clatto Country Park** is to the north of the city, and is centred on a 24-acre former reservoir. It has facilities for water sports and fishing. The ruins of **Mains Castle**, sometimes called Mains of Fintry, is in Cairds Park, and was once owned by John Graham, a cousin of Viscount Dundee.

To the east of the city is

Broughty Ferry, once called the "richest square mile in Europe" because of the many fine mansions built there by the jute barons. The **Broughty Ferry Museum** is at Castle Green, and housed within a castle built by the Earl of Angus in 1496 as a defence against marauding English ships. It has displays on local history, and tells the story of Dundee's former whaling fleet, at one time Britain's largest. If you visit Broughty Ferry at New Year, you can see the annual **N'erday Dook** ("New Year's Day Dip") held on January 1st, when swimmers enter the waters of the Firth of Tay. It is organised by Ye Amphibious Ancients Bathing Association, one of the country's oldest swimming clubs, and is done for charity. It attracts about 100-150 bathers a year, and it is not unknown for the crowd of spectators, which can be over 2,000 strong, to be wrapped up in warm woollens, scarves and gloves as the swimmers enter the water dressed only in swimsuits.

To the west of Dundee, on the north bank of the Tay, is the Carse of Gowrie, one of the most fertile areas of Scotland.

AROUND DUNDEE

BALGRAY

5 miles N of Dundee off the A90

Four miles north of the city centre, near Balgray, is the **Tealing Souterrain** (Historic Scotland), an underground dwelling dating from about AD 100. It was accidentally discovered in 1871, and consists of

118 MILLS OBSERVATORY

Dundee

The UK's only full time public observatory where you have the opportunity to view stars and planets through an impressive telescope.

 see page 417

119 THE GLASS PAVILION

Broughty Ferry

Stunning "art deco" restaurant beside the River Tay offering a critically acclaimed menu.

see page 419

Angus Folk Museum, Glamis

•

Within the village of Glamis, at Kirkwynd, is the Angus Folk Museum (National Trust for Scotland), housed in a row of 18th century stone cottages. It contains one of the finest folk collections in Scotland, including a "Life on the Land" exhibition based in an old courtyard, and a restored 19th century hearse.

•

a curved passage about 78 feet long and seven feet wide with a stone floor.

GLAMIS

10 miles N of Dundee on the A94

With its Disneyesque towers and turrets, cupolas and bartizans (look-out towers) **Glamis Castle** has an enchanting fairy-tale appearance. The name (pronounced Glahms) is indissolubly linked with Macbeth's murder of King Duncan as presented in Shakespeare's play. In fact, the Bard was playing fast and loose with history since Macbeth actually killed his cousin in a battle near Elgin, some 50 miles away.

All the same, when you step into the 15th century Dunce's Hall, among the oldest and eeriest parts of the castle, it seems an appropriately grim setting for such a dreadful deed. Glamis continued to have close associations with royalty right up to the present day. Mary, Queen of Scots stayed in August 1562 and was "never

merrier"; her son, James VI became a close friend of the 9th Lord Glamis whom he elevated to the rank of Earl of Kinghorne.

The Lyon family, now Earls of Strathmore and Kinghorne, have lived at Glamis since 1372. It was to be the childhood home of their most famous descendant, the late Queen Mother who was the second daughter of the 14th earl. After her marriage to the Duke of York in 1923, the couple spent much of their time at Glamis and it was here that the late Princess Margaret was born.

The richly furnished apartments in which the Yorks lived are open to the public and contain notable collections of Dutch and Chinese porcelain, and a dazzling portrait by de Laszlo of the young Duchess of York which hangs in the Queen Mother's Bedroom.

It was the 3rd Earl in the mid-1600s who did nost to give Glamis its present appearance, inspired by his love of French chateaux architecture. He transformed the 15th century Great Hall into a sumptuous Drawing Room which is still the most splendid apartment in the castle. It is 60 feet long and 22 feet wide with a fine arched ceiling of delicate plasterwork. A complete west wing was added as well as a lovely Chapel whose ceiling and walls are covered with devotional paintings. A generation later when the Old Pretender, James VIII, was staying at Glamis he came to this Chapel to touch people against the "King's Evil", or scrofula. All those whom the king touched, it was reported, were cured.

The 3rd Earl also laid out the lovely gardens where the formal vistas are enhanced by some fine statuary and a huge baroque sundial with 84 faces. There are some delightful walks and a nature trail through the extensive landscaped park.

A few miles north of the village is Pictish **St Orland's Stone**, with, on one side, the carving of a cross and on the other a carving of a boat containing several men.

FORFAR

14 miles N of Dundee on the A932

Once the county town of Angus, Forfar is now a small royal burgh and market town. It gives its name to one of Scotland's culinary delights - the **Forfar Bridie**, the local equivalent of a Cornish pasty. This confection of meat and vegetables within a pastry crust was created by Mrs Bridie, a farmer's wife, so that the farm workers could eat it with work-soiled hands. The crust was simply thrown away. It used to be popular with the farm workers of Angus as it was a self-contained and easily portable meal. Appropriately enough, the Bridie plays a prominent role in the **Forfar Food Festival** which takes place annually at the beginning of July.

The town stands on what was once the centre of the kingdom of the Picts and the surrounding countryside is scattered with solitary stones carved deep with mysterious shapes. Some of them, along with Neolithic and Celtic examples, are on display at the **Meffan Museum and Art Gallery** in West High Street which also has an interactive computer archive logging every known Pictish stone in Angus. Visitors can also walk down an old cobbled street and peer into shops and workshops. A more unusual display is one about witchcraft in Angus - Forfar was the only town in Angus where witches were executed.

Five miles east of Forfar is **Balgavies Loch**, a Scottish Wildlife Trust reserve, where you can see great crested grebe, whooping swans, cormorant and other birds. Keys to the hide are available from the ranger at the Montrose Basin Wildlife Centre. There is a hide which is open on the first Sunday of each month. **Forfar Loch Country Park**, to the west of the town, has viewing platforms where wildfowl can be observed feeding.

The ruins of **Restenneth Priory** (Historic Scotland) stand about a mile-and-a-half from the town, on the B9113. The priory once stood on an island in Restenneth Loch but this was drained in the 18th century. The priory was founded by David I for Augustinian canons on the site of a much earlier church and its square tower, which is surmounted by a later spire, has some of the earliest Norman - and possibly Saxon - work in Scotland. The priory was sacked by Edward I but under the patronage of Robert the Bruce it

120 DROVERS INN

Memus, by Forfar

Interesting pub and restaurant serving excellent fresh home-made food.

see page 419

A few hundred yards from the town square, the Kirriemuir Aviation Museum has a private collection of World War II memorabilia. It was established in 1987, and largely confines itself to British aviation history.

soon regained its importance. Prince John, one of Bruce's sons, is buried here.

A few miles north of Forfar, near Tannadice, is the **Mountains Animal Sanctuary**, for rescued ponies, horses and donkeys.

DUNNICHEN

*14 miles N of Dundee
on minor road off the B9128*

Close to the village was fought, in AD 685, the **Battle of Nechtansmere** between the Picts, under King Nechtan, and the Northumbrians. It was a turning point in early Scottish history, as it was decisive in establishing what was to become Scotland as an independent nation, and not part of an enlarged Northumbria and later England. At the crossroads in the village is a cairn, which commemorates the battle. A newer one was erected in 1998 close to the actual battlefield.

The picturesque village of Letham, which is close by, was founded in 1788 by George Dempster, the local landowner, as a settlement for farm workers who had been forced to leave the land because of farming reforms. It became a centre of weaving and spinning, though the introduction of power looms in nearby towns killed it off.

KIRRIEMUIR

17 miles N of Dundee on the A926

This handsome little town is often called the "Gateway to the Glens" with roads leading directly to the magnificent scenery of Glen Clova

and Glen Prosen. Another, Glen Isla, was frequently visited by Kirriemuir's most famous son, the creator of the eternally youthful Peter Pan. JM Barrie was born here in 1860 in what is now **JM Barrie's Birthplace** (National Trust for Scotland) at 9 Brechin Road. Here, from an early age, Barrie dragooned his brothers and sisters into performing his "plays" in the family wash-house. The wash-house is till there, looking much as it did 150 years ago. Barrie was later to use it as the model for the house that Peter Pan built for Wendy in Never-Never-Land.

Barrie's most famous creation is commemorated in the little town square by a winsome **Statue of Peter Pan.** In 1930, when he was given the freedom of the town, Barrie donated a **Camera Obscura** (National Trust for Scotland) to the town, one of only three such cameras in the country. It is situated within the cricket pavilion on top of Kirriemuir Hill, and is open to the public. Although Barrie was offered burial in Westminster Abbey, he chose to be interred in Kirriemuir's Episcopal Church, just along the road from his birthplace.

Kirriemuir is the gateway to many of the beautiful Angus glens, and in the **Gateway to the Glens Museum** in the former town hall in the High Street you can find out about life in the glens and in Kirriemuir itself. The glens lie north of the town, and go deep into the Cairngorms. They are extremely beautiful, and well worth a visit. The B955 takes you into

Glen Clova, then, at its head, forms a loop, so you can travel along one side of the glen and return along the other for part of the way. A minor road at the Clova Hotel takes you up onto lonely Glen Doll before it peters out. At Dykehead you can turn off the B955 onto a minor road for Glen Prosen and follow it as it winds deep into the mountains. A cairn close to Dykehead commemorates the Antarctic explorers Robert Falcon Scott and Edward Adrian Wilson. Wilson was born in Cheltenham, the son of a doctor, but lived in Glen Prosen, and it was here that some of the Antarctic expedition was planned. He died along with Scott in Antarctica in March 1912.

Glen Isla is the southernmost of the Angus glens, and you can follow it for all of its length along the B951, which eventually takes you onto the A93 at Glenshee and up to Braemar if you wish. You will pass the **Lintrathen Loch**, which is noted for its bird life. A couple of miles further up the glen a minor road takes you to lonely Backwater Reservoir and its dam.

ARBROATH

17 miles NE of Dundee on the A92

The ancient town of Arbroath is special to all Scots. It was here, in 1320, that the nobles of Scotland met and signed the **Declaration of Arbroath**, which stated that the country was an independent kingdom, and not beholden to England. It was sent to a sceptical Pope John XXII in Rome and in it they claimed that they were not

fighting for glory, riches or honour, but for freedom. They also, in no uncertain terms, claimed that they would remain loyal to their king, Robert the Bruce, only as long as he defended Scotland against the English. It was a momentous declaration to make in those days, when unswerving loyalty to a sovereign was expected at all times.

The Declaration was drawn up in **Arbroath Abbey** (Historic Scotland) which was then one of the wealthiest and grandest churches in the country. Today, the pink sandstone ruins of the abbey are a melancholy sight but the remnants of its massively proportioned West Front, the Abbot's House and the Gatehouse testify to its former glory. Dr Johnson described the ruins as "fragments of magnificence". A Visitor Centre tells the story of the abbey and the Declaration and occasionally a re-enactment of the signing is held there.

The award-winning **Arbroath Museum**, at Ladyloan, is housed in the elegant signal tower for the Bellrock Lighthouse, and brings Arbroath's maritime and social history alive through a series of models, sounds and even smells.

Arbroath has had a harbour at the "Fit o' the Toon" (Foot of the Town) since at least the 14th century, and it supported a great fishing fleet. The town gave its name to that delicacy called the **Arbroath Smokie** (a smoked haddock) though the supposed origins of the delicacy are to be found not in the town, but in

In 1446 the Battle of Arbroath took place around Arbroath abbey. It had been the custom for the abbot to nominate a baillie to look after the peacekeeping and business side of Arbroath. He appointed Alexander Lindsay to the lucrative post but later dismissed him for "lewd bahaviour", appointing John Ogilvie in his place. Lindsay took exception to this and arrived at the abbey with an army of 1000 men. The ensuing battle, fought in the streets of the town, killed more than 600 people with Lindsay's army emerging triumphant. However, it was a hollow victory, as Lindsay himself was killed.

Auchmithie, a fishing village four miles to the north. The story goes that long ago it was the practice to store fish in the lofts of the fishermens' cottages. One day, a cottage burned down, and the resultant smoked fish was found to be delicious. Not only that - it preserved them.

The **Cliffs Nature Trail** winds for one and a half miles along the red sandstone cliffs towards Carlinheugh Bay. There is plenty of birdlife to see, as well as fascinating rock formations. The town is also a holiday resort, and at West Link Parks is the 10¼ inch gauge **Kerr's Miniature Railway**, always a favourite with holidaymakers. It operates during the summer months and is Scotland's oldest miniature railway, having been built in 1935. It runs for over 400 yards alongside the main Aberdeen to Edinburgh line.

ST VIGEANS
18 miles NE of Dundee off the A92

When the 12th century parish

Pictavia Visitor Centre, Brechin

church of St Vigeans was being refurbished in the 19th century, 32 sculptured Pictish stones were discovered. They are now housed in the **St Vigean's Museum**, converted cottages close to the small knoll where the church stands. The most important stone is the St Dristan Stone, dating from the 9th century.

St Fechan, or St Vigean, was an Irish saint who died in about AD 664. The village of Ecclefechan in Dumfriesshire is also named after him.

ABERLEMNO
18 miles NE of Dundee on a minor road off the B9134

Within the village are the Pictish **Aberlemno Sculptured Stones** (Historic Scotland). One is situated in the kirkyard of the parish church, the others are within a stone enclosure near the roadside north of the church. The one in the kirkyard shows a fine cross on one side surrounded by intertwining serpents and water horses, and a typical Pictish hunting scene on the other. It dates from the 8th or 9th century. The other two have crosses, angels, and battle or hunting scenes. Because of possible frost damage, the stones are boxed in between October and May.

BRECHIN
27 miles NE of Dundee off the A90

If the possession of a cathedral makes a town a city, then Brechin is indeed a city, even though it has a population of only 6000. **Brechin**

Cathedral dates from the 12th century, though most of what we see today is 13th century and later. In 1806 the nave, aisles and west front were remodelled, and between 1901 and 1902 were restored to their original design. Adjacent to the cathedral, and now forming part of its fabric, is an 11th century **Round Tower**, which rises to a height of 106 feet. These towers are common in Ireland but this is one of only two to have survived in Scotland. From the top a monk rang a bell at certain times during the day, calling the monks to prayer. It was also used as a place of refuge for the monks during troubled times which is why the doorway is 6 feet above the ground. In Maison Dieu Lane is the south wall of the chapel of the **Maison Dieu** almshouses founded in 1267 by Lord William de Brechin.

Brechin Museum has exhibits and displays about the cathedral, the ancient city crafts and local archaeology. Brechin Castle (private) is the seat of the Earls of Dalhousie, and within the **Brechin Castle Centre** are a garden centre, walks and a model farm. There is also **Pictavia**, an exhibition that explores the enigmatic Picts who occupied this part of Scotland for centuries. One of the displays explains the Battle of Nechtansmere. Their name means the "painted people", and they fought the Romans, the Vikings and the Angles.

At Menmuir, near the town, are the White and Brown **Caterthuns**, on which are the well-preserved remains of Iron Age forts. The hills also give good views across the surrounding countryside.

The **Caledonian Railway** runs on Sundays during summer and on Saturdays also during the peak season, when passengers can travel the 4-mile route between the Victorian Brechin Station on Park Road and the Bridge of Dun. The railway has ten steam engines and 12 diesels, and is run by the Brechin Railway Preservation Society. The Brechin branch line, on which the trains run, was closed in 1952.

To the north west of Brechin is **Glen Lethnot**, one of the beautiful Angus glens. Flowing through it is the West Water, and near the head of the glen is an old trail that takes you over the Clash of Wirren into Glen Esk. Illicit distillers used this as a route in days gone by, and hid their casks in the corries among the hills. For this reason it became known as the Whisky Trail.

MONTROSE

31 miles NE of Dundee on the A92

Montrose stands on a bulbous peninsula with the North Sea washing into its natural harbour on the east, and the 2-mile wide **Montrose Lagoon** defining its western boundary. The Lagoon is a wildlife sanctuary of international importance, its mussel and reed beds providing a natural reserve for migrant birds. Seals, thousands of ducks and geese are regular visitors; osprey and kingfishers have also been spotted here. At the

Though not born in Montrose, George Wishart the religious reformer has close associations with the town. He attended the grammar school here in the 1520s, and went on to Aberdeen University. He later returned and taught at the grammar school where he used the Greek translation of the Bible while teaching his pupils. For this he was accused of heresy, and had to flee to England. In 1546 he was burnt at the stake in St Andrews on the orders of Cardinal Beaton.

261

To the west of Montrose, overlooking the Basin, is the House of Dun (National Trust for Scotland), an imposing Georgian mansion designed by William Adam and built in 1730 for David Erskine, Lord Dun. Outside, the house has an elegant, restrained appearance but inside there's a riot of baroque plasterwork and sumptuous furnishings. At one time, an illegitimate daughter of William IV lived here, Lady Augusta Kennedy-Erskine by name. A collection of her embroidery is on display in the house. Within the grounds there are formal gardens and woodland walks.

Montrose Basin Wildlife Centre you can join in one of the regular guided walks or view the wildlife through powerful binoculars or on live remote-control television.

At the old Montrose Air Station, where some of the Battle of Britain pilots trained, is the **Montrose Air Station Heritage Centre**. In 1912, the government planned 12 such air stations, to be operated by the Royal Flying Corps, later called the Royal Air Force. Montrose was the first, and became operational in 1913. Now it houses a small collection of aircraft, including a full size replica of the famous Sopwith Camel, plus mementoes, documents and photographs related to flying.

The **William Lamb Studio** is in a close off Market Street and is open to the public during the summer. The working studio of the famous Montrose sculptor who

Montrose Basin Wildlife Centre

died in 1951 includes displays of his sculptures, etchings, paintings and drawings. Also featured are his workroom and tools and his living room with furniture he designed and made. In 1932, Lamb was commissioned by the Duchess of York to make busts of her daughters, Princess Elizabeth and Princess Margaret. So impressed was she that she then commissioned a bust of herself.

EDZELL
32 miles NE of Dundee on the B966

Described as the "jewel in the crown of Angus", this pretty village right on the Grampian border is always winning "best kept village" awards. It's approached through the much-photographed **Dalhousie Arch,** erected in 1887 in memory of the 13th Earl of Dalhousie and his Countess who died within a few hours of each other.

Edzell is an estate village, created in the 1840s to a regular plan with trim Victorian houses lining the straight-as-an-arrow main road. About a mile to the west stand the ruins of **Edzell Castle** (Historic Scotland), an important 15th century tower visited by Mary Stuart and James VI, and also used by Cromwell's troops as a garrison. Much of the 16th century castle is ruined, but the beautiful walled garden has survived for more than 350 years and is one of Scotland's unique sights. The garden was created in 1604 by Sir David Lindsay, Lord Edzell: enclosed by rosy-coloured sandstone walls it still retains its elegant symmetry with sculptured stone panels on the walls and an immaculate box hedge spelling out the family motto: *Dum spiro spero* - "While I breathe I hope".

Edzell is the gateway to Glen Esk, the longest and most northerly of the Angus glens. You can drive the 19 miles to Invermark Lodge, close to Loch Lee, where the road peters out. Along the way you can stop at the Retreat, where you will find the **Glen Esk Folk Museum**, which traces the life of the people of the glen from about 1800 to the present day.

ST CYRUS
32 miles NE of Dundee on the A92

St. Cyrus is a small village boasting 3 miles of glorious sandy beaches and an adjacent Nature Reserve. Fishing is still a significant element in the local economy with lobster being particularly important.

Back in the mid-1800s a certain John Orr, the **Laird of Bridgeton.** saw a young couple struggling through snow drifts near St Cyrus and, rather curiously, this inspired him to establish a dowry valued at £1000. The interest was to be divided into five equal parts with one part devoted to helping old folk. The remaining four amounts were to be paid to the youngest, oldest, tallest and shortest brides of the year who had married in St. Cyrus. The dowry is still in place.

MONIFIETH
7 miles E of Dundee on the A930

This little holiday resort sits at the entrance to the Firth of Tay, and has some good sandy beaches. Its golf courses were used in the qualifying rounds of the British Open. At one time it was an important Pictish settlement, and some Pictish stones were discovered at **St Rule's Church** that are now in the National Museum of Scotland in Edinburgh.

CARNOUSTIE
11 miles E of Dundee on the A930

Golf is king in Carnoustie. Every street in this coastal town seems to lead down to a fairway and a bunker is in the foreground of almost every sea view. This small holiday resort on the North Sea coast hosted the British Open Championships in 1931 and 1999, and is a favourite destination for golfing holidays.

But it has other attractions. **Barry Mill** (National Trust for Scotland) is a 19th century working corn mill, though a mill has stood here since at least the middle of the 16th century. You can see the large

Carlungie Souterrain, Carnoustie

263

water wheel turning, and also find out how corn is ground. There is an exhibition explaining the historical role of the mill, as well as a walkway along the mill lade, or mill-race.

Three miles north west of the town are the **Carlungie and Ardestie Souterrains** (Historic Scotland), underground earth houses dating from the 1st century AD.

FOWLIS EASTER

*6 miles NW of Dundee
on a minor road off the A923*

This small village has one of the finest small churches in Scotland. The **Parish Church of St Marnan** dates from about 1453 and still has part of its rood screen as well as medieval paintings dating to around 1541 and a sacrament house that is reckoned to be the finest in Scotland.

North East Scotland

Northeast Scotland is centred on Aberdeen, and consists of the counties of Aberdeenshire, Kincardineshire, Banffshire and Morayshire. High mountains, wooded glens, cityscapes, beaches, rich farmland, towering cliffs and moorland - it's got the lot. And yet it is relatively unknown by those outside Scotland, apart from the city of Aberdeen and along Deeside. The beaches are quiet and uncrowded, the country lanes are a joy to

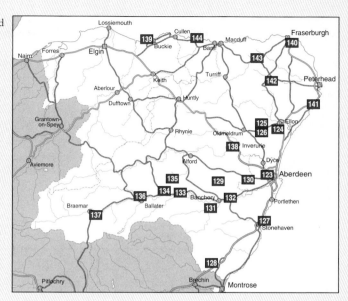

265

drive in, and there is history and heritage aplenty.

To go off the beaten track in the North East is to be rewarded with some wonderful discoveries. Few, for example, have explored the farmlands of Buchan with their rich soil which, even though they are above the Highland line, have more of a Lowland feel about them. How many people stop in Kincardineshire, with its fishing villages and its literary connections? Nowhere else in Europe is there such a concentration of historic castles - around 1000 at the last count. And then there are the distilleries. The industry is centred mainly on Banffshire and Moray where the streams are swift flowing and the water pure.

The inland villages are quiet and peaceful, and the market towns such as Inverurie, Forres and Huntly, are packed with history and charm. The coastline is as dramatic as anywhere in Britain. For all its crowds (especially in late summer when the Queen is there), Deeside cannot be missed.

Aberdeen is Scotland's third largest city and Europe's oil capital. The oil industry has brought money to the city, and it has also brought a cosmopolitan lifestyle that includes smart restaurants, boutiques, nightclubs and stylish pubs. The other city in the region is Elgin, at one time one of the most important places in Scotland. It has lost some of that importance now, but has not lost any of its charm.

ABERDEEN

Aberdeen is well-known as the Granite City which makes it sound rather dour but in fact this granite is of a rather special kind. In sunlight, the millions of specks of mica embedded in each block produce a distinctive sparkle to the city's handsome buildings. Another quirk of nature has endowed the area with the kind of soil beloved by roses. You see them everywhere in the city - in the splendid parks, brightening up the roadsides and filling private gardens. No wonder Aberdeen was barred from the "Britain in Bloom" competition - it was winning too regularly.

One of the most striking floral displays can be seen in the Old Town, at the University's **Cruikshank Botanic Gardens,** laid out in 1898. There are more dazzling displays at Johnston Gardens, Hazelhead Park, Union Terrace Gardens and Duthie Park.

The Cruikshank Gardens provide a superb foreground for **St Machar's Cathedral** which was reputedly founded by Machar, a disciple of St Columba, in AD 580. The present 15th century building, part church, part fortress, is notable for its sumptuous stained glass windows and the equally colourful nave whose oak roof is ablaze with heraldic coats of arms.

Nearby, **King's College Chapel** is the oldest of the university's buildings, completed in 1495. The chapel contains a wealth of exquisite medieval wood-carving, with especially fine work in

the rood screen and the canopied stalls. The **King's College Centre** explains the college's history.

Aberdeen University was founded by Bishop Elphinstone in 1494 under a Papal Bull from Pope Alexander IV. **Marischal College,** another university, was founded in 1593, which meant that the city had two universities - exactly the same number as the whole of England at the same time, as locals gleefully point out. It was founded by George Keith, 5th Earl Marischal of Scotland, as a Protestant alternative to the Catholic-leaning King's College. The present imposing granite building in Broad Street dates from the 19th century, and is the second largest granite building in the world. In 1860 the two universities united to form Aberdeen University. The **Marischal College Museum,** founded in 1786, houses a collection of classical and Egyptian objects, as well as local collections.

The **Brig o' Balgownie** over the Don near the cathedral, dates from the early 14th century and has

123 GORDON HIGHLANDERS MUSEUM

Aberdeen

The heroic story of the 200-year history of the Gordon Highlanders, is illustrated with displays and re-creations.

 see page 422

Provost Skene's House, Aberdeen

Aberdeen prides itself on being Scotland's most prosperous city, due to the oil fields that lie beneath the North Sea. For this reason it is also known as the "Oil Capital of Europe", and the docks and harbours, which were once full of fishing boats, now pulse with supply ships ferrying men and machines out to the oil rigs. It also has the ferry terminal for the Shetland ferry.

a single, pointed arch. It is said to have been built using money given by Robert the Bruce, and is reckoned to be the finest single arch structure in Scotland. Aberdeen's other old bridge, to the south of the city, is the **Bridge of Dee**, built by Bishop Dunbar in the early 1500s.

The **Church of St Nicholas** stands in St Nicholas Street. Of the original church only the transepts and the crypt survive. Its carillon of 48 bells is the largest of any church in Britain. There are six entrances to the kirkyard, the grandest being the granite colonnade in Union Street, designed in 1830 by John Smith, Aberdeen's city architect.

Just off St Nicholas Street, **Provost Skene's House** dates from 1545 and is now a museum

illustrating the life and times of the rich Aberdonian merchant, Sir George Skene who lived here in the late 1600s. It is a tall, solid building of turrets and chimneys, and has wonderful painted ceilings and period furniture, as well as displays on modern history. **Provost Ross's House** is in Shiprow, said to be Aberdeen's oldest street still in use. The house was built in 1593, but is named after its most famous owner, John Ross, lord provost of Aberdeen in the 18th century. It now houses the **Aberdeen Maritime Museum**, with exhibits and displays on Aberdeen's maritime history, plus a re-created "helicopter ride" out to an offshore oilrig.

Union Street, Aberdeen's main thoroughfare, is more than a mile long, and thronged with shops. It was laid out in the early 1800s to celebrate the union of Britain and Ireland. At one end, in Castle Street, is the city's 17th century **Mercat Cross**.

The **Aberdeen Art Gallery and Museums** are at Schoolhill, near Robert Gordon's College. Apart from a fine collection of paintings and sculpture by such artists as Degas, Reynolds, and Epstein, it houses displays on Aberdeen's history, including finds made at various archaeological digs throughout the city. James Dun's House, dating from the 18th century, forms part of the museum.

The Planetarium at Aberdeen College in the Gallowgate Centre is a star dome, which shows the

River Dee, Aberdeen

planets and stars as they "move" through the heavens. And the **Gordon Highlanders Museum** on Viewfield Road tells the story of what Sir Winston Churchill called "the finest regiment in the world". There is an audiovisual theatre, gardens, a children's "handling area", a shop and a café.

One of Aberdeen's newest attractions is **Stratosphere** in The Tramsheds in Constitution Street, a hands-on science centre where children can explore all aspects of science, and watch a science show that explains things like colour and bubbles.

In King Street is the Aberdeen and North East Scotland Family History Society, which has a wide range of reference material for family and genealogical research. At Blairs, on South Deeside Road, there was once a catholic seminary, which closed in 1986. The **Blairs Museum** now holds the Scottish Catholic Heritage Collection, and is open to the public. There are objects connected with the Stuart line (including Mary Stuart and Charles Edward Stuart) on display, as well as a collection of rich vestments, church plate and paintings.

At Bridge of Don is **Glover House,** the family home of Thomas Blake Glover, the Scotsman who, it is said, inspired Puccini's opera *Madame Butterfly*. Born in Fraserburgh in 1838, his family moved to Bridge of Don in 1851, when he was 13 years old. When he left school, he began working for a trading company, and

got a taste for overseas travel.

When he first went to Japan at 21, he was entering a feudal society that had been closed to the west for over 300 years. However, within one year he was selling Scottish-built warships and arms to Japanese rebels during the country's civil war. At the same time he sent young Japanese men to Britain to be educated.

He was called the "Scottish Samurai", and helped found the Mitsubishi shipyards, the first step Japan took to becoming a great manufacturing power. He also helped found the famous Kirin Brewery, and his picture still appears on Kirin labels to this day. A grateful government presented Glover with the Order of the Rising Sun, Japan's greatest honour. He later built himself a house at Nagasaki, and married a Japanese woman called Tsura, who invariably wore kimonos decorated with butterfly motifs. When Puccini came across a short story and subsequent play based on this relationship, it sowed the seeds for *Madame Butterfly*.

AROUND ABERDEEN

ELLON

17 miles N of Aberdeen on the A920

Situated within an area known as the Formartine, Ellon is a small burgh or barony, which was granted its charter in 1707. It sits beside the River Ythan with a **Parish Church** that dates from 1777. Ellon is also one of the stops on the **Formartine Buchan Way**,

124 EAT ON THE GREEN

Udny Green, Ellon

Eat on the Green is a superb restaurant serving a good selection of contemporary and classic dishes, using the freshest of local produce.

see page 421

125 LINSMOHR HOTEL

Pitmedden, nr Ellon

Stylish and friendly this family run hotel offers comfort, relaxation and quality along with its very own popular Bronie Brasserie.

see page 422

126 PITMEDDEN GARDEN

Pitmedden, nr Ellon

Dating from the 17th century, this beautiful garden is filled with 40,000 plants. Adjacent to the Garden is the Museum of Farming Life with an extensive collection of domestic and agricultural artefacts.

 see page 424

based on disused railway tracks from Dyce, just outside of Aberdeen, to Fraserburgh. The **Moot Hill Monument** stands on Moot Hill, from where justice was dispensed by the Earls of Buchan in the 13th and early 14th centuries.

Five miles west of the town, on the A920 is the **Pitmedden Garden** (National Trust for Scotland). The centrepiece is the Great Garden, laid out by Sir Alexander Seton, 1st Baronet of Pitmedden, in 1675. In the 1950s the rest of the garden was re-created using elaborate floral designs. Four parterres were created, three of them being inspired by designs possibly used at the Palace of Holyrood in Edinburgh, and the fourth based on Sir Alexander's coat-of-arms. There is also a visitor centre and a **Museum of Farming Life,** which has a collection of old farming implements once used in this largely farming area.

Near the gardens are the substantial ruins of **Tolquhon Castle**, built by William Forbes, 7th Lord of Tolquhon in the 1580s. In 1589 James VI visited the house,

and both his and the Forbes' coats-of-arms were carved over the doorway. William Forbes and his wife Elizabeth were buried in an elaborately carved tomb in the south aisle of the parish church at Tarves. The church has since been demolished, but the **Forbes Tomb** in the churchyard has been preserved.

Haddo House (National Trust for Scotland), one of the grandest stately homes in Aberdeenshire, lies six miles northwest of Ellon. It was designed by William Adam for the 2nd Earl of Aberdeen in the early 1730s, and restored in the 1880s. It is noted for its Victorian interiors within an elegant Georgian shell, and features furniture, paintings and objets d'art. It also has a terraced garden with rose beds and a fountain. In the grounds is Kelly Lake, one of the few natural (as opposed to man made) sheets of water called "lake" rather than "loch" in Scotland.

STONEHAVEN
15 miles S of Aberdeen off the A90

Set around a sheltered bay, this popular holiday resort has a picturesque harbour overlooked by the town's oldest building, the Tolbooth. Originally built in the 1500s as a storehouse, it later served as the town jail and is now a museum of local history and fishing.

Near the harbour stands the 18th century **Mercat Cross**, and the **Steeple**, from where James VII was proclaimed king in 1715 after landing at the town's harbour.

The High Street links the

Forbes Tomb, Ellon

harbour to the 18th century New Town set around a Market Square with a striking Market Hall topped by an impressive steeple. One of the houses in the square bears a plaque identifying it as the birthplace of Robert Thomson (1822-1873), inventor of the pneumatic tyre, the fountain pen and the dry dock.

Each year at Hogmanay the traditional **Fireball Festival** is held in Stonehaven. It takes place in the "Auld Toon" area of the town, with up to 60 men parading at midnight while swinging huge fireballs on the end of stout wires. The origins are rooted in paganism, with the light from the balls supposedly attracting the sun, ensuring its return after the dark days of winter.

Two miles south of the town is **Dunnottar Castle**. It is magnificently sited, as it stands on a promontory 160 feet above the sea and is guarded on three sides by the North Sea and on the fourth by St Ninian's Den, a steep ravine. It dates from the 13th century and later, and has seen some gruesome episodes in Scotland's history. In 1297 William Wallace torched it, burning to death every English soldier within its walls. In 1652 Cromwell's troops laid siege to it to capture Scotland's Crown Jewels. However, they were foiled by the wife of the minister of Kinneff Church, who smuggled them out under the very noses of the troops.

INVERBERVIE

25 miles S of Aberdeen on the A92

Though no bigger than a village, Inverbervie is in fact a royal burgh, having been granted its charter in 1341 by David II who, along with his queen, was shipwrecked off the coast as he returned from imprisonment in France, and was "kindly received" by the people of the village. John Coutts, whose son Thomas Coutts founded the famous bank, was born here in 1699. The village's **Mercat Cross** dates from 1737.

Three miles north, at Kinneff, is **Kinneff Church**, built in 1738. The previous church on the site, built in about 1242, has a unique place in Scotland's history. In 1651 the Scottish Crown Jewels were used at the coronation of Charles II at Scone, then hidden in Dunnottar Castle so that Parliamentarian troops could not find them. But when their whereabouts became known to Cromwell, they were smuggled out by the wife of Kinneff's minister, and placed within the church. There they lay for ten years, beneath the floor. Every three months the minister and his wife dug them up, cleaned them and aired them before a fire. With the Restoration of Charles II in 1660, they were taken to Edinburgh Castle. Though no longer used for worship, the church is still open to the public and under the care of the Kinneff Old Church Preservation Trust.

ARBUTHNOTT

27 miles S of Aberdeen on the B967

The village of Arbuthnott lies in what is called The Mearns, the area celebrated by the author Lewis Grassic Gibbon in his novels. His

127 THE SHIP INN

Stonehaven

18th century inn overlooking the harbour and offering excellent cuisine, en suite rooms and seaview terrace.

see page 423

128 CLATTERIN' BRIG

Clatterin Bridge, nr Fettercairn

Excellent traditional home-made Scottish fare in restaurant occupying wonderfully scenic location.

see page 424

dark brooding stories about Mearns farm life were far removed from the couthy stories about simple Scottish country folk that had been published before. **The Lewis Grassic Gibbon Centre**, next to the parish hall, traces the life and works of a man who became one of the most important British writers of the 20th century. His ashes are buried in the Kirk yard of Arbuthnott Collegiate Church.

The area has other literary associations. Robert Burn's father was born here before setting up home in Ayrshire, and in the kirkyard of the church at Glenbervie four miles to the northwest is the grave of Burns's great grandfather, James Burnes (the "e" in the name was dropped after Burns's father moved to Ayrshire).

Arbuthnott House, home to the Arbuthnott family for 800 years, dates mainly from the 18th and 19th centuries, and is open to the public on certain days of the year. The gardens, including a formal 17th century walled garden, are open all year round.

PETERCULTER

7 miles SW of Aberdeen on the A93

One mile west of the village is **Drum Castle** (National Trust for Scotland), built in the late 13th century, probably by the wonderfully named Richard Cemantarius, king's master mason and provost of Aberdeen. In 1323 it was given to William de Irwyn by Robert the Bruce, and the Irvines lived in it from that date right up until 1975. It was enlarged in 1619 by the creation of a grand Jacobean mansion and later by some Victorian additions.

MARYCULTER

7 miles SW of Aberdeen on the B9077

Storybook Glen is a 28-acre children's park set in spectacular scenery where more than 100 fairy tale and nursery rhyme characters can be found. Also on site are a restaurant, gift shop and garden centre.

FETTERCAIRN

29 miles SW of Aberdeen on the B974

In September 1861, Queen Victoria and Prince Albert paid an unheralded visit to the attractive village of Fettercairn, taking over the local inn, the Ramsay Arms. Their identity having been

Old Town Mercat Cross, Fettercairn

discovered by the next morning, the royal couple were loyally cheered on their way and the local people erected the impressive **Fettercairn Arch** at the entrance to the village. Today, the Arch marks the start of the **Victorian Heritage Trail** linking the many locations associated with the queen during that visit.

Fettercairn Distillery, the second oldest in Scotland, lies to the northwest of the village and has guided tours (with a free dram at the end) and a visitor centre.

About a mile north of the town is **Fasque**, the family home of the Gladstones since 1829. The most famous of them, William Ewart, served four times as prime minister to Victoria but he was not a royal favourite. The queen complained that he addressed her like "a public meeting". The interior of the Gladstones' stately Georgian house has changed little since the late 19th century and provides a fascinating insight into the life-style of the upper middle class in those days. The house is open for groups of more than 12 by prior arrangement.

GARLOGIE

10 miles W of Aberdeen on the B9119

The **Garlogie Mill Power House Museum** has a rare beam engine - the only one to have survived intact in its location - which used to power this wauk mill, which finished off woven cloth. The mill is open to the public and there are displays about its history and machinery.

The **Cullrelie Stone Circle**, close to the village just off the B9125, dates from the Bronze Age, and consists of eight stones placed in a 33-feet diameter circle. The shallow **Loch of Skene**, to the north of the village, is a special protection area and supports an important colony of Icelandic greylag geese. Three miles to the west of the village, near Echt, is the **Barmekin of Echt**, an ancient fortified hill settlement.

MONYMUSK

17 miles W of Aberdeen off the B993

Monymusk was once the site of an Augustinian priory, founded in 1170 by the Earl of Mar. The Monymusk Reliquary, in which was kept a bone of St Columba, was one of its treasures. It dates from the 8th century and lies in a small wooden box covered in silver and bronze and decorated in semi-precious stones. It was paraded before Bruce's troops at the Battle of Bannockburn and is now in the Museum of Scotland.

The **Parish Church of St Mary**, which formed part of the priory, dates from the early years of the 12th century. In 1929 it was restored to its original condition, and it is now one of the finest parish churches in Scotland. Inside it is the Monymusk Stone, on which are carved Pictish symbols.

ALFORD

27 miles W of Aberdeen on the A944

Alford (pronounced "Afford" locally, with the accent on the first syllable) is a pleasant village within

129 THE MILLERS VISITOR AND RETAIL CENTRE

Midmar

A great family day out with all your different shopping needs under one friendly roof. Open 7 days.

 see page 425

130 RED STAR INN

Kirkton on Skene

A modern and fresh pub welcomes you with traditional values; serving great home cooked meals, real ale and en suite accommodation.

see page 425

273

131 FEUGHSIDE INN

Strachan

A superior Scottish inn that makes the perfect base for exploring Deeside and its royal connections.

see page 426

132 CRATHES CASTLE AND GARDENS

Banchory

A 16th century tower house, standing in beautiful grounds, that still retains some original features and holds interesting collections of furniture and portraits.

 see page 426

a fertile area known as the Howe of Alford. The **Grampian Transport Museum** has displays and working exhibits about transport in the Grampian area. Major exhibits include the world's oldest Sentinel Steam Wagon from 1914, a giant Mack Snowplow and the Jaguar XKR used in the James Bond film, *Die Another Day*. Visitors can even clamber aboard some of the exhibits. Each year the Eco Marathon takes place at the museum, where vehicles have to travel as far as possible on a set amount of fuel. The current record, established in 2008, is 6030 miles per gallon of petrol.

The **Alford Valley Railway** is a two-mile long narrow gauge passenger railway with steam and diesel locomotives that runs between the Transport Museum and **Haughton House Country Park**, where there are woodland walks, a wildflower garden and a caravan park.

Four miles south of Alford on the A980, the massive 7-storey high **Craigievar Castle** has to be seen to be believed. This exuberant wedding cake confection in pink granite was completed in 1626 and is so popular with visitors that the National Trust for Scotland sometimes has to restrict the numbers allowed to enter. But you can always enjoy the chocolate box exterior from the grounds, for which there is no admission charge. The castle is currently closed for major renpvation work but is scheduled to re-open some time in 2010.

BANCHORY

18 miles W of Aberdeen on the A93

This attractive little 19th century burgh stands at the point where the River Freugh enters the Dee, and is often called the "Gateway to Royal Deeside". It once stood on the Deeside railway line that closed in 1966. and there are now plans to re-open a section between the town and Crathes, three miles to the east. In Bridge Street is the **Banchory Museum**, which has collections featuring tartans, royal commemorative china and the natural history of the area. The Scottish musician and composer James Scott Skinner, "the Strathspey King", was born at Arbeadie, just outside the town, in 1843, and a further display in the museum is dedicated to his life.

About three miles east of Banchory is **Crathes Castle** (National Trust for Scotland), one of the most appealing old buildings in the country. Built between 1550 and 1590, its sturdy outline is sprinkled with fairytale-like turrets and fantastic gargoyles. The interior is no place for claustrophobics but the low ceilings of the small rooms are dazzlingly decorated with wonderful early-17th century paintings. The Nine Muses and Seven Virtues are depicted in the Muses' Room, while the Room of the Nine Nobles portrays great heroes of the past, amongst them Julius Caesar and King Arthur. In the Great Hall hangs the ancient Horn of Leys, made of ivory and encrusted with jewels. It was presented to the then owners by Robert the Bruce. Outside, eight themed gardens separated by yew hedges, have been laid out within the old walled garden, There is also a shop and restaurant.

KINCARDINE O'NEILL

26 miles SW of Aberdeen on the A93

This little village, with its Irish-sounding name, claims to be the oldest village on Deeside. It is in fact a small burgh, having been granted its charter in 1511. It was here, in 1220, that the first bridge was constructed across the Dee beyond Aberdeen, so it became an important place. The ruins of the **Kirk of St Mary** date from the 14th century.

LUMPHANAN

27 miles W of Aberdeen on the A980

Lumphanan was founded when the Deeside railway was constructed, and was the highest point on the line. The **Peel Ring of Lumphanan** (Historic Scotland) is a huge motte and bailey where a castle built by the Durward family once stood.

ABOYNE

29 miles W of Aberdeen off the A93

This small Royal Deeside town is famous for the **Aboyne Highland Games**, held in August each year. The village prospered with the coming of the railway in the 19th century, and is now a quiet settlement, popular with tourists. It is also the home of the **Aboyne and Deeside Festival**, held in July and August, which features music,

drama and art. There is a lovely, but in places difficult, walk up **Glen Tanar**, two miles west of Aboyne.

Five miles north of the town, and two miles north east of Tarland is the **Culsh Earth House**, a souterrain, or underground chamber, which is more than 2000 years old. It is a long, dog-legged tunnel which was probably not used as a house, but as a store for foodstuffs. A torch is needed to explore it. The **Tomnaverie Stone Circle** (Historic Scotland) is a mile to the south west, and dates to about 1600 BC.

BALLATER

38 miles W of Aberdeen on the A93

Queen Victoria was particularly fond of the valley of Glen Muick (pronounced "Mick") which runs southwest from Ballater and it's still popular with walkers and cyclists. Whichever direction you travel from this trim little town, the River Dee and the pine-clad hills provide superb vistas at every turn. Victoria often arrived by train at Ballater but she vetoed plans to extend the railway to Balmoral itself. The railway service petered out many years ago but the elegant station still stands and has been restored to show what it would have looked like in Victorian times.

There is plenty of good walking country around the village, and **Glen Muick** has a narrow road that takes you up towards Loch Muick (the road ends before the loch is reached, so you have to

133 GLEN TANAR HOLIDAY COTTAGES

Aboyne

Exclusive hideaway for all in the heart of Royal Deeside and the Cairngorms National Park.

🛏 *see page 427*

134 VICTORIA RESTAURANT

Dinnet

A tasteful restaurant with a subtle theatrical theme that serves relaxed yet truly delicious lunches and dinners to guests in the heart of Royal Deeside.

🍴 *see page 428*

135 STRACHAN COTTAGE

Tarland

A superior self-catering cottage that makes the ideal base from which to explore Royal Deeside and all it has to offer.

🛏 *see page 427*

Ballater

Handsome Victorian property set in lovely gardens and offering both en suite B&B and self-catering accommodation.

see page 429

walk part of the way). The loch lies in the shadow of Lochnagar which, notwithstanding its name, is a mountain rising to a height of 3786 feet. It provided the title of Prince Charles's book, *The Old Man of Lochnagar*. The drive is a particularly fine one, and takes you past Birkhall (not open to the public) which was bought by Edward VII before he became king. It was the Deeside home of the late Queen Mother.

CRATHIE

46 miles W of Aberdeen off the A93

This neat and tidy village has 'model' cottages built by Victoria and Albert for workers on the Balmoral Estate, and a grey granite church of 1895 whose building was funded by the proceeds of a bazaar held at Balmoral Castle. Many of the fittings and furnishings have been donated over the years by members of the Royal Family. John Brown, Queen Victoria's controversial ghillie, lies in the adjoining cemetery.

The **Royal Lochnagar Distillery**, established in 1845, is near the kirk, and has a visitors centre. It was given a Royal Warrant by Queen Victoria in 1864.

Balmoral Castle nearby is a full-blooded example of Scottish Baronial style of architecture, beautifully set in a wooded landscape beside the River Dee. Victoria and Albert bought the estate in 1852 for £31,000, demolished the rather poky mansion that stood there, and replaced it with a gracious building

of white granite, dominated by a tower 80 feet high. Royalists will be disappointed to discover that access to the castle is restricted to the ballroom and grounds - and only when there are no members of the Royal Family in residence.

Queen Victoria made her first visit to Scotland in 1842 and was immediately captivated by the scenery - *"so wild and grand"* she wrote. She was to return as often as her numerous pregnancies permitted and after Prince Albert's death she spent so much time at Balmoral that her ministers became increasingly fretful that she chose to spend up to 4 months a year 500 miles away from the capital.

In her early years Victoria was an indefatigable explorer, braving storms and mountain passes with equanimity. In her diary she noted *"I seldom walk less than four hours a day, and when I come in I feel as if I want to go out again"*. A **Victorian Heritage Trail** has been laid out (with distinctive brown signs) which traces the footsteps of Queen Victoria not just on Deeside, but throughout the area, and a leaflet is available from most tourism offices.

BRAEMAR

55 miles W of Aberdeen on the A93

Braemar sits high in the Cairngorms and is officially Britain's coldest place. Between 1941 and 1970 its average temperature was only 6.4 degrees Celsius. On two occasions, in 1895 and 1982, it experienced the lowest temperature ever officially recorded in Britain - minus 28.2 degrees Celsius.

It sits at an altitude of 1100 feet, and is famous for the **Braemar Highland Games**, held every September, and usually attended by the Royal Family. The Gathering has its origins in the athletic contests initiated by Malcolm III (1031-93) to find "his hardest soldiers and fleetest messengers". The games lapsed in medieval times but were revived in 1834 and featured such traditional contests as Putting the Stone, Throwing the Hammer and, the most distinctive of the Highland Games, Tossing the Caber - a 20 feet long pole of stripped pine weighing 132 pounds. The Gathering is held on the first Saturday in September but if you want to attend, make sure you get a ticket well in advance.

The event takes place close to **Braemar Castle,** a small but forbidding fortress occupying a strategic position where three mountain passes meet. Built in 1628, it was badly damaged during the first Jacobite rising of 1689, re-fortified by the English in the wake of the 1745 Rebellion, and in 1797 passed to the Farquharson family, now Lairds of Invercauld. They began converting the castle into a family home and the result is an intriguing blend of uncompromising military architecture and elegant features such as Hepplewhite chairs and Chippendale mirrors. In the drawing room can be seen the world's largest Cairngorm (a semi-

precious stone) weighting 52 pounds. And in the morning room display is a collection of Native American items from the Great Lakes area of Canada. They were sent to this country by two members of the family who went there seeking their fortunes.

The 72,598-acre **Mar Lodge Estate** (National Trust for Scotland) lies five miles west of Braemar on a minor road, and is part of the Cairngorms National Park which came into being in September 2003. The estate has been described as the most important nature conservation landscape in Britain, and contains four out of its five highest mountains. In medieval times, when the estate was owned by the Earls of Mar, it was one of Scotland's premier hunting estates. It displays many of the features normally associated with Highland landscapes and has a wealth of wildlife, plants, trees and archaeological sites. The estate is open daily, and the Lodge itself has special open days that are well advertised.

To the south of Braemar, on the A93, is one of Scotland's most popular winter sports areas, **Glenshee**. The snowfields stretch over three valleys and four Munros, with about 25 miles of marked pistes as well as off-piste skiing.

KINTORE

11 miles NW of Aberdeen off the A96

This tiny Royal Burgh has an elegant **Tolbooth** of 1747 with a two-winged outside staircase. The

137 MOORFIELD HOUSE HOTEL

Braemar

Charming family-run hotel, recently refurbished and offering exceptional cuisine and en suite rooms.

see *page 429*

NORTH EAST SCOTLAND

138 BLACK BULL INN

Inverurie

Family-run town centre
hostelry offering impressive
malt whisky collection,
regular entertainment and
comfortable en suite rooms.

🍴 🛏 see page 430

---

*The Battle of Harlaw
was fought near the town
of Inverurie in 1411, and
a monument now marks
the spot. A Lowland
army fought a Highland
army under Donald,
Lord of the Isles, and
while the result was an
honourable draw, it did
stop the Highlanders
from moving into the
Aberdeenshire lowlands
and controlling them. It
was one of the bloodiest
battles ever fought on
Scottish soil, which
earned it the nickname
of "Red Harlaw".*

town is well-known to
archaeologists because of the
ancient Ichthus Stone in the
churchyard which is carved with a
fish on one side and what may be
an elephant on the other. On the
surrounding hills are many remains
of prehistoric forts and stone
circles, most of which have
probably entered their fifth
millenium.

INVERURIE

17 miles NW of Aberdeen off the A96

One of the few sizeable
communities in the Aberdeenshire
heartland, this flourishing farming
town hosts the thrice-weekly
Thainstone Mart, the largest
livestock auction in Europe.

A royal burgh, Inverurie sits
where the River Urie meets the
Don. A legend tells of how a
Roman soldier who came to this
area exclaimed "urbi in rure!" (a
city in the countryside) when he
first saw the settlement. The town
adopted the words as its motto and
it is inscribed on the coat of arms
of the burgh. However, in reality
the town's name has a more prosaic
meaning - the "mouth of the
Urie".

In 1805, the Aberdeenshire
Canal was opened which linked
Inverurie with Aberdeen. Designed
by John Rennie, it was never a great
success, and in 1845 it was sold to
the Great North of Scotland
Railway Company, who drained it
and used part of its route to carry
their railway line. Port Elphinstone,
to the south east of the town,
recalls the canal, and part of its

channel can still be seen there. It
was the only canal in Britain to be
closed down every winter in case
of ice and snow. Within the
Carnegie Inverurie Museum in
the Square is a small display
dedicated to the canal, as well as
displays on local history.

To the west of the town is the
area's best-known hill, Bennachie.
Though not particularly high (1600
feet) it has a distinctive conical
shape and is sometimes called
"Aberdeenshire's Mount Fuji" as it
can be seen from all round the
area. Near the Chapel of Garrioch
is the **Bennachie Visitors Centre,**
where the natural and social history
of the hill is explained.

Two miles south of the town
are the ruins of the 16th century
Kinkell Church, which has a
particularly fine sacrament house.
The ornate grave slab of Gilbert de
Greenlaw, who was killed at the
Battle of Harlaw, can also be seen.

Castle Fraser (National Trust
for Scotland) lies six miles south
west of the town, near the village
of Craigearn. Work started on it in
1575 by Michael Fraser, the sixth
laird, and was finished in 1636. It
has a traditional "Z" plan, and
contains many Fraser portraits, fine
carpets, linen and curtains.

OYNE

23 miles NW of Aberdeen on the B9002

More than 7000 ancient sites have
been identified in Aberdeenshire,
from Pictish carvings to stone
circles, and these form the basis for
the **Archaeolink Prehistory Park,**
which bridges the gap between

278

ancient history and modern times by way of exhibits and hands-on displays, both indoor and out. It has some of the finest collections of ancient remains in Europe.

FYVIE

26 miles NW of Aberdeen off the A947

The oldest part of **Fyvie Castle** (National Trust for Scotland) dates from the 13th century and was once a royal stronghold. There are 17th century panelling and plaster ceilings, as well as a portrait collection that includes works by Raeburn, Romney and Gainsborough. One of the legends attached to the castle is that its five towers were built by the five great families in the northeast who owned it - the Gordons, the Leiths, the Meldrums, the Prestons and the Setons. Both Robert the Bruce and and his descendant Charles I stayed here.

The **Parish Church** dates from the 19th century and has a fine laird's pew and wine glass pulpit. In Fyvie Old Manse in 1864 was born Cosmo Gordon Lang, who became Archbishop of York in 1908 and Archbishop of Canterbury in 1928.

HUNTLY

40 miles NW of Aberdeen on the A96

Huntly is an attractive market town surrounded by pleasant, open countryside. It lies in an area called Strathbogie and is famous for the ruins of **Huntly Castle** (Historic Scotland) which are beautifully set overlooking a gorge of the River Deveron. Until the mid-1500s, the castle belonged to the "Gey

Gordons", a term which was later corrupted into the name of a popular Scottish dance. "Gey" meant prominent or influential which the Gordons certainly were from medieval times until the Civil War when the Marquess of Huntly supported Charles I. He was shot against the walls of his own castle. From about the early 18th century the castle fell into decay. But even today you can see just how stately and comfortable the place must have been in its heyday. It entertained many famous people, including Mary of Guise, mother of Mary Stuart, and Perkin Warbeck, pretender to the English throne.

In the town square is a statue to the 4th Duke of Richmond, and beneath it are the **Standing Stones of Strathbogie**, or as they are known in Huntly, the "Stannin Steens o Strahbogie". At one time they formed part of a stone circle.

The **Brander Museum** in the Square has collections dealing with local history, arms and armour and the works of local author George MacDonald, who died in 1905. His most popular stories were of fantasy and fairies, with a strong religious message. He rejected the Calvinist view, still held by some people in the Church of Scotland at the time, that art was self-indulgent and iconoclastic. Instead he argued that God could be understood through art and imagination.

Six miles south of Huntly, on the B9002 near Kennethmont, is **Leith Hall** (National Trust for

Scotland), an appealing 17th century mansion house set in the middle of a 286-acre estate. The Leith family, who lived here for some 300 years, produced a long line of distinguished soldiers and the Hall contains a unique collection of military memorabilia.

ELGIN

This charming city developed around the River Lossie in the 1200s and still retains its medieval street plan. The bustling High Street gradually widens to a cobbled Market Place where the architectural focus is an elegant neo-classical building, the **Church of St Giles**, erected in 1828. Eight years later, at the top of the High Street, the citizens of Elgin subscribed funds to build one of the first municipal museums in Britain. The **Elgin Museum** offers a good display of local artefacts, some fine Pictish stones and pre-Columbian pottery. It also displays an eclectic anthropological collection which includes a shrunken head from Ecuador and a gruesomely grinning mummy from Peru. Another museum worth visiting is the **Moray Motor Museum** in converted mill buildings in Bridge Street. Its collection of old cars and motorcycles spans the period from 1904 to the 1960s. The centrepiece of the collection is a 1928 Rolls-Royce Phantom I.

Just off the High Street is the **Thunderton Hotel**, housed in what was a grand medieval town house. It was once the royal residence of the town, and was where the monarch stayed when he visited. It was surrounded by orchards, gardens and a bowling green. In 1746 Charles Edward Stuart stayed here while on his way to Culloden.

During his 11-day stay, the Bonnie Prince visited the ruins of **Elgin Cathedral** which is possibly the most accident-prone ecclesiastical building in the country. Founded in 1224, barely fifty years later it was severely damaged by fire. When rebuilt, the cathedral was described as "the ornament of the district, the glory of the kingdom and the admiration of foreigners". Then in 1390 the "Wolf of Badenoch", (the epithet applied to the lawless Earl of Buchan), with his "wyld, wykked Helendmen" set fire to the building along with the rest of the town. It was the earl's way of expressing his displeasure with the Bishop of Moray who had excommunicated him for leaving his wife. Rebuilt

Elgin Cathedral

once again, the cathedral flourished for a century and a half until the Reformation. Then it was stripped of all its priceless treasures, the lead was salvaged from the roof in 1667, and on Easter Sunday 1711, the central tower collapsed. The ruins were cannibalised as "a common quarry" until 1807 when steps were taken to preserve what remained. And what remains is still remarkably beautiful.

To the north west of the cathedral are the ruins of the so-called **Bishop's Palace**. It had nothing to do with the bishop but was instead the manse of the cathedral's preceptor who looked after the sacred music. It was one of about 20 such manses around the cathedral which housed the cathedral staff. To the north east of the cathedral is the Brewery Bridge, built in 1798 and so called because a brewery stood close by until 1913.

Off Greyfriars Street stands the restored **Greyfriars Monastery**, now reckoned to give the best idea of what a medieval Scottish friary looked like. It was built n 1479, then, in the late-19th century, was restored by John Kinross, who built new walls on the foundations of the old ones.

At the west end of the high street is the imposing façade of Dr Gray's Hospital, the town's main infirmary. It was founded by Dr Alexander Gray, who amassed a fortune in India, and built itbetween 1816 and 1819.

Johnston's Cashmere Visitor Centre is at Newmill. There are

tours round the mill where visitors can watch the whole process by which raw cashmere from China and Mongolia is transformed into luxury garments. There is also a shop where Johnston products can be bought, and a coffee shop.

The **Old Mills** is the last remaining meal mill on the River Lossie. Its history goes back to the 13th century, when it was owned by Pluscarden Abbey.

AROUND ELGIN

LOSSIEMOUTH

6 miles N of Elgin on the A941

Elgin's nearest seaside resort is Lossiemouth with two sandy beaches swept by invigorating breezes. Once important for its herring fishing, the town is generally known as Lossie and its

•

North of Elgin are the impressive ruins of Spynie Palace (Historic Scotland), built in the 1460s as a residence for the Bishop of Moray, David Stewart. Taking into account the less-than-respectful attitude at that time to the established church, the bishop decided that a well-fortified building might be appropriate. The colossal, four-square David's Tower, named after the bishop, is the largest tower house in Scotland - a clear indication from His Grace that the meek would not be inheriting the earth for a while.

•

The 'Biblical Garden', Elgin

residents as "Lossie loons". The town's most famous loon was James Ramsay MacDonald, the first labour prime minister. The cottage in which he was born illegitimately still stands at 1, Gregory Place, identified by a plaque. The interior is not open to the public but, curiously, there is a reconstruction of MacDonald's study in the **Lossiemouth Fisheries and Community Museum** which is otherwise devoted to the town's fishing industry and includes some interesting small scale models of fishing vessels.

FOCHABERS

9 miles E of Elgin on the A96

Fochabers is one of many Scottish villages which were re-sited from their original location when the Laird, embarking on a programme of improving his property, decided to remove his tenants' unsightly hovels from view. Normally, an 18th century laird could achieve his aim with a few strokes of a lawyer's pen but at Fochabers the ancient contract of "feu tenancy" involved the Duke of Gordon in a quarter of a century of expensive litigation before he finally removed the last blot on his landscape in 1802. The duke's gracious Georgian residence, Gordon Castle, overlooking the now-sanitised view, is not open to the public.

A century or so after the building of the castle, one of the 50 gardeners who tended its extensive grounds made a momentous decision. Gordon Baxter resigned his job, borrowed £100 and together with his eife Margaret, an inspired cook, opened a small grocery shop in Spey Street, Fochabers. In the back of the shop, Margaret magicked the fruits of local hedgerows into unbelievably tasty jams and jellies. George's former employer, the Duke of Gordon, was captivated by them. They graced his breakfast and tea tables, and so introduced his many rich and aristocratic friends to these very Scottish specialities. As a result of the duke's patronage George and Margaret Baxter's business thrived. But it was their daughter-in-law, Ethel, who in 1929 created the firm's most famous product, Baxter's Royal Game Soup, still savoured by gastronomes around the world. Today, the Baxter's Visitor Centre at Fochabers welcomes almost a quarter of a million visitors each year, drawn here by its historic appeal, its Old Shop Museum (a re-creation of George Baxter's original establishment), and its constellation of other attractive speciality shops.

Other places of interest in Fochabers include the **Fochabers Folk Museum,** housed within the former Pringle Church in the High Street; and the elegant, porticoed **Bellie Church** in the square. Its rather quaint name comes from the Gaelic "beul-aith", meaning "the mouth of the ford". There's also the imposing Milne's High School which dates from 1844 and was built using money gifted by a native of the town who made his fortune in New Orleans.

BUCKIE

16 miles E of Elgin on the A990

Buckie is a major fishing port, based in Cluny Harbour. In the **Buckie District Fishing Heritage Museum** in Clunie Place and the **Buckie Drifter** in Freuchny Road are displays that tell the story of the fishing industry on the Morayshire coast. The **Peter Anson Gallery** is within the town's library, and has a collection of paintings by the maritime artist Peter Anson.

The small fishing communities round about, such as Findochty and Portnockie are very attractive, and well worth visiting. Five miles southwest of the town are the ruins of **Deskford Church**, within the village of the same name. It is noted for its ornately carved sacrament house.

One of the most dramatically situated castles in the area is **Findlater Castle**, which sits on a small promontory jutting into the sea. The ruins you see now date from the 15th century and were built by the Ogilvie family. The name comes from the Norse "fyn", meaning "white" and "leitr" meaning "cliff", as the cliffs in this part of the country are studded with quartz.

Cullen, a former fishing village, gives its name to one of Scotland's best known dishes - Cullen skink, a fish soup enriched with potatoes, onion and cream. The word "skink" comes from the Gaelic word for "essence".

In the village of Fordyce, south east of Cullen, is the **Fordyce Joiner's Workshop and Visitor Centre** in Church Street, dedicated to the skills and tools of carpentry in northeast Scotland. Fordyce Castle was built in 1592 by Sir Thomas Menzies of Durn, a provost of Aberdeen. It is an L-plan tower, and is not open to the public.

KEITH

17 miles SE of Elgin on the A96

Keith is divided into two communities, separated by the River Isla. The old Keith was founded in the 12th century on the west bank of the river as a market centre for the selling of cattle. The newer, and larger, Keith was laid out in 1755 by the Earl of Findlater on the east bank.

The old **Packhorse Bridge** dates from 1609, though the town's oldest building is **Milton Tower**, dating from 1480. There is a **Scottish Tartans Museum** in Keith's Institute Hall and the town is the eastern terminus of the Keith and Dufftown Railway.

CRAIGELLACHIE

12 miles S of Elgin off the A95

The **Craigellachie Bridge** dates from 1814, and is Scotland's oldest iron bridge. It was designed by Thomas Telford, and has one single graceful arch spanning the Spey. The village sits in the heart of the Malt Whisky Trail, and most of the distilleries organise tours round the premises, with a tasting at the end. Craigellachie Distillery lies within the village, as does the Macallan

139 HIGHLANDER HOTEL

Buckie

Recently renovated hotel in small fishing village offering good home-made food and en suite accommodation.

🛏 ❚ *see page 431*

Keith is home to the Strathisla Distillery, famous for its Chivas Regal whisky which is exported all over the world. Founded in 1786, Strathisla is the oldest working distillery in the Highlands and, with its curious twin pagodas serving as vents, one of the most architecturally interesting.

Distillery, and four miles north is the Glen Grant Distillery. The Glenfarclas Distillery is seven miles southwest.

In Craigellachie itself, at the **Speyside Cooperage** on the Dufftown road, visitors can see highly skilled coopers practising their ancient craft, Each year, they prepare some 100,000 oak casks which will be used to mature many different whiskies. It's like watching an industrial ballet as the coopers circle the casks, rhythmically hammering the iron bands into place.

DUFFTOWN

17 miles S of Elgin on the A941

Founded in 1817 by James Duff, the 4th Earl of Fife, Dufftown was built to provide employment after the Napoleonic wars. Its four main streets converge on the town's most prominent feature, the **Clock Tower**, originally built in 1839 as the town jail. The clock itself came from Banff, where it was known as the "Clock That Hanged MacPherson". McPherson of Kingussie had been sentenced to death in 1700, but was later pardoned. While the pardon was on its way to Banff, Lord Braco put the clock forward to ensure that MacPherson would hang.

This small town is home to another famous distillery, **Glenfiddich,** which is still owned and managed by the Grant family who established it more than a century ago. They take great pride that Glenfiddich is the only "chateau-bottled" malt whisky made in the Highlands.. Bottling at the distillery, using a single source of water, gives their whisky, they believe, a unique purity of taste. In the early years of the 20th century when successive British governments imposed increasingly savage duties on whisky, Glenfiddich cannily advertised the medicinal properties of their malt, *"manufactured under the Careful and Personal Supervision of a Fully qualified Doctor"*.

Clock Tower, Dufftown

Standing beside the distillery, overlooking great piles of whisky barrels, are the substantial and picturesque ruins of **Balvenie Castle** (Historic Scotland), a moated stronghold originally built by the "Black" Comyn Earls of Buchan in the 1200s. In the 15th century the great round tower was added which still looks formidable.

Mortlach Church (Scottish Heritage), was founded on a much earlier church and is thought to have stood here since the community began in AD 566 and to have been in regular use as a place of worship ever since. Although much of the church was reconstructed in the 19th century, parts of the original building still survive. In the graveyard is an old Pictish cross, and inside the church is the Elephant Stone, again with Pictish associations.

The Keith and Dufftown Railway connects Dufftown to the market town of Keith, 11 miles away. It was reopened in 2000/2001 by a group of enthusiasts, and runs services between the two towns.

The 18-hole Dufftown Golf Club boasts the highest hole in the UK. Besides golf, the town caters for all types of outdoor activities including walking, fishing, shooting and cycling.

BALLINDALLOCH

22 miles S of Elgin on the A95

Ballindalloch Castle is not just one of the most beguiling ancient houses in Strathspey but in the whole of Scotland. The charm, as always, derives from the fact that the same family has lived here since 1546 - the McPherson-Grants who have managed to preserve their heritage intact. According to family legend, its original builder back in the 16th century, the Laird of Ballindalloch, intended his new castle to crown a nearby hill. But each morning, when his masons returned to their work, they found the previous day's construction strewn across the ground. So, one stormy night, the Laird, accompanied by his masons, kept vigil on the hill site. Great gusts of wind swept across them, each blast somehow conveying the repeated message, "*Build it in the coo haugh* (cow pasture)". Deeply impressed by this wind-borne supernatural advice, the Laird complied and so his new castle was built on a level plain beside the river Spey, a location which also happened to provide one of the most picturesque settings for any inland Scottish castle.

A vigorous stream of supernatural events continued to flow through the castle's history. General James Grant inherited Ballindalloch in 1770, died here in 1806, and was buried in his favourite spot overlooking the river. From his grave, the General, who was a noted bon viveur, rises each evening and "walks to the dungeon passage to refresh himself from his beloved wine cellar".

Inside the castle itself, a vaporously beautiful lady, dressed in a pink crinoline gown and wearing a large straw hat, is said to regularly visit the Pink Bedroom.

About four miles south of Ballindalloch is the Glenlivit Distillery, which again has organised tours. And a couple of miles south west is the village of Aberlour, where there is the Aberlour Distillery which also has a visitor centre.

About 8 miles southeast of Tomintoul, at Cockbridge, is Corgarff Castle (Historic Scotland), a tower house set within a curious star-shaped walled enclosure. It was built in about 1550 by John Forbes of Towie. There was a long running feud between the Forbes and the Gordons. During a siege of the castle in 1571, John Forbes's wife Margaret held out against a force led by Adam Gordon. Eventually the castle was burned down, killing everyone within it, including Margaret.

These spectral appearances cannot be guaranteed but you can certainly see an extraordinary collection of 16th and 17th century Spanish paintings acquired by Sir John Macpherson during his tenure as Secretary of the British Legation in Lisbon. Painted on a small scale, these fine and delicate paintings provide an interesting cultural contrast with the grandiose portraits by Allan Ramsay of George III and Queen Charlotte on display in the Great Hall. In the grounds outside roams the famous herd of Ballindalloch Aberdeen Angus cattle, the oldest registered herd of its kind in existence. Other attractions include extensive gardens and grounds, river walks and a tea room.

TOMINTOUL

31 miles S of Elgin on the A939

Surrounded by bleak moorland, Tomintoul (pronounced *Tom-in-towel*) sits 1160 feet above sea level, the highest village in the Highlands although, strangely, not the highest in Scotland. (That distinction belongs to Wanlockhead in "lowland" Dumfries & Galloway). The village was plonked down in this raw countryside by the Duke of Gordon in 1779. Fifteen years later a visitor noted that 37 families lived here "with not a single manufacture to employ them, but all of them sell whisky and all of them drink it". A century later, Queen Victoria, passing through, described it as "the most tumble-down poor looking place I ever saw". She was told that it was the "dirtiest, poorest village in the whole of the Highlands". Things have changed greatly since those days, particularly in recent years when Tomintoul has become a base for skiers on the nearby area known as **The Lecht.** Here there is dry ski-slope skiing all year and snow-making equipment helps to extend the snow season in winter.

The small **Tomintoul Museum**, in the village square, has displays on local history and wildlife.

PLUSCARDEN

5 miles SW of Elgin on a minor road

Pluscarden Priory was founded in 1230 by Alexander II and settled firstly by the Valliscaulian and then the Benedictine monks. In the 19th century the Bute family acquired the ruined buildings and in 1943 presented them to the monks of Priknash in England, who took up residence in 1948. This means that it is the only medieval abbey in Britain still used for its original purpose. At first it was a priory, but became an abbey in its own right in 1974. It is open to the public, and has a small gift shop.

FORRES

12 miles W of Elgin on the A96

This small royal burgh, which was granted its charter in the 13th century, was once one of the most important places in Scotland, and is mentioned in Shakespeare's *Macbeth*. The ground plan of the medieval settlement still forms the basis of the town today, though it is much more open and green than it was then, thanks to some large areas of parkland.

The 20-feet high **Sueno's Stone** (Historic Scotland) dates from the 9th or 10th century, and is the largest known stone with Pictish carvings in Scotland. One side shows a cross, while the other shows scenes of battle. One of the scenes might be the battle fought at Forres in AD 966 where the Scottish king, Dubh, was killed. It is now floodlit, and under glass to protect it from the weather.

The Falconer Museum in Tolbooth Street was founded in 1871, and highlights the history and heritage of the town and its surroundings. It was founded using money from a bequest left by two brothers who left Forres for India. One was Alexander Falconer, a merchant in Calcutta, and the other was Hugh Falconer, a botanist and zoologist.

Dominating the town is the **Nelson Tower**, opened in 1812 in Grant Park to commemorate Nelson's victory at Trafalgar seven years before, the first such building to do so in Britain. If you're fit enough to climb its 96 steps, you'll get spectacular views over the surrounding countryside and the Moray Firth.

Brodie Castle (National Trust for Scotland) lies four miles west of the town. It is a 16th century tower house with later additions which give it the look of a comfortable mansion. In about 1160 Malcolm IV gave the surrounding lands to the Brodies, and it was their family home until the late 20th century. It contains major collections of paintings, furniture and ceramics, and sits in 175 acres of ground. Within the grounds is Rodney's Stone, with Pictish carvings.

On the coast north of Forres is perhaps Scotland's most unusual landscape, the **Culbin Sands**. In 1694 a storm blew great drifts of sand - some as high as 100 feet - over an area that had once been green and fertile, causing people to flee their homes. The drifts covered cottages, fields, even a mansion house and orchard, and eventually created eight square miles of what became known as "Scotland's Sahara". Occasionally, further storms would uncover the foundations of old cottages, which were then covered back up again by succeeding storms. The sands continued to shift and expand until the 1920s, when trees were planted to stabilise the area. Now it is a nature reserve.

At Findhorn, on the Moray Firth coast, is the Findhorn Foundation, one of the most successful centres in Britain for exploring alternative lifestyles and spiritual living. It was founded by Dorothy Maclean and Peter and Eileen Caddy in 1962 in a caravan park. The **Findhorn Heritage Centre and Museum** has displays on the history and heritage of the place. The village of Findhorn itself was once a busy port, trading with the Low Countries and Scandinavia. Now it is a sailing and wildlife centre.

Dallas Dhu Distillery

(Historic Scotland) sits to the south of Forres, It was built between 1898 and 1899 to produce a single malt for a firm of Glasgow blenders called Wright and Greig. This picturesque distillery ceased production in 1983 and is now a living history museum explaining the making of whisky.

DUFFUS

5 miles NW of Elgin on the B9012

The ruins of the **Church of St Peter** (Historic Scotland) stand near the village. Though mainly 18th century, it incorporates work that is much older. Opposite the porch is the medieval Parish Cross.

Close by are the ruins of **Duffus Castle (**Historic Scotland**)** which owe their present dramatic appearance to some Norman builders who didn't get their calculations exactly right. The great earthen mound on which they erected their huge castle eventually gave way under the massive weight of the stone, undermining the impressive 14th century tower which has sunk, split open and now leans at an ominous angle.

Just outside Duffus is Gordonstoun School, founded in 1933 by Kurt Hahn, a refugee from Nazi Germany who, by manic force of character, established a dire educational establishment. Gordonstoun managed to incorporate the worst

elements of the English public school ethos Hahn so greatly admired, along with a glorification of physical prowess borrowed from the Nazi movement he so much detested. Prince Philip was happy as a pupil here; his son, Prince Charles, much less so.

FRASERBURGH

Fraserburgh sits on the coastline just at that point where the Moray Firth becomes the North Sea. It is one of the main fishing ports in northeast Scotland and the largest shellfish port in Europe. It was founded in the 16th century by Alexander Fraser, eighth laird of Philorth, who built the first harbour in 1546. Between 1570 and 1571 he also built Fraserburgh Castle. A powerful lantern was built

Kinnaird Lighthouse, Fraserburgh

on top of it in 1787 and it became a lighthouse known as **Kinnaird Lighthouse** (Historic Scotland). It is now a museum dedicated to Scotland's lighthouses.

The **Old Kirk** in Saltoun Square isn't as old as its name would suggest. It was built in 1803 to replace the original church built by Alexander between 1570 and 1571. Beside it is the Fraser Burial Aisle.

One of Alexander's grander schemes was the founding of a university in the town, and he even went so far as to obtain James VI's permission to do so. The Scots Parliament gave it a grant, and the Revd Charles Ferme became its first principal. Unfortunately, the Revd Ferme was later arrested for attending a general assembly of the Church of Scotland in defiance of the king. The embryonic university subsequently collapsed, though one street in the town, College Bounds, still commemorates the scheme.

In Quarry Road is the **Fraserburgh Heritage Centre**, which has exhibits about the history of the town, including some haute couture dresses designed by the late fashion designer Bill Gibb, who hailed from Fraserburgh. The most unusual building in Fraserburgh is the **Wine Tower**, next to the lighthouse. It too was built by Alexander Fraser, possibly as a chapel. It has three floors, but no connecting stairways. The Tower probably got its name because it was the wine-cellar of those who at one time lived in the nearby castle. Under the tower is a cave more than 100 feet long.

At Sandhead, to the west of the town, is the **Sandhaven Meal Mill**, dating from the 19th century. Guided tours and models show how oatmeal used to be ground in Scotland. At Memsie, three miles south of Fraserburgh on the B9032, is the **Memsie Burial Cairn**, dating from about 1500 BC. At one time three stood here, but only one is now left.

AROUND FRASERBURGH

PETERHEAD

16 miles SE of Fraserburgh on the A982

Peterhead is the largest town (as opposed to city) in Aberdeenshire, and in the mid-1980s more white fish was landed here each year than at any other port in Europe. Now that fishing has declined, it benefits from being one of the ports that services the offshore gas industry. The **Arbuthnot Museum** in St Peter Street tells the story of the town and its industries, and has a large collection of Inuit artefacts. It was given to the town of Peterhead in 1850 by Adam Arbuthnot, a local man who had acquired a huge collection of antiquities.

In South Road, in a purpose-built building, is **Peterhead Maritime Heritage Museum**. This tells of the town's connections with the sea over the years, from its fishing fleet (which went as far as the Arctic in search of fish) to its whaling fleet (in its day, the second largest in Britain) and finally to the modern offshore gas and oil industries. The building was shaped

140 BAYVIEW GUEST HOUSE

Fraserburgh

Good choice of comfortable rooms, all en suite, and a truly hearty breakfast.

see page 432

289

141 KILMARNOCK ARMS HOTEL

Cruden Bay

A historic and beautiful hotel just 5 minutes from the beach, harbour and golf course, with superb restaurant and bar attached serving the freshest local produce.

 see page 432

142 MARGARET & JIMMY'S B&B

Maud

A pleasant and homely B&B with great facilities, views across the pretty Aberdeenshire countryside and the warmest of welcomes.

see page 432

to resemble a "scaffy", a kind of fishing boat once used in the area.

The town's most ancient building, dating back to 1585, is still fulfilling its original purpose. At **Ugie Salmon Fishings** in Golf Road visitors can watch salmon and trout being smoked over oak chips in the traditional way, and can purchase the finished product.

A few miles south of the town, at Cruden Bay, are the ruins of **Slains Castle**, built by the 9th Earl of Errol in 1597. Perched on top of the cliffs looking out over the North Sea, the castle has been rebuilt and refurbished several times since then, and the ruins you see now date from the early 19th century. Now there are plans to restore it yet again, this time as holiday flats. It has literary associations of an unusual kind. While staying at the nearby village of Cruden Bay in 1895, Bram Stoker began writing *Dracula*, and based the vampire's Transylvanian castle on Slains. In an early draft of the novel he even has the Count coming ashore at Slains rather than Whitby.

MINTLAW

12 miles S of Fraserburgh on the B9030

In the village you'll find the 230-acre **Aberdeenshire Farming Museum** (free) which sits within Aden Country Park. The museum traces the history of farming in this fertile area of Aberdeenshire through three separate themes - the Aden Estate Story, the "Weel Vrocht Grun" ("well worked ground") and the country park itself. Hareshowe Farm has been

restored to what it would have been like in the 1950s.

OLD DEER

14 miles S of Fraserburgh on the B9030

In a beautiful location on the banks of the River South Ugie are the ruins of **Deer Abbey** (Historic Scotland), founded in 1219 by William Comyn, Earl of Buchan, for the Cistercian order of monks. Little remains of the abbey church, but the walls of some of the other buildings are fairly well preserved. It is said that it was built on the site of a Celtic monastery founded by St Columba and his companion St Drostan in the 6th century.

MAUD

16 miles S of Fraserburgh on the B9029

Maud grew up around a junction in the railway line that once connected Aberdeen to Fraserburgh and Peterhead. In the **Maud Railway Museum**, housed in the village's former station, you can relive the days of the Great North of Scotland Railway through exhibits, sound effects, photographs, artefacts and displays.

TURRIFF

22 miles SW of Fraserburgh on the A947

Set on the River Deveron in the heart of the Buchan farmlands, Turriff is an ancient burgh that was given its charter in 1512 by James IV. **Turriff Parish Church** was built in 1794 and there are some good carvings on its belfry and walls from the previous kirk that stood on the site.

Delgatie Castle, close to the

town, was founded in about 1050, though the castle as you see it today dates from the 16th century. It is the ancestral home of Clan Hay and has been in the Hay family for just under 700 years. Attractively set amidst parkland and woods, the castle has some marvellous painted ceilings from around 1590, a magnificent turnpike stair with 97 steps, and some interesting paintings including one of Mary, Queen of Scots who stayed at the castle for three days in 1562 after the Battle of Corrichie, which took place to the west of Aberdeen. The Queen's troops easily defeated a force of men led by the 4th Earl of Huntly who was killed in the battle.

Turriff was the scene of a famous incident concerning the **Turra Coo** ("Turriff Cow"), which received widespread publicity throughout Britain. New National Insurance Acts were passed in 1911 and 1913 which required employers to pay 3d per week for each of their employees. The farmers of Aberdeenshire, in common with others all over Britain, did not want to pay, as they reckoned that farm workers had a healthy lifestyle, and would not need much medical treatment. Curiously enough, the farm workers themselves supported the farmers on this issue.

One Turriff farmer in particular, Robert Paterson, refused to comply with the new regulations, so one of his cows was taken to be sold at auction to pay off his arrears. However the auction, held in Turriff, turned into a fiasco, as the cow, which had slogans painted all over its body, took fright and bolted through the streets of the town. Meanwhile, the auctioneer was pelted with raw eggs and bags of soot. Three days later the cow was taken to Aberdeen where it was sold for £7.

It was a hollow victory for the authorities, which had spent nearly £12 in recovering the sum. And they were further annoyed to hear that Paterson's neighbours had clubbed together and bought the cow so that it could be returned to him. So, while the authorities were out of pocket over the whole affair, it had not cost Robert Paterson a penny. There are now plans to erect a statue of the "Turra Coo" to commemorate the event.

Seven miles south west of Turriff along the B9024 is the Glendronach Distillery, situated on the banks of the Dronach Burn. Tours are available, and there is a visitor centre and shop.

PENNAN

10 miles W of Fraserburgh on the B9031

Pennan is possibly the most spectacular of the little fishing villages on the northern coast of Aberdeenshire. It is strung out along the base of a high cliff, with many of the cottages having their gable ends to the sea for protection. It is a conservation village, and is famous as being the setting, in 1983, for the film *Local Hero*. The red telephone box, famously used in the film, was a prop. However, Pennan's real red telephone box, about 15 yards away

143 THE PITSLIGO ARMS HOTEL

New Pitsligo

Handsome late-Georgian listed building offering outstanding cuisine and recently refurbished en suite rooms

🛏 🍴 *see page 433*

144 SEAFIELD ARMS

Whitehills

A friendly hotel & Maitlands bar in Whitehills with an open coal fire and years of local history and heritage on display.

🍴 🛏 *see page 434*

from where the prop stood, is still a favourite place for photographs, and is now a listed historic monument.

BANFF

22 miles W of Fraserburgh on the A98

A small fishing port close to the mouth of the River Deveron, Banff was once the county town of Banffshire. It is an ancient royal burgh, having been granted its charter in 1163 by Malcolm IV. The **Banff Museum** in the High Street is one of Scotland's oldest, having been founded in 1828. It has a nationally important collection of Banff silver.

Duff House is a unique country house art gallery run by a unique partnership between Historic Scotland, the National Galleries of Scotland and Aberdeenshire Council. It houses a fine collection of paintings by such artists as Raeburn and El Greco as well as tapestries and Chippendale furniture. The house was designed by William Adam and built between 1735 and 1740 for William Duff of Braco who later became Earl of Fife. After a bitter wrangle with Adam, William Duff abandoned it, and it was left to James, the 2nd Earl Fife, to complete the grand plan, including the grounds. Over the years it has had a chequered career, having been a hotel, a

sanatorium, a prisoner-of-war camp and the scene of an attempted murder when a Countess of Fife tried to do away with her husband.

The small town of Macduff sits on the opposite shore of the small bay where the Deveron enters the Moray Firth. The lands were bought by the 1st Earl of Fife in 1733, and in 1783 the 2nd Earl founded the town as a burgh or barony. It contains the **Macduff Marine Aquarium** at High Shore, which has a central tank open to the sky surrounded by viewing areas so that you get a good view of fish and marine mammals from all angles. This deep central exhibit, which displays a living kelp reef, is the only one of its kind in Britain and divers hand feed the fish on a regular basis. The aquarium has a wave-making machine which adds to the experience of seeing underwater life in its true condition.

Six miles west of Banff, on the A98, is the attractive little fishing port of Portsoy, which is well worth visiting if only to soak in the atmosphere. Though its burgh charter dates from 1550, it was Patrick Ogilvie, Lord Boyne, who realised its potential and developed it as a port to export marble from the nearby quarries. Portsoy marble, or serpentine, a dark green stone resembling marble, was used on Louis XIV's palace at Versailles.

The Highlands

When people talk of Scottish scenery, they inevitably mean the scenery of the Highlands - mountains, dark, heather-clad glens and deep, brooding lochs. And though other areas can also claim their fair share of these features, this is the one that has them in abundance.

The Highlands area has no set boundaries, and some places described in earlier chapters, such as Aberdeen and Grampian, Argyllshire and parts of Perthshire, can lay claim to being in the Highlands as well. But the area described in this chapter has the same boundaries as the local government area, and can legitimately be called the true Highlands. It stretches from the northernmost coast of mainland Scotland down to Perthshire, and from the borders of Aberdeenshire and Moray to the rugged west coast, taking in one or two of the Inner Hebridean islands on the way.

It is mostly wild country, with fewer roads than other parts of Scotland. Some areas are totally inaccessible unless you go by foot over difficult terrain, and if you do decide to take to the hills or moors, remember that Highland weather can be unpredictable, even in summer. Take the correct clothing, and always tell someone about your intended route and your estimated times of arrival at various stages.

The capital of the Highlands is Inverness. It is a thriving city with an enviable quality of life, and its environs are reckoned to be one of the most rapidly growing areas in Britain, if not Europe. The recently announced plans for a large development (in essence a "new town") to the east of the city will see it grow even more.

Seen from the A9 as you head over the Kessock Bridge, Inverness has all the appearance of a large metropolis, with suburbs that sprawl along the Moray and Beauly Firths. But in fact its population is no more than 50,000, though this is growing daily. And some of the countryside surrounding it looks more like the Lowlands than the Highlands, with neat fields, villages and winding country roads. However, if you head southwest along the A82 towards Loch Ness, or south along the A9, you'll soon find yourself in what is undoubtedly Highland scenery.

Within the Highlands you'll find Scotland's most famous features. Ben Nevis, Scotland's highest mountain, is here, as is Loch Morar, the country's deepest loch. Loch Ness, undoubtedly the most famous stretch of water in Europe, is a few miles from Inverness's city centre, and the last full battle on British soil was fought at Culloden. Here too is Glencoe, scene of

Glen Carry, Lochaber

the famous massacre, as well as John O' Groats, Aviemore, Monarch of the Glen Country, Skye, Fort William, Cape Wrath and Plockton, the setting for the books and TV series *Hamish Macbeth*.

The west coast is rugged, with sea lochs that penetrate deep into the mountains. Settlements are few and far between, and most of them are to be found right on the coast. Some visitors to the west coast of the Highlands are amazed at the sub-tropical plants that seem to thrive here. It's all down to the Gulf Stream, which warms the shores and keeps snow at bay.

The east coast, from Nairn to Inverness then north to John O' Groats, is gentler, with many more settlements. Dornoch, though small, has a medieval cathedral, so is more of a city than a town, and at Fortrose there are the remains of another cathedral. Strathpeffer was once a thriving spa town, with regular trains connecting it to Edinburgh and London.

And between the east and west coasts are the mountains, the lochs, the tumbling streams and the deep glens. The scenery can be austere and gaunt, but never anything less than beautiful. No Gulf Stream here, and in some sheltered corners, snow lies well into May or even June. Glencoe/Nevis and Aviemore take advantage of this by being skiing centres, though in recent years snow has been in short supply.

In Caithness and Sutherland - Scotland's

two northernmost counties - you will find the Flow Country, mile upon mile of low peaks, high moorland and small, shallow lochans. This is not the dramatic scenery of the West Highlands where mountain seems to pile on mountain, but it has a ruggedness and grandeur of its own.

The Highlands takes the breath away at every turn. There are areas that are all mountains, lochs and glens, and there are areas that are as green and intensely cultivated as the Lowlands. There are lonely places, where another human being is likely to be miles away, and there are crowded holiday towns such as Fort William and crowded cities such as Inverness. All these qualities ensure that the Highlands is one of the most rewarding areas in Britain to visit.

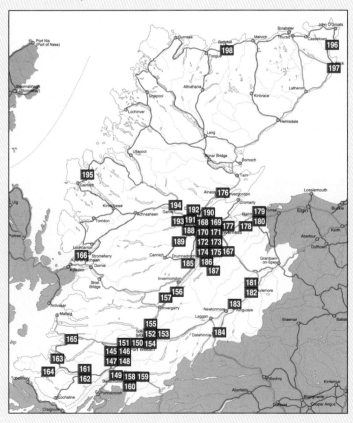

THE HIGHLANDS

145 THE WEST END HOTEL

Fort William

Long established and well appointed family-run hotel offering good food, regular live entertainment and quality en suite rooms.

see page 434

146 THE GANTOCKS

Fort William

Superbly located 5-star premises offering both en suite B&B accommodation and self-catering cottage.

see page 435

147 HUNTINGTOWER LODGE

Fort William

Offering the very best in 21st century comfort Huntingtower Lodge, with its stunning views overlooking Loch Linnhe, boasts some of the finest accommodation in the Highlands.

see page 435

FORT WILLIAM

With its excellent road, rail and waterway links, Fort William has become the business and tourism capital of the western Highlands. It occupies a glorious position overlooking Loch Linne (although an ill-conceived dual carriageway has blocked off access to the shore). The town is the main shopping centre for a huge area and the High Street, with inviting little squares set back from it, gets very busy during the season. Paradoxically, many in the throng are visitors seeking the genuine, uncrowded Highlands.

The major attraction for tourists is, of course, **Ben Nevis,** at 4406 feet Britain's loftiest mountain and with a base which is said to be 24 miles in circumference. Despite its height, there are several undemanding and well-worn routes to the top. The record time achieved during the annual race to the summit is one hour and twenty-five minutes, but for those walking at a more realistic pace between four and five hours should be allowed. The views from the top are incredible, extending halfway across Scotland to the distant Hebrides.

Before tackling the mountain, a visit to the **Glen Nevis Visitors Centre** is recommended. It has exhibits about local heritage and wildlife and, importantly, information about the weather on the mountain. Aonach Beag (4058 feet) and Aonach Mor (3999 feet) are Ben Nevis's little brothers, rising just over a mile to the east. In the winter this is a skiing area, but it is equally popular in the summer. Britain's only mountain gondola system offers an exhilarating ride to a height of 2150 feet in just 15 minutes. The views, needless to say, are staggering. At the gondola station there's a restaurant and bar, and several walks start here.

Back in Fort William, the

Inverlochy Castle, Fort William

West Highland Museum has collections covering almost every aspect of Highland life. The museum's most popular exhibit is the secret portrait of Bonnie Prince Charlie, a meaningless smudge of colour until viewed against a curved mirror when a charming miniature of the Prince wearing a brown wig and an elaborate satin coat comes into focus. The portrait comes from the time when the penalty for anyone possessing an image of the Prince was death. Another interesting exhibit is the long Spanish rifle used in the assassination of a local facot in 1752, the notorious "Appin Murder" that inspired Robert Louis Stevenson's *Kidnapped*. A more specialised museum can be found on the A830 at Corpach, northwest of the town. The award-winning **Treasures of the Earth** holds one of Europe's finest collections of crystals and gemstones.

A highly recommended excursion from Fort William is a day trip on the **Jacobite Steam Train** to Mallaig. The 42-mile journey passes alongside Loch Eil and on to the west coast through some of the most spectacular scenery in the country. En route, it crosses the massive 21-arch **Glenfinnan Viaduct** (featured in the Hogwarts Express in the Harry Potter films) and makes an extended stop at Glenfinnan Station, allowing time to visit the Station Museum. The trip was voted *Top Railway Journey in the World 2009* by Wanderlust Magazine and takes passengers past Britain's highest mountain, deepest loch, shortest river and most westerly station.

Fort William is the northern terminus of the 95-mile long **West Highland Way** which snakes through Western Scotland from Milngavie on the outskirts of Glasgow. It is also the starting point of the **Great Glen Way** which runs between Fort William and Inverness. Fort William is also where the Caledonian Canal begins. It is not one uninterrupted canal, but a series of canals connecting Loch Lochy, Loch Oich and Loch Ness. **Neptune's Staircase** at Banavie, near Fort William, was designed and built by Thomas Telford in the early 1800s. It takes the canal through a series of eight locks while raising it over 60 feet.

The fort referred to in the town's name was built by General Monk in the 1650s, then rebuilt during the reign of William III to house a garrison of 600 troops to keep the Highland clans in order. At that time it was renamed Maryburgh, after William's queen. Only parts of the town wall survive, as most of it was dismantled in the 19th century to make way for the West Highland Railway.

The **Underwater Centre,** on the banks of Loch Linnhe. was opened in 2003, and cost £2.3m. It features marine life (including more than 42 species of fish) and diving shows in a large aquarium. You can even take dives yourself

148 WESTHAVEN

Fort William

The popular Westhaven B&B is a relaxing home-from-home boasting stunning loch and hill views.

see page 436

149 THE WOOLLY ROCK B&B

Fort William

A family, and dog friendly, B&B with magnificent panoramic views overlooking Loch Leven and the surrounding mountains

see page 436

150 MAYFIELD B&B

Torlundy

Four-star B&B in peaceful rural location enjoying grand views of Ben Nevis.

see page 437

297

and get guided tours around the adjacent diver training centre.

The impressive ruins of 13th century **Inverlochy Castle** (Historic Scotland) stand 1½ miles north east of Fort William. It was built by the Comyn family in the 13th century on the site of an even earlier fort, though the ruins you see now date from much later.

Not far away, on the A82, is the 174-year-old **Ben Nevis Distillery and Whisky Centre** which has conducted tours. One of its products is a blend of whiskies called The Dew of Ben Nevis.

AROUND FORT WILLIAM

ACHNACARRY

10 miles N of Fort William on a minor road off the B8005

A 17th century white-washed single storey croft house now houses the **Clan Cameron Museum**, which has displays, charts and exhibits relating to the history of the clan and to the commandos who trained here during the Second World War. A minor road takes you past the museum and along the lovely banks of **Loch Arkaig,** finally petering out near its western end.

SPEAN BRIDGE

8 miles NE of Fort William on the A82

There are in fact two bridges at Spean Bridge: Thomas Telford's elegant structure of 1819 and, a couple of miles downstream, the older High Bridge built by general Wade in 1736. One hundred feet high, it spans a deep gorge in the river. In 1913 one of its arches collapsed into the river and the bridge has never been repaired.

Spean Bridge offers some excellent views of the Nevis Range, especially from the **Commando Memorial** atop a hill just outside the village. This much-admired bronze sculpture, designed by Scott Sutherland depicts three commando soldiers in combat gear looking west to Lochiel where they trained during World War II. **The Spean Bridge Mill,** which is nearby, has demonstrations of tartan weaving as well as a clan tartan centre.

Near the tiny village of Roybridge was fought the **Battle of Mulroy** in 1688 between the MacDonnells and the Macintoshes, with the MacDonnells being the victors. It was the last great inter-clan battle fought in the Highlands, and the last one on British soil where bows and arrows were used. A cairn marks the spot.

LAGGAN

20 miles NE of Fort William on the A82

Laggan sits between Loch Lochy and Loch Oich, two of the lochs that make up the Caledonian Canal. It was here, in 1544, that the **Battle of the Shirts** took place, fought between Clan Fraser and the combined forces of Clan Ranald and Cameron. It was fought on a hot summer's day, and the clansmen removed their plaids and fought in their shirts. There were many casualties, including the chief of Clan Fraser and his son.

FORT AUGUSTUS

30 miles NE of Fort William on the A82

This modest village on the shore of Loch Ness takes its imposing name from the military base established here in the wake of the 1715 Jacobite rising. The fortress was built by General Wade and named after George II's younger son, Augustus. At that time, Augustus was a plump lad just 8 years old but he would be later reviled as the Duke of Cumberland, the "Butcher of Culloden". Following that battle, it was at Fort Augustus that the Duke expressed his gratification at receiving the head of Roderick Mackenzie, a young Edinburgh lawyer who had maintained the pretence of being Bonnie Prince Charlie in order to help the real prince escape.

After Culloden the fort no longer had any useful purpose and in 1876 it was demolished, giving way to a Benedictine abbey. The community of monks was unable to sustain itself and left in 1998. Surrounded on three sides by waters of the Caledonian Canal, Loch Ness and the River Tarff, the abbey has recently been converted into self-catering holiday apartments.

Fort Augustus is bisected by the Caledonian Canal and within the village itself is a flight of locks, designed by Thomas Telford, that provide a fascinating place to watch the world go by. The **Caledonian Canal Heritage Centre** is located in a converted lock keeper's cottage near these locks through which boats pass into Loch Ness. The centre explains the history and uses of the canal. Incidentally, Fort Augustus is one of few places where you are guaranteed a sighting of the Loch Ness monster, "Nessie". A "life-size" model of the mythical beast sits beside one of the locks here.

Real creatures can be encountered at the **Highland and Rare Breeds Croft** on Auchterawe Road where you can see Highland cattle, red deer and rare breeds of sheep. At the **Clansman Centre**, housed in a former school, there are presentations on ancient Highland life.

KINLOCHLEVEN

24 miles SE of Fort William on the B863

This little town sits at the head of Loch Leven and is on the West Highland Way. It was developed as an industrial village in the early 20th century when the North British Aluminium Company built the Blackwater reservoir and a hydro electric scheme to power an aluminium smelter which was the largest in the world at the time. Before that, it had been two small villages called Kinlochmore and Killochbeag. The **Aluminium Story Visitor Centre** at the library on Linnhe Road tells the story of the smelting works right up until the year 2000. Outside the centre is a giant sundial designed by blacksmith Robert Hutcheson that takes its inspiration from the area's history and scenery.

The **Ice Factor** on Leven Road is Britain's premier indoor

155 RIVERSIDE LODGES

Invergloy

These three lodges boast their own beach and magnificent views over simply stunning scenery.

see page 439

156 AUCHTERAWE COUNTRY HOUSE

Loch Ness, Fort Augustus

Rustic country guest house, with a backdrop of the Great Glen mountain range.

see page 440

157 HILLSIDE BED & BREAKFAST

Fort Augustus

A B&B with rooms of the highest standard overlooking the surrounding forests and mountains.

see page 440

•

There are actually two villages in Ballachulish, separated by the waters of Loch Leven - North Ballachulish and Ballachulish itself. They were once connected by ferry which stopped running in 1975 when a bridge was built.

•

158 GLENCOE COTTAGES

Torren, Glencoe

Three stunning cottages in beautiful surroundings, perfect for groups of 6 to 8.

see page 441

159 GLENCOE B & B

Torren, Glencoe

This B & B boasts two comfortable double rooms with magnificent mountain views.

see page 441

160 ALLTBEAG B&B

Glencoe

A newly built modern B&B with spectacular views across the loch side and surrounding area

see page 441

mountaineering centre, and features the world's largest indoor ice climbing wall as well as Britain's largest articulated rock climbing wall. There is also a children's activity zone, audiovisual lecture theatre, steam room, plunge pool and hot tub, and a cafeteria and restaurant.

BALLACHULISH

12 miles S of Fort William on the A82

On her way to visit Glencoe, Queen Victoria noted the village of Ballachulish "where the slate quarries are". The miners had "decorated every house with flowers and bunches or wreaths of heather and red cloth". The slate quarries at Ballachulish had provided a living for the villagers since 1693 and at the time of Victoria's brief visit were at the height of their productive life with some 26 million slates being shaped and shipped in 1875. The quarries finally closed in 1955 but their legacy lives on in the slate gravestones in the churchyard, many of them elegantly engraved, and in the unique loch-side boat sheds constructed almost entirely of slate, their survival now guaranteed by preservation orders.

Ballachulish straggles along the southern shore of Loch Leven. To the west of the village a cairn marks the spot where Jacobite sympathiser **James of the Glen** was hanged for a crime he did not commit. He was found guilty of the murder of Colin Campbell, known as the "Red Fox", a government agent, by a Campbell

judge and jury. Robert Louis Stevenson used the incident in his book *Kidnapped*. Another cairn marks the site of the murder.

On the edge of town, **Highland Mysteryworld** promises to take you back in time to a world of bogles, kelpies, fachans and the Blue Man of the Minch with the help of energetic actors in costume, special effects and lots of models. Children garbed in Viking helmets and cloaks can have great fun in the adventure playground, and there's also a loch side trail, a gift shop specialising in herbal mixtures and books of legends, and a restaurant.

GLENCOE

15 miles S of Fort William on the A82

To the east of Ballachulish opens up one of the starkest and most sombre glens in Scotland, Glen Coe. In Gaelic, the name means "Valley of Weeping". Here, in the early hours of 13th February 1692, during a howling blizzard, some 40 men of the Clan MacDonald were slaughtered by soldiers under the command of Campbell of Glenlyon. It was a heinous crime, "murder under trust", since for the previous ten days Campbell's soldiers had been entertained with traditional Highland hospitality by the MacDonalds. The legal pretext for the government-ordered massacre was that the MacDonalds had failed to meet the deadline of New Year's Day, 1692 for signing an oath of loyalty to William III. In fact, the necessary papers had been signed but, because of bad weather, arrived a few days late in Edinburgh. Secretary of State Sir James Dalrymple seized on the opportunity of making an example of the MacDonalds who, besides being notorious for their thievery, were known Jacobite sympathisers. The MacDonalds may have been unpopular but the treachery of their slaughter outraged the whole country. Three years later, an official enquiry confirmed that the killings were indeed murder. The massacre at Glencoe poisoned the history of western Scotland for generations and even now a sign on the door of an inn in the village still proclaims "*Nae Campbells*".

Today, most of this gloomy, melancholy glen is owned by the National Trust for Scotland which has set up the **Glencoe Visitor Centre** which tells the story of the massacre. In Glencoe village itself is the **Glencoe and North Lorn Folk Museum**, which has exhibits about the history of the area and its people.

About 9 miles east of Glencoe, on a minor road off the A82, is the Glencoe skiing area with a chair lift that is open in the summer months, and gives wonderful views over Glencoe and Rannoch Moor.

STRONTIAN
20 miles SW of Fort William on the A861

Strontian (pronounced "*Stron-teeh-an*", and meaning "point of the fairies") sits in an area known as Sunart which lies to the south of Loch Shiel. The village gave its name to the metal strontium which was discovered in 1791 in the local lead mines by a chemist called Adair Crawford. A few years later Sir Humphrey Davie gave it its name.

To the north of the village are the **Ariundle Oakwoods**, a national nature reserve.

ARDNAMURCHAN PENINSULA
44 miles SW of Fort William

The B8007 leaves the A861 at Salen (where a small inlet of Loch Sunart is usually crowded with picturesque yachts) and takes you westwards onto the Ardnamurchan Peninsula. The single track road heads for Ardnamurchan Point and its lighthouse, the most westerly point of the British mainland, and in doing so passes through some wonderful scenery.

At Glenborrodale you can see the late-Victorian Glenborrodale Castle, the home from 1933 to 1949 of Jesse Boot, founder of the chain of chemists. The castle was built in the early 20th century for CD Rudd, who made his fortune in diamonds in South Africa. The castle is now available for weddings and other functions.

At Kilchoan are the ruins of **Mingary Castle**, a stronghold of Clan MacIan before passing to the Campbells. It was visited by James IV in 1493 on one of his expeditions to subdue the Western Isles. It was briefly used in the 2002 movie *Highlander: Endgame*. Kilchoan is Britain's most westerly mainland village, and up until 1900, when the B8007 was constructed, it was also Britain's most inaccessible

161 BEN VIEW HOTEL

Strontian

The 2700 feet high Corbett of Ben Resipole is the breathtaking backdrop of this friendly hotel, which is an ideal base for visitors wanting to take in the local history and culture.

see page 442

162 TEA ROOM

Strontian

A popular restaurant serving everything from a hearty breakfast or morning coffee to a light lunch or candle lit supper.

see page 442

163 ARDSHEALACH LODGE

Acharacle

Fantastic B&B restaurant with the freshest home grown home cooking and views across Loch Shiel.

see page 443

164 LOCHSIDE FOLLIES

Acharacle

Two unique and character-filled holiday homes set in eighty acres of rugged countryside and boasting some of the best views in the area.

see page 444

165 LOCHAILORT INN

Lochailort

High quality food and drink, open log fires and cosy rooms nestled amongst some of the highlands best attractions.

see page 445

•

Purpose-built in 1999, the Land, Sea and Islands Centre in a stunning location in Arisaig has exhibits and displays about the history and wildlife of the area. Crofting, fishing, church history, marine life, the SOE and the films made here - Local Hero being one of the most famous - are amongst the contents.

•

as it could only be reached by boat. Nowadays, in summer, a ferry connects it to Tobermory on Mull.

A few miles North of Salen, on the edge of the area known as Moidart, are the ruins of **Castle Tioram** (pronounced "Chirrum"). The castle stands on a small island and was originally built in the 14th century by Lady Anne MacRuari, whose son Ranald gave his name to Clan Ranald. It was burnt by the Jacobites in 1715 to prevent it being used by Hanoverian forces, and has been a ruin ever since.

At the head of Loch Moidart is a line of five beech trees. Originally there were seven, and they were known as the **Seven Men of Moidart**. They commemorate the seven men who landed with Charles Edward Stuart and sailed with him up Loch Shiel. They were originally planted in the early 19th century.

SALEN

44 miles SW of Fort William on the A861

Salen sits on the shore of Loch Sunart. There miles east (not accessible by road) is **Claish Moss**, a good example of a Scottish raised bog. Water is held in the peat and the landscape is dotted with lochans, or pools. The peat has preserved seeds and pollen for thousands of years so it is of great interest to biologists researching the flora of the Western Highlands.

GLENFINNAN

14 miles W of Fort William on the A830

It was here, at the northern tip of Loch Shiel, Scotland's fourth

longest freshwater loch, that Charles Edward Stuart raised his standard in 1745, watched by 1200 Highland followers, after having been rowed a short distance up the loch from the house of MacDonald of Glenaladale on the western shores. The **Charles Edward Stuart Monument** (National Trust for Scotland) was erected in 1815 by Alexander MacDonald of Glenaladale to commemorate the event. A small visitors centre nearby tells the story.

The **Glenfinnan Station Museum**, which lies on the Fort William - Mallaig line, tells of the building of the famously scenic line by Robert McAlpine (known as "Concrete Bob") in the late 19th and early 20th centuries. The museum's restaurant and tearoom is a restored 1950s railway carriage.

ARISAIG

35 miles W of Fort William on the A830

The tiny village of Arisaig has wonderful views across to the islands of Rum and Eigg. Southeast of the village is Loch nan Uamh where, on 25th July 1745, Charles Edward Stuart first set foot on the Scottish mainland. After his campaign to restore the Stuart dynasty failed, he left for France from the same shore. A cairn now marks the spot.

MALLAIG

44 miles NW of Fort William on the A830

Mallaig, Britain's most westerly mainland port, is a busy fishing port and the terminal of a ferry connecting the mainland to Armadale on Skye. It is also the end of the "Road to the Isles" and the western terminus for the Jacobite Steam Train. The **Mallaig Heritage Centre** on Station Road has displays and exhibits that tell the story of the districts of Morar, Knoydart and Arisaig. The **Mallaig Marine World Aquarium and Fishing Exhibition** sits beside the harbour and tells the story of Mallaig's fishing industry and the marine life found in the waters of Western Scotland. Most of the live exhibits were caught by local fishermen.

Southeast of the town is water of another sort - **Loch Morar,** which is Britain's deepest fresh water loch. It plunges to a depth of 1077 feet - if you were to stand the Eiffel Tower on the bottom, its top would still be 90 feet below the surface. A minor road near Morar village, south of Mallaig, takes you to its shores. Like Loch Ness, it has a monster, nicknamed Morag which, judging by people who have claimed to see it, looks remarkably like Nessie.

KYLE OF LOCHALSH

77 miles NW of Fort William on the A87

Until the Skye Bridge was opened in 1995, Kyle of Lochalsh was a busy little place with a constant stream of traffic rolling in to line for the ferry to the fabled Isle of Skye. The elegant new bridge put the ferry out of business and the traffic-clotted streets of the past are no more and Kyle is an inviting place to stay.

Three miles east of the village on the A87 is the Balmacara Estate and **Lochalsh Woodland Garden** at Lochalsh House with sheltered walks beside the shores of Loch Alsh as well as mature woodlands and a variety of shrubs, such as rhododendrons, bamboo, ferns, fuchsias and hydrangeas. There is a small visitors centre at the square in Balmacara, just off the A87. Also centred on Kyle of Lochalsh is **Seaprobe Atlantis**, a glass-bottomed boat that takes you out into the Marine Special Area of Conservation and shows you the rich diversity of marine life in the waters surrounding Scotland.

Six miles east of the village is one of the most photographed castles in Scotland, **Eilean Donan Castle,** which stands on a small island connected to the mainland by a bridge. Its name ("Donan's Island") comes from the legend that St Donan lived on the island as a hermit. He was killed during a Viking raid on the island of Eigg in

166 SOLUIS MU THUATH GUEST HOUSE

Braeintra

Family-run guest house in a peaceful location noted for its high standards and keen prices.

see page 446

Eilean Donan Castle, Kyle of Lochalsh

303

167 DALVOURN HOLIDAY COTTAGES

Inverarnie

Situated on the 200 acre Dalvourn Farm, these self-catering cottages are set in secluded birch woodland and offer the perfect retreat.

see page 447

168 THE PHOENIX

Inverness

Traditional Victorian hostelry offering good pub grub, real ales and regular live music sessions.

see page 448

169 CROWN COURT TOWN HOUSE HOTEL

Inverness

Former residence for Crown Court judges offering stylish accommodation, great food and first class service.

see page 449

AD 617. Parts of the castle date back to 1220 when it was built by Alexander II and given to an ancestor of the Mackenzies who fought beside him at the Battle of Largs. The castle was left in ruins for 200 years until it was purchased in 1911 by Lt-Col. John Macrae Gilstrap who spent some 20 years carrying out a complete restoration before opening it to the public in 1932. It is now the ancestral home of Clan MacRae and has a small clan museum. The castle has also featured in many films, most notably *The World is Not Enough* and *Highlander*.

If you continue eastwards along the A87 you will eventually arrive at Shiel Bridge, at the head of Loch Duich. To the southeast is Glen Shiel, where five peaks, called the **Five Sisters of Kintail** (National Trust for Scotland) overlook the picturesque glen. Close by is the site of the **Battle of Glen Shiel**, fought in 1719 between a Hanoverian Army and a force of Jacobites (which included 300 Spaniards). It was the last battle fought on British soil between British and foreign soldiers, and it had no clear victor. There is a Countryside Centre (National Trust for Scotland) at Morvich Farm, off the A87, and it makes a good starting point for walking on some of the surrounding hills and mountains.

Northeast of Kyle of Lochalsh is the conservation village of Plockton, with its palm trees and idyllic location. This was the Lochdubh of *Hamish Macbeth* fame,

as it was here that the TV series was filmed. It sits beside Loch Carron. On the opposite bank, a few miles inland off a minor road, are the ruins of **Strome Castle** (National Trust for Scotland). It was built in the 15th century, and was a stronghold of the MacDonalds, Lords of the Isles. On **Craig Highland Farm**, near the village, you can view rare breeds, as well as feed the farmyard animals

Kyle of Lochalsh is the western terminus for the famous Dingwall - Kyle of Lochalsh railway line (see Dingwall).

INVERNESS

Long known as the "Capital of the Highlands", Inverness is a cosmopolitan town attractively sited around the River Ness where it flows into Beauly Firth. The town's history stretches back to the 6th century when it developed as a trading port serving what was then, and still is, the most populated part of the Highlands with some 50,000 residents. It has all the feel and bustle of a much larger place, and its shopping - especially in the pedestrianised High Street, where the Eastgate Shopping Centre is located - is superb.

There have been three castles, all occupying the same dominating position above the town. The present **Inverness Castle** dates from 1835, a striking mock-medieval building in red sandstone which today houses the Sheriff Court. On the terrace outside the castle, the **Flora MacDonald Memorial** commemorates the strong-character clanswoman who rowed Bonnie Prince Charlie over the sea to Skye after his defeat at Culloden.

Near the castle, in Bridge Street, is the **Town House** built in Victorian Gothic style and completed in 1882. It was in the council chamber here, in 1921, that the only cabinet meeting ever held outside London took place when Lloyd George, the Prime Minister, wanted to discuss the worsening Ireland situation. Across from the Town House is the **Tolbooth Steeple**, dating from the late 18th century. In Castle Wynd, in a modern building, is **Inverness Museum and Art Gallery**, which has a large collection relating to the history of the Highlands and the town in particular. Within the library is the Highland Archives and Genealogy Centre, where you can research your forebears.

The oldest buildings are to be found around Church Street. The Steeple, built in 1791, is notable for having had its spire straightened out after an earthquake in 1816. **Abertarff House** (National Trust for Scotland) is even older, dating from 1593 and distinguished by its round tower staircase and stepped gables. It was built as a town house for the Frasers of Lovat, and is now the local headquarters for the National Trust for Scotland. **Dunbar's Hospital** is also on Church Street, and dates from 1668. It was founded by Provost Alexander Dunbar as a hospital for the poor. It has now been divided into flats.

Inverness Cathedral, dedicated to St Andrew, is a gem of a building in pink sandstone designed by Alexander Ross and consecrated in 1874. It was supposed to have had two large spires, but these were never built. The interior is more spacious than the exterior suggests and is notable for a beautiful oak choir

Inverness

Superb, centrally located bar/restaurant just minutes from Eastgate shopping centre and the river Ness.

🍴 *see page 450*

171 THE STEAK ACADEMY

Inverness

With a truly unique menu, this chic and contemporary restaurant is great for those special occasions.

🍴 *see page 451*

172 THE ROOM

Inverness

A popular music venue that serves great food and drink all week long.

🍴 *see page 451*

Glen Carry, Lochaber

screen separating the nave from the choir. The Eden Court Theatre, next to the cathedral, incorporates parts of the old Bishop's Palace.

The Old High Church in Church Street, dedicated to St Mary, is Inverness's parish church and was built in 1770, though parts of the tower may date from medieval times. After the battle of Culloden, the church was used as a jail for Jacobite soldiers, some of whom were executed in the kirkyard. Bullet marks left on the gravestones by the firing squads can still be seen. The **Old Gaelic Church** was originally built in 1649, though the present building dates from a rebuilding of 1792.

Inverness is one of the few Scottish towns to have retained its traditional market. The indoor **Victorian Market** in the Academy Street building dates from 1890 when it was rebuilt after a disastrous fire.

Anyone of Scottish descent will be interested in the **Clan Tartan Centre** at James Pringle's Holms Mills on Dores Road where traditional tartans and tweeds have been produced since 1798. Visitors can watch the centuries-old craft of tartan weaving on impressive Hattersley power looms, trace their own links to a Scottish clan through a data base of more than 50,000 names, or browse in a shop stacked with a huge range of woollen clothes. On a similar theme, the unique Scottish Kiltmaker Visitor Centre in Huntly Street is devoted entirely to the kilt and offers audio-visual displays on its history. Visitors

can watch kilt makers at work and there's even a short film, *Kilted Hall of Fame*, which features famous people who have worn a kilt.

The magnificent Kessock Bridge, opened in 1982, carries the A9 over the narrows between the Moray and Beauly Firths and connects Inverness to the Black Isle. At North Kessock is the **Dolphins and Seals of the Moray Firth Visitor and Research Centre**. The Moray Firth is famous for its bottlenose dolphins, and boats leave from many small ports so that you can observe them. This visitor centre gives you one of the best opportunities in Europe to learn about the creatures, and to listen to them through underwater microphones.

A few miles west of the town at Kirkhill is the Highland Wineries, based around Moniack Castle, an old Fraser stronghold dating from 1580. There are country wines, liqueurs, preserves and sauces.

AROUND INVERNESS

TAIN

34 miles N of Inverness on the A9

The most distinctive building in Tain is the **Tolbooth,** built in the 1500s and restored in 1707. It's an attractive sight with its conical spire and corner turrets, but at the time of the Clearances this "sharp-pointed house" struck fear into the hearts of the local crofters. It was then the administrative centre from which notices of dispossession were issued and also the jail for anyone who tried to resist the order.

Tain's history goes back to Viking times when it was the "capital" of the area, its name a corruption of the Norse word *"Thing"*, meaning a council. The town became a royal burgh in 1066 and the 900 Roses Garden commemorates the town's nine centuries of existence.

In medieval times, Tain was a great Christian centre, drawing pilgrims from all over Europe to the shrine of St Duthac within St Duthac Collegiate Church. King James IV made an annual pilgrimage here every year between 1492 and 1513, combining this act of piety with a visit to his mistress, Janet Kennedy, whom he had installed in nearby Moray. He made many offerings to the shrine including, on one particularly parsimonious occasion, some broken silver plates for the adornment of St Duthac's relics. One of the finest medieval buildings in the Highlands, the church is now an exhibition and visitors centre called **Tain Through Time.** The exhibits explain about St Duthac himself, the pilgrimage, and the people who made it. Half a mile north of the town, off the A9, is the Glenmorangie Distillery which operated illegally for many years before acquiring a licence in 1843. Guided tours are available, with a tasting at the end of the tour, and there's also a museum and shop.

DORNOCH

43 miles N of Inverness on the A949

With miles of sandy beaches, and near the top of Scotland's listings for hours of sunshine, Dornoch is a trim holiday resort with flowers everywhere and a celebrated championship golf course. The town overlooks Dornoch Firth with fine views across the estuary to the Tain peninsula.

In the spacious main square, **Dornoch Cathedral,** dating back to 1224, dominates the town. The church as we see it today is largely a rebuilding of the early 19th century, though there are some old features still to be seen, mostly in the chancel and crossing. Sixteen Earls of Sutherland are said to be buried within it. It was also where, in December 2000, the son of pop star Madonna and her husband Guy Ritchie was baptised. **Dornoch Castle** stands opposite the cathedral, and was built in the 15th century with later additions. It is now a hotel.

Incongruously, the attractive little town of Dornoch witnessed the last burning of a witch in Scotland. The year was 1722 when a misfortunate old woman named Janet Horne was accused of transforming her daughter into a pony, riding her to a witches' coven and having her shod there by the Devil. During her trial, Janet was judged to have confirmed her guilt of these improbably crimes because she incorrectly quoted the Gaelic version of the Lord's Prayer. She was sentenced to be roasted alive in a barrel of oil. This gruesome event is commemorated by the Witch's Stone, just south of the Square on Carnaig Street.

176 THE SHIP INN

Invergordon

Comfortable B&B accommodation in former Temperance Hotel.

see page 453

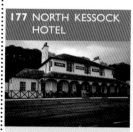

177 NORTH KESSOCK HOTEL

North Kessock

A popular hotel offering some of the best accommodation and cuisine in the area

see page 454

Cawdor

Set in the old workshop for the nearby castle, the Cawdor Tavern provides excellent food and drink for regulars and visitors alike.

🍴 *see page 455*

CULLODEN

4 miles NE of Inverness on the B9006

The **Battle of Culloden** was fought in April 1746, and was the last major land battle to take place in Britain. It lasted less than an hour and left 349 Government troops dead and 1000 Jacobites. The casualty figures reflect how hopelessly outnumbered were the forces of Bonnie Prince Charlie against those of the Duke of Cumberland. Culloden became the graveyard for all hope of the Stuart dynasty ever recovering the throne. Immediately after the battle, Cumberland ordered that none of the wounded should be spared, a brutal command that earned him the bitter nickname of "Butcher" Cumberland. Culloden marked the end of a distinctive Highland way of life. The clan leaders, forbidden to maintain private armies, became mere landlords, seeking rents rather than service. The English government passed a series of punitive laws designed to obliterate the Highlanders very culture: speaking Gaelic became a crime; wearing the tartan and playing the bagpipes were also banned.

Today, there is still a sadness about the place, and it was once said that no birds ever sang here. That's not quite true, but no one who visits can fail to be moved. You can still see the stones that mark the graves of various clans, and there is a huge memorial cairn at the centre of the battlefield. **Leanach Cottage**, outside which 30 Jacobite soldiers were burnt alive in the aftermath of the battle, has been restored, and

the **Culloden Visitors Centre** (National Trust for Scotland) has displays and exhibits which explain the battle. The Cumberland Stone marks the place where the 25-year-old Duke of Cumberland, third son of George II and commander of the Royalist troops, watched the battle.

Not far from the battlefield are the **Clava Cairns** (Historic Scotland), a fascinating group of three burial cairns of the early Bronze Age.

CAWDOR

12 miles NE of Inverness on the A96

The lovely conservation village of Cawdor is best known for **Cawdor Castle,** home of the Thanes of Cawdor for more than 600 years. A fairy-tale building of turrets and towers, it must surely be the only castle built around a tree. A family tradition asserts that in a dream the 3rd Thane of Cawdor was told to load his donkey with gold and wherever the beast settled for the night, there to build his castle. The donkey chose to rest beside a tree. The tree still stands, bare and limbless now, in the great vaulted room at the base of the central tower. It is a holly tree, one of the seven sacred trees of Celtic mythology, and has been carbon dated to 1372. The presence of such a mystic tree was probably intended to ward off evil influences, but in the late Middle Ages it would have needed more than a tree to preserve the Cawdors from the intrigue, murder and mayhem of the time. A typical (and true) story tells of

Muriel, the 9th Thaness. She inherited the title at birth in 1510, her father having died a few months before. As a rich heiress, the infant girl was promptly kidnapped by the most powerful man in Scotland, the Earl of Argyll, and "for future recognition, the babe was branded on the hip by her nurse with a key, and the top joint of her left little finger was bitten off". The rest of Muriel's long life (she lived to be 77 years old), is strewn with similarly striking incidents.

Fort George

The castle is well worth visiting for its remarkable collection of tapestries, paintings (Reynolds, Lely, Lawrence, Romney, Stanley Spencer and John Piper amongst them), Chippendale furniture and a wealth of family memorabilia. The grounds are especially satisfying, with superb gardens (first laid out in the 1720s), a 9-hole mini-golf course, a topiary maze, picnic spots and several nature trails.

Many visitors are drawn to Cawdor because of its associations with Shakespeare's *Macbeth* although the present castle wasn't built until more than 300 years after Macbeth's death. Still worse, Macbeth never was Thane of Cawdor - the title was retrospectively bestowed on him by the 16th century historian Boethius to give the old story more dramatic spice.

FORT GEORGE

15 miles NE of Inverness on the B9006

Fort George (Historic Scotland) was designed by Major General William Skinner, the King's Military Engineer for North Britain (the name given to Scotland after the Jacobite Uprising). He originally wanted to build it at Inverness but the councillors of the town objected, saying it would take away part of the harbour. The fort was named after George II and stands on a headland that guards the inner waters of the Moray Firth near Ardersier. Work started on building it in 1748 as a direct result of the Jacobite Uprising of 1745 and it was subsequently manned by government troops. It covers 42 acres, has walls a mile long, and the whole thing cost over £1bn to build at today's prices. It has been called the finest 18th century fortification in Europe, and has survived almost intact from that time. The **Queen's Own Highlanders Museum** is within the fort.

NAIRN

16 miles NE of Inverness on the A96

Nairn is a small, picturesque holiday and golfing resort on the Moray Firth. Local people will tell

Nairn

A warm and friendly traditional bar with a big open fire to make winter evenings all the more cosy

see page 455

180 AURORA HOTEL

Nairn

Town centre hotel offering a restaurant serving authentic Italian cuisine and comfortable en suite rooms.

 see page 456

Near Fortrose at Chanonry Point is one of the best places to observe the Moray Firth dolphins. Here, where the Firth is at its narrowest, you can sometimes see up to 40 of these graceful creatures glide through the waters or put on a fine display of jumping and diving. It was at Chanonry Point that Kenneth Mackenzie, better known as the Brahan Seer, was executed in 1660. He had the gift of second sight, and when he was asked by the 3rd Countess of Seaforth why her husband was late returning home from Paris, he said that he was with a lady. She was so enraged that she had Kenneth executed. A cairn marks the spot.

---

you that the name is a shortened version of "nae rain" ("no rain"), and indeed this area is one of the driest in Britain. It has a fine, clean beach and a large caravan park. The River Nairn, which flows through the town, is supposed to mark the boundary between the English speaking areas to the east and the Gaelic speaking areas to the west. This divide was made abundantly clear to King James VI when he visited in the late 1590s. He boasted sardonically that his kingdom was so extensive that people at one end of a town's main street could not understand those who lived at the other.

The **Nairn Museum** on Viewfield Drive has collections on local history, archaeology and wildlife. There is also the **Fishertown Museum**, in the heart of the fisher town area. As its name implies, this is where the fishermen that manned the town's former fishing fleet lived. There are displays and artefacts highlighting the industry.

At Auldearn, two miles east of the town (now bypassed), is the **Boath Doocot** (National Trust for Scotland), which stands within what was a small medieval castle built in the late 12th century by William the Lion. The **Battle of Auldearn** was fought here in 1645 between 1500 Royalist troops of the Marquis of Montrose and a 4000-strong Covenanting army under Sir John Hurry. Even though they outnumbered the Royalist troops, the Covenanters were routed, and some of the dead were

buried in the kirkyard of Auldearn Parish Church, built in 1757.

FORTROSE

16 miles NE of Inverness on the A832

Fortrose Cathedral (Historic Scotland) was founded by David I as the mother church of the diocese of Ross. Building began in the 1200s, though the scant remains you see nowadays date from the 14th century. One of the three fine canopied tombs is of Euphemia Ross, wife of the Wolf of Badenoch (see also Dunkeld, Grantown-on-Spey and Elgin). The other two are of bishops, possibly Robert Cairncross and John Fraser.

In nearby Rosemarkie is the **Groam House Museum,** with exhibits and displays that explain the culture of the Picts, those mysterious people who inhabited this part of Scotland in the Dark Ages.

CROMARTY

26 miles NE of Inverness on the A832

No-one travelling in these parts should fail to visit the enchanting little town of Cromarty, an almost perfect example of an 18th century seaport. Narrow streets and old cottages are interspersed with handsome Georgian houses built during the period of prosperity from the 1770s to the 1840s. In 1772, the Laird of Cromarty, George Ross, founded a hemp mill here in which imported Baltic hemp was spun into cloth and rope. The business was spectacularly successful and the profits helped to build some of Scotland's finest Georgian houses. Also dating from those affluent days is the elegant **Cromarty Courthouse** of 1782. It is now a museum with a reconstruction of an 18th century trial in the courtroom itself, plus you can see the old cells, children's costumes, a video presentation giving 800 years of Cromarty history and an audio tape tour of the old part of the town.

The tour takes in **Hugh Miller's Cottage (NTS),** a charming thatched building of 1711 where the celebrated geologist and prolific man of letters was born in 1801. It has a collection of fossils and rock specimens, as well as some of his personal possessions, including his geological hammer and microscope. The major part of his fossil collection of more than 6000 specimens provides the core of today's Scottish national collection in the Royal Scottish Museum in Edinburgh.

GOLSPIE

50 miles NE of Inverness on the A9

This straggling red-sandstone village is the administrative centre for Sutherland and also the "capital" of the Dukes of Sutherland who still own vast tracts of northeast Scotland.

A steep hill path takes you to the summit of Beinn a'Bragaidh, on which there is a 100 feet high monument by Chantry to the first **Duke of Sutherland** who died in 1833. It was this duke who evicted some 15,000 crofters from his land during the infamous Clearances of the early 1800s. However, the inscption on his monument, "erected by a mourning and grateful tenantry", refers only to "a judicious, kind and liberal landlord who would open his hands to the distress of the widow, the sick and the traveller". There have been continued calls to have the statue removed, and in some cases blown up. Others have argued that the statue should stay as a reminder of those terrible times.

Dunrobin Castle, the seat of the Dukes of Sutherland, is the most northerly of Scotland's stately homes and one of the largest in the Highlands. The core is 14th century, but in 1840 it underwent a spare-no-expense remodelling by Sir Charles Barry, designer of the Houses of Parliament. Queen Victoria described it very accurately as "a mixture of an old Scotch castle and a French chateau". The treasures on show include paintings by Landseer, Allan Ramsay, Reynolds and Canaletto. There are some exquisite Mortlake tapestries, Louis Quinze furniture, and wonderfully ornate ceiling in the drawing-room; and a library lined with sycamore wood. Some of the castle's 189 rooms are open to the public and outside there are magnificent formal gardens modelled on those at Versailles, and a museum housed in a gracious 18th century summerhouse. It contains an astonishing collection that includes archaeological remains and hunting trophies from all over the world, Pictish stones, one of John o'Groats bones, a "picnic gong from the South Pacific", and mementoes of Queen Victoria who

311

Three miles north of Brora, on the seaward side of the A9, Kintradwell Broch is an impressive example of these circular, prehistoric forts, with an interior measuring some 30 feet in diameter. A little further north, in a lay-by near Lothbeg, the Wolf Stone marks the spot where the last wolf in Sutherland was killed, around 1700.

One of Carrbridge's prime attractions is its imaginative Landmark Forest Heritage Park which has as its focus a striking modern building surrounded by pine trees. Inside, you can watch a dramatic audio-visual history of the highlands. Outdoors, you can wander through the Red Squirrel Trail, venture onto the Tree Top Trail where you take a walk through the high branches of the trees, or climb the 65 feet high Timber Tower which provides amazing views over the surrounding countryside.

was a great chum of the 3rd Duke and Duchess.

Dunrobin Castle Station is one of the most exclusive railway halts in Scotland, It was built as a private stop for the duke and his guests and last used regularly in the 1960s.

North of Golspie, on the road to Brora, is **Carn Liath** ("the Grey Cairn"). It overlooks the sea, and is all that is left of a once mighty broch. The walls are still 12 feet high in places.

BRORA

55 miles NE of Inverness on the A9

Brora is a picturesque coastal village at the mouth of the River Brora. The **Brora Heritage Centre** on Coalpit Road has a hands-on guide to the history and wildlife of the area. At one time it was the location of the Highland's only coal mine, with the coal being shipped out from the local harbour until the railways took over.

A mile or so north of the town is the **Clynelish Distillery** which offers guided tours culminating in a complimentary dram and also has a visitors centre and shop.

TOMATIN

13 miles SE of Inverness off the A9

Tomatin sits on the River Findhorn, just off the A9. The **Tomatin Distillery**, north of the village, is one of the highest in Scotland, and was founded in 1897. Now owned by a Japanese company, it has 23 stills, and draws its water from the Alt-na-Frithe burn. It has tours, a visitor centre and tastings.

CARRBRIDGE

19 miles SE of Inverness on the A938

The stone bridge that gave Carrbridge its name still survives, an elegant, single high-arched span. It was built in 1717 following the deaths of two men who drowned here while attempting to cross the treacherous ford over the River Spey.

At Dulnain Bridge, six miles east of the village, visitors can acquire a living memento of their stay in Scotland at the **Speyside Heather Centre** which has more than 300 varieties of a plant that has become synonymous with Scotland. Its Heather Heritage Centre houses an exhibition on the varied historical uses of the plant in thatching and rope making, for doormats and baskets, as well as in medicine, cooking, drinks and dyeing wool. In the heather craft shop you can buy the plants themselves and gifts associated with them - including heather wine.

NETHY BRIDGE

26 miles SE of Inverness on the B970

Dell Wood National Nature Reserve is in Abernethy Forest. It is famous for its rare bog woodland, which has largely disappeared from the area because of drainage and agricultural improvements.

GRANTOWN-ON-SPEY

27 miles SE of Inverness off the A939

One of Queen Victoria's favourite little towns, Grantown-on-Spey was originally laid out in 1776 with wide, tree-lined streets leading to a central square. This traditional Highland resort grew in stature when doctors began to recommend its dry, bracing climate for those "requiring rest and quiet on account of nervous overstrain and debility". The town stands close to several busy tourist routes and is a popular centre all year round - many winter visitors prefer Grantown's elegant Georgian and Victorian appeal to the rather functional facilities at Aviemore.

The 15,000-acre **Revack Country Estate** lies to the south of the town, on the B970 to Nethy Bridge. It has gardens, woodland trails, an adventure playground, gift shop and restaurant.

Six miles north-west of the town are the ruins of **Lochindorb Castle**, built on an island in Lochindorb, on bleak Dava Moor. This was the home of the infamous Alexander Stewart, son of Robert II, and known as the Wolf of Badenoch.

AVIEMORE

30 miles S of Inverness off the A9

Once a quiet Inverness-shire village, Aviemore has now expanded into one of the main winter sports centres in the Highlands. The skiing area and chair lifts lie about 9 miles east of the village, high in the Cairngorms. This is also the starting point of Cairngorm Mountain Railway which carries passengers all year round to the Ptarmigan Station, within 400 feet of the summit of the 4084 feet high Cairngorm itself.

On the road to the skiing area is the **Cairngorm Reindeer Centre**, where Britain's only permanent herd of reindeer can be seen.

The **Rothiemurchus Highland Estate** is a magnificent area with spectacular views, deep forests and woodland trails. You can try hill walking and mountain biking, and there are guided walks and safari tours in Land Rovers. The estate contains some of the last remnants of the great, natural Caledonian Pine Forest, which once covered all of the Highlands. Parts of *Monarch of the Glen* are filmed here (see also Kingussie). Details of all the activities are available from the Visitor Centre on the B970 south east of the village.

Aviemore is one of the termini of the **Strathspey Steam Railway** which runs through Boat of Garten to Broomhill, ten miles away. The railway's vintage rolling stock includes a functioning restaurant car that was once part of the *Flying Scotsman* express train. Depending on the time of year there are from five to eight return trips each day. The Aviemore station is worth visiting just to see its engine shed full of burnished locomotives. The shed itself is original but the other station buildings were imported from Dalnaspidal, and the turntable from Kyle of Lochalsh. The line was once part of the Aviemore to Forres line which closed in 1965. Devotees of the TV drama series *Monarch of the Glen* will probably recognise Broomhill station which

181 SPEYBANK GUEST HOUSE

Aviemore

Town centre guest house offering en suite rooms, excellent breakfast and amenities such as a drying room.

see page 456

182 PINEBANK CHALETS

Aviemore

Quality self-catering accommodation in secluded setting surrounded by some of the finest scenery in the Highlands.

see page 457

183 GREYSTONES B&B

Kingussie

Quality B&B
accommodation in
handsome stone building set
in *Monarch of the Glen*
country.

see page 457

184 THE INN AT DALWHINNIE

Dalwhinnie

"The coolest hotel in the
Highlands" offering
scrumptious food and
quality en suite
accommodation.

see page 458

has featured as 'Glenbogle Station'
in the series.

KINGUSSIE

37 miles S of Inverness off the A9

Southwest of Aviemore, the A9,
the B9152 and the railway run
alongside each other to the resort
village of Kingussie (pronounced
King-you-see). The B9152 will give
you better views of Loch Alvie and
Loch Insh , where there's a
watersports centre, and also bring
you to the excellent **Highland
Wildlife Park** near Kincraig.
Owned and run by the Royal
Zoological Society of Scotland, a
registered charity which also owns
Edinburgh Zoo. Visitors drive
around the huge reserve where
herds of secretive roe deer,
enormous bison, ancient breeds of
sheep and wild Przwalski horses,
one of the world's rarest mammals,
can all be seen. The rest of the
park can be explored on foot,
wandering through themed habitats
such as the Wolf Territory where a
raised walkway takes visitors right
into the heart of the enclosure.

About a mile south of
Kingussue stand the substantial
remains of **Ruthven Barracks**
(Historic Scotland). They were built
in 1719 to keep the Highlanders in
check following the 1715 Rising.
After the tragedy of Culloden in
1746, some 3000 Jacobite survivors
rallied here hoping that Bonnie
Prince Charlie might once again
take to the field. When they
received a brusque message that
every man should seek his safety in
the best way he could, they blew up

the barracks and fled. The stark
ruins of the once-mighty military
outpost look best at night when
they are floodlit.

A mile or so from Ruthven
Barracks in Kingussie is the RSPB
reserve at **Insh Marshes,** one of
the most important wetlands in
Britain. In spring, lapwings,
redshanks and curlews all nest here,
and in the winter when the marshes
flood, they attract flocks of
whooper swans and greylag geese.
The best months for visiting are
from November until June.

A few miles south west of
Kingussie, along the A86, is Loch
Laggan where scenes for the BBC
series *Monarch of the Glen* were
filmed. The Adverikie Estate, with
its large house, played the part of
Glenbogle.

NEWTONMORE

40 miles S of Inverness on the A9/A86

Newtonmore boasts a major visitor
attraction in the **Highland Folk
Museum.** Here, across an 80-acre
site, are displayed a fascinating
collection of buildings. They
include a reconstructed Lewis
"black house", an old smokehouse,
a water-powered sawmill, a 19th
century school, and a clock maker's
workshop. Indoors, the farming
museum has a stable, barn, dairy
and a large range of old carts,
ploughs and other farming
implements. On most days during
the summer there are
demonstrations of various
traditional crafts.

In the village itself is the **Clan
Macpherson House and Museum**

which, as its name implies, recounts the history of the Macphersons. One of the prize exhibits is a black chanter allegedly presented to the Macphersons by the "little People". On the first Saturday in August, clan members from around the world gather here for the Newtonmore Highland Games.

DRUMNADROCHIT

15 miles SW of Inverness on the A82

Drumnadrochit sits on the shore of Loch Ness at Drumnadrochit Bay. It is a quaint place though it can get overcrowded in the summer due to tourists flocking here to catch a glimpse of the Loch Ness Monster, nicknamed **"Nessie".** Whether a monster actually exists or not has never been proved, but that has never deterred the crowds. The loch measures just less than 23 miles long by a mile wide at its widest, and contains more water than any other loch in Britain.

Two exhibitions vie for attention in the village, the **Original Loch Ness Exhibition** and the **Loch Ness Exhibition Centre.** They each have displays about the Loch Ness Monster but the latter was designed by scientist Adrian Shine who has spent more than 30 years investigating the Loch Ness phenomenon.

The first mention we have of a monster - though in this case it was in the River Ness and not in the loch - occurs in Adamnan's *Life of St Columba*, written in the 7th century. In the year AD 565 St Columba was heading up the Great Glen towards Inverness when he

encountered a monster attacking a man in the River Ness at the point where it enters the loch. He drove it back by prayer and the man's companions fell on their knees and were converted to Christianity.

Nowadays the monster is a bit more timid. Most sightings have been made at **Urquhart Castle** (Historic Scotland), about a mile from Drumnadrochit. Curiously enough, this is where the loch is at its deepest at 754 feet. The castle is one of the largest in Scotland and stands on a promontory that juts out into the water. A fortification has stood here for centuries, but the present ruins date from the 16th century. After the Jacobite Uprising of 1689 the castle was blown up and never rebuilt. A visitor centre contains a model of the castle which shows what it was like in its heyday.

BEAULY

11 miles W of Inverness on the A862

Within this picturesque village are the ruins of **Beauly Priory** (Historic Scotland), founded by the Bisset family in 1230 for monks of the Valliscaulian order, though what can be seen nowadays dates from between the 14th and 16th centuries. The north transept, which is more or less complete, is the burial place of the MacKenzies of Kintail.

The **Beauly Centre**, next to the priory, has displays about the history of the area. There is also a reconstructed village store, a weaving centre and a Clan Fraser exhibition.

185 GLENURQUHART HOUSE HOTEL

Drumnadrochit

A beautiful hotel nestled on a secluded wooded hillside

see page 459

186 THE DORES INN

Dores

Quality pub serving wonderful food and drink on the banks of the world famous Loch Ness.

see page 459

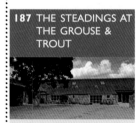

187 THE STEADINGS AT THE GROUSE & TROUT

South Loch Ness

A great hotel in stunning surroundings, steeped in history and charm, the perfect place to relax.

see page 460

188 ARCHDALE GUEST HOUSE

Beauly

Welcoming family-run bed & breakfast accommodation in peaceful Beauly village.

see page 461

189 CULLIGRAN COTTAGES

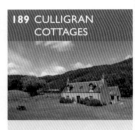

Struy

Self-catering accommodation in traditional cottage or Norwegian style chalet

see page 461

190 CULBOKIE INN

Culbokie

A traditional inn at the heart of community life, with spectacular views across the Cromarty Firth and Ben Wyvis.

see page 462

To the southwest is **Strathglass**, one of the most beautiful glens in the area. It was here, in the early 19th century, that the Sobieski Stuarts lived in some style, claiming to be the legitimate grandsons of Charles Edward Stuart. Their claims were believed by many people, notably the Earl of Moray, Lord Lovat and the Earl of Dumfries. There is no doubt, however, that they were charlatans.

The **Wardlaw Mausoleum**, built on to the east end of Kirkhill Parish Church, is one of the burial places of Clan Fraser. It was built in 1634, and in 1998 was restored by Historic Scotland.

DINGWALL

14 miles NW of Inverness on the A862

Dingwall's name derives from the Norse "thing vollr", meaning "the place of the parliament", which shows that even in ancient times it was an important settlement. It is a royal burgh, and received its charter from Alexander II in 1227. Its castle, now long gone, was the birthplace of Macbeth in 1010. Another famous son is **Sir Hector MacDonald**, a crofter's son who was born in 1853 and joined the army as a private, rising through the ranks to become a major general and national hero. He was known as "Fighting Mac", and eventually commanded the British Army in Ceylon. In 1903, on his way back to Ceylon after a trip to London, he committed suicide in Paris after unproved accusations of homosexuality from those who objected to his lowly birth. After his death, his accusers were stunned to discover that he had a secret wife and child. A monument to him, known as the Mitchell Tower, stands on a hill to the south of the town on Mitchell Hill.

Within the old Tolbooth of 1730 is the award-winning **Dingwall Museum**, where the town's history is explained by way of displays and exhibits.

Dingwall is the eastern terminus for the famous Dingwall - Kyle of Lochalsh railway line, which runs through some of the most beautiful scenery in Scotland as it crosses the country.

The Dingwall Canal (now closed) is Britain's most northerly canal, and was designed by Thomas Telford in 1817, though by 1890 it had closed. It is just over a mile in length. At the end of the canal is the Ferry Point, which has a picnic area.

Eight miles west of the town, off the A835, are the **Rogie Falls** on the Blackwater, reached by a footpath from a car park on the main road. A fish ladder has been built to assist salmon to swim upriver. There are also woodland walks in the surrounding area.

STRATHPEFFER

19 miles NW of Inverness on the A834

At one time, this small village was one of the most famous spa resorts in Britain, and trains used to leave London regularly carrying people who wanted to "take its waters". For this reason, it is full of hotels, B&Bs and genteel guesthouses. So fashionable was it

that the local paper used to publish a weekly list of the crowned heads and aristocratic families who were "in town".

The spa days are over now, though the **Spa Pump Room** has been refurbished and re-creates the halcyon days of the village when the cream of society flocked here. You can even sample the curative waters yourself. The adjacent Victorian gardens, where Victorian society used to promenade and play croquet, have also been restored.

Other attractions in the town include the restored Victorian railway station where there are no trains but an interesting collection of craft shops and a superb museum, **Highland Museum of Childhood.** It tells the story of childhood in the Scottish Highlands through a series of well-presented displays, each exploring a different theme - education, health, home life, folklore and recreation. Artefacts on show include toys, games, puppets, cradles, a school desk, slate and strap, as well as a number of rare dolls from the Angela Kellie Collection. Particularly engrossing are the historic photographs of Highland children at work and play from late-Victorian times to the recent past.

Eagle Stone, Strathpeffer

There's also a gift shop and coffee shop.

On the eastern outskirts of the village is the **Eagle Stone.** It is carved with an eagle, the crest of the Clan Munro, and commemorates their victory over the MacDonalds in 1411. A local visionary, the Seer of Brahan, predicted that if the stone fell over three times, the waters of the Cromarty Firth, five miles to the east, would rise so that ships could drop anchor near where the stone stood. The stone has fallen over twice so far, so it is now embedded in concrete. The precaution seems wise since many other of the Seer's prophecies have come to pass since his death in 1660. He is credited with

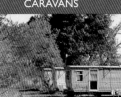

194 BIRCH COTTAGE

Garve

Traditional Highland cottage, prided on the hospitality and delightful locally sourced home-cooked menu.

see *page 464*

foreseeing the building of the Caledonian Canal, the Clearances, World War II, as well as predicting that Strathpeffer "uninviting and disagreeable as it now is, the day will come when crows of pleasure and health seekers shall be thronging its portals".

LAIRG

59 miles NW of Inverness on the A836

Lairg is an old village that sits at the south-eastern tip of Loch Shin, which, since the 1950s, has been harnessed for hydroelectricity. The loch, which is famous for its fishing, is over 18 miles long by no more than a mile at its widest, with the A838 following its northern shoreline for part of the way. Due to the hydroelectric scheme, it is 30 feet deeper than it used to be.

The village became important because it stands at the meeting point of various Highland roads

that head off in all directions. Five miles south are the picturesque **Falls of Shin** which has a visitor centre and a Harrod's shop. **Ord Hill**, west of the town, has an archaeological trail, which takes you round a landscape rich in ancient sites. **Ferrycroft Countryside Centre** explains land use in this part of Sutherland since the end of the last Ice Age.

ULLAPOOL

The most northerly settlement of any size on the northwest coast is Ullapool, embarkation point for ferries to Stornoway. This appealing little town was purpose-built in 1788, to a design by Thomas Telford, by the British Fisheries Society which hoped to capitalise on the herring boom of the time. Ullapool's streets are laid out in a grid design, their regularity enlivened by brightly-painted houses and a wonderful variety of busy little shops. Despite its smallness, the town has the feeling of a cosmopolitan port: your next-table neighbours in one of its cosy pubs may well be speaking in strange tongues - fishermen from Eastern Europe as likely as not celebrating their catch of Atlantic fish.

The town's comparatively short history is amply recorded at the award-winning **Ullapool Museum and Visitor Centre**, housed in a former church designed by Thomas Telford. In 1773, before the town was established, the very first settlers bound for Nova Scotia left Loch Broom in the *Hector*, and there

Ullapool Harbour

is a scale model of the ship within the museum.

From Ullapool there are frequent boat trips during the season to the **Summer Isles** whose only inhabitants are colonies of seabirds. In the surrounding waters, dolphins and porpoises can be seen larking about; there are seals greedy for travellers tit-bits and, if you are really lucky, you may get a sighting of an elusive otter.

One of the hidden jewels of the West Highlands are the **Leckmelm Gardens**, three miles south of the town just off the A835. They were planted in about 1870, but by 1985 had become overgrown. In that year work began in re-establishing them and revealing the beauty that had been lost for so long.

The area surrounding Ullapool is famous for its golden beaches, the best ones being at Achnahaird, Gruinard Bay and Achmelvich.

AROUND ULLAPOOL

LOCHINVER

37 miles N of Ullapool on the A837

This small fishing port sits on Loch Inver, at the end of the A837. A few miles east is Loch Assynt on whose shore you will find the ruins of **Ardvreck Castle**, built in the 16th century by the MacLeods of Assynt. It was here, in 1650, that Montrose was kept prisoner before being taken to Edinburgh for execution. The **Assynt Visitor Centre** has small displays and exhibits about local history.

Four miles south east of the village is what has been called "the

most beautiful mountain in Scotland" - **Suilven**. At a mere 2389 feet, it is not even a Munro, nor is it the highest in the area. Seen from Lochinver, it appears to be a solitary mountain that rises sheer on all sides. It's name comes from the Norse, and means the "Mountain Pillar". However, it is the western end of a high ridge, and makes for some superb walking and climbing country.

At Achiltibuie, 10 miles south of Lochinver, and reached by a narrow road, is the **Hydroponicum**, a "garden" where plants grow without soil. It calls itself the "garden of the future" and kits are available so that you too can start growing plants without soil. It was set up in the mid-1980s to show that some of the problems found in this part of Scotland -- poor soil, a short growing season and high winds - could be overcome. It now provides high quality produce (from lettuces to bananas) for homes and businesses in the area. It also now features renewable sources of energy and green technologies.

DURNESS

70 miles N of Ullapool on the A838

Durness, in Sutherland, is one of the most northerly villages in Scotland, and sits close to Cape Wrath - one of only two "capes" in Great Britain, the other being Cape Cornwall. To reach it, you have to cross the Kyle of Durness from Durness itself on a small ferry and walk or take a minibus to the cape itself, ten miles away.

There are many clean, golden

South of Ullapool, Corrieshalloch Gorge is one of the most spectacular, and accessible, sights in the Highlands. A mile long and 200 feet deep, this awesome ravine is additionally watered by the Falls of Measach which plunge 150 feet down the hillside. The best view of them is from the Victorian suspension bridge across the gorge, but do take note of its prominent warning that no more than two people at a time should stand on its vertigo-inducing boards.

The peculiarly named Smoo Cave is in the cliffs a mile-and-a-half west of Durness. It consists of three chambers, and goes underneath the coast road. The name may come from the Old Norse smjugga, meaning "rock". A walkway with railings takes you down to the cave, which has had lights fitted.

319

Smoo Cave, Durness

Poolewe itself is a picturesque crafting village set around the pool formed where the River Ewe flows into the loch of the same name. Loch Ewe is as pretty as any in Scotland but blemished in parts by bunkers, pillboxes and gun sites, an unlovely legacy of World War II when the loch was a loading base for convoys to Russia.

195 POOLEWE HOTEL

Poolewe

Former coaching inn in magnificent setting offering outstanding cuisine and 3-star en suite rooms.

 see page 465

beaches in the area, most of them uncrowded. The best ones are Balnakeil, Ceann na Beinne, Sango Beag and Sango Mor.

The village has associations with John Lennon of the Beatles, who used to spend holidays here with his family when he was young. The **John Lennon Memorial Garden** commemorates his stays, and there is a small display of Lennon letters in the village hall.

POOLEWE

51 miles SW of Ullapool via the A835/A832

Just to the north of Poolewe, on the banks of Loch Ewe, **Inverewe Gardens** (National Trust for Scotland) are one of the "must-not-miss" attractions of the Highlands. In 1862, young Osgood Mackenzie inherited a huge, 12,000 acre estate. The legacy wasn't as valuable as it sounds since almost all of those sprawling acres were barren, covered with beach gravel and sea grass. A dedicated botanist, Osgood made it his life's work to make this desert bloom. He

purchased tons of the rich soil which Irish ships carried as ballast to Gairloch and smothered his arid domain with inches-deep layers of this unusual import. He planted a protective break of trees and began his project by filling a walled garden, (which is still the centrepiece of the gardens), with plants from all over the world. Over the course of more than half a century until his death in 1922, he transformed this infertile peninsula into one of the great gardens of the world. Even though the gardens lie further north than some parts of Greenland, the benign influence of the Gulf Stream allows exotic plants from the Far East, South America, Australasia and the Himalayas to flourish. Mid-May to mid-June is the best time to see the rhododendrons and azaleas in their full glory; during July and August the herbaceous garden is at is most colourful.

GAIRLOCH

56 miles SW of Ullapool on the A832

This little village, on the shores of Loch Gairloch, has one of the loveliest settings in Scotland, enjoying stunning views to distant Skye and the Torridon mountains. There are facilities for almost every kind of outdoor activity here and should the weather be inclement, the **Gairloch Heritage Museum,** housed in old farm buildings, provides plenty of interest. Amongst the many fascinating items on display are two sturdy fishing boats constructed locally in the early 1900s; a huge lantern from Rudha Reidn lighthouse just up the coast; and an "illicit" still.

From Gairloch's small harbour, a passenger ferry service runs two return crossings daily to Portree on the Isle of Skye.

WICK

In Old Norse "Vik" means a bay, and Wick is indeed set around a bay although its spread of dull grey houses makes the setting far from picturesque. Robert Louis Stevenson was scathing about the town, describing it as "the meanest of man's towns, situated on the baldest of God's bays". Like Budapest, Wick is really two towns, with the original settlement on the north bank of the Wick River, and Pulteneytown on the south.

The latter was named after the president of the British fisheries Society which in 1806 commissioned Thomas Telford to design a new town to house crofters who had been evicted during the Clearances. The society was motivated by the humane intention of providing work for them as fishermen and the herring boom of the mid-1800s fulfilled their wishes. Wick became the busiest herring port in Europe with more than 1000 boats registered here, exporting tons of the silvery fish around the world.

The town's chequered history is well presented at the award-winning **Wick Heritage Centre** in Bank Row which, among many interesting exhibits, displays an excellent collection of

photographs dating back to the 1880s.

In Huddart Street in Pulteneytown is the **Pulteney Distillery,** which makes the world-famous "Old Pulteney" single malt whisky. It has a visitor centre and shop, and there is a tour of the distillery plus tastings.

The **Old Parish Kirk,** dedicated to St Fergus, dates from 1830, though a church has stood here since medieval times. In the kirkyard is the Sinclair Aisle, burial place of the old Earls of Caithness.

On the northern edge of the town is Wick Airport, Scotland's most northerly mainland commercial airport. It currently has scheduled flights to and from Aberdeen and Edinburgh.

One mile south of the town, on a cliff top, are the ruins of the **Castle of Old Wick** (Historic Scotland), built by Harald Maddadson, Earl of Caithness, in the 12th century.

On a hill to the south of Wick Bay is a memorial to the engineer James Bremner who was born in Wick and who died in 1856. He collaborated with Brunel, and salvaged the *SS Great Britain* when it ran aground off Ireland.

North of Wick, the two castles of **Girnigoe** and **Sinclair** stand above Sinclair Bay. They were strongholds of the Earls of Caithness. Girnigoe is the older of the two, dating from the end of the 15th century; Sinclair Castle dates from about 1606.

196 SINCLAIR BAY HOTEL

Keiss

Small, popular family-run hotel offering excellent food, real ales and quality en suite rooms.

see page 465

197 BREADALBANE HOUSE HOTEL

Wick

Great accommodation in the heart of Wick, recently voted as one of the top six music venues in Scotland.

see page 466

The Strath of Kildonan near Helmsdale, through which flows the River Helmsdale, was the scene of a famous Gold Rush of 1868. A local man called Robert Gilchrist, who had been a prospector in Australia, began searching for gold in the river. He eventually found some, and once his secret was out, the Duke of Sutherland began parcelling off small plots of land to speculators. At its height, more than 500 men were prospecting in the area, and a shanty town soon sprung up. But in 1870, when sportsmen complained that the prospectors were interfering with their fishing and hunting, the Duke put a stop to it all, and the gold rush was over. There is still gold there today, and it is a favourite spot for amateur gold panners.

AROUND WICK

LATHERON

17 miles S of Wick on the A9

Latheron, unlike other villages in the area, has a name derived from Gaelic, "làthair roin", meaning "resort of seals". Within the old church, which dates from 1735, is the **Clan Gunn Heritage Centre**. It traces the history of the clan from its Norse origins right through to the present day. At Dunbeath, three miles south of Latheron, is the thatched **Laidhay Croft Museum**, which shows a typical Highland house, with living quarters, byre and stable all under the one roof. And in an old schoolhouse at Dunbeath is the **Dunbeath Heritage Centre**, managed by the Dunbeath Preservation Trust. It has displays, photographs and documents about the village.

Neil Gunn (1891-1973), one of Scotland's finest writers was born in Dunbeath and attended the very school in which the Heritage Centre is located. In books such as *The Grey Coast* and *Morning Tide* he drew on his intimate knowledge of the Caithness area and its people to create highly readable tales.

HELMSDALE

37 miles SW of Wick on the A9

Within this little fishing port is **Timespan**, a visitor centre that tells the story of Helmsdale and its surrounding communities. There are exhibits about the Clearances, Picts, Norse raids, witches and much more.

In 1567 a famous tragedy - said to have inspired Shakespeare to write *Hamlet* - was enacted here. Isobel Sinclair had hopes that her son would claim the earldom of Sutherland. She therefore invited the then earl and countess and their heir to dinner one evening and poured them poisoned wine. The earl and countess died, but the heir survived. Unfortunately, Isobel's own son drank the wine and also died.

ALTNAHARRA

82 miles SW of Wick on the A836

Sitting close to the western tip of Loch Naver, Altnaharra is a small village famous as a centre for game fishing. Loch Naver is the source of the River Naver, one of the best salmon rivers in Sutherland, which flows northwards through Strathnaver to the sea.

On a narrow, unclassified road from Altnaharra to Strath More and Loch Hope are the remains of the **Dun Dornaigil Broch**. Some of its walls rise to 22 feet, and over the entrance is a strange triangular lintel. A few miles beyond the broch is Ben Hope, at 3041 feet Scotland's most northerly Munro.

The B873 strikes east from Altnaharra along Strathnaver, following the loch and then the river, until it joins the B871, which joins the A836 south of Bettyhill. It is a superb run, with magnificent scenery.

THURSO

21 miles NW of Wick on the A9

Thurso is a former fishing port on Caithness's northern coast and is the most northerly town on mainland Britain. It was once a Norse settlement, with its name meaning "river of the god Thor". The ruins of **St Peter's Church** stand in the old part of the town and date from the 16th century. It was once the private chapel of the Bishop of Caithness, whose summer retreat was **Scrabster Castle**, of which only scant remains survive.

The **Thurso Heritage Museum** is located within an old cottage in Lyn Street and has displays and mementos relating to the town's past. It is open during the summer. At the mouth of the river are the ruins of the mock-Gothic **Thurso Castle**, built in 1878 by Sir Tollemarche Sinclair on the site of a much older castle. At Crosskirk, a few miles west of the town, are the ruins of **St Mary's Chapel**, dating from the 12th century. All that remains is the nave. At Holborn Head is the Clett Rock, a huge natural pillar, or stack, situated just offshore.

Eight miles west of the town, on the A836, is Dounreay, where Scotland's first operational nuclear reactor was built. The **Dounreay Visitor Centre** explains about nuclear power and the history of the site.

BETTYHILL
53 miles NW of Wick on the A836

Within the old St Columba's Church at Bettyhill is the **Strathnaver Museum**, with exhibits about local history, most notably the Clearances and Clan

Mackay. Strathnaver was probably the most notorious area in the Highlands for the eviction of tenants so that they could be replaced with the more profitable sheep. Between 1811 and 1821, some 15,000 people were cleared from this area which formed part of the estate of the Countess of Sutherland. Unusually for the time, she then had a new village built which she named after herself.

The whole area abounds with prehistoric archaeological sites, and within the kirkyard of the museum is a burial stone dating to the 8th or 9th century. The £190,000 **Strathnaver Trail** to the east of the village opened in May 2003 and takes you round 16 sites which date from 5000BC to the 20th century.

TONGUE
65 miles NW of Wick off the A838

Tongue is a small village situated near the shallow Kyle of Tongue. It's name means exactly what it says, as it comes from the Norse *tunga*, meaning a tongue, in this case a tongue of land. In 1972 a causeway was built across it to take the A838 westwards towards Loch Eribol and Durness.

The ruins of **Varrich Castle** (Caisteal Bharraich in Gaelic) sit on a rise above the loch, with a footpath taking you to them. It dates from the 14th century, and was once a Mackay stronghold.

The 16th century House of Tongue, overlooking the Kyle of Tongue, was also a Mackay stronghold. It was destroyed in the 17th century, with the Mackays

198 FARR BAY INN

Bettyhill
Former Manse in delightful village offering quality home-cooked food and spacious en suite rooms.

‖ ⊨ *see page 467*

•

In 1746 a ship - the Hazard - carrying gold coinage for Charles Edward Stuart's Jacobite army tried to take shelter in the Kyle of Tongue to escape HMS Sheerness, a government frigate. The crew took the coinage ashore for safekeeping but were followed and captured by some Mackay clansmen, who were supporters of the government. The crewmen threw the coins into a loch, but most were later recovered

•

building a new house sometime in the 18th century. The gardens are open to the public.

The A836 south from Tongue to Lairg passes alongside beautiful **Loch Loyal** for part of the way, and has some beautiful views.

JOHN O'GROATS

13 miles N of Wick on the A99

John O' Groats is 873 miles by road from Land's End in Cornwall, and 290 miles from Kirkmaiden in Wigtownshire, Scotland's most southerly parish. It is believed to be named after a Dutchman called Jan de Groot who, in 1496, paid a handsome sum to James IV for the exclusive right to run a ferry from here to the Orkney Islands. The business prospered but Jan, it appears, was burdened with a dysfunctional family - eight sons who constantly quarrelled over who should take precedence after Jan's death. In an inspired attempt to secure domestic harmony, Jan built an octagonal house so that each of his fractious children could enter by his own door and sit at (his) head of the table. A much less appealing version of the story is that Jan erected an eight-sided shelter for his ferry customers to protect them from the North Sea's gusting winds, whatever their direction. Whichever interpretation is true, a mound with a flagstaff marks the supposed site of the house/shelter, and nearby is a much-photographed sign pole, its arms pointing in all directions, each inscribed with the number of miles from John O'Groats to far-flung places.

Nearby, the **Last House in Scotland Museum** contains displays and artefacts about the area.

To the west is Dunnet Head, the most northerly point on the British mainland. Between the two is the **Castle of Mey**, the late Queen Mother's Scottish home. Built in the 16th century by the 4th Earl, it is a fairy story castle with a picturesque jumble of towers, turrets and castellations. As far as possible, the castle is still set out very much as when the Queen Mother stayed here.

Mary-Ann's Cottage in the village of Dunnet shows how successive generations of one crofting family lived and worked over the last 150 years. The cottage is named after its last owner, Mary-Ann Calder, whose grandfather had built the house in 1850. Mary-Ann lived in the house until 1990 when she was 93 years old. She then entered a nursing home in Wick where she died

The **Northlands Viking Centre** in the Old School House at Auckengill, five miles south of John O'Groats, tells the story of the Vikings and Norsemen in the area, as well as recounting the life of John Nicolson, a local artist and mason. Ten minutes away are the remains of the **Nybster Broch**, built between 200 BC and AD 200.

The Western Isles

Also known as the Outer Hebrides, the Western Isles stretch for 130 miles from north to south, a string of islands which in most places rise no more than a few hundred feet. Battered by the full force of Atlantic storms, the nearest landfall to the west is Labrador. It sounds desolate but there are miles of empty beaches with dazzling white sands, unbelievably clear water and breathtaking sunsets. There is also a fascinating range of flora and fauna here with most islands having at least one Nature Reserve. Deer and otters abound, and the machair (the meadows bordering the sandy beaches) brim with flowers in summer. The seas are home to dolphins, basking sharks, whales and seals. In fact, some people claim that the waters surrounding the Western Isles are the most populated in Britain.

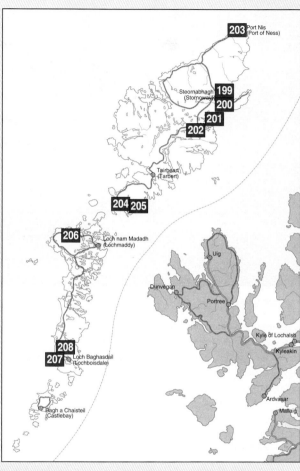

Sunset, Outer Hebrides

Humans have inhabited the islands for more than 6000 years and there are numerous prehistoric remains, most notably the Callanish Standing Stones - the second largest stone circle in Britain - and the Carloway Broch.

These islands are the last bastion of true Gaeldom in Scotland. In some places English, though spoken and understood perfectly, is still a second language. Some are also bastions of Free Presbyterianism, where the Sabbath is strictly observed, and work or leisure activities of any kind on a Sunday is frowned upon. To complicate the position further there are some islands that are almost wholly Roman Catholic, never having been influenced by the Scottish Reformation in 1560.

Of the main southern islands, Berneray, North Uist, Benbecula, South Uist and Eriskay are joined by causeways. North Uist connects to Harris by a ferry between An t-Obbe and Berneray, and Barra has a ferry connection with Eriskay. Each island in the chain has its own flavour, and all are noted for their quality of light, especially in summer.

ISLE OF LEWIS AND HARRIS

The main island is divided into two parts, Lewis and Harris, an ancient arrangement going back as far as the 13th century. Though joined geographically, they are usually considered to be two separate islands, and indeed the differences between them are marked. A natural boundary of mountains and high moorland runs between Loch Resort on the west and Loch Seaforth on the east, explaining the differences.

Lewis is the northern, and larger part, and up until the mid 1970s was within the county of Ross and Cromarty. Harris (and the smaller islands to the south) came under Inverness-shire. Now they all form one administrative area, with the capital being Stornoway.

The underlying rock of Lewis is gneiss, one of the oldest in the world. It is largely impermeable, so does not absorb water. For this reason the interior of the island is a large, empty peat moorland dotted with shallow lochs, while most of the settlements are on the coast. Harris is more mountainous, and has peaks reaching 2500 feet. It is also an area where the underlying rocks break through to the surface like bones, giving an essentially bleak but nevertheless attractive landscape.

Various attempts have been made over the years to encourage industry, most notably when Lord Leverhulme bought both Lewis and Harris in 1918 and tried to promote fishing. Today, the islands rely on fishing, crofting and tourism, with the weaving of Harris Tweed being an important industry on Lewis and Harris, although currently under threat.

STORNOWAY

With a population of about 6000, Stornoway is by far the largest community on the island, the political and commercial centre of the Western Isles. The town has a fine natural harbour and a small airport serving Glasgow, Inverness and Benbecula. Its harbour is no longer busy with the thousand or more fishing boats registered at Stornoway a century ago, but there are regular ferries to and from Ullapool, and a small active fishing fleet whose catches are sold at the fish markets on Tuesday and Thursday evenings.

The town's architecture is generally functional rather than attractive but there are two notable exceptions. **Lews Castle** was built in the 1840s and 50s by James Matheson, a businessman who earned a fortune in the Far East trading in tea and opium. The castle later became part of the University of the Highlands but is currently disused but with plans to convert it into a hotel and museum. The other building of interest is the former town hall, built in full-blooded Scottish Baronial style. It now houses the **Museum nan Eilean** which has artefacts and exhibits highlighting the history

199 THE FLAT AIGNISH

Stornoway

A self catering property in an ideal location for exploring the Isle of Lewis

see page 466

200 THE CALEDONIAN HOTEL

Stornoway

Close to the quayside with an outstanding restaurant, bar food, regular entertainment and en suite rooms.

see page 468

201 LOCHS HOUSE

Ranish, Isle of Lewis

A fantastic bungalow offering Bed, Breakfast and Evening Meals all year round. The perfect get away!

see page 469

202 BORISHADER COTTAGE

Habost

This three star holiday cottage offers the very best in comfortable accommodation and enjoys some fantastic views over Loch Erisort.

see page 469

and archaeology of both the island of Lewis and Stornoway itself,

Other buildings of some interest include **The Parish Church of St Columba**, dating from 1794, and **St Peter's Episcopal Church** (1839) whose two main treasures are David Livingstone's Bible and an old font from a chapel on the Flannan Isles, about 33 miles west of Lewis in the Atlantic. Its bell, which was made in 1631, was once the town bell that summoned townspeople to important meetings. The Gothic-style **Free Church** in Kenneth Street has the distinction of being the best attended church in all of Britain, with the Sunday evening congregation regularly exceeding 1500. Many visitors to Stornoway are taken aback by the Sabbaticalism of the Free Church, the "Wee Free", which imposes a strict observance of Sunday as a day of rest. Shops, pubs, cafés, garages and public transport all close down and even the swings in the children's playgrounds are padlocked.

Another building of interest is the modern **An Lanntair Arts Centre** which sits across from the ferry terminal and has contemporary and traditional exhibitions, as well as varied programmes of music and drama highlighting the Gaelic culture. In mid-July each year, it is at the heart of the Hebridean Celtic Festival celebrating traditional folk and Celtic music,

One of Stornoway's most famous sons was the 18th century explorer and fur trader Sir Alexander Mackenzie, who gave his name to the Mackenzie River in Canada. In Francis Street, on the site of his house, is Martins Memorial, built in 1885.

More than 1150 men of Lewis died in the two world wars, and the **Stornoway War Memorial** must be the most imposing in Britain. It stands on the 300-feet high Cnoc nan Uan, and itself rises to a height of 85 feet.

The Western Isles are synonymous with Harris tweed, and at the Lewis **Loom Centre** on Bayhead you can find out about its history and about how it is woven. To attain the "orb" symbol of genuine Harris tweed, the cloth needs to be woven from "virgin wool produced in Scotland", then spun, dyed and hand woven in the Outer Hebrides.

West of Stornoway, on the Eye Peninsula, are the ruins of **St Columba's Church**, built in the 14th century on the site of a small monastic cell founded by St Catan in the 6th century. It is said that 19 MacLeod chiefs are buried here.

AROUND STORNOWAY

CALLANISH (CALANAIS)

15 miles W of Stornoway off the A858

Dating back at least 4000 years, the **Callanish Stone Circle** (Historic Scotland) is second only to Stonehenge in importance in Britain. It is more than just a circle of upright stones. Four great arms made up of monoliths radiate from it to the north, south, east and west, with the northern arm (which veers slightly to the east) having a double row of stones as if enclosing an approach way. And in the middle of the circle is the tallest stone of them all, measuring more than 15 feet in height.

It is a mysterious place, and has attracted many stories and myths over the years. One story tells of a race of giants who met to discuss how to defeat the new religion of Christianity that was spreading throughout the islands. This so incensed St Kieran, a Celtic monk and missionary, that he turned them all to stone. Another says that the stones were brought to Lewis by a great priest king who employed "black men" to erect them. The men who died building the circle were buried within it.

A visitors centre next to the stones tries to uncover the truth behind them, which may have something to do with primitive ritual and predicting the seasons for agricultural purposes.

SHAWBOST

16 miles W of Stornoway on the A858

Housed within a former church, the **Sgoil Shiaboist Museum** (Shawbost School Museum) has artefacts and objects collected by school pupils 30 years ago as part of a project that illustrates the way people used to live in Lewis. Nearby is the thatched **Norse Mill and Kiln**, a restored water mill of the type used in Lewis up until the mid-20th century.

The Shawbost Stone Circle, near the shores of the small Loch Raoinavat, only has two stones left

standing. They are difficult to find, and good walking gear is recommended if you want to find them.

CARLOWAY (CÀRLABHAGH)

19 miles W of Stornoway on the A858

The 2000-year-old **Dun Carloway Broch,** overlooking Loch Roag, is one of the best-preserved brochs in Scotland. It is more than 47 feet in diameter, and its walls are 22 feet high in places. Some of the galleries and internal stairways are still intact. The Doune Broch Centre has displays explaining what life must have been like within fortifications such as this.

GREAT BERNERA (BEARNARAIGH)

22 miles W of Stornoway off the B8059

The small island of Great Bernera measures only six miles long by three miles wide at its widest. It is connected to the mainland by the Great Bernera Bridge, opened in 1953 and the first bridge in the

One-and-a-quarter miles north of Carloway is the Gearrannan Blackhouse Village. It faces the Atlantic and is a huddle of traditional thatched cottages dating from the 19th century. They have two distinctive features: there is no chimney and they housed animals as well as people. The animals made the house warmer and meant fewer buildings were needed. The smoke rising from the peat fire into the roof was also practical - it killed bugs and the smoke-enriched thatch made excellent fertiliser for the fields. These cottages were lived in up until 1974 and were restored, complete with box beds, by the Garenin Trust between 1991 and 2001.

Dun Carloway Broch, Carloway

During archaeological excavations at Barvas, a 200-year-old Iron Age cemetery was uncovered. One of the finds was a beautiful iron and copper alloy bracelet, the first of its kind to be found anywhere in Scotland.

203 THE CROSS INN

Port of Ness

A comfortable hotel, which is in a fantastic location for the perfect get-away.

see *page 470*

country made from pre-stressed concrete girders. The **Community Centre and Museum** has displays about the island, and also sells tea, coffee and cakes. On the lovely beach at **Bostadh** an Iron Age village has been excavated, and a reconstruction of an Iron Age house built.

A cairn commemorates those men who took part in the Bernera Riot of 1874, when crofters stood up for their right of tenure. Three of them eventually stood trial, though a later Act of Parliament gave them the rights they were fighting for.

BARVAS (BARABHAS)

13 miles NW of Stornoway on the A858

At one time, most of the population of Lewis lived in small cottages known as blackhouses. On the west coast of the island, at Arnol, is the **Arnol Blackhouse** (Historic Scotland) which shows what life was like in one of them. People and animals lived under the one roof, separated by thin walls, with the roof usually being of thatch and turf. They had tiny windows because of the seasonal gales and rain and the fact that glass was very expensive. The thick, dry stone walls (with a central core of clay and earth) kept the cottage cool in summer and warm in winter.

The Arnol house has been furnished in typical fashion, with a clay floor. There is no fireplace, the fire being placed centrally, with no chimney. The houses got their name in the mid-19th century to distinguish them from the more

modern white houses, which had mortar binding the stones. There is also an interpretation centre in a nearby cottage, which has a model of a typical blackhouse showing how they were made.

SHADAR (SIADAR)

16 miles NW of Stornoway on the A857

The **Steinacleit Stone Circle and Standing Stones** sit on a low hill, and date from between 2000 and 3000 BC. The stones are placed more in the shape of an oval than a circle, and archaeologists are unsure whether it is indeed a stone circle, a burial cairn or the remains of a settlement of some kind.

A mile or so up the road is the **Borgh Pottery,** owned and run by Alex and Sue Blair whose work is on display in the showroom. A range of carefully selected gifts is also available to compliment the ceramics including locally made Harris Tweed items and soaps.

BALLANTRUSHAL (BAILE AN TRUISELL)

15 miles NW of Stornoway on the B857

The **Clach an Trushal** (Historic Scotland), at 18 feet high, is the tallest standing stone in Scotland. It is said to mark the site of an ancient battle. In the 19th century several feet of peat were cut away from around its base, revealing the true height.

TARBERT (TAIRBEART)

37 miles S of Stornoway on the A859

The small village of Tarbert has a ferry connection with Uig on Skye.

This is the starting point of South Harris where an isthmus no more than half a mile wide separates East Loch Tarbert, which is an arm of the Minch, from West Loch Tarbert, which is an inlet of the Atlantic. In fact, *Tairbeart* in Gaelic means "isthmus" or "place of portage", where boats were dragged across land from one stretch of water to another. **Amhuinnsuidhe Castle** was built in 1868 by the Earl of Dunsmore who owned Harris. It was the earl's wife who introduced the weaving of Harris tweed to the island. The castle was subsequently owned by the Bulmer family, which founded the cider firm. It was here that J.M. Barrie wrote his play *Mary Rose*. It is now used as an upmarket conference centre.

SCALPAY (SCALPAIGH)
42 miles S of Stornoway

The tiny island of Scalpay, measuring three miles by two, lies off Harris's east coast. It is connected to the mainland by the £7m Scalpay Bridge, the biggest civil engineering project ever undertaken in the Western Isles. It was opened in 1998 by Tony Blair, the first serving prime minister ever to visit the Western Isles. The visit is also remembered because of the biting attack he received from some of the island's more militant inhabitants - *culicoides impunctatus*, more commonly known as the midge. The first official crossing of the bridge was made in December 1997, when the island's oldest inhabitant, 103-years-old Kirsty Morrison, was taken across it in a vintage car.

RODEL (ROGHADAL)
61 miles S of Stornoway on the A859

Rodel sits near the southern tip of Harris and is famous for **St Clement's Church**, burial place of the MacLeods. It was built in 1500 by Alasdair Crotach ("hunchback") McLeod, who lived in the church's tower from 1540 to his death in 1547. He is still within the church, in a magnificent tomb that shows carvings of his home at Dunvegan on Skye. By 1784 the church was ruinous, but in that year Alexander MacLeod of Berneray, a captain with the East India Company, restored it.

OTHER WESTERN ISLES

BARRA (BARRAIGH)
105 miles S of Stornoway

Barra ("Barr's Island") is the southernmost of the Western Isles and despite its small area, just 4 miles wide and 8 miles long, has been described as the "Western Isles in miniature". There are sandy beaches and peaks that rise to 1260 feet, prehistoric relics and even a medieval fortress, **Kisimul Castle** (Historic Scotland). It stands on a small island in the bay and is the ancestral home of the MacNeils, once notorious for their piracy and vanity. The old chiefs of Clan Macneil had the reputation of being haughty and proud. When one Macneil Chief had finished his dinner, he would send a servant up to the ramparts of Kisimul Castle and announce to

204 CARMINISH HOUSE

Leverburgh

An award-winning B&B boasting stunning panoramic views over the Sound of Harris and the Carminish Islands.

see page 471

205 CNOC NA BA

Finsbay

A beautiful self-contained, four bedroom, property, Cnoc Na Ba is perfect for those wanting to explore the Western Isles.

see page 471

●

The ruined Cille-bharraidh (Church of St Barr) is located at the north end of Barra, and was the burial place of the MacNeils. Also buried here is Sir Compton Mackenzie, who wrote Whisky Galore *(see also Eriskay). The island is predominantly Catholic, and at Heaval, a mile north east of Castlebay, is a marble statue of the Madonna and Child called* Our Lady of the Sea.

●

the world: "as the MacNeil has dined, the other kings and princes of the world may now dine also."

After many years of neglect, the 45th chief of the MacNeil clan bought the castle back in 1937 and it has since been restored to its original appearance. The castle is reached by ferry from Castlebay, the only settlement of any size on the island and the proud possessor of the only airfield in Britain that disappears under water twice a day - scheduled flights to the tiny island land on the beach here.

NORTH UIST (UIBHIST A TUATH)

59 miles SW of Stornoway

Like most of the Western Isles, North Uist is low lying, with more water than land making up its total area of 74,884 acres. Loch Scadavay is the biggest of the lochs and although it only has an area of eight square miles, it has a shoreline measuring 51 miles in length. The island was given to the MacDonalds of Sleat in 1495 by James IV. They sold it in 1855, having cleared many of the tenants to make way for sheep. The highest point on the island, at 1127 feet, is Eaval, near the southeast corner. The island has a ferry service to An t-Obbe in Harris from Berneray, and one to Skye from Lochmaddy, the island's capital where most of the hotels and B&Bs are to be found.

Taigh Chearsabhagh, a museum and arts centre is housed in an old inn dating from the early 18th century. Near the village is **Barpa Langais,** a Neolithic burial cairn with its burial chamber almost complete. Half a mile south east of it is the **Pubull Phinn Stone Circle**.

The stark ruins of **Teampull na Trionaid** ("Trinity Temple") stand on the south west shore. This was once a great place of learning in the Western Isles and some people claim that it was Scotland's first university with scholars and students making their way here from all over the country, one of them being Duns Scotus (see also Duns). The temple was founded in the early 13th century by one Beathag, a prioress from the priory on Iona and daughter of Somerled, Lord of the Isles. By the end of the 15th century, however, its influence began to wane, and during the Reformation it was attacked. Valuable books, manuscripts and works of art were tossed into the sea and much of the island's heritage was lost. The other building on the site is Teampull MacBhiocair, (MacVicar's Temple), where the teachers were buried.

It was in this area, in 1601, that the **Battle of Carinish** took place, the last battle on British soil not to have involved firearms. A troop of MacLeods from Harris was raiding the island and took shelter in the Trinity Temple buildings when attacked by the MacDonalds. The MacDonalds ignored the status of the temple, and slaughtered every MacLeod clansman except two, who escaped.

On the island's west coast, off the A865, is the RSPB's **Balranald Nature Reserve**, where you can see waders and seabirds in various habitats.

BENBECULA
(BEINN NA FAOGHLA)

80 miles SW of Stornoway

Benbecula is sandwiched between North and South Uist, with a landscape that is low and flat and dotted with shallow lochans. Rueval, its highest peak, soars to all of 403 feet. The island marks the boundary between the Protestant islands to the north and the Roman Catholic islands to the south. There is no ferry terminal on the island as it is connected to South Uist and North Uist by causeways.

To the south of the village, on the B892, are the ruins of **Nunton Chapel**, supposed to have been a nunnery built in the 14th century. It was Lady Clanranald from nearby Nunton House (built from the stones of Nunton Chapel) who gave Charles Edward Stuart his disguise as a serving girl when he escaped from Benbecula to Skye in 1746.

Borve Castle, about three miles south of Balivanich, was owned by Ranald, son of John of Islay, in the 14th century. The ruins show a typical tower house of the period. Within the school at **Lionacleit**, three miles south of Balivanich, is a small museum.

SOUTH UIST
(UIBHIST A DEAS)

87 miles SW of Stornoway

Running down the east side of South Uist is a range of low mountains, with Beinn Mhor being

the highest at 2034 feet. The west side of the island is gentler, with fine white sandy beaches. Lochboisdale, in the southeast corner, is the largest village on the island, and has a ferry connection to Mallaig, Oban and Castlebay on Barra.

The island is one of the few places in Scotland never to have fully embraced the Reformation, and is predominantly Roman Catholic. To the northwest of the island, at Rueval, is the famous statute of **Our Lady of the Isles**, overlooking Loch Bee. Standing 30 feet high it was erected in 1957 and sculpted by Hew Lorimer of Edinburgh. At the **Loch Druidibeag Nature Reserve**, which is close by, many birds such as greylag geese and mute swans, can be observed.

It was in South Uist, near Milton on Loch Kildonan, that **Flora MacDonald** was born in 1722. Her house is now completely ruinous, though the foundations can still be seen. She was no simple Gaelic lass, but the daughter of a

> •
>
> *The main settlement in Benbecula is Balivanich, or Baile na Mhanaich, meaning "Monk's Town". It stands on the west coast and beside it is a small airstrip. The scant ruins of Teampall Chaluim Cille, founded by St Torranan, lie close to the village.*
>
> •

Borve Castle, Benbecula

207 ARD NA MARA

South Uist

A delightful, modern and spacious B&B located in a rural setting with views of lochs and the sea.

see page 472

208 298 KILPHEDER

South Uist

A wonderful self catering property with 3 bedrooms, a lounge, kitchen and spacious garden. Local amenities are a short drive away.

see page 472

prosperous landowning farmer who died when she was young. Her mother then married Hugh MacDonald, a member of the great MacDonald of Sleat family. She was brought up in Skye and went to school in Sleat and Edinburgh.

Kildonan Museum, north of Lochboisdale on the A865, has displays and exhibits on local history, as well as a tearoom and shop. The basis of the museum is a collection of artefacts gathered by the island priest, Father John Morrison, in the 1950s and 60s. Further north along the A865 are the ruins of **Ormiclate Castle**, built between 1701 and 1708 as a sumptuous residence for the chief of Clanranald. Alas, the chief's stay there was short lived, as it burnt down in 1715 after a rowdy Jacobite party.

Off the south coast of South Uist is the small island of Eriskay (from the Norse for "Eric's Island"), which is joined to South Uist by a causeway opened in 2002 and costing £9.8m. It is noted for one of the most beautiful of Gaelic songs, the *Eriskay Love Lilt*. It was here, on 23rd July 1745, that Charles Edward Stuart first set foot on Scottish soil when he stepped off a French ship to reclaim the British throne for the Stuarts. The beach where he landed is now called Prince's Beach, and legend says that his first action was to plant the sea convolvulus which now thrives here.

It was in February 1941 that another event took place which was to make Eriskay famous. The **SS Politician** was heading towards the United States from Liverpool with a cargo of 260,000 bottles of whisky when it was wrecked off Calvey Island in the Sound of Eriskay. Legend has it that as soon as the seamen were removed from the ship to safety, work began on "rescuing" the cargo. Eventually Customs and Excise men appeared on the island but by this time the bottles had been spirited away into peat bogs and other hidey-holes. Only 19 people were charged with illegal possession.

Sir Compton Mackenzie used the incident as the basis for his novel *Whisky Galore*, made into a film in 1948. The wreckage can still sometimes be seen at exceptionally low tide. In the late 1980s an attempt was made to get at the rest of the cargo but this proved unsuccessful.

The highest point on the island is Ben Scrien, at 609 feet. It is an easy climb, and gives magnificent views. The island's native pony, the grey and black Eriskay pony, was at one time used to carry seaweed and peat on panniers slung across their back. In the 1950s they nearly died out but now are on the increase again. They are the last surviving examples of the once common Hebridean ponies which were popular all over the islands.

Orkney & Shetland

For more than 400 years, the Orkney and Shetland archipelagos were governed by Norsemen and the islands still maintain strong links with Scandinavia. Many of the place names are pure Norse and the ancient Norn language was still in use on Shetland until about one hundred years ago. Even today, the local accent is much closer to Scandinavian rhythms and inflections that it is to Scottish English.

Orkney has some 70 islands although only 19 of them are inhabited. But they have been inhabited for more than 5000 years and can boast northern Europe's greatest concentration of

prehistoric monuments. Shara Brae on the Mainland (the largest island, some 20 miles long), is one of the best preserved Stone Age settlements in Europe and across the islands there are literally hundreds of chambered tombs, stone circles and Iron Age brochs, or fortified dwellings.

Whaling and fishing have been the most important industries of the Orkney Islands and Orcadians were at one time the preferred employees of the Hudson Bay Company. During both World Wars the naval base at Scapa Flow brought much-needed prosperity, a role performed nowadays by the North Sea oil industry. The generally flat and treeless but fertile land produces an abundance of wildflowers in the summer and the coastal scenery is magnificent with towering cliffs supporting a huge bird population during the breeding season.

On Orkney, says the local tourist board, "the commonplace if frequently extraordinary". Where else would you find a road sign asking you to give way to otters, or discover that your beach picnic has been raided by a seal? Killer whales patrol the surrounding waters and on Hoy colonies of mountain hares study passers-by with an inquisitive interest. As the Orcadian poet, Edwin Muir, recorded:

> *The Orkney I was born into was a place*
> *Where there was no great distinction between*
> *The ordinary and the fabulous; the lives of*
> *living men turned into legend.*

KIRKWALL

Kirkwall has a population of about 4800 and was granted its charter as a royal burgh in 1486. It sits almost in the centre of Mainland, and divides the island into East Mainland and West Mainland. It is a lively, busy place of old stone buildings and streets paved in flagstones with a shopping centre that serves all of the islands.

The most imposing building in Kirkwall is **St Magnus Cathedral,** founded in 1127 in honour of Magnus, Earl of Orkney, who had been assassinated by his cousin ten years earlier. As Magnus was buried, a heavenly light irradiated the sky, divine confirmation it was thought of the earl's sanctity. The cathedral attracted pilgrims from across the extensive Earldom of Orkney, their donations helping to fund the building of the present, immensely impressive church with its pink, sandstone columns and arches of exposed brickwork. During restoration work back in 1911, a skull and some bones were found concealed in one of the pillars. The skull was cleft as if by an axe, exactly the way Magnus was said to have met his death. These relics are now on display in the cathedral along with a monument to the dead of the Royal Oak (torpedoed in Scapa Flow in 1939 with the loss of 833 men), and a collection of 16th and 17th century tombstones engraved with cheerful inscriptions such as "Remember death waits us all, the hour none knows".

A mere 100 yards away is **Earl Patrick's Palace** (Historic Scotland) which has been described as one of the finest examples of Renaissance architecture to have survived in Scotland. Built around 1600 by the tyrannical Earl Patrick Stewart, the palace is now roofless but the superb central hall, the colossal fireplaces and the dismal dungeons evoke a powerful impression of upper-class Orcadian life in the early 17th century.

Also in ruins, the **Bishop's Palace** (Historic Scotland) dates mainly from the 12th century when it was built for Bishop William the Old. The Round Tower (called the "Moosie Too" by locals), however, was built by Bishop Reid between 1541 and 1548. It was within the palace, in 1263, that King Haakon IV of Norway died, having just been defeated at the Battle of Largs (see also Largs). He was buried in Kirkwall Cathedral, but his body was later taken back to Bergen in Norway.

Standing in its own courtyard opposite the cathedral with an ornamental garden to the rear, Tankerness House is a fine 16th century town house, considerably enlarged in the early 1700s and now home to the interesting **Orkney Museum** which celebrates some 5000 years of Orkney history. Look out for the Pictish board games, an Iron Age bone shovel and antique bowls made from the vertebrae of whales. The Baikie Drawing room within the museum shows what a typical late 18th and early 19th century drawing room would have

209 WEST END HOTEL

Kirkwall

Popular town centre hotel serving delicious food and offering comfortable en suite accommodation.

see page 473

210 ALBERT HOTEL

Kirkwall

Town centre hotel with good traditional food and boutique style en suite guest rooms.

see page 474

211 EAST BANK HOUSE

Kirkwall

Overlooking the town and harbour, and offering quality en suite B&B or self-catering accommodation.

see page 474

looked like.

More specialised interests are catered for at the **Orkney Wireless Museum** which has examples of wartime and domestic wireless sets used on the islands. It was founded by local man Jim MacDonald who had a lifetime's fascination with wireless and radio sets, and amassed a huge collection.

Also recommended is a visit to the **Highland Park Distillery,** Scotland's most northerly distillery, where you can tour the lovely old buildings and enjoy a complimentary dram.

AROUND KIRKWALL

MINE HOWE

5 miles SE of Kirkwall on the A960

This deep, subterranean structure within a large mound was examined by the TV programme *Time Team* but they were unable to establish its real purpose. It was originally uncovered in 1946 and then reburied to preserve it. It consists of a chamber accessed by a stone-lined tunnel with steps. The latest thinking is that it dates from the Iron Age and had a religious significance.

LAMB HOLM

7 miles S of Kirkwall on the A961

After the sinking of the *Royal Oak* by a U-boat in 1939 a string of islands to the south of Mainland were joined by causeways called the Churchill Barriers to prevent submarines from slipping through again. On the 99-acre Lamb Holm, one of the islands, is the ornate

Italian Chapel. It was built by Italian prisoners-of-war who had been captured in North Africa in 1942 and were working on the causeways. The work is remarkable considering its basis is two Nissen huts and various pieces of cast-off metal and wood. In 1960 some of the ex-POWs were invited to return to the island to restore it. Mass is still said here every day during the summer months.

KIRBISTER

8 miles SW of Kirkwall on the A964

Kirbister Museum is the last un-restored example of a traditional 'firehoose' in Northern Europe. Dating back to at least the 16th century, the house has a central hearth and a stone bed (neuk), a unique survival. Astonishingly, Kirbister was occupied up until the 1960s. Outside, there's an 'implement shed' containing a collection of farming memorabilia, a lovely Victorian walled garden and a putting green.

ORPHIR

9 miles SW of Kirkwall off the A964

During early Norse rule, Orphir was one of the main Orcadian settlements. Orphir Church was built in the 11th or 12 century and dedicated to St Nicholas, some say by Haakon, who murdered St Magnus, possibly as an act of penance after a pilgrimage to Jerusalem. It was a circular church about 18 feet in diameter, with a small apse at its eastern end, and was the only such medieval church in Scotland. All that remains now is the apse and some of the east wall. An Interpretation Centre, next to the church, explains the ruins.

HOY

17 miles SW of Kirkwall

Scapa Flow, the vast expanse of water between Hoy and Mainland, is one of the best natural harbours in the world. After World War I the German fleet was brought to Scapa Flow while a decision was made about its future. However, the German officers decided the fleet's future themselves - they scuttled the ships. Most still lie at the bottom of the sea, a constant attraction for divers. The **Scapa Flow Visitor Centre** at Lyness houses an important record of the role the Royal Navy played in Orkney during both World Wars. Occupying a former pump house, the centre provides a comprehensive series of interpretative displays, while outside there's a fascinating collection of vintage military equipment. World War I displays include a propeller and other artefacts from *HMS Hampshire,* mined off Orkney in 1916 with the loss of Lord Kitchener. Guns salvaged from the German High Seas Fleet form part of the display along with railway engines on tracks.

The **Old Man of Hoy** is Great Britain's tallest and most famous sea stack. Made of sandstone, it is more than 445 feet high and rises off the island's north west coast, a constant challenge to climbers. The first successful climb was in 1966 and TV cameras were there to record it. At the southwest end of

the island is a **Martello Tower,** erected between 1813 and 1815 to protect the island from the French.

The **Dwarfie Stone** is unique in the United Kingdom - a burial chamber dating from at least 3000 BC cut into a great block of sandstone. Some people claim, however, that it was not a tomb, but an ancient dwelling. The most amazing thing about it is that it was hollowed out using nothing but horn tools, antlers and pieces of rock.

216 MURRAY ARMS HOTEL

St Margaret's Hope

Traditional inn at the heart of quaint fishing village offering good home-made cooking and en suite accommodation.

see page 476

The Old Man of Hoy

217 FOINHAVEN B&B AND SELF-CATERING

Orphir

Choice of B&B or self-catering in spacious modern house in superb location with spectacular views.

🛏 see page 477

218 STROMNESS CAFÉ BAR

Stromness

Fully licensed café bar with waterside terrace serving appetising home-made fare based on local produce.

🍴 see page 477

219 ORCA GUEST HOUSE

Stromness

Family-run harbourside guest house offering both comfortable B&B and self-catering accommodation.

🛏 see page 478

MAES HOWE

9 miles W of Kirkwall off the A965

Maes Howe (Historic Scotland) lies within the Heart of Neolithic Orkney World Heritage Site, an astonishing collection of prehistoric sites. Excavated in 1861, Maes Howe is Britain's largest chambered cairn. In 1910 it was taken into state care, at which time the mound was "rounded off" to give it the appearance we see today. When archaeologists reached the main chamber, they discovered that the Vikings had beaten them to it, as there was Norse graffiti on the walls. The name "Maes Howe" comes from the Old Norse meaning "great mound". It is indeed a great, grassy hill, 36 feet high and 300 feet in circumference, and was built about 2700 BC. A long, narrow passage leads into a central chamber with smaller side chambers, which are roofed and floored with massive slabs.

One of the most evocative of the prehistoric monuments in Maes Howe is the **Ring of Brodgar**. Also dating from about 2700 BC, it still has 27 of its estimated original 60 stones. They are smaller than the Stenness Stones, around 7 feet high, and stand on a strip of land between two small lochs. Legend says that long ago a group of giants came to this spot during the night, and that one of their number began playing the fiddle. The giants began to dance in a circle, and so carried away were they that they never noticed the sun starting to rise. When the light struck them,

they were turned to stone.

Also looked after by Historic Scotland are the four **Stenness Standing Stones**, the largest such stones in Orkney and dating from about the same time as Maes Howe. Originally there were 12 of them and they formed a circle 104 feet in diameter. The tallest stone in this group is 16 feet high but not far away is an even taller stone, the **Watch Stone**, which is eighteen-and-a-half feet tall.

To the north of the Stenness Stones, near the shore of Harray Loch, is the **Barnhouse Settlement**, a neolithic village discovered in 1984. Agricultural activity over the years has destroyed much of it, though it is reckoned there were 15 dwellings on the site.

STROMNESS

16 miles W of Kirkwall on the A965

When Sir Walter Scott visited Orkney in 1814, he complained that Stromness: "cannot be traversed by a cart or even by a horse, for there are stairs up and down even in the principal street..."

Like Kirkwall, Stromness is basically one long winding road - simply known as "the street". From this street a great number of narrow lanes and closes branch off. This gives the town a convoluted character with steep narrow paths climbing the hillside on the north side of the street, while on the south, the houses and shops back onto the shore.

Orkney's second largest settlement, Stromness is also the home port of the vehicle ferry that plies between here and Scrabster in Caithness. Though it looks old and quaint, the town was founded in the 17th century and only received its burgh charter in 1817. The **Stromness Museum** in Alfred Street has displays on Scapa Flow, whaling, lighthouses and the Hudson's Bay Company which had a base here and employed many Orcadians.

Housed in a complex of buildings that sit on one of the town's many piers, **The Pier Arts Centre** was established in 1979 to provide a showcase for an important collection of British fine art donated to 'be held in trust for Orkney' by the author, peace activist and philanthropist Margaret Gardiner (1904-2005). Alongside the permanent collection the Centre curates a year round programme of changing exhibitions and events.

CLICK MILL
16 miles NW of Kirkwall on the B9057

Click Mill (Historic Scotland), with its turf covered roof, is the islands' last surviving example of a horizontal watermill, and got its name from the clicking sound it made when turning. They were once common throughout Scandinavia.

At Harray, a couple of miles south of the mill, is the **Corrigall Farm Museum**, housed in a 19th century farmhouse. Exhibits include a working barn with grain kiln and a loom.

SKARA BRAE
18 miles NW of Kirkwall on the B9056

In 1850, at the Bay of Skaill, a

Stone Age Village, Skara Brae

storm uncovered the remains of a village which was at least 5000 years old - older even than the Pyramids. It is the oldest known prehistoric village in Europe and the remains are now looked after by Historic Scotland. The remains show that the people who built it from stone were sophisticated and ingenious, and that the houses were comfortable and well appointed, with beds, dressers and cupboards made of stone, as wood was hard to come by. Archaeological evidence tells us that it was built by neolithic people who farmed, hunted and fished. When it was built, it stood some distance from the sea, but due to erosion over the years the sea is now on its doorstep.

Only 300 metres from the village is **Skaill House** (see panel), the finest mansion in Orkney. The

220 SKAILL HOUSE

Sandwick

A popular 17th century mansion, located in a secluded spot between the sea and the Loch of Skaill, Skaill House provides both the ideal get-away and perfect wedding venue.

see page 479

341

main part of the house was originally built in 1620 for George Graham, Bishop of Orkney, though it has been extended over the years. It houses a fine collection of furniture, including Bishop Graham's bed, on which are carved the words *GEO. GRAHAM ME FIERI FECIT* ("George Graham caused me to be made").

When Skaill House was being built, 15 skeletons were uncovered to the south of the South Wing. In the 1930s skeletons were also uncovered under the house itself. It is now thought that the house was built on the site of a Christian Pictish cemetery. It is no wonder that Skaill is said to be haunted.

BROUGH OF BIRSAY
20 miles NW of Kirkwall off the A966

This little island, which is connected to the mainland at low tide by a narrow causeway, has the remains of a Norse settlement and an early medieval chapel dedicated to St Peter (once the cathedral of the diocese of Orkney). After he was killed, St Magnus was possibly buried here until such time as his body could be taken to the newly built St Magnus Cathedral in Kirkwall. When visiting the island, the times of tides must be taken into account. The tourism office at Kirkwall can advise.

The area on Mainland opposite the island is also called Birsay and here you can see the ruins of **Earl Stewart's Palace.** It was built about 1574 by Robert, Earl of Orkney, a cruel, unpopular man and father of Patrick, who was even more cruel and unpopular.

South of the island, at Marwick Head, is a squat tower - the **Kitchener Memorial**. It was erected in memory of Kitchener of Khartoum who was killed when *HMS Hampshire*, on which he was travelling to Russia to discuss the progress of the war, struck a German mine near here in June 1916. Only 12 people survived the sinking of the ship.

ROUSAY
12 miles N of Kirkwall

This island is sometimes known as the "Egypt of the North", as it brims with archaeological sites. The **Taversoe Tuick Chambered Cairn** has two chambers, one above the other. The Blackhammer Cairn, the Knowe of Yarso Cairn and the Midhowe Cairn can also be seen. **The Broch of Midhowe** has walls that still stand 13 feet high.

On Egilsay, a small island to the east, are the superb ruins of the 12th century **St Magnus's Church**, with its round tower. It was on Egilsay in 1115 that Magnus was killed. A cairn marks the spot of his martyrdom.

WESTRAY
20 miles N of Kirkwall

The substantial ruins of **Noltland Castle** stand to the north of the island. It was built by Gilbert Balfour, who was Master of the Household to Mary Stuart and also Sheriff of Orkney. At Pierowall, the island's main settlement, are the ruins of the **Ladykirk**. To the east of Westray is the smaller island of

Papa Westray. It is connected to Westray by air, the flight (which lasts two minutes) being the shortest scheduled air flight in the world.

SHETLAND ISLES

The Shetland Isles are closer to Bergen in Norway than they are to Edinburgh; the Arctic Circle nearer than Liverpool. In midsummer there is virtually no night, just a dimming of the sky around midnight, a phenomenon known locally as "simmer dim". The islands' northerly location is rewarded with one of the most spectacular light shows on earth - the Aurora Borealis, or Northern Lights which shimmer across the night sky in September and October.

The sea is part of every day life and such was the reputation of the Shetlanders' sea-faring skills that 3000 of them were serving with Nelson's fleet during the Napoleonic wars. Today, around 22,000 people live in the islands but they are vastly outnumbered by some 30,000 gannets, 140,000 guillemots, 250,000 puffins, 300,000 fulmars and at least 330,000 sheep. Despite lying so far north, Shetland enjoys the benefit of the Gulf Stream which creates a temperate, oceanic climate. It doesn't however protect the islands from ferocious winter storms which have battered the coastline into a frazzled hem of caves, blow-holes and rock stacks.

Shetland has recently gained European and Global Geopark Status. From the highest sheer cliffs in Britain to the best 'hands on' exposure of the Great Glen Fault, Shetland is packed with an incredibly varied geology spanning almost 3 billion years. Best of all, due to Shetland's size, you can visit all of these geological features in a few days. Geopark Shetland is leading a number of initiatives to interpret Shetland's fascinating geology and how it has influenced life in the isles.

LERWICK

There are about 100 Shetland islands, with fewer than 20 being inhabited. The largest of them, as in Orkney, is again called Mainland, and it is here that Lerwick, the island's capital, is situated.

The name "Lerwick" comes from the Norse for "muddy bay", and up until the 17th century that's all it was - a muddy bay surrounded by a handful of crude dwellings. The town was originally developed by the Dutch in the early 17th century to service their herring fleet, and from there gradually grew into a small town. It is the most northerly town in Britain with a population of about 9000.

The most imposing building in the town is **Fort Charlotte**, named after George III's wife. It was built in the 1780s to protect the town from the Dutch whom, the British government felt, had too much power in the area due to its large herring fleet which was based here.

•

Shetland is, of course, the home of the hardy ponies of that name, and of the distinctive black and brown native sheep, said to be descended from a Siberian breed, which are seen everywhere. Until the 1970s most Shetlanders were either fishermen or crofters but with the arrival of North Sea oil the economic pattern has changed dramatically. Most of the development however has been contained within the Sullom Voe area so those seeking unspoilt scenery, peace and quiet will not be disappointed.

•

221 BYDEST SELF-CATERING

Lerwick

Well-appointed town centre house offering quality self-catering accommodation.

see page 478

222 SHETLAND LIGHTHOUSE HOLIDAYS

Lerwick

Self-catering holidays with a choice of three spectacularly sited lighthouse keepers' cottages.

🛏 *see page 480*

223 HAY'S DOCK CAFÉ RESTAURANT

Lerwick

Set within Shetland Museum and Archives, this popular café restaurant showcases quality local produce.

🍴 *see page 480*

The fort is built on a rock that drops sheer to the shore and has a long seaward-facing side with emplacements for up to 12 guns. These looked out across Bressay Sound. The remaining four sides of the pentagon have well-preserved bastions at the corners. Inside the fort many of the original buildings are still standing These include the "piles": barrack blocks capable of housing a garrison of 270 men. The original powder magazine, designed to be proof against all forms of accidental ignition, is also still in place.

Shetland Museum and Archives at Hay's Dock tells Shetland's story, from its geological beginnings to the present day. Two floors of displays contain a wealth of treasures, including world famous textiles, boats suspended in mid air and bog butter - a commodity once used to pay the tax man. The archives house documents from the 15th century to the present day. There is also a large collection of music and oral history material and access to a substantial photographic archive. Other facilities include a café restaurant, shop, boat building shed, auditorium and temporary exhibition space, which regularly hosts art exhibitions.

Every year, on the last Tuesday in January, the festivaerwick **Up Helly Aa** is held. After being hauled through the streets of the town accompanied by men carrying torches, a Viking longboat is set on fire. The ritual is thought to date back to pagan times, when the

darkest days of winter were feared. It was thought that the light from celebrations of this kind attracted the light of the sun, which would then gradually return, lengthening the days. The introduction of a Viking ship, however, was a Victorian idea. Before that tar barrels were used.

The wonderfully named Böd of Gremista is located north of the town, and was the birthplace in 1792 of Arthur Anderson, co-founder of the P&O line. He joined the Royal Navy, and subsequently fought in the Napoleonic wars. In 1833 he co-founded the Peninsular Steam Navigation Company, which, in 1937, became the Peninsular and Oriental Steam Navigation Company. The 18th century building has been restored as a small museum and interpretation centre highlighting the island's maritime history.

AROUND LERWICK

BRESSAY

1 mile E of Lerwick by ferry

The island of Bressay lies opposite Lerwick and shelters its harbour. The **Bressay Heritage Centre**, close to the ferry terminal, illustrates through displays and exhibits what life was like on the island in former times. The tiny island of **Noss**, off its west coast, is a nature reserve, one of the oldest on the Shetlands. Boat trips to the island are available. Bressay has some fine walks, notably on its east coast. Its highest point is

Ward Hill, at 742 feet.

The ruined **St Mary's Chapel** is at Cullingsbrough Voe, on the island's east coast. It may date back to Norse times and is the only cruciform church on the Shetland Islands.

MOUSA

13 miles S of Lerwick

A broch is a prehistoric round, fortified tower and there are about 120 probable sites in Shetland. The best preserved is on Mousa, a tiny uninhabited island off Sandwick on the east coast of Mainland. The **Broch of Mousa** (Historic Scotland) was built sometime during the Iron Age from local stone, and is more than 40 feet high and 49 feet in diameter. It has lost its uppermost courses but is still in a remarkable state of preservation and shows the typical layout of these curious buildings which are found nowhere else but in Scotland. The double walls slope inwards as they get higher and embedded in them are staircases (which you can use to climb to the top) and defensive galleries. Like other brochs, no mortar was used in its construction.

BODDAM

21 miles S of Lerwick on the A970

The **Crofthouse Museum** comprises a thatched house, steading and water mill, and illustrates what life was like in a 19th century Shetland Island croft. It is furnished with home-made furniture of the type in use at that time. The croft would have housed an extended family of children, parents and grandparents, and the men would have earned their living from the sea while the women worked the land. In the summer months the museum hosts a programme of traditional music and stories.

JARLSHOF

23 miles S of Lerwick on the A970

Lying close to Sumburgh Airport on Mainland, Jarlshof is one of the most important historical sites in Europe and was continuously occupied from the Bronze Age right up until the 17th century. There are Bronze Age huts, Iron Age earth houses, brochs, wheelhouses from the Dark Ages, Norse longhouses and medieval dwellings. It is managed by Historic Scotland which also runs the small museum and interpretation centre.

At **Old Scatness**, close to Jarlshof, is an archaeological site centred on an Iron Age broch and village. There is a living history area with demonstrations that reproduce ancient technologies using authentic materials. The site was discovered in 1975 when a road was cut through what was thought to be a natural mound. Old walls were discovered and work began on excavating the site in 1995.

The **Ness of Burgi**, a small promontory jutting out into the sea, lies to the west of Jarlshof, and has an Iron Age fort.

FAIR ISLE

46 miles S of Lerwick

The most southerly of the Shetland

345

226 EASTERHOULL CHALETS

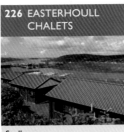

Scalloway

Well-appointed self-catering accommodation enjoying grand sea and island views.

 see page 482

227 BUSTA HOUSE HOTEL

Busta, Brae

A superb country house hotel with 22 comfortable en-suite rooms and fine food served in the restaurant.

 see page 482

Just off the Scalloway - Tingwall Road is the Murder Stone, a prehistoric standing stone. It got its name from a local legend which states that murderers were made to run between Law Ting Holm and the stone pursued by relatives of the murdered person. If the murderer made it to the stone unscathed, he wasn't executed, if he didn't, his pursuers killed him.

Islands lies almost half way between Shetland and Orkney. It is owned by the National Trust for Scotland and is one of the remotest inhabited islands in the country with a population of about 70. It was originally called Fridarey, meaning "island of peace", by Norse settlers. In 1558 one of the Spanish Armada vessels, the *El Gran Grifon*, was shipwrecked here. About 200 men managed to struggle ashore, and they were looked after by the islanders as best they could. However, the sailors, hungry and exhausted, began killing the islanders' animals for food, and they were eventually shipped off to Shetland from where they were sent home. In 1948 a Spanish delegation dedicated a cross on the island to those Spaniards who had died.

The island was once owned by George Waterston, the Scottish Director of the Royal Society for the Protection of Birds who founded a bird observatory in 1948. **The George Waterston Memorial Centre and Museum** has displays about the history and wildlife of the island. The **Feely Dyke**, a turf wall separating common land from modern crofting land, may date from prehistoric times.

Fair Isle knitting is famous the world over, and it is a craft that is still carried out to this day, using traditional patterns.

SCALLOWAY

7 miles W of Lerwick on the A970

Though only six miles from Lerwick, this small village sits on the Atlantic coast while its larger neighbour sits on the coast of the North Sea. Its name comes from the Norse "Scola Voe", which means the "Huts by the Bay".

Up until 1708 it was Shetland's capital, but as Lerwick expanded so the centre of power shifted eastwards. **Scalloway Castle** dates from around 1600, and was built by Patrick Stewart, who was executed 15 years later in Edinburgh for treason.

During World War II Scalloway was a secret base from where Norwegians were ferried across to their country in fishing boats (nicknamed "Shetland buses") to mount sabotage operations and bring back resistance fighters who were on the run from German troops. The Scalloway Museum in Main Street tells the story of these men, as well as the story of Scalloway itself. There are plans to move this museum to larger premises, next to the castle, for summer 2011.

TINGWALL

6 miles NW of Lerwick on the A970

Law Ting Holm near Tingwall was where the ancient Shetland Islands parliament, or Althing, used to meet. It sits on a small promontory (which in Norse times was an island) jutting out into the Loch of Tingwall.

TANGWICK

39 miles NW of Lerwick on the B9078

The **Tangwick Haa Museum**, in Northmavine, has displays and artefacts about the local history of the northern part of Mainland. The haa ("hall") itself dates from the 17th century and was built by the Cheyne family, the local landowners. It was restored by Shetland Amenity Trust and opened as a museum in 1988.

WHALSAY

18 miles NE of Lerwick

This small island, no more than six miles long by two miles wide, is connected to Mainland by a ferry from Laxo or Vidlin (depending on weather). There are superb coastal walks and many ancient remains. The 393-feet high **Ward of Clett** is its highest point, and from here a good view of the east coast of Mainland can be enjoyed. The granite **Symbister House**, in the island's ferry port, is the finest Georgian house in Shetland. It was built by the Bruce family who nearly bankrupted themselves in doing so, something that did not trouble the people of the island as the family had oppressed them for years. The house now forms part of the local school.

FETLAR

40 miles NE of Lerwick

The small island of Fetlar is no more than seven miles long by five miles wide at its widest and lies off the east coast of Yell to which it is connected by ferry. **The Fetlar Interpretive Centre** at Beach of Houbie has displays on the island's history, wildlife, and folklore, as well as genealogical archives. There is also an archive of more than 3000 photographs.

In the middle of the island are three mysterious stone circles known as **Fiddler's Crus**, which almost touch each other. Close by is the **Haltadans**, another stone circle, where 38 stones enclose two stones at its centre. The story goes that the two inner stones are a fiddler and his wife who were dancing with 38 trolls in the middle of the night. As the sun rose in the morning, its light turned them all to stone.

The island is a bird sanctuary with the highest density of breeding waders in Britain. As well as being the best place in Britain to find Red-Necked Phalarope and Whimbrel, you can see the Red-Throated Diver, Eider, Dunlin, Great and Arctic Skua, Wheatear, Curlew, Merlin and Snipe.

YELL

30 miles N of Lerwick

The second largest island in Shetland is about 20 miles long by seven miles wide at its widest, and is connected to Mainland by ferry. Though its population is close to 1000, it still has lonely moorland and a varied coast that lend themselves to hill walking and bird watching.

The whitewashed **Old Haa of Burravoe** ("Old Hall of Burravoe"), at the island's south east corner, is the oldest complete building on the island and dates from 1637. It now houses a small museum and interpretation centre, and has a digital recording studio. A tapestry commemorates the crashing of a

228 BUNESS HOUSE

Unst

Great accommodation on Britains most northerly island. Burness House offers a fantastic base to explore the local area.

see page 483

Catalina aircraft in 1941 close to Burravoe with only three out of the crew of ten surviving.

UNST

46 miles N of Lerwick

Unst is the most northerly of the Shetland Isles and here, packed into an area just 12 miles long by 5 miles wide, you'll find some of the most spectacular scenery in Scotland - stupendous cliffs, sculpted sea stacks, sheltered inlets, golden beaches, heather-clad hills, fertile farmland and even a unique sub-Arctic stony desert. Unst also offers standing stones, brochs, ruined Muness Castle (built in 1598), two important National Nature Reserves, Hermaness and Keen of Hamar, as well as an abundance of wild-life. It seems fitting somehow that in Robert Louis Stevenson's *Treasure Island* the map showing where the treasure is hidden closely resembles the shape of Unst. The author visited the island in 1869, following in the footsteps of his father, Thomas, who built the spectacularly sited lighthouse on Muckle Flugga rocks in 1857-8. The nearby Out Stack is the very last speck of northern Britain.

At Haroldswick, in the north of the island, is **Harald's Grave,** an ancient burial cairn that is supposed to mark the grave of Harold the Fair of Norway. **Burra Firth**, on the northern coast, is one of Britain's tiniest firths, and certainly its most northern. Everything here is Britain's "most northern" something or other. The Post Office is Britain's most northerly post office, and **Wick of Shaw** is the most northerly dwelling house. The village's Methodist church is the county's most northerly church, and was built between 1990 and 1993, with a simple layout based on a traditional Norwegian design.

Unst has the highest concentration of rural longhouse sites in the world, making it the ideal place to interpret Shetland's Viking past. Shetland Amenity Trust set up the **Viking Unst** project in 2006, which now consists of a series of sites around the isle, including three excavated Viking longhouses and a full size replica Viking longship. There are also plans to create a reconstruction of one of the excavated longhouses.

Accommodation, Food & Drink and Places to Visit

The establishments featured in this section includes hotels, inns, guest houses, bed & breakfasts, restaurants, cafés, tea and coffee shops, tourist attractions and places to visit. Each establishment has an entry number which can be used to identify its location at the beginning of the relevant chapter.

In addition full details of all these establishments and many others can be found on the Travel Publishing website - **www.findsomewhere.co.uk**. This website has a comprehensive database covering the whole of Britain and Ireland.

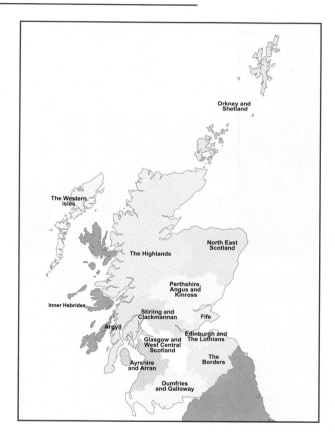

1 SIAMESE KITCHEN & PEWTER PLATE

12 Murray Street, Duns,
Berwickshire TD11 3DE
Tel: 01361 883470

Located just off the main square of this pretty little town, the **Siamese Kitchen & Pewter Plate** occupies a handsome listed building and is both a charming tea room and an excellent restaurant serving authentic Thai cuisine.

The Restaurant/Tearoom serves a good selection of teas, coffees and light snacks. Thai food is of course the speciality including Thai one-plate quick lunches for busy people. The full evening menu is available throughout the day. On Sundays a Thai Buffet is served from 12.30pm to 4.30pm after which the full evening menu is served. All food, including the Buffet, is cooked freshly as customers order, and is also available as takeaway. The premises are fully licensed.

The Restaurant is open 10.00am Tuesday to Sunday in summer, Monday to Saturday in winter. It closes at 10.00 pm Monday to Saturday and 9.00pm on Sunday. Booking is recommended.

2 WHEATSHEAF HOTEL

Main Street, Reston,
Berwickshire TD14 5JS
Tel: 01890 761219

Located in the small village of Reston, just off the A1 and close to the St Abb's Diving Centre. **The Wheatsheaf Hotel** is a popular spot for divers as well as many walkers and cyclists following The Southern Upland Way.

Within a short drive the river tweed offers some of the finest salmon and trout fishing around. Other outdoor pursuits include quad biking, 4x4 driving, horseriding to name a few point to point meetings as well as Kelso races are held regularly.

The Borders is alive with many historical sites of interest from Melrose & Kelso Abbeys to Alnwick Castle (Hogwarts in Harry Potter).

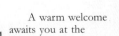

A warm welcome awaits you at the Wheatsheaf and they will endeavour to make your stay as comfortable as possible.

The hotel offers a range of quality pub meals and snacks throughout the day, along with a range of wines and spirits to enjoy in the bar or beer garden.

Although not all rooms are en-suite, they are all equipped with T.V and Tea/Coffee making facilities. Included in the B&B price is also a light bedtime snack.

Children and well behaved pets are most welcome.

3 NEW INN

Bridge Street, Coldingham,
Berwickshire TD14 5NG
Tel: 018907 71315

Conveniently located close to the A1 and the Berwickshire coast, the **New Inn** is a handsome stone building in traditional style that was built some 200 years ago.

Andrew Penman, who is a local man, took over here as chef/patron in the winter of 2008, bringing with him some 24 years experience in the hospitality business.

The friendly and welcoming bar has a real fire for chilly days, and for fine weather days there's a pleasant sheltered beer garden. Andrew's menu offers a good choice of traditional pub food with dishes based wherever possible on fresh locally sourced produce. As

we go to press, a new restaurant area is almost completed and should be operating by the time you read this.

The inn is open from 10am to 12 midnight, Sunday to Thursday, and from 10am to 1am on Friday and Saturday. There is good wheelchair access throughout. And if you are thinking of staying in this delightful part of Berwickshire, the inn has 3 comfortable standard rooms available.

5 THE BLACK BULL HOTEL

13-15 Market Place, Lauder,
Berwickshire TD2 6SR
Tel: 01578 722208
Fax: 01578 722419
e-mail: enquiries@blackbull-lauder.com
website: www.blackbull-lauder.com

Dating back to the 18th century when it was built as a coaching inn on the road to Edinburgh, the **Black Bull Hotel** is a traditional family-run hotel full of charm and character. Many 18th century features remain, amongst them the high ceilings, wood-panelled walls and polished wood flooring.

There's an inviting bar, the Harness Room, with cosy armchairs and log fires where you can enjoy a fine malt whisky, a locally-brewed ale or your choice from the extensive wine list. The inn offers great food in a number of dining areas, from the informal comfort of the bar to the elegant surroundings of the Georgian dining room. Only the best quality local beef, lamb, fish and seasonal game is used in the preparation of the dishes on offer.

The accommodation at the Black Bull comprises 8

attractively decorated rooms furnished with antiques and original artwork and dressed with crisp white linen.

The rooms retain period style along with modern comforts such as the en suite facilities. Awarded 4-stars by the AA and 3-stars by Visit Scotland, the hotel has its own parking, a disabled toilet downstairs, and accepts credit cards apart from American Express.

4 WATERLOO ARMS HOTEL

Allanton Road, Chirnside, Duns, TD11 3XH
Tel: 01890 818034
e-mail: info@chirnsideinn.co.uk
website: www.chirnsideinn.co.uk

A traditional Scottish welcome awaits guests at the **Waterloo Arms**, a delightful old coaching inn dating back to the 1820s. It stands just outside the pretty Borders village of Chirnside, on the Coldstream side. Owners Brian McLintock and Agnes Sinclair arrived at this cosy wayside inn in the spring of 2009, bringing with them more than 50 years experience in the hospitality business. They have upgraded the amenities of the inn while maintaining its welcoming atmosphere and traditional style. With its roaring log fire, real ales and ice cold beers, this is a pub to savour.

The inn serves bar lunches and evening meals all year round. The food is locally produced and freshly cooked in the kitchens by the helpful and friendly staff under the eye of head chef John. He does his best to ensure that wherever possible the ingredients are locally produced and grown. Brian and Agnes take pride in offering good home-cooked food at reasonable prices. There's a very popular bar lunch menu and the bar suppers are renowned for their fresh, local ingredients. With its cosy atmosphere and local chit-chat you can dine in the refurbished restaurant. It has a relaxed bistro atmosphere, but is away from the bar area.

There's a selection of fine wines to accompany your meal and our bar stocks over 100 different spirits, over 30 malt whiskies, various real ales, including guest ales and ice cold beers including draught Magners, ice cold Carling, other ciders, heavy beer and ice cold Guinness.

The inn also offers comfortable accommodation in five attractively furnished and decorated bedrooms, including 2 four poster suites, all of which have been individually designed with your total comfort in mind.

So, whether you're visiting for a few hours, a few days or a few weeks, Waterloo Arms has everything you need to relax, unwind and enjoy a stress-free break. There's a host of activities on the doorstep ranging from golf, fishing, and hiking to other, more restful pursuits. And the inn makes an ideal base for exploring other parts of Scotland and the North of England - the perfect haven to return to after a day's excursion.

42 Abbotsford Road, Galashiels TD1 3HR
Tel: 01896 754050
e-mail:
enquiries@maplehurstguesthouse.co.uk
website:
www.maplehurstguesthouse.co.uk

Maplehurst Guest House was originally built in 1906 for Andre Fairgrieve and his Canadian wife. Mr Fairgrieve was the grandson of a local Mill Owner. Maplehurst is a striking building with the architecture and interior design bearing witness to the best of the Scottish Arts and Crafts style, but with an intriguing incorporation of many Canadian features. For instance, there is a wonderful and original tapestry that adorns the wall above the rich oak wood panelling in the reception hall, and many and varied stained glass windows of differing designs and sizes. These include maple leaves, hence the name "Maplehurst".

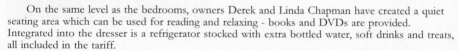

Outside, the garden extends to just over an acre and contains sweeping lawns, large rhododendron bushes which, when in flower, are the talk of the town, and forty-five listed trees, many of them Canadian species. A new terraced garden and a large patio area are available for guests to use and relax in, and for chillier evenings a summerhouse is available.

The accommodation at Maplehurst comprises 3 bedrooms which have been recently decorated in keeping with the arts and crafts theme of the house. The rooms, along with the library seating area, have been tastefully and individually styled to a very high standard. The amenities include central heating, DVD/TV/radio; wireless internet access, hairdryer, robes and slippers, hospitality tray and organic toiletries from Purdie's Highland Soap Company to pamper you.

On the same level as the bedrooms, owners Derek and Linda Chapman have created a quiet seating area which can be used for reading and relaxing - books and DVDs are provided. Integrated into the dresser is a refrigerator stocked with extra bottled water, soft drinks and treats, all included in the tariff.

Breakfast at Maplehurst is definitely something to look forward to. Derek and Linda strive to provide a varied choice of healthy food using, as far as possible, fresh locally sourced ingredients. There's a wide variety that includes full Scottish, Continental and vegetarian breakfasts, all freshly cooked on the Aga. If you have any special dietary requirements, just give advance notice and the Chapmans will do their best to accommodate your needs.

Maplehurst offers a very central location from which to explore the Borders and Lothian regions with many historic houses, castles and abbeys all within easy reach.

7 CLOVENFORDS COUNTRY HOTEL

1 Vine Street, Clovenfords,
Galashiels TD1 3LU
Tel: 01896 850203
e-mail: info@clovenfordshotel.co.uk
website: www.clovenfordshotel.co.uk

Nestled in the heart of the Borders region, the family-run **Clovenfords Country Hotel** is a beautiful establishment surrounded by rolling hills. The luxurious rooms have everything you could want from a modern hotel, while retaining plenty of charm and character. The hotel is finished to a high standard throughout and offers the very best in comfort and service. The owners really have made this place a perfect home from home experience and pride themselves on their range of fine foods and beverages.

Guests have a choice of three eating areas – The Vineyard, Scott Lounge and Public Bar. They all provide a different eating experience and on brighter days there is a large, seated outdoor sun terrace for people to make the most of. The Vineyard Restaurant offers a pleasurable dining experience, serving a wide range of fresh, local ingredients that are blended into traditional and ultra modern dishes to tempt every palate. The extensive menu boasts all home made dishes that reflect the flavours of the countryside the hotel nestles in. The Borders region has a worldwide reputation for its hill and pasture grazed beef, lamb and game. All of the dishes are made with the finest ingredients and the mouth watering desserts are extremely tempting. Children's portions of any main dish can be purchased, but they might like to choose from the special children's menu. The restaurant is open seven days a week and serves meals and snacks from 12 noon to 9.30pm. Such is its popularity booking is advised to avoid disappointment.

In a tranquil, village location, the hotel is the ideal get-away for those wanting to escape the hustle and bustle of city life. The main town of Galashiels is just two miles away and the Border towns of Melrose, Kelso, Selkirk, Hawick, Duns and Berwick are all within easy reaching distance, with the city of Edinburgh just a 40 minute drive away. There is plenty to explore in the area with rolling hills, river walks and woodlands all within a few miles of the hotel. Activities such as fishing, cycling and golf can be enjoyed and there are many historical sites to be seen, including Abbotsford, Traquair, the Border Abbeys and Floors Castle.

The hotel offers locked boxes for rods and fishing equipment and can arrange storage for bicycles. Clovenfords Country Hotel is also available for private parties and weddings and welcomes bus parties and tours.

8 CLINT LODGE COUNTRY HOUSE

St Boswell's, nr Melrose TD6 0DZ
Tel: 01835 822027
Fax: 01835 822656
e-mail: clintlodge@ aol.com
website: www.clintlodge.co.uk

Dating back to 1869, **Clint Lodge Country House** is a splendid former sporting lodge which enjoys outstanding views over the magnificent Borders countryside. Its the home of Bill and Heather Walker who have been welcoming guests here since 1996.

The house has 5 beautifully furnished guest bedrooms, 4 of them en suite, 1 with a private bathroom. If you prefer self-catering, just across the yard is a well appointed cottage that sleeps up to six people. Heather and Bill also offer a superb 3-course evening meal which is highly recommended. Credit cards are accepted.

9 HAZEL LODGE TEA ROOM

20 Horsemarket, Kelso TD5 7HA
Tel: 01573 226909
e-mail: tearoom@hazellodge.co.uk
website: www.hazellodge.co.uk

Occupying a building more than 150 years old, **Hazel Lodge Tea Room** is set back from the cobbled Horsemarket, just yards from Kelso's huge French-style Market Place which is also cobbled.

Owners Ian and Kay Burton took over the Tea Room in the spring of 2009 and have quickly established a reputation for serving wholesome and appetising food.

Hazel Lodge Tea Room is the ideal spot for a cup of tea or coffee, light lunch or snack, offering tasty treats including home made soup, sandwiches, paninis, burgers and salads. However if you prefer something more substantial they offer a full menu available all day. Most of the dishes are hand-made and based on locally sourced ingredients such as the

Fresh Eyemouth haddock and home-made steak pie.

Children have their own menu. In good weather, customers can enjoy their refreshments in the garden at the front where pets are also welcome. The tearoom is licensed and also offers an excellent choice of non-alcoholic drinks. There's good disabled access and disabled toilets.

10 FINDLAY'S RESTAURANT

I North Bridge Street, Hawick,
Renfrewshire TD9 9BD
Tel: 01450 375195
e-mail: simon@findlaysrestaurant
website: www.findlaysrestaurant.co.uk

Occupying a prime position in the centre of Hawick, **Findlay's Restaurant** is a quaint, modern rustic restaurant with a relaxed atmosphere that customers love. It is owned and run by Simon and Ruth Findlay who both have a passion for good food.

Simon, born and bred in Hawick, is the chef and boasts a glittering CV that includes a spell working as a freelance when he had the great pleasure of cooking for the Duke of Westminster, Her Grace the Duchess of Roxburgh, Prince Andrew and the late Princess Diana to name just a few. At Hawick he offers a menu that changes seasonally and is based on top quality fresh local produce. Simon and Ruth are so enthusiastic about fresh produce that they have also opened

"Simply Scrumptious", a deli just across the road selling all kinds of Borders delicacies. But Simon's repertoire is far from parochial: twice a month he puts on a tapas or pasta evening.

Findlay's is open for breakfasts and lunches from 9.30am to 2.30pm, and for dinner from 6.30pm to 9pm, Monday to Saturday. All major credit cards are accepted, apart from American Express, and there is good disabled access.

11 BRYDON'S BAKERY RESTAURANT

16 High Street, Hawick TD9 9EH
Tel: 01450 372672
e-mail: nick.powolny@sky.com

Nick and Jackie Powolny have owned and run **Brydon's Bakery Restaurant** since 1993 and have established an outstanding reputation for quality and service. Their restaurant lies behind a striking Art Nouveau shop front of 1902 which still displays the name of the original bakery. The interior features high ceilings and wooden beams, and at the front of the shop is a counter selling cakes, pastries, sweets and preserves. At the back of the premises are two cast iron bread ovens set into the wall, a leftover from the days when this was a bakery.

Today, the cooking is done by Nick, while Jackie looks after the front of house. Nick's menu offers an appetising selection of snacks, light meals and cakes as

well as main courses which are listed on the specials board. A popular Scottish dish here is "Stovies", a kind of hash of meat and vegetables whose name originates from the fact that it was indeed cooked in a stove.

The restaurant is open from 8.30am to 4pm, Monday to Saturday; credit cards are not accepted.

356

12 THE STEADINGS

Roundabouts Farm, Chesters,
Hawick TD9 8TH
Tel: 01450 860730
e-mail:
steadings@scottishbordersbandb.co.uk
website: www.scottishbordersbandb.co.uk

Set in two acres of garden and conveniently located between Hawick and Jedburgh, **The Steadings** offers quality B&B accommodation in beautifully converted farm steadings (outbuildings). Guests have the use of a large separate sitting room with a log-burning stove. This room opens out onto a large patio with access to the mature garden grounds where guests can sit and children can entertain themselves in the play area. DVDs, games, books, local maps and a Wii console are all in the sitting room. There's also free broadband connection in all the rooms. All three guest bedrooms are of a high standard with en suite bath or shower room and views of the stunning Borders hills. One twin room is on the ground floor and has an en suite shower room. There's guest controlled central heating, tea making facilities and TVs in all rooms.

Breakfast at The Steadings is served in the dining room at the time of your choice. The selection includes a full Scottish breakfast and options such as Scottish smoked salmon with scrambled local free range eggs on a toasted muffin.

If you prefer self-catering, a charming cottage sleeping 4 people is available.

13 THE SHIELING GUEST HOUSE

Eshiels, nr Peebles, Borders EH45 8NA
Tel: 01721 722577
e-mail: the-shieling@hotmail.com

Located in a beautiful rural area, this modern, three storey house is still in close proximity to Peebles and other Border towns. Situated at the gateway to the Glentress Forest, there are some fantastic views to be enjoyed in the surrounding area. **The Shieling Guest House** is popular with walkers and those wanting to explore the Borders. An idyllic stream runs through the spacious garden of the house and there is a summer house and decking area for guests to make the most of on brighter days. The views really are superb and the area is popular with cyclists and walkers as well as tourists. The guest house has storage for mountain bikes.

There are three tastefully decorated and comfortable bedrooms, all boasting TVs, WiFi and hospitality trays;

two of which boast king size

beds. Two of them are en suite and the other has its own private facilities. Open all year round, evening meals can be ordered and all of the produce is sourced locally from the farmers market, butchers and bakers.

Owned by Pauline McHugh, the gay friendly guest house also welcomes children; some pets can stay by prior arrangement. There is off road parking. No credit cards are taken.

357

14 ST RONANS HOTEL

High Street, Innerleithen,
Peeblesshire EH44 6HF
Tel: 01896 831487
e-mail: stronanshotel@hotmail.co.uk
website: www.stronanshotel.co.uk

St Ronans Hotel has a history that goes back to 1827 when it was officially opened by the then Earl of Traquair. The novel by Sir Walter Scott, *St Ronan's Wells* (a Victorian spa half a mile from the hotel) had made the area popular and people were coming from far and wide to "take the waters".

This fine old hostelry has a public bar with a solid fuel stove, pool table, and dartboard. Cask-conditioned ales are on tap here (the hotel is featured in the *Good Beer Guide*) and bar meals are served only by prior arrangement. There's also a lounge bar where breakfasts are served as well as meals for those who would rather not be in the public bar.

Outside, overlooked by the hills Lee Pen and Caerlee, there is a large enclosed beer garden with a children's activity area. The garden provides a great setting for various activities throughout the year - live bands, BBQs, folk sessions, some events connected with the Innerleithen music festival in August, and even weddings. And if you are planning to stay in the area, the hotel has 7 comfortable guest bedrooms, all with en suite facilities and TV.

15 UNKY DUNKS

5 St Andrew Street, Dumfries DG1 1BS
Tel: 01387 249249

Unky Dunks is very much at home in Dumfries town centre, adding to the already cosy and village-like atmosphere in this narrow cobbled street. A brief but considered menu, Unky Dunks goes for the classic café fare and they serve up hearty portions with the emphasis on traditional home made food. There's a simple menu of light meals & snacks, such as baked potatoes, ciabattas, toasties, panini's & salads, as well as a good selection of Bellagio coffee and cakes. In fine weather breakfasts and lunches can be enjoyed outside in a roped off area on the quaint cobbled street.

The café is licensed with wine and bottled beer (Wychwood Breweries) and is open 6 days a week. The relaxed management will happily welcome those simply looking for an afternoon coffee or a quick bite from the snack menu right up to closing time.

16 ANNANDALE ARMS HOTEL

High Street, Moffat,
Dumfries & Galloway   DG10 9HF
Tel: 01683 220013
Fax: 01683 221395
e-mail:
reception@annandalearmshotel.co.uk
website: www.annandalearmshotel.co.uk

Located right in the heart of Moffat, behind the Georgian facade, the **Annandale Arms Hotel** has been a major local landmark for more than two hundred and fifty years. Inside, the public rooms are stylishly furnished and decorated in contemporary style and the hotel throughout has a peaceful and relaxed atmosphere.

A listed building, the hotel was also the recipient of the 2009 Real Food Award in Scotland's national hotel awards, and the restaurant reviewer in the *Hotel Review Scotland* declared himself "most impressed by the food, especially superb char-grilled organic lamb and steaks, and delicious homemade puddings". In December 2008 *The Restaurant Magazine* voted the Annandale Arms

among the Best of the Rest in the Game-to-Eat competition for stuffed loin of red deer venison in a red wine jus. More praise for the food on offer here came from Les Routiers' Gold Key Award which lavished praise on the Scotch beef, game and salmon and also recommended the steak, stout and mushroom pie served with hand cut potato chips. In addition to the regular menu, a large selection of home-produced dishes are offered throughout the year subject to seasonal changes. And do look out for Annandale's very own "Moffat Munchie". To accompany your meal, there's an excellent selection of fine wines, ales and whiskies.

Over a period of ten years good professional relationships have been nurtured between the kitchen and their local Scottish suppliers. Great care has been taken to find just the right quality, whether it be for wild Scottish salmon, scallops, organic lamb or well hung beef. For example, all the beef is traceable from farm to mouth. Source codes are checked and recorded in line with the stringent stipulations of the Scotch Beef Club.

The accommodation at the Annandale Arms maintains the same high standards evident throughout the hotel. All the 16 rooms have been recently refurbished in a modern contemporary style yet with sympathy for the building's history. They overlook the private courtyard at the rear of the hotel, away from the bustle of Moffat High Street. All the rooms have en suite bath or shower rooms, complimentary tea and coffee making facilities, Wifi, digital television, telephone and hair drier as standard. To ensure a comfortable night's sleep, there are pocket sprung mattresses on the beds.

17 BUCCLEUCH ARMS HOTEL

High Street, Moffat DG10 9ET
Tel: 01683 220003 Fax: 01683 221291
e-mail: enquiries@buccleucharmshotel.com
website: www.buccleucharmshotel.com

Dating back to 1760, this multi award winning, privately run hotel set in the heart of Moffat; famously frequented by Scots poet Robert Burns, provides warm and comfortable accommodation to all who visit this picturesque town. Originally from

Zimbabwe, owner David has just won a prestigious award (amongst many others) for staff training - and quality service really shows at every level. This outstanding Georgian coaching inn is listed and has retained many of its original features, the most popular has to be the open fireplace that provides warmth and comfort during the colder parts of the year.

With 16 en suite rooms, the **Buccleuch Arms Hotel** manages to offer an accommodation option for

everyone, and balances the oldness of the hotel bedrooms with immaculate housekeeping. As well as the bedrooms, the Buccleuch Arms also boasts a popular bar or the 'Bucc' as it is known locally, a function room for those special occasions, a lounge for guests to unwind and relax in and a boardroom, available for hire for meetings and small dining groups. Local facilities include a sports centre, a tennis court and many golf courses just a short distance away.

19 SAVINGS BANK MUSEUM

Ruthwell, Dumfries DG1 4NN
Tel: 01387 870640
e-mail: info@savingsbankmuseum.co.uk
website: www.savingsbankmuseum.co.uk

Dr Henry Duncan was an accomplished artist and some of his work is displayed in the museum, but he is best remembered as the man who

identified the first fossil footprints in Britain. Minister of the Ruthwell parish church for 50 years, he opened the world's first commercial savings bank in 1810. The museum also houses a large collection of early home savings boxes, coins and bank notes from many parts of the world. Open 10am-1pm and 2pm-5pm, Tuesday to Saturday 1st October to Easter and every day Easter to 30th September. Admission free.

20 SHAMBELLIE HOUSE

Museum of Costume, New Abbey,
Dumfries DG2 8HQ
Tel: 01387 850375

The house was designed by Scottish architect David Bryce and built in 1856 for the Stewart family. In 1977 Charles Stewart, the great grandson of the

original owner, donated the house and his costume collection to the National Museums of Scotland. Charles Stewart was in his own words 'that obsessed and demented being, a collector.' He searched through market stalls, friends' attics and forgotten trunks for interesting items of clothing. Browse through the gift shop and choose from our unique range of Victorian style gifts. Picnic on the lawn or take a stroll through the wooded grounds. You can also enjoy delicious homebaking in the below stairs tearoom.

Market Place,
High Street, Langholm,
Dumfries & Galloway DG13 0JH
Tel: 013873 80357 / 81178
e-mail: enquiries@eskdalehotel.co.uk
website: www.eskdalehotel.co.uk

Located in the heart of the Scottish borders, in "The Muckle Toon" of Langholm, the **Eskdale Hotel** is a family run hotel occupying a prominent position in the centre of one of Scotland's most attractive Border towns. A former coaching inn and now a listed building, the Eskdale offers a wide variety of amenities. The relaxed atmosphere of the bright, airy, 'quiet' bar provides an ideal venue for chatting with friends over drinks and a bar meal, or perhaps a freshly brewed coffee and scones. Then there's another lively bar with

a comfortable and friendly ambience and with plasma TV to watch the sport of the day. Pool and darts are available and the weekends offer a selection of live music, karaoke, quizzes and competitions for customers' entertainment. A wide choice of home cooked snacks and bar meals are available in both bars daily at lunch (12noon - 2pm) and in the evening (6pm-8pm).

For more formal dining, the restaurant caters for all from breakfast to evening dining with comprehensive table d'hôte and à la carte menus offering dishes based on home-grown local produce as much as possible. The beef and lamb served, for example, comes from the owners own farm in the next village of Eskdalemuir.

If you have any special dietary or culinary requirements, the kitchen will cater accordingly, given notice. The venue for Langholm Rotary Club's weekly meetings, this room can be opened up to twice its size for small functions (80 for seated meals) and has its own private bar. It also has direct access to the 'beer deck' and so can happily accommodate any smokers in the party.

There's also a larger function room that caters for parties of up to 120 with a disco / stage area for bands; it also has its own private bar. The hotel can provide a selection of buffets ranging from sandwiches to plated meals for this number.

If you are planning to stay in this lovely part of Scotland, the Eskdale has 14 newly decorated en suite rooms available, offering single, twin, double and family accommodation for up to 5 persons. Each room is equipped with tea/coffee making facilities, direct dial telephone, internet access and colour television. The fully central heated rooms are provided with shaver points, hairdryers and complimentary toiletries.

21 STEAMBOAT INN

Carsethorn, Dumfries DG2 8DS
Tel: 01387 880631
e-mail: steamboatinn01@aol.com
website:
www.steamboatinncarsethorn.co.uk

Set in the delightful old fishing village of Carsethorn, **The Steamboat Inn** overlooks the Solway Firth, with magnificent views to the Lake District Peaks. Dating back to the 1800's, the Inn would have been the last watering hole for many of the emigrants who left these Scottish shores, in order to seek a better life in New Scotia.

A free house, the Inn has a selection of forty malt whiskies and a good variety of beers, including the excellent Belhaven Best. There is a range of reasonably priced wines, which are sold by the glass, carafe or bottle. The Steamboat is renowned for its excellent food; visitors and guests can choose their favourite bar lunch or evening meal from the extensive menus. Meals are served in the public bar with its real fire, in the lounge or in the dining room. The spacious and tastefully decorated dining room can accommodate fifty covers and is the ideal setting for an evening meal or social event.

Whether in for a pint or for a meal, to relax and chat with friends or to play pool or darts, you can be sure of friendship and a warm welcome at the Steamboat.

The bed and breakfast accommodation is set behind the Inn, with it's own entrance and ample parking. The accommodation consists of double and twin en suite rooms, which are centrally heated and double-glazed. The bedrooms are furnished to a high standard and have colour TV, tea and coffee making facilities, hair dryer, shaver points, complimentary snacks and mineral water.

The self-catering accommodation, named the "Auld Byre" is fitted out to an extremely high standard with wheelchair access and can accommodate 2/4 people. Weekly lets are available throughout the year and short breaks at specified times.

Coach loads of visitors come from as far away as Liverpool to see the birds wheel above the Solway during their migrations and at nearby Nature Reserves. Birdwatchers can expect a wide variety of seabirds at Carsethorn. Waders and other seabirds can be seen on the foreshore and the marsh.

22 BARNSOUL FARM

Shawhead, Dumfries,
Dumfries & Galloway DG2 9SQ
Tel: 01387 730249
e-mail: barnsouldg@aol.com
website: www.barnsoulfarm.co.uk

Just off the A75 Dumfries to Stranraer road you will find **Barnsoul Farm**, a superb caravan and camping park that has everything for the tourist. Passing through, or looking for a base from which to explore beautiful Dumfries and Galloway, the place has everything.

It has 50 pitches for tents and caravans as well as 8 Wigwam timber mountain bothies. The site has electricity and water throughout, plus a modern comfortable shower unit with basins, mirrors and seats. The unit is open 24 hours a day. There is also a kitchen equipped with gas cookers, fridges and microwaves. Laundry facilities are available with hot water day and night.

The compact, comfortable and cosy mountain bothies have been described as 'camping without a tent', and are compact. Constructed from timber, they have bunks for four to six people.

They are heated, and come with basic furniture, cushions, mattresses, pillows, kettle toaster and fridge. Each one has an exterior patio with bench table and stone barbecue. People using the bothies still have full use of the site kitchen and its appliances.

23 GLENLEE HOLIDAY HOUSES

New Galloway, Castle Douglas DG7 3RN
Tel: 01664 430212 Fax: 01644 430430
e-mail: agnew@glenlee-holidays.co.uk
website: www.glenlee-holidays.co.uk

Located two miles from the villages of New Galloway and St John's Town of Dalry, **Glenlee Holiday Houses** are set in quiet secluded woodland well away from the road. Set around a central courtyard, the five cottages have been imaginatively converted from the old Home Farm buildings of the Glenlee Estate.

Each cottage is well-equipped and comfortably furnished yet retains its own individual character. Each has its own open hearth fire, its own front door, privacy and car parking. The cottages can sleep from 4 to 7 people and taking all five cottages at one time makes a great base for family gatherings and reunions. Pets are welcome (at no extra charge) provided they are house-trained and respect the countryside. From the cottages, there is a special woodland walk – the Glen – past two spectacular waterfalls and some fine tall trees.

Owners Cathy and Richard Agnew also offer guests free trout fishing on their stretch of the River Ken and other fishing is available locally. The cottages are open from March to October for weekly lets (Friday-Friday) and also short breaks. Winter lets by special arrangement.

24 THE CATSTRAND

High Street, New Galloway,
Castle Douglas DG7 3RN
Tel: 01644 420374
e-mail: rachel@catstrand.com
website: www.cat strand.com

The CatStrand is Scotland's newest and most exciting contemporary performance and meeting space. Set in the heart of the Glenkens community, it is named after the very small stream that used to run beneath it. The name also reflects the stream of activities that flow through the building. Not only does The CatStrand promote a varied music, arts and exhibition programme, it also boasts up-to-date training and conference facilities, offers local information and runs regular computer and exercise classes. The centre is also home to the CatStrand Cinema and a café serving Fairtrade coffee and home baking daily; during the week it also serves freshly prepared lunches made with locally sourced ingredients. The Gift Shop stocks a good range of arts & crafts, prints, cards and local

produce and there's also an information centre centre with free internet access. A central focal point for the whole of Dumfries and Galloway, the CatStrand welcomes individuals, groups and businesses wanting to hire its fully equipped meeting rooms. The CatStrand aims to offer a range of high quality events, activities and facilities, with full disabled access, to suit every taste and every visitor - all under one roof.

25 GALLOWAY HYDROS

Tongland Power Station, Kirkudbright DG7 3SF
Tel: 01557 330114
e-mail: visit.galloway@scottishpower.com

A guided tour of **Galloway Hydros** will give you an insight into the force of nature that is captured, channelled and released back into the environment, enabling Scottish Power to produce pure, clean energy. The Visitor Centre tells the story of the construction of the Galloway Hydros in the 1930s and the tour takes you into the power station, the control room and the turbine hall. You will learn about the operation of the power stations and how they

contribute to the national electricity grid system. Close by is the impressive Tongland Dam and Reservoir - the power source. Here, you might catch a glimpse of a migrating salmon. A picnic area and refreshments room allow you to relax and enjoy the tranquility.

26 THREAVE ESTATE & GARDENS

Castle Douglas,
Dumfries & Galloway DG7 1 RX
Tel: 01556 502575 Fax: 01556 502683
Ranger/naturalist: tel (01556) 503702
e-mail threave@nts.org.uk
website: www.nts.org.uk

Threave Garden is delightful in all seasons. At 26 ha (64 a), it is best known for its spectacular springtime daffodils (nearly 200 varieties), but herbaceous beds are colourful in summer and trees and heather garden are striking in autumn. The Victorian house is home to the Trust's School of Practical

Gardening. The principal rooms in **Threave House** opened to the public for the first time in 2002 and have attracted great interest ever since. The interiors have been restored to their appearance in the 1930s, and from the house visitors can enjoy impressive vistas of the Galloway countryside. Guided walks. Maxwelton Collection of local bygones in the Visitor Centre on show. Plant Centre.

Threave Estate is a wildfowl refuge and is designated a Special Protection

Area for its breeding waders and wintering wildfowl. The important wetlands are designated an Area of Special Scientific Interest. Threave provides a good example of integrated management of the land, taking account of agriculture, forestry and nature conservation. Marked walks include a 2.5 km estate trail through this variety of landscapes, and hides provide good cover to observe bird activity. A Countryside Centre in the old stables highlights nature conservation, forestry and agriculture at Threave.

27 MAD HATTER

53 King Street, Castle Douglas, Dumfries
& Galloway DG7 1AE
Tel: 01556 502712

Castle Douglas is Scotland's 'food town', with many small outlets selling fresh, local produce. In the main street you will find the **Mad Hatter**, the place to visit for a delightful lunch or snack. It is owned and run by Neill Walker, who has been here since 2007. All the food is prepared on the premises and represents good, honest Scottish fare, some with a Continental hint to make it that little bit different. Try the filled paninis, the baked potatoes or the all day breakfast! The café has an attractive frontage on the town's main thoroughfare, and it is cosy with 75 seats, while still giving a feeling of spaciousness. It is a café with a difference - they serve Fair Trade Coffee and have a Takeaway service, whilst also placing great emphasis on the quality of the ingredients and the way they are prepared and cooked. Wheelchair access and disabled toilet available. Coach parties welcome.

28 GELSTON CASTLE HOLIDAYS

Gelston, Castle Douglas DG7 1QE
Tel: 01556 502211
Fax: 01556 504183
e-mail: holidays@gelstoncastle.com
website: www.gelstoncastle.com

For nearly 40 years **Gelston Castle Holidays** has provided some of the most popular self-catering accommodation in southwest Scotland. Some 80% of guests return again and again, with some families now on the third generation! One of the key advantages is that families can come on holiday together, and yet each can have their own house: there are 4 houses in the former stable courtyard of Gelston Castle, and for those who want even greater seclusion there is the romantic and luxurious Kirkmirren Cottage just down a delightful lane(pictured below).

It's easy to see why people return. First, there's the standard of the accommodation itself. Owners Alexander and Lucinda Scott concentrate on the things that matter: comfy beds with crisp cotton bedlinen; properly lined curtains; efficient central heating; log fires; quality crockery, cutlery and glassware; well-equipped kitchens; bathrooms with big cast-iron baths as well as showers - so, after a stormy day walking the Balcary cliff-top path, you can then have a hot soak in a full-length bath. Or you could have a sweat in the new steam room. This place never rests on its laurels!

Second, there's the outstanding leisure facilities. In a sheltered courtyard is a wonderful large heated swimming pool (open May to September), with proper quality deckchairs and sun loungers. There's also a tennis court, giant chess and in a garage are bike racks - this is a great area for cycling.

Third, there's the location, right at the midpoint of Dumfries & Galloway. Gelston is far from the madding crowd and yet only 3 miles from the thriving small market town of Castle Douglas. The town was founded by Sir William Douglas who built Gelston Castle as his home in 1800.

Fourth, there's the 4500 acre estate, one of the prettiest in southern Scotland: hills, pasture, woodlands and the magical Solway coast. It stretches 6 miles from Gelston village to Almorness peninsula, a beautiful and wild place where the small Galloway oaks grow and naturalists count rare bugs and butterflies. At the end of the peninsula is one of the most idyllic beaches in Britain, looking out to Hestan Island where a king of Scotland lived in the 14th century. You can walk to the island by a mussel-encrusted causeway at low tide.

29 BALCARY MEWS BED & BREAKFAST

Balcary Bay, Auchencairn, nr Castle
Douglas DG7 1QZ
Tel: 01556 640276
e-mail: pamelavaughan@yahoo.com
website: www.balcarymews.co.uk

Lying in Dumfries and Galloway in Scotland's South West, **Balcary Mews** is a beautiful home on the sea front. Slightly elevated, Balcary Mews commands magnificent uninterrupted views across Balcary Bay, with the Galloway Hills and coastline beyond and Hestan Island to the fore. It is beautifully appointed, adjacent to spectacular coastal walks and ideal for exploring glorious Galloway.

Balcary Mews has a large, welcoming reception area with seating and ample space for walking boots and coats along wth an abundance of local tourist information. The accommodation is superb and consists of three spacious bedrooms individually designed and beautifully co-ordinated and all with fabulous sea views. All rooms are well appointed

with a television and complimentary trays. Your host, Pamela Vaughan serves a delicious Scottish cooked breakfast. The guest sitting room has spectacular panoramic frontage with Patio doors opening onto the terrace and into a large, colourful landscaped garden which guests are welcome to enjoy.

Adjoining Balcary Mews is a very comfortable, well-appointed semi-detached cottage, which sleeps four and is available for letting throughout the year. All prices quoted are inclusive of linen, towels, fuel and electricity.

Ample private parking, non-smoking, 4 Tourist Board stars.

30 BOBBIN GUEST HOUSE

36 High Street, Gatehouse of Fleet,
Kirkcudbrightshire DG7 2HP
Tel: 01557 814229
e-mail: bobbinguesthouse@sky.com

From a professional catering background and with two years at the **Bobbin Guest House** under her belt, Helen Findlay certainly has the credentials for running a successful inn. Based in the area for a long time, Helen has built up a well deserved reputation for fine service, comfortable accommodation and fine food. Originally constructed in 1770, and adorned with colourful window boxes, the Bobbin guest house is one of the oldest buildings in Gatehouse of Fleet, a pretty

town on the edge of the Galloway Forest Park.

The warm and comfortable accommodation takes the form of five en suite rooms, comprised of three doubles, one twin and one family, all of which are available at very reasonable rates that include a delicious breakfast cooked by Helen herself who is a fine cook. In house facilities include a well decorated guest lounge, a securer area for storing bicycles and a drying area for wet clothes from walkers exploring the vicinity. Local facilities include opportunities for a variety of sporting activities: golf, sailing, mountain biking and fishing.

367

ACCOMMODATION, FOOD, DRINK AND PLACES TO VISIT

31 THE SMUGGLERS GRILL

12-14 Castle Street, Stranraer DG9 7RT
Tel: 01776 706195
e-mail: thesmugglersdg9@btconnect.com

Located on the first floor above a craft bakery, **The Smugglers Grill** is owned and run by Jane Kennedy and Kenny Walker who opened their restaurant in 2006. Their aim was to provide appetising home-made food using traditional recipes and locally sourced ingredients. Most items on the menu, including the sausages, are made in the kitchen here.

The extensive menu, which varies according to the seasons, includes lots of old favourites such as steak pie, haddock and chips, and home-made chicken curry. Vegetarian options include home-made macaroni, spicy veggie burger, and various omelettes. Also on offer are an all day Scottish breakfast, baked potatoes, and a good range of sandwiches, wraps and baguettes.

Special dietary requirements can be catered for if advance notice is given.

The Smugglers Grill also provides a comprehensive selection of outside catering and is available for private hire for weddings and other celebrations. The restaurant is open from 9.15am to 3pm, Monday to Saturday; all major credit cards except American Express are accepted.

32 CAFÉ CREE

48 Victoria Street, Newton Stewart,
Wigtownshire,
Dumfries & Galloway DG8 6BT
Tel: 01671 404203
e-mail: enquiries@cafecree.co.uk
website: www.cafecree.co.uk

If you are passionate about food and using local produce, then **Café Cree** is your kind of eating place. It only opened in May 2006 but in 2008 was named as one of the 5 Scottish finalists in the Gary Rhodes search for Local Food Heroes.

Owners Jan and Chris Cole are passionate about where their food comes from - they know their suppliers and name them on the menu. They prepare really home-made soups, carrot, sage and cashew, for example, and their bread is handmade. Their smoked salmon, cream cheese, fresh lemon and black pepper sandwich provides the opportunity to sample the excellent Marrbury smoked salmon as served to world leaders at the Gleneagles G8 summit. And their gently scrambled or properly poached duck eggs are made from fresh, free range duck eggs laid beside the River Cree.

This is an outstandingly customer-friendly café - children are welcome and so are dogs; and the cafe is on one level with a disabled toilet provided. Jan and Chris understand vegetarians and vegans, and can usually offer gluten/wheat-free bread, pasta and cakes, and non-dairy butter substitutes. Café Cree is open from 10am to 5pm, but closed on Mondays during the winter months.

368

33 FLOWERBANK GUEST HOUSE

Millcroft Road, Minnigaff,
Newton Stewart DG8 6PJ
Tel: 01671 402629
e-mail: enquiries@flowerbankgh.com
website: www.flowerbankgh.com

Flowerbank Guest House is an attractive 18th century listed building set on the picturesque bank of the River Cree. It stands in more than an acre of private landscaped gardens with a summerhouse, numerous flowerbeds and rockeries, a pergola and fountain, and an extensive central lawn that runs to a tree-lined riverbank with seating areas. The vegetable plots and greenhouse allow owners Michael and Diane Reynolds to grow a wide range of fresh ingredients.

Guests have the use of a spacious south-facing lounge overlooking the garden and with a coal/log fire for cooler days. The house has 5 guest bedrooms, four of which have en suite facilities. Three of the rooms enjoy

views of the garden and river while the other two have pleasant views over neighbouring gardens to the Minnigaff hills in the distance. A hearty Scottish breakfast is included in the tariff and evening meals which make extensive use of home-grown and local produce are available on request. Flowerbank is open from March to November; dogs are accepted; and payment is by cash or cheque only.

34 LOCHANCROFT

24 Lochancroft Lane, Wigtown,
Wigtownshire DG8 9JA
Tel: 01988 402499

This beautifully restored two bedroom croft is the ideal base for exploring Galloway. Situated on a quiet residential road in Wigtown, the apartment contains a mix of antique furniture and modern appliances. Within a two minute walk are pubs, shops, a golf course, and miles of stunning countryside. The surrounding area is described as Scotland in miniature, with beaches, mountains, forests, lochs and rolling green landscapes dotted with stone circles, ancient monuments, castles and pretty towns.

The double bedroom has a superking size bed and a twin room has two single beds; there's also a folding bed in the sitting room. In the bathroom the roll-top Victorian bath is perfect for a long soak and the kitchen has all the essentials with the added luxury of a dishwasher and a cappuccino maker. There's a TV, DVD player and stereo in the sitting room, and downstairs in the hall there's a small laundry

room with washing machine. The flat has a wireless broadband connection free of charge.

In the south-facing garden you'll find a range of plants which flourish here thanks to the warming influence of the Gulf Stream , as well as a paved area with a barbecue, and a lawn.

ACCOMMODATION, FOOD, DRINK AND PLACES TO VISIT

35 KIRKINNER INN

5 Main Street, Kirkinner,
Wigtownshire DG8 9AN
Tel: 01988 840252
e-mail: muira86@aol.com

At the heart of the pleasant village of Kirkinner stands an impressive Victorian building that hosts the warm and welcoming **Kirkinner Inn**. The colourful window boxes and hanging baskets adorn the exterior and create the feeling that this inn is well looked after. Owners Alex and Jane have been the proprietors for four years now and the reputation of the Kirkinner Inn has certainly improved in that time. Alex is a keen fisherman and a fly-fishing instructor whilst Jane enjoys walking, reading and collecting whiskies.

Frequented by locals and tourists alike, the Kirkinner Inn provides sumptuous food on a daily basis, the excellent chefs producing delicious fresh meals from a well thought out, extensive menu. Using only the finest of locally sourced ingredients, the chefs

have created a menu that manages to cater for every taste. The kitchens will also produce breakfasts by appointment and have a popular takeaway service.

The good sized restaurant has space for 30 covers and the well stocked bar boasts a large TV for those special events and a pool table. Open all year round from 12 till 12, the Kirkinner welcomes dogs and children on family days out.

36 THE HARBOUR INN

18 South Crescent, Garlieston DG8 8BQ
Tel: 01988 600685

Occupying a superb position looking out across Wigtown Bay, the hamlet of Garlieston has only one hostelry which, happily, is a very good one. A Grade II listed building, **The Harbour Inn** has been owned and run since 1992 by Margaret (Maggie) Harrison, a local lass who was born in the nearby town of Whithorn. Her inn is interestingly decorated with a nautical theme and the walls and ceilings are of wooden boarding.

Garlieston is also very fortunate in that the inn serves excellent home-made food every lunchtime and evening. The extensive menu offers dishes such as Maggie's home-made soup of the day, or crispy coated Camembert among the starters. The main course choices include some perennial favourites such as home-made steak pie or battered haddock, while

vegetarians are well-catered for with dishes like a creamy vegetable Kiev, or a spicy bean burger. Desserts range from home-made apple pie to a delicious chocolate & hazelnut meringue roulade. Children have their own menu. Food is served from 12 noon until 2pm; and from 6pm to 8pm.

The inn has a charming beer garden and also offers accommodation in 2 en suite rooms.

37 THE ROYAL CAFE

11 New Rd, Ayr KA8 8DA
Tel: 01292 263058
e-mail: philipmancini1@hotmail.com
website: www.mancinisicecream.co.uk

Producing high quality products ranging from dairy and non-dairy ice cream, fresh fruit sorbets and Italian high quality frozen desserts, M B Mancini & Co has been at **The Royal Café**, Ayr since 1925 with the company being 96 years old. The highly recommended company can produce more than 200 different flavours of ice cream and operates Ayr's only Italian style café. Owner, Philip Mancini, is the *UK's Champion of Champions* in ice cream making and his family has been making ice cream in the town since 1913. Having been voted, *Scottish Ice Cream Champions* and winning many awards, such as *Champion of Champions Vanilla, Champion of Champions, Flavour Class, Chocolate and Mango Sorbet Class* at the *National Ice Cream Championships 2009/2010*, the Mancini's are well known for their ability to produce high quality ice cream and people travel from all over to sample the delights on offer. Mancini's are also highly recommended in *Scotland, the best guide 2010* by Peter Irvine.

From the outside the stone building has a traditional shop front and is located close to the town's amenities. Inside, it is tastefully decorated and can seat 40 people, many who return time and time again to enjoy the offerings of the traditional fish and chip shop and ice cream parlour. cakes are made to order and there are hot and cold snacks and meals available as well as teas and coffee. The café is open from 9am-10pm seven days a week and also operates a take away service. Twenty flavours of ice cream are available for take-away or take-home packs to the retail trade.

The cafe trades under the name of 'The Royal Café' and is currently undergoing refurbishment, with the fourth generation of Mancinis already taking an active part. The company is being run today by Anna and Philip Mancini. Philip has 30 years experience in ice cream manufacturing and spent eight years on the national executive committee of the Ice Cream Alliance Ltd and had the great honour of being national president of the association in the year of 1993/94. He is in charge of all production of Mancini's Ice Cream on a daily basis which is now being wholesaled through the West of Scotland by the company's own refrigerated vehicle. For a small company, Mancini's has a big name for ice cream in Scotland and has won many national awards. In the thirties to the fifties Mancini made ice cream for many outlets in Ayr and serviced the Ayr Promenade with their high quality ice cream. The company is almost 90 years old and is still under the Mancini family and four generations later is still producing high quality products with Philip's son Mark now in charge of production . Mancini's also operate a little cafe on Prestwick Promenade, 1mile from Glasgow Prestwick Airport.

38 ARRAN GARDENS B&B - SHELLDUN

36 Arran Gardens, Troon KA10 6TE
Tel: 01292 679 532
website: www.shelldun.co.uk

Attention to detail makes the **Shelldun B&B** a comfortable and ideal get-away for those wanting to explore the west coast of Scotland. The large detached corner bungalow is situated to the north

of Troon in a quiet residential area. It offers ground floor, level accommodation in two en-suite twin/double bedrooms and one single bedroom. The two twin bedrooms face the front of the property, the single bedroom boasts a door into the secluded south facing garden. The guest lounge is light and spacious with French doors which open onto a level patio within the walled garden. Linda maintains high standards of comfort, quality and privacy for guests throughout. Breakfast is served in the conservatory, so that guests can enjoy the view over the garden. Produce is organic, free range and from local

farms or suppliers when possible. Snacks and picnic lunches along with evening meals are available with prior notice.

Shelldun is only 100 yards from Barassie Beach and boasts views over the Firth of Clyde to the Isle of Arran. It is conveniently located for all road, rail, air and sea links to the West Coast of Scotland and the many places of interest and golf courses the area has to offer.

39 CROWN HOTEL

24 Cunningham Street, Tarbolton,
Ayrshire KA5 5QG
Tel: 01292 541222

The small village of Tarbolton is well known to fans of Robert Burns as it was here he founded the Tarbolton Bachelors Club in 1780. Another good reason for visiting is to call in at The **Crown Hotel**, a small family run business where you are sure of a welcome in the friendly bar, where you can sample one of the many malts on offer. Why not stay over night? Rooms are en-suite and you are sure of a hearty breakfast. (The pleasant beer garden where families are very welcome is nice and quiet.) The Crown is open until 12.30am, Monday to Saturday; and until midnight on Sunday.

HIDDEN PLACES GUIDES

Explore Britain and Ireland with *Hidden Places* guides - a fascinating series of national and local travel guides.

Packed with easy to read information on hundreds of places of interest as well as places to stay, eat and drink.

Available from both high street and internet booksellers

For more information on the full range of *Hidden Places* guides and other titles published by Travel Publishing visit our website on

www.findsomewhere.co.uk or ask for our leaflet by phoning **01752 697280** or emailing **info@travelpublishing.co.uk**

Maybole, Ayrshire KA19 7DD

website: www.maybole.org

Maybole Castle is the oldest inhabited house in the town having been built about the middle of the sixteenth century (believed to be around 1560). It was the town house of the Earls of Cassillis who spent most of the winter months in Maybole, and was the largest and finest of the twenty-eight lairds' houses written about by Abercrummie in 1696. It was built in the style of a typical Scottish castle, with square tower and round turrets, and strong enough to protect its occupants from unfriendly neighbours, of whom there were many at that time. The main hall was above vaulted cellars which still remain and above the hall were the sleeping apartments. The retainers' quarters were on the other side of a gateway which gave entrance into the castle yard, built round the well, locally known as "The Pump".

The tower is capped by a lovely little oriel window with heads carved round it which local people wrongly believe represent the heads of Johnnie Faa and his gypsies. The corbels to the roof of the little room at the top of the tower (known as the Countess's Room) are carved with male and female heads and symbols of fertility. The walls are extremely thick (in some places about seven feet) and it must have been a safe retreat in troublesome times when the Earls lived in it, with their own men around them in the small township clustered on the hillside below it.

It was from Maybole Castle that the Earl of Cassillis and his men sallied forth to the fight at Ladycross in December 1601, when young Bargany was killed in the bitter feud between the Cassillis and Bargany families. Locally there is an old tale of the Countess of Cassillis being imprisoned at the top of the tower, after she had allegedly eloped with Johnnie Faa, King of the Gypsies, but while the story is a delightful one, facts disprove it.

As years passed the Earls spent less of their time in Maybole, and gradually the old Castle fell into disrepair and was practically abandoned except for a few old retainers who lived in outbuildings. In 1805 the Earl of Cassillis agreed with the town council that the part sited where the Post Office now stands could be demolished to allow a road to be formed from the foot of the High Street to Duncanland Toll at the bottom of Redbrae. When the old buildings were removed the Earl decided to repair the Castle and in 1812 re-roofed it and built some additions. The gardens and park had walls erected round them and from 1812 the Castle has remained as it is now, apart from repairs to the roof following a fire in 1919.

The Historical Society has been very active in promoting Maybole Castle since May-Tag (founded by the Community Council in 1986 as a training company to promote local unemployment) moved out and has said, "The Castle goes from strength to strength and we have a very good relationship with the factor and through him the Estate and Trustee. We are putting together proposals and plans for opening the castle regularly to the public; improving and expanding the display material in the castle; and the future of the castle as a heritage centre".

40 KIRKTON INN

Main Street, Dalrymple,
Ayrshire KA6 6DF
Tel: 01292 560241 Fax: 01292 560835
e-mail: kirkton@com.co.uk

Located in the picturesque village of Dalrymple, the **Kirkton Inn** occupies a charming stone building dating back to 1879. Part of it used to serve as the village hall. Vicki Fairfoull and Joyce Hislop took over here in the spring of 2009 when the premises were completely refurbished in traditional style. They offer their customers a good choice of appetising "pub grub" which is served every lunchtime (noon until 2.30pm) and evening (5pm to 9pm), Monday to Saturday, and from noon until 8pm on Sunday. In good weather, enjoy your meal in the beer garden at the rear where there's also a kids play area.

The inn stocks an excellent selection of wines and spirits, and even has a special Malt Room for sampling the various whiskies. If you are staying in this lovely part of Ayrshire, the inn offers ground floor, level accommodation in 2 en-suite twin/double bedrooms and one single bedroom. The 2 twin bedrooms face the front of the property, the single bedroom boasts

a door into the secluded south facing garden. The guest lounge is light and spacious with French doors which open onto a level patio within the walled garden. Linda maintains high standards of comfort, quality and privacy for guests throughout. Set in the heart of Burns Country, the inn is just 3 miles from the Burns Heritage Museum and Cottage, and close to Turnberry and the Royal Troon golf course.

42 CORRA-LINN

20 Louisa Drive, Girvan,
Ayrshire KA26 9AH
Tel: 01465 712178
e-mail: corra-linn1@tiscali.co.uk
website: www.corra-linn.co.uk

Facing the sea and with an uninterrupted view of the Ailsa Craig bird sanctuary, **Corra-Linn** is a handsome Victorian property dating back to the 1850s. It's the home of Carol and Eddie Williams who have been welcoming guests here since 2002.

Inside, the rooms are high-ceilinged with original cornices and roses, and impressive crystal chandeliers adorn the dining room and hallway. There are 8 guest bedrooms in all - 5 twins, 2 doubles and one single. All the rooms are attractively furnished and decorated in traditional style, and all have en suite facilities, TV and hospitality tray. Some rooms enjoy that spectacular view of Ailsa Craig; the others command a view of the surrounding hills. In the morning, a traditional Scottish breakfast is served in the newly renovated dining room and will certainly set you up for the day.

There's plenty to see and do, whether visiting Culzean Castle or Burns Heritage; golfing, swimming, walking, touring - or just relaxing by the sea. Corra-Linn is open all year; pets are welcome; and payment is by cash or cheque only.

43   ROYAL HOTEL

36 Montgomerie Street,
Girvan, KA26 9HE
Tel: 01465 714203
e-mail: info@royalhotelgirvan.com
website: www.royalhotelgirvan.com

Paul and Nancy offer a warm welcome to all who visit the **Royal Hotel**, a friendly family-run establishment located in a residential area close to the centre of this pleasant seaside resort. The hotel is fully licensed and its bar food has a justified reputation for excellence. Enjoy one of the appetising dishes with a pint of real ale, perhaps, and in good weather take advantage of the beer garden. The menu at the Royal (available daily from 12.30pm - 8.30pm) offers plenty to choose from, with Hickory chicken, chicken with a cheese & chive sauce, haggis neeps & tatties and steaks among the favourites. A daily specials board is available and there is a mouth-watering choice of desserts to finish off a meal. During the summer months, regular barbeques are held in the large garden with comfortable seating and a water feature.

The hotel is disabled-friendly with good access throughout and disabled toilets. Accommodation at the Royal comprises 7 rooms each with flat screen TV, five of which have en suite facilities, and most have views over the town to the Firth of Clyde and Ailsa Craig which is known locally as 'Paddy's Milestane'.

Girvan lies in the heart of an area of outstanding natural beauty. A 5-minute walk from the Royal will bring you to the charming and picturesque harbour and miles of clean sandy shore. The world famous championship course at Turnberry is only 5 miles away, and this is only one of more than 20 golf courses within easy reach. Colsean Castle is only 10 miles away for those who are interested in local history, and the amazing optical illusion Electric Brae is only 15 miles away.

44 PORTHEAD TAVERN

2/4 High Street, Irvine KA12 0AY
Tel: 01294 274640
e-mail: stuart@porthead.co.uk
website: www.porthead.co.uk

A fine old traditional hostelry, the **Porthead Tavern** is set in the heart of Irvine's town centre. There's a spacious and comfortable bar offering a full range of beers, wines and spirits, as well as having full satellite subscription for all major sporting events. The lounge area provides a stylish and relaxing environment in which to enjoy a few drinks with friends or enjoy a bar meal from the very popular menu featuring a great range of cooked to order and locally sourced produce. Chef Lynn O'Donoghue prepares all meals freshly each day and his repertoire ranges from fresh haddock in batter, through chicken hoi sin parcels to steak pie and a vegetarian cheese salad.

On the first floor, the inn's cocktail lounge ABuV the

main bar and lounge offers a luxurious, sophisticated environment to enjoy an extensive range of fine wines and cocktails at very reasonable prices. This truly is a great place to spend an evening out with friends.

The Porthead also caters for a range of private functions, whether it be a christening, special birthday celebration or any other function, they can satisfy all your catering requirements.

45 SCOTTISH MARITIME MUSEUM

Harbourside, Irvine KA12 8QE
Tel: 01294 278283 Fax: 01294 313211
website:
www.scottishmaritimemuseum.org

The museum is sited in three locations - the **Scottish Maritime Museum** at Irvine, Clydebuilt at Braehead and the Denny Ship Model Experiment at Dumbarton. At Irvine you will have the opportunity for a guided tour which includes a restored 1920's

shipyard workers 'Tenement Flat' and a collection of moored vessels in the harbour, some of which can be boarded. Trips are occasionally available for visitors. The museum shop stocks a wide selection of souvenirs and light meals, snacks and drinks are served at the Puffers Coffee Shop on the wharf. Check website for opening times.

48 THE TALL SHIP AT GLASGOW HARBOUR

100 Stobcross Road, Glasgow G3 8QQ
Tel: 0141 222 2513
e-mail: info@thetallship.com
website: www.thetallship.com

Sail through 100 years of maritime history at the **Tall Ship at Glasgow Harbour**. Follow the remarkable restoration of the Glenlee from an abandoned hulk in Seville harbour to her fullyrigged splendour today and learn about the living conditions aboard a deep sea trading ship.

Explore the cargo hold where you will see what goods she carried, the deck house where the crew lived, the poop deck and the galley. Also in the harbour is the Pier 17 restaurant, a gift shop and various exhibitions and events. Phone for details.

Largs Yacht Haven, Largs,
Ayrshire   KA30 8EZ
Tel: 01475 689198
website: www.thebosunstable.co.uk

Beautifully located within the bustling and picturesque Largs Yacht Haven in the popular seaside holiday town of Largs, **The Bosun's** enjoys a fine and growing reputation for quality food, freshly prepared on the premises and served with efficiency and a friendly manner. It is very much a family-run business, owned and run under the personal supervision of David and Margaret Rennie, their son Douglas and daughter Linda.

Formerly known as The Bosun's Table, the restaurant occupies a spacious, light and airy conservatory looking out to an extensive outside seating area surrounded by rock gardens. Here customers can enjoy a wide selection of meals ranging from hearty all day breakfasts and lunches, to lighter fare such as burgers, baked potatoes, toasties and sandwiches. The main course dishes include old favourites such as chicken curry, macaroni cheese, breaded haddock and, of course, haggis and neeps. Under 10's can choose from the Cadet's Corner menu, whilst over 60's have their own Senior Sailor Special menu. In the evenings, a different menu is available which changes every week. Your choice here might include chili and ginger mussels, or cajan breaded mushrooms among the starters; prime Scotch steak, whole grilled lemon sole, or a vegetable, tomato and basil tagliatelli as a main course.

The Bosun's is fully licensed from 8am and serves a range of beers and whiskeys along with its own range of wines from all around the world, some of which are available by the glass. There's something to suit every taste and budget and even the most discerning guests will find something to excite their palate.

During the summer months, The Bosun's is open from 9am to 7pm, Monday to Thursday; from 8am until late, Friday and Saturday; and from 8am to 5pm on Sunday. In winter, the restaurant closes at 5pm, Monday to Thursday.

47 POLLOK HOUSE

Pollok Country Park,
2060 Pollokshaws Road,
Glasgow G43 1AT
Tel: 0141 616 6410 Fax: 014) 616 6521
e-mail pollokhouse@nts.org.uk
website: www.nts.org.uk

Visit **Pollok House** and capture the flavour of one of Scotland's grandest Edwardian country houses. It is the ancestral home of the Maxwells of Pollok, who have lived on this site for 700 years. The present house, which replaced three earlier structures, was begun in 1747. It was extended from 1890 by Sir John Stirling Maxwell Bt, KT, a founder member of The National Trust for Scotland.

The house contains much original furniture as well as some of the finest Spanish paintings in Britain. A rare survival is the magnificent suite of servants' quarters, which shows the scale of country house life around 1900. These contain the popular Edwardian Kitchen Restaurant, renowned for

its lunch menu and home baking, and the shop in the Housekeeper's Room. At weekends, visitors can see a reconstruction, of the way the house might have been run at the turn of the last century. Pollok House is set amid formal and walled gardens at the heart of **Pollok Country Park**.

50 CONSERVATORY BAR

Cloch Caravan Park, Cloch Rd,
Gourock PA19 1AY
Tel: 01475 659033
e-mail: conservatory@the-cloch.co.uk
website: www.the-cloch.co.uk

This popular venue is located on the outskirts of Gourock and overlooks the Firth of Clyde. The bar is located in Cloch Caravan Park, and has a strong reputation with those who live in the surrounding area. The bar's owners, Alan and Rosemary Lyall, have been there since February 2008. Having visited the caravan park for years, when the bar became available it seemed like the ideal opportunity for the couple.

The Conservatory Bar is tastefully decorated and full of character, with many pictures and memorabilia on the walls. The lounge area, which boasts comfortable leather armchairs, provides the perfect place for people to relax with a drink. All of the food served is cooked on site by Rosemary and there is a strong focus on local produce.

 Around 40 people can be seated in the dining area and children are more than welcome.

Once a month there is live entertainment at the bar and every Saturday it is the customers who provide the entertainment with Karaoke and Disco. The Conservatory Bar is open seven days a week from 11am-11pm and on a Saturday it opens an hour longer. Food is served until 8pm. There is full disabled access, with a ramp to the rear of the premise, and ample parking.

Whistlefield, Garelochhead G84 OEP
Tel: 01436 810000
e-mail: sandramartin46@yahoo.com

Nestled in the hills of Whistlefield, the **Green Kettle Inn** is a real hidden gem. The impressive establishment, surrounded by countryside, boasts some spectacular hill views and has four tastefully decorated en-suite rooms. There are two doubles, a family room and a twin room, all boasting en-suite facilities, TV, and a complimentary selection of beverages. The rooms really are lovely and this delightful B&B is in an ideal location for those wanting to explore Loch Lomond and the surrounding area. The B&B is beautifully furnished throughout and has a wealth of charm and character.

The views from the Green Kettle Inn stretch over Loch Lomond and many visitors return again and again to get away from the hustle and bustle of city life and enjoy the relaxation the place has to offer. That said, there are plenty of activities in the area if sports is more your thing. Outdoor activities range from golf, hill walking, horse riding, clay pigeon shooting, bird watching and fishing. There really is something for everyone and there are plenty of opportunities to get out on the water of Loch Lomond, sailing or canoeing. The area is extremely popular with walkers and those interested in wildlife. Trossachs National Park and the Highland Whiskey Trail are just some of the beautiful places to visit in the area and there are some stunning views to be enjoyed.

With so much exploring to do, it is a good job owners Sandra and George (who have owned the Green Kettle Inn since February 2009) cook up a hearty Scottish full cooked breakfast. Home cooking and local produce is at the heart of the food served and with a newly refurbish restaurant, finished to a high standard, guests and visitors are guaranteed a good evening. On brighter days many guests like to make the most of the outside seating area and with the surrounding views of the countryside it is obvious why.

Whether it is a relaxing break, family holiday or sporting/adventure weekend you are after, Loch Lomond is certainly a good choice. With a warm welcome waiting to greet you, the Green Kettle Inn, which offers accommodation and dining of a high standard, is an ideal place to stay. The B&B has a really friendly atmosphere, providing a home from home and has a growing reputation in the area.

379

51 | THE SHAWLANDS PARK HOTEL

Ayr Road, Shawsburn, Larkhall,
Lanarkshire ML9 2TZ
Tel/Fax: 01698 791111
e-mail: reception@shawlandshotel.co.uk
website: www.shawlandsparkhotel.co.uk

Recently re-opened following extensive refurbishment, **The Shawlands Park Hotel** is tucked away in rural Lanarkshire within the picturesque Clyde Valley. The hotel stands in its own grounds on the A71, half-way between Glasgow and Edinburgh, and is the epitome of luxury. This stunning hotel has a uniquely intimate atmosphere, making it the ideal setting for special occasions and perfect breaks.

Arrange to meet your family and friends in the public bar to enjoy the relaxed atmosphere, sample one of the bar meals and snacks, or have a session on the pool table. An interesting feature of the bar is an organ and pulpit brought here from Broomhill Parish Church. Every Thursday, from 8.30pm, the bar is the venue for a lively karaoke evening - the hotel boasts a state-of-the-art sound and lighting system.

The hotel's commitment to quality catering can be experienced in the Ash Grill Restaurant & Carvery where, using only fresh, local produce, the dedicated team of chefs has created an exquisite menu with something to suit everyone. With a passion for food and the desire to delight every guest, the team strive to make every mouthful delicious.

The restaurant caters for all special dietary requirements and food is served all day, every day.

The accommodation at Shawlands maintains the same high standards evident throughout the hotel. There are 48 rooms and suites with a choice that includes standard and premier rooms, premier suites and premier family suites with 2 bedrooms and 2 bathrooms making them the ideal family retreat. The standard rooms are equipped with a private bath/shower, satellite TV, hospitality tray, hair dryer and direct dial telephone. The suites have private balconies with stunning views over the picturesque Clyde Valley, a large lounge area with double sofa bed, mini bar, large plasma TV, power shower and bath robes.

For special occasions, there's the hotel's function room which is the largest in South Lanarkshire, capable of catering for up to 300 guests, and there's also a 200-space car park. Naturally, the hotel is a popular venue for weddings and has a highly experienced management team to help and guide you through every aspect of your special day.

52 THE ROYAL YACHT BRITANNIA

Ocean Terminal, Leith, Edinburgh, Scotland
EH6 6JJ
Tel: 0131 555 5566
e-mail: enquiries@tryb.co.uk
website: www.royalyachtbritannia.co.uk

For over forty years **The Royal Yacht *Britannia*** served the Royal Family, travelling over one million miles to become the most famous ship in the world. Travelling to every corner of the globe, in a career spanning 968 royal and official visits, she played a leading role in some of the defining moments of recent history. To Her Majesty The Queen and the Royal Family, *Britannia* proved to be the perfect royal residence for glittering State Visits, official receptions, honeymoons and relaxing family holidays. Since her decommissioning *Britannia* has now made Edinburgh's historic Port of Leith her final home and is open to the public throughout the year. Now owned by The Royal Yacht *Britannia* Trust, a non profit making charity, any proceeds go towards *Britannia's* maintenance.

Your tour of *Britannia* starts in the Visitor Centre on the second floor of Ocean Terminal. Here you can learn about *Britannia's* fascinating history through exhibits and photographs before you collect your complimentary audio handset and step on board *Britannia,* a privilege previously reserved for guests of Her Majesty The Queen and the Royal Family. Starting at the Bridge and finishing at the gleaming Engine Room, come and discover the reality behind life and work on board this Royal Yacht. Viewing five decks, using the lift or stairs for easy access, you will tour *Britannia* at your own pace and enjoy highlights that include the State Dining Room, the Drawing Room, the Sun Lounge, the Wardroom and the Chief Petty Officers' Mess. *Britannia* is furnished with artefacts from The Royal Collection, which are on loan from Her Majesty The Queen.

53 MUSEUM OF SCOTLAND

Chambers Street, Edinburgh EH1 1JF
Tel: 0131 247 4422
website: www.nms.ac.uk

The **Museum of Scotland** tells the remarkable story of a remarkable country. From the geological dawn of time to modern day life in Scotland, you'll discover the roots of a nation - a land steeped in fascinating cultures and terrible wars, passionate religion and scientific invention. A land of creative struggle - and occasionally of glorious failure. In a unique and purpose - built museum are gathered together the treasured inheritance and cultural icons which tell Scotland's many stories. The people, the land, the events that have shaped the way they live now.

If you weren't aware of the extraordinary history and impressive achievements of this small country, then it's time to find out. Because after more than 3,000 million years of Scotland's story, there is the perfect place in which to celebrate it - the Museum of Scotland. The exhibits include the earliest known fossil reptile found in Bathgate, dating back to 338 million years BC, artefacts from around 8,000 BC when the first settlers arrived and a tiny shrine thought to date from AD 750.

The museum shop sells a wide variety of souvenirs and a café and restaurant ensure that all appetities are catered for. Guides are available and there is a rooftop garden with spectacular views. Open Monday to Saturday 10am-5pm and Sunday 12 noon-5pm. Disabled access.

54 THE VOLUNTEER ARMS

17 Victoria Street, Dunbar,
East Lothian EH42 1HP
Tel: 01368 862278
e-mail: doniw@btconnect.com

With views overlooking Dunbar Harbour,
The Volunteer Arms is a small family-run
pub specialising in good homemade food at
reasonable
prices. There is
an extensive
menu offering
the very best in
traditional
cuisine and food
is served from
12pm-9pm.

Homemade steak & ale pie and seafood pie
are among the favourite dishes served and
there is a special children's menu for younger
diners. At the front of the establishment, the
delightful patio area boasts views of the
harbour and many locals and visitors like to
enjoy a meal or drink there on brighter days.
Pre-arranged small functions can be catered
for. All major credit cards accepted.

57 IVY TEA ROOM

68 South Street, Bo'ness EH51 9HA
Tel: 01506 823389

The **Ivy Tea Room** is a quaint coffee shop
located in the heart of the Scottish town of
Bo'ness (Borrowstounness). The exterior of
the premises is dominated by beautiful
Georgian
windows,
adding to the
character and
charm of the
place. Inside,
the tables are
spaciously laid

out, allowing people to enjoy one of the
many drinks or homemade fare on offer.
Situated on the south bank of the Firth of
Forth the town was formerly a major port
and the centre of the coal mining industry in
the area. Now a commuter town, The Ivy Tea
Room is extremely popular with locals and
visitors with a number of attractions nearby
such as a railway museum, car museum and
the Hippodrome (the oldest purpose built
cinema in Scotland).

55 THE GARVALD INN

Garvald, nr Haddington,
East Lothian EH41 4LN
Tel: 01620 830311
e-mail: garvald_inn@garvald.org

Dating back to the 18th century, **The Garvald Inn**
is a welcoming purpose-built hotel in a beautiful,
rural setting. Located in the hidden village of
Garvald, on the Hill Foots Trails, the family-run
establishment is extremely popular with walkers
and cyclists who frequent the area and it is open all year round. Owners, Peter and Elaine
McQuade are friendly hosts and the multi fuel stove
makes for a cosy bar area. Although there is a separate
restaurant area, food can be enjoyed at one's leisure in
the bar too. The bar area used to be a Drapers Store and
its south facing beer garden is a real sun trap on brighter
days. Many visitors to The Garvald Inn enjoy sitting
outside the inn with a cold drink and something to eat.

The menu
has a lot to offer,
serving mostly
traditional food,
including a lot of
fish and game. All
of the produce is of the highest quality and local produce
is used where possible. Among the most popular dishes are
the seafood platter and traditional Sunday lunches, as well
as the numerous vegetarian options available. Closed all day
on Mondays, as well as Sunday evenings. There is
wheelchair access.

56 THE OLD FARM HOUSE

Redshill Farm, Gifford, Haddington,
East Lothian EH41 4JN
Tel: 01620 810406
e-mail: redshill@btinternet.com
website:
www.haddingtonaccommodation.com

Offering a choice of B&B or self-catering accommodation, **The Old Farmhouse** is an imaginatively converted former cart shed, now the home of Ian and Gill Tait who run the surrounding farm with their son. The farm is mainly arable, growing barley for malting, but there are also some sheep grazing on the permanent pasture. Guests have the use of an attractively decorated lounge overlooking the garden and there's a cosy fire for chilly days. The house has 3 guest bedrooms, all ensuite and equipped with TV, DVD player, hospitality trays, toiletries, bathrobes and hair dryer. Business travellers can take advantage of a WiFi connection.

Breakfast is something to really look forward to. There's

a buffet style selection of juice, fruit, cereals and so on followed by your choice of freshly prepared cooked breakfast, complemented by home-made preserves.

If you prefer self catering, there's a charming cottage available which has its' own enclosed garden and can sleep up to 4 people. It has spacious bedrooms, a comfortable lounge/dining room, modern bathroom and a well equipped kitchen.

59 ROYAL PALACE OF FALKLAND

Falkland, Cupar, Fife KY15 7BU
Tel: 01337 857397 Fax: 01337 857980
Tel shop: 01337 857918
website: www.nts.org.uk

The **Royal Palace of Falkland** was the country residence of Stuart Kings and Queens when they hunted deer and wild boar in the Fife forest. Mary, Queen of Scots spent some of the happiest days of her tragic life here, 'playing the country girl in the woods and parks'. The Palace was built between 1501 and 1541 by James IV and James V, replacing earlier castle and palace buildings dating from the 12th century, traces of which can still be seen in the grounds. The roofed South Range contains the Chapel Royal, and the East Range the King's Bedchamber and the Queen's Room, both restored by the Trust. The Keeper's Apartments in the Gatehouse are now also on display. The palace contains fine portraits of the Stuart monarchs and two sets of 17th century tapestry hangings.

The garden, designed and built by Percy Cane between 1947 and 1952, contains three herbaceous borders enclosing a wide lawn with many varieties of shrubs and trees. Here also is the original Royal Tennis Court, the oldest in Britain still in use, built in 1539. There is also a small herb garden border featuring quotations from John Gerard's book *Herboll (1597)*. Exhibitions at Royal Tennis Court and at Town Hall.

58 THE ELGIN HOTEL

Charlestown, by Dunfermline,
Fife KY11 3EE
Tel: 01383 872257
Fax: 01383 873044
e-mail: info@theelginhotel.com
website: www.theelginhotel.com

Located in the tranquil and picturesque village of Charlestown, only a ten minute drive from Dunfermline, **The Elgin Hotel** is a beautiful country house hotel enjoying beautiful views over the Firth of Forth,

the Pentland Hills and the world famous Forth Bridges.

Over many years the Elgin Hotel has gained a reputation for quality service, fine food and warm hospitality. If you are looking for a good nights sleep, fine food with fresh locally sourced produce or simply a drink with friends in the welcoming bar, you'll find them all here. During the summer months you can sit outside and enjoy the beautiful gardens while your children play in the well-equipped adventure area and play park. The hotel was recently voted one of Scotland's best wedding venues, its beautiful chapel providing an intimate and idyllic setting for that special day. The secluded self-contained function suite is perfect for weddings, conferences and all types of private functions, catering for up to 160 people with its own private bar and complete with substantial car parking.

Naturally, good food is a priority here with a strong emphasis on dishes featuring top quality Scottish produce. So, in the table d'hôte menu you'll find Elgin steak pie made with prime Aberdeen Angus beef, and chicken Glen Royal - breast of chicken stuffed with haggis in a creamy whiskey and Stilton sauce.

The accommodation at the Elgin maintains the same high standards evident throughout the hotel. There's a choice of single, double and family rooms with special rates for weekend breaks as well as weekday breaks for golf, fishing, walking and shooting.

Charlestown itself is an interesting place. It was created in the 1750s a planned village by Charles Bruce, the 5th Earl of Elgin. The original layout of the village, still visible, with the houses built in the form of the letters 'CE', from Bruce's formal title of Charles Elgin. The village was all part of Charles' grand design to make most effective use of his estate's main assets: the coal and the limestone that lay under it. The Elgin Hotel was added in 1911, and a little to the north the granary and stables still stand, with the granary now converted into the village shop.

Close by, in the Charlestown Workshops, is the Scottish Lime Centre, which celebrates the heritage of the industry around which Charlestown was created.

REF: 2010

60 BALHOUSIE FARM

Upper Largo, Leven, Fife,
Scotland KY8 5QN
Tel/Fax: 01333 360680
e-mail: anneyjack@aol.com

Balhousie Farm offers guests a peaceful stay in a comfortable, warm modern farmhouse (built 2002) with

patio, large garden and duckpond. This family run bed and breakfast is set at the base of Largo Law and above the River Forth. There are a range of great golf courses to

be found in the local area in addition to many pleasant walks and of course, the farmhouse is an ideal touring base for St Andrews and the East Neuk. The rooms are complete with Freeview TV, radio alarm and tea and coffee making facilities. Open all year.

63 THE SCOTTISH FISHERIES MUSEUM

Harbourhead, Cellardyke, Anstruther,
Fife KY10 3AX
Tel: 01333 310628
website: www.scotfishmuseum.org

Situated in Anstruther, at the heart of the East Neuk fishing villages of St Monans, Pittenweem,

Cellardyke and Crail, the centre of local crab and lobster fishing, the Museum tells and researches the story of the Scottish fishing industry and its people from the earliest times to the present. The comprehensive Collection includes ships, models, paintings, photographs, equipment and the written word.

Apr-Sept 10.00-5.30 (4.30 Sun) March 10.00-4.00 (12-4.00 Sunday)

61 BRITISH GOLF MUSEUM

Bruce Embankment, St Andrews,
Fife KY16 9AB
Tel: 01334 460046
website: www.britishgolfmuseum.co.uk

*Award Winning Museum
at the Heart of the Home of Golf*

The British Golf Museum sits at the heart of the Home of Golf. Just yards from the front doors of the Museum sits The Royal and Ancient Golf Clubhouse, overlooking the 1st tee and 18th hole of the Old Course. The Clubhouse and the links of St Andrews are probably the two most emotive symbols of golf anywhere in the world. From the roof of the Museum, breathtaking views help evoke the sense of history that makes this corner of St Andrews so special.

Once inside the British Golf Museum, the history of golf unfolds before your eyes. Imaginative displays are enhanced by stunning interactives, which add to the exciting and varied ways of looking at golf's past. A unique opportunity awaits at the end of your visit to practice putting with replica clubs and balls from the last 175 years.

A visit to the British Golf Museum is the perfect break from playing golf.

385

4 High Street, Crail, Fife KY10 3TD
Tel: 01333 450206
e-mail: info@thegolfhotelcrail.com
website: www.thegolfhotelcrail.com

The award winning Golf Hotel is situated in the heart of the historic town of Crail. Famed for its quiet and unspoiled charm, the Royal and Ancient Borough of Crail has a beautiful old harbour, which alongside the traditional houses have

attracted artists and photographers for many years.

Reputed to be one of the oldest licensed inns in Scotland, The Golf Hotel is privately owned and managed by Graham Gutherie. It is extremely popular for its good food, good company and good service. Among the most reputable dishes is the Golfer's Breakfast as well as the seafood options. The restaurant seats 120 people and on brighter days meals can be enjoyed in the beer garden. Local produce is at the heart of the extensive menu and there are some good quality wines and spirits to sample too. The inn has won the Scottish Tourist Board 3 Crowns Small Inn Award and it is its growing reputation that has guests visit and revisit. The Golf Hotel is tastefully decorated throughout and the homely feel of the place continues into the comfortable residents' lounge, which has satellite TV. There are five en-suite rooms, which each have colour TV and coffee and tea making facilities as well as central heating throughout. The inn is full of character and has low ceilings with original features including beams and wooden floors. There has been an inn on the site since the early 14th century and overlooking the High Street The Golf Hotel has a warm and friendly atmosphere. Graham prides himself on the quality of produce and drinks served and the high standard of service. The lounge bar and public bar are well-known for their unique olde worlde atmosphere and tasteful decor

in keeping with the age and character of such a historic inn.

There are many places of interest to visit in the vicinity of The Golf Hotel, including the famous Fisheries Museum, Kellie Castle and Balcaskie House. Activities include bowling, pottery, tennis, golf and water sports at Ellie. There are many scenic walks to be enjoyed and there is a beach nearby. The inn, which is open all year round, has live music nights and there is private parking.

For those wanting to travel further afield, Edinburgh, Dundee, Glasgow, Stirling and the Western Highlands can all be visited on a day trip by car, using the excellent road links throughout central Scotland.

16 High Street West, Anstruther,
Fife KY10 3DL
Tel: 01333 310727
website: www.thedreeltarvern.co.uk

The **Dreel Tavern,** set in the heart of the East Neuk of Fife, is one of Anstruther's oldest and most frequented public houses. As soon as you enter the Dreel Tavern, you can feel the warm friendly atmosphere. An old tale associates the inn with a royal visitor. King James V (1513-1542) travelling incognito through Fife as the 'Guid Man O'Ballengiech', coming to the Dreel Burn and fearful of wetting his hose, was carried across at the Dreel Tavern by a stout Gaberlunzie woman who was rewarded with the king's purse.

Filled with charm and history, the Dreel Tavern offers customers a warm and friendly atmosphere along with a wide variety of beers, including guest cask conditioned ales. If you would prefer a wee dram, then there is a selection of fine Malts from around Scotland.

Customers can wine and dine in the old part of the tavern where there are old oak beams, stone walls and an open fire, or in the bright conservatory. The menu is extensive and mouth-watering, and the chef takes pride in using locally sourced sustainable produce, particularly fish, crab and lobster harvested in the Firth of Forth. Amongst the starters you'll find tasty home-made soup, hummus and chicken liver pâté, while the main courses range from home-made steak pie or lasagne, to fresh hot smoked salmon, freshly caught local dressed crab salad, or local haddock. Vegetarian dishes include a dish of stir fry vegetables and there are special meals for children. The dessert menu offers some enticing choices, amongst them sticky banoffee pie and "chocolate junk yard"! In good weather, enjoy your refreshments in the peaceful gardens to the rear of the inn, overlooking the Dreel Burn.

The Dreel Tavern is open all year round from 11am to midnight every day. Children and dogs are welcome, and all major credit cards apart from American Express are accepted. Such is the restaurant's popularity that booking is advisable at all times and when you make your booking you can also pre-order your meal using the detailed menu available on the Dreel Tavern's website.

65 THE WATERFRONT RESTAURANT

20 Shore Street, Anstruther,
Fife KY10 3EA
Tel: 01333 312200
website:
www.anstruther-waterfront.co.uk

Described as "One of the treasures of the East Neuk", **The Waterfront Restaurant** was proudly opened in May 2003 after an extensive refurbishment program to alter what was once the local bakery and then a Co-operative supermarket. It occupies Anstruther's finest location, situated just a few steps from the harbour and marina and enjoying superb views over the Firth of Forth. The restaurant was developed with a modern glass and timber frontage bringing a stylish but contemporary note to Anstruther shore front. The stylish theme continues inside where the decor in the bar and restaurant is dark chocolate complemented by oak panelling and natural slate floors, giving an overall effect of luxury and comfort.

But the main attraction that draws customers back time and time again is the extensive menu offering something for all tastes. If you wish, you could start your meal with traditional cullen skink, featuring Scotland's wealth of top-quality fresh fish. This is a strong favourite with the regulars to The Waterfront and not to be missed. However, sweet chilli tiger prawns make an exciting alternative depending on your mood, but everything on the menu is cooked and presented to the highest of standards. The main courses include a wide range of dishes varying from haggis-stuffed chicken to Mexican fajitas, with many other tempting dishes in between! A speciality at the Waterfront is its seafood selection which boasts freshly delivered fish from local markets including oriental scallops, citrus salmon, stuffed sea bass, and steamed mussels. There are also chef's specials, a children's menu, as well as delicious coffee and cakes. During the warmer months, enjoy al fresco dining at the front of the restaurant or in the mature courtyard to the rear.

If you are planning to stay in this delightful little town, The Waterfront can accommodate you in its cool and stylish 4-star en suite guest rooms. The rooms have been furnished and decorated to the highest of modern standards, and are all provided with private bathrooms, TV/DVD, hospitality tray, laundry facilities and a spacious lounge with a dining area to relax in. The Waterfront also offers a luxury self-catering apartment which enjoys views of the harbour and can sleep up to 8 persons, including a sofa bed.

66 THE SHIELING

4 East Road, Cupar, Fife KY15 4HQ
Tel: 01334 653268

Offering friendly and welcoming bed & breakfast accommodation, **The Shieling** is an attractive detached bungalow built in the 1930s with gardens to both the front and rear. The interior still has the feel of that Art Deco era with bright spacious rooms, good quality furnishings and fittings, and dark mahogany furniture. Your host is Elizabeth Cunningham who has been welcoming B&B guests since 2001.

An excellent cook, Elizabeth offers the choice of either a full Scottish or a continental breakfast, and will cater for special diets by prior arrangement. Evening meals are also available by arrangement. Alternatively, guests may use the dining room to consume takeaway

meals and to enjoy drinks of their choice.

The accommodation at The Shieling comprises 2 tastefully decorated bedrooms, (1 twin, 1 double) which currently share bathroom facilities but planning permission has recently been granted for their conversion to en suite rooms, with the work scheduled for completion by February 2010. Children are welcome; there are no special disabled facilities and payment is by cash or cheque only.

67 EDENSHEAD STABLES B&B

Gateside, by Cupar, Fife KY14 7ST
Tel: 01337 868500
e-mail: info@edensheadstables.com
website: www.edensheadstables.com

Hidden behind trees in spectacular countryside, **Edenshead Stables B&B** offers comfort, peace, good food and warm hospitality. The house is on one level with a colourful courtyard, garden and patio for guests to use and enjoy, as well as a residents' lounge. Just 3.5 miles from Jct 8 on the M90, the converted stables has 3 attractively furnished guest bedrooms, all with en suite facilities and hospitality tray. And for an evening meal, there's an inn within easy walking distance that serves good food .

68 HILLPARK HOUSE

96 Main Street, Leuchars, St Andrews
Fife KY16 0HF
Tel: 01334 839280 Fax: 01334 839051
e-mail: enquiries@hillparkhouse.com
website: www.hillparkhouse.com

Built in 1906 as a family home, **Hillpark House** now offers splendid accommodation in five comfortable and spacious rooms, three of which are fully en suite. It sits five miles from St Andrews in open countryside, and offers the very best in Scottish hospitality. The breakfasts - ranging from full Scottish to vegetarian, can be served in an airy conservatory.

389

70 THE GRAEME HOTEL

40 Grahams Road, Falkirk, FK1 1HR
Tel: 01324 628576 Fax: 01324 636340
e-mail: info@graemehotelfalkirk.co.uk
website: www.graemehotelfalkirk.co.uk

Perfectly located between the heart of Glasgow, Edinburgh and Stirling, **The Graeme Hotel** offers 14 extensively refurbished bedrooms of which 9 are en-suite and 5 with fully equipped bathrooms with shower or bath adjacent to rooms. In addition, our rooms are inclusive of sky tv, tea & coffee making facilities and ironing facilities on request.

Our newly refurbished elliot's Restaurant allows you to choose from our New Char-Grill Steak Menu and extensive range of wines in relaxed, modern surroundings. Our revised main menu and traditional Sunday Roast can either be served in elliot's Restaurant, or if you prefer you can dine within the lounge area situated within our public bar. Whether you need accommodation, a light lunch or a venue for all the family to celebrate, you can be assured that we can accommodate you here at The Graeme Hotel.

FREE CAR PARKING

71 THE PLOUGH HOTEL

507 Main Street, Stenhousemuir, FK5 4EY
Tel: 01324 570010   Fax: 01324 882545
e-mail: info@ploughhotel.com
website: www.ploughhotel.com

Perfectly located between the heart of Glasgow, Edinburgh and Stirling, **The Plough Hotel** offers 7 standard bedrooms which offer sky tv, tea & coffee making facilities, iron, shower cubical and wash hand basin. We offer breakfast, lunch and dinner which is served in our lounge from 9am - 8pm, ranging from your traditional favourites to our own daily specials. The Macallan Function Suite holds 160 guests for any event. We can provide conferencing facilities on request, so please ask our team for more details. Our new Wedding Package boasts of taking care of every aspect of your anticipated wedding day and is the least expensive venue within the Falkirk and Stirling area. Whether you need accommodation, a light lunch or a venue for all the family to celebrate your marriage, you need to contact us here at The Plough Hotel.

FREE CAR PARKING

72 THE RED LION HOTEL

2 Stirling Road, Larbert, FK5 4AF
Tel: 01324 562886   Fax: 01324 553627
e-mail: info@redlion-hotel.co.uk
website: www.redlion-hotel.co.uk

Located in the heart of Larbert Cross, we are close to Falkirk, the local shopping area and vital road links through central Scotland. **The Red Lion Hotel** offers14 comfortable, elegant and relaxed en-suite accommodation for those who require to stay in the area for either business or pleasure. Availability includes Single, Double, Twin and Family rooms which ensures we can comfortably cater for any group size. In addition to en-suite facilities, our rooms are inclusive of Sky TV, LCD screens, tea & coffee making facilities and ironing facilities on request.

Situated within the hotel is our very own Chinese Restaurant, where we pride ourselves in offering the best Chinese cuisine. Our restaurant is supplied daily with the freshest foods from carefully chosen suppliers, ensuring that all of our dishes taste delicious. Situated at the front of the hotel is our elegant Wine & Champagne bar which is perfect if you wish to relax or unwind at the end of the evening.

FREE CAR PARKING

390

69 ALLOA TOWER

Alloa Park, Alloa,
Clackmannanshire FK10 1PP
Tel: 0 1259 211701 Fax: 01259 218744
website: www.nts.org.uk

Alloa Tower, the largest surviving keep in Scotland, dates from the 14th century. It was home to successive generations of the Earls of Mar, who played host to and were guardians of many Scots monarchs. Here, so legend has it, Mary, Queen of Scots was reconciled with Darnley and shortly thereafter granted the 5th Lord Erskine the much coveted earldom in 1565. One tradition holds that Mary's infant son, later James VI and I, died shortly after his birth and was replaced by the baby son of the Earl of Mar. The Tower has seen six major alterations, the most dramatic being the sweeping Italianate staircase and dome added in the early 1700's by the 6th Earl of Mar. But it still retains original medieval features such as the dungeon, first floor well and magnificent oak roof timbers.

75 THE HAWTHORNS

The Square, Drymen,
by Loch Lomond G63 OBH
Tel: 01360 660916
e-mail: info@thehawthorns-drymen.com
website: www.thehawthorns-drymen.com

Built in 1873, **Hawthorns B&B** is located in the picturesque Scottish Village of Drymen. There are some excellent pubs and amenities in the area and the B&B is located near Loch Lomond and Trossachs  National Park. The family-run B&B overlooks the village square and the rooms are large and tastefully decorated, boasting en-suite facilities. The traditional B&B is an ideal place to stay for those wanting to explore Loch Lomond and the surrounding area. Drymen is close to the West Highland Way and the beginning of the Rob Roy Way and is only 30 minutes from Glasgow and Stirling.

73 ALLANWATER CAFÉ

15 Henderson Street, Bridge of Allan,
Stirlingshire FK9 4HN
Tel: 01786 833060

With seating for 80, the **Allanwater Café** is bright and spacious, being decorated in the "ice cream parlour" style. It is popular with visitors and locals alike and offers a menu which includes many freshly made Scottish dishes, as well as a large selection of ice-creams and ice-cream sundaes.

HIDDEN PLACES GUIDES

Explore Britain and Ireland with *Hidden Places* guides - a fascinating series of national and local travel guides.

Packed with easy to read information on hundreds of places of interest as well as places to stay, eat and drink.

Available from both high street and internet booksellers

For more information on the full range of *Hidden Places* guides and other titles published by Travel Publishing visit our website on

www.findsomewhere.co.uk
or ask for our leaflet by phoning
01752 697280 or emailing
info@travelpublishing.co.uk

Carron Valley, Stirlingshire, FK6 5JG
e-mail:
enquiries@carronbridgehotel.co.uk
website: www.carronbridgehotel.co.uk

Carronbridge Hotel is a small cosy family-run former Coaching Inn steeped in history, situated on what used to be the main Glasgow to Stirling road, but is now a rural single track road which runs mainly through foresty(Campsies). It is approximately 6 miles from Kilsyth and at one time could only serve alcohol to people who had travelled 6 miles or more, many people walked from Kilsyth to Carronbridge thus became bonafide travellers, as from 1920 Kilsyth town went "dry" (prohibition era) and stayed dry until 1967! This tradition of walking to the 'Brigg' is still alive today.

The Battle of Bannockburn in 1314 - is celebrated at the Bannockburn Heritage Centre, just four miles away . . Robert the Bruce prepared to meet Edward 11 with six thousand spearmen, five hundred light horse and a few archers and it is well documented that he travelled through Carronbridge.

Just up the road from the 'Brigg' on the B818 is Duncarron Fort, The Clanranald & Bailey fort, where the Clanranald Trust is building an early Medieval Motte, typical of a Scottish Clans Chief residence.

Next to the fort are the **Carron Valley Mountain Bike Trails** where you can enjoy an action packed ride on the mountain trails. These are man-made for use all year round, plus you can see the fabulous scenic views as you traverse the bumpy trails and head up or down the high hills.

The **Carron Valley Reservoir** (Venue for the Fips Mouche World Fly Fishing Champs for 2009 Scotland) stocked with hard fighting Browns and Rainbow trout, plus a good head of Wild Brown trout, is a favourite among Scottish anglers. Many clubs use Carron for club competitions and days out, and the well maintained fleet of boats and lovely surroundings make for a pleasant days fishing. Horse riding/trekking through the forestry tracks can be arranged through the local riding school, or if you want to bring your own horse a stable can be supplied on the premises. Dogs are also.welcome. Traditional music evenings are a regular occurrence, as are darts nights.

Our rooms are all ensuite, and have wifi, sky television and tea and coffee making facilities. All meals are home cooked using the best possible fresh ingredients; packed lunches can also be provided on request and there is private secure parking available

We are 6 miles from Stirling, 15 miles from Glasgow and 30 miles from Edinburgh. You can be assured of a warm welcome to our wonderful country oasis.

76 BRIDGEND HOUSE HOTEL

Bridgend, Callander FK17 8AH
Tel: 01877 330130
e-mail:
enquiries@thebridgendhouse.co.uk
website: www.thebridgendhouse.co.uk

Located by the Red Bridge over the River Teith in one of the oldest parts of Callander, **Bridgend House Hotel** looks very inviting with its half-timbered frontage, hanging baskets and dormer windows. Inside the 15th century Grade B listed building, there's an informal and relaxed atmosphere in the cosy bar with its wood-burning stove.

During the summer months, there are regular live music performances at weekends. You can see why the *Daily Telegraph* included Bridgend House in its 70 Great British Inns. *The Scotsman* also recommended the great pub food on offer here, complemented by a good selection of real ales, fine wines and a full range of other beverages.

In good weather, enjoy your refreshments in the lovely beer garden looking out across Callander

meadows and the River Teith towards Ben Ledi and the Trossachs. Those same views can also be enjoyed from the five guest bedrooms available, all of them recently refurbished and equipped with en suite facilities, TV and hospitality tray. The hotel also has a spacious function room, good disabled access and toilet, and ample parking.

78 THE SWALLOW CAFE

172 Argyll Street, Dunoon, PA23 8HA
Tel: 01369 707942
e-mail: jenni333@btinternet.com

Attracting plenty of locals, tourists and walkers **The Swallow Café** is located in the popular Clyde coastal resort of Dunoon. It is the largest town in Argyll and has some fantastic views because it is built around two bays. The café is very traditional and has home baking is at its heart.

The ice cream it serves is made on the premise and hot and cold snacks can be enjoyed inside or taken away. The wooden floors add to the character of the café, which can seat 36 people and is often busy with people relaxing with a tea or coffee.

Located on the main thoroughfare, The Swallow Café is popular with locals and visitors to the area. It is close to the ferry and the town's many amenities. Many

visitors to the area like to visit the historic site, where Dunoon Castle, which was built in the 11th century, used to stand.

Jenni Harrison and Tony Watkins have owned The Swallow Café since July 2009. Well known in the area, the child-friendly café is open seven days a week from 8am-6pm and during the winter months from 8am-4pm. Access for disabled customers is not a problem. No credit cards are taken.

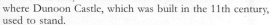

393

Kilmahog, Callendar,
Perthshire FK17 8HD
Tel: 01877 330152
e-mail: info@theladeinn.com
website: www.theladeinn.com or
www.scottishrealales.com

The Lade Inn is a family run business situated at Callander in the Loch Lomond & the Trossachs National Park, a wonderful location near the foot of Ben Ledi with tremendous scenery, beautiful wildlife and masses of history. Our passion is to create a wonderful Scottish experience for our customers with excellent service and entertainment, built on a foundation of superb food and drink. Frank and Rita Park (Mum & Dad) look after the customers, well supported by Laura (Daughter in Law), her bar and restaurant team.

Our food is the creation of Stephen (Son), whose CV includes Turnberry, the Ritz and Landmark Hotels. Stephen can indulge his passion for creating interesting dishes, however as he points out the menu must address "what the customer is looking for" and many of our customers enjoy good hearty eating. The Smiley faces on our menu indicate where smaller portions are available for kids and our young at heart over 60s. We cater for the entire family including dogs in our Bothy Bar with its log fire or in our beautiful garden in summer.

Quality starts at the food source, so we have selected a group of excellent local suppliers: Stephen's great talent is to create a brilliant taste by carefully selecting the best ingredients for his recipes, and then through his cooking skills produce an amazing dish. Recognition came from Forth Valley Food Links with our award Winner of the Best Informal Eating Place in the Forth Valley. A cornerstone of our business is our very own Lade Inn Real Ale - Waylade, Ladeback and award winning Ladeout, only available in draught at the Lade Inn. Excellent ales, superb food, fine malts followed by a sing along with one of our bands – a great Scottish Experience.

In 2008 we opened the **Scottish Real Ale Shop** stocking over 130 different Scottish Real Ales from 30 Micro Breweries across Scotland. Now, visitors do not have to travel the length and breadth of Scotland to find interesting real ales, simply, visit the Scottish Real Ale Shop @ the Lade Inn or buy on line from our website, either select one of our special cases, or if you prefer, create your own mixed cases. Annually, at the end of August we host the Trossachs Beer Festival a ten day celebration of Scottish Real Ale.

Our customers enjoy a true Scottish experience of good food, real beer and good cheer.

79 ABBOT'S BRAE HOTEL

West Bay, Dunoon PA23 7QJ
Tel: 01369 705021
e-mail: info@abbotsbrae.co.uk
website: www.abbotsbrae.co.uk

Nestled high up in the tranquil seaside town of Dunoon, Abbot's Brae Hotel offers the perfect romantic get-away. It boasts spectacular views over the Firth of Clyde and is surrounded by some of the most breathtaking scenery you will ever see.

The hotel has an extremely high reputation and with luxurious rooms in an idyllic setting it isn't hard to see why. Providing a home from home Abbot's Brae is a family run hotel standing in its own woodland garden. There are eight spacious and comfortable bedrooms, all finished to the

highest of standards. Each are individually named after places within the stunning Cowal Peninsula, with each room displaying photographs and the history related to the place-name. Guests always comment on the sensational views of the sea and hills and the hotel's peaceful secluded setting. Despite being hidden away, the hotel is only a mile away from the centre of Dunoon, home to the world's most spectacular Highland Games. The town is located close to the Loch Lomond National Park, only one hour from Glasgow International Airport and is an ideal base for those wanting to explore this area of the Scottish Highlands.

There are plenty of places to visit in the area, including Fyne Studios, Kilmartin House Museum, Millcroft Lavender, Inveraray Castle, Benmore Botanical Gardens, Strachur Smiddy, Mount Stuart House and the Castle House Museum. Abbot's Brae Hotel is a perfect venue for those wanting to escape from the hustle and bustle of city life.

Whether it is a short weekend stay, a romantic break or a one night stay, you will not be disappointed. If it is just one night you are staying for you can opt for a VIP night, where you will be treated to a bottle of chilled Champagne and a box of chocolates in your room followed by a three course dinner in the restaurant and a full Scottish breakfast in the morning.

Small corporate events and weddings can be held at the hotel. Catering for parties up to 24 people, it provides the perfect setting for a small and intimate wedding. The ceremony can take place within the hotel and gardens or at the historic, picturesque Castle House, Dunoon's Registry Office, situated on the hill overlooking the Victorian Pier and located only one mile away. The owners are happy to assist in any arrangements for the wedding and can provide contact details for local ministers, photographers etc.

80 BENMORE BOTANIC GARDEN

Dunoon, Argyll **PA23 8QU**
Tel: 01369 706261
website: **www.rbge.org.uk**

In the natural woodland setting of the Eachaig Valley lies Benmore, a Garden famous for its magnificent collections of trees and shrubs including some of the tallest trees in Britain. Surrounded by dramatic scenery, the Garden's west coast climate provides the ideal growing conditions for the cultivation of some of the finest Himalayan rhododendrons.

On entering the Garden, visitors are welcomed by an impressive Avenue of Giant Redwoods, arguably one of the finest entrances to any Botanic Garden in the world. Established in 1863, these majestic giants are over 40 metres tall! Benmore also contains one of the finest living collections of rhododendron, with over 250 species represented, from the rare to the familiar.

The recently renovated Courtyard Gallery has diverse programme of exhibitions and events throughout the year, from craft displays to planned activities.

With its delicious home baking, the James Duncan Café is a welcome resting place for visitors. Keen gardeners will also appreciate the selection of books, gifts and plants on offer at the Botanics Shop, some of which can be seen growing in the garden.

81 MUASDALE HOLIDAY PARK

Muasdale, Tarbert, Argyll **PA29 6XD**
Tel: 01583 421207
Fax: 01583 421137
e-mail: enquiries@muasdaleholidays.com
website: www.muasdaleholidays.com

Voted "Best Small Site in the Top 100 Parks, 2009" by *Practical Caravan* magazine, **Muasdale Holiday Park** is a peaceful, relaxing, family-run site located on the west coast of the Kintyre peninsula enjoying a panoramic outlook over the Atlantic and the islands of Jura, Gigha and Islay.

The park offers a good and varied choice of accommodation, ranging from caravan holiday homes to a spacious, first floor holiday apartment for 5 people. A large ground floor apartment suitable for couples, young families or those with mobility limitations is also available. A well-maintained level grass field by the beach provides berths for touring caravans, motor homes and tents. There are electric hook-ups, a toilet/shower block with

continuous hot water, and a washing-up area. Other amenities include washing, drying and ironing facilities; table tennis and pool.

Muasdale village has a licensed shop catering for everyday needs. The site itself provides abundant opportunities for viewing wildlife - otters, seals, dolphins, cormorants, herons, swan, various seagulls and buzzards are frequent visitors. The park is conveniently located on the A83 at the southern end of Muasdale village.

82 INVERARAY JAIL 🏛

Church Square, Inveraray,
Argyll PA32 8TX
Tel: 01499 302381 Fax: 01499 302195
e-mail: info@inverarayjail.co.uk
website: www.inverarayjail.co.uk

Inveraray Jail, the former County Courthouse and prison for Argyll, tells the story of the men, women and children who were tried and served their sentences here. Fascinating displays give an insight into the harshness of prison life in the 19th century, including cells where murderers, madmen and children were crammed in together, the courtroom where trials took place and the airing yards where prisoners were allowed to take an hours exercise each day. An exhibition of items such as branding irons and thumb screws illustrates punishments inflicted before the days of prisons. There is an excellent range of gifts and souvenirs available at the Jail Shop.

83 BANK HOUSE GUEST HOUSE ⊨

Church Square, Inveraray,
Argyll PA32 8TX
Tel: 01499 302442
e-mail: the.bank.house@btinternet.com

Located right next door to Inveraray Jail, one of Scotland's top tourist attractions, **Bank House Guest House** is a striking building which was built in 1745 for the brother of the 3rd Duke of Argyll - the man who designed and funded the creation of this, the first planned town in Europe. Your host at Bank House is Norina Coupar, a friendly and welcoming lady with some 30 years experience in the hotel business. There are 3 guest bedrooms available, all with en suite facilities and all individually furnished and decorated.

Norina is a keen gardener and her walled garden has been designed to provide year-round colour to

complement the mature trees. During the summer months, there are more flowers in hanging baskets and in planters at the front of the house.

Inveraray itself is a pleasant place to explore. It sits on the shore of Loch Fyne, has an outstanding Maritime Museum which occupies a 3-masted schooner and, of course, there's the jail for which guests at Bank House receive a 10% discount on the entry price.

397

84 SGEIR MHAOL GUEST HOUSE

56 Soroba Road, Oban, Argyll PA34 4JF
Tel: 01631 562650
e-mail: info@sgeirmhaol.co.uk
website: www.sgeirmhaol.co.uk

Located at the southern end of Oban, this family-run guest house offers the very best in hospitality and comfort. There is double, twin and family accommodation (all on the ground floor), with all rooms finished to an extremely high standard. Tastefully decorated, they all have colour televisions, mini fridges, electronic safes among other things. Visitors can be sure to find a traditional full Scottish breakfast on the morning menu and can enjoy it in the dining room, which like the lounge, overlooks the front garden.

Owners, Ishbell and Jamie also offer two self catering flats, which are located 100 yards from can also, Sgeir Mhaol and have two bedrooms, toilet, sitting room and kitchen. There is a garden to the front and to the rear of the building and parking for three cars.

There is plenty to do in the surrounding area, with many visitors taking walks and soaking up the natural beauty of the place. Pronounced 'Sgeir Vole', the name of the guest house means 'A Bare Rock', in Gaelic and is derived from that of a lighthouse with a family connection off the Isle of Jura. It is open all year round and has a spacious private car park within the grounds.

86 ARDBRECKNISH HOUSE

South Lochaweside, Dalmally, Oban, Argyll PA33 1BH
Tel/Fax: 01866 833223
e-mail: enquiries@loch-awe.co.uk
website: www.loch-awe.co.uk

Occupying a superb position overlooking Loch Awe, **Ardbrecknish House**, is the ideal base for exploring scenic Argyll with access to limitless outdoor pursuits. Extending some 26 miles, Loch Awe is the longest freshwater loch in Britain set in some of the most outstanding scenery in the Highlands, Glen Coe being just over an hour away. Loch Awe holds the Brown Trout record at 31lb 12oz and is renowned for trout and pike fishing.

Boat hire and launch facilities are available 300 yards away. There are many historical sites on and around the loch including Kilchurn Castle and Innishail Burial Isle all accessible by either foot or boat. Oban, gateway to the Isles, is only 45 minutes away and Inveraray is 20 minutes.

Ardbrecknish House offers ten self catering properties varying in size sleeping from 2 to 12. There is a friendly bar, restaurant and games room with pool, darts and carpet bowls. There are laundry facilities and a children's play area. Open all year and pets are welcome.'

85 BARCALDINE HOUSE HOTEL & COTTAGES

Barcaldine, near Oban, Argyll PA37 1SG
Tel: 01631 720 219
Fax: 01631 720540
e-mail: enquiries@barcaldinehouse.co.uk
website: www.barcaldinehouse.co.uk

Located near Oban, the heart of the west coast of Scotland, **Barcaldine House Hotel & Cottages** are set in stunning Argyll countryside and offer only the finest in hospitality.

The idyllic country house, dating back to 1709, is surrounded by enchanting forests and secret gardens - a joy for children and adults alike. The hotel is well known for its outstanding restaurant which offers the very best in local Scottish cuisine. A typical menu might offer a mini goat's cheese tart or venison burger as canapés; stuffed quail with pistachio & apricot or hand-dived scallops served with a carrot and pea puree with butter foam as an entrée. For the main course, how about pan-seared venison with fondant potato, Victorian cabbage and red currant jus, or grilled halibut with lobster tail bisque? Round off your meal with an exquisite dessert - sticky toffee pudding, perhaps, or chocolate ganache & raspberry tart with lemon possette, or a selection of Scottish cheeses with Arran oaties.

The accommodation at Barcaldine House is particularly welcoming with just eight attractively furnished and decorated bedrooms and spacious common areas. The country mansion provides an exceptionally romantic Scottish wedding venue and is available for private bookings and sporting parties.

For those who prefer self-catering, the hotel has six holiday cottages arranged around a bright, colourful courtyard situated within the beautifully maintained gardens of Barcaldine House. The spacious and comfortable cottages sleep between 2 to 6 guests and cater for all your holiday needs. The facilities include a fully equipped modern kitchen, a separate living area with 26" screen LCD TV, DVD and CD player; bright, spacious bedrooms offering comfortable double and twin rooms, central heating and wired Internet access. The bathroom is equipped with Egyptian cotton luxury bath towels along with complimentary toiletries, and there's a free laundry service. Room service is available and guests have the full use of the hotel facilities including the bar, restaurant and the oak-panelled billiard room.

Barcaldine House makes a convenient base when exploring Argyll and Bute and the Highlands and Islands of Scotland. It is just 9 miles from Oban with easy access to spectacular mountains, beaches, lochs and glens in the stretch between Oban and Fort William.

87 DALAVICH SHOP & WILD ROWAN CAFÉ

39 Dalavich, by Taynuilt PA35 1HN
Tel: 01866 844256
e-mail: grace_well@hotmail.com

Truly hidden away, the tiny village of Dalavich is reached by an unlisted single track road that skirts the western shore of Loch Awe. Set beside the loch, **Dalavich Shop & Wild Rowan Café** is at the very heart of this small community. As well as running the shop and café, owners Hayati and Grace Gok also run the Post Office and bicycle hire facility.

Open every day, the café offers a hearty all day breakfast as well as an extensive choice of main meals, light snacks, hot and cold

rolls, toasties and sandwiches. Ingredients such as the fresh haddock are locally sourced wherever possible. There's also a home-made soup of the day and a choice of Kiddies Lunches. The extensive range of hot drinks includes aromatic coffees made using top quality Lavazza Italian espresso beans. Most of the items are available to take away.

Dalavich itself is wonderfully peaceful and noted for its interesting wildlife, which includes wild osprey, red squirrels and even the rare and elusive pine marten.

88 CLAN COTTAGES

Thatched Holiday Cottages
Oban, Argyll, Gateway to the Isles
Affordable Luxury Accommodation

Fàilte

A warm welcome awaits you at Clan Cottages. A newly built self catering holiday village built within five acres of ground. The five cottages are newly built in traditional stone and thatch, with modern, high quality interiors. Situated on the shores of Loch Nell and the River Nell - within 6 minutes drive of Oban - each cottage can accommodate 2-6 visitors. The village includes a one bedroom cottage with a beautiful mezzanine lounge, three two bedroom cottages, one of which has been designed and built to suit anyone who has mobility problems and one three bedroom cottage.

To make an enquiry or booking please contact
John or Mary MacKinnon on
Tel 01631 770 372 or
Email info@clancottages.com
www.clancottages.com

SEE INSIDE FRONT COVER

89 THE BARN AT SCAMMADALE FARM

Kilninver, Oban PA34 4UU
Tel: 01852 316282
e-mail: scammadale@hotmail.com

The delightful **Scammadale Farm** is owned and run by Neil and Hazel and accommodation is offered in the recent barn conversion and in a wing of the farmhouse itself. The working farm breeds Scottish Blackface sheep and Luing cattle. Neil and Hazel also breed Arab horses for competing in endurance races.

Both forms of accommodation are self catering, will sleep 6 people in 3 rooms and are homely and comfortable. The farm grounds include the side of the local Loch, and fishing is very popular here; there are brown trout and salmon.

90 CUILFAIL HOTEL

Kilmelford, by Oban, Argyll PA34 4XA
Tel: 01852 200274
Fax: 01852 200264
e-mail: mail@cuilfail.com
website: www.cuilfail.co.uk

Located close to the shore of Loch Melfort and dating from 1840, the **CUILFAIL HOTEL** is a splendid former coaching inn, one of the oldest hotels on the west coast. Part of the hotel was originally an old drovers' inn and is at least 250 years old, however the majority of the hotel was built during the Victorian era and many features of that period have been preserved. The name Cuilfail (pronounced "cool-fail") in Gaelic appropriately means "Sheltered Corner".

Outside, the magnificent display of ivy bedecks the hotel with quite amazing colour for most of the summer and autumn months.

As soon as you enter this charming little hotel you will be struck by its homely highland feel. This rather infectious highland ambience provides a superbly stress-free, unhurried environment.

For the owners Yvonne O'Shea and Simon Fletcher, excellent cuisine is a top priority. Two contrasting dining areas provide the perfect setting for enjoying delicious uncomplicated Scottish cuisine. The Ceann Mòr restaurant is a spacious light room which gets its name from the surrounding hillside visible through the large sash windows and the amazing bar with its stone walls and large collection of notes from around the world. On offer at the Cuilfail is a good range of real ales, beers, aperitifs and malt whiskies naturally specialising in those originating from the west coast of Scotland and the western Isles.

The inn is one of the area's most popular and favourite country eating out experiences. Much of the produce used, including wonderful Scotch beef, comes from the surrounding farms and the local farmers are very discerning about how their endeavours are presented and flavoured on the plate. They are some of the inn's most regular customers so there is a local recommendation if ever there was one!

The public rooms, while deceptively spacious and plentiful, preserve the intimacy and easy friendliness of the place. There's an authentic village bar with its real fire, imposing fireplace and stone walls, a cosy "snug" lounge area, a games room, the residents "whisky lounge" and a grand function room with wood panelling and vaulted ceiling.

Accommodation at the Cuilfail comprises 12 very individual rustic in style and spacious bedrooms, most having a good view of the surrounding countryside. All have en suite facilities, individually controlled heating, hospitality tray and colour television.

2 Bridgend Street, Rothesay PA20 0HU
Tel: 01700 502922
e-mail: tim@brechins-bute.com
website: www.brechins-bute.com

Serving the very best in fine local produce, **Brechin's Brasserie** is well known for its quality food and good service. The Mediterranean style brasserie is located in the centre of Rothesay, the main town of the Isle of Bute and has a growing reputation for its healthy eating choices since opening in 2004. Brechin's Brasserie has won a second healthy living award from Consumer Focus Scotland and prides itself on providing excellent home cooked dishes of the highest standard. Among the most popular dishes on the extensive menu are those using locally smoked fish and Bute lamb and beef. The dishes are homemade and freshly prepared,

using top quality ingredients that will tantalise the fussiest of taste buds.

The Brasserie, located

in the town centre just a short walk from the ferry and marina, offers occasional themed menus and music evenings on Fridays & Saturdays. Many visitors to the town go to see Rothesay Castle, which dates back to the 13th century and visit and revisit the Brasserie to sample the delights on offer and enjoy the friendly atmosphere. Freshly ground coffee and home baking are available throughout the day.

Brechin's Brasserie is open Tuesday – Saturday between 10.30am and 2.30pm and from 7pm on Friday and Saturdays for dinner.

Kilbride Croft, Balvicar,
Isle of Seil PA34 4RD
Tel: 01852 300475
e-mail: kilbridecroft@ aol.com
website: www.kilbridecroft.co.uk

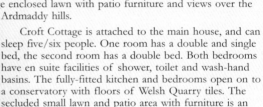

The Isle of Seil near Oban is reached by "the only bridge over the Atlantic", an elegant structure built in 1792 with a high arch to allow sailing ships to pass beneath it. The island's major settlement is Balvicar and it's here you'll find **Kilbride Croft Cottages** which offer quality self-catering accommodation in two properties, both of which enjoy breath-taking views. Kilbride Cottage is detached and built of stone, has a log-burning stove and full central heating, and will sleep four in one twin room and one double room, each with en suite bathrooms. The lounge and dining area adjoins a modern open plan, well-equipped kitchen which also has a wood-burning stove. The cottage is set in a large enclosed lawn with patio furniture and views over the Ardmaddy hills.

Croft Cottage is attached to the main house, and can sleep five/six people. One room has a double and single bed, the second room has a double bed. Both bedrooms have en suite facilities of shower, toilet and wash-hand basins. The fully-fitted kitchen and bedrooms open on to a conservatory with floors of Welsh Quarry tiles. The secluded small lawn and patio area with furniture is an ideal place for relaxing.

402

93 MULL POTTERY

Baliscate Estate, Tobermory,
Isle of Mull PA75 6QA
Tel: 01688 302347
e-mail: info@mullpottery.com
website: www.mullpottery.com

Located just outside the picturesque town of Tobermory, **Mull Pottery** makes high-fired, hand-thrown ceramics the designs of which are inspired by the landscapes and seascapes of Scotland's rugged west coast.

All the pottery is made by skilled craftspeople who are dedicated to producing pieces that are both beautiful and unique. The pottery makes all its own glazes and refines its own clay to a recipe that was first used in 1982. When you visit the well-stocked gallery you can see the pots being made in the workshop before choosing a pot from the complete range of products on display. Seconds at bargain prices, and the work of other crafts people can also be purchased.

Crafts showcased here include glassware, textiles, jewellery, prints, original paintings and other ceramics. The gallery was recently awarded a 4-star shopping award from Visit Scotland.

After you've made your purchase, why not relax in the Mull Pottery's licensed Café/Restaurant which has an outdoor balcony with fantastic views overlooking the Sound of Mull. The restaurant serves great snacks, meals and drinks using the pottery's own tableware. There is local seafood, game and farm produce, as well as aromatic Costa coffee, tea and home baking.

403

94 IONA ABBEY & NUNNERY

Isle of Iona PA76 6SQ
Tel: 01681 700512
website: www.historic-scotland.gov.uk/
properties

One of Scotland's most historic and sacred sites, **Iona Abbey** was founded by St Columba and his Irish followers in AD 563. A celebrated focus for Christian pilgrimage, Iona retains its spiritual atmosphere and remains an enduring symbol of worship.

Over a century ago, the abbey and monastic buildings were restored and, in 1938, The Iona Community was founded to continue the tradition of worship in the abbey through daily services and teaching.

Iona's historical and religious attractions include the abbey church and cloisters, St Columba's shrine, the site of St Columba's writing cell, and a superb collection of over 180 medieval carved stones and crosses

In the Abbey graveyard, many early Scottish kings and chiefs, as well as kings from Ireland, Norway and France are buried, and nearby are the remains of the 13th century nunnery. There is a gift shop in the Abbey cloister featuring locally made original arts and crafts along with a wide range of souvenirs specific to Iona and Mull.

95 BEINN NA CAILLICH CAFÉ

Ford Road, Broadford, Isle of Skye,
Inverness-shire IV49 9AB
Tel: 01471 822616
e-mail: beinn@fsmail.net

Named after the nearby mountain, the **Beinn na Caillich Café** is much more than just a café. It is a superb restaurant serving some of the best food in the Broadford area. The extensive menu is based on only the freshest produce and no artificial additives or preservatives are used. The day starts with a good choice of breakfasts ranging from filled rolls to a Mega Breakfast with more than a dozen items, including a slice of haggis, a tattie scone and fruit pudding. Breakfasts are served until 11.45am. Throughout the day, you'll find an appetising selection of main meals (including vegetarian options), salads, snacks and desserts. The regular menu is supplemented by daily specials - a seafood platter, perhaps.

Owner Linda Armstrong is passionate about food quality and wherever possible sources her ingredients in Scotland. Children have their own menu and a range of hot and soft drinks is available. Linda also owns the adjacent Gift & Craft Shop which stocks an enticing selection of local pottery, pictures, photographs and prints, along with aromatics, children's toys and cards.

96 LUIB HOUSE BED & BREAKFAST

Luib, Broadford, Isle of Skye IV49 9AN
Tel: 01471 820334
e-mail: luibhouseb_b@btinternet.com
website: www.luibhouse.co.uk

A warm welcome awaits you at **Luib House**, nestling in the shadow of the Red Cuillins, with wonderful views over Loch Ainort and the surrounding countryside. The family

room and one of the double rooms are en suite, the other double room has a private bathroom. All rooms have tea and coffee-making facilities, satellite television, clock radio and hairdryer. There is a large, comfortable residents' lounge as well as a fully equipped kitchen where guests can prepare an evening meal for themselves. A full Scottish breakfast is served in the dining room. Well-behaved dogs are welcome by prior arrangement.

97 SAUCY MARY'S LODGE

Mense Lane, Kyleakin,
Isle of Skye IV41 8PH
Tel: 01599 534845
website: www.saucymarys.com

The majority of rooms at **Saucy Mary's Lodge** have sea or mountain views, which may be why it is so popular among visitors. The hostel occupies two buildings and has a good reputation among backpackers, walkers, couples, families, youth groups and motorcycle clubs. There are 20 rooms, which sleep two, three, five and six people.

Located in the village of Kyleakin the surrounding area is extremely picturesque and is on the main bus routes from Glasgow and Inverness. Saucy Mary's Lodge is ideal accommodation for those travelling to the Outer Hebrides. Inside there is a shop, café, self catering kitchens and a bar.

All of the rooms are modern, comfortable and tastefully decorated. In brighter weather guests can make the most of the lovely garden.

Breakfast can be eaten in the Sun Lounge and lunch and evening homemade meals can be enjoyed in the bar, which often has live music. The hostel, which has wheelchair access, baby changing facilities and a play room for young children, is open all year round apart from Christmas day. Visitors can check in after 3pm unless other arrangements are made prior to arrival. All credit and debit cards accepted. There is ample free parking.

98 THE MACKINNON COUNTRY HOUSE HOTEL

Kyleakin, Isle of Skye IV41 8PQ
Tel: 01599 534180
Fax: 01599 534460
e-mail: info@mackinnonhotel.co.uk
website: www.mackinnonhotel.co.uk

The MacKinnon Country House Hotel was built in 1912 by Major Archie MacKinnon and was originally named Dunringell after his clan's old fort near Elgol. Respected as an ideal example of a Scottish country house hotel, it is overlooked by the magnificent Sgurr na Coinnich mountain range and set in more than four acres of magnificent gardens.

Surrounded by magnificent gardens boasting rhododendrons and azaleas, the hotel has been awarded three stars by the Scottish Tourist Board.

Good food is taken very seriously at the MacKinnon. As one visitor wrote about the Fountain Restaurant: 'One of the loveliest restaurants I have ever eaten in. What stunning views and great food.' The Fountain is indeed a huge favourite with both guests and local customers alike. The Head Chef, while renowned for creating fine food and tantalising menus, will always be delighted to prepare your favourite dish if it doesn't appear on the menu. An excellent wine list specially created for the Fountain Restaurant will ensure your meal is a complete success. As part of his efforts to make your stay simply perfect, all of the produce is delivered fresh every morning from Inverness on the mainland. The Fountain is open from 7pm till late every day. Should you prefer a less formal evening, another enchanting room houses the Garden Restaurant. You will find all kinds of popular bar foods on the menu and some that are just that bit special! The Garden Restaurant is open every day from 12 noon, last orders are taken at 6pm with the restaurant closing at 7pm.

The accommodation at the MacKinnon maintains the same high standards evident throughout the hotel. You can choose to stay in the main building or in the delightfully secluded Hunting Lodge less than a minute's walk from the main building. There are ten rooms in the main building and a further eight rooms in the Hunting Lodge provide the perfect setting for the romantic at heart! All 18 rooms benefit from central heating, an en suite bathroom, direct dial telephone, colour television, hair drier and tea and coffee making facilities. A very special feature in every en suite bathroom is the fine array of beautiful toiletries made especially for you on the Isle of Arran.

99 CAFÉ ARRIBA

Portree, Isle of Skye,
Inverness-shire IV51 9DB
Tel: 01478 611830
e-mail: arriba@cafearriba
website: www.cafearriba.co.uk

Café Arriba is a lively café/bistro located in the heart of Portree. Traditional on the outside and modern, funky and smart on the inside, it is more than just a café - it is a great eating place where good food and value for money go hand in hand. By day you can relax and enjoy great teas and coffees, as well as light snacks and lunches. In the evening, from 6pm onwards during the summer, the ambience changes and it becomes an intimate yet spacious restaurant serving some of the best food on the island.

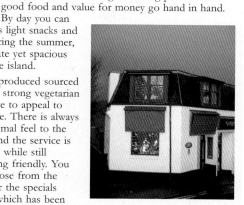

The cuisine is always imaginative, with the produced sourced locally wherever possible, and though there is a strong vegetarian influence to many of the dishes, the food is sure to appeal to

everyone. There is always an informal feel to the place, and the service is efficient while still remaining friendly. You can choose from the menu or the specials board, which has been known to change two or three times a day as popular dishes run out and are replaced by something else!

Café Arriba is open every day from 7am to 10pm in the summer, and from 8am to 5 or 6pm in the winter.

100 THE ISLES INN AND THE PORTREE HOTEL

Somerled Square, Portree,
Isle of Skye IV51 9EH
Tel: 01478 612511
e-mail: info@accommodationskye.co.uk
website: www.accommodationskye.co.uk

Decorated in a Jacobean Style the **Isles Inn** restaurant & bar encompasses the best of Highland hospitality. Good food, using locally sourced ingredients wherever possible served in a true Celtic atmosphere by staff dressed in the family tartan. Guests are invited to enjoy freshly prepared dishes using langoustines landed on the pier perhaps ten minutes earlier or Sconser scallops hand dived just down the road. Vegetarians are most certainly not forgotten with choices ranging from creamy home-made lasagne to mushroom tagliatelle and goats cheese & onion flan. Sit in the thatched traditional Skye Black Crofthouse bar in front of the roaring open fire and contemplate your day or perhaps listen to the live Ceildh music which is played throughout the year. The inn is situated in Somerled Square, only minutes away from the shops, harbour and swimming pool.

The Portree Hotel is also in Somerled Square with 24 ensuite bedrooms. The Clansman restaurant, upstairs with a new menu created by the head chef. All the ingredients are sourced locally to provide a real taste of Skye. The upstairs restaurant depicts some famous local Clans such as the MacLeods and the MacDonalds, and is a cosy and intimate setting to spend an evening enjoying fine food and wine. The Claymore Suite has been recently upgraded and is available for functions for up to 100 people. All needs can be catered for including invitations, entertainment, food and accommodation. Downstairs there is Cappucinos Bistro, where meals can be enjoyed next to a welcoming coal fire; or pop into the Camanachd bar where you can have a game of pool and enjoy the craic from the locals.

101 URQUHART CALEDONIAN HOTEL

Wentworth Street, Portree, Isle of Skye,
Inverness-shire IV51 9ET
Tel: 01478 612641
e-mail: celedonianhotel@quista.net
website: www.urquhartcaledonianhotel.co.uk

The **Urquhart Caledonian Hotel**, right in the heart of Portree, has recently been refurbished to a high standard to give some of the best tourist and business accommodation on the Isle of Skye. It is a friendly, family-run establishment that puts informality and a warm welcome first, without compromising high standards of service or outstanding value for money.

There are eight rooms on offer, each one extremely comfortable and furnished and decorated to a high standard. They are fully en suite, as you would expect, and have a colour TV, tea/coffee making facilities, a hair drier, radio alarm clock and a telephone. The Caley Bar is a favourite haunt of local people, and it is the ideal place to meet people, relax and have a quiet drink. Sit by the open fire and enjoy one of the many blended whiskies and single malts, or have a game of darts, pool or one of the board games.

And when it's eating time, enjoy one of the no-frills meals that are cooked on the premises. There is an extensive menu, and most of the dishes are prepared from fresh local produce. The bar is a child friendly area up until about 9 pm, so the whole family can eat here.

Skye is a wonderful place for sightseeing and outdoor activities such as walking and fishing, so ironing and laundry facilities are always available.

103 THE BOTHY & BARN

Staffin, Isle of Skye IV51 9JS
Tel: 01470 562204

Looking out to the isles of Staffin and Frodigarry and with grand views of the Quirang Mountain Range, **The Bothy & Barn** offers quality self-catering accommodation in exhilarating surroundings. The Bothy is a former farm building which owner John Mackenzie has professional converted to holiday accommodation with lots of character. It has a lounge/dining area with a wood-burning stove, a fully equipped kitchen, shower room, and 2 bedrooms - 1 double and one with 2 single beds. The lounge is equipped with colour TV, DVD and radio/CD player. Other amenities include a washing machine, fridge freezer and microwave. All linen is provided. The Bothy also has its own patio area.

John is currently converting another farm building, The Barn, and this will be ready for guests from March 2010.

The area around Staffin provides some superb fishing, great climbing and walking, and of course some of the most spectacular scenery in the Highlands. And if you want to venture further afield, there are vehicle ferries nearby travelling to the outer island's and Skye's main settlement, Portree, with its shops, pubs and restaurants is just 16 miles away.

102 GRESHORNISH HOUSE

Edinbane, by Portree,
Isle of Skye, IV51 9PN
Tel: 01470 582266
e-mail: info@greshornishhouse.com
website: www.greshornishhouse.com

Greshornish House, a traditional Skye manor house on its own remote peninsula between Portree and Dunvegan, is now run as a small country house hotel well deserving its four star accreditation. Secluded in a charming loch-side setting of 10 acres and surrounded by a belt of beautiful trees, Greshornish was once owned by the popular and influential laird Kenneth MacLeod and the house dates back to the early 18th century.

Now owned by Neil & Rosemary Colquhoun, Greshornish can best be summed up as a quintessential retreat: a comfortable home from home, where one can snuggle down into the squashiest of sofas or toast ones toes in front of a warming log fire whilst enjoying a dram of Scotland's finest; a grand piano and full-sized billiard table are available for residents' use, along with tennis court and croquet lawn. Upstairs there are eight en-suite bedrooms, each distinctive and wonderfully relaxing. Where food is concerned our kitchen seeks to serve the very best of Skye's expansive larder: seafood lunches are a must in the summer months as are traditional afternoon teas. In the evening candle-lit dinners complete the culinary experience. For non-residents, advance booking is essential. Perfect for long or short stays, weddings or other occasions, Greshornish is a truly memorable and special destination.

Open March – November; restricted winter opening. (Always closed for Christmas.) We look forward to welcoming you.

Uig, Isle of Skye IV51 9XP
Tel: 01478 611216
Fax: 01478 611224
e-mail: info@ferryinn.co.uk
website: www.ferryinn.co.uk

The Ferry Inn at Uig occupies a superb position on the south west facing amphitheatre of Uig Bay with magnificent views over the bay towards the Waternish Peninsula. The inn's bars are small and friendly and provide a welcoming atmosphere for both locals and visitors. The main bar, having its

own access, is ideal for that quiet pint to reflect on the day's excursions or enjoy old fashioned 'bar games', of dominos, chess or a game of cards. The reception bar, with its access from the hotel, has a selection of malt whiskies to sample. Teas and specialty coffees are available from either bar. In good weather, refreshments can be enjoyed in the beer garden at the front of the inn with its commanding views over the bay. The lounge provides comfortable leather seating in which to relax with a selection of newspapers, magazines and books or to plan the next day's itinerary with the help of the available information brochures.

Also in the lounge is the broadband internet connection to a catch up with friends and relatives around the world.

The inn's restaurant is very popular and the varied menu incorporates, where possible, locally sourced ingredients. The beef is Scottish beef and is fully traceable; seafood is sourced from Mallaig and, during the growing season, the salad ingredients are organically grown on the Isle of Skye by Glendale Salads. To complement the meal, there is a small selected wine list and during the season cask conditioned ales are served in the bar.

The inn provides comfortable 3 star accommodation consisting of one single, two twin and three double bedded rooms. All six bedrooms have ensuite facilities, individual heating, television, coffee/tea making facilities and are attractively furnished and decorated.

Uig, on the Trotternish peninsula, is an ideal location for exploring the top end of Skye, with it's spectacular scenery, walks, castles, art studios, wildlife including otters, golden eagles and corncrakes.

From Uig, Caledonian MacBrayne operates daily sailings to Lochmaddy on North Uist and Tarbet on Harris. With the ferry terminal just one mile away, the inn is ideally situated for an overnight stop before continuing to the Outer Isles.

105 MEIKLEOUR HOTEL

Meikleour, nr Blairgowrie,
Perthshire, PH2 6EB
Tel: 01250 883206
Fax: 01250 883406
e-mail: visitus@meikleourhotel.co.uk
website: www.meikleourhotel.co.uk

The beautiful ivyclad building of the **Meikleour Hotel**, which dates back some 200 years once used as a coaching house, sits in the countryside near the peaceful Blairgowrie village. The area, and the hotel, is popular with cyclists, walkers, anglers

and country sports enthusiasts. The owners Kia and Andrew have an abundance of knowledge and experience (Andrew has 30 years of experience and Kia was raised in hotels) which, when they took over the hotel in Nov 2006, translated into amazing service, sumptuous menus and comfortable accommodation.

The food – which is best described as "imaginative bistro fare with the accent on home made" – can be enjoyed in the dining room or less formally (with a glass of "The lure of Meikleour" ale brewed especially for the hotel) in the cosy bar. The entire menu is made from the highest quality locally sourced produce: fish from Aberdeen, meat from a local butchers, fruit and vegetables delivered fresh daily. The menu includes dishes such as the signature *fresh haddock coated in the hotel's own beer and spring water batter*. Open for lunch and dinner, families welcome, booking is advisable due to the popularity of the restaurant. An experience at the Meikleour is not complete without a stay in one of their luxury fully en-suite rooms, equipped with all the conveniences to allow you to really relax – including TV (with DVD player and free view) and Wi-Fi.

106 THE OLD CROSS INN & RESTAURANT

Alyth Road, Rattray, Blairgowrie, Perth &
Kinross PH10 7DT
Tel: 01250 875502
e-mail: theoldcrossinn@tiscali.co.uk
website: www.theoldcrossinn.co.uk

The Old Cross Inn & Restaurant occupies a Victorian sandstone building in the heart of Perthshire, amidst some glorious Scottish scenery and within striking distance of a host of tourist attractions and leisure activities. It's a family-owned business run by the husband and wife team of

Claire and Liam Leask; and it's also a family-friendly enterprise - children are welcome and baby-changing facilities are also available.

The inn is noted for its excellent home-made food which places great emphasis on fresh, locally sourced ingredients. The bar always has at least one real ale available on draught (usually from the Inveralmond Brewery in Perth), and the bar has been selected for

the 2010 good beer guide by CAMRA. There is a pleasant

beer garden at the rear of the inn where barbecues are occasionally held, weather permitting.

Claire and Liam also cater for small functions, private parties or special occasions. As well as the bar and restaurant, the inn offers accommodation on a bed and breakfast basis, with two double rooms, a twin room and a family room available.

411

107 DRUMELLIE MEADOW

Drumellie Meadow, Wester Essendy,
by Blairgowrie, Perthshire PH10 6RD
Tel: 01250 884282
e-mail: patanddondevine@btinternet.com
website: www.drumellie-meadow.com

Providing 4 star Bed and Breakfast close to Blairgowrie, in Perthshire, **Drumellie Meadow** is a ranch style home set in three acres of wooded gardens. There are two patio areas, an orchard and a duck pond where you may see kingfishers, red squirrels, herons and the occasional red deer. Our bed and breakfast accommodation is ideal for use as a base for touring the Central Highlands. **Royal Deeside**, **Glamis Castle** and the Angus coast, **St Andrews and the East Neuk of Fife**, **Loch Lomond and the Trossachs**, Loch Tayside and Queen's View, **Dunkeld Cathedral**, **Blair Castle** and **Scone Palace** are all within an easy day's return trip. The cosmopolitan cities of Glasgow and Edinburgh are only just over an hour's drive away.

Your hosts, Pat and Don Devine, look forward to welcoming you to Drumellie Meadow. We are open all year.

108 SMIDDY HAUGH HOTEL

Main Road, Aberuthven,
Perthshire PH3 1HE
Tel: 01764 662013
e-mail: enquiries@smiddyhaughhotel.co.uk
website: www.smiddyhaugh.co.uk

A favourite with golfers, tourists, anglers and businessmen the **Smiddy Haugh Hotel** provides a quality and friendly service. Once a traditional coaching inn the family-run hotel is now a warm and hospitable resting spot for visitors, with plenty of character. Located in the village of Aberuthven, on the east side of the Ruthven Water, the hotel is in the ideal location for visitors to explore the area, which has many things to do. With a growing reputation it is easily one of the most popular hotels in Perthshire.

The owners and staff offer an efficient and courteous service and work hard to make sure every visitor has an enjoyable and memorable experience. With seven spacious rooms, three of which are en-suite the Smiddy Haugh

Hotel provides a comfortable and relaxing stay for guests. The superb

and varied cuisine the hotel serves is popular with visitors and guests who are able to enjoy lunch and evening meals in the hotel's dining room or bar. Whether it is a bar meal or an à la carte dinner you are after the menu offers a traditional selection of dishes, which are made using the freshest fish, local game, meat and locally sourced seasonal produce.

109 THE GREEN HOTEL

2 The Muirs, Kinross, KY13 8AS
Tel: 01577 863467
Fax: 01577 863180
e-mail: reservations@green-hotel.com
website : www.green-hotel.com

Having started in the eighteenth century as a popular coaching inn on the main route north from Edinburgh the family-owned **Green Hotel** has retained its reputation for warm hospitality and excellent service.

Dine in style in the award-winning Basil's Restaurant. An elegant setting in which to enjoy our varied menus that feature a subtle blend of Modern International cuisine with some Scottish influences. Jock's Bar offers a fine selection of traditional fayre in a relaxed atmosphere from hot and cold snacks to filling bar lunches and suppers.

You can try your hand at curling on the 4-sheet curling rink (open September-March). The Shop at the Green offers clothes for all occasions and is an Aladdin"s Cave for unique and original gifts. There are two 18-hole Golf Courses – The Montgomery and The Bruce Both courses deemed by many to be amongst Scotland's hidden gems.

The hotels and golf courses lie in a quiet corner of the small country town of Kinross, which has many historic connections with Scotland's glorious past. With Loch Leven and the bordering hills it is an idyllic place to escape. Just of the M90 junction 6, we are centrally located in the heart of Scotland with St Andrews, Edinburgh, Glasgow, Stirling and Perth – all within an hour's drive.

110 THE WINDLESTRAE

The Muirs, Kinross, KY13 8AS
Tel: 01577 863217
Fax: 01577 864733
e-mail:
reservations@windlestraehotel.com
website: www.windlestraehotel.com

The Windlestrae is situated in beautiful landscaped grounds just a 5 minute walk from the town centre. A host of leisure opportunities are guaranteed to help you relax and unwind. When you stay at The Windlestrae Hotel you can expect a great night's sleep and a hearty full Scottish breakfast. Each of our spacious 47 bedrooms have been designed and created with your lifestyle and comfort in mind.

The Fairway Restaurant offers a menu selection that reflects Scotland's wonderful local ingredients and the comprehensive wine list will compliment any meal. Relax in Rushes Bar which offers an extensive selection of drinks from cocktails to malt whiskies and has a light menu available.

Gravity Health & Leisure Club offers an indoor pool, gymnasium, sauna, steam room, and invigorating jacuzzi. There are two 18-hole Golf Courses – The Montgomery and The Bruce Both courses are deemed by many to be amongst Scotland's hidden gems.

Kinross-shire is a beautiful county bordered by Perthshire, Fife and Clackmannanshire. Set amidst gently rolling hills it is the ideal location for hill walking, golf, cycling, fishing, bird watching or just relaxing and enjoying the beauty of Scotland. The county town of Kinross can be found just off junction 6 on the M90 providing easy access from Edinburgh, Glasgow, Dundee and Perth.

111 THE MUIRS INN

Kinross, Perth & Kinross KY13 8AU
Tel: 01577 862270
e-mail: themuirsinn@fsmail.net

Located on the outskirts of Kinross, just off the M90, **The Muirs Inn** is a picturesque listed building dating back to the 1800s. It was originally a small farmhouse where the blacksmith of the area lived and serviced travellers' horses, carts and carriages. At that time the house was just a small, single level cottage of croft type design – this is now the Mash Tun public bar. Next to the cottage was a byre which now houses the Wee Still Lounge. Later, the original building was extended by the addition of another floor above for accommodation along with a single storey extension for use as stables. These in turn became a garage and today the Maltings and Cellar Food Parlour Rooms occupy the space. Around 1900 the property became a small hotel where the owners initially served drink and refreshments through the living room window to mounted horse riders outside. The owners lived on the premises – and this is the case today.

The Mash Tun Bar still features the original – and much admired – custom-built gantry constructed by a local craftsman around 1909. Also still in place are the much coveted and now scarce original hand-etched ornamental glass porch windows and bar mirrors. The Wee Still Lounge features its own "wee still" which was used in the now defunct Stronachie Distillery in nearby Milnathort. Later it was used by a local chemist for the distillation of water before being acquired by the Muirs' innkeeper of the day.

The extensive menu offers a wide choice of traditional Scottish dishes and pub favourites. Amongst the starters there's a Bothy Broth – the inn's own home-made traditional kitchen soup, and Smokehouse Scotia – a hot smoked fish which is an established favourite. As a main course, choose between a selection of grills, succulent home oven roasted joints and country classics such as the Muirs Steakhouse Pie or the Chicken Cleish – tender breast of chicken marinated in white wine and mushroom cream sauce. Many of the dishes are available in petite and pensioner's portions at reduced prices. To accompany your meal there's a choice of wines, real ales, spirits and Scottish fruit wines, all at very reasonable prices.

The Muirs Inn also offers comfortable accommodation in 5 guest bedrooms. Four of them have en suite facilities; the fifth is a family room with its own private bathroom.

112 THE JOLLY BEGGARS HOTEL

3 New Road, Milnathort,
Kinross KY13 9XT
Tel: 01577 862473

Having been a traditional inn since the 1700's, **The Jolly Beggars Hotel** is a charming find in central Scotland. Located in the small area of Milnathort, in the Perth and Kinross region, the hotel has been owned by Anne Rowse for six years.

The hotel has three good sized bedrooms and two bathrooms as well as a bar, lounge and restaurant. There is a splendid outside seating area, which guests are often eager to enjoy in the summer months.

Guests are welcome to bring their dogs with them, and dog walkers and cyclists will find the hotel a haven, because it is close to the Loch Leven heritage trail, which is the ideal place to spend hours exploring.

Milnathort is a hive of activity with many activities for tourists and locals to enjoy including a nine-hole golf course. There is a large park area nearby and guests can also enjoy fishing in the vicinity. On a main bus route to all of the major towns and cities the hotel is situated in an ideal location for exploring what the surrounding area has to offer. It is also close to a range of traditional pubs and cafés.

114 DRUMNAKYLE FARMHOUSE

Foss, Pitlochry, Perthshire PH16 5NJ
Tel: 01882 634281
website: www.come.to/drumnakyle

Drumnakyle Farmhouse is an historic highland farmhouse offering every traditional homely comfort with some tasteful modern touches. The setting is superb and all the rooms enjoy spectacular views from every window, with Schiehallion in the west and Ben-y-Vrackie to the east. The house can sleep up to 8 people and one of the four bedrooms is on the ground floor and has its own shower and toilet en suite. There's a large living/dining room area with an open-plan modern kitchen equipped with fridge-freezer, ceramic hob cooker, dishwasher, washing machine/drier, food processor and microwave oven. A very efficient wood-burning stove is set on a hearth against the ancient stone wall, redolent of Jacobite bygones. Other features

include a spacious conservatory, Laura Ashley bedrooms, TV, DVD and Hi Fi.

From the conservatory one visitor noted an abundance of wildlife: "2 nests of ospreys, a family of buzzards, the occasional red deer, owls at night, and a wonderful array of small birds, including great spotted woodpeckers, that come to the bird table." An impressive testament to the peacefulness of the spot which lies ¼ mile off the B846 nestling on the hillside looking north over Loch Tummel

113 FASGANEOIN COUNTRY HOUSE

Perth Road, Pitlochry,
Perthshire PH16 5DJ
Tel: 01796 472387
Fax: 01796 474285
e-mail: sabrina.fasganeoin@surfree.co.uk
website: www.fasganeoincountryhouse.co.uk

Fasganeoin Country House stands in one acre of ground overlooking lovely Glen Tummel in Pitlochry and surrounded by low Highland hills. It has real "home-from-home" atmosphere and people return to it again and again for its relaxed atmosphere, its warm friendly welcome and its amazing value for money. Its owner, Mrs Turk, is determined to keep up the high standards she has set since opening the Country House Hotel and as a result Fasganeoin has three coveted stars from Visit Scotland. The year 2007 was the 40th

anniversary of Mrs Turk, her son Norbert and daughter Sabrina and her family running this small gem, something of which they are all justifiably proud.

The guest bedrooms at Fasganeoin are either fully en suite, or have private bathrooms, and each one is immaculately furnished and decorated, meaning that your stay here is comfortable and fuss free - just the place to recharge your batteries. Not only that - Sabrina and her brother speak perfect German and they have an extensive knowledge of the area around Pitlochry, so can recommend places to go and things to see. Incidentally, Fasganeoin is the nearest country house to the famed Pitlochry Festival Theatre.

As you might expect, food is very important in Fasganeoin. A full Scottish breakfast is served every morning - just the thing to set you up for a day exploring the area or taking part in one of the many activities available. All the produce used in the kitchen is fresh and locally sourced whenever possible.

The house itself has some history attached to it. It is a picturesque stone villa built in Victorian times and was once the home of the architect Thomas Renny whose great friend was a famous Japanese poet called Suseki Natsume. Renny was also a timber merchant who traded with Japan and Russia and had a fleet of ships on the Clyde. The house has, over the years, been tastefully renovated to make it an oasis of calm and friendliness.

There is, of course, so much to see and do in and around Pitlochry. Apart from the theatre, there is great fishing on the Tummel, the Tay and Loch Faskally; bird watching; climbing, walking, tennis and so much more. The surrounding countryside is rich in heritage and history, and from here you can have great days out in Inverness, Perth, the Trossachs and Aviemore.

Sabrina invites you to stay at Fasganeoin and help her celebrate those 40-odd great years of welcoming guests to this small, friendly establishing. She is looking forward to continuing welcoming people - make sure you are one of them!

115 KILLIECRANKIE

Pitlochry, Perthshire PH16 5LG
Tel/fax: 01796 473233 (Visitor Centre)
e-mail killiecrankie@nts.org.uk
website: www.nts.org.uk

On 27 July 1689, the Pass of Killiecrankie
echoed with the sound of battle cries and
gunfire when, nearby, a Jacobite army led by
'Bonnie Dundee' defeated the government
forces. One soldier evaded capture by making
a spectacular jump across the River Garry at
Soldier's Leap. The magnificent wooded
gorge, much admired by Queen Victoria in
1844, is tranquil now, and is designated a Site
of Special Scientific Interest because it is a
fine example of an oak and mixed deciduous
woodland. The Visitor Centre exhibition
features the battle, natural history and ranger
services.

118 MILLS OBSERVATORY

Glamis Road, Balgay Park,
Dundee DD2 2UB
Tel: 01382 435967 Fax: 01382 435962
e-mail: mills.observatory@dundeecity.gov.uk
website: www.dundeecity.gov.uk

Mills Observatory, housed in a classically
styled sandstone building, is the UK's only
full time public observatory. Here you can see
the stars and planets for yourself through an
impressive Victorian telescope and look at
safe projected images of the sun. The
planetarium has an
artificial night sky giving
you the chance to view
constellations and
planets. More can be
learnt through the
changing displays, audio
and visual presentations
and an interactive
computer. The shop
offers a range of gifts
and educational items.
Admission to the
observatory is free.

116 THE COUNTRY BAKERY

26 Atholl Street, Dunkeld,
Perthshire PH8 0AR
Tel: 01350 727343
e-mail: iaincboyd@tiscali.co.uk
website: www.countrybakerydunkeld.co.uk

Customers of **The Country Bakery**, located in the
small town of Dunkeld, have a wide selection of
mouth-watering cakes to choose from as well as
the other appealing delights on offer. Inside the
bakery, which is clean and modern, has a wonderful
ambience. The place is fresh and bright with
contemporary, pine furniture. Customers sitting by the window can enjoy a peaceful bite to eat,
while watching village life go by.

The current owner, Iain Boyd, has been in charge for more than three years and with over
eight years experience in the catering industry he takes an approach that has customers returning
for more. He took over the bakery after deciding to seek a quieter life, away from Edinburgh,
where he moved from. Iain has built up a growing reputation with locals and visitors.

Located in the main street of the village, it is open six days a week 9am-3.30pm. The bakery,
which welcomes special dogs, is closed on Sundays and also for two weeks in November.

The Country
Bakery is a delightful
little find in the centre
of the village, where
customers can enjoy a
pleasant rest, while
making the most of
the tasteful treats
being served.

117 LOCH TAY LODGES

Remony, Aberfeldy, Perthshire PH15 2HR
Tel: 01887 830209
e-mail: remony@btinternet.com
website: www.lochtaylodges.co.uk

Set in the heart of Scotland, **Loch Tay Lodges** are beautiful self catering holiday accommodation. They boast some stunning views overlooking Loch Tay towards Ben Lawers and Schiehallion and there is some spectacular scenery to be enjoyed in the surrounding area. The six, tastefully decorated, lodges have been converted from a stone built Grade B listed building dating back to the 1800s and now form part of Remony Estate, which surrounds the picturesque village of Acharn. The lodges are rated three stars by Visit Scotland and are of a high quality, retaining many original features, while providing everything a modern family needs.

The lodges are popular with walkers, sports enthusiasts and those wanting to visit the castles and distilleries in the area. Menzies Castle, the historic home of the Menzies Clan, and Blair Castle, the home of Scotland's only private army, are nearby. The breathtaking Acharn Falls Walk starts minutes from Loch Tay Lodges and there is other scenic, countryside walks in the area for all abilities.

Located between the village and the loch, there is good parking and a safe play area for children and easy access down to the loch where dogs may be walked. A secluded beach and jetty with access to a private boat shed and moorings are a temptation to those wishing to use the estate boats, sail their own, fish or simply paddle or have a picnic.

The nearby town of Aberfeldy has everything you may need and there are many activities available locally, including hill walking, bird watching, horse riding, golfing, fishing, sailing and white water rafting. There are plenty of restaurants and bars in the area, offering dishes made with the very best of local produce.

The lodges are available for weekly lets with a Saturday change over and there is one lodge that allows for shorter stays. All are fully equipped with colour television, washing machine, microwave, electric cooker and oven and fridge. Bed linen, duvets and towels are all provided and electric blankets are also available. A 'starter pack' of groceries can be ordered from the village shop and will be delivered to your lodge prior to your arrival.

Most parts of Scotland's east and west coast are easily accessible for day trips by car and if you want to go further afield Edinburgh, Inverness, Oban and Glasgow are all about two hours away by car.

119 THE GLASS PAVILION

The Esplanade, Broughty Ferry,
Dundee DD5 2EP
Tel: 01382 732739
e-mail: info@theglasspavilion.co.uk
website: www.theglasspavilion.co.uk

The Glass Pavilion is situated on the banks of the beautiful River Tay in the one-time fishing village of Broughty Ferry. Originally constructed as a bathing shelter in the 1930s, this listed building has been totally transformed to provide one of the most stunning dining venues in Scotland. The restaurant has an "art deco" theme throughout and the glass-fronted restaurant offers spectacular views over the Tay Estuary.

The menu at the Glass Pavilion offers everything from a tearoom fayre of speciality teas and coffees with fresh home-baked cakes, to bistro lunches served from Tuesday until Sunday. (The

restaurant is closed on Mondays except for Public and Bank Holidays). The dishes on offer are prepared using only the best locally sourced produce to create an imaginative menu and "specials" board. On Friday and Saturday evenings, à la carte dining is on offer with a superb, critically acclaimed menu freshly prepared by the young and talented chefs. On Sundays, the Scottish

favourite of "high tea" is served consisting of a main course, followed by home-baked scones, toast, tea or coffee.

120 DROVERS INN

Memus, by Forfar, Angus DD8 3TY
Tel: 01307 860322
Fax: 01307 860300
e-mail: info@the-drovers.com
website: www.the-drovers.com

Drovers Inn is set beside an old drovers' road along which cattle were herded to markets in the south. This interesting pub and restaurant combines the traditional Scottish inn atmosphere with contemporary and unusual decoration. The inn stands within a hunting estate so the walls are adorned with a variety of striking antlers and two open fires blaze away during the cooler months.

Good food is a top priority here. Everything is freshly made and based on locally sourced seasonal produce. There's fish from the east coast and, of course, plenty of game from the estate. The menu, which changes weekly, offers a selection of old favourites as well as more modern

dishes. So, typically, you will find haggis, neeps & tatties or an Angus rib-eye steak as well as baked goats cheese with toasted brioche and a caper dressing. Half portions are available for children and those with a smaller appetite.

Everything is home-made and that includes the bread with your soup, and the after dinner chocolates. The excellent food is complemented by an extensive wine list full of variation and quality, as well as a large selection of whiskeys and cognacs to complete the experience.

121 THE KINLOCH ARMS HOTEL

27/29 High Street, Carnoustie, DD7 6AN
Tel: 01241 857008
website: www.kinlocharms.co.uk

A former coach house, dating back to the early 1800's, **The Kinloch Arms Hotel** is located in the heart of one of the world's most popular golfing areas. The family-run hotel boasts a large restaurant, traditional bar, beer garden and games room.

Located in the picturesque town of Carnoustie, on the east coast of Scotland, the hotel is just a two minute walk from the seafront and main line train station. With miles of beautiful sandy beach on its doorstep visitors can enjoy a relaxing and comfortable stay in one of the many en-suite bedrooms.

HIDDEN PLACES GUIDES

Explore Britain and Ireland with *Hidden Places* guides - a fascinating series of national and local travel guides.

Packed with easy to read information on hundreds of places of interest as well as places to stay, eat and drink.

Available from both high street and internet booksellers

For more information on the full range of *Hidden Places* guides and other titles published by Travel Publishing visit our website on

www.findsomewhere.co.uk
or ask for our leaflet by phoning
01752 697280 or emailing
info@travelpublishing.co.uk

122 RISTORANTE BELMONTE

2 Burnside Street, Carnoustie, DD7 7EU
Tel: 01241 853261
website: www.ristorantebelmonte.co.uk

Serving the real taste of Italy in the picturesque seaside town of Carnoustie, on the east coast of Scotland, **Ristorante Belmonte** is popular among locals and visitors. Close to the town's famous championship golf course the restaurant welcomes a wide variety of clientele throughout the year including golfers from around the world who choose to dine there. Since 1996, owners Lucuiano and Maria have built up a great reputation for the fresh ingredients they use and the fun, casual, laid back atmosphere Ristorante Belmonte has. The pasta, bread and desserts are all made on the premises and are complimented by an extensive wine list and range of Italian beers and liqueurs. Catering for everyone, the menu is vegetarian friendly and there is a large al fresco for diners who smoke to eat.

Just a short walk to the seafront, main line train station, golf course and town the restaurant is in the perfect spot for diners to enjoy a pleasant night out. With miles of beautiful sandy beach on its doorstep and located in the heart of one of the most popular golfing areas in the world it is no wonder people visit and revisit Ristorante Belmonte.

124 EAT ON THE GREEN

Udny Green, Ellon,
Aberdeenshire AB41 7RS
Tel: 01651 842337   Fax: 01651 843362
e-mail: enquiries@eatonthegreen.co.uk
website: www.eatonthegreen.co.uk

EAT on the GREEN

Eat on the Green brings a new dining experience to the picturesque village of Udny Green, tucked away in the green Aberdeenshire countryside between Oldmeldrum and Ellon. Owned and managed by Craig Wilson, it has earned a fine reputation for its imaginative range of contemporary and classic dishes using only the finest and freshest of specially selected local produce. Craig is an award-winning chef who brings a wealth of experience to the superb food served in the restaurant, and you will be looked after 'front of house' by the restaurant staff who ensure that your dining experience takes place in a relaxed and informal atmosphere while still retaining the hallmarks of a great restaurant – high standards of service coupled with value-for-money prices.

Eat on the Green seats up to 70 in absolute comfort, while the adjoining lounge offers light snacks and fresh coffee in a warm and inviting ambience. A sample lunch or dinner menu might include Parsnip, Honey & Ginger Soup, Thai-style Smoked Haddock Fishcakes, Seared Fillets of Salmon with Lime Hollandaise and Wok-Fried Greens or Chargrilled Sirloin of local Aberdeen Angus with Roasted Shallots and Homemade Chunky Chips. Desserts might include: Caramelised Lemon Tart, Banana and Cinnamon Pavlova, or Iced Terrine of White & Dark Chocolate.

Eat on the Green is closed on Monday and Tuesday.

123 GORDON HIGHLANDERS MUSEUM

St Lukes, Viewfield Road,
Aberdeen AB15 7XH
Tel: 01224 311200
e-mail: museum@gordonhighlanders.com
website: www.gordonhighlanders.com

The story of The Gordon Highlanders spans 200 years of world history and is packed with tales of courage and tenacity on the field of battle. At the museum you can re-live the compelling and dramatic story of one of the British Army's most famous regiments, through the lives of its outstanding personalities and of the killed soldiers of the North East of Scotland who filled its ranks.

The spectacular exhibition includes a unique collection of the finest of the regiments treasures, including a remarkable display of Victoria Crosses; strikingly detailed life size and scale reproductions of some of the Regiment's finest moments in battle; state of the art touch screens to let you explore the deeds and values that made the Regiment great and stunning film presentations which convey the story of the 'Gordons'.

A stroll in the delightful museum gardens can be rounded off with light refreshments in The Duchess Jean Tea Room. A range of souvenirs are available at The Gordon Gift Shop. Open April to October, Tuesday to Saturday 10.30am-4.30pm and Sunday 12.30pm-4.30pm; November, February and March Thursday to Saturday 10am-4pm.

125 LINSMOHR HOTEL

Oldmeldrum Road,
Pitmedden AB41 7NY
Tel: 01651 842214 Fax: 01651 842800
e-mail: info@linsmohrhotel.co.uk
website: www.linsmohrhotel.co.uk

Found off the B999 road just 15 minutes from Aberdeen and Dyce Airport sits the **Linsmohr Hotel** in Pitmedden. This small family run establishment is ideally situated for keen golfers, fishing, shooting, bird watching and those eager to try out the famous Castle and Whiskey trails.

Run by William and Karen Berry and their team of hard working staff, they create an atmosphere that is both friendly and refined, dedicated to making sure any stay is a memorable one.

All six bedrooms are spacious and comfortable with simple quality furnishings, en suite and tea and coffee facilities. All rooms are due to be refurbished during 2009/2010.

Guests can relax further in a large comfy sofa beside the log burning stove to enjoy a pre or post dinner drink with an extensive choice of over 90 malts and a healthy wine list. Inventive and exquisite food is served here daily at lunch and dinner in the stylishly furnished Bronie Brasserie, with original stone walling and soft lighting. All dishes are prepared freshly by talented chefs using the finest of local and seasonal produce around. Guests are offered the highest standards at good value.

127 THE SHIP INN

5 Shorehead, Stonehaven,
Kincardineshire AG39 2JY
Tel: 01569 762617
Fax: 01569 767074
e-mail: enquiries@shipinnstonehaven.com
website: www.shipinnstonehaven.com

Dating back to 1771 and one of the oldest inns in the area, **The Ship Inn** occupies a superb position overlooking Stonehaven harbour. In 2009, the property next door was acquired and converted to add 5 new modern bedrooms and an extension of the restaurant, adding new windows to provide stunning views while you eat. The new restaurant seats

40 (up from 26) and offers a wide range of freshly cooked dishes using the finest ingredients. Fresh, locally caught fish and seafood are a speciality but you'll also find fine steaks, chicken dishes, pasta, home-made burgers, vegetarian options - something for everybody in fact! Meals are also served in the bar and - weather permitting - outside on the terrace. Enjoy a glass of wine with your meal? Well, have a look at the extensive wine list. There's also a good selection of malt whiskies and liqueurs to round off your meal. The restaurant is open from 12 noon to 2.15pm, and from 5.30pm to 9.30pm, Monday to Friday; and from 12 noon to 9.45pm on Saturday and Sunday.

The hotel bar stocks a good selection of keg beers and two guest real ales which are changed regularly - plus a range of more than 100 malt whiskies to make your mouth water.

The Ship Inn has eleven bedrooms, all with private facilities. There are 6 double rooms (4 with harbour views), 1 single room with harbour view, 2 twin bedded rooms (without harbour view) and 2 family rooms.

The family rooms both have harbour views. One has a double and a single bed and the other has a king size bed and 2 full size single bunk beds. All the rooms are equipped with private showers and toilets, and two of the rooms have full private bathrooms with bath and shower. Two of the bedrooms have four-poster beds. All the rooms are provided with tea and coffee making facilities, colour television with teletext, radio alarm clock and hairdryer. Wi-fi internet connection is available at no charge to all guests. The tariff includes a hearty breakfast with plenty of choice.

Stonehaven itself is a popular holiday resort and its attractions include a scenic golf course and historic Dunottar Castle nearby which starred as Elsinore Castle in Mel Gibson's film of *Hamlet*.

423

126 PITMEDDEN GARDEN

Ellon, Aberdeenshire, AB41 0PD
Tel: 01651 842352
website: www.nts.org.uk

The heart of this property is the formal walled garden originally laid out in 1675 by Sir Alexander Seton. In the 1950s, the Trust set about re-creating the gardens following designs dating from the 17th century. Today, **Pitmedden** features over 5 miles of box hedging arranged in intricate patterns to form six parterres. Each parterre is filled with some 40,000 plants bursting with colour in the summer months.

Extensive herbaceous borders provide an abundance of colour and texture throughout the season and the spectacular lupin border is not to be missed. Honeysuckle, jasmine and roses create a succession of fragrances, while fountains, topiary, sundials, and a fascinating herb garden add to the sense of discovery around the walled garden. There are over 80 varieties of apple trees offering a spectacular show of blossom and scent in spring. On the last Sunday in September the garden holds harvest celebrations with dancing and music, and visitors can buy fruits harvested from the gardens.

The adjacent Museum of Farming Life boasts an extensive collection of domestic and agricultural artefacts of a bygone era. For the more adventurous, the woodland walk extends for a mile and a half round the estate and takes in ponds, rhododendrons, a lime kiln and a nature hut with information about the wider estate. The picnic area is an ideal spot to stop for lunch, and visitors can even enjoy a game of boules on the petanque piste.

128 CLATTERIN' BRIG RESTAURANT

nr Fettercairn, Kincardineshire AB30 1HB
Tel: 01561 340297
e-mail: jltaylor123@aol.com

Set in wonderfully scenic countryside, the **Clatterin' Brig** takes its name from the sound of horse-drawn carriages rattling across the nearby brig, or bridge. Inside, the restaurant has a very Scottish feel with tartan-clad walls, a high ceiling with trusses visible, a full wall fireplace and windows offering amazing views along Drumtochty Glen.

Jane Taylor took over here in 2008 and her menu lists a good selection of traditional Scottish fare ranging from a hearty Scottish breakfast to traditional high teas. Everything is home-cooked and all the ingredients are sourced locally wherever possible. Jane is happy to cater for functions, private parties and bus parties. The restaurant is disabled-friendly with ramp access and a disabled toilet. Outside, there's ample parking, including spaces for touring caravans, and plenty of outdoor seating for balmy days. During the summer months, the restaurant is open from 10am to 5pm, Monday to Friday; and from 10am to 7pm at the weekend.

129 THE MILLERS VISITOR AND RETAIL CENTRE

North Lurg, Midmar,
Aberdeenshire AB51 7NB
Tel: 01330 833462
website: www.millersmidmar.co.uk

Open 7 days a week and just 10 minutes from Westhill on the B9119 Aberdeen to Tarland road you will find the **Millers Visitor and Retail Centre** of Midmar. It's the perfect place to spend an enjoyable day out with friends or family with something for everyone at every turn.

With a wide range of local and luxury goods you will find a range of departments for every occasion including equestrian, agricultural, pets, hardware, DIY, gardening, footwear and animal feeds amongst much, much more. The upper floor has a fashion and country clothing department which houses a fantastic range of clothing, footwear and accessories for ladies, gents and kids. For the homemakers there is also an impressive selection of kitchenware

products and gifts and for those book worms a massive book room with a good collection of both hardback and paperback books. Those interested in the area's history can pop into the local Interpretation centre which details a great view of all the facts.

After an afternoons happy shopping, visitors can retire to the Acorn restaurant which serves quality food throughout the day all made in its own kitchen with the very best produce and if you like the food served there visit the Fine Food Shop serving a tempting selection of goods to take home.

130 RED STAR INN

Kirkton of Skene, Westhill,
Aberdeenshire AB32 6XE
Tel: 01224 743264
e-mail: redstarinn@google.com
website: www.redstarinn.co.uk

Owners Margaret and James have been extending the warmest of welcomes to their fine pub, the **Red Star Inn** for over 8 years now. This fine establishment originally started life as a garage in the 1930's and has also experienced life as a shop before it became the splendid pub it is today over forty years ago. Located just 10 minutes from the airport and 15 minutes from the vibrant city centre of Aberdeen the Red Star is ideally located for guests of all kind, those wanting to stay for a pleasant short break, cyclists or ramblers just after a final drink after a day walking the nearby Whiskey Trails.

By early 2010 there will be 6 new rooms for guests to choose from, all of which are en suite and one with disabled facilities. Guests have access to wi-fi, Sky TV and all other modern facilities.

The pub itself has a modern and fresh appeal also but offers good real ale on a weekly rotation and excellent traditionally home-cooked meals made with the freshest local produce around. If guests remember to quote "Hidden Places" to their generous landlords they will receive a free bottle of wine with every second night's stay – an offer too good to refuse! Occasionally traditional live music is played here too, adding to the great atmosphere that families (and their dogs!) come to enjoy all year round.

131 FEUGHSIDE INN

South Deeside Road, Strachan,
Aberdeenshire AB31 6NS
Tel: 01330 850225

Sitting no more than five miles from Banchory in Royal Deeside, the **Feughside Inn** is a superior hotel close to the River Feugh, and boasts ten rooms, four of which are fully en suite. Each one is well furnished and from most of the rooms there are great views over the surrounding countryside, especially the 1,932 feet high Clachnaben. The inn is the perfect base from which to explore one of the most scenic and historic areas of Scotland. It is also the ideal place to stay if you want to indulge in some of the many activities in the area, such as fishing, shooting, pony trekking, motor biking, hill walking, bird watching (there are ospreys in the district), and so on.

The restaurant and carvery serve some of the finest food in Deeside. Only the freshest of local produce is used wherever possible, guaranteeing you a gastronomic experience you will long remember for all the right reasons. The wine list is comprehensive, and there is sure to be something to suit your taste. The cuisine is Scottish/European, specialising in game, fish, local beef and locally grown vegetables. Special dietary requirements can be accommodated by prior arrangement.

The Feughside Inn prides itself on its Scottish high teas, which are available by arrangement. Afternoon teas are served during the season, and the bar serves a great range of drinks - real ales, beer, malt whisky, spirits, wine, liqueurs and soft drinks.

132 CRATHES CASTLE AND GARDENS

Banchory, Aberdeenshire AB31 5QJ
Tel: 0870 118 1951
Ranger service: 01330 844810
e-mail: crathes@nts.org.uk
website: www.nts.org.uk

King Robert the Bruce granted the lands of Leys to the Burnett family in 1323: the ancient Horn of Leys, which can be seen today in the Great Hall, marks his gift. The castle, built in the second half of the 16th century, is a superb example of a tower house of the period. Some of the rooms retain their original painted ceilings and collections of family portraits and furniture.

A visit is enhanced by the walled garden, which

incorporates herbaceous borders and many unusual plants, providing a wonderful display at all times of the year. The great yew hedges, fascinating examples of the art of topiary, date from as early as 1702. Explore the estate on the seven

waymarked trails (including one suitable for wheelchairs) that lead through the mixed woodlands, along the Coy Bum and past the millpond. In the Visitor Centre a new exhibition, *A Walk on the Wild Side*, explores the wildlife on the Crathes Estate.

133 GLEN TANAR HOLIDAY COTTAGES

Glen Tanar Estate, Aboyne,
Aberdeenshire AB34 5EU
Tel: 013398 86451 Fax: 013398 86047
e-mail: info@glentanar.co.uk
website: www.glentanar.co.uk

Glen Tanar Estate offers an exclusive hideaway for all, from action-packed family holidays to romantic breaks for two. Set in the heart of Royal Deeside and the Cairngorms National Park, **Glen Tanar Holiday Cottages** provide a wealth of activities for visitors, including walking, cycling, horse-riding and trout and salmon fishing amidst a glorious 25,000-acre landscape. You will feel right at home in one of the 6 self-catering cottages on the estate which can cater for two up to eleven guests. Each cottage is individually designed, from the bothy tradition of the Rowan to the style of the Butler's Lodge. Guests can sample the true taste of Royal Deeside at Liz's Larder, run by Glen Tanar Housekeeper Liz Peck who provides home-made quality meals using locally sourced produce.

Explore the diverse areas of open moorland, forest and farmland where red deer roam, eagles fly and the elusive capercaillie and Scottish crossbills live. The stunning surroundings of Glen Tanar Estate, combined with its exquisite accommodation, make this Deeside retreat a supremely relaxed place to stay.

135 STRACHAN COTTAGE

9 Strachan Cottages, Tarland, Aboyne,
Aberdeenshire AB34 5PG
Tel: 01339 881401

In the charming village of Tarland, four miles northwest of Aboyne, you will find **Strachan Cottage**, a stone-built cottage that offers the very best in self-catering accommodation. It sleeps six in three bedrooms, and has a spacious and comfortable lounge, a well-equipped kitchen and a bathroom. It is owned and run by Evelyn Smith, who keeps it spotlessly clean so that guests have a memorable holiday.

It is the ideal place for people who want a quiet holiday close to Royal Deeside, or for the more energetic, such as anglers, golfers or ramblers. Tarland nestles at the centre of The Howe O'Cromer, close to the boundary of the Cairngorms National Park. This natural hollow of land on the eastern edge of the Grampian Mountains, between the rivers Dee and Don is an area of exceptional beauty with much to interest the walker and the naturalist. It is a very special part of Scotland, rich in historic and prehistoric sites to delight the visitor.

134 VICTORIA RESTAURANT

Dinnet, Aboyne, Aberdeenshire AB34 5JY
Tel: 013398 85337
website: www.victoriarestaurant.co.uk

The **Victoria Restaurant** is set at the gateway to the Caingorm National Park in the heart of Royal Deeside. Sometimes described as 'the first restaurant in the highlands,' it has developed a popular reputation with both locals and visitors alike who find it the perfect start or end to exploring the nearby countryside which is filled with many local attractions including castles Balmoral, Fraser, Craigievar and Crathes, fishing spots, golf courses, forest trails and routes along Loch Nagar, Glen Muick and Glen Tanar for the more ambitious walkers. Visitors will not find themselves short of things to do around here, yet many find themselves whiling away the evening within the relaxing walls of the Victoria – a favourite for a wide range of customers including families, senior citizens, tourists, locals, day-trippers and of course 'ladies who lunch.'

The Victoria is located on the main A93 road from Aberdeen to Braemar halfway between Aboyne and Ballater near the A97 junction. A traditional pink granite cottage in its own grounds, the restaurant is tastefully and neutrally decorated inside which complements the owner's passion for the theatre which is reflected in the framed posters and art work from their previous life spent working in London's West End for nearly two decades. Their retreat here in Dinnet is as enjoyable for them as it is for their clients who benefit from the relaxing atmosphere, spacious design, comfy seating and log stove in the winter. Guests can dine inside, in the Garden Room (the conservatory) or al fresco in the summer months. A wide range of light lunches and evening meals are on offer - all delicious, all home cooked to taste. Food here is honest and generous and is made from largely locally sourced produce. This place prides itself on creating a no hassle evening for you, allowing guests to enjoy the good company, good music and good food in their own time. As an added bonus tables can be decorated for special occasions and cakes prepared if arranged in advance. Owing to its popularity and reputation for a few timeless special dishes we recommend booking, especially at weekends.

The restaurant is open Wednesday - Sunday from 11am (noon on Sundays) and lunches are served from noon - 2.30pm, with evening meals served from 5.30pm - 8pm (7pm on Sundays) Also open Tuesdays over the Easter holidays, July and August and December.

136 TANGLEY HOUSE

41 Braemar Road, Ballater,
Aberdeenshire AB35 5RQ
Tel: 01339 755624
e-mail: info@tangleyhouse.co.uk
website: www.tangleyhouse.co.uk

Set in lovely gardens overlooking Craigendarroch (the 'Hill of Oaks'), **Tangley House** is a handsome Victorian property which has been renovated to a very high standard. Owners Shirley and Tom Oliver offer their guests the choice of either bed & breakfast or self-catering accommodation. Bed & breakfast guests stay in the main house where there are 2 rooms available, a twin and a double, both of them with en suite facilities and fully equipped with colour TV, hospitality tray and hair dryer. Both rooms enjoy magnificent views of Craigendarroch.

For those who prefer self-catering, Tangley Cottage is situated within the grounds of Tangley House, in quiet pleasant surroundings yet close to the village centre and all amenities. It has one double bedroom, a sitting/dining room with an open coal fire, colour TV and CD/

radio player. There's also a fully equipped kitchen and shower room. Please note that payment at Tangley House is by cash or cheque only.

Both properties are within easy walking distance of Ballater village centre which has some excellent shops, art galleries and restaurants.

Many outdoor activities are also available locally such as golf, walking, fishing, cycling, ski-ing etc.

137 MOORFIELD HOUSE HOTEL

Chapel Brae, Braemar AB35 5YT
Tel: 01339 741244
e-mail: hairhotels@btconnect.com
website: www.moorfieldhousehotel.com

A charming family-run hotel, **Moorfield House Hotel** occupies a peaceful location overlooking the famous 'Braemar Gathering' arena, just a few yards from the Queen's Pavilion. Recently refurbished to a high standard, the hotel offers a warm and friendly welcome, comfortable accommodation, a first class dining experience, and an ideal base for outdoor activities all year round.

The hotel has a growing reputation for the exceptional quality of its meals, all of which are cooked to order using fresh local produce. The dishes are beautifully presented and served in a relaxed and friendly environment. You may also want to enjoy a fine malt whiskey, or one of the local real ales. Sample your drink beside the log fire in the cosy bar.

The hotel also offers quality accommodation with 3 doubles, a single, a twin and

a ground level family bedroom all available. All the rooms have en suite facilities and are equipped with a hair dryer and hospitality tray. Pets are allowed in the family room only. Visitors will find plenty to see and do in the area, and your hosts Iain and Elspeth Hair will be happy to put you in the picture.

50-52 North Street, Inverurie,
Aberdeenshire AB51 4RS
Tel: 01467 621242
e-mail: inn.blackbull@yahoo.co.uk

Dating back to the mid-1800s, the **Black Bull Inn** is one of the oldest pubs in Inverurie. It is situated across from the former sheep and cattle market whose drovers met to do their business at the inn, thus giving it the name. "The Bull", as it is affectionately known by the locals is easily accessible from the north and south via the A96.

After having been in the Christie family for more than 150 years, the Black Bull Inn found a new lease of life when it was bought by Judy and Les Stuart in 2007. A local family, the Stuarts were determined to keep the character and family-run atmosphere that came with the pub. The open coal fire and dark-wood finishings date back to the 1950s and, along with the ever-welcoming locals, give the inn a cosy and friendly feeling that is lacking in most modern bars. The bar has undergone a few changes in the recent past, with an open lounge being added as well as a games room and beer garden for those summer days. Disability access has also been greatly improved and the Bull is a most welcoming place for those with wheelchairs.

The bar, run by son Mike, boasts an impressive Malt Whisky collection with more than 40 Malts for all tastes. Along with a fine rum and gin selection, all your premium labels are available.

With pool, darts, Quiz nights every week and regular live music, as well as Sky Sports, there is rarely a night goes by that the Bull isn't a hive of activity.

The brand new bed & breakfast, "The Bennachie View", also run by the Stuarts is situated above the inn, with access to the large rear car park. The B&B provides a most comfortable stay in the "Heart of the Garioch" with 3 en suite rooms consisting of 2 twin rooms and a double room. With a hearty breakfast provided by Judy, including a ten-item full breakfast, kippers and porridge, every day can be planned in the knowledge that a full stomach is guaranteed. All the rooms are non-smoking; credit cards are welcome.

With the family living in the North East, they have an extensive knowledge of outings available, ranging from the Whisky (and CastleTrails) to adventure days - there is something available for everyone.

The Black Bull is open from noon until 3pm, and from 5pm to 11pm, Monday to Thursday; until 1am on Friday; from 11am to 12.30am on Saturday; and from noon until 11pm on Sunday.

430

139 HIGHLANDER HOTEL

75 West Church Street, Buckie,
Banffshire AB56 1BQ
Tel: 01542 834008

Located in the small fishing village of Buckie, the **Highlander Hotel** is a sturdy stone building dating from the 1880s which became a hotel in the 1940s and was extensively refurbished in the winter of 2007/8. Highly popular with local people, the hotel has a public bar, lounge bar and a separate small dining room. Bar snacks and meals, including daily specials, are served throughout the day, and in the evening there's another menu which features some more exotic dishes. Everything on offer is based on fresh, local produce and a speciality of the kitchen is delicious fresh haddock served in a special beer batter. In good weather, refreshments can be savoured in the pleasant beer garden with a covered area at the rear, where there is also a car park for residents. Children are welcome throughout the hotel.

Accommodation at the Highlander comprises 6 comfortable guest bedrooms, all stylishly furnished and well-equipped. Five of them have recently modernised en suite facilities; the 6th has its own modern private bathroom. The hotel has good access for wheelchairs and disabled toilets; all major credit cards are accepted.

431

140 BAYVIEW GUEST HOUSE

63 Saltoun Place, Fraserburgh AB43 9RY
Tel: 01346 515353
e-mail: neilinesimpson@msn.com
website: www.fraserburghguesthouse.co.uk

An excellent base for exploring northeast Scotland, **Bayview Guest House** offers a good choice of comfortable single, double,

twin or family rooms, all with flat screen TV and hospitality tray as well as en suite facilities. Your hosts, Neiline and Fergie, believe that breakfast is the most important meal of the day so you'll find a appetising range of options available and servings hearty enough to set you up for the day. Vegetarians can be catered for and evening meals are also available by arrangement. As one visitor wrote: "You couldn't ask for more!"

142 MARGARET & JIMMY'S B&B

Pond View, Brucklay,
Maud, nr Peterhead AB42 4QN
Tel: 01771 613675
e-mail: mhepburn@lineone.net
website: www.pondview.co.uk

Margaret and Jimmy Hepburn run this pleasant bed and breakfast with beautiful views. This modern bungalow holds three tastefully decorated and spacious rooms, two

double ensuite rooms and one twin room with its own private bathroom. Each room also has TV, wi-fi and tea and coffee making facilities. Margaret and Jimmy are happy to accommodate families and are willing to add an extra bed to each room if necessary. Just fifteen miles from the coastal towns of Fraserburgh and Peterhead this B&B is the ideal location to explore this lovely area. The surrounding area is filled with outstanding natural beauty and top tourist attractions.

141 KILMARNOCK ARMS HOTEL

Bridge Street, Cruden Bay,
Aberdeenshire AB42 0HD
Tel: 01779 812213
website: www.kilmarnockarms.com

Passionate owners of the **Kilmarnock Arms** Martin and Lucy Taylor are dedicated to exceeding expectations in this finely run historic hotel. An ideal place to stay for golf, business or on your tour of the east coast, there are 14 en-suite well decorated and comfortable rooms to choose from. The hotel was built in the 1880's from Peterhead granite and retains many beautiful original features such as large sash and bay windows in all front-facing rooms, large open fireplaces, ceiling roses and a slate roof. Bram Stoker himself was a regular guest of the hotel with the nearby Slains Castle being the inspiration for Dracula's own castle. The local area has many other historic attractions and tourist spots including one of the top 100 golf courses in the world and Cruden Bay beach, home to many native seals.

Local area aside the hotel itself has plenty to entertain you with a varied locally-sourced menu that can include lobster if you give them a days notice! Whether you choose to dine in the restaurant, the well-stocked lounge bar that carries a selection of 65 malts or in the warmer months dine al fresco in the hotels own charming garden complete with its very own babbling brook, there really is something for everyone at the Kilmarnock Arms Hotel.

143 THE PITSLIGO ARMS HOTEL

51 High Street, New Pitsligo,
Aberdeenshire AB43 6NF
Tel: 01771 653208
e-mail: info@thepitsligoarms.co.uk

A handsome late-Georgian listed building, **The Pitsligo Arms Hotel** has recently been sympathetically refurbished and now offers a warm and welcoming atmosphere where guests can unwind and enjoy a truly relaxing experience. It is particularly noted for the quality of the cuisine served in the dining room where all the dishes on the menu are based on the best locally produced and freshly prepared ingredients. This is Scottish cuisine at its finest.

The hotel also caters for all in the morning, serving a Full Scottish breakfast for those with a big day ahead or a continental breakfast for those with a lighter appetite. In the evening you may want to relax in the lounge where there's an ample selection of fine wines and malt whiskies.

The accommodation at The Pitsligo Arms consists of 5 en suite rooms which are larger than average and furnished in keeping with the simple modern style of the hotel. Each offers total comfort with many added extras such as a power shower in every bathroom, colour TV, Internet connection and hospitality tray. The hotel is located within a short drive to many local amenities and tourist attractions.

144 SEAFIELD ARMS HOTEL

5 Chapel Street, Whitehills, Banff AB45 2NB
Tel: 01261 861209
e-mail:
enquiries@seafieldarmshotelwhitehills.co.uk
website:
www.seafieldarmshotelwhitehills.co.uk

Located in the North East of Scotland, Whitehills is central to the Banffshire Coast – an area of outstanding natural beauty boasting the opportunity to spot Minke Whales, dolphins and porpoises Also nearby is Scotland's only mainland gannet colony. The area is also the only location in Scotland to have two Royal golf courses; Royal Tarlair in Macduff and Duff House Royal in Banff as well as a great selection of other courses in the area. There is a rich maritime history along the coastline and Whitehills itself boasts one of the finest Marinas in the North.

Seafield Arms Hotel & Maitlands Bar in Whitehills is a friendly, traditional village pub with an open coal fire and years of local history and heritage on display with all the pictures and photos on the walls, and the bar counter itself together with lots of instruments and equipment having come from local fishing boats. Described as "a local institution" the bar is a focal point for the community with some customers still involved in the fishing or farming industries and others in the newer fields of oil and gas. As well as the well stocked bar, there is a restaurant on the same level with the menu offering classic favourites such as lasagne and steak & ale pie as well as varying special dishes using great quality fish, seafood, Scottish beef and game from local suppliers. With 3 en-suite bedrooms available for bed & breakfast upstairs there's hardly any reason to ever leave!

145 THE WEST END HOTEL

Achintore Road, Fort William PH33 6ED
Tel: 01397 702614 Fax: 01397 706279
e-mail: welcome@westend-hotel.co.uk
website: www.westend-hotel.co.uk

Offering the best of Highland hospitality and personal service to make sure your stay is relaxed, carefree and competitively priced, the **West End Hotel** boasts a tastefully furnished restaurant, lounge bar and delightful patio. It is well known for offering good food with excellent service. The choice includes a wide variety of menus from bar meals to private parties and functions. The main dining room is particularly comfortable for occasional dinner or for those requiring a special dinner evening.

During the season there is regular live entertainment that takes place in the large lounge bar which often provides a very enjoyable and relaxing evening for guests and locals. There's a well stocked bar with a large choice of wines, spirits and, of course, fine whiskies from around the Highlands.

The hotel's bedrooms are comfortable with many having a view of the loch and surrounding mountains. All rooms are en suite with central heating and TV. Tea and coffee making facilities as well as direct dial telephone are also included.

146 THE GANTOCKS

Achintore Road, Fort William,
Inverness-shire PH33 6RN
Tel: 01397 702050 Fax: 01397 705954
e-mail: thegantocks@hotmail.co.uk
website: www.fortwilliam5star.co.uk

Occupying a superb position, **The Gantocks Bed and Breakfast** enjoys stunning, unrestricted views across Loch Linnhe to the Ardgour hills. But it is also on the edge of Fort William town centre - just a pleasant 15 minute walk along the shore and through Achintore gardens. Prepare to be pampered at this 5-star establishment with 6 feet wide super king beds, power showers/ spa bath, not to mention breakfast, catered entirely to your needs, in a dining room that will make you think you are on a boat without the waves.

The Gantocks is an ideal centre for your Highland holiday in Fort William, the Outdoor Capital of the UK. There are ferries for the Isles of Skye, Eigg, Rum and Canna; glorious silver sands at Morar where the film *Local Hero* was shot. Loch Ness, Cairngorm National Park and Oban are all only approximately 1 pleasant hour away.

If you prefer self-catering, the adjacent architect-designed three bedroom luxury cottage, Ard Na Faire, enjoys the same wonderful loch views. It has 3 elegantly furnished and decorated bedrooms, two of them on the ground floor; a large lounge area and kitchen, and two bathrooms.

147 HUNTINGTOWER LODGE

Druimarbin, Fort William,
Inverness-shire PH33 6RP
Tel: 01397 700079
e-mail: enquiries@huntingtowerlodge.com
website: www.huntingtowerlodge.com

With stunning and ever-changing views of Loch Linnhe, **Huntingtower Lodge** boasts some of the finest accommodation in the Highlands. Chris and Jackie Clifford offer the very best in 21st Century comfort and a warm welcome to all their guests.

The lodge, just two miles south west of Fort William, has a light and bright feel to it and is tastefully decorated throughout. Each room has fantastic views over the loch and guests can often see a wide range of wildlife in the area, including roe deer and red squirrels. Set in four acres of woodland there is plenty of exploring to be done and if you want to take things a bit slower there is always the wild flower garden for guests to amble around.

Run as a 'green' establishment Huntingtower Lodge uses the very finest locally sourced or British produce and

the owners are keen supporters of fair-trade. Bread, biscuits and cakes are baked by Jackie and the varied breakfast menu is extremely popular with guests. Whether you are visiting the area for leisure or work Chris and Jackie do their very best to help you relax and enjoy your time in the Highlands.

148 WESTHAVEN

Auchintore Road, Fort William,
Inverness-shire PH33 6RW
Tel: 01397 705500
e-mail: westhaven888@hotmail.co.uk
website: www.westhaven.co.uk

With stunning views of the Ardgour Hills, **Westhaven B&B** is the ideal base for those wanting to explore the Highlands. The relaxing home-from-home has five spacious bedrooms (four en-suites) - all tastefully decorated and finished to a high standard and all boasting fantastic loch views.

Richard and Rose Sliwinski have owned Westhaven for five years and Rose's hearty breakfasts are served in the dining room, which has unbeatable views of the surrounding loch and hills. Located on the shores of Loch Linnhe the popular B&B is about two miles from the

historic town of Fort William and close to Ben Nevis. If you don't fancy climbing Britain's highest mountain there are plenty of other activities in the vicinity, including sailing, fishing, golf, walking, cycling and horse riding.

Open all year round the traditional villa, with real wood floors, serves only the finest of fresh local produce and early breakfast is available from 7.30am by arrangement or packed breakfast for early checkout. Packed lunches and a laundry service are also available. As well as a beautiful, well-maintained garden, there is secure parking at the rear of the house and lockable storage for cycles and outdoor equipment. No children under 10 years. No pets.

149 THE WOOLLY ROCK B&B

North Ballachulish, Fort William,
Inverness-shire PH33 6SA
Tel: 01855 821338
e-mail: rogerlucas@woollyrock.co.uk
website: www.woollyrock.co.uk

Boasting magnificent panoramic views of Loch Linnie and surrounding mountains **The Woolly Rock B&B** is an ideal place to stay for visitors to the area. Owned by Roger Lucas for the past three years the B&B is a family home where everyone is made to feel welcome.

There are three comfortable ground floor bedrooms – and one room on the first floor. Disabled access is not a problem. Open all year round The Woolly Rock B&B is a unique place to stay with the living quarters situated upstairs to make the most of the superb views of the loch. Located in the village of North Ballachulish, which is centred around former slate quarries, the dog-friendly B&B is popular with cyclists and there is a golf course nearby as well as loch fishing. Walkers will be in their element with several excellent local walks.

There are plenty of hotels a short walk away from the B&B, which serve good evening meals and Roger can arrange table bookings. To get to the B&B, north of Loch Leven, turn right off the A82 onto the B836, just north of the bridge at North Ballachulish. Turn immediately right into drive by school. There is off street parking.

150 MAYFIELD B&B

Happy Valley Torlundy,
Fort William   PH33 6SN
Tel: 01397 703320
e-mail: enquiry@torlundy.co.uk
website: www.torlundy.co.uk

Occupying a peaceful rural location, **Mayfield B&B** is situated in the settlement of Torlundy, close to the Highland town of Fort William, which along with the Lochaber area has now been designated the **"Outdoor Capital of the UK"**.

Mayfield sits in the shadow of Ben Nevis (making it an excellent base for the climb) and is only a short distance from the winter skiing area and mountain gondola of Aonach Mhor. Walking, fishing, horse trekking and water sports can all be arranged locally and wildlife including deer, golden eagles, ospreys, otters, seals, migrating whales and dolphins can all be spotted in the Lochaber area. We provide an excellent base for touring the area.

The dining room at Mayfield enjoys glorious views of Ben Nevis, and it is here you can enjoy a hearty Scottish breakfast to include fruit juice, cereals, porridge, bread, toast, tea, coffee, and a full cooked breakfast including among other things locally made black pudding and sausages, bacon, tomato, mushrooms and eggs. Where possible all our breakfast ingredients are sourced locally.

Accommodation at Mayfield has been awarded 4 Stars by the Tourist Board and comprises 3 attractively furnished and decorated bedrooms – 2 Double ensuites and 1 Single with its own Private Bathroom. Wi-Fi internet access is available.

151 SNOWGOOSE MOUNTAIN CENTRE & SMIDDY BUNKHOUSE

Station Road, Corpach,
Fort William   PH33 7SH
Tel: 01397 772467
e-mail: info@highland-mountain-guides.co.uk
website: www.highland-mountain-guides.co.uk

Family-run hostel & bunkhouse accommodation plus self catering apartments on the Caledonian Canal from

£13.50 ppnt. Accomodation includes s/c kitchens, two drying rooms, ample parking & storage, hot showers, and laundry.

Adventure available includes river & sea kayaking, open canoeing on lochs, rivers & coastal water, rock climbing & abseiling, high mountain walking and dinghy sailing. Wilderness expeditions by water, sail, bike or on the mountains and Winter mountain courses are also available.

152 COINACHAN GUEST HOUSE

Gairlochy Road, Spean Bridge PH34 4EG
Tel/Fax: 01397 712417
e-mail: info@coinachan.com
website: www.coinachan.com

Located just outside the village of Spean Bridge, **Coinachan Guest House** is a 250-year-old shepherd's cottage set in magnificent countryside.

Owner Dorothy Gibb offers visitors top quality bed & breakfast accommodation with 3 guest rooms available, all with en suite facilities, Sky TV and WiFi access. Guests have the use of a comfortable residents' lounge which commands grand views of the mountains. Breakfast at Coinachan is really something special with a menu that includes smoked salmon, venison sausage, fresh waffles with maple syrup and, in season, home-grown strawberries. Evening meals and packed lunches are also available on request. All major credit cards apart from American Express and Diners are accepted.

In the spring and autumn, Dorothy also operates Textile Tours and Trails which are designed to introduce participants to some of the area's great textile personalities - and some of Scotland's spectacular scenery. These small group tours have their own dedicated coach, driver and guide, and as well as meeting local craftspeople include visits to local attractions such as Glenfinnan, Glencoe, Glen Nevis and the Caledonian Canal.

153 SPEAN BRIDGE HOTEL

Spean Bridge, Inverness-shire PH34 4ES
Tel: 01397 712250
e-mail: info@speanbridgehotel.co.uk
website: www.speanbridgehotel.co.uk

This 17th century coaching house has been extended and added to several times over the years, but it has never lost the spirit of hospitality that you now find in the **Spean Bridge Hotel**.

The well kept and welcoming exterior boasts a traditionally Scottish interior, which is clean, comfortable and homely. The 28 en suite rooms are all attractively decorated and contain all of the basic amenities expected. There are also chalets and bunkhouses for larger groups and families. The hotel also has a spectacular restaurant and function room which can play host for those special occasions.

HIDDEN PLACES GUIDES

Explore Britain and Ireland with *Hidden Places* guides - a fascinating series of national and local travel guides.

Packed with easy to read information on hundreds of places of interest as well as places to stay, eat and drink.

Available from both high street and internet booksellers

For more information on the full range of *Hidden Places* guides and other titles published by Travel Publishing visit our website on

www.findsomewhere.co.uk
or ask for our leaflet by phoning
01752 697280 or emailing
info@travelpublishing.co.uk

154 INVEROUR GUEST HOUSE

Spean Bridge, Inverness-shire PH34 4EU
Tel: 01397 712218
e-mail:
enquiries@inverourguesthouse.co.uk
website: www.inverourguesthouse.co.uk

Attractively located in the centre of Spean Bridge village, close to Fort William and Ben Nevis, **Inverour Guest House** is surrounded by stunning views of the Nevis Range and the Grey Corries. Originally the village post office and schoolmaster's house, Inverour is now the home of Lesley and Ian

Brown who have been welcoming bed & breakfast guests here since 2002. There are 8 bedrooms, most of them with en suite facilities, and all are equipped with colour TV, tea and coffee making facilities, hair dryer and radio alarm. The Browns pride themselves on their hearty breakfasts which are served in the attractive dining room – guests can choose from traditional Scottish, continental or vegetarian. They will also provide packed lunches for

your days out and about. Inverour has a heated drying room for those of you who do enjoy the outdoors should you need it, a garage for safe storage of mountain bikes, canoes etc, and lots of private parking.

The area around Spean Bridge is a paradise for outdoor lovers and many activities are available such as golf, pony trekking, quad biking, fishing and even white water rafting.

155 RIVERSIDE LODGES

Riverside, Invergloy,
Spean Bridge PH34 4DY
Tel: 01397 712684
e-mail: enquiries@riversidelodge.org.uk
website: www.riversidelodge.org.uk

The three stunning cottages that comprise **Riverside Lodges** are set in 12 acres of beautiful woodland gardens and boast a private beach onto Loch Lochy. Other natural attractions here include a river gorge, waterfalls and more than 300 species of Rhododendron to create a bird watchers

paradise. Centrally located in the Great Glen, this is known to many as the heart of the Highlands and is the ultimate Highland getaway.

The cottages are all timber built with enclosed decking overlooking the gardens and lochside; the beach is a mere 100 metres away. Each cottage will sleep 6 people in 3 bedrooms, the heavy insulation and double glazing mean that even during the snows of winter, you will be warm and cosy inside! In addition to the lodges, there is also a room

available in the owners Steve and Marilyn's bungalow. It can be used as a family room, a twin or a double; exactly the same facilities are available with the added bonus of a cooked Scottish breakfast every morning!

The lodges are available for hire all year round and the B&B during the main season. Pets are very welcome in the lodge and while there aren't full disabled facilities, one of the lodges is more suited to the less able than the others.

156 AUCHTERAWE COUNTRY HOUSE

Auchterawe, Loch Ness, Fort Augustus,
Inverness-shire, PH32 4BT
Tel: +44 (0)1320 366228
e-mail: auchterawe@talktalk.net
website:
www.fortaugustuscountryhouse.co.uk

It would be hard to find a better situated guest house than the **Auchterawe Country House** set in the woods of Auchterawe forest, and just 2 miles from the award winning village of Fort Augustus, Loch Ness and the Caledonian Canal, and with the dramatic backdrop of the Great Glen mountain range. This makes the Auchterawe Country House a perfect retreat for walkers, with many riverside and mountain tracks just outside your door. Along with climbers, travellers and families – which are attracted to this spectacular location all year round.

The bed and breakfast accommodation offered ranges from intimate double rooms, to rooms to accommodate families of four - and all come with their own en-suite. The rooms are decorated and furnished with a beautiful style combining crisp modern and rustic, and with open log fires in the colder

months, make for a cosy and relaxing visit. Facilities include

communal lounge area for guests with sofas and a pool table.

In addition to the breakfast (a hearty Scottish cooked breakfast, or continental fare from the antique breakfast bar), they now offers evening meals in their lively dining room with chandelier and mountain views. Special dietary requirements are catered for by prior arrangement, from dairy- and gluten-free to vegetarian and vegan. Packed lunches can also be arranged prior to your stay.

157 HILLSIDE BED & BREAKFAST

I The Steadings, Auchterawe,
Fort Augustus PH32 4BT
Tel: 01320 366253
e-mail: hillside.fortaug@btinternet.com

Surrounded by forests and mountains there are some stunning views to be enjoyed at **Hillside Bed & Breakfast**. There are three rooms, one en-suite and two with private facilities. All of the rooms have TVs and hospitality trays and all are finished to an extremely high standard. The full cooked breakfasts are made using the freshest local produce and served in the spacious dining room, which boasts open views over the garden and adjoining farmland.

Built in 2001 Hillside Bed & Breakfast is owned by Helen and Peter Butler and is in an ideal location for visiting Inverness, Fort William and exploring The Highlands of Scotland. Popular among walkers, cyclists,

hill climbers, bird watchers and wild life enthusiasts, packed lunches are available for those wanting to go on day trips.

The B&B is just two miles from Fort Augustus, which is famous for its flight of lochs allowing boats to pass between the Caledonian Canal and Loch Ness. There are plenty of opportunities to take a boat trip on Loch Ness as well as river walks and outdoor activities. The area has many good quality pubs, cafés and restaurants. The B&B is open between April and October and has off-road parking for guests. No credit cards.

158 GLENCOE COTTAGES

Torren, Glencoe PH49 4HX
Tel: 01855 811207
e-mail: victoria@glencoe-cottages.com
website: www.glencoe-cottages.com

The three **Glencoe Cottages** are situated amongst some of the most breath taking scenery in the UK; millions of people will see the surrounding mountains and countryside as they watch the latest Harry Potter film; Warner Bros return to film here regularly.

Each sleeping 6 – 8 people in style and comfort, the cottages are slate roofed and traditionally built, with views of the river from a patio.

The cottages are heated using under-floor heating with carbon neutral wood being burnt. The cottages are open plan and are very well equipped for that short break away from the hustle and bustle of the city.

159 GLENCOE B & B

Torren, Glencoe PH49 4HX
Tel: 01855 811207
e-mail: victoria@glencoe-cottages.com
website: www.glencoe-cottages.com

Recently finished in 2008, Signal Rock Cottage has been constructed to the highest green standards and in amongst the most famous of Scottish Glens. It is here that **Glencoe B & B** is found, and the two double rooms with en suite facilities are fabulous.

Breath taking mountain views create a feeling of serenity and calm; this intensifies as you explore the fifty acres of woodland

surrounding the B & B. There is a great pub just 15 minutes walk through the woods if you crave human contact but this place is brilliant for a short break away.

160 ALLTBEAG B&B

Tighphuirt, Glencoe, Argyll PH49 4HN
Tel: 01855 811719

Built just three years ago by owners Anne and David Thomson the Alltbeag B&B in the delightful village of Glencoe has three lovely bedrooms. All of them are tastefully decorated and have a television, hospitality tray and en-suite facilities. Guests can enjoy some spectacular views across the surrounding area including views over the loch side.

The B&B has been built to a high quality and has a real homely feel to it, making guests feel at ease. A traditional Scottish breakfast is served and there is a good selection of organic alternatives. Local produce and home-baking is at the heart of the food served, which is extremely popular with guests. The unique open plan lounge, kitchen and dining room adds to the

modern feel of the house. Designed by Anne and David the house, which has plenty of off road parking, has top fixtures and fittings throughout.

Having worked in the B&B industry for 25 years the owners are the perfect hosts and are more than happy to give guests information on the local area, suggesting walks and climbs. Many people arrive as guests and leave as friends. No pets. No credit cards.

161 BEN VIEW HOTEL

Strontian, Acharacle, Argyll PH36 4HY
Tel: 01967 402333
e-mail: benviwehotel@aol.com
website: www.benviewhotel.co.uk

Located just 2km from the scenic, peaceful village of Strontian – the main village in Sunart – the **Ben View Hotel** has nine guest bedrooms, all with en-suite facilities. Overlooking Loch Sunart, the hotel's garden was once part of the old Caledonian Forest and is surrounded by stunning scenery, history and wildlife.

Owners Graham and Joanne McMenemy have been at Ben View for nine years and pride themselves on their warm welcome and friendly staff. The finest food and drink is served in the hotel's restaurant and well-stocked bar and there is a daily changing menu for guests to make the most of. Evening meals are served to non-residents every day. The 2,700 feet high Corbett of Ben Resipole is the breathtaking backdrop of the hotel, which also has

superb views to Ben Garbhein, Loch Sunart and the Morvern Hills.

Strontian is on the Ardnamurchan Peninsula, close to the most westerly point on the UK mainland, making Ben View Hotel the ideal base for visitors wanting to take in the local history and culture. At the end of a busy day exploring the area guests can relax in the hotel's relaxing spa bath and sauna. Pets allowed. There are off road parking facilities.

162 TEA ROOM

Ariundle Centre, Strontian,
Argyll, PH36 4JA
Tel: 01967 402279
e-mail: ariundle@aol.com
website: www.ariundle.co.uk

Located in the village of Strontian the light and spacious **Tea Room** can be found in the Ariundle Centre - a small friendly family-run business with many activities to attract visitors. Owner Kate Campbell has lived in the area for 40 years and owned the restaurant for 20 years.

Whether it is a hearty breakfast, morning coffee, light lunch or snack you are after the Tea Room serves it all and in the evening candle lit suppers can be enjoyed. It is a place people visit and revisit and with its daily changing menu, which has local produce at its heart and is freshly prepared and individually cooked in the kitchen, it isn't hard to see why. Such is its popularity it is advisable to book.

Completed at the beginning of 2006 the centre's Bunk House sleeps up to 26 people and is 100m from the main

centre. Popular with walkers and climbers there is a mix of dormitories, family rooms with en suite facilities and self catering to choose from. Packed lunches can be made on request.

The Tea Room also has a craft shop selling hand-made gifts produced locally, books and maps. Live specialist workshops in Batik art, stained glass products and spinning yarn are also popular with visitors.

163 ARDSHEALACH LODGE

Acharacle, Argyll PH36 4JL
Tel: **01967 431399**
Fax: **01967 431546**
e-mail: ardshealach@btconnect.com
website: www.ardshealach-lodge.co.uk

Located on the edge of Loch Shiel, this bed and breakfast with attached restaurant has been running for 6 years under the ownership of Jill Gosney. Ardshealach Lodge offers three double rooms and one twin room, all exceptionally comfortable with views out to the islands off the coast and two rooms offering full sky TV. Guests are welcome to bring their dogs along, as Ardshealach welcomes all, tourists, locals, hikers and walkers, families and couples.

Attached to the fresh and comfy bed and breakfast is a truly fantastic restaurant serving a wide variety of food from daily changing menus. A wonderful qualified chef cooks up a storm in the kitchen with food available from 6:30-8:30pm Mon-Sat. Dishes are all cooked to order and use the freshest produce imaginable as they grow the vegetables in the back garden, picking them fresh for each meal. Local fresh venison and shellfish are also used in the fine home cooking served here. Popular dishes include Moules Marinere, fillet steak, pan fried scallops and Greshingham duck. The bar stocks 14 fine Highland malts to warm you and as this B&B is the perfect location for exploring the rugged coast with Castle Tioram and beaches just 5 miles away - you'll need one!

findSOMEWHERE.co.uk

For people who want to explore Britain and Ireland

Places to Stay

Our easy-to use website contains details and locations of places to stay, places to eat and drink, specialist shops and places of interest throughout England, Wales, Scotland and Ireland.

Places to Stay:	**Places to Eat and Drink:**	**Places of Interest:**	**Specialist Shops:**	**Gardens:**
Hotels, guest accommodation, bed & breakfast, inns, self-catering accommodation	Restaurants, pubs, inns, cafes, tea rooms	Historic buildings, gardens, art galleries, museums, nature parks, wildlife parks, indoor and outdoor activities	Fashion shops, art and craft shops, gift shops, food and drink shops, antique shops, jewellery shops	Garden centres and retail nurseries

164 LOCHSIDE FOLLIES

Greenwood, by Ardslignish, Acharacle,
Argyll PH36 4JG
Tel: 01972 500201
e-mail: loislivett@ardnamurchan.com
website: www.selfcateringardnamurchan.co.uk

Nestling in the lee of Ardslignish Point on Loch Sunart, **Lochside Follies** are cosy, romantic self-catering properties primarily for two people, equipped in excess of STB 4 star standard.

The Ruin is a very peaceful, delightful natural stone hideaway close to the shore. A few years ago a tumbledown croft house, hence the name, now a gem with hand crafted woodwork and every comfort. The nearby Byre houses the utility items and can accommodate 2 children if required.

The Tower is totally self-contained on the west side of our home, has a circular living room and a circular bedroom, with a unique ceiling. From the windows and the balcony splendid views over our gardens and Loch Sunart can be enjoyed.

The Folly which will be completed during 2011 will have elevated panoramic views of the Loch and the Morvern hills beyond. It will be spacious, unique and very comfortable.

Our properties have plenty of hand crafted woodwork, interesting features, cosy wood burning stoves and under floor heating. A snooker table, table tennis, mini gym, bicycles and a mini putting course are provided to add to your enjoyment of your holiday in beautiful, peaceful Ardnamurchan.

165 LOCHAILORT INN

Lochailort, Invernesshire PH38 4LZ
Tel: 01687 470208 Fax: 01687 470203
e-mail: enquiries.lochailort@btinternet.com
website: www.lochailortinn.co.uk

Lochailort Inn is beautifully located on the famous 'Road to the Isles' and is renowned across the country for its great hospitality and the stunning views from each room. Owners John and Ellen Ferguson have been in residence here for 6 years now with a wealth of experience from across the globe behind them. They offer a quiet, peaceful yet warm welcome to all guests including hikers, cyclists, tourists, special interest groups, families and dogs. Lochailort is still the perfect place to stay today for weary walkers, deer stalkers, fishermen as it was once for cattle drivers many years ago on the long road to market between Fort William and Mallaig. The place also draws in a large oversees crowd as just minutes from the

inn is the famous highland railway viaduct made popular by its appearances in the Harry Potter films.

Guests can choose from eleven cosy, fresh and modern en suite rooms available all year round apart from boxing day and Christmas. The hotel was completely rebuilt in 1997 after a bad fire brought it to the ground, but much good has come of the rebuild as the hotel now sports full central heating and insulation – essential for any highland living! Although the rooms don't have the reception for TV's guests will find themselves truly relaxing in this cosy environment without the hassles of today's mindless programming. Guests can unwind by an open log fire in the well stocked bar or sample some of the fine home cooked food on offer in the 24 seater restaurant, with more al fresco dining in the summer. The food is all locally sourced with a daily changing specials board: popular dishes include seared venison steak, pan-fried breaded pork fillet, squat lobsters and beefsteak pie. Food is served from 12-8pm daily, but if you're really hungry and ask nicely you might find someone to rustle you up a little special something out of hours! Priding themselves on fine real ales, there is a varied choice including Tradewinds along with other Scottish and Newcastle lagers and plenty of other wines, spirits and soft drinks to be enjoyed throughout the day. With high quality service, comfort and spectacular views who needs a TV?!

445

166 SOLUIS MU THUATH GUEST HOUSE

Braeintra, by Achmore,
Lochalsh IV53 8UP
Tel: 01599 577219
e-mail: soluismuthuath@btopenworld.com
website: www.highlandsaccommodation.com

Soluis Mu Thuath is a five bedroom, family-run guest house set in peaceful Strath Ascaig, a wooded glen in one of the loveliest parts of the West Highlands. The name means "Northern Lights" and if the conditions are right, the Aurora Borealis can be viewed from here.

The owners are Margaret and Gerry Arscott who have established a fine reputation for their high standards and keen prices. This is Scottish hospitality at its best! All the rooms are spacious and extremely comfortable, with en suite shower rooms, central heating and hospitality tray. Two of the rooms are on the ground floor and are suitable for the accompanied disabled. Visitors can relax in the elegant guests' lounge and enjoy the superb views, or consult some of the tourist brochures and leaflets kept there to plan your exploration of an area that is rich in wonderful scenery, history and heritage.

The hearty breakfast will set you up for the day and is served in the dining room which also has beautiful views out over the nearby hillsides. Evening meals from a limited menu are available if booked before 6pm, and you are welcome to bring your own bottle.

167 DALVOURN HOLIDAY COTTAGES

Dalvourn Farm, Farr, Inverness IV2 6XJ
Tel: 01808 521467 / 521747
e-mail: info@dalvourn.com
website: www.dalvourn.com

Situated on the 200 acre Dalvourn Farm, Farr in the beautiful Strathnairn glen, south of Inverness and east of Loch Ness, our self-catering cottages are set in secluded birch woodland. There are over three miles of on-farm riverside and woodland walks connecting with extensive forest walks/ roads within Forest Enterprise woods. Mountain bikes are available on site.

The cottages sleep 2 to 6 people and are ideal for families, couples or other parties seeking an idyllic base for their holiday in the Highlands of Scotland. Whatever your interests or leisure pursuits there is lots to do and see – Cairngorm National Park, Culloden Battlefield, the Whisky Trail, Ben Nevis, Landmark Adventure Park to name but a few.

Much thought has gone into the positioning of the cottages to provide the best views of the mountains and landscape. The cottages have large windows for watching the numerous varieties of wild birds and wildlife that inhabit the surrounding woodland.

Mountain View, Rowan Ridge and Woodpecker Pad each have three bedrooms (one en suite) with lounge, kitchen/dining area and bathroom. The Haven, classified as Category 1 Unassisted Wheelchair Access, has two large bedrooms, a wet room, lounge and kitchen with dining area. Cathie's Cottage, opened in 2009, has three bedrooms (one en suite) with lounge, sun room, kitchen/dining area and bathroom.

Comfortable, modern and double glazed, each cottage has everything you need for your stay. The spacious lounges are equipped with TV, DVD player and CD player with IPod dock. The cottages have free wireless broadband.

All cottages have patios with outdoor furniture and gas barbeque. We also accept up to two well behaved pets, except in Cathie's Cottage which is pet free.

We look forward to welcoming you to our cottages at Dalvourn and are confident you will be refreshed and revitalized by your time in the Highlands.

Credit and debit card payments are accepted at no extra charge.

106-110 Academy Street,
Inverness IVI ILX
Tel: 01463 245990
e-mail: rich@therichorg.co.uk

A spacious old stone-built inn with lots of atmosphere, **The Phoenix** was built more than 100 years ago and still in place are many of the Victorian fittings such as the traditional horseshoe bar. Mine host at this welcoming hostelry is Richie Gaston who took over here in the summer of 2009, bringing with him 18 years experience of the hospitality business. The Phoenix is well-known for the quality of its beers and offers no fewer than 9 real ales. It also serves a good choice of pub grub, all based on local produce, cooked on site and sold at value-for-money prices. Highly popular with both locals and visitors alike are the regular live music sessions.

The inn has good disabled access throughout and a disabled toilet, and all major credit cards are accepted. The Phoenix is open from 11am to 1am, Monday to Friday; from 11am to 12.30am on Saturday; and from noon until midnight on Sunday.

169 CROWN COURT TOWN HOUSE HOTEL

25 Southside Road, Inverness IV2 3BG
Tel: 01463 234816 Fax: 01463 714900
e-mail:
reception@crowncourthotelinverness.co.uk
website:
www.crowncourthotelinverness.co.uk

If stylish accommodation coupled with first class service, great food, friendly staff, and the personal touch appeal, all mixed in with a great Highland welcome, then the **Crown Court Town House Hotel** is the place to be. This small, intimate hotel originates from the 1700s when it was used as a residence for Crown Court judges. Now, after a complete restoration, it provides a peaceful retreat from the hustle and bustle of the city centre, simply a great place to relax, unwind and absorb true Highland hospitality. Perfect for a leisure break, the business traveller or your Highland wedding, the Crown Court Hotel boasts nine en suite rooms all of which are tastefully furnished to a high standard. Dining is available at the hotel's Bistro where guests can be assured of delicious food, fine wines and a

warm, personal and attentive service.

Inverness, and indeed the whole Highland region is renowned for providing the warmest of welcomes to visitors, so for those choosing to stay, explore, relax and enjoy the craic (Gaelic for chat and light hearted conversation) the city, and indeed the Crown Court Hotel will make your time here a memorable one, which is why the hotel's guests return time and time again.

449

27 Castle Street, Inverness IV2 3DU
Tel: 01463 241999
e-mail: number27@btinternet.com
website: www.theroomandno27.co.uk

With a prime view of Inverness Castle in the centre of this gateway to the highlands, **No 27** is a quality dining and drinking establishment in a great location. A two minute walk will bring you to the shoreline of the river Ness and just 200 yards away is the popular Eastgate shopping centre. The place has been recently refurbished since opening 12 years ago and sees guests from all over the country as well as established locals. Bob Gray has been the manager for 6 years now and has seen the No 27 grow into a huge success.

Inverness is known as the capital of the Scottish Highlands and boasts art galleries, theatres and a thriving night life, the perfect location for this cosmopolitan and contemporary restaurant/bar. On approach, the building is impressive; with floor to ceiling windows interspaced with stone columns in the style of build much seen around the city. Inside the high ceilings and large windows create a light and airy ambiance that is enhanced by the smiling staff's warm welcome. The refurbishment has been carried out well; comfortable seating dotted around enable guests the opportunity of just sitting and watching the world go by with a well earned drink.

Stocked with a truly extraordinary range of beverages, the bar is well known for having the largest selection of draught beers in Inverness, accompanied by a huge range of malt whiskies, wines and spirits. There really is a drink for every occasion, supported by regular special offers; double measure spirits for an extra 99p or pitchers of beer. With the premises aimed at 21 years and over, evenings are a more sedate affair than other centrally located bars and promote the special night out feel to the place.

Eating at No 27 is always an exciting event; the chefs work overtime to ensure that the menu is jam packed with sumptuous choices created using locally sourced produce. With 30 covers in the bar and 42 in the restaurant, reservations are recommended to avoid disappointment, especially in the evening times. The extensive menu is full of those popular pub classics, plus more exotic and unusual selections, for e.g. monkfish tail roasted in parma ham. Always well liked is the large range of steaks available, cooked just how you like it with a vast array of accoutrements. No 27 is open all day every day, all year round.

171 THE STEAK ACADEMY

8 Queensgate, Inverness IV1 1DA
Tel: 01463 709409
e-mail: info@thesteakacademy.com
website: www.steakacademy.com

Owner Stuart is very well known in the area for his culinary expertise; 24 years as a chef of the highest quality working in restaurants all over England and Europe have crafted an unbeatable reputation. **The Steak Academy** is a truly unique dining experience, marketed as "the only genuine steakhouse in the Highlands", there are large expectations placed on this popular restaurant. These expectations are easily met; inside the Brooklyn style bar area sets the tone for the place, beautiful furnishings are matched by the high quality table settings and chic atmosphere.

The menu is the main selling point though, offering the unusual choices of Zebra, Kangaroo and Springbok steaks alongside the more common beef variety. Accompanied by a brief description, these

unique steak options are very popular and draw custom from all over the place. The rest of the menu is by no means to be ignored; only the finest of locally sourced ingredients are used to create sumptuous dishes made fresh to order.

Close to the station, Eastgate shopping centre and the river Ness, the Steak Academy is in a prime position for a light bite or for those special occasions.

172 THE ROOM

73 Queensgate, Inverness IV1 1DG
Tel: 01463 233077
e-mail: theroom@hotmail.co.uk

A popular venue in the centre of Inverness, **The Room** is situated in a great location; just 2 minutes away from the river Ness and a stone's throw from the Eastgate shopping centre. The stone built building boasts a large bar and restaurant with high ceilings creating a light and airy atmosphere that is hard to beat. Managed for the last 3 years by Tina who has almost 10 years experience in hospitality management, The Room benefits from a long term staff who know the place inside out and provide simply superb service.

Late opening all week long, the bar does a roaring trade thanks to its great wine menu and excellent range of malt whiskies. Enhancing the visitor's experience is

the magnificent 'pub grub' on offer from the hard working chefs who take the finest of local ingredients and create sumptuous food, fresh to order.

Live music on Friday and Saturday nights draw in a huge crowd every time as local and visiting bands alike play till late in this awesome music venue. Add to that the Sky TV that shows big sporting events and it is clear that The Room is well worth a few visits!

173 RIVERVIEW GUEST HOUSE

2 Moray Park, Island Bank Road,
Inverness IV2 4SX
Tel: 01463 235557
e-mail: s-n@cults15fsnet.co.uk
website: www.accommodationinverness.com

Ideally located overlooking the Cavell Gardens and the River Ness, **Riverview Guest House** is the home of Susannah and Neil Robertson who assure visitors of a warm Highland welcome to their 150-year-old house. The high ceilings make for a fresh, airy atmosphere and the full central heating guarantees a warm and comfortable stay. All rooms have en suite shower facilities, remote-controlled TV, radio and CD player, hairdryer and a well-stocked hostess tray. A tourist pack is provided in each room containing details of local eating houses, places to go and things to do. Breakfast at Riverview is definitely something to look forward to. There's a choice of anything from a light breakfast to a full cooked plateful. Vegetarian options are available,

special dietary needs can be catered for given notice, and packed lunches are available.

Riverview is just a short walk from the city centre and railway station. The Great Glen Way starts nearby but there is plenty of opportunity for a more leisurely stroll just outside the door by the river or in the adjacent park. Reserved parking is available for guests directly opposite the house.

174 CEDAR VILLA GUEST HOUSE

33 Kenneth Street, Inverness IV3 5DH
Tel: 01463 230477
e-mail:
enquiries@guesthouseinverness.co.uk
website: www.guesthouseinverness.co.uk

Built in 1893, the **Cedar Villa Guest House** is a perfect example of a Victorian villa, complete with several stunning features: high ceilings, large bay windows and even a mezzanine floor. Close to the bustling city centre of Inverness, gateway to the Scottish Highlands, Frank and Lisa are there to ensure that your stay is as comfortable and enjoyable as possible. Just a few minutes' walk from the many sights and sounds of Inverness, Cedar Villa makes a great base for exploring the area; highlights include the historical castle and Loch Ness.

Accommodation takes the form of six extremely well appointed rooms, three en suite family rooms, 1 single, 1 double and a twin; all of which boast reasonable rates with a hearty breakfast thrown in for good measure. Taking the form of a full Scottish, with vegetarian and vegan alternatives, it is the perfect way to start your day, and with the option of eating whenever suits you, late home comers or early risers are catered for.

175 DOW'S BAR AND RESTAURANT

Balloon Park, Inverness IV2 4PF
Tel: 01463 719960
website: www.dowsbar.co.uk

This family friendly bar offers the very best in hospitality and comfort. Aileen Black took over in October 2009 and is adding to the good reputation of the establishment, which is open all year round. Located in the Hilton area of the city it is an ideal place to meet

family or friends and there is ample car and coach parking. The community pub boasts a recently refurbished sports bar, lounge bar, conservatory restaurant and a conference/business suite on the first floor. The service is excellent and good value for money and home cooking and local produce is at the heart of the menu. Good disabled access.

176 THE SHIP INN

33 Shore Road, Invergordon IV18 0ER
Tel: 01349 852427
e-mail: the.ship.inn@btconnect.com

Situated in the heart of Invergordon, **The Ship Inn** dates back more than 200 years and served for a long time as a Temperance Hotel. It is now the home of Allan and Sue who have been welcoming bed & breakfast guests here since 2003. It's a very popular establishment with a large part of its custom being repeat visitors. Guests are welcome all year round except at Christmas and the New Year.

There are 7 comfortable guest bedrooms – 2 singles, 3 twins, 1 double and a room with 3 single beds. Allan and Sue are very hospitable hosts and you'll find that the hearty breakfast served between 8.30am and 9.30am will truly set you up for the day. Children are welcome. Cash or cheques are accepted. The Ship Inn is located about 5 minutes off the main A9 road.

177 NORTH KESSOCK HOTEL

Main Street, North Kessock,
by Inverness IV1 3XN
Tel: 01463 731208
e-mail: stay@northkessockhotel.com
website: www.northkessockhotel.com

With individually styled en-suite bedrooms, the **North Kessock Hotel** offers some of the best accommodation and cuisine in the area. With its waterfront location, overlooking Inverness, many of the rooms have views of the sea or garden. The bedrooms at the North Kessock hotel are tastefully decorated and offer the usual refinements as well as a slim vision TV, DVD player and binoculars for a bit of dolphin spotting. Refurbished in 2004 they are spacious with good quality furniture. With a choice of sea or garden views, all rooms at the hotel were refurbished in 2004. There is a large garden, terrace and patio area for guests to make the most of on dry days and there are some beautiful views to enjoy.

In the kitchen, the team strives to produce imaginative menus from locally sourced produce. The starters are all reasonably priced and include garlic mushrooms bound in a tarragon cream with garlic bread; and breaded king prawn served with a sweet chilli mayonnaise. Vegetarians are well catered for at The North Kessock Hotel. Among the tasty main courses diners can choose steak and mushroom pie; and smoked haddock & prawn fishcakes with a sweet chilli mayonnaise. For those wanting to opt for something a little less filling there is a range of tempting salads, filled baked potatoes and fresh sandwiches.

The hotel is child-friendly and there is a 'small eaters menu' to satisfy younger customers. The service is professional and efficient and the staff members have good knowledge on the local area and are happy to suggest places for visitors to go.

The area boasts plenty of restaurants, cafes and bars providing a cosmopolitan nightlife as well as a developing street cafe culture. There is plenty to keep visitors busy in North Kessock, with a range of mountain activities to have a go at. Information is available at the hotel's reception alongside details on the wide range of golf clubs and courses throughout the Highlands and Islands. Activities in and around the area include fishing, hillwalking, cycling and a choice of boat trips along the Caledonian canal for Loch Ness or the Moray Firth for Bottle nose dolphin spotting. Day trips to Cairngorn National Park, Culloden Battlefield are popular as well as local whisky distillery tour and tasting trips. Inverness is within easy reaching distance and is an area renowned for its spectacular landscape, proud history and vibrant culture.

178 CAWDOR TAVERN

Cawdor, Nairn IV12 5XP
Tel: 01667 404777 Fax: 01667 493678
e-mail: enquiries@cawdortavern.info
website: www.cawdortavern.info

Originally the workshop for nearby castle, **Cawdor Tavern** has a sweet cottage style about it from the exterior, pretty bay windows, slate roof and colourful hanging baskets all around. Inside couldn't be more welcoming; smiling staff create a convivial atmosphere, enhanced by the open fires, hand crafted woodwork and wooden panelling, a gift from a former laird of Cawdor. Christine and Norman have owned the Cawdor Tavern for 15 years now and have truly perfected the art of good food, well kept ales and splendid service, all day every day.

Norman is the proud owner of two breweries, and the results of both are on sale in the bar, real ales that are very popular with regular and visiting guests. As well as the good

selection of beer, an extensive wine list and over 60 malt whiskies mean there is a drink for every occasion, dining or otherwise. Serving food all week long, the chef has created a sumptuous menu with locally sourced ingredients providing the backbone of each well thought out dish.

Easy access from Nairn, just 7 miles away, and Inverness, 12 miles, means the Cawdor Tavern is rarely quiet, with a warm and friendly ambience that would be tough to equal anywhere else.

179 JACKO'S

44 Hardovr Street, Nairn IV12 4NU
Tel: 01667 455422
e-mail: deborah@jacksonline.com
website: www.jacksonline.com

A warm welcome is ready to greet any visitor to **Jacko's**, a traditional style bar with a big open fire. Built in 1896, the place is filled with character, and the low ceilings, wooden floors, wooden panelled walls and stone wall feature really add to the atmosphere of the bar. Debbie Anderson has been the licensee of Jacko's since April and has really contributed to its growing reputation in the area.

With a background in interior design, you can be guaranteed that the bar is stylish and tastefully decorated. Inside, it is warm and cosy with seating in hidden away nooks and comfy sofa areas around the open fire, to keep you warm on a colder day. If you want something to eat, there is an excellent menu to choose from, brimming with dishes made from local produce. The central bar serves

from all angles creating a good social atmosphere. It is extremely popular with locals and visitors and customers vary in age groups.

The venue is ideal for hosting live music on weekends and the style of entertainment changes to cater for all tastes. Street parking. Wheelchair access and disabled toilet facilities. Credit cards accepted.

180 AURORA HOTEL

2 Academy Street, Nairn IV12 4RJ
Tel: 01667 453551 Fax: 01667 456577
e-mail: aurorahotelnairn@aol.com
website: www.aurorahotelnairn.com

When staying at the **Aurora Hotel** in the heart of this seaside town, guests can be assured of a warm welcome and comfortable surroundings with the added bonus of the personal attention of the resident proprietors. The hotel is close to all the local amenities including the award winning beach, harbour and championship golf courses and the local leisure centre whose facilities include a swimming pool, gym and squash courts.

The hotel's restaurant is renowned for its extensive menu of traditional Italian dishes and wide variety of Italian wines. Guests can enjoy pre-dinner drinks in the bar before dining in either the elegant dining room or the less formal conservatory, each with its own unique atmosphere. Traditional Scottish dishes are also on the menu - make sure you try the steaks, chicken dishes or fresh Scottish

salmon. Whichever cuisine you prefer, all the dishes are prepared to order from fresh ingredients.

The accommodation at the aurora comprises 10 bedrooms, all tastefully decorated and equipped with en suite facilities, Freeview colour television, DVD player and hospitality tray. Overseas visitors can feel at home at the Aurora since the owners speak several languages including Italian, Spanish and Portuguese and are happy to try new ones too!

181 SPEYBANK GUEST HOUSE

Dalfaber Road, Aviemore PH22 1PU
Tel: 01479 810058
e-mail: christine-orr@btconnect.co,
website: www.speybank.com

Located close to the centre of Aviemore and the railway station, and just a short walk from shops and restaurants, **Speybank Guest House** nevertheless enjoys views of woodland and hills. Speybank is the home of Christine Orr, a painter on canvas, who has been welcoming bed & breakfast guests here since 1992. The house makes an ideal base for skiers and other devotees of outdoor life,

and has a drying room with humidifier available. The accommodation comprises two attractively furnished and decorated double en suite rooms with shower rooms, and a twin room with adjacent shower/bath room. All rooms are equipped with TV, hair dryer and hospitality tray. Discounted rates are available for longer and off peak stays; children are welcome but no pets apart from guide dogs.

At breakfast time Christine serves a full Scottish breakfast or a Continental, both based on local produce, and is happy to cater for vegetarians. Other amenities at Speybank include Wifi access and off road parking. Rooms are available all year round.

182 PINEBANK CHALETS

Dalfaber Road, Aviemore,
Inverness-shire PH22 1PX
Tel: 01479 810000
e-mail: pinebankchalets@btopenworld.com
website: www.pinebankchalets.co.uk

Delightfully situated within the grounds of Craigellachie House by the River Spey, **Pinebank Chalets** are approached along a sweeping cobbled driveway. The 14 chalets and cabins occupy a secluded setting, nestling amongst mature Scots Pines and surrounded by some of the finest

scenery in the Highlands. With the impressive backdrop of the Cairngorm Mountains, they represent the ideal base from which to explore this area of outstanding beauty.

With occupancy ranging from 2 to 6 people, all units on site are double glazed and well insulated, offering a high standard of comfort with quality furnishings, fully equipped kitchens (most with microwaves) and colour TV with selected 'Sky' channels and video. Between October and April background heating is included in the tariff. In

some units lighting, water, heating, cooking and additional heating are metered. Bed linen is included and towel hire is available.

Pinebank Chalets provide a superb base for a variety of activities in and around Aviemore and the Highlands of Scotland. Activities to enjoy in this beautiful and unique region include fishing, golfing, skiing, walking, hill climbing, bird watching, touring, Highland gatherings and much more.

183 GREYSTONES B&B

Acres Road, Kingussie,
Inverness-shire PH21 1LA
Tel: 01540 661052
e-mail: info@greystonesbandb.com
website: www.greystonesbandb.com

Devotees of the popular TV series Monarch of the Glen will find the area in and around Kingussie rather familiar as many scenes for the series were filmed here. One of the locations was **Greystones B&B** (The Glenbogle Boutique Hotel) a handsome stone building dating back to 1901, set in the heart of the Cairngorm National Park, with the Cairngorm and Monadhliath mountains on its doorstep.

Greystones is the home of Anne & Mark Johnstone who bought the property in 1990 and restored it with a subtle mix of period character, warmth, comfort and modern facilities. With its 4 poster double bedrooms and traditional Scottish single and twins, Greystones is the perfect place for family gatherings and exploring the

highlands. In the morning you will enjoy a delicious home cooked breakfast with

eggs from their own chickens. You have your own lounge where you can snuggle up to the open fire, make yourself tea and coffee and relax with a DVD, TV, board games and the library of books. Computer and Wi-Fi internet are also available. There are a wealth of outdoor activities and places of interest available locally.

457

184 THE INN AT DALWHINNIE

Perth Road, Dalwhinnie PH19 1AG
Tel: 01528 522257 Fax: 01738 511296
website: www.theinndalwhinnie.com

Regarded by many as the coolest hotel in the Highlands, **The Inn at Dalwhinnie** is located in the magnificent Cairngorms National Park on the banks of the River Truim, opposite Loch Ericht; truly a perfect spot from which to explore the Highlands. The bar/restaurant is mellow and relaxed with fat comfy leather sofas, and tables overlooking the river. From here you can enjoy

spectacular views, unwind to the cool languid sounds, sip organic fairtrade coffee or maybe a Dalwhinnie malt from our village distillery. The menu is scrumptious and the daily specials board is quite legendary.

The team who will look after you are upbeat and friendly and more than happy to pull a pint of draught beer for you if you've built up a thirst walking, climbing or biking. The inn rents mountain bikes too and have drying facilities for any wet clothes you might have after a hectic day out. Also, don't forget your laptop so you can enjoy the free Wi-Fi and send those photos back home of the day you kite surfed, climbed Ben Alder or hand-fed the Loch Ness Monster.

The hotel has 27 en suite bedrooms with full guest facilities, including TV and radio/alarm clock. The rooms command fantastic views of the surrounding countryside, and all of them provide a peaceful haven in which to read, relax and dream.

Dalwhinnie itself sits at the head of Loch Ericht where it meets Glen Truim, at a height of 358m or 1160 feet. This makes it a few metres higher than the Highlands' officially highest village at Tomintoul, 40 mountainous miles to the north east. While Dalwhinnie's altitude may not always gain the recognition it deserves, Dalwhinnie Distillery is without challenge Scotland's highest. This beautifully kept white-painted complex of buildings stand out for miles as you approach Dalwhinnie on the A9, which bypassed the village in the late 1970s.

Although Dalwhinnie's malting has been done elsewhere since 1968, the distillery has thankfully kept its two distinctive pagodas. Its origins date back to 1897, though in its early years it traded under the very misleading name of the Strathspey Distillery. The distillery was largely rebuilt following a fire in 1934 and today Dalwhinnie is one of UDV's "Classic Malts". In common with other distilleries in the group it has invested in a high quality visitor centre and offers distillery tours.

Mention that you saw our advertisement in "Hidden Places of Scotland" and enjoy a 10% discount on your room.

185 GLENURQUHART HOUSE HOTEL

Marchfield, Drumnadrochit IV63 6TJ
Tel: 01456 476234
e-mail: info@glenurquhart-house-hotel.co.uk
website: www.glenurquhart-house-hotel.co.uk

Nestled on a secluded wooded hillside, **Glenurquhart House Hotel** provides an ideal escape for those longing for a relaxing break. The hotel stands in a six acre estate and boasts scenic views of Loch Meikle and Glen Urquhart.

The centrally heated accommodation is first class and consists of six individually designed en-suite bedrooms (two with four poster beds), a cosy lounge bar with log fire and an intimate restaurant serving quality freshly cooked meals. Breakfast and dinner is served in the restaurant which has stunning views of Loch Meikle. It has an Eatscotland award and is graded a four star restaurant with rooms by the Scottish tourist Board. There is a wide and varied menu of freshly cooked food available and special diets can be catered for with prior notice.

The area has many attractions for those visiting the area. The village of Drumnadrochit is only four miles away and has Loch Ness exhibitions, shops and galleries and Loch Ness cruises.

The establishment is popular with walkers and cyclists with the Glenurquhart forest opposite the hotel and Cannich (which leads to the Glen Affric National Nature Reserve) just five miles away. There are also self-catering lodges available.

186 THE DORES INN

Dores, Loch Ness, nr Inverness IV2 6TR
Tel: 01463 751203
e-mail: info@thedoresinn.co.uk
website: www.thedoresinn.co.uk

Quintin and Michelle have years of experience in the beautiful Highlands, as they currently own and run a restaurant at Foulis Ferry near Evanton called the Storehouse. This however, is the newly refurbished **Dores Inn**, situated on the shore of the world famous Loch Ness and on the south side of Inverness. The pub has been extensively renovated, with a new kitchen, dining area and cellar, as well as opening up the pub restaurant to allow views of the Loch. Quintin says that they wanted to create a traditional pub with an emphasis on food, beer and wine; the menu is certainly packed with local dishes.

The Dores Inn is situated on the eastern shore of the Loch and commands views over a wonderful crescent beach, ideal for a walk before eating to whet the appetite. The pub now serves food all day, from morning coffee and cakes to lunch, afternoon teas and an evening meal. The popular venue has become a firm fixture of music lovers who flood into the village for the annual 'Rockness' festival.

The Storehouse is also well worth a visit, it is both a restaurant/tea room and a farm shop selling a huge range of quality produce along with local crafts, gifts and souvenirs.

459

187 THE STEADINGS AT THE GROUSE & TROUT

Flichity by Farr, South Loch Ness,
Inverness IV2 6XD
Tel: 01808 521314 Fax: 01808 521741
e-mail: david@steadingshotel.co.uk
website: www.steadingshotel.co.uk

The world famous Loch Ness attracts thousands of visitors every year and if you are looking for a friendly and welcoming place to stay, then you can do no better than at **The Steadings at the Grouse & Trout**. Set in the idyllic setting of the Scottish Highlands, close to the highland capital of Inverness and in the south Loch Ness area, this tranquil spot creates the perfect base. All kinds of people are drawn to this area: ramblers, climbers, monster hunters and bird watchers for the nearby RSPB reserve at Loch Ruthen. The Upper Strathnairn countryside is the home of this charming hotel full of rustic character, with ancient stone walls and beamed ceilings creating a real olde world feeling.

The warm and friendly hosts are David and Mary Allen, who boast a wealth of experience between them in the hospitality industry, having owned and operated Country House three star hotels since the seventies. There are eight excellently appointed rooms available, all decorated in a manner that compliments the rural surroundings, image and property. Tariffs for double rooms start from £95 per night and from £68 for single; these very reasonable prices include a hearty Scottish breakfast.

Along with the excellent rooms, there are also places to sit awhile; the cosy lounge bar with its sloping beamed ceiling and stone walls brings an atmosphere of olde world charm, the ideal place to relax with a tot of whisky from the excellent array on offer, or for an aperitif before dinner. A varied selection of Scottish beers and lagers may also quench the thirst of the avid traveller. The comfortable main lounge situated along the rear of the property has wonderful panoramic views of the Strath and the hills of Strathnairn, from here much wildlife can be admired. Often the resident hare family play on the lawn; or you may be privileged to see the Osprey collecting a trout from the Flichity Loch.

On site is the wonderful Grouse & Trout restaurant, Scottish and international cuisine is on offer and it is all prepared where possible using the best of local and Scottish produce.

460

188 ARCHDALE GUEST HOUSE

High Street, Beauly,
Inverness-shire, IV4 7BT
Tel: 01463 783043
e-mail: racjohn42@hotmail.com
website: www.archdaleguesthouse.co.uk

Proprietors John and Rachel have been running the **Archdale Guest House**, situated in the pretty village of Beauly, for five years and pride their establishment on being clean, comfortable and affordable. It is hard to dispute this at the price of £22 per night per person!(at time of publication)

Beauly offers much in the way of conveniences, from banks and shops to free parking through the whole village.

Accommodation at the Archdale comes in the form of single, twin or double rooms, and one which can provide a family room. All of the rooms are spacious and light, with lovely simple traditional decoration and furnishing. In addition to the regular conveniences (including iron and hairdryer), guests are welcome to use the communal lounge area, which includes TV and DVD player, literature on local attractions,

sofas, games and hot drink making facilities – all perfect for a relax after a busy day.

The price of the rooms also includes a breakfast; a hearty cooked or continental breakfast, both of which are served with toast, a selection of jam and marmalade, cereal, fresh fruit and juice, daily between 8 – 9.30am. Evening meals can be provided by prior arrangement; alternatively you are more than welcome to eat take-away food in the dining room. The guest house is licensed, pet friendly and non-smoking throughout.

189 CULLIGRAN COTTAGES

Glen Strathfarrar, Struy, nr Beauly,
Inverness-shire IV4 7JX
Tel: 01463 761285
e-mail: info@culligrancottages.co.uk
website: www.culligrancottages.co.uk

The **Culligran Cottages** are situated in one of the most beautiful areas of Scotland – Strathfarrar, to the west of Inverness. All around is striking scenery, historical places to visit and plenty of opportunities for activities such as fishing, golf, climbing, walking or indeed just relaxing away from the hustle and bustle of everyday life.

One of the cottages would make the ideal base from which to explore the area. Owned and run by Juliet and Frank Spencer-Nairn, the accommodation consists of a traditional stone built cottage and four Norwegian style chalets on the banks of the beautiful river Farrar, and within a naturally wooded area in the Culligran estate. The cottage sleeps up to 7 people and has three bedrooms, a spacious sitting room, a large, well equipped kitchen, bathroom and a shower room.

The chalets have an open plan living room with kitchen/dining area, a bathroom and either two or three bedrooms. A sofa bed in the living room means that they can sleep up to five in a two bedroom chalet and up to seven in a three bedroom chalet. All are comfortable and extremely well appointed, with double glazing, electric heaters, cookers and fridge. Frank offers Land Rover tours of Culligran Deer Farm, and a daily permit allows you to fish the river Farrar. Culligran Cottages are open between mid March and mid November each year. There is now WiFi access on site and full laundry facilities are available.

Culbokie, Ross-shire IV7 8JH
Tel: 01349 877280

Popular among locals and tourists the **Culbokie Inn**, on the north coast of the Black Isle, boasts spectacular views across the Cromarty Firth and

Ben Wyvis.

Just ten miles north west of Inverness the traditional inn is the ideal resting spot for people wanting to tour the Highlands and Islands and enjoy the attractions and outdoor activities there are on offer.

Catherine and David Fraser are the new owners of the Culbokie Inn, having taken charge in March 2008. The restaurant seats 26 guests and there is a traditional bar, which is wood-paneled, with an open log fire, for customers to enjoy. There is a wide selection for visitors to choose from, including additional options on the daily specials board. Offering a seasonal menu the dishes are created using locally sourced products. Catherine and David are passionate about all of the food served being cooked fresh to order, adding to the quality of the inn which is at the heart of the village. Having enjoyed a splendid meal, diners with an eager appetite can choose from one of the many homemade desserts on offer.

Local ales are popular among visitors, as is the malt whiskey collection. Drinks and food can be enjoyed in the beautiful, spacious beer garden which boasts magnificent views of the Cromarty Firth and spectacular mountains beyond.

Made of old stone with sash windows the inn is very traditional and has a white-wash finish. At the centre of community life the pub has a football team, as well as a ladies and gents darts team, and customers can also make the most of the inn's pool room. Disabled customers are well catered for with disabled parking on site and wheel chair access throughout the building, including a disabled toilet. For smoking customers there is an external smoking shelter where they can relax, enjoying their favourite tipple and socialize.

Lunch is served between 12.30 and 2.30pm Monday-Sunday and dinner every day between 5.30pm and 9pm. The inn is closed on Mondays from November through until February. The bar is open from Monday-Sunday 12pm-11pm. If it is a quality, traditional inn you are searching for, to have a drink or appealing meal in, the Culbokie Inn, which has customers returning again and again, is a must. With unbeatable views and plenty of amenities in the surrounding area locals and tourists alike can make the most of the peacefulness with a drink in hand.

191 CONON BRIDGE HOTEL

High Street, Conon Bridge, Dingwall,
Ross-shire IV7 8HD
Tel: 01349 861500
website: www.cononbridgehotel.co.uk

Situated in beautiful highland countryside alongside the river Conon, **The Conon Bridge Hotel** provides an excellent base from which to explore this rugged and charming part of Scotland. Close to Inverness, the capital of the highlands, there is no shortage of things to see and do, no matter what the weather is doing. The attractive stone building dates back to the 18th century and was originally a coaching inn; the hospitality and warmth of the welcome remaining a constant throughout the years.

Inside there are 12 rooms available for hire in a mixture of shapes and sizes, most have en suite and all are warm and comfortable. Room prices start from a very reasonable £30 and include a hearty Scottish breakfast to start the day.

Facilities in this great hotel are wonderful; there is a large TV for those sporting events, a bar, a large welcoming log fire, pool table and darts in the lounge bar.

The hotel restaurant is very popular amongst the locals and is open for breakfast, lunch, bar meals and dinner; the menu being packed full of local dishes and meats. The hotel recently became a member of the Scotch Beef Club, a prestigious organisation, the patron of which is HRH Princess Anne.

192 WESTER BRAE HIGHLAND LODGES

Culbokie, Dingwall, Ross-shire IV7 8JU
Tel: 01349 877609 Fax: 01349 877221
e-mail: westerbrae@btconnect.com
website:
www.westerbraehighlandlodges.co.uk

The **Wester Brae Highland Lodges** are comprised of six, fully self contained lodges that have been awarded a Four Star rating by the Scottish Tourist Board. Whilst comfort and practicality are paramount in these high quality lodges, the location has to be the main draw. Set on the Black Isle peninsula, the lodges have views overlooking the Cromarty Firth, popular with Dolphin watchers and the entire location is overlooked by the Ross-shire Mountains.

The lodges have either two or three bedrooms, the two bedroomed lodges having separate lounges and kitchens and the three bedroomed lodges boasting a more open plan design. Fully heated and double glazed, there is no chance of inclement weather affecting your visit. On site is a games room, complete with a pool table and table tennis, open between 9 am and 10.30 pm, the games room is free to guests.

All sorts of activities are available to guests here; the Millbuie Forest, immediately behind the lodges has a vast network of quiet roads and paths suitable for cycling and walking. Facilities for horse riding, hiking, water sports, fishing and many others are on your doorstep.

463

193 DRUIMORRIN CARAVANS

Orrin Bridge, Urray, Muir of Ord,
Ross-shire, IV6 7UL
Tel: 01997 433566
Fax: 01997 433566
e-mail: info@druimorrin-caravans.co.uk
website: www.druimorrin-caravans.co.uk

The **Druimorrin Caravan** site has been a family run business since 1974, and can provide the perfect tranquil retreat away from the hustle and bustle of the crowded tourist areas; a real hidden gem. The site, which lies within the quaint parish of Urray, attracts a variety of people, including fishers (there is a fishery right across the road where you can fish for blue trout), walkers, cyclists, families, and bird enthusiasts. Sightings of ospreys and red kites are a regular occurrence, and other birds of prey including kestrels & buzzards, and many species of wildlife which live here in happy abundance.

There are three self-catering caravans on the site – the Conon 1 and 2 which each sleep 6 people, or the Orrin which sleeps 3 and is suitable for those with mobility difficulties – an unusually small number ensuring an intimate and quiet holiday

(a world away from the tourist sites brimming at the sides!). They are all provided with WC and shower, kitchen, gas heating, cooker & fridge, and you are provided with all of the bedding, utensils, crockery, etc that you could need. Every caravan is provided with a picnic table. Pets are welcome, and will no doubt enjoy the many lovely walks there are to explore here as much as you will. Hillwalkers particularly appreciate how easily some of Scotland's most stunning landscapes are reached from here.

194 BIRCH COTTAGE

7 Station Road, Garve,
Ross-shire, IV23 2PS
Tel: 01997 414237
e-mail: raywalt4@aol.com
website: www.bedandbreakfastgarve.co.uk

Ray and Linda have been welcoming customers to their traditional Highland bed & breakfast **Birch Cottage** for 6 years; the epitome of wonderful Scottish hospitality. The refurbished cottage is nestled in Garve – a central location to explore the Highlands and east & west coasts, which attracts a variety of tourers, walkers, wildlife enthusiasts and families every year.

At Birch Cottage you have the option of cosy double or twin-bed rooms, all with en-suite and hospitality tray, and the price of which includes a delicious breakfast. Served between 8 – 9am (earlier times can be arranged on request), breakfast includes cooked traditional or continental breakfast along with omelettes, kippers and scrambled eggs with smoked salmon. They can also cater for food allergies

and special dietary requirements.

The evening meals here, the real pride of Birch Cottage home-cooked by Ray with his 40 years of catering experience, are a delightful feast of locally sourced produce and seasonal vegetables from the garden. Served in the intimate candle-lit dinning room, you can enjoy such mouth-watering dishes as breast of chicken wrapped in bacon stuffed with haggis and with a whisky sauce, and strawberry and cointreau cocotte.

464

195 POOLEWE HOTEL 🛏 🍴

Poolewe, Ross-shire IV22 2JX
Tel: 01445 781241
Fax: 01445 781405
e-mail: info@poolewehotel.co.uk
website: www.poolewehotel.co.uk

Standing at the head of Loch Ewe, the **Poolewe Hotel** dates back to 1570 and was originally a coaching inn. It boasts a long history of providing quality accommodation with the best in Scottish Highland hospitality. The setting is magnificent: the hotel looks both down the loch to the open sea, and across to the world famous gardens at Inverewe.

The hotel's elegant and spacious restaurant has rapidly established a reputation for itself as one of the best in the area. Ania leads in the kitchen where locally supplied and selected produce are part of every meal. You'll find langoustines and hand-dived scallops from Loch Ewe, salmon from Loch Duart, haddock, halibut and sole from the east coast; Highland beef and lamb and local venison. Ania's own daily special dishes, soups and Cullen skink, have become great favourites with visitors, along with local steak & ale pie, venison pie, panfried

halibut, fresh crab gateau and local black pudding.

Scoring very high in the three star category award, all the guest bedrooms have an individual character and are en suite. Most have wonderful sea or mountain views. If the hotel is fully booked, well equipped traditional cottages next to the Hotel are used as an over-flow, and are available on a B&B or D, B& B rate. This allows guests to relax in 'home-from-home' comfort with a wood burner in the sittingroom.

Scottish
TOURIST BOARD
★★★
SMALL HOTEL

196 SINCLAIR BAY HOTEL 🛏 🍴

Main Street, Keiss, Caithness KW1 4UY
Tel: 01955 631233
Fax: 01955 631492
e-mail: sinclairbayhotel@tiscali.co.uk
website: www.sinclair-bay-hote

A small, popular, family run hotel, the **Sinclair Bay Hotel** offers a warm Caithness welcome to everyone, including children. The food is excellent - with lunch, evening and children's menus - and there is a good selection of wines, beers (including real ales), and spirits, all contributing to a value for money package. The attractively furnished bedrooms are cosy and equipped with colour television and hospitality tray. Most have en suite facilities and enjoy attractive views over Sinclair Bay. There is an attractive lounge bar, a public bar, games room, an intimate breakfast room and a residents lounge for quiet relaxation.

465

197 BREADALBANE HOUSE HOTEL

20 Breadalbane Crescent,
Wick KW1 5AQ
Tel: 01955 603911 Fax: 01955 604532
e-mail:
reservations@breadalbanehousehotel.co.uk
website: www.breadalbanehousehotel.co.uk

With an in house bar that was recently voted one of the top six music venues in Scotland, the **Breadalbane House Hotel** is extremely popular both with the locals and visitors to the area. Local lad Ryan Cook is your gracious host and has run the Breadalbane Hotel for four years now, perfecting the great service associated with this handsome Victorian villa. Boasting high ceilings, original cornices and large, bright and airy rooms, all of the best features remain from the late 19th century build. In fact, most of the interior woodwork, including the door and window frames and the staircase, were reputedly built personally by the owner, a local furniture maker.

The hotel is a mere 2 minutes walk from Wick's historical town centre. Other nearby facilities offer many activities, including golf, fishing, swimming and tennis. There are ten very well appointed rooms available, eight with en suites and two with private bathrooms, other bonuses in the rooms are 20" LCD televisions and wireless internet access.

The in-house pub use locally sourced ingredients to provide sumptuous food on Saturdays and Sunday lunches while during the week playing host to a range of live entertainment that draw visitors from all over the place.

199 THE FLAT AIGNISH

21 Aignish, Stornoway,
Isle of Lewis HS2 OPB
Tel: 01851 870258
e-mail: kenny@aignishfsnet.co.uk

Situated in a rural location, but in easy reaching distance of the nearest town and airport **The Flat Aignish** is a self contained property popular among visitors to the Isle of Lewis. The property is reasonably modern and has two bedrooms, consisting of one single and one double. Kenneth has owned the property since 1982 and welcomes back visitors year on year. Open all year round there are some fantastic views to be enjoyed in the area with the property overlooking Croft Land and Minch. It is in an ideal location for those wanting to explore the scenic island, which has plenty to offer, including many outdoor activities.

Dining out isn't a problem because there are many good quality cafés and restaurants in the vicinity. The Flat Aignish is just 4.5 miles from Stornoway and 3 miles to the airport. Due to its sheltered location Stornoway is the main port on the Isle of Lewis. The town has plenty of facilities, including a museum, art gallery, swimming pool, golf course, go karting and there are also many boat trips that can be had during the summer months. The place is child friendly and popular among families, walkers, cyclists, golfers and fishermen.

No pets.

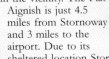

198 FARR BAY INN

Clachan, Bettyhill, Sutherland KW14 7SZ
Tel: 01641 521230
e-mail: info@farrbayinn.co.uk
website: www.farrbayinn.co.uk

The delightful **Farr Bay Inn** started life in
1819 as the Manse attached to the adjacent
Church of Scotland church. A listed building,
it was converted to an inn in 1983 and is now
owned and run by the family team of Karan,
Steve, Terry and Luke who extend a warm
Highland welcome to all their guests.

Nestled amongst the dunes of Farr Bay
close to the beautiful village of Bettyhill on
Scotland's North Coast, The Farr Bay Inn (or
the FBI as it is known locally) offers a superb
location for a relaxing getaway from the hustle and
bustle of everyday life. It is within easy walking
distance of secluded Farr Bay and close to the other
amenities offered in the centre of the village. With
its welcoming atmosphere, log fire, lovely rooms and
a well-stocked bar, it is popular amongst locals and
holiday-makers alike.

The bar, with its wood-burning stove, offers a
number of single malt whiskies, wines, spirits,
draught beers, and soft drinks. For those wishing to
drink outside, the inn has a delightful garden and
stone seated beer garden. Live arranged or
impromptu music is a regular occurrence at the inn,
and people are encouraged to bring musical
instruments and whip up a tune whenever the mood
takes them.

The FBI has built up a strong local reputation
for good food at affordable prices. Where possible
the chef cooks with locally farmed produce, meats,
and fish. Food is served between 12pm and 2pm,
then between 6pm and 8pm, with light snacks
available in between. Non-residents are more than
welcome.

The rooms at the FBI are all spacious,
comfortable, and well heated. Whilst maintaining the
original features of the old building, the decor is
modern and bright. All four rooms have en suite
showers and each is equipped with a colour
television, DVD player, tea and coffee making
facilities. Breakfasts are always cooked to order, and
can be enjoyed in the sunny dining room, setting you
up for the day ahead.

The inn is open from noon until 11pm, Monday
to Thursday; from noon until midnight on Friday;
and Saturday; and from 12.30pm to 11pm on Sunday.
The Farr Bay inn is open all year round.

467

South Beach Street, Stornoway,
Isle of Lewis HS1 2XY
Tel: 01851 702411 Fax: 01851 701680

Located just across the road from the quayside and enjoying spectacular views of the harbour, **The Caledonian Hotel** was built in 1968 after two previous hotels on the site had been destroyed by fires. It's now owned by Allan and Manna, who purchased it in December 2006. Allan, who has been a chef for 27 years, had previously worked at the hotel before buying it. Naturally, good food is a priority for him and the hotel restaurant enjoys a high reputation for quality cuisine. Allan's imaginative dinner menu offers his own classic Chicken Liver, Bacon, Garlic & Red Wine Parfait as one of the starters; Haddock fillet and fresh crab roulade on a crisp bed of leeks amongst the main courses; and a delicious roasted coffee tiramisu on a mandarin orange fruit coulis as one of the desserts. The restaurant is open from 5pm to 9pm, Tuesday to Saturday and such is its popularity it is advisable to make a booking. Food is also available in the bar areas from noon until

2pm, and from 5pm to 9pm every day including Sunday when it is available all day – very unusual in Stornoway where most places close on the Lord's Day. The extensive menu ranges from old favourites such as Steak & Kidney Pudding or Fish & Chips, through "hot'n'spicy" Tortilla Wraps or Mexi Burgers, to light bites of filled baguettes and burgers. If you are still hungry, return for a High Tea, served from 5pm to 6.30pm, Tuesday to Saturday. Dishes on offer include homemade lasagne served straight from the oven, and "Pigs in a Pond" – sausage and mash inside a Yorkshire pudding served with onion gravy. All food served at the Caledonian has been sourced locally wherever possible.

The hotel has a full on licence and its

popular draught keg beers are Tennant's lager and Tennant's 70sh. On Friday evenings, starting around 9.30pm, a local duo entertains customers with a programme of all types of music, and on Saturday evenings there are occasional live entertainment performances.

Accommodation at the Caledonian comprises 10 comfortable guest bedrooms of varying sizes, all with en suite facilities, telephone, TV, trouser press, hairdryer and hospitality tray. Rooms are available all year round. Children are welcome; all major credit cards except American Express and Diners are accepted.

201 LOCHS HOUSE

41 School Hill, Ranish, Isle of Lewis HS2 9NW
Tel: 01851 860514
e-mail: asinclair4@toucansurf.com
website: www.lochshouse.co.uk

Sitting amidst the breathtaking scenery of the hills, lochs and islands of Lewis, **Lochs House** is a large detached bungalow offering the perfect get-away. Located around 8 miles from the main town of Stornoway, in a rural setting, the bungalow enjoys spectacular views to the mountains in the south, the rugged coastline and in the distance, the vast mountains of mainland Scotland. Lochs House is an ideal staging point to explore both Lewis and Harris as it is located around half way between the top and bottom of the 'joined' islands.

Lochs House has four comfortable bedrooms with En-Suite Toilet / Wash-hand basins, Colour TVs with Freeview, and the usual Tea/Coffee making facilities. There is a large shared Guest Shower Room and a separate Guest TV Lounge for visitors to relax in, take advantage of WiFi Internet access or simply make the most of the amazing views. 2010 brings with it the exciting opening of an onsite Tearoom/Diner where snacks and meals will be available. Lochs House is open all year round and is perfect for winter Astronomers as star-gazing with the naked eye can be as enjoyable in the zero light polluted skies as using the on-site 10" Dobsonion Telescope.

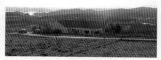

The area boasts some of the finest scenery, beaches and wildlife in Scotland and there are plenty of historical sites of interest for visitors to explore. Outdoor activities are extremely popular and many visitors return time and time again to surf, hill-walk, cycle, climb, photograph, paint or just relax on one of the many beautiful beaches. Whether you want to explore the area, or simply relax, Lochs House is highly recommended.

202 BORISHADER COTTAGE

16 Habost, South Lochs,
Isle of Lewis HS2 9QB
Tel: 01851 830328
website: www.borishadercottage.co.uk

Offering the very best in picturesque surroundings and accommodation, **Borishader Cottage** can be located in the quiet village of Habost. The cottage, which was recently awarded three stars by The Scottish Tourist Board following a major refurbishment, has been finished to an extremely high standard throughout. There are two comfortable bedrooms (one single and one double) and the option of sleeping another two on a sofa bed. There is a spacious living room and a fully fitted kitchen with an open fire and dining area. The cottage enjoys fantastic views over Loch Erisort and the surrounding countryside and is in an ideal location for exploring the Isle of Lewis.

Port of Ness, Isle of Lewis H52 0SN
Tel: 01851 810152
e-mail: info@crossinn.com
website: www.crossinn.com

Located on the northern tip of the Isle of Lewis, **The Cross Inn** is a warm and friendly hotel where attention to detail matters. Allan and Maureen are welcoming hosts and having been residents of the local area for generations have a lot of local knowledge that they are willing to share with guests. The hotel is located in Port of Ness, which is just north of the island's capital, Stornoway. Located in a beautiful area of peace and tranquility it is the perfect get-away for those wanting to forget the stresses of modern day living.

There are six rooms for guests to choose from – and all of them have been recently refurbished and tastefully decorated. Each of the rooms has been individually furnished and there are family, double and single options. All of them have ensuite facilities, a TV/video, coffee and tea making facilities among other things. One of the rooms located downstairs has disabled facilities.

Food is served throughout the day and can be enjoyed in the comfortable lounge or in the restaurant in the evening. Both are spacious and brimming with character. The produce used is sourced locally and the dishes on the extensive menu are made fresh to order. The menu features a good selection of seafood dishes, including salmon, lobster and other shellfish. The beef, lamb, pork and venison are all sourced locally and cooked to perfection. Visitors to The Cross Inn return time and time again to explore the area.

The islands look over the Atlantic Ocean and if you travel eastwards from the Western Isles of Scotland, the next stop is North America. Many visitors enjoy discovering The Butt of Lewis Lighthouse and the Callanish Stones. Apart from plenty of scenic walks, there are many other things for visitors to do aside from relaxing. The area is well known for the outdoor activities available and among the most popular are sea fishing, river fishing, cycling and golf.

At The Cross Inn there is also the opportunity to hold special events, from wedding celebrations to business meetings. Its function room can entertain up to 100 guests and the evening can be tailor made to suit the occasion. There is also a meeting room that can host up to 12 people and with accommodation on site Allan and Maureen can sort out all the plans for you. The Cross Inn has it all, comfortable rooms, a lovely location and fantastic hosts.

204 CARMINISH HOUSE

1A Strond, Leverburgh,
Isle of Harris, HS5 3UD
Tel: 01859 520400
e-mail: info@carminish.com
website: www.carminish.com

With a big focus on the comfort of guests, the award winning **Carminish House** is in a secluded location in the rolling countryside and by the sea. Built in a traditional style, the impressive establishment is a quarter of a mile away from its nearest neighbour. The house is in an ideal central position for those wanting to explore the Outer Hebrides.

There is one double room and two twin rooms available (all ensuite) for guests and the twin beds can be converted to super king size doubles on prior request. Two of the rooms are located at the front of the house and boast magnificent views and the resident's lounge also has stunning panoramic views over the Sound of Harris and the Carminish Islands. The third room looks East

with views towards Skye. Although there is central heating available in the rooms year round, an open fire in the lounge in colder months gives a warm and homely feel to the place.

The B&B has been awarded four stars by the Scottish Tourist Board for the excellent service and facilities offered including the breakfasts so popular with guests. In addition to the familiar full Scottish breakfast fayre, there is a choice of fish dishes, and various Scottish grilled puddings.

205 CNOC NA BA

Finsbay, Isle of Harris HS3 3JD
Tel: 01859 530232
website: www.cnocnaba.co.uk

Meaning 'Hill of the Cow' in Gaelic, **Cnoc Na Ba**, is located on the rocky east coast of South Harris, known as The Bays. Situated in Finsbay, the self-contained, four bedroom property, is in the ideal location for exploring the surrounding hills, moorland, inland lochs and sea.

Available all year round, many people who stay find it an ideal get-away and often return to enjoy the peace and tranquility of the area. The accommodation is of an extremely high standard. There is a large open plan sitting room, dining room and well equipped kitchen. Views overlooking moorland and Mount Roineabhal can be enjoyed and on brighter days so can the enclosed garden and patio area, which has access to the moorland.

Cnoc Na Ba is an ideal place to stay for those who want to explore the Western Isles and there are plenty of outdoor activities to be tried, including water sports, cycling and fishing. Keen walkers and bird watchers will be in their element because the surrounding terrain is ideal and there are many rare flowers to be found. The owners, who live in the property adjoining Cnoc Na Ba, are happy for children to stay, but not pets.

471

206 BALARD

9 Malaclate, Sollas, North Uist HS6 5BX
Tel: 01876 560242

Popular with fishermen, cyclists, birdwatchers and families, **Balard** is just a two minute walk from the beach. There are five comfortable bedrooms, consisting of two doubles, two twins and a single room. There is also a bathroom

with bath and shower.
Balard has a living/dining room and a sitting room and is tastefully decorated

throughout. The traditional croft house has a fully equipped kitchen and there is electrical heating. There are plenty of scenic routes for keen walkers and there is a unique golf course, which moves depending on the ploughing. For disabled customers there is a ground floor bedroom, but the bathroom is located upstairs.

208 298 KILPHEDER

Daliburgh, South Uist HS8 5SS
Tel: 01878 700204
e-mail: maureenpeteranna@hotmail.com

298 Kilpheder is a 3 bedroom self catering cottage with a separate lounge and breakfasting kitchen with laundry facilities within. The bathroom is fully equipped with a power shower and heated towel rail. All linen and towels are provided. There is a spacious garden front and rear as well as ample parking at the front of the property. Amenities are a short 5 minute drive or a leisurely 15 minute walk. Access to the beach is also the same distance. Golf is a short 10 minute drive away. For any further information please feel free to call proprieter or e-mail.

207 ARD NA MARA

Kilpheder, South Uist HS8 5TB
Tel: 01878 700452
e-mail:
rosemaryrobinson334@btinternet.com

Located in a rural setting there are some fantastic views to be enjoyed from **Ard Na Mara**. Since 2006 the property has undergone extensive refurbishments and it has been finished to an extremely high standard. All of the rooms are en-suite, including a twin room and the deluxe suite

has triple aspect offering views of the surrounding sea, lochs and hills. Built in 1985 the property is modern and spacious and there is free Wi-fi internet access available for guests. Ard Na Mara is popular with walkers because there are many scenic routes in the area, which are also popular among bird watchers and cyclists. Within two miles of the B&B there is a golf course and there are also many other outdoor activities that can be tried, including fishing.

There is a beach nearby, which stretches for miles and on brighter days visitors often like to go hill walking to the east of the island. Open all year round the B&B caters for vegetarians. Each of the rooms has tea and coffee facilities and Sky TV. There is disabled access, with a room on the ground floor, but there is no ramp. There is off road parking for guests with a spacious car park. No pets.

209 WEST END HOTEL

Main Street, Kirkwall, Orkney KW15 1BU
Tel: 01856 872368
e-mail: info@westendkirkwall.co.uk
website: www.westendkirkwall.co.uk

Popular with both locals and visitors, the **West End Hotel** is, in many ways, the ideal blend of old and new. Its history goes back to 1824 when a retired sea captain built his new house just outside Kirkwall. Some twenty years later, it became Orkney's first hospital. Today, as a hotel it offers simple comforts and is among the finest places to stay in Orkney with owners Gifford Leslie and Robert Dawson providing a warm welcome to all their guests. The property has been refurbished in the past few years and is now fresh and inviting with the intriguing blend of both old and new to cater to all tastes.

The hotel's guest rooms are both elegant and comfortable with an understated style that will help you relax both body and mind at the end of any day. Each is equipped with a modern shower-only bathroom and for that special occasion you could sleep in a four-poster bed.

The hotel is well-known for its cost-conscious meals which are served in both the small restaurant and the bar. Customers can feast from the wide variety of the delicious menu which is based on freshly obtained produce, transformed into dishes to satisfy any discerning appetite. All

the food is home-cooked and freshly prepared using organic produce wherever possible. Vegetarian and special diets can be catered for.

Or you can just satisfy your thirst in the warm and friendly atmosphere of the West End Hotel bar. The finest wines, beers, spirits and soft drinks are served the way you like.

The hotel also offer facilities for small conference retreats or workshops, concerts, lectures, weddings and courses.

210 ALBERT HOTEL

Mounthoolie Lane, Kirkwall,
Orkney KW15 1JZ
Tel: 01856 876000 Fax: 01856 875397
e-mail: enquiries@alberthotel.co.uk
website: www.alberthotel.co.uk

The **Albert Hotel** in Kirkwall occupies a superb location in the town centre only a short distance from the local tourist information centre and within walking distance of the central bus station and the harbour, cathedrals and nearby museum. Guests can unwind in the relaxing atmosphere of

the Cosy Bothy Bar which is adorned with old memorabilia and photos. Here you'll find an excellent choice of traditional Orkney ales, whiskies a large selection of other alcoholic drinks, soft drinks and tea & coffee. Warm yourself by the fire while you eat from the hearty traditional British menu based on fresh local produce.

The hotel offers modern, boutique style guest bedrooms with luxury furnishings and a contemporary

design. All of the guest rooms are en suite and have flatscreen televisions and central heating. Each room has tea and coffee making facilities and is equipped with broadband Internet access, ideal for business travellers.

The hotel also has a variety of dining options and conference facilities. So, whether you are staying for business or looking for a weekend leisure break, you'll find all your requirements fully met at The Albert.

211 EAST BANK HOUSE

East Road, Kirkwall, Orkney KW15 1LX
Tel: 01856 870179
e-mail: eastbankhouse@yahoo.co.uk
website: www.eastbankhouse.co.uk

Situated on a hill overlooking Kirkwall and its harbour, **East Bank House** is just a five minute walk from the city and all its amenities. Its location makes it an ideal base for exploring the Orkney Islands. Standing in its own grounds and dating

back to 1824, the house was completely refurbished in 2005. It now provides comfortable en suite accommodation with 7 double/twin rooms, 3 family and 3 single rooms - all of them with en suite facilities. The ground floor consists of a large, fully fitted kitchen for the use of guests in the evening, a dining room and adjacent conservatory. Guests are served a generous breakfast based on the very best of Orkney produce. Vegetarian or special diets can be catered for on request

and everything is served in a friendly, informal atmosphere. Dogs are welcome.

East Bank House also offers self-catering options, as well as group and long stay reductions by negotiation. Accommodating up to 26 guests, the house is eminently suitable for small to medium sized groups.

212 SANDERLAY GUEST HOUSE

2 Viewfield Drive, Kirkwall,
Orkney KW15 1RB
Tel: 01856 875587
e-mail: enquiries@sanderlay.co.uk
website: www.sanderlay.co.uk

Located in a residential area on the outskirts of Kirkwall, **Sanderlay Guest House** is a smart modern property to which Elma and Ronald Tulloch have welcomed guests for many years.

The two largest rooms on the first floor are used as self-contained flats outwith the tourist season and have their own lounge seating, colour TV and en suite shower/toilet. Also available are family, double and single rooms, all but one with en suite facilities. A full breakfast is included and the guest's lounge has basic kitchen facilities for the additional convenience of guests.

214 AVALON GUEST HOUSE

Carness Road, Kirkwall KW15 1UE
Tel: 01856 876665
e-mail: jane@avalon-house.co.uk
website: www.avalon-house.co.uk

Avalon Guest House is a purpose built property which is owned and run by Jane and Alastair MacDonald who have years of experience in the tourism industry. Home cooking, home comforts and a warm welcome await

you at their home. All rooms are en suite with king size beds and memory foam mattresses and every room has digital TV and wireless broadband access. Avalon House is only 20 minutes walk from the historic town centre of Kirkwall while offering a quiet location with views across Kirkwall Bay and north to the isles of Rousay, Wyre and Gairsay only a minutes walk away.

213 LYNNFIELD HOTEL

Holm Road, St Ola, Kirkwall,
Orkney KW15 1SU
Tel: 01856 872505
e-mail: office@lynnfield.co.uk
website: www.lynnfieldhotel.com

The **Lynnfield Hotel** has had an interesting history. It was originally built as a second manse for St Magnus' Cathedral and during World War II was requisitioned as an Officers' Mess. Located next to the famous Highland Park Distillery and overlooking Kirkwall town and the sea, enjoys a glowing reputation for fine food with all the ingredients being locally sourced wherever possible. Fish comes from local boats, and the beef, lamb and seasonal vegetables are all from Orkney farms. Typical dishes include roast loin of North Ronaldsay ewe, and baked darne of organic Westray salmon. The owners are proud to offer Orkney's leading wine list with more than 70 bins available. The bar also stocks 60 malt whiskeys including 20 variants from neighbouring Highland Park. This ties in with the whiskey theme in the dining room.

The 4-star accommodation at Lynnfield comprises two suites whose lounges enjoy grand views; two large deluxe rooms with antique beds - one William IV four-poster, and one with a Half-Tester. There are also superior doubles, two twin rooms and a ground floor suite with twin beds and facilities for the less able-bodied. All the rooms are equipped with 37" TV with Sky, free wi-fi, telephone and hospitality tray.

475

215 COMMODORE CHALETS

St Mary's, Holm, Orkney KW17 2RU
Tel: 01856 781319
e-mail:
christine@commodorechalets.co.uk
website: www.commodorechalets.co.uk

Offering the very best in B&B and self catering accommodation **Commodore Chalets** is a popular choice among visitors. Located 300 yards from the village of St Mary's the chalets are close to several diving sites. Just six miles from Kirkwall on the south coast of the Orkney mainland the business has nine self catering chalets and six overnight lodges all boasting spectacular views over St Mary's Bay and the Churchill Barriers.

The double glazed self catering units are built to a high standard and the open plan design adds to the relaxing and friendly feel of the place. The chalets, which provide a comfortable home-from-home, are on the main bus route to Kirkwall and in walking distance of the famous Italian chalet, a play park and football pitch. If it is a peaceful holiday exploring the

tranquil islands you are longing for then staying at the Commodore Chalets, with its adjacent bar and restaurant, is an ideal choice.

Open all year the accommodation is on the ground floor and there is a ramp available for use if required. The chalets are available from 2pm on arrival and guests are asked to vacate them by 10am on the morning of departure.

216 MURRAY ARMS HOTEL

Back Road, St Margaret's Hope,
South Ronaldsay, Orkney KW17 2SP
Tel: 01856 831205
e-mail: info@murrayarmshotel.com
website: www.murrayarmshotel.com

St Margaret's Hope is a quaint fishing village on the beautiful island of South Ronaldsay. It boasts a craft shop, small museum, post office, café, grocery shop and, in the heart of the village, a welcoming inn, the **Murray Arms Hotel**. It's a typically solid stone Scottish building, set in a conservation area, which was taken over in the summer of 2009 by a local couple, Heather and Graeme Brown.

Graeme used to be a dairy farmer; Heather was the village postmistress so between them they possess a wealth of local knowledge. Both enjoy meeting and greeting people and their bar is a lively place with darts and pool, and a large screen TV for live football. You can also eat here or in the separate restaurant and the menu

offers a good choice of home-cooked food prepared on the premises using local produce. Lunch is served daily from noon until 2pm, (Sunday from 12.30pm to 2pm), and dinner from 6pm to 8.30pm. Children and pets are all welcome but because this is a traditional stone building there is no disabled access. The hotel also offers comfortable B&B accommodation in 5 attractive rooms, all with en suite facilities.

217 FOINHAVEN B&B AND SELF-CATERING

Germiston Road, Orphir, Stromness,
Orkney KW16 3HD
Tel: 01856 811249
e-mail: margaret.wishart@btinternet.com
website: www.foinhaven.co.uk

Foinhaven B&B and Self-Catering is run by Orcadians Margaret and Raymond Wishart whose aim is to make your stay in Orkney a happy and memorable one. With a wealth of local knowledge, they are always happy to suggest suitable activities and places to visit. Foinhaven is a modern spacious house, built in 1997 and located on a quiet country road on elevated ground overlooking Kirbister Loch, Waulkmill Bay and Scapa Flow.

The house has 3 family/twin rooms, each consisting of a double and single bed and full en suite facilities. There's also a double with bath. Each room also has a colour television and enjoys lovely unspoilt views across open countryside. Guests are welcome to relax in the spacious lounge which also commands stunning views. Self-catering guests have the choice of 3 recently opened apartments

with 1, 2 or 3 bedrooms, all beautifully furnished and decorated, comprehensively equipped, and with spectacular views from every window.

All guests have the use of a boat on Kirbister Loch, there are ferries to the island of Hoy from Houton a few miles away, and Waulkmill Bay - one of the Orkney Mainland's finest sheltered beaches, is a short distance away.

218 STROMNESS CAFÉ BAR

22 Victoria Street, Stromness KW16 3AA
Tel: 01856 850551

Stromness Café Bar occupies a superb position at the pier head in the heart of the town and its waterside terrace is the only place in the town where you can eat outside at the waterfront, enjoying the view of the harbour. Chris and Rosie Dambach took over here in the spring of 2009 and their appetising menu quickly became highly popular. They offer a wide range of meals, everything from breakfast to dinner with the emphasis on local produce, especially local seafood. Their home-made pizza is also very popular and is also available, along with other dishes, to take away. As well as the terrace seating for 30 people, there are 40 more places inside where there is also a convenience store. Open all year round, the café is fully licensed, welcomes children and has good disabled access and disabled toilets.

477

219 ORCA GUEST HOUSE

76 Victoria Street, Stromness KW16 3BS
Tel: 01856 850447
website: www.orcahotel.com

Located right on the harbour just a few minutes walk from the ferry terminal, **Orca Guest House** is ideally situated for exploring Orkney by land and sea. This family-run guest house offers a choice of B&B or self-catering accommodation. The 6 comfortable en suite rooms range from single to family rooms, with double beds and solid pine bunk beds for children or friends. Each room is equipped with a modern toilet and shower unit, TV, radio alarm and hospitality tray. The recently refurbished breakfast room also serves as a residents' lounge with comfortable seating, TV, video and tape facilities. At breakfast time there's an extensive buffet of fresh fruit, juices, cereals, yoghurts, tea and coffee, followed by a full breakfast prepared by the chef exactly to your

liking. For self-catering, groups of up to 16 can book exclusive use of the hotel and facilities, including the fully fitted kitchen, and from November to March self-catering is available as an option for all guests at a reduced rate.

Within walking distance of the guest house are some spectacular cliff walks and unspoilt moorlands abound with birds and wildflowers.

221 BYDEST SELF-CATERING

19c St Magnus Street, Lerwick ZE1 0JT
Tel: 01950 431496
Mobile: 07741 008296
e-mail: cairnlea.smith@btinternet.com

Conveniently located in the heart of Lerwick, **Bydest Self-Catering** offers quality accommodation in a well-appointed town house. Owners Leslie and Jennifer Smith have taken great care to provide everything you might need for your stay. An ideal base for exploring Shetland's countryside and attractions, Bydest can accommodate up to 4 people, is available all year round, but does not have disabled facilities.

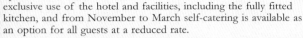

220 SKAILL HOUSE

Breckness Estate, Sandwick,
Orkney KW16 3LR
Tel: 01856 841501
e-mail: malcolm@skaillhouse.co.uk
website: www.skaillhouse.co.uk

Steeped in 5000 years of history **Skaill House** is an impressive establishment, which stands proudly on the Atlantic coast of Orkney. The mansion is located just 200m from the world famous Neolithic village of Skara Brae. Open to the public from April to September the house is available all year for weddings and private functions and there are two self-catering apartments.

Skaill House is an excellent base for exploring Orkney and is six miles from Stromness and 16 miles from Kirkwall. Built in 1620 the mansion provides a fantastic get-away, located in a secluded spot between the sea and the Loch of Skaill. The name 'Skaill' is the Old Norse for hall and most of the farmsteads north and south of the Bay of Skaill have Norse names, suggesting that the area has been continuously farmed for at least a thousand years. The

house is more than 400 years old, and was built and first owned by Bishop George Graham (Bishop of Orkney 1615-1638) on the site of a farmstead thought to date to the Norse period. Since then all of its 12 Lairds have been related, including the seventh Laird William Graham Watt who discovered Skara Brae in 1850. Today the house is one of Okney's top tourist attractions and visitors can explore the family home and artiefacts, which date back to the 17th century.

In the North Wing of Skaill House there are two apartments available as self-catering holiday accommodation and guests can enjoy free access to the house. The southern wing of the house stands on an early Norse burial ground and the remains of a broch and another Iron Age building can still be seen on the shoreline of the Bay. Both apartments are spacious and well-equipped, with Langskaill sleeping six and boasting stunning views across Skaill Bay. Guests to Langskaill can enjoy private use of the 'Long Room' and table tennis table, providing children with plenty of room to play. Peerieskaill is situated downstairs in the north wing of Skaill House and is a very comfortable and cosy apartment – sleeping five. Both apartments have access to a payphone and utility room with a washing machine and tumble dryer.

Surrounded by vast gardens Skaill House is licensed to hold civil marriage ceremonies. Providing a romantic and intimate venue there are some perfect backdrops for wedding photographs to be taken. The ceremonies are held in the drawing room or dining room and can accommodate up to 40 people.

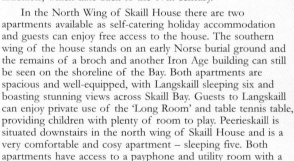

222 SHETLAND LIGHTHOUSE HOLIDAYS

Shetland Amenity Trust, Garthspool,
Lerwick, Shetland ZE1 0NY
Tel: 01595 694688
e-mail: info@shetlandamenity.org
website: www.lighthouse-holidays.com

Shetland Lighthouse Holidays offers high quality, affordable, self-catering accommodation at three of the islands' most spectacularly situated buildings, Sumburgh, Bressay and Eshaness lighthouses. Staying in the former lighthouse keepers' cottages you will discover breathtaking scenery and stunning coastal walks whatever time of year.

They are all Stevenson lighthouses, built by ancestors of the famous author Robert Louis Stevenson, and with a fascinating history. **Sumburgh Lighthouse**, built in 1821 by Robert Louis Stevenson's grandfather, is situated on a headland at the southern tip of the Mainland. The surrounding cliffs and shores are teeming with wildlife and the RSPB Reserve at Sumburgh Head is one of the best places in Britain to see puffins and whales. **Bressay

Lighthouse,** built in 1858, overlooks the entrance to Lerwick

Harbour and is ideally located for visiting the nature reserve at Noss and for exploring the archaeology on Bressay. A short 10-minute ferry ride from Lerwick, this lighthouse is rural while close to town. **Eshaness Lighthouse** is set amongst some of the most spectacular cliff top scenery in the UK and is surrounded by fascinating geology. Eshaness and Bressay can accommodate up to 6 people, and Sumburgh 7.

223 HAY'S DOCK CAFÉ RESTAURANT

Hay's Dock, Lerwick, Shetland ZE1 0WP
Tel: 01595 695057
e-mail: sita@shetlandamenity.org

Every trip to Shetland should start with a visit to its Heritage Hub, the Shetland Museum and Archives where you can discover Shetland's story from its geological beginnings to the present day as well as finding out about the network of high quality heritage and cultural sites throughout the isles. Set in a restored 19th century dock, this new building - opened in 2007 - offers a beautiful location, a wide range of facilities and a host of special events and exhibitions throughout the year. Within the building, you will find two floors of displays, learning and research rooms, a temporary exhibition gallery, auditorium, shop and a

restored boatshed where you can watch boats being built and restored using traditional techniques.

Set within the Shetland Museum and

Archives, **Hay's Dock Café Restaurant** commands superb views over Lerwick Harbour and showcases quality local produce throughout the year. Seals and other wildlife are often seen outside in hay's Dock so you can watch them while enjoying your meal. Through the day, the café restaurant offers light snacks and lunches whilst in the evening there is fine dining in a relaxed atmosphere. If the weather is fine you can enjoy your meal out on the balcony.

224 SHALDERS GUEST HOUSE

Levenwick, Shetland   ZE2 9HX
Tel: 01950 422229
e-mail: ann@shalders.co.uk
website: www.shalders.co.uk

Shalders Guest House is a fabulous 4-star B&B situated in the south mainland of Shetland in the picturesque village of Levenwick. The old croft-style house has

been extended and lovingly improved with modern facilities and it commands magnificent sea views as far as Bressay and Noss to the north. In the evening, guests can relax in the comfortable lounge which has panoramic sea views, television and broadband internet access. The attractively furnished and decorated guest rooms consist of an en suite double bedroom and adjoining room with bunk beds for two children.

HIDDEN PLACES GUIDES

Explore Britain and Ireland with *Hidden Places* guides - a fascinating series of national and local travel guides.

Packed with easy to read information on hundreds of places of interest as well as places to stay, eat and drink.

Available from both high street and internet booksellers

For more information on the full range of *Hidden Places* guides and other titles published by Travel Publishing visit our website on

www.findsomewhere.co.uk
or ask for our leaflet by phoning
01752 697280   or emailing
info@travelpublishing.co.uk

225 THE SPIGGIE HOTEL

Scousburgh, Shetland   ZE2 9JE
Tel: 01950 460409
e-mail: spiggiehotel@gmail.com
website: www.thespiggiehotel.co.uk

Occupying a wonderful position overlooking tranquil Spiggie Loch, **The Spiggie Hotel** provides a perfect base for exploring all that Shetland has to offer, including breathtaking views, wildlife, archaeology and stunning sunsets. The hotel's restaurant, which also overlooks the loch, serves quality home-made cuisine based on local produce wherever possible. Freshly caught fish and shellfish dishes are the speciality of the house, along with delicious Shetland lamb. There's a good selection of fine wines to complement your meal and the bar stocks a variety of real ales, including ales from the local Valhalla Brewery in Unst. The accommodation offers a choice of single, double, twin and family rooms, all with en suite facilities.

Spiggie Loch is a Nature Reserve owned by the RSPB and is one of the finest trout fishing lochs in the Islands. Fishing is by permit only which can be purchased at the hotel, which may also be able to arrange the use of a boat and Ghillie. Scousburgh Sands with its gleaming white sand and rocky Spiggie beach, both with crystal-clear seawater are ideal for fishing, picnics or just relaxing. Both beaches are within five minutes walk from the hotel.

226 EASTERHOULL CHALETS

East Voe, Scalloway, Shetland ZE1 0UR
Tel: 01595 880526 Mobile: 0781 8845385
e-mail: info@easterhoull.co.uk
website: www.easterhoull.co.uk

Enjoying grand sea and island views, **Easterhoull Chalets** have been providing excellent self-catering accommodation since 1980. The 9 individual chalets have been furnished and decorated to a high standard and each comprises 1 twin bedroom and 1 double. There's a comfortable sitting room equipped with TV, DVD and Wi-Fi, and a kitchenette with microwave, fridge and cooker. Each has its own shower room and dedicated car parking. Bed linen and towels are provided, the rates are very competitive and there's no minimum stay.

The chalets are a 10-minute walk from the main street of Scalloway which offers 2 licensed grocery shops, a hotel, post office, swimming pool, museum and local pub, the Kiln Bar. There are purpose-built steps from the chalets leading into the town and passing the excellent local fish shop which also sells grocery items. Lerwick, the capital of Shetland, is just 5 miles away and boasts a wide range of shops, cafés, pubs, hotels, a sports centre and an award-winning museum.

Shetland is a paradise for bird watchers, with vast cliff-face colonies of gannets and puffins at various nearby locations. The fishing too is outstanding with hundreds of secluded lochs and voes (small bays) abounding in brown and sea trout.

227 BUSTA HOUSE HOTEL

Busta, Brae, Shetland ZE2 9QN
Tel: 1806 522506 Fax: 01806 522588
e-mail: reservations@bustahouse.com
website: www.bustahouse.com

With 22 en-suite rooms, the **Busta House Hotel** is the leading hotel in Shetland. The house is an historic building dating back hundreds of years, with a 16th Century Long Room (built during the reign of Elizabeth the 1st of England), where the present Queen, Elizabeth the II had tea in 1961 and the Gifford Library, dates from 1710. But for all it's age, the hotel is firmly in the 21st Century, where high standards of service, great cuisine, comfort and value of money are concerned. All the rooms are named after Shetland Islands, and all have direct dial telephones, modem ports, complimentary WI-FI, Tea/Coffee making facilities, Electronic Safe, Satellite Television and Hairdryer. They are well furnished and decorated and have a comfortable, welcoming feel to them. Regrettably none are on the ground Floor and lifts or elevators were not invented in the 16th, 17th or 18th Centuries.

Food is important at the Busta House Hotel. The Pitcairn restaurant serves only the finest dishes all prepared from fresh local produce wherever possible and bar meals are also available. The menu has been put together with imagination and flair, and this, with a fine wine and malt whisky list, means that you will have a dinner to remember.

You can relax in the lounge or bar area and Busta House has something which is a rarity in Shetland – A garden, where you can relax or stroll on a Summers evening. The hotel makes a perfect base and staff are knowledgeable about what to do and see. There's even a Ghost in the Hotel – but don't worry! It's a warm, friendly one, and it will leave you alone to enjoy your stay.

Baltasound, Unst, Shetland ZE2 9DS
Tel: 01957 711315 Fax: 01957 711815
e-mail: buness-house@zetnet.co.uk
website:
www.users.zetnet.co.uk/buness-house

On Britains most northerly island, **Buness House**, is a listed building, a family home occupied since Norse times, with comfortable sea facing bedrooms ensuite or with private bathroom.

Dine well on seafood and fresh local/home grown produce and relax in the conservatory savouring the long summer evenings and wildlife along the shore beneath the house.

Two nearby Nature Reserves, lovely walks, striking cliffs where Puffins abound, rare plants, beaches, heather moors, wild flowers, archaeological sites, otters, seals, tranquility and clean air are all to be enjoyed by lovers of unspoilt countryside and the outdoors.

Tourist Information Centres

ABERDEEN

23 Union Street, Aberdeen, Aberdeenshire,
Grampian AB11 5BP
Tel: 01224 288 828 Fax: 01224 252 219
e-mail: aberdeen@visitscotland.com
website: www.aberdeen-grampian.com

ABERFELDY

The Square, Perth & Kinross, Aberfeldy,
Central Scotland PH15 2DD
Tel: 01887 820276 Fax: 01887 829495
e-mail: aberfeldy@visitscotland.com
website: www.perthshire.co.uk

ABERFOYLE

Trossachs Discovery Centre, Main Street, Aberfoyle,
Stirlingshire FK8 3UQ
Tel: 08452 255 121
e-mail: aberfoyle@visitscotland.com

ABINGTON

Welcome Break Service Area, Junction 13, M74,
Lanarkshire, Crawford, Strathclyde ML12 6RG
Tel: 01864 502 436
e-mail: abington@visitscotland.com
website: visitscotland.com

ALFORD

Railway Museum, Old Station Yard, Main Street, Alford,
Aberdeenshire, Grampian AB33 8FD
Tel: 019755 62052
e-mail: alford@visitscotland.com
website: www.aberdeen-grampian.com

ALVA

Mill Trail Visitor Centre, West Stirling Street, Alva,
Stirlingshire FK12 5EN
Tel: 08707 200 605 Fax: 01259 763100
e-mail: info@alva.visitscotland.com
website: www.visitscottishheartlands.org/

ANSTRUTHER

Scottish Fisheries Museum, Harbourhead, Anstruther, Fife,
Central Scotland KY10 3AB
Tel: 01333 311073
e-mail: anstruther@visitscotland.com
website: www.standrews.co.uk

ARBROATH

Harbour Visitor Centre, Fish Market Quay, Arbroath,
Angus and Dundee, DD11 1PS
Tel: 01241 872 609 Fax: 01241 878 550
e-mail: arbroath@visitscotland.com
website: www.angusanddundee.co.uk

ARDGARTAN

Forestry Car Park, Glen Croe, by Arrochar,
Dunbartonshire, Ardgartan, Strathclyde G83 7AR
Tel: 08707 200 606 Fax: 08707 200 606
e-mail: ardgartan@visitscotland.com

AUCHTERARDER

90 High Street, Perth & Kinross, Auchterarder,
Central Scotland PH3 1BJ
Tel: 01764 663450 Fax: 01764 664235
e-mail: auchterardertic@perthshire.co.uk
website: www.perthshire.co.uk

AVIEMORE

Unit 7, Grampian Road, Inverness-shire, Aviemore,
Highlands and Islands PH22 1RH
Tel: 0845 22 55 121
e-mail: aviemore@visitscotland.com
website: www.visithighlands.com

AYR

22 Sandgate, Ayr, Ayrshire and Arran,
Strathclyde KA7 1BW
Tel: 01292 290 300
e-mail: ayr@visitscotland.com
website: www.ayrshire-arran.com

BALLACHULISH

Albert Road, Ballachulish, Argyll and Bute,
Strathclyde PH49 4JR
Tel: 08452 255 121
e-mail: ballachulish@visitscotland.com
website: www.visithighland.com

BALLATER

Old Royal Station, Station Square, Ballater, Aberdeenshire,
Grampian AB35 5QB
Tel: 013397 55306
e-mail: ballater@visitscotland.com
website: www.aberdeen-grampian.com

BALLOCH

Balloch Road, Dunbartonshire, Balloch,
Strathclyde G83 8LQ
Tel: 08707 200 607 Fax: 01389 751704
e-mail: balloch@visitscotland.com

BALLOCH (PARK)

National Park Gateway Centre, Balloch,
West Dunbartonshire, G83 8LQ
Tel: 08707 200 631 Fax: 01389 722 177
e-mail: info@lochlomond.visitscotland.com
website: www.visitscottishheartlands.com

BANCHORY

Bridge Street, Banchory, Aberdeenshire,
Grampian AB31 5SX
Tel: 01330 822000
e-mail: banchory@visitscotland.com
website: www.aberdeen-grampian.com

BANFF

Collie Lodge, Banff, Aberdeenshire, Grampian AB45 1AU
Tel: 01261 812419
e-mail: banff@visitscotland.com
website: www.aberdeen.grampian.com

BETTYHILL

Clachan Bettyhill, by Thurso, Sutherland, Bettyhill,
Highlands and Islands KW14 7SS
Tel: 01845 22 55 121
e-mail: info@visitscotland.com
website: www.visithighlands.com

BIGGAR

155 High Street, South Lanarkshire, Biggar,
Strathclyde ML12 6DL
Tel: 01899 221 066 Fax: 01899 221 066
e-mail: biggar@visitscotland.com
website: www.seeglasgow.com

BLAIRGOWRIE

26 Wellmeadow, Perth & Kinross, Blairgowrie,
Central Scotland PH10 6AS
Tel: 01250 876 825 Fax: 01250 876 825
e-mail: blairgowrie@visitscotland.com
website: www.perthshire.co.uk

BO'NESS

Bo'ness and Kinneil Railway Station, Union Street,
Bo'ness, Lothian EH51 9AQ
Tel: 08452 255 121
e-mail: boness@visitscotland.com

BORDERS

Shepherd's Mill, Whinfield Road, Selkirk,
Scottish Borders TD7 5DT
Tel: 0870 6080404 Fax: 01750 21886
e-mail: bordersinfo@visitscotland.com
website: www.scot-borders.co.uk

BOWMORE

The Square, Isle of Islay, Bowmore,
Highlands and Islands PA43 7JP
Tel: 08707 200 617 Fax: 01496 810 363
e-mail: islay@visitscotland.com

BRAEMAR

The Mews, Mar Road, Braemar, Aberdeenshire,
Grampian AB35 5YP
Tel: 01339 741 600 Fax: 01339 741 643
e-mail: braemar@visitscotland.com
website: www.aberdeen-grampian.com

BRECHIN

Pictavia Visitor Centre, Haughmuir, Brechin,
Angus and Dundee, Central Scotland DD9 6RL
Tel: 01356 623 050
e-mail: brechin@visitscotland.com
website: www.angusanddundee.co.uk

BRECHIN TOWN CENTRE

Brechin Town House Museum, 28 High Street, Brechin,
Angus and Dundee, Central Scotland DD9 6ER
Tel: 01356 625 536
e-mail: enquiries@angusanddundee.co.uk
website: www.angusanddundee.co.uk

BROADFORD

The Car Park, Broadford, Isle of Skye,
Highlands and Islands IV49 9AB
Tel: 01845 22 55 121
e-mail: info@visitscotland.com
website: www.visithighlands.com

BRODICK

The Pier, Isle of Arran, Brodick, Ayrshire and Arran,
Strathclyde KA27 8AU
Tel: 01770 303 776
e-mail: brodick@visitscotland.com
website: www.ayrshire-arran.com

BRORA

Cunninghams of Brora Newsagents, Brora,
Highlands and Islands KW9 6NU
Tel: 01408 621 204

CALLANDER

Rob Roy and Trossachs Visitor Centre, 10 Ancaster Square,
Callander, Stirlingshire FK17 8ED
Tel: 08452 255 121
e-mail: callander@visitscotland.com

CARNOUSTIE

Carnoustie Library, High Street, Carnoustie,
Angus and Dundee, Central Scotland DD7 6AN
Tel: 01241 859 620
e-mail: enquiries@angusanddundee.co.uk
website: www.angusanddundee.co.uk

CASTLE DOUGLAS

Market Hill, Castle Douglas,
Dumfries and Galloway DG7 1AE
Tel: 01556 502611
e-mail: castledouglas@visitscotland.com
website: www.visitdumfriesandgalloway.co.uk

CASTLEBAY

Pier Road, Isle of Barra, Castlebay,
Highlands and Islands HS9 5XD
Tel: 01871 810336 Fax: 01871 810336
e-mail: castlebay@visitscotland.com
website: www.visithebrides.com

TOURIST INFORMATION CENTRES

CLUANIE
Cluanie Inn, Glenmoriston,
Highlands and Islands IV63 7YW
Tel: 01320 340 238

CRAIGNURE
The Pier, Isle of Mull, Craignure, Strathclyde PA65 6AY
Tel: 08452 255 121
e-mail: craignure@visitscotland.com

CRAIL
Crail Museum & Heritage Centre, Marketgate, Crail, Fife,
Central Scotland KY10 3AB
Tel: 01333 450869
e-mail: crail@visitscotland.com
website: www.standrews.co.uk

CRATHIE
The Car Park, by Braemar, Crathie, Aberdeenshire,
Grampian AB35 5UL
Tel: 01339 742 414
e-mail: crathie@visitscotland.com
website: www.aberdeen-grampian.com

CRIEFF
Town Hall, High Street, Perth & Kinross, Crieff,
Central Scotland PH7 3HU
Tel: 01764 652 578 Fax: 01764 655 422
e-mail: crieff@visitscotland.com
website: www.perthshire.co.uk

DAVIOT WOOD
Picnic Area (A9), by Inverness, Daviot Wood,
Highlands and Islands IV2 5ER
Tel: 01845 22 55 121
e-mail: daviotwoods@visitscotland.com
website: www.visithighlands.com

DORNOCH
Sheriff Court House, Castle Street, Sutherland, Dornoch,
Highlands and Islands IV25 3SD
Tel: 01845 22 55 121 Fax: 01506 832 222
e-mail: dornoch@visitscotland.com
website: www.visithighlands.com

DRUMNADROCHIT
The Car Park, Inverness-shire, Drumnadrochit,
Highlands and Islands IV63 6TX
Tel: 0845 22 55 121 Fax: 01506 832 222
e-mail: drumnadrochit@visitscotland.com
website: www.visithighlands.com

DRYMEN
Drymen Library, The Square, Dunbartonshire, Drymen,
Strathclyde G63 0BD
Tel: 08707 200 611 Fax: 01369 660 751
e-mail: info@drymen.visitscotland.com
website: www.visitscottishheartlands.org

DUFFTOWN
2 The Square, Dufftown, Moray, Grampian AB55 4AD
Tel: 01340 820501
e-mail: dufftown@visitscotland.com
website: www.aberdeen-grampian.com

DUMBARTON
7 Alexandra Parade, A82 Northbound, Dunbartonshire,
Milton, Strathclyde G82 2TZ
Tel: 08452 255 121
e-mail: dumbarton@visitscotland.com

DUMFRIES
64 Whitesands, Dumfries,
Dumfries and Galloway DG1 2RS
Tel: 01378 245 555 Fax: 01378 245 555
e-mail: dumfries@visitscotland.com
website: www.visitdumfriesandgalloway.co.uk

DUNBAR
143a High Street, Dunbar, Lothian EH42 1ES
Tel: 0845 22 55 121 Fax: 01506 832 222
e-mail: dunbar@visitscotland.com

DUNBLANE
Stirling Road, Dunblane, Stirlingshire,
Central Scotland FK15 9EP
Tel: 08707 200 613 Fax: 08707 200 613
e-mail: info@dunblane.visitscotland.com
website: www.visitscottishheartlands.org

DUNDEE
Discovery Quay, Dundee, Angus and Dundee,
Central Scotland, Scotland DD1 4XA
Tel: 01382 527 527
e-mail: dundee@visitscotland.com
website: www.angusanddundee.co.uk

DUNFERMLINE
1 High Street, Dunfermline, Fife,
Central Scotland KY12 7DL
Tel: 01383 720 999 Fax: 01383 625 807
e-mail: dunfermline@visitscotland.com
website: www.standrews.co.uk

DUNKELD
The Cross, Perth & Kinross, Dunkeld,
Central Scotland PH8 0AN
Tel: 01350 727688 Fax: 01350 727688
e-mail: dunkeld@visitscotland.com
website: www.perthshire.co.uk

DUNNET HEAD
Caithness, Brough, Highlands and Islands KW14 8YE
Tel: 08452 255 121 Fax: 01605 225 5121
e-mail: info@visitscotland.com
website: www.visithighlands.com

DUNOON
7 Alexandra Parade, Dunoon, Argyll and Bute,
Strathclyde PA23 8AB
Tel: 08452 255 121
e-mail: dunoon@visitscotland.com

DUNVEGAN
2 Lochside, Dunvegan, Isle of Skye, Highlands and
Islands IV55 8WB
Tel: 01845 22 55 121 Fax: 01506 832 222
e-mail: dunvegantic@visitscotland.com
website: www.visithighlands.com

486

DURNESS

Durine, by Lairg, Sutherland, Durness,
Highlands and Islands IV27 4PN
Tel: 01845 22 55 121 Fax: 01506 832 222
e-mail: durnesstic@visitscotland.com
website: www.visithighlands.com

EDINBURGH

Edinburgh and Scotland Information Centre,
above Waverley Shopping Centre, 3 Princes Street,
Edinburgh, Lothian EH2 2QP
Tel: 0845 22 55 121 Fax: 01506 832 222
e-mail: info@visitscotland.com
website: www.edinburgh.org

EDINBURGH AIRPORT

Edinburgh Airport, Edinburgh, Lothian EH12 9DN
Tel: 0870 040 0007 Fax: 01506 832 222
e-mail: edinburgh.airport@visitscotland.com

ELGIN

17 High Street, Elgin, Moray, Grampian IV30 1EG
Tel: 01343 542 666 Fax: 01343 552 982
e-mail: elgin@visitscotland.com
website: www.aberdeen-grampian.com

EYEMOUTH

Auld Kirk, Market Place, Eyemouth,
Scottish Borders TD14 5HE
Tel: 08706 080 404 Fax: 01750 21886
e-mail: eyemouth@visitscotland.com
website: www.visitscottishborders.com

FALKIRK

Lime Road, Tamfourhill, Falkirk, Stirlingshire,
Central Scotland FK1 4RS
Tel: 08452 255 121
e-mail: falkirk@visitscotland.com

FORFAR

The Meffan Museum & Art Gallery, Forfar,
Angus and Dundee, Central Scotland DD8 1BB
Tel: 01307 464 123
e-mail: enquiries@angusanddundee.co.uk
website: www.angusanddundee.co.uk

FORRES

116 High Street, Forres, Moray, Grampian IV36 1NP
Tel: 01309 672 938
e-mail: forres@visitscotland.com
website: www.aberdeen-grampian.com

FORT AUGUSTUS

Car Park, Inverness-shire, Fort Augustus,
Highlands and Islands PH32 4DD
Tel: 01845 22 55 121
e-mail: info@visitscotland.com
website: www.visithighlands.com

FORT WILLIAM

Cameron Centre, Cameron Square, Inverness-shire,
Fort William, Highlands and Islands PH33 6AJ
Tel: 01845 22 55 121 Fax: 01506 832 222
e-mail: fortwilliam@visitscotland.com
website: www.visithighlands.com

FORTH BRIDGES

c/o Queensferry Lodge Hotel, St Margaret's Head,
North Queensferry, Fife, Central Scotland KY11 1HP
Tel: 01383 417759
e-mail: forthbridges@visitfife.com

FRASERBURGH

3 Saltoun Square, Fraserburgh, Aberdeenshire,
Grampian AB43 9DA
Tel: 01346 518315
e-mail: fraserburgh@visitscotland.com
website: www.aberdeen-grampian.com

GAIRLOCH

Achtercairn, Ross-shire, Gairloch,
Highlands and Islands IV22 2DN
Tel: 01445 712 071
e-mail: info@visitscotland.com
website: www.visithighlands.com

GATEHOUSE OF FLEET

Mill on the Fleet, High Street, Gatehouse of Fleet,
Dumfries and Galloway DG7 2HS
Tel: 01557 814 099
e-mail: millonthefleet@btopenworld.com
website: www.visitdumfriesandgalloway.co.uk

GIRVAN

Bridge Street, Girvan, Ayrshire and Arran,
Strathclyde KA26 9HH
Tel: 01465 715500 Fax: 01465 715500
e-mail: info@girvanvisitorcentre.co.uk

GLASGOW

11 George Square, Glasgow, Strathclyde G2 1DY
Tel: 0141 204 4400 Fax: 0141 221 3524
e-mail: glasgow@visitscotland.com
website: www.seeglasgow.com

GRANTOWN ON SPEY

54 High Street, Inverness-shire, Grantown on Spey,
Highlands and Islands PH26 3EH
Tel: 01845 22 55 121 Fax: 01506 832 222
e-mail: grantown@visitscotland.com
website: www.visithighlands.com

GRETNA GREEN

Unit 38, Gretna Gateway Outlet Village, Glasgow Road,
Gretna, Dumfries and Galloway DG16 5GG
Tel: 01461 337 834
e-mail: gretna@visitscotland.com
website: www.visitdumfriesandgalloway.co.uk

HAMILTON

Road Chef Services, M74 Northbound, South Lanarkshire,
Hamilton, Strathclyde ML3 6JW
Tel: 01698 285 590
e-mail: hamilton@seeglasgow.com
website: www.seeglasgow.com

HARESTANES

Ancrum, Jedburgh, Harestanes,
Scottish Borders TD8 6UQ
Tel: 01835 863170 Fax: 01750 21886
e-mail: bordersinfo@visitscotland.com
website: www.scot-borders.co.uk

HAWICK

1 Tower Mill, Heart of Hawick Campus, Hawick,
Scottish Borders TD9 0AE
Tel: 08706 080 404 Fax: 01750 21886
e-mail: hawick@visitscotland.com
website: www.visitscottishborders.com

HELENSBURGH

Clock Tower, The Pier, Dunbartonshire, Helensburgh,
Strathclyde G84 7PA
Tel: 08452 255 121
e-mail: helensburgh@visitscotland.com

HUNTLY

9a The Square, Huntly, Aberdeenshire,
Grampian AB54 8AD
Tel: 01466 792255
e-mail: huntly@visitscotland.com
website: www.aberdeen-grampian.com

INVERARAY

Front Street, Inveraray, Argyll and Bute,
Strathclyde PA32 8UY
Tel: 08452 255 121
e-mail: inveraray@visitscotland.com

INVERNESS

Castle Wynd, Inverness-shire, Inverness,
Highlands and Islands IV2 3BJ
Tel: 01845 22 55 121 Fax: 01506 832 222
e-mail: inverness@visitscotland.com
website: www.visithighlands.com

INVERURIE

Book Store, 18a High Street, Inverurie, Aberdeenshire,
Grampian AB51 3XQ
Tel: 01467 625800 Fax: 01467 625800
e-mail: inverurie@visitscotland.com
website: www.aberdeen-grampian.com

ISLAY

The Square, Main Street, Isle of Islay, Bowmore,
Strathclyde PA43 7JP
Tel: 08707 200 617
e-mail: bowmore@visitscotland.com
website: www.visitscottishheartlands.org

JEDBURGH

Murray's Green, Jedburgh, Scottish Borders TD8 6BE
Tel: 08706 080 404 Fax: 01750 21886
e-mail: jedburgh@visitscotland.com
website: www.visitscottishborders.com

JOHN O'GROATS

County Road, Caithness, John O'Groats,
Highlands and Islands KW1 4YR
Tel: 01845 22 55 121
e-mail: info@visitscotland.com
website: www.visithighlands.com

KELSO

Town House, The Square, Kelso,
Scottish Borders TD5 7HF
Tel: 01835 863 170 Fax: 01750 21886
e-mail: kelso@visitscotland.com
website: www.visitscottishborders.com

KILCHOAN

Kilchoan Community Centre, Pier Road, Acharacle,
Kilchoan, Argyll and Bute PH36 4LJ
Tel: 01845 22 55 121
e-mail: info@visitscotland.com
website: www.visithighlands.com

KILLIN

Breadalbane Folklore Centre, The Old Mill,
Falls of Dochart, Killin, Stirlingshire FK21 8XE
Tel: 08707 200 627 Fax: 01567 820764
e-mail: killin@visitscotland.com

KINGUSSIE

Highland Folk Museum, Inverness-shire, Kingussie,
Highlands and Islands PH21 1JG
Tel: 0845 22 55 121
e-mail: info@visitscotland.com
website: www.visithighlands.com

KINROSS

Heart of Scotland Visitor Centre, Junction 6, M90,
Perth & Kinross, Kinross KY13 7NQ
Tel: 01577 863680 Fax: 01577 863370
e-mail: kinrosstic@perthshire.co.uk
website: www.perthshire.co.uk

KIRKCALDY

The Merchant's House, 339 High Street, Kirkcaldy, Fife,
Central Scotland KY1 1JL
Tel: 01592 267 775 Fax: 01592 203 154
e-mail: kirkcaldy@visitscotland.com
website: www.standrews.co.uk

KIRKCUDBRIGHT

Harbour Square, Kirkcudbright,
Dumfries and Galloway DG6 4HY
Tel: 01557 330 494 Fax: 01557 332 416
e-mail: kirkcudbright@visitscotland.com
website: www.visitdumfriesandgalloway.co.uk

KIRKWALL

West Castle Street, Kirkwall, Orkney,
Highlands and Islands KW15 1GU
Tel: 01856 872 856 Fax: 01856 875 056
e-mail: info@visitorkney.com
website: www.visitorkney.com

KIRRIEMUIR

Kirriemuir Gateway to the Glens Museum, The Town
House, 32 High Street, Kirriemuir, Angus and Dundee,
Central Scotland DD8 4BB
Tel: 01575 575 479
e-mail: enquiries@angusanddundee.co.uk
website: www.angusanddundee.co.uk

KYLE OF LOCHALSH

Car Park, Ross-shire, Kyle of Lochalsh,
Highlands and Islands IV40 8AQ
Tel: 01845 22 55 121
e-mail: info@visitscotland.com
website: www.visithighlands.com

LAIRG

Ferrycroft Countryside Centre, Sutherland, Lairg,
Highlands and Islands IV27 4AZ
Tel: 01845 22 55 121
e-mail: info@visitscotland.com
website: www.visithighlands.com

LANARK

Horsemarket, Ladyacre Road, South Lanarkshire, Lanark,
Strathclyde ML11 7LQ
Tel: 01555 661 661 Fax: 01555 666 143
e-mail: lanark@visitscotland.com
website: www.seeglasgow.com

LARGS

Railway Station, Main Street, Largs, Ayrshire and Arran,
Strathclyde KA30 8AN
Tel: 01475 689 962
e-mail: largs@visitscotland.com
website: www.ayrshire-arran.com

LERWICK

Market Cross, Lerwick, Shetland,
Highlands and Islands ZE1 0LU
Tel: 08701 999 440 Fax: 01595 695 807
e-mail: info@visitshetland.com
website: www.visitshetland.com

LINLITHGOW

County Buildings, High Street, Linlithgow,
Lothian EH49 7EZ
Tel: 01506 775 320
e-mail: linlithgow@visitscotland.com
website: www.edinburgh.org

LOCHBOISDALE

Pier Road, Isle of South Uist, Lochboisdale,
Highlands and Islands HS8 5TH
Tel: 01878 700286 Fax: 01878 700286
e-mail: lochboisdale@visitthebrides.com
website: www.visitthebrides.com

LOCHCARRON

Main Street, Ross-shire, Lochcarron,
Highlands and Islands IV54 8YB
Tel: 01520 722357 Fax: 01520 722324

LOCHGILPHEAD

Lochnell Street, Lochgilphead, Argyll and Bute,
Strathclyde PA31 8JL
Tel: 08452 255 121
e-mail: lochgilphead@visitscotland.com

LOCHINVER

Assynt Visitor Centre, Main Street, by Lairg, Sutherland,
Lochinver, Highlands and Islands IV27 4LX
Tel: 01845 22 55 121 Fax: 01506 832 222
e-mail: lochinver@visitscotland.com
website: www.visithighlands.com

LOCHMADDY

Pier Road, Isle of North Uist, Lochmaddy,
Highlands and Islands HS6 5AA
Tel: 01876 500 321 Fax: 01876 500 321
e-mail: lochmaddy@visitthebrides.com
website: www.visitthebrides.com

MALLAIG

The Pier, Inverness-shire, Mallaig,
Highlands and Islands PH41 4SQ
Tel: 01845 22 55 121
e-mail: info@visitscotland.com
website: www.visithighlands.com

MELROSE

Abbey House, Abbey Street, Melrose,
Scottish Borders TD6 9LG
Tel: 08706 080404 Fax: 01750 21886
e-mail: melrose@visitscotland.com
website: www.visitscottishborders.com

MOFFAT

Churchgate, Moffat, Dumfries and Galloway DG10 9EG
Tel: 01683 220 620
e-mail: moffat@visitscotland.com
website: www.visitdumfriesandgalloway.co.uk

MONIFIETH

Monifieth Library, High Street, Monifieth,
Angus and Dundee, Central Scotland DD5 4AE
Tel: 01382 533 819
e-mail: enquiries@angusanddundee.co.uk
website: www.angusanddundee.co.uk

MONTROSE

Montrose Museum, Panmure Place, Montrose,
Angus and Dundee, Central Scotland DD10 8HE
Tel: 01674 673232 Fax: 01674 671 810
e-mail: enquiries@angusanddundee.co.uk
website: www.angusanddundee.co.uk

NAIRN

The Library, 68 High Street, Inverness-shire, Nairn,
Highlands and Islands IV12 4AU
Tel: 01845 22 55 121
e-mail: info@visitscotland.com
website: www.visithighlands.com

NEWTON STEWART

Dashwood Square, Newton Stewart,
Dumfries and Galloway DG8 6EQ
Tel: 01671 402 431
e-mail: newtonstewart@visitscotland.com
website: www.visitdumfriesandgalloway.co.uk

NEWTONGRANGE

Scottish Mining Museum, Lady Victoria Colliery,
Newtongrange, Lothian EH26 8HB
Tel: 0845 22 55 121 Fax: 01506 832 222
e-mail: newtongrange@visitscotland.com
website: www.edinburgh.org

NORTH BERWICK

Quality Street, North Berwick, Lothian EH39 4HJ
Tel: 0845 22 55 121 Fax: 01506 832 222
e-mail: info@visitscotland.com
website: www.edinburgh.org

NORTH KESSOCK

Picnic Site, Ross-shire, North Kessock,
Highlands and Islands IV1 3UB
Tel: 01845 22 55 121 Fax: 01506 832 222
e-mail: northkessock@visitscotland.com
website: www.visithighlands.com

OLD CRAIGHALL

Old Craighall Service Area (A1), Musselburgh,
Lothian EH21 8RE
Tel: 0845 22 55 121
e-mail: info@visitscotland.com
website: www.edinburgh.org

PAISLEY

9a Gilmour Street, Renfrewshire, Paisley,
Strathclyde PA1 1DD
Tel: 0141 889 0711 Fax: 0141 848 1363
e-mail: paisley@visitscotland.com
website: www.seeglasgow.com

PEEBLES

23 High Street, Peebles, Scottish Borders EH45 8AG
Tel: 08706) 080 404 Fax: 01750 21886
e-mail: peebles@visitscotland.com
website: www.visitscottishborders.com

PERTH

Lower City Mills, West Mill Street, Perth & Kinross, Perth,
Central Scotland PH1 5PQ
Tel: 01738 450 600 Fax: 01738 444 863
e-mail: perth@visitscotland.com
website: www.perthshire.co.uk

PERTH (INVERALMOND)

Caithness Glass, Inveralmond, Perth & Kinross, Perth,
Central Scotland PH1 3TZ
Tel: 01738 638481

PITLOCHRY

22 Atholl Road, Perth & Kinross, Pitlochry,
Central Scotland PH16 5BX
Tel: 01796 472215/472751 Fax: 01796 474046
e-mail: pitlochry@visitscotland.com
website: www.perthshire.co.uk

PORTREE

Bayfield House, Bayfield Road, Portree, Isle of Skye,
Highlands and Islands IV51 9EL
Tel: 01845 22 55 121 Fax: 01506 832 222
e-mail: portree@visitscotland.com
website: www.visithighlands.com

ROTHESAY

Isle of Bute Discovery Centre, Winter Garden,
Isle of Bute, Rothesay, Argyll and Bute PA20 0AH
Tel: 08707 200 619 Fax: 01700 505 156
e-mail: rothesay@visitscotland.com

SELKIRK

Halliwells House, Selkirk, Scottish Borders TD7 4BL
Tel: 08706 080 404 Fax: 01750 21886
e-mail: selkirk@visitscotland.com
website: www.visitscottishborders.com

SPEAN BRIDGE

The Kingdom of Scotland, by Fort William, Inverness-
shire, Spean Bridge, Highlands and Islands PH34 4EP
Tel: 01845 22 55 121
e-mail: info@visitscotland.com
website: www.visithighlands.com

ST ANDREWS

70 Market Street, St Andrews, Fife,
Central Scotland KY16 9NU
Tel: 01334 472 021 Fax: 01334 478 422
e-mail: standrews@visitscotland.com
website: www.visitfife.com

STIRLING (DUMBARTON ROAD)

41 Dumbarton Road, Stirling, Stirlingshire,
Central Scotland FK8 2QQ
Tel: 08452 255 121
e-mail: stirling@visitscotland.com

STIRLING (PIRNHALL)

Motorway Service Area Junction 9 M9/M80, Pirnhall,
Stirling, Stirlingshire, Central Scotland FK7 8ET
Tel: 08452 255 121
e-mail: pirnhall@visitscotland.com

STIRLING (ROYAL BURGH)

Royal Burgh of Stirling Visitor Centre, Castle Esplanade,
Stirling, Stirlingshire FK95LF
Tel: 08707 200 622 Fax: 01786 451 881

STONEHAVEN

66 Allardice Street, Stonehaven, Aberdeenshire,
Grampian AB39 2AA
Tel: 01569 762806

STORNOWAY

26 Cromwell Street, Isle of Lewis, Stornoway,
Highlands and Islands HS1 2DD
Tel: 01851 703088 Fax: 01851 705244
e-mail: stornoway@visithebrides.com
website: www.visithebrides.com

STRANRAER

Burns House, 28 Harbour Street, Stranraer,
Dumfries and Galloway DG9 7RA
Tel: 01776 702 595 Fax: 01776 889 156
e-mail: stranraer@visitscotland.com
website: www.visitdumfriesandgalloway.co.uk

STRATHPEFFER

Square Wheels, The Square, Ross-shire, Strathpeffer,
Highlands and Islands IV14 9DW
Tel: 01845 22 55 121
e-mail: info@visitscotland.com
website: www.visithighlands.com

STROMNESS

Ferry Terminal Building, Pier Head, Stromness, Orkney,
Highlands and Islands KW16 3AA
Tel: 01856 850 716 Fax: 01856 850 777
e-mail: stromness@visitorkney.com
website: www.visitorkney.com

STRONTIAN

Acharacle, Strontian, Argyll and Bute,
Strathclyde PH36 4HZ
Tel: 01845 22 55 121 Fax: 01506 832 222
e-mail: strontian@visitscotland.com
website: www.visithighlands.com

SUMBURGH AIRPORT

Sumburgh Airport, Wilsness Terminal, Sumburgh,
Shetland, Highlands and Islands ZE3 9JP
Tel: 08701 999 440 Fax: 01950 460 807
e-mail: info@visitshetland.com
website: www.visitshetland.com

TARBERT

Pier Road, Isle of Harris, Tarbert,
Highlands and Islands HS3 3DJ
Tel: 01859 502 011 Fax: 01859 502 011
e-mail: tarbert@visithebrides.com
website: www.visithebrides.com

TARBERT (LOCH FYNE)

Harbour Street, Tarbert, Argyll and Bute,
Strathclyde PA29 6UD
Tel: 08452 255 121
e-mail: tarbert@visitscotland.com

TARBET (LOCH LOMOND)

Main Street, Loch Lomond, Tarbet, Argyll and Bute,
Strathclyde G83 7DE
Tel: 08707 200 623
e-mail: tarbet@visitscotland.com

THURSO

Riverside, Caithness, Thurso,
Highlands and Islands KW14 8BU
Tel: 01845 22 55 121 Fax: 01506 832 222
e-mail: thurso@visitscotland.com
website: www.visithighlands.com

TOMINTOUL

The Square, Tomintoul, Aberdeenshire,
Grampian AB37 9ET
Tel: 01807 580285
e-mail: tomintoul@visitscotland.com
website: www.aberdeen-grampian.com

TYNDRUM

Main Street, Tyndrum, Stirlingshire,
Central Scotland FK20 8RY
e-mail: tyndrum@visitscotland.com

ULLAPOOL

20 Argyle Street, Ross-shire, Ullapool,
Highlands and Islands IV26 2UB
Tel: 01845 22 55 121 Fax: 01506 832 222
e-mail: ullapool@visitscotland.com
website: www.visithighlands.com

VISIT ORKNEY

Orkney, Highlands and Islands Scotland
e-mail: info@visitorkney.com
website: www.visitorkney.com

WICK

McAllan's, 66 High Street, Caithness, Wick,
Highlands and Islands KW1 4NE
Tel: 01955 602 547

Towns, Villages and Places of Interest

493

501

505

506

TRAVEL PUBLISHING ORDER FORM

To order any of our publications just fill in the payment details below and complete the order form. For orders of less than 4 copies please add £1.00 per book for postage and packing. Orders over 4 copies are P & P free.

Name:

Address:

Tel no:

Please Complete Either:

I enclose a cheque for £ _____ made payable to Travel Publishing Ltd

Or:

Card No: _____ Expiry Date: _____

Signature:

Please either send, telephone, fax or e-mail your order to:

Travel Publishing Ltd, Airport Business Centre, 10 Thornbury Road, Estover, Plymouth PL6 7PP

Tel: 01752 697280   Fax: 01752 697299   e-mail: info@travelpublishing.co.uk

	Price	Quantity		Price	Quantity
HIDDEN PLACES REGIONAL TITLES			**COUNTRY LIVING RURAL GUIDES**		
Cornwall	£8.99	....	East Anglia	£10.99	....
Devon	£8.99	....	Heart of England	£10.99	....
Dorset, Hants & Isle of Wight	£8.99	....	Ireland	£11.99	....
East Anglia	£8.99	....	North East	£10.99	....
Lake District & Cumbria	£8.99	....	North West	£10.99	....
Lancashire & Cheshire	£8.99	....	Scotland	£11.99	....
Northumberland & Durham	£8.99	....	South of England	£10.99	....
Peak District and Derbyshire	£8.99	....	South East of England	£10.99	....
Yorkshire	£8.99	....	Wales	£11.99	....
HIDDEN PLACES NATIONAL TITLES			West Country	£10.99	....
England	£11.99	....			
Ireland	£11.99	....			
Scotland	£11.99	....			
Wales	£11.99	....	**TOTAL QUANTITY:**		
OTHER TITLES			**POST & PACKING:**		
Off the Motorway	£11.99	....			
Garden Centres & Nurseries	£11.99	....	**TOTAL VALUE:**		

HIDDEN PLACES GUIDES

Explore Britain and Ireland with *Hidden Places* guides - a fascinating series of national and local travel guides.

Packed with easy to read information on hundreds of places of interest as well as places to stay, eat and drink.

Available from both high street and internet booksellers

For more information on the full range of *Hidden Places* guides and other titles published by Travel Publishing visit our website on

www.travelpublishing.co.uk
or ask for our leaflet by phoning **01752 697280** or emailing **info@travelpublishing.co.uk**

Our easy-to use website contains details and locations of places to stay, places to eat and drink, specialist shops and places of interest throughout England, Wales, Scotland and Ireland.

Places to Stay:	**Places to Eat and Drink:**	**Places of Interest:**	**Specialist Shops:**	**Gardens:**
Hotels, guest accommodation, bed & breakfast, inns, self-catering accommodation	Restaurants, pubs, inns, cafes, tea rooms	Historic buildings, gardens, art galleries, museums, nature parks, wildlife parks, indoor and outdoor activities	Fashion shops, art and craft shops, gift shops, food and drink shops, antique shops, jewellery shops	Garden centres and retail nurseries

508

READER REACTION FORM

The *Travel Publishing* research team would like to receive reader's comments on any visitor attractions or places reviewed in the book and also recommendations for suitable entries to be included in the next edition. This will help ensure that the *Hidden Places series of Guides* continues to provide its readers with useful information on the more interesting, unusual or unique features of each attraction or place ensuring that their visit to the local area is an enjoyable and stimulating experience. To provide your comments or recommendations would you please complete the forms below and overleaf as indicated and send to:

The Research Department, Travel Publishing Ltd,
Airport Business Centre, 10 Thornbury Road, Plymouth PL6 7PP

Your Name:

Your Address:

Your Telephone Number:

Please tick as appropriate:

Comments ☐   Recommendation ☐

Name of Establishment:

Address:

Telephone Number:

Name of Contact:

READER REACTION FORM

COMMENT OR REASON FOR RECOMMENDATION:

....
....
....
....
....
....
....
....
....
....
....
....
....
....
....
....
....
....
....

READER REACTION FORM

The *Travel Publishing* research team would like to receive reader's comments on any visitor attractions or places reviewed in the book and also recommendations for suitable entries to be included in the next edition. This will help ensure that the *Hidden Places series of Guides* continues to provide its readers with useful information on the more interesting, unusual or unique features of each attraction or place ensuring that their visit to the local area is an enjoyable and stimulating experience. To provide your comments or recommendations would you please complete the forms below and overleaf as indicated and send to:

**The Research Department, Travel Publishing Ltd,
Airport Business Centre, 10 Thornbury Road, Plymouth PL6 7PP**

Your Name:

Your Address:

Your Telephone Number:

Please tick as appropriate:

Comments ☐   Recommendation ☐

Name of Establishment:

Address:

Telephone Number:

Name of Contact:

READER REACTION FORM

COMMENT OR REASON FOR RECOMMENDATION:

....
....
....
....
....
....
....
....
....
....
....
....
....
....
....
....
....
....
....
....

READER REACTION FORM

The *Travel Publishing* research team would like to receive reader's comments on any visitor attractions or places reviewed in the book and also recommendations for suitable entries to be included in the next edition. This will help ensure that the *Hidden Places series of Guides* continues to provide its readers with useful information on the more interesting, unusual or unique features of each attraction or place ensuring that their visit to the local area is an enjoyable and stimulating experience. To provide your comments or recommendations would you please complete the forms below and overleaf as indicated and send to:

**The Research Department, Travel Publishing Ltd,
Airport Business Centre, 10 Thornbury Road, Plymouth PL6 7PP**

Your Name:

Your Address:

Your Telephone Number:

Please tick as appropriate:

Comments ☐   Recommendation ☐

Name of Establishment:

Address:

Telephone Number:

Name of Contact:

READER REACTION FORM

COMMENT OR REASON FOR RECOMMENDATION:

READER REACTION FORM

The *Travel Publishing* research team would like to receive reader's comments on any visitor attractions or places reviewed in the book and also recommendations for suitable entries to be included in the next edition. This will help ensure that the *Hidden Places series of Guides* continues to provide its readers with useful information on the more interesting, unusual or unique features of each attraction or place ensuring that their visit to the local area is an enjoyable and stimulating experience. To provide your comments or recommendations would you please complete the forms below and overleaf as indicated and send to:

The Research Department, Travel Publishing Ltd,
Airport Business Centre, 10 Thornbury Road, Plymouth PL6 7PP

Your Name:

Your Address:

Your Telephone Number:

Please tick as appropriate:

Comments ☐   Recommendation ☐

Name of Establishment:

Address:

Telephone Number:

Name of Contact:

READER REACTION FORM

COMMENT OR REASON FOR RECOMMENDATION:

....
....
....
....
....
....
....
....
....
....
....
....
....
....
....
....
....
....
....

READER REACTION FORM

The *Travel Publishing* research team would like to receive reader's comments on any visitor attractions or places reviewed in the book and also recommendations for suitable entries to be included in the next edition. This will help ensure that the *Hidden Places series of Guides* continues to provide its readers with useful information on the more interesting, unusual or unique features of each attraction or place ensuring that their visit to the local area is an enjoyable and stimulating experience. To provide your comments or recommendations would you please complete the forms below and overleaf as indicated and send to:

**The Research Department, Travel Publishing Ltd,
Airport Business Centre, 10 Thornbury Road, Plymouth PL6 7PP**

Your Name:

Your Address:

Your Telephone Number:

Please tick as appropriate:

Comments ☐   Recommendation ☐

Name of Establishment:

Address:

Telephone Number:

Name of Contact:

READER REACTION FORM

COMMENT OR REASON FOR RECOMMENDATION:

....
....
....
....
....
....
....
....
....
....
....
....
....
....
....
....
....
....
....
....
....

Index of Advertisers

FOOD AND DRINK

PLACES OF INTEREST